Communication Technology and Society

Audience Adoption and Uses

THE HAMPTON PRESS COMMUNICATION SERIES
New Media: Policy and Social Research Issues
Ron Rice, supervisory editor

Telecommunications and Development in China
Paul S.N. Lee (ed.)

Communication Technology and Society: Audience Adoption and Uses
Carolyn A. Lin and David J. Atkin (eds.)

Foundations of Communication Policy: Principles and Process in the
Regulation of Electronic Media
Philip M. Napoli

Virtual Politicking: Playing Politics in Electronically Linked Organizations
Celia T. Romm

forthcoming

Culture and Design: The Case of Computer-Supported Cooperative Work
Lorna Heaton

The Privatization of Greek Television: Economics, Regulations, and Policy
Theomary Karamanis

Media Policy for the 21st Century in the United States
Yaron Katz

Impact and Issues in New Media: Toward Intelligent Societies
Paul S.N. Lee, Louis Leung and Clement Y.K. So (eds.)

Global Trends in Communication Research and Education
Kenneth W.Y. Leung, James Kenny, and Paul S.N. Lee (eds.)

Computer Mediated Group Processes
Tom Postmes

Automating Interaction: Economic Reason and Social Capital in
Addressable Networks
Myles A. Ruggles

Communication Technology and Society

Audience Adoption and Uses

edited by

Carolyn A. Lin
David J. Atkin
Cleveland State University

 HAMPTON PRESS, INC.
CRESSKILL, NEW JERSEY

Printed in the United States of America

Library of Congress Cataloging-in-Publication Data

Communication technology and society / audience adoption and uses /
edited by Carolyn A. Lin, David J. Atkin
    p. cm.
    Includes bibliographic references and index.
    ISBN 1-57273-362-4 (cl) -- ISBN 1-57273-363-2 (ppb)
        1. Information society. 2. Information technology--Social
aspects. 3. Telecommunications--Social aspects. I. Lin, Carolyn A.
II. Atkin, David J.

HM851.C653 2002
303.48'33--dc21

2001059367

Hampton Press, Inc.
23 Broadway
Cresskill, NJ 07626

To my parents, who were the most generous people I have ever known
Carolyn Lin

To Kenward and Jane Atkin, who guided me with love and support
David Atkin

Contents

Preface

This book addresses a subject that has received great popular press attention in recent years—mass media and information technology integration. The authors hope to expand on a communication literature that has either overlooked the influence of new media like the Internet, or focused on speculative, anecdotal, or "gee-whiz" accounts of likely influences of the new media. In particular, we apply empirically based, social scientific research to better understand how the incredible proliferation of media and communication forms are diffusing though society. By applying such perspectives as diffusion of innovations and uses and gratifications in this context, we can gain a better understanding of how these new communication technologies shape our daily lives, at home as well as in the workplace.

As Dholakia's compendium on the marketing of new media suggests, "several details change daily but the basic issues retain their importance and centrality" (1996, p. vii). In a similar vein, this book offers an innovative, current, scholarly and industry-relevant approach, providing readers with a solid understanding of emerging wired/wireless entertainment and information media. It features the work of leading scholars in interpersonal, organizational, and mass communication, as well as telecommunication, investigating adoption and diffusion of new communication technology at home and in the workplace.

The present book is designed to help academicians and practitioners alike meet those challenges. But even in a fast-moving field like telecommunication, where technology can transform the competitive landscape in the time it takes to even print a book like this, our understanding of new media adoption can be informed by the concepts developed here. In particular, the overarching focus on communication theory applications—particularly the Diffusion of Innovations perspective—provides a useful framework for understanding how audiences assimilate other media innovations into their daily lives.

Past work on new telecommunication media has developed irregularly, having originated from diverse disciplinary frameworks (e.g., political science and economics), and is not widely accessible. This volume brings together, in a unified format, the most thoughtful and current empirical research addressing new media and their influences on users.

Although several academic and popular books cover general or specific communication technology topics, few explore the phenomenon of converging media and information communication technology environments and their implications for society (Baldwin, Steinfield, & McVoy, 1996; Straubhaar & LaRose, 1999). The present volume will overcome limitations of past work in this area while reaching out to scholarly and professional audiences.

To help chart our path into the new millennium, we're fortunate to have the world's foremost authority on Diffusion theory occupy our honorary "Captain's chair"—Everett Rogers. Our list of contributors, each highly accomplished in their own fields of expertise, boasts names that should be well-known to scholars of mediated communication. We thank them all for their contributions. We're also indebted to Dr. Ronald Rice, Professor of Communication at Rutgers, for the encouragement he offered in developing, editing, and ultimately contributing to this book project.

This volume aims to organize research on adoption patterns for new media into logical component parts, focusing upon: (a) a thorough "user-friendly" overview of technical features for each medium; (b) a review of regulatory and economic trends and issues; (c) a summary of past work addressing audiences/adopters, uses, and social effects for that medium; (d) presentation of data profiling aggregate uses of the technology or traits of adopters in terms of social locators, media uses, and technology adoption; and (e) a summary of key findings and directions for later work that should help the narrative "come alive" for the reader.

The book is designed for use in advanced undergraduate and graduate coursework in any academic disciplines offering courses in communication, information marketing, technology management, organizational or consumer technology, technology studies, or any readers who wish to examine—in whole or in part—the functions and dynamics of an integrated communication environment. It also serves as a supplementary text in communication-related fields, where new media and the ongoing information revolution are an important focus. In addition, communication professionals should find the book useful for keeping up with developments both within and adjacent to their fields. Whether readers reside in the public or private sector, we hope that the book will serve as an indispensable learning instrument for those seeking a better understanding of new media features, adoption prospects, and uses.

—CL and DA

REFERENCES

Baldwin, T.F., Steinfield, C., & McVoy, D.S. (1996). *Convergence*. Newbury Park, CA: Sage.

Dholakia, R., Mundorf, N., & Dholakia, N. (1996). *New infotainment technologies in the home: Demand side perspectives*. Hillsdale, NJ: Erlbaum .

Straubhaar, J., & LaRose, R. (1999). *Communications media in the information society* (2nd ed.). Belmont: Wadsworth.

About the Authors

Kendra Albright has extensive experience in management and knowledge of the information industry. She holds a Master's degree in Library and Information Science and is finishing her Ph.D. in Communications at the University of Tennessee. She serves as Manger of Research Services at Information International Associates, Inc.

David Atkin (Ph.D., Michigan State University) is Distinguished Professor of Communication at Cleveland State University. His research interests include the diffusion of new media and program formats, media economics and telecommunication policy. He's also co-authoring a forthcoming book on television audiences, *The Televiewing Audience,* at Hampton Press.

Benjamin J. Bates (Ph.D., Michigan) is an Associate Professor in the Department of Broadcasting at the University of Tennessee. His research focuses on information and telecommunications policy and economics, and how they influence the development of telecommunications and information systems and those systems' social impacts.

Shawn Boyd currently attends the University of St. Thomas in St. Paul, Minnesota, where he is pursuing a Master of Arts in English.

Elizabeth Burch (Ph.D., Michigan State University) is an Assistant Professor in the Department of Communication at California State University, Sonoma.

Tamar Charney (M.A., Michigan State University) is a Senior Broadcast Producer and Journalist for the University of Michigan's Public Radio Network. Much of her master's degree research work centered around the social effects of new media technologies.

Luiz G. Duarte was a graduate student at Michigan State University and now works for Hughes Corporation.

Michel Dupagne's (Ph.D., Indiana University) research interests include new communication technologies, international communication, and media economics. With Peter B. Seel, he co-authored *High Definition Television: A Global Perspective* (Iowa State University Press, 1998).

Keren Eyal (M.A., Kent State University) is a Ph.D. student in the Department of Communication at the University of California, Santa Barbara. Her research interests include media effects, especially on children and adolescents.

August E. Grant (Ph.D., Annenberg School, USC) is a Senior Consultant for Focus 25 Research & Consulting in Columbia, South Carolina. His consulting practice focuses on consumer adoption and use of communication technologies. He has written numerous articles and conference papers dealing with adoption and use of emerging communication technologies, broadband services, audience behavior, and theories of new media. He is the editor of the Communication Technology Update (now in its 7th edition), a semi-annual review of the latest developments in communication technologies.

Bradley Greenberg (Ph.D., University of Wisconsin) is University Distinguished Professor of Communication & Telecommunication at Michigan State University. His primary research examines the social influence of mass communication.

Leo Jeffres (Ph.D., University of Minnesota, is Professor in the Department of Communication at Cleveland State University. His interests include media effects, neighborhoods and urban communication systems, ethnic communication, and communication technologies. He has a new book, *Urban Communication Systems: Neighborhoods and the Search for Community* (Hampton Press, in press).

Bruce C. Klopfenstein (Ph.D., Ohio State University) is professor of telecommunications and director of the Dowden Center for New Media Studies in the Grady College at the University of Georgia. Klopfenstein did his graduate work at The Ohio State University an has authored numerous publications of new communication media. He co-authored *The Whole Internet: Academic Edition* (Wadsworth and O'Reilly, 1996).

Carolyn A. Lin (Ph.D., Michigan State University) is Professor of Communication at Cleveland State University. Her research interests include the economic and sociocultural impact of communication technology and advertising. She is also co-authoring *International Communication: Issues and Cases* (Wadsworth, forthcoming).

Kimberly Neuendorf (Ph.D., Michigan State University) is Professor of Communication at Cleveland State University. Her research interests include media and race/ethnicity, new media technologies, and affective correlates of media use. She has a book, *The Content Analysis Handbook* (Sage, in press).

Kristine Nowak (Ph.D., Michigan State University) is as Assistant Professor at the University of Connecticut in the Department of Communication Sciences. Her research interests focus on the design and use of interfaces, particularly how the interface influences interactions and the processes involved in person perception in mediated interactions.

Joey Reagan (Ph.D., Michigan State University) is Professor in the School of Communication at Washington State University and owner of Reagan Market Research. He does research about predicting technology adoption, and assessing the relative credibility of the Internet and traditional media as information sources.

Ronald E. Rice (Ph.D., Stanford University) is Professor and Chair of the Department of Communication, at the School of Communication, Information, & Library Studies, Rutgers University. His research interests include diffusion of innovations, communication networks, communication campaigns, information seeking, and evaluation of new organizational media. He has co-authored or co-edited a number of recent publications: *The Internet and Health Communication* (2001; *Accessing and Browsing Information and Communication* (2001); and *Public Communication Campaigns* (3rd ed., 2001).

Everett M. Rogers (Ph.D., Iowa State University) is Regents' Professor in the Department of Communication and Journalism, University of New Mexico, where he is also appointed by courtesy in the three research centers in which he collaborates in conducting health communication research. Rogers is best known for his book, Diffusion of Innovations, which was published in its fourth edition in 1995; the fifth edition will appear in 2003.

Alan M. Rubin (Ph.D., University of Illinois at Urbana-Champaign) is Professor and Interim Director in the School of Communication Studies at Kent State University. His research interests include the uses and effects of communication media, including broadcast news and entertainment, the links among personal and mediated communication and new communication technologies. He is past editor of *Journal of Broadcasting & Electronic Media* and *Journal of Communication.*

Patrice Sheffer is a faculty member in Communication at Brigham Young University.

Charles Steinfield (Ph.D., Annenberg School, USC) is a Professor in the Department of Telecommunication at Michigan State University. His current research is in the area of organizational uses of information technology and focuses on business strategy and electronic commerce.

Joseph Straubhaar (Ph.D., Tufts University) is Professor in the Department of Radio-Television-Film at the University of Texas-Austin.

Joseph B. Walther (Ph.D., University of Arizona) is an associate professor of communication, social psychology, and information technology at Rensselaer Polytechnic Institute (Troy, NY). His research interests include computer-mediated communication, virtual groups and organizations, online relationships, theory development and research methods for online behavior.

Kadesha D. Washington (Ph.D., University of Tennessee) is currently a Presidential Management Fellow, working for the Department of the Interior and The Department of Commerce.

Jane Webster (Ph.D., New York University) is a Professor Queen's School of Business in Canada. Her research investigates the impacts of technologies to support distributed work, organizational communication, employee recruitment and selection, and training and learning.

PART ONE

INTRODUCTION

1

Communicating in the Information Age

Carolyn A. Lin
Cleveland State University

At the dawning of the 21st century, the advances made in communication technology stand among the most notable achievements in human history. As interconnecting peoples and cultures at different points across distance has never been made easier and more expedient, Marshall McLuhan's (1962) vision of a "global village" seems to have arrived, primarily in a technical sense. It is fair to say that a true global village of shared meaning and understanding of human expressions between peoples and cultures remains a utopian notion. Yet, without this technical infrastructure in place, the global village will forever exist as an unattainable ideal.

This book visits this "technical global village" to explore how its residents utilize all of the different technology devices to communicate with each other across distance—in an interpersonal context, an organizational setting and a mass communication milieu as well as an intermedia mode. The concept of *intermedia mode*, introduced here, refers to a fluid technology unit (Lin, 2000a) that embodies the technical functions that are designed primarily to suit a particular or unique communication purpose (i.e., interpersonal, organizational, or mass communication). A good example of such an intermedia device is the Internet. In essence, the Internet's fluid nature enables it to "morph" itself from one communica-

3

tion modality into another or to simultaneously operate in different communication modalities.

Before each of these communication technologies is discussed, I will first explain the basics of analog versus digital transmission methods as well as wired versus wireless transmission channels utilized by various communication technologies via a "communication technology primer." Then, I introduce the chapters that explore the theoretical and empirical applications of these technologies.

A COMMUNICATION TECHNOLOGY PRIMER

Electromagnetic Spectrum

The electromagnetic spectrum contains a range of electromagnetic radiation frequencies, partially visible to human eyes in the form of a rainbow (whose colors are always arrayed in the order of Red-Orange-Yellow-Green-Blue-Indigo-Violet). Electromagnetic radiation frequencies, in mediated form, embody such physical energy forms as sound, light, electrical energy, and so on, that can be tapped for communication purposes via a communication device (e.g., cellular phone) and proper signal amplification units (e.g., an antenna). We measure these electromagnetic radiation frequencies in the unit of Hertz (Hz), or wave cycles per second. One Hz thus equals one cycle per second, and the prefixes kilo, mega, and giga, respectively refer to thousands, millions, and billions of cycles per second. Each type of communication device is designated to piggyback on a range of frequencies in the spectrum to perform its information transmission task. For an overview of the frequencies utilized for communication purposes, see Table 1.1.

Spectrum Use and Technical Standards

Although domestic use of this spectrum is regulated and often licensed by the Federal Communications Commission (FCC), this government agency is also a technical standard selection entity. Its international parallel, the International Telecommunications Union (ITU), is a signatory organization comprised of 189 nations. As the FCC sometimes prefers to let the marketplace determine the best de facto technical standard for a communication technology device, its technical standard selection decision is often the result of open warfare between different technology manufacturers and industry players. The ITU's decisions in setting global technical standards for communication technology devices and spectrum use, too,

Table 1.1. Electromagnet Spectrum and Radio Communication Bands.

Band	Frequency Range	Communication Applications
Ultra Low Frequency (ULF)	300-3,000 Hz	Human voice, musical instruments
Very Low Frequency (VLF)	3-30 KHz	Sea-shore submarine communication
Low Frequency (LF)	30-300 KHz	Shortwave radio
Medium Frequency (MF)	300-3,000 KHz	AM radio
High Frequency (HF)	3-30 MHz	CB radio
Very High Frequency (VHF)	30-300 MHz	FM radio, TV channels (2-13)
Ultra High Frequency (UHF)	300-3,000 MHz	TV channels (14-69), cell phones, PCS, Police/fire, FRS satellites
Super High Frequency (SHF)	3-30 GHz	Satellite communications
Extremely High Frequency (EHF)	30-300 GHz	Point-to-point microwave communication

can often turn into a geopolitical or a geoeconomic battle. These battles can sometimes continue for decades without a resolution, as with the case of satellite orbital spectrum allocation (Lin, 2000b) and high definition television (HDTV; see DuPagne, chap. 10, this volume).

Analog Signal

When an energy form such as a sound wave (e.g., speaking voice) is converted into an electrical signal (via a device such as a microphone), the electrical signal containing continuous electrical currents—measured in amplitude—tends to take the shape that is "analogous" to (or resembling) the original sound wave patterns. As the sound wave pattern changes (due to variation in the pitches and tone of the voice), so does the shape of the amplitudes contained in the electrical signal; a wave's amplitude is related to its strength. The way analog signals travel can be compared to ocean waves that are washed ashore by the forces of continuous subsequent waves.

A wave can also be characterized by its vibration rate, which is related to bandwidth. The other major broadcasting method based on this principle, frequency modulation (FM), holds the wave-height constant and alters the wavelength. Both AM and FM modulation can be implemented via analog or digital transmission techniques.

Digital Signal

When the same energy form (e.g., speaking voice) is converted into an electrical signal (via a microphone) and then converted into a stream of noncontinuous binary numerical codes (of 1s and 0s) to reflect the electrical current or amplitude levels, this binary code signal is called a digital signal. For instance, an electrical signal with amplitude levels at 5 and 10 volts, when converted into a digital signal, will appear as two numerical strings of: 0 0 0 0 1 0 1 and 0 0 0 1 0 1 0. The seven-bit code is considered a byte (an eight-bit code contains a "parity bit" for checking transmission error). Unlike analog signals, a digital signal does not resemble the original sound wave. But, unlike analog signals (e.g., a photocopy), a digital signal can be retransmitted with minimal error.

Analog-to-Digital and Digital-to-Analog Conversion

An analog signal can be converted into a digital signal for transmission. But, at the receiving end, the digital signal is often converted back to analog signal and then back to the original form of physical energy (e.g., sound wave) such as a speaking voice, so the person receiving it can decipher the voice. By contrast, data communication involving text and graphic material, when transmitted as digital signals, also needs to be converted back to the letters, pixels, and light/shape patterns for human consumption.

Wired Channels

A wired channel contains a physical "wire" or "cable" as the tool to transport a communication signal, utilizing a certain range of electromagnetic radiation frequencies as the physical force for signal propagation. Examples of a wired channel can include copper wires, coaxial cables, optical fiber cables (i.e., fiber-glass cables) and metallic pipes (or waveguides). The most commonly used wired channel remains the copper wire network, as the majority of the public telephone networks around the world still use the copper wire due to its economic value. Coaxial cables, a more costly alternative, are installed primarily for providing cable TV services and broadband communication (capable of sending volumes of data, voice, and video information via the same cable). The even more costly optical fiber channels, primarily installed for high-speed and broadband communication purposes, have been popular with institutional users in both public and private sectors. These channels convert electrical signals into light signals for transmission purposes; the received light signal is then converted back to the original electrical signal (and then back to its original energy form such as speaking voice) for end reception. Waveguides, primarily installed for "protected" communication and high speed and volume transmission, provide the most secure type of communication due to their relatively low external electromagnetic activity influence. These channels are typically deployed by government intelligence or military units and air traffic control communication units.

Wireless Channels

These channels, by definition, are over-the-air communication channels that are easily susceptible to the interference of any electromagnetic radiation activity, weather conditions and physical obstacle (e.g., terrain or tall buildings). The most commonly employed wireless channels include (a) radio and television broadcasting, (b) cellular phone and personal communications services, (c) multichannel multipoint distribution service (MMDS; transmits scrambled cable network signals and data to group living quarters such as hotels), and (d) satellite communication (relays voice, video, and data signals from signal sources to various ground receiving stations). The most recent development in wireless technology involves inventive uses of satellites to help provide wireless Internet services, global positioning systems, and satellite telephone services (Lin, 2000b).

Communication Network

There are two basic types of communication networks—local area network and wide area network. A local area network typically serves a geographically contiguous area to interconnect different buildings and personnel working for the same institution (e.g., a college campus). By comparison, a wide area network often serves people and locations that spread across long distances and wide geographic regions (e.g., Ford Motor Company's private global satellite network). A large modern wide area communication network may contain a chain of local area networks linked by both wired and wireless transmission channels, computer networks, telephone networks, fax machines, Intranet and Internet as well as a series of analog-to-digital and digital-to-analog transmission conversions.

COMMUNICATION TECHNOLOGY AND INFORMATION SOCIETY

This section (chapters 2 through 4) explores the social impact of communication technology diffusion in terms of technology and the information society, interpersonal communication, organizational communication, mass communication, and intermedia communication. Examining the meaning of "convergence" requires examining the changing nature of communication networks. The most noticeable difference between today's "nimble" intelligent network/broadband communication era and the "rigid" network/narrowband communication age of yesteryear exists in the former's ability to efficiently route signals to available channels and manage traffic flows to prevent system breakdowns. This intelligent communication network has the ability to splice a signal into different segments, transmit the signal segments through different available channels (or in a timed sequence on the same channel) and reassemble the signal at the receiving end. Such capabilities heavily depend on the convergence of various communication networks and transmission methods, because of the digitization of all information, regardless of its analog mode (sound, images, text, numbers, video, etc.).

The end product of this intelligent communication network ideally is a well-connected, cost-efficient as well as high-speed communication capability (e.g., Forrest, 2000). Individuals who utilize this network are able to communicate with others as well as send and receive information in ways unimaginable only a few years ago. A nearly limitless capacity of information "bytes"—containing a dynamic interactive encyclopedia of ideas, data, and so on—are readily available at our fingertips. This phenomenon of "digital convergence" has been dubbed the 5Cs of convergence (i.e., communications, computers, cable TV, content and consumer electronics), and the "ICE Age"—an acronym for information, communications and entertaining (Pelton, 2000). In other words, network and transmission facets—combined with the ongoing digitization of content—are the means by which different media are converging. This technology convergence phenomenon then presages our entry to an information society.

Even as our information society has been progressing steadily, the task of technology forecasting or technology market prediction is a very risky business, because the rate of technology innovation often outpaces the rate of innovation diffusion (see Reagan, chap. 4, this volume). These market uncertainties, in turn, highlight the importance of technology market research that address human communication motivations, needs, adoption decision-making process, and so on. In essence, it is human communication research that is at the heart of technology market research.

Convergence Across Media

Atkin (chap. 2, this volume) examines the technology convergence phenomenon from several different perspectives. From the perspective of technology, it is clear that telephony, broadcasting, video, and computer technologies have now been integrated into a single network that is capable of transmitting voice, video, and data simultaneously (e.g., the Internet). Alternatively, from an economic and marketing perspective, the development of such "converged" technology as the Internet also has created new outlets for advertising, direct marketing, consumer/market research, direct corporate-consumer, and corporate-corporate communication. From a regulatory and policy dimension, both the Telecommunication Act of 1996 and the FCC's policies in recent years strongly reflect a deregulatory philosophy that aims to help "foster" further technological convergence by tearing down the technical and market barriers between different communication technology sectors (Aufderheide, 1999).

Finally, the tradition of communication research often demarcates interpersonal, organizational, and mass communication literature into three distinctive and disconnected areas. Technological convergence, however, has brought cross-fertilization of these three bodies of research and literature, as seen by the effort put forth in this book. For instance, electronic mail can be a form of interpersonal, organization or even mass communication, depending on the address and the purpose of one's communication task.

Technology Diffusion Prediction

Reagan (chap. 4, this volume) points out that most scientific and market research tend to focus on explaining the diffusion rates and patterns of those innovations that have already achieved a certain level of market diffusion success. Equally important in diffusion research is the issue of market failure (i.e., how and why certain innovations failed to reach widespread market acceptance). Nevertheless, even though technology convergence seems to be an unstoppable trend, the market successes of these functionally converged technology devices and industries are far from being certain. A number of economic, political, as well as technological reasons, along with market timing and demographic/psychographic shifts in the consumer population, all may interfere with the timely diffusion success of a technology product.

These market uncertainties are symptomatic of the difficulties associated with making technology market predictions. And such predictions now seem riskier than ever, as the progress toward technology convergence speeds up and brings along a host of products and services that can look promising today and outdated tomorrow in the rapidly changing communications technology marketplace. The need for technology market prediction research is hence stronger than ever. It is thus essential to conduct diffusion research by addressing the reasons behind market success and failures, developing valid theoretical frameworks and empirical measures, as well as research typologies that are comprehensive in nature to avoid a singular innovation market prediction approach.

Information Society

Rogers (chap. 2, this volume) addresses when and how scholarly communication research on new media technology began and flourished, riding on the revolutionary "computer-as-communication" conceptualization (Andersen, 1986). It traces the root of the current technology-driven culture and explains the concepts of diffusion of innovation and critical mass. As a critical mass is necessary to propel further technology diffusion and later mobilize social changes, social development in an information society is perhaps a product of both "technological determinism" (Williams, 1974) as well as "social determinism." This sociotechnological development can have several implications for life in the 21st century, including technopolis and information workers who exemplify the social transformation of our workforce in this brave new world.

TECHNOLOGY AND INTERPERSONAL COMMUNICATION

The oldest forms of electromagnetic communication technology—the telephone and telegraph—provide people with an instantaneous means to communicate interpersonally. Although the telegraph remains what it was, as when it was first invented, the technology of telephony has been completely transformed to suit the needs of a multifunctional telecommunication medium. As Bates et al. (chap. 5, this volume) note, telephony played an important role in contributing to the economic as well as social development of an industrialized society in the past and an information society of today. One example of using a telephone to communicate between strangers or for information-seeking purposes involves the use of an audiotext service. An audiotext service allows for an interpersonal chat or individualized searches for database information. Just as the art of letter writing was nearly pronounced dead due to the dominance of telephony as a means for interpersonal communication, the emergence of electronic chat and mail have altered interpersonal communication dynamics. Much like an audiotext service, electronic chat and mail allow an individual to communicate interpersonally with friends and strangers alike. The social implications of these types of interpersonal communication are numerous and are just beginning to emerge. Chapters 5 through 7 present variegated approaches to examine the relationship between technology and interpersonal communication.

Telephony

Bates et al. (chap. 5, this volume) take us onto a journey of how telephony technology evolves over time to become what it is today—a multifunctional wired and wireless interpersonal communication network that is capable of transmitting voice, data, and video signals. Explaining the development of telephony from a systems approach, the authors turn to the "macrosocial perspective." This perspective suggests that the "access" (to the communication system by users), "bias" (within the industry that favors certain content or use types for the system) and "control" (embedded in the system's structure that allows for external groups such as the competition or regulation to exert control over the system) mechanisms are influential in defining the characteristics of the communication system and its users. In essence, social and technological factors help guide communication system development, which in turn decides how the system will be used and what the subsequent social and technological factors may be in reshaping the system and its uses.

Hence, faster and better access demand, advances in digital and fiber optics transmission technology, competition from the wireless phone industries, and government deregulation, all helped push the telephone industry to transform itself from yesterday's "plain old telephone service" (POTS) into the "pretty amazing new stuff" (PANS) of today. In other words, the expanded telephony services now can utilize such digital transmission systems as Integrated Services Digital Network (ISDN), Asynchronous Transfer Mode (ATM), or Asymmetrical Digital Subscriber Line (ADSL) to provide high-speed transmission of voice, data, and video via an "intelligent" value-added network.

Government deregulation of the telecommunication industry also helped telephone companies to acquire and provide cable TV and wireless phone service operators in addition to being Internet service providers. In face of the increased competition from the Internet telephony industry (that can either bypass local or long-distance telephone system) and computer (or desktop) videoconferencing, we may yet see another round of telephony reinvention in lieu of continuous convergence between computer-based, video broadcast, wireless communication and telephone technologies. It is entirely possible that the future of telephony services will evolve around Internet-based telecommunications services, as the Internet network structure is one that embraces open-hierarchy, flexibility and versatility to achieve high efficiency.

Audiotext Communication

Neuendorf, Atkin, and Jeffres (chap. 6, this volume) address an interesting technology "reinvention" phenomenon where a regular telephone service finds an innovative new use—audiotext service—one that opens a different venue for interpersonal communication and hence a new set of social implications. Fundamentally, this service enables a user to dial a telephone number with either an 800 or a 900 area code prefix to express their opinions, thoughts, and feelings as well as solicit similar information or ideas from others (that are employed to provide such interpersonal communication services). Examples of this reinvented use of a telephone service range from telephone polling, psychic chat lines, sports trivia to dial-a-porn and dial-a-prayer.

From a theoretical perspective, the authors introduce the concept of "bridge technology" to describe audiotext service, suggesting that an audiotext service bridges a gap between telephony and the Internet. Although both the telephone and the Internet services are interactive in nature, audiotext service adds an odd touch of interpersonal communication and physical intimacy that a regular telephone communication with friends and families and the Internet chat may not reveal.

Electronic Mail Communication

Walther and Boyd (chap. 7, this volume) introduce us to the world of "virtual communication" that is intended to comfort, heal, and advise those in need of such consolation. This type of "non-real time" delayed communication has succeeded to form interpersonal communication networks resembling social support networks and shaping interpersonal relationships. Such a virtual interpersonal communication channel could be as effective as face-to-face (FtF) communication for various purposes.

As social support groups typically function to provide informational support, esteem support, and social network support through dyadic and group settings, the drawbacks stemming from these communication settings—such as "mismatching," "dependency," "cost of giving" and "cost of receiving"—seem to lessen with virtual communication settings. This is due to the fact that computer-mediated social support groups reflect "weak tie" social relationships between their group members. Within this weak tie social network, concerns over interpersonal communication factors such as "stigma management" are minimal compared to a "strong tie" interpersonal social network.

Hence, the major factors that help solidify the role of the Internet as an effective interpersonal communication channel for social support could be both technical as well as social. For instance, from the technical perspective, the delayed communication allows the individuals who visit the site time to think about how best to respond. From the social perspective, the anonymity between individuals communicating online allows more free exchange of inner thoughts and feelings as well as a more diversified number of individuals to participate in such social support networks. Virtual social support networks have thus far been proven as a good alternative to face-to-face social support networks for some.

TECHNOLOGY AND ORGANIZATIONAL COMMUNICATION

Historically, the corporate world often was the first civilian sector to adopt new communication technologies, before these technologies were deemed viable in the consumer market. Adoption of new communication technologies was seen as the major means for achieving office automation—a cost-cutting and cost-efficient way for corporate America to help facilitate their "downsizing" strategies (e.g., Atkin, 1998). This became a widespread trend in the 1980s. Large-scale adoption of computer-based communication technology utilizing multiple networking channels greatly improved communication efficiency and worker productivity; these techniques range from the local office phone systems (e.g., private branch exchange), workstation (e.g., personal computers), and local area networks (e.g., networked workstations) to wide area networks (e.g., private satellite network computer links). Chapters 8 through 10 address corporate communication networks from an intra-organizational perspective via a local area network as well as interorganization via a wide area network and organization-to-consumer, via an electronic commerce context.

Intraorganizational Communication

Rice and Webster (chap. 8, this volume) introduce us to a comprehensive body of literature that lays the foundation for explaining what kinds of new communication technology corporations adopt and why they adopt them as well as how they use them. The chapter carefully distinguishes the concepts of adopters, adoption, use types, and levels of adoption. Such differences are crucial in explaining why certain new communication technologies are adopted by some corporations, but not others, and why the same technologies adopted by corporations are used differently—either for their functionalities or degrees of usage. To further explicate this complex phenomenon of how technologies are used for enhanced organizational communication, the authors also illustrate how a corporation can "reinvent" an adopted technology and integrate it with an existing or newly adopted communication technology "platform" to optimize the efficiency of its uses.

This chapter further explains the adoption, use patterns, and statistics for each of the most commonly adopted intraorganizational technologies, including e-mail, voice mail, desktop conferencing, fax, Internet, and Intranet as well as "integrated communication media." The adoption of integrated communication media, for instance, can involve the wired and wireless technologies such as the usage of both an office computer and a palm-sized computer or even a cellular phone. Other examples can include the usage of "groupware" such as Lotus Notes, which combines network sharable e-mail as well as other data communication utilities. The chapter closes with a discussion of organizational communication theories or constructs developed around adoption of innovations within the following frameworks: individual influences, task influences, contextual influences, social influences, organizational influences and perceived characteristics (of the technology).

Interorganization Communication

Steinfield (chap. 9, this volume) looks at the theories and practice of new communication adoption in an inter-organizational communication context. To achieve a competitive edge in the marketplace, a company must be able to effectively communicate with all other structurally interdependent companies, such as suppliers and distributors that help contribute to its market success. The major theoretical explanations behind why and how a company chooses to adopt certain communication technologies include whether the perceived characteristics of the new media can achieve the desired levels of "social presence" deemed desirable for different intercorporate communication tasks (e.g., Short, Williams, & Christie, 1976). Moreover, social influences—transferred either through intraorganizational peers or interorganizational networks—serve as additional organizational forces for bringing about technology adoption and uses.

    But such adoption and uses are also dependent on whether a critical mass of peer organizations have also become adopters; without them, a company can't take advantage of the networking benefits it intends to enjoy. In essence, "virtual" enterprises that heavily rely on external networking of both "upstream" and "downstream" modular units—comprised of interdependent companies—to help produce or distribute goods, are increasing in number. This type of virtual organization brings forth an "electronic market" or "electronic commerce" phenomenon, where the Internet plays an increasingly important role in carrying out commercial transactions between organizations. Such a "web-based" interorganizational communication structure may produce different economic outcomes, which may, in turn, help "revolutionize" the traditional industrial structure for companies.

Electronic Commerce

Another example of this "electronic market" is the fast-growing direct-to-consumer electronic shopping channels offered either offline or online. Grant and Meadows (chap. 10, this volume) look at this electronic commerce phenomenon by examining the two common modes of electronic commerce—shopping via a TV channel and the Internet. At present, shopping via a TV channel is a $5 billion industry—representing a fraction of the $150 billion plus catalogue industry. By the same token, the online shopping revenue in 1999—approximately $30 billion—also represents only 1% of the U.S. consumer spending of the same year. Even though the dollar statistics appear to be small at present for direct-to-consumer electronic commerce, the growth potential for this marketplace is nonetheless virtually unlimited.

This chapter differentiates the nature of these two types of electronic shopping from a theoretical as well as empirical point of view. Although shopping via a television channel is considered a technically noninteractive experience, there are often human interactions involved when the consumer orders a product promoted on TV. By contrast, online shopping is considered a technically "interactive" experience, whereby a consumer can directly order the product desired without any human interaction. Another form of interactive shopping is done via a two-way interactive digital TV system, one that will allow TV viewers to click on the shopping icon on screen to directly order products seen in a program or a commercial in real time. This shopping venue is regarded as a "brave" new marketing channel that will be developed alongside the implementation of a digital television broadcast system in the United States.

The major consumer motivations behind TV versus online shopping channel use appear to parallel each other, for the most part. This assertion is drawn from past research findings (Lin, 1999) that indicate the parallel between general TV viewing and online use motives (although specific content use motives may differ). It appears that the motives for both TV and online shopping channel use are rooted in hedonic as well as utilitarian motives, as both types of shopping activities can be seen as ritual events that contain an instrumental dimension. Although TV shopping provides a parasocial interaction and viewers/shoppers may eventually develop a media dependency relationship with the TV medium, online shopping channels also intend to emulate these user/consumer relationships by using product-spokesperson chat rooms and other tactics. In this way, the online shopping experience goes beyond organizational commercial communication to embody a form of mass communication as well.

TECHNOLOGY AND MASS COMMUNICATION

Mass media traditionally have been the main source for keeping society informed and entertained at the same time. Although much about the mass media is "old" when it comes to content and genre offerings, much else can also be considered "new" if one looks at the technologies that deliver these media offerings. The essence of the "newness" of these technologies is in their capabilities to allow better audience control of their media use choice and environment, broaden the audience's cultural scope through media content-sharing across the globe and provide the audience an "interactive" TV viewing experience. Chapters 11 through 13 discuss the mass communication technologies, which are also rapidly converging, with an emphasis on these changing media roles.

Home Video Technology

As different media technologies converge, audience choices also widen. Yet, the origins of audience choice and hence audience control over their media use environment afforded by media technology can be found in the advent of the videocassette recorder (VCR). Rubin and Eyal (chap. 14, this volume) provide a thorough examination of how and why the VCR is used at home by the audience and the social impacts the VCR has created.

First and foremost, the VCR is utilized to help the audience schedule and thus program their TV viewing lineups and video playback preferences. The VCR's technical capability to record and replay a TV program or a prerecorded video frees the audience from the constraints of TV program schedules and allows them to enjoy a wider range of program and video offerings. The practice of time-shifting, prerecorded tape playback, and home video library building has by now become commonplace.

The social effects of VCR use are also multifaceted. It appears that, although there are no verifiable cultivation effects here, video viewing reinforces the existing cultivated beliefs. The VCR's role in family viewing illustrates that the VCR can be a conduit for family communication via negotiating time-shifting and video choice preferences, a tool for enforcing "parental mediation" of children's TV viewing and a centerpiece for planning social gatherings. By contrast, VCRs are primarily utilized for video playback in countries that either have limited TV program fare—or heavily censored media systems—to broaden their viewing choices or "circumvent" cultural and political prohibitions against "undesirable" viewing content.

Satellite Communication

One of the most marvelous inventions in the 20th century is satellite communication. No means of communication is more inclusive when it comes to reaching the maximal number of "sites" covered within the "footprint" of the satellite networks around the world. Hence, satellite communication is the most natural choice when it comes to delivering the traditionally labeled "mass communication" contexts such as news, educational, and entertainment content aimed at the masses.

Straubhaar (chap. 13, this volume) examines the impact of the global effects stemming from the distribution of international satellite television programs. The chapter traces the origins and development of satellite TV program genres and flows around the world. As media imperialism is considered a direct outcome of an imbalanced flow of media content between economically developed and underdeveloped nations, a "dependency" relationship is said to exist from the latter to the former economically, culturally, and politically as well. Nonetheless, this type of "dependency" relationship between these two groups of nations seems to have been altered over time, in the case of "cultural dependency."

In essence, even though industrialized nations such as the United States have successfully developed television programs for global satellite distribution, regional and national satellite networks have also flourished to both create culturally and/or linguistically based television networks and programs in recent years. This development signifies a desire from economically underdeveloped nations to take hold of and thus reinforce their own cultural identity in light of an ever growing flow of foreign cultural products. The end result of this parallel development is a phenomenon of "asymmetric interdependency," whereby the Western styles of media management models and program genres are often emulated and adapted to create regionally or locally appealing cultural products.

High Definition Television

Dupagne (chap. 12, this volume) illustrates that high definition TV (HDTV), first demonstrated in the United States in 1981, was designed to upgrade the U. S. TV transmission standard of 525 lines per second resolution to 1,080 lines and to enlarge the screen size ration from 4:3 to 16:9. After years of intense competition between different players from the United States, Europe, and Japan—each of which developed their unique technical standards—the FCC finally approved a digital television (DTV) standard that can accommodate the carriage of one single HDTV signal or multiple standard-definition TV (SDTV) within a 6 Mhz bandwidth. Subsequently, the FCC issued a schedule for DTV broadcast compliance for all television stations in the United States, designating the year 2006 as the time to phase out the current analog TV broadcast system.

The chapter reviews quantitative HDTV-related consumer studies conducted between 1987 and 1998. These studies found that although just over half of the public surveyed had heard something about HDTV or digital TV in 1998, the participants in lab tests demonstrated only a minor preference in HDTV over the current TV standard in the areas of screen size and shape as well as picture and color resolution. By the same token, the affective results (e.g., emotional responses toward the program content) are also mixed. The major broadcast networks, well aware of the low consumer interest in purchasing new digital TV sets, also choose to stall any regular broadcast of DTV signals. Hence, the speculation game begins, not in terms of if but when and how fast the diffusion of digital TV sets will occur, in light of the FCC's DTV broadcast implementation deadlines and the high costs associated with these sets.

TECHNOLOGY AND INTERMEDIA COMMUNICATION

It is clear that, even though the Internet and its World Wide Web platform remains a very "young" public communication medium, it has already been transformed into a "communication appliance." The main reasons why the Internet has quickly become a communication appliance is due to its ability to allow users to send and receive messages and information or data, retrieve and store messages and information or data, and pursue mass media entertainment content (Lin, 1999). In other words, the Internet is an embodiment of an intermedia channel that is capable of performing interpersonal, organizational, and mass communication objectives.

Another type of intermedia medium examined in this volume involves virtual reality (VR; Rheingold, 1991). By definition, VR communication refers to projecting a mediated embodiment of a human body (or a virtual body) into a digitally constructed sociophysical reality to feel, sense, act, and react toward objects, events, and other virtual bodies encountered in that setting. Of interest here are the communication patterns manifested by these virtual communication experiences, as such experience is artificially created by the computer-human interface and interaction in a multimedia animated 3-D environment. Hence, a VR communication experience can encompass any digitally constructed communication settings designed for performing any intended communication tasks. VR communication applications have thus been adopted by corporate America, the U.S. military, scientific community, and the video media industry for training, research, and entertainment purposes. However, the social scientific effects of VR communication remain an untamed communication research frontier to date.

Internet Communication: An Overview

Klopfenstein (chap. 14, this volume) visits the Internet phenomenon from a historical, technical, diffusion, and scientific research point of view. Born first as a cold-war technology innovation, the Internet grew into a scientific research tool for universities and research institutions and then was reshaped into a consumer-oriented mediated communication medium. Once the personal computer diffusion in American homes hit the critical mass around 1997, the use of the Internet—especially the World Wide Web platform—also started to spread, following the proliferation of Internet service providers (ISPs). With the popularity of web portal services such as Yahoo and the success of such ISPs as America Online, advertisers also started to launch online marketing and shopping—making e-commerce the newest corporate marketing frontier.

Internet users still tend to be more upscale and younger but their demographic profile is moderating to include average middle-class families and middle-income households; it is also reaching younger generations, who "grow up" with computers and the Internet at school. In fact, it is predicted that by year 2002, nearly half of all children ages 1 through 12 will be online. At present, the majority of the Internet users have some college education and are males, although the gender gap is fast vanishing.

The major problems facing Internet use measurement remain the lack of a standardized scientifically valid and reliable methodology that can accurately assess online use activities and patterns of all online users. Without a standard Internet use measurement methodology, it is difficult for corporate America to closely monitor whether their online marketing endeavors are worth the effort. It also makes setting online advertising rates a less-than-scientific process, compared to the ways advertising rates are set for traditional mass media outlets. The still nascent social scientific research outputs on such fundamental questions as Internet use motives (e.g., Lin, 1999), for instance, also make the infantile Internet medium—albeit a strapping adolescent—remain a little understood medium of information, entertainment, communication, and commerce.

Internet Communication Motives and Uses

With the Internet medium sweeping across the information-age landscape like a massive storm, reaching users of diverse demographic backgrounds, the questions of why users access the Internet and what they do with it remain largely unanswered. As some researchers have adopted the uses and gratifications perspective to study these questions, the existing literature does indicate that the Internet use motives have been found to parallel television use motives and gratifications to a large extent (e.g., Lin, 1999). This suggests that the uses and gratifications perspective—a proven theory for explaining media use motives and predicting media use behavior—can also be a valid theory for studying Internet use motives, gratifications and behaviors.

Charney and Greenberg (chap. 15, this volume) set out to explore the variables that are predictive of online uses and gratifications. The online use aspects explained (by predictor variables) include the amount of time spent online and the reasons for "surfing" the Internet as well as frustrations with online use. Similarly, the online use gratifications dimensions examined include surveillance, diversion/entertainment, peer identity, good feelings (about oneself), communications (to stay in touch), sights and sounds (of visual elements), and career-related site use. These dimensions encompass both psychological as well as physiological gratifications in addition to cognitive learning. The overall study findings suggest that most users do not yet spend a lot of time online on a daily basis. As the reasons for online use differ, so do the online use frustration levels. Most interestingly, online use is perceived as best-equipped to provide entertainment or diversion gratification instead of the much ballyhooed "information utility"—a finding nevertheless consistent with existing literature.

Virtual Reality

Biocca and Nowak (chap. 16, this volume) challenge readers to comprehend how they can use the human body as a communication medium in a virtual communication environment. This mediated communication environment represents an interface between computers, visual display technology, and an animated "human body" reflective of (and controlled by) computer-encoded human senses and motor actions. In essence, the human body is "reincarnated" in the form of a mediated embodiment or a "virtual body" that "intends" to act, react, and thus communicate in a digitally constructed VR system that can project various physical settings, physical activities, or physical presence of various objects and events.

This virtual body, also called an *avatar*, is a digital representation of a person that can, in a networked immersive VR system, perform actions and motions that extend beyond "earthly physical restraints" such as flying. One of the most intriguing questions to communication researchers here involves how the differences in the appearance of virtual body types may communicate different symbolic meanings about the persons "hiding" inside of those virtual bodies. For instance, conceptualizing the virtual body as a social construction, we once expected that it can play roles freely as a social being and thus escape from gender and class identities or limitations. Research findings nevertheless discovered that, when virtual bodies meet in VR, aspects like gender and race continue to be attributes that interaction partners intend to assess from each other. Another question of intense research interest is how the morphology of the virtual body can lead to intersensory conflicts, for an individual, when they "reenter" the physical environment from the virtual environment.

At this nascent stage of VR communication research, as there are a number of different forms of VR immersiveness, a number of technical design and system platform issues remain unresolved. Nonetheless, the human-computer interaction in a virtual reality world offers us many mysteries and clues concerning how communication cues—exchanged between humanoid virtual bodies—can help humans (re)interpret the meanings of human communication outside of the physical constraints of a physical world. VR communication between virtual bodies then represents a form of mediated communication that can help in understanding the meanings of co-presence accompanying a human-to-human and human-to-artificial intelligence interaction. It also opens the door to further psycho-physiological research on the virtual body communication experience.

THEORETICAL SYNTHESIS AND RESEARCH IMPLICATIONS

The final chapter of this book endeavors to synthesize the various theoretical perspectives and applications and propose a research paradigm for communication and information technology adoption and uses. In particular, this research paradigm illustrates an open hierarchical and horizontally integrated model that links micro-system factors to macro-system factors. The paradigm components include systems, technology, audience, social, adoption, and use factors.

As the chapter conceptually defines each of these factors and their interrelationships, it also provides a list of theories and constructs as proposed theoretical foundations to study each factor. These interrelationships between factors represent critical theoretical links that enable the paradigm to form a dynamic interactive system where each factor is dependent on each other for input, output, and feedback at varying degrees. The paradigm's emphasis on interdependence is formulated to affirm the notion that communication is a social behavior that is facilitated by the adoption and uses of communication technology.

The chapter then reviews each theory or construct and their respective empirical evidence to demonstrate each's theoretical vigor in

conjunction with their study subject. It closes with a discussion of the
need for social science theories to keep pace with technology innovation
and diffusion, by exploring the mechanisms for generating theories.
Although research implications for each of the theories and constructs
included in the research paradigm are explicated, potential obstacles for
future-oriented communication technology research are also explored.

REFERENCES

Andersen, P. B. (1986). Semiotics and informatics: Computers as media.
In P. Ingversen, L. Kajberg, & A. M. Peitersen (Eds.), *Information
technology and information use. Towards a unified view of informa-
tion and information technology* (pp. 64-97). London: Taylor
Graham.
Atkin, D. J. (1998). Local and long distance telephony. In A. E. Grant &
J. Meadows (Eds.), *Communication technology update* (pp. 329-
340). Boston, MA: Focal Press.
Aufderheide, P. (1999). *Communication policy and the public interest:
The Telecommunications Act of 1996.* New York: Guilford.
Forrest, J. (2000). Communication networks for the new millennium.
Intermedia, 28, 24-28.
Lin, C. A. (1999). Online-service adoption likelihood. *Journal of
Advertising Research, 39,* 79-89.
Lin, C. A. (2000a). *Programming localism via online broadcasting*
(Research report). National Assocation of Broadcasters,
Washington, DC.
Lin, C. A. (2000b). Satellite communication. In A. E. Grant & J.
Meadows (Eds.), *Communication technology update* (7th ed., pp.
223-233). Boston, MA: Focal Press.
McLuhan, M. (1962). *The Gutenberg galaxy: The making of typographic
man.* Toronto: University of Toronto Press.
Pelton, J. N. (2000). *E-sphere: The rise of the world-wide mind.* Westport,
CT: Quorum Books.
Rheingold, H. (1991). *Virtual reality.* New York: Touchstone.
Short, J., Williams, E., & Christie, B. (1976). *The social psychology of
telecommunications.* London: Wiley.
Williams, R. (1974). *Television, technology and cultural form.* New York:
Schocken Books.

2

Convergence Across Media

David J. Atkin
Cleveland State University

A NEW FERMENT IN THE FIELD

Much as been written about the emerging information society, where press accounts describe a society in transition at several levels (e.g., Stipp, 1998; Williams, 1988). As Rogers (chap. 3, this volume) outlines, labor-intensive smokestack industries are gradually giving way to a computer-literate workforce equipped with wired and wireless communication channels. By one measure, America has been in the information age since 1991. That was the first year that companies spent more on computing and communications—the "capital goods of the new era"—than on industrial, mining, farming, and construction machines (Stewart, 1994, p. 70).[1]

At the heart of this ongoing media-information revolution now lies the Internet, which has crystallized the nation's attention on media convergence. The very year that Web (hypertext) applications were introduced on the Internet, Vice President Al Gore jumped on the information technology bandwagon by unveiling plans to remove regulatory barriers between voice, video, and data providers (IITF, 1993). These measures

---

[1]According to economist Mark Porat's (1977) analysis, America was in an information society as early as 1952—the year when services accounted for the plurality of American economic output.

were largely incorporated into the highly deregulatory Telecommunications Act of 1996, discussed later.

As this example illustrates, politicians and civic leaders regard the Internet as the potential "Holy Grail" media application, unifying the previously disparate realms of voice, video, and data communication. President Bill Clinton, for instance, articulated a national goal that every high school student know how to log onto the Internet before graduation. Others (Stoll, 1995) are less sanguine about the Internet's staying power and social significance, questioning whether it simply might be a more technologically savvy reincarnation of the 1970s CB radio fad.

Along those lines, naysayers can point to periodic diffusion lags that accompany the introduction of new communication technologies. As Biocca (1993) noted, after a series of "false starts" in which an "information revolution" and "wired city" were proclaimed, the consumption of personal computers increased by approximately 900% during the 1980s. But, even though roughly half of U.S. homes now have a computer, fewer than two thirds of these users receive an online service that might facilitate e-mail. And as early failures were widely publicized (e.g., Booker, 1988)—and even heralded as the death of online computing—the continuing growth of the Internet provides contrary evidence to these naysayers.

It remains to be seen whether or not the Internet proves to be the next CB fad or the next revolution in media, on a scale with television, the telephone, or some combination of the two. What is clear, however, is that changes in technology, policy, and audience receptivity to new media all point to the day when previously distinct applications are all delivered through the same wire or wireless channels.

The dawning of the new millennium has also ushered in the longest economic expansion in U.S. history, going on 10 years without a recession. As this "new" economy takes root, with a rare dual blessing of low (4%) unemployment and minimal inflation, economists give much of the credit of this prosperity to increases in production efficiency wrought by communication technologies (e.g., e-mail; see chapters by Rice and Webster, chap. 7, as well as Steinfield, chap. 8).

As we approach the dawn of the digital television revolution, the convergence between television and online services continues along technological as well as content dimensions. Only time will tell whether that wire is ultimately controlled by broadcasters, cablecasters, telephone companies, newspapers, computer companies, or someone else. But the chapters in this volume can enhance understanding of how audiences assimilate these new media applications into their present patterns of work and leisure, factors driven by convergence on several levels.

This chapter explores the dimensions of this ongoing convergence of communication technologies. I focus, in particular, on covergence in the following realms: technology, regulation, marketing, function, economics, culture and research. In the context of reviewing the latter, I outline how this book investigates emerging diffusion patterns for various communication technology innovations (Rogers, 1995). I focus on the American experience because the United States represents the most "wired," computer-literate nation in the world.

TECHNOLOGICAL CONVERGENCE

As Lin's (chap. 1, this volume) overview suggests, the Internet perhaps represents the clearest, most pervasive example of a medium that consolidates voice, video, and data functions.[2] The Internet now boasts more than 60 million users in the United States, who account for 60% of the global online population. Forming the heart of that network, computer-mediated communication (CMC) services enhance one's ability to gather, process, filter, organize and disseminate information. In 1997, Anderson Consulting defined the medium as a

> hypertext multimedia system that links computer resources around the world. Innovative uses of the Internet/Web and online services involve interactive databases, three-dimensional graphics, virtual reality, animation, audio/video, Java applets, and other emerging technologies. (p. 173)

Only a few years earlier, nationwide interest in this emerging "information superhighway" was spurred by Executive and Legislative branch initiatives to remove regulatory barriers between voice, video, and data providers, as mentioned earlier. These measures were designed to facilitate a nationwide integrated systems digital network—the Internet (IITF, 1993; Telecommunication Act of 1996). The Internet is arguably the most significant development in communications to emerge in the past century, carrying a promise to revolutionize workplace, education, politics, and leisure pursuits (e.g., Kiesler, 1997).

Few could dispute that the Internet's growth rate has been meteoric. As Klopfenstein (chap. 14, this volume) details, the Internet has grown dramatically since 1995, when 8 million Americans were using their computers to telecommute, and more than 20 million accessed the Internet each week (Lewis, 1995). As of early 1999, there were an estimated 140 million Internet users worldwide, as the medium experienced a

---

[2]Note that other converging media functions are also explored in this volume, including television (Dupagne, chap. 10) and the telephone (Bates et al., chap 4; Neuendorf et al., chap. 5).

100% annual growth rate since 1989 (or 1,000% during the 1990s!). Roughly 75% of that activity was World Wide Web traffic—a network of hypertext links that did not even exist in the early 1990s. Despite the recent explosion of market research on the Web (e.g., Anderson Consulting, 1997), the understanding of psychological factors that lead to its adoption and use remains incomplete.

MARKETING CONVERGENCE

Even with the potential for revenue growth on the Internet, it seems that advertisers remain perplexed about how to reach consumers in this new medium (Lin, 2001). As a medium presently characterized by limited reach, available to only one third of U.S. households, the Internet has yet to take off as an advertising medium. Market research suggests that most online ad messages are rarely accessed, sporting a click-through rate of 1% or lower (Andres, 1998). Stipp (1998) concluded that exotic "electronic superhighway" conceptions of the Internet are being replaced by a new paradigm: "the 'old' media will converge with the computer" (p. 16). Television, for example, will not disappear as an advertising medium; it will be enhanced by computer functions.

Even so, as researchers (Krugman, 1985) note, these viewers are nevertheless more desirable targets for advertisers, owing to their greater exposure opportunities and high levels of purchasing power. As a study commissioned by Ted Turner confirms, this upscale subscriber profile reinforces the justification for higher cable cost per thousand (CPM) rates due to increased reach (see Eighmey, 1997).

In the beginning of the new millennium, advertisers are looking for the releasing touch that will help them harness the potential of the Internet. This nascent medium's capability encompasses a continuum, ranging from interactive information retrieval, to one-on-one interpersonal, group, and mass communication modes. As Lin (1999) noted, television allows the audience to gaze into a "visual window" on the world initially, but the Internet enables them to reach beyond that window threshold and communicate with the world within.

It is clear that the unique nature of the Internet, as a multifaceted communication medium, may have far-reaching political, economic, and social consequences for society. Even though the marketing applications accompanying Internet diffusion present one of the best opportunities for communication research to help inform public and private policy decisions in recent years, remarkably little work has explored this phenomenon, in either theoretical or empirical terms (Atkin, Jeffres, & Neuendorf, 1998; Ducoffe, 1996; Eighmey, 1997; Lin, 1999; Morris & Ogan 1996).

According to market studies, the Web is an excellent medium for conducting a successful one-to-one marketing campaign, via such vehicles as personalization, push, interactivity, telephone, virtual community and e-mail (e.g., Allen, Kania, & Yaeckel, 1998). Perhaps the most widely reported Internet study, conducted at Carnegie Mellon, suggests that users become lonely and socially withdrawn (Kiesler, 1997). Yet, as Perse and Dunn (1998) noted, a focus on social impacts may be "premature" until we understand how and why people use computer technology.

Pioneer online information services were first marketed under the rubric of videotext during the mid-1980s. More recent "compunications" applications involve such features as home utility management (e.g., meter reading), telephone, cable television, pay-per-view, video libraries, radio programs and electronic newspapers, magazines, and books to serve users (Lin, 1994b).

Amidst the heady "blue sky" predictions offered by Gore and others, it must be recalled that pioneer online information services such as videotext generated little interest during the 1980s (e.g., Booker, 1988; Rice, 1984). Only a relatively small, upscale segment of the population adopted videotext services in communities where it was offered on an experimental basis (Ettema, 1989), whereas Knight Ridder's Viewtron business collapsed before decade's end. This latter failure, combined with the removal of Times-Mirror's Gateway service in 1986 struck some as a death knell for electronic text modalities. Videotext's rocky start has perplexed academic and industry commentators (e.g., Atkin & LaRose, 1994), especially when one considers success stories in the United Kingdom and France (Greenberg & Lin, 1988).

In that regard, the slow growth of online services in the United States is less related to diffusion lag and more a function of marketing or investment lag (Ettema, 1989). Thus, only time will tell whether popular entertainment and news services represent "trigger" innovations (Dozier, Valente, & Severn, 1986) that can stimulate the adoption of more advanced information services (Jeffres & Atkin, 1996). In gaining a better understanding of this adoption dynamic, it is useful to assess why such services have generated so little interest in some contexts (e.g., advertising), while enjoying great success in others (e.g., e-mail, surfing; see Charney & Greenberg, chap. 15, this volume).

REGULATORY CONVERGENCE

As Grant and Meadows (1998) noted in their "umbrella model of communication," the origins of separate media sectors can be found in technical and regulatory domains. As for global deregulation of state-supported media monopolies and protectionist policies (Pelton, 1996), it seems that many nations are following America's lead in opening up their media systems to competition (see Straubhaar, chap. 11, this volume). For instance, telephony and broadcasting in the United States were treated under separate titles of the Communication Act of 1934 (Titles 2 and 3, respectively). Not even envisaged at that time, cable was finally acknowledged by Congress as a distinctive medium under the 1984 Cable Act, which also upheld FCC prohibitions on telco-cable crossownership (Pub. L. No. 98-594, 98 Stat 2785 S. 533[b], 1984).

As technology enabled a merging of these functions, Congress amended several provisions of the Communications Act of 1934 to allow broadcasters, telecommunications providers, and cable companies to compete against each other in the Telecommunications Act of 1996 (Pub. L. No. 104-104, Section 292, 119 Stat. 56). Thus, as Collette (1998) concluded, "we have witnessed an evolutionary shift in regulatory thinking, one culminating in a final leap meant to accommodate competition and to lessen the technological barriers encountered by competitors wishing to provide one type of service" (p. 4).

Yet now, in the early years succeeding the act's passage, Congress remains perplexed by the lack of cross-media competition in telecommunications industries and some are even seeking a reconsideration of the Act. Rather than spurring expected dividends in job growth, improved service, and lower rates via competition, the deregulatory Telecommunication Act has been widely attacked in the press as anticompetitive (e.g., Lipin, 1997).

Preliminary analyses (Atkin, 1999) document a sharp increase in industry consolidation in cable since the Act was passed, as the top four exhibitors (e.g., TCI) now command nearly three fifths of subscribership, and the top pay channels (e.g., HBO) control an even steeper (80%) market share. Local telephony has been characterized by record merger and acquisition activity, as five of the seven Baby Bells are combining forces (e.g., Ameritech and SBC Communications). Not to be outdone, long distance players have also been rapidly combining forces with other industry segments, including cable (AT&T-TCI) and long distance (GTE-Bell Atlantic; MCI-World Com and MCI-Sprint). In addition, cellular telephone giant AirTouch Communications is moving to acquire a unit of U.S. West. And all of these mergers were dwarfed by AOL's merger with Time-Warner, the largest merger in history.

That same analysis documented efforts by cable companies to pull back from telephone operations, and similar measures by telcos to scale down their video dialtone operations. McChesney's (1997) volume is representative of several critical analyses concluding that major media/telecommunication firms are more interested in cooperating than competing. As Atkin (1999) noted:

> A cynic might conclude that these players knew full well of the infeasibility of cross-media competition on the eve of the Act's passage, but sought to play up prospects for competition as a ruse to encourage government elimination of longstanding public-interest based ownership limitations and regulations. (p. 54)

Thus, although the convergence has yet to assume the form of active cross-media competition, the foundation for such an infrastructure can be found in enhanced merger activity and co-ventures such as MSNBC. The full range of these synergies, centered largely in telephony, is outlined by Bates et al. (chap. 4, this volume).

As technology continues to redefine market boundaries, it is important to consider Bill Gate's admonition that even IBM—once thought invincible—fell from grace after missing a few turns in the road. As he suggested in response to antitrust proceedings against Microsoft, now trying to leverage its market dominance in operating systems to capture the Web browser market, prospects for competition obviate the need for government regulation. Of course, it is easier to make such arguments when one is a monopolist, as Microsoft is in operating systems. What's different in the present Microsoft situation, however, is that the Internet enables the merging of voice, video and data applications about which programmers have dreamed for decades (e.g., Noll, 1994).

FUNCTIONAL CONVERGENCE

Just as the emerging media have evolved from separate domains, the literature addressing their adoption and influence is reflected in a pedagogy that is focused narrowly on entertainment media or information technology. But, as the major sections of this book underscore, ongoing technological change presages a convergence of applications in interpersonal and organizational as well as mass communication contexts. As Stipp (1998) maintained, in the few short years since the Web was conceived as a hypertext-based medium, popular conceptions of new media have changed dramatically.

No longer do we envision an inexorable progression toward ever more complex media, with all wires necessarily leading to a computer, per earlier prognostications (e.g., Negroponte, 1995). Today, electronic superhighway sounds oddly old-fashioned. The term has been replaced by a new, equally ubiquitous one: *convergence* (Stipp, 1998).

In this manner, computer technology may perhaps be used to enhance the functions of television—as with PC-TV's or TV-PCs—but no large scale revolution in media behaviors can be expected. But, just as television gradually challenged radio in the 1950s we can expect that technological change can yield market turbulence, and eventually a retrenchment, as new media niches evolve.

Even so, as Web services diffuse to the larger population, Internet promotions represent an opportune vehicle to foster market product or media promotions. Such an archetype is consistent with the Media Substitution Hypothesis, which suggests that the introduction of a new outlet encourages a restructuring in the way consumers view established media (e.g., Krugman 1985; Lin, 1994a).

This idea stems from Lasswell's (1948) early work, which foretold television's success in competition with radio for audiences, programming, and advertising revenues. Research on advertising, for instance, suggests that the arrival of new cable channels has displaced viewership of traditional TV viewing (Henke & Donohue, 1989; Lin, 1994a). Such a dynamic underscores the need to move beyond global media substitution conceptions and focus on specific (e.g., channel-specific) functional equivalence, as done in this volume.

In that regard, communication technologies are rapidly affecting the organizations and contexts in which students work and live. Meanwhile, the boundaries between print, broadcast, film, wire, and online media are blurring in editing systems that pool content and images—in print as well as video formats—to construct messages that may emerge in several forms (e.g., Baldwin, Steinfield, & McVoy, 1996; Straubhaar & LaRose, 1999).

For instance, as the gateways to a wide variety of new interactive services, phone, cable, and computer delivery systems are a major contributing factor to an understanding of attendance to 21st century information technologies. A key facet of this transition involves the blurring of distinctions between mass and telecommunication media, as Atkin and LaRose (1994) noted:

> Telephony and television . . . can no longer be associated exclusively with point-to-point audio or one-way mass media applications. Newly emerging audiotext systems (e.g., public announcement services providing entertainment or information services) and videotext reach mass audiences via the telephone network. Nor can we classify pay-per-view cable, video teleconferences, and video phones solely as mass communications media. Researchers must also contemplate future phone company entry into information services, continued development of high-capacity fiber distribution networks as well as electronic mail and end-to-end Integrated Services Digital Networks (ISDNs). (pp. 91-92)

Such changes, which allow for the delivery of voice, video, and data services through a single wire, suggest a need to reconceptualize diffusion and other theories in an ever-widening telematic domain. That these different distribution technologies are delivering each other's services blurs the technological and regulatory lines, which had been drawn so neatly for much of this century. It also reinforces the need for comparative analysis.

As Lin (1998) noted, concerns regarding this potential media substitution phenomenon have prompted expert predictions that online or PC-TV services could gradually displace the traditional ways that television services are received, due to their added interactive capabilities and highly targeted reach. These future market scenarios, although not completely speculative, seem to rest on one or both of the following assumptions: (a) television and online content is mutually substitutable, and (b) television-use motives are similar to online service use motives. Will McLuhan's aphorism, "The medium is the message," hold true in coming years? Now that technology is increasingly delivered through the same channel, currency of this observation may have passed with the 20th century.

It may be that audience motives for media-use decisions could be similar across both television and online media. However, despite their similarities, these motives are perceptually distinct from each other when actual use or adoption decisions are made. In other words, the perceptual links between the medium and audience motives for media use may dictate medium adoption choice. The question remains, however, as to what if any, Internet communication services might be considered as attractive applications that could encourage adoption among nonadopters and thus widen the medium's reach.

As the media content offerings on an online service emulate the characteristics of print and electronic media, several chapters in this volume address the extent to which audiences seek to gratify media-use needs with online service use. Moreover, as the audience's media use level and the breadth of home communication technology ownership both may compete for online access time, their interrelationships—such as the potential for functional displacement—could be indicative of one's likelihood of adopting online services.

CONVERGENCE OF RESEARCH TRADITIONS

Rogers (1995) noted that all innovations are not equivalent units, evidenced by the fact that some new products fail and others succeed; indeed, U.S. Department of Commerce estimates that 90% of all new products fail within 4 years of their release.

In the marketing literature, Dholakia, Mundorf, and Dholakia (1996) attributed the high rate of failure of media innovations to an overemphasis on supply-side forces, labeling it "The Field of Dreams approach: If we build it, they will come" (p. 3). Their own framework divides these applications into business and home domains, each of which is characterized by supply- and demand-side components. The authors further maintained that the demand-side of information technology in the home is the most commonly neglected component of that typology, which serves as the focus for their analysis.

Several volumes have investigated uses of new media generally, although most empirical analyses were done during the 1980s (e.g., Rice, 1984; Salvaggio & Bryant, 1989). A line of other work, extending to the present, has addressed uses of such individual media innovations as cable (Heeter & Greenberg, 1988), VCRs (Dobrow, 1990; Levy, 1989), virtual reality (Biocca & Levy, 1995), HDTV (Dupagne & Seel, 1998) and the Internet (Kiesler, 1997).

Although we agree that the literature has been prejudicial to the case of sweeping supply-side prognostications (e.g., the "Wired city"), it is likely that changing technologies have further merged these functions since Dholakia et al.'s (1996) initial research was presented at a 1993 marketing conference. In particular, the World Wide Web—a medium that did not even exist in 1990—grew to encompass 1.5 million Web sites by 1998. As Klopfenstein's chapter details, that number is expected to double as the new millennium begins, but even these projections may be conservative, as not all are successfully queried by Web search engines.

What is clear in this rapidly changing landscape is that the larger Internet merges many of the functions that had previously supported distinctions between home and business applications. For that reason, we consider both home and business domains for information technology—encompassing mass, organizational, and interpersonal applications—within the larger context of technology convergence.

More generally, the computerization of society can be seen as an inexorable evolution driven by market forces. The diffusion of innovations paradigm is arguably the most influential framework brought to bear in the study of technology adoption. At the level of individual users, diffusion research suggests that adoption of technological innovations is a function of one's innovativeness, or willingness to try new products (Rogers, 1995). Adopters of text and computer services, for instance, approximate the demographic profile of general "innovators," inasmuch as they are typically younger and better educated (e.g., Ettema, 1989).

Pioneering work on computer adoption addressed the compatibility between innovations and the existing values, past experiences and needs of potential users (e.g., Dutton, Rogers, & Jun, 1987). Research reveals that the adoption of new text services is related to the adoption of other innovations (Ettema, 1989), as experience with technology encourages adoption of new media (e.g., Dutton et al., 1987; LaRose & Atkin, 1992; Neuendorf, Atkin, & Jeffres, 1998).

Diffusion research suggests another type compatibility—involving a need for greater information—is related to the adoption of protypical online services (Ettema, 1989). To that we might add compatibility with beliefs or attitudes, as exemplified by the "lifestyle" explanation (Jeffres & Atkin, 1996; LaRose & Atkin, 1992). According to that perspective, true "innovators" would likely adopt any technology, without regard to its compatibility with one's past beliefs or technology uses. Market studies (e.g., Andres, 1998) point to innovation clusters (Rogers, 1986), whereby adoption of various high technology items is interrelated. In either case, adopters are more comfortable with new technologies, relative to non-adopters (Dutton et al, 1987; Neuendorf et al., 1998; Rogers, 1986).

Although diffusion research is typically applied to study an innovation in its early stages of diffusion, more mature media are often the subject of uses and gratifications research (see, e.g., Charney & Greenberg, chap. 15, this volume). The latter perspective suggests that different audience needs are associated with different media. Broadcast media, for instance, have been widely linked with entertainment needs, whereas newspapers primarily serve surveillance needs (e.g., Jeffres, 1994). However, although the literature on "receiver" needs, uses and gratifications is extensive, there is little parallel literature on "sender" needs—the extent to which people are fulfilled by sending messages and expressing themselves to others using existing channels or new technologies. When investigating "public goods" explanations of collaborative media use, Rafaeli and LaRose (1993) found that the diversity of content and the symmetry of exchange between participants were the most important predictors of bulletin board success. Surveillance needs met by newspapers seem most functionally similar to information services, as Lin (1998) found that users of newspapers had more favorable perceptions of computers. Heikkinen and Reese (1986) discovered that similar information needs predicted videotext adoption, whereas heavy television viewers were less likely to adopt videotext. Such needs are even more significant given that attitudinal variables (e.g., perceived benefits) were more predictive than demographics or media use patterns in explaining adoption of interactive telephone and cable services (LaRose & Atkin, 1988, 1992; O'Keefe & Sulanowski, 1995), as well as videotext (Reagan, 1987, 1989).

Given the crucial role that computer-based information services will play as part of an electronic newspaper and communication pathway, it is important to consider how background variables, media-use patterns, and perceived benefits shape user evaluations of online technology. As new media reach a certain "critical mass" of users, the value of being hooked up to their networks (e.g., for computing or electronic text) should increase. Most businesses have reached that "critical mass" of utility for information services. But the potential for home use remains unfilled. Further work is needed to address the human dimensions of technology adoption as international information grids expand their reach, and more home users come online.

ECONOMIC CONVERGENCE

As several futurists note, the ongoing convergence of telecommunication media defines a "communications" or "information" revolution that is based on collecting, storing, processing, and communicating information (e.g., Dizard, 1994; Williams, 1988). According to some estimates, more than half of American employees today are part of the "knowledge class" in an "information age" (Porat, 1977). In this emerging postindustrial society, communication is increasingly replacing transportation as the major means of connecting people. The energy core of this new social framework involves the new technologies of communication (Bell, 1976, 1980).

Pelton (1996) noted that this convergence is bringing about a new age of consolidation in information, communication and entertainment (ICE age). These various services help define a $4 trillion global ICE industry, spurred by changes in technology and deregulation, which presently accounts for $1 of every $12 spent worldwide.

This ferment in the communications industry can be seen in the recent spate of media mega-mergers. Even aside from the telecommunication deregulation reviewed earlier, mergers in the entertainment industry have focused the country's attention on media convergence, including Disney-Cap Cities and Time Warner (TW)-Turner, TCI-AT&T, and so on. But nowhere will the pace of economic growth be faster than the telecommunications field, which now accounts for one sixth of America's gross domestic product. In fact, the President's Council of Economic advisers recently noted that job offerings in telecommunication will increase from 3.5 million in 1994 to 4.5-5.5 million by 2003, as economic activity in that area doubles ("Gore stumps," 1994).

Those job offerings will extend beyond the natural offerings in computer design and repair, encompassing software innovation and computerized page layout for magazines and newspapers. Thus, even traditional media industries such as printing and publishing are expected to be among the top 20 career growth areas for the next century, along with advertising, film, and broadcasting industries (Berko, Brooks, & Spielvogel, 1995).

An extended research focus on how these media are transformed by technology is needed if communications programs are to meet the needs of students in America's increasingly "hi-tech" job market, where journalism and promotional communication professionals rely increasingly on the Internet as an information source. Moreover, America Online's (AOL) move to acquire an "upsteam" traditional media counterpart— Time Warner—attests to the perceived synergy between content providers and emerging Internet distribution channels.

For instance, commentators emphasize how the emerging information grid (Dizard, 1994; Jeffres & Atkin, 1996) deliver traditional media content (e.g., an unlimited menu of movies) and marketing services (e.g., ordering books and merchandise, making plane reservations, buying stock). These ongoing mergers—which reached a record level in the mid-1990s—reflect a belief that the new technologies will be successful in meeting people's needs in a variety of domains (Lipin, 1997). In particular, service providers like AOL realize that they will fail if they don't capture and provide content, which helps explain the company's willingness to acquire a much less profitable (but content savvy) Time Warner company. As the frenetic pace of these mergers suggests, we're only in the first stages of this new information age, and our present understanding of the uses and social impact of emerging media technologies remains incomplete.

CULTURAL CONVERGENCE

As the revolution in new media has unfolded, Hollywood has solidified its position as the center of global popular culture. The "media imperialism" that the United States enjoys throughout the world, including 90+% of world box-office receipts, now constitutes her largest export sector (e.g., "B.O. numbers," 1997; Waxman, 1998). Media product exports recently contributed $50 billion to an otherwise bleak balance of trade for the United States ("An entertaining trade," 1993). This expansion hence marks a new "communications" age for the United States—just as steam technology heralded the industrial age some 300 years ago. Although critics of one-sided media flows decry this dependency as a form of cultural hegemony, Straubhaar et al. (chap. 11, this volume) maintain that even Third World nations are beginning to successfully express themselves in the emerging "global media village."

As mentioned earlier, the strong growth in America's rapidly converging new and traditional media sectors played a key role in insulating her from the global economic displacements of the 1990s. This economic ferment accompanying the convergence of media is perhaps best illustrated by the film industry, once known as a job-scarce sector for communications graduates. But the number of jobs in the U.S. film industry jumped 50% from 1992 to 1995 alone, with film revenues approaching $40 billion in recent years and accounting for the majority of global box office (e.g., Vogel, 1995).

A consideration of cultural implications of America's global media power, as reflected in the literatures on "media imperialism" (e.g., Anokwa, Lin, & Salwen, in press) exceeds the scope of this book. But it is important to note that the United States has continued to dominate both the form and substance of media content. Some commentators (e.g., Dizard, 1994) even maintain that America's strength in media content was pivotal in helping her in the Cold War, as media were used to purvey such values as capitalism, democracy, and ethnic pluralism to strengthen her influence in the world. Now it can be said that this influence extends far beyond the traditional realms of news agencies, advertising, and television, to embrace such new media as the Internet. As Dizard's (1994) review suggests, America has been writing the story of the 21st century, as most global data traffic is in an ASCII format developed in the United States, and English remains the dominant language of telecommunications exchange.

All told, more than 70 countries are directly connected to this latest of American media progeny—the Internet—with more than 120 reachable via e-mail. (As Klopfenstein, chap. 14, details, foreign networks are expanding rapidly.) More than 40,000 networks are now connected, and a new one is connected every 30 minutes, facilitating 3,500,000 Internet hosts. At the turn of the millennium, the global user population was estimated in excess of 100 million, with annual growth rates approaching 15%.

Thus, after years of decline in several industrial sectors, America now turns to intellectual copyright (i.e., Hollywood) as a primary export commodity, serving the world's growing appetite for U.S. movies, TV series, news, and music. The production process itself has been transformed by technology, with such advances as "filmless" multimedia editing techniques. Traditional and emerging media now allow instant information access, storage and retrieval, embedded as they are within an increasingly automated technology environment.

CONCLUSION

Despite the ongoing ferment that new technologies present, the current level of scholarship addressing such new telecommunication technologies at most U.S. universities remains modest. Researchers (Atkin & Jeffres, 1998; Vincent, 1991) note that new media technology accounts for only a small portion (below 10%) of all research addressing telecommunication in communication journals. Most scholars choose to focus instead on traditional applications in broadcasting and telephony.

Even as the information superhighway comes to fruition, we have only a crude understanding of who uses the new media, why, and to what effect. In order to gain a better understanding of this dynamic, this volume seeks to profile Internet and other new media users in terms of social locators, media use habits, and attitudes toward technology adoption.

As Dizard (1994) noted, the emerging "communication grid" ultimately will allow for a wider range of communication behaviors than those originally envisioned. Researchers (Jeffres & Atkin, 1996) note that the traditional media audience activities (as receivers of messages) need to be separated from sender roles, and both of these need to be distinguished from consumer activities. Past work, in focusing on technologies and hardware interfaces, casts people into the role of "consumers" more than as participants in symbolic activity as senders and receivers of messages. Emerging telematic networks facilitate the convergence of three technology blocks: traditional mass media, the telephone, and the computer. Having evolved from separate domains—associated with a different set of delivery systems, skills, uses, and images among the general population—these media may now engender different uses for the "same" information grid. It is useful, then, to investigate new patterns of diffusion based on needs beyond those traditionally associated with conventional or emerging media.

This book revisits some of the earlier work on technology adoption, in the context of the broader domain of communication needs fulfilled by technology adoption and use. After investigating predictors of adoption for a range of emerging "infotainment" services, the focus is shifted away from hardware variables and toward those involving communication processes. Individual contributions will address perceptions of interest, perceived benefits, and pitfalls concerning the use of emerging communication technologies. Specific emphasis is placed on wire-based applications for sending and receiving information, along with uses of technologies for consumer purposes.

The chapters then discuss how these various communication technologies are converging and reshaping the ways information and entertainment content are produced and transmitted. Each chapter is designed to broaden the traditional study focus of the source-channel-receiver process, typically cast in sociocultural effects of mass media content, to include an "integrated communication paradigm." In this paradigm, the study of legislative directives, public policies, marketplace dynamics, and economic factors—which directly impact how information and entertainment content is constructed and distributed—is examined alongside the content and sociocultural effects of media. Such an integrated approach is necessitated by recent regulatory and technical changes in the communications field, including the Telecommunication Act of 1996, which have dramatically widened the range of potential players.

These various and several impediments to adoption are addressed in turn in a variety of different technology contexts in the chapters that follow.

REFERENCES

Allen, C., Kania, D., & Yaeckel, B. (1998). *Internet worldguide to one-to-one web marketing.* New York: Mecklermedia.

Andres, G. (1998, November 30). Wide open space: Internet advertising, just like its medium, is pushing boundaries. *The Wall Street Journal,* pp. A1, A6.

Anderson Consulting. (1997). *Technology forecast: 1997.* New York: Author.

Anokwa, K., Lin, C., & Salwen, M. (in press). *Mass media around the globe.* New York: Wadsworth.

Atkin, D. (1999). Video dialtone reconsidered: Prospects for competition in the wake of the Telecommunications Act of 1996. *Communication Law & Policy, 4,* 35-38.

Atkin, D., & Jeffres, L. W. (1998). An analysis of research article productivity by telecommunication scholars in the U.S. over the past decade. *Journal of the Association of Communication Administration, 27,* 18-29.

Atkin, D., Jeffres, L. W., & Neuendorf, K. (1998). Understanding Internet adoption as telecommunications behavior. *Journal of Broadcasting & Electronic Media, 42,* 475-490.

Atkin, D., & LaRose, R. (1994). An analysis of the information services adoption literature. In J. Hanson (Ed.), *Advances in telematics* (Vol. 2, pp. 91-110). Norwood, NJ: Ablex.

Baldwin, T., Steinfield, C., & McVoy, D. S. (1996). *Convergence.* Newbury Park, CA: Sage.

Bell, D. (1976). *The coming post-industrial society.* New York: Basic Books.

Bell, D. (1980). *The winding passage: Essays and sociological journeys, 1960-1980.* Cambridge, MA: Abt.

Berko, R., Brooks, M., & Spielvogel, J. C. (1995). *Pathways to careers in communication.* Annandale, VA: Speech Communication Association.

Biocca, F. (1993, August). *A human factors approach to the study of computer adoption.* Paper presented at the Association for Education in Journalism and Mass Communication, Kansas City.

Biocca, F., & Levy, M. (1995). *Communication in the age of virtual reality.* Mahwah, NJ: Lawrence Erlbaum Associates.

B.O. numbers sizzle. (1997, January 14). *Variety,* p. 1.

Booker, E. (1988). Consumer videotex: The perilous path. *Telephony, 214,* 30.

Collette, L. (1998, April). *Phony ambitions: Economic analysis of telco competitive entry into the multichannel video market after the 1996 Telcom Act.* Paper presented at the Broadcast Education Association, Las Vegas.

Dholakia, R., Mundorf, N., & Dholakia, N. (1996). *New infotainment technologies in the home: Demand side perspectives.* Mahwah, NJ: Lawrence Erlbaum Associates.

Dizard, W. (1994). *Old media, new media.* New York: Longman.

Dobrow, J. (1990). *Socio-cultural aspects of VCR use.* Hillsdale, NJ: Lawrence Erlbaum Associates.

Dozier, D. M., Valente, T. M., & Severn, J. J. H. (1986). *The impact of interconcept networks on perceived attributes and projected adoption of discontinuous innovations.* Paper presented at the International Communication Association, Chicago.

Ducoffe, R. H. (1996). Advertising value and adversing on the web sites. *Journal of Advertising Research, 36,* 21-35, 59-66.

Dupagne, M., & Seel, P. (1998). *High definition television: A global perspective.* Ames: Iowa State University Press.

Dutton, C., Rogers, E., & Jun, S. H. (1987). Diffusion and social impacts of personal computers. *Communication Research, 14*(2), 219-250.

Eighmey, J. (1997). Profiling user responses to commercial web sites. *Journal of Advertising Research, 37,* 59-66.

An entertaining trade surplus. (1993, July 13). *Cleveland Plain Dealer,* B4.

Ettema, J. S. (1989). Interactive electronic text in the United States: Can videotex ever go home again? In J. Salvaggio & J. Bryant (Eds.), *Media use in the information age* (pp. 105-124). Hillsdale, NJ: Lawrence Erlbaum Associates.

Gore stumps for info superhighway bill. (1994, June 14). *Broadcasting & Cable,* p. 38.

Grant, A., & Meadows, J. (1998). *Communication technology update* (6th ed.). Boston: Focal Press.

Greenberg, B. S., & Lin, C. (1988). *Patterns of teletext use in the United Kingdom.* London: IBA.

Heeter, C., & Greenberg, B. (1988). *Cableviewing.* Norwood, NJ: Ablex.

Heikkinen, K., & Reese, S. D. (1986). Newspaper readers and a new information medium. *Communication Research, 13,* 19-36.

Henke, L., & Donohue, T. (1989). Functional displacement of traditional TV viewing by VCR owners. *Journal of Advertising Research, 29*(2), 18-23.

Information Infrastructure Task Force (IITF). (1993, September 15). *The national information infrastructure: Agenda for action* (Vol. 1). Washington DC: U.S. Government Printing Office.

Jeffres, L. (1994). *Mass media processes.* Prospect Heights, IL: Waveland.

Jeffres, L. W., & Atkin, D. (1996). Predicting use of technologies for communication and consumer needs. *Journal of Broadcasting & Electronic Media, 40,* 318-330.

Kiesler, S. (Ed.). (1997). *Culture of the Internet.* Mahwah, NJ: Lawrence Erlbaum Associates.

Krugman, D. (1985). Evaluating the audiences of the new media. *Journal of Advertising, 14,* 21-27.

LaRose, R., & Atkin, D. (1988). Satisfaction, demographic and media environment predictors of cable subscription. *Journal of Broadcasting & Electronic Media, 32,* 403-413.

LaRose, R., & Atkin, D. (1992). Audiotext and the re-invention of the telephone as a mass medium. *Journalism Quarterly, 69*(2), 413-421.

Lasswell, H. (1948). The structure and function of communication in society. In L. Bryson (Ed.), *The communication of ideas* (pp. 37-51). New York: Harper.

Levy, M. (1989). *The VCR age.* Newbury Park, CA: Sage.

Lewis, P. H. (1995, May 29). Technology. *The New York Times,* p. 21.

Lin, C. A. (1994a). Audience fragmentation in a competitive video marketplace. *Journal of Advertising Research, 34,* 1-17.

Lin, C. A. (1994b). Exploring potential factors for home videotext adoption. *Advances in Telematics, 2,* 111-121.

Lin, C. A. (1998). Exploring personal computer adoption dynamics. *Journal of Broadcasting & Electronic Media, 42,* 95-112.

Lin, C. A. (1999). Online service adoption likelihood. *Journal of Advertising Research, 39*(2), 79-89.

Lin, C. (2001). Audience attributes, media supplementation, and likely online service adoption. *Mass Communication & Society, 4,* 19-38.

Lipin, S. (1997, January 27). Gorillas in our midst: Megadeals smash records as firms take advantage of favorable climate. *The Wall Street Journal,* p. R8.

McChesney, R. W. (1997). *Corporate media and the threat to democracy.* New York: Seven Stories Press.

Morris, M., & Ogan, C. (1996). The Internet as mass medium. *Journal of Communication, 46*(1), 39-50.

Negroponte, N. (1995). *Being digital.* New York: Knopf.

Neuendorf, K., Atkin, D., & Jeffres, L. (1998). Understanding adopters of audio information services. *Journal of Broadcasting & Electronic Media, 42,* 80-94.

Noll, M. (1994). *Highway of dreams.* Hillsdale, NJ: Lawrence Erlbaum Associates.

O'Keefe, G., & Sulanowski, B. (1995). More than just talk: Uses, gratifications, and the telephone. *Journalism & Mass Communication Quarterly, 72*, 922-933

Pelton, J. (1996). *Wireless and satellite telecommunication.* Upper Saddle River, NJ: Prentice-Hall.

Perse, E., & Dunn, D. (1998). The utility of home computers and media use: Implications of multimedia and connectivity. *Journal of Broadcasting & Electronic Media, 42*, 435-456.

Porat, M. (1977). *The information economy: Definition and measurement* (Vol. 1). Washington, DC: Office of Special Publications.

Rafaeli, S., & LaRose, R. (1993). Electronic bulletin boards and "public goods" explanations of collaborative mass media. *Communication Research, 20*, 277-297.

Reagan, J. (1987). Classifying adopters and nonadopters for technologies using political activity, media use and demographic variables. *Telematics & Informatics, 4*, 3-16.

Reagan, J. (1989, November). *Technology adoption: Is satisfaction the best predictor?* Paper presented at the Midwest Association of Public Opinion Research, Chicago, IL.

Rice, R. (1984). *The new media.* Newbury Park, CA: Sage.

Rogers, E. M. (1986). *The new communications technology.* New York: The Free Press.

Rogers, E. M. (1995). *The diffusion of innovations.* New York: Free Press.

Salvaggio, J., & Bryant, J. (Eds.). (1989). *Media use in the information age.* Hillsdale, NJ: Lawrence Erlbaum Associates.

Stewart, T. A. (1994, April 4). The information age in charts. *Fortune,* 70-74.

Stipp, H. (1998). Should TV marry PC? *American Demographics,* 16-21.

Stoll, C. (1995). *Silcon valley snake-oil: Second thoughts on the information highway.* New York: Doubleday.

Straubhaar, J., & LaRose, R. (1999). *Communications media in the information society* (2nd ed.). Belmont, CA: Wadsworth.

Technology Forcecast: 1997. (1997, January). Menlow Park, CA: Price Water House World Technology Center.

Vincent, R. (1991). Telecommunication research productivity of U.S. communication programs: 1984-1989. *Journalism Quarterly, 68,* 840-851.

Vogel, T. (1995, September 22). There's no stimulus like show business. *Wall Street Journal,* p. B1.

Waxman, S. (1998, December 7). Letting exports write the script. *Washington Post,* p. 8.

Williams, F. (1988). *Measuring the information society.* Newbury Park, CA: Sage.

3

The Information Society in the New Millennium: Captain's Log, 2001

Everett M. Rogers
University of New Mexico

> In a few years, men will be able to communicate more effectively
> through a machine than face to face.
> —Licklider and Taylor (1968, p. 24)

In the mid-1980s, when I wrote a book, *Communication Technology: The New Media in Society* (Rogers, 1986), the Internet had not yet been established, and there were only a few million users of computer networks in the world. According to the latest estimates, by 2000 more than 100 million North American adults were using the Internet, and the rate of adoption continued to increase steeply. The impacts of the new media are felt throughout U.S. society, and in certain other nations like India (Singhal & Rogers, 2001). How will the new communication technologies change nature of daily life change in the decades ahead?

The purpose of this chapter is to trace the history of communication research on the new communication technologies such as the Internet, showing how the diffusion of innovations model has provided a useful framework for understanding this process. The theme of this chapter is that communication research on the diffusion of new communication technologies initially borrowed heavily from the model of the diffusion of technological innovations, but in the past decade or so has made important contributions in return. The most important of these contributions is the notion of the critical mass, which is especially prominent in the case of interactive new media (Rogers, in press).

BACKGROUND OF THE NEW MEDIA

The rate of adoption of the Internet and the World Wide Web was exceedingly rapid during the 1990s. As of 2001, an estimated 100 million individuals aged 15 and over in the United States and Canada were using the Internet, a doubling over the previous 12 months (Fig. 3.1). By early 2001, more than 100 million adults were using the Internet. This rate of adoption during the 1990s was perhaps one of the most rapid diffusions of an innovation in the history of humankind. It was so rapid that the rate of adoption must begin to level off in the early 2000s, as the number of individuals who could potentially adopt, decreased.

However, as shown in Fig. 3.2, this overnight success in the adoption of the Internet actually occurred after a 20-year delay, with the original computer network (ARPANET)—from which the Internet evolved—created in 1968 (Hafner & Lyon, 1996). Similar long delays have occurred for the fax machine, which was invented 125 years before its rate of adoption took-off in 1986; and for the laptop computer, which was envisioned 20 years before the first models were sold by Toshiba in 1986. Why does this long-time lag, followed by a very rapid rate of adoption, occur for new communication technologies?

Visionaries for the New Paradigm

The origins of the Internet trace to the visions of engineers like Vannevar Bush and Douglas C. Engelbart and psychologists like J. C. R. Licklider and Robert W. Taylor who foresaw the use of computers as communication devices (Rogers & Malhotra, 2000). At the time of these visionaries, in the 1950s and 1960s, mainframe computers were only used for number crunching. Licklider and Engelbart were ridiculed by the computer establishment of their day for predicting that computers would become a means for people to exchange information.

A key event in the evolution of computers-as-communication was the establishment of the Advanced Research Projects Agency (ARPA) in the U.S. Department of Defense in the early 1960s, in response to the

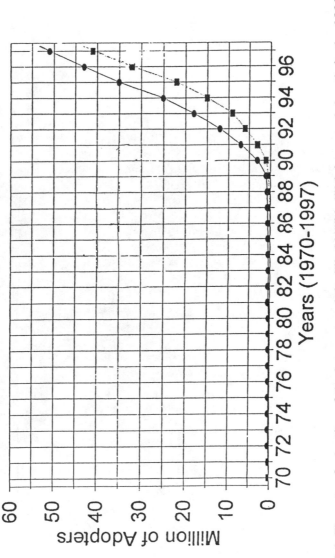

Figure 3.1. The rate of adoption of the Internet and the World Wide Web increased sharply in the 1990s

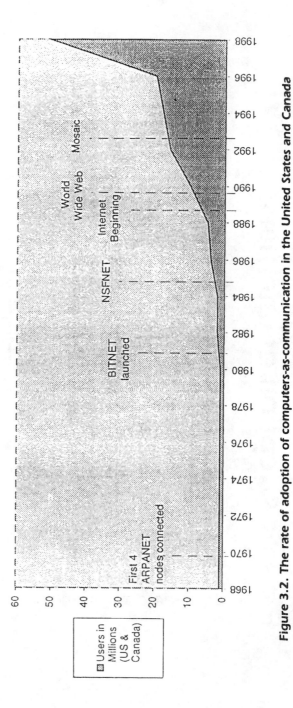

Figure 3.2. The rate of adoption of computers-as-communication in the United States and Canada

Soviet Union's technological success in orbiting Sputnik. ARPA was a high-technology research and development (R&D) unit within the Pentagon. It invested millions of dollars in the advancement of computer science, an ARPA program managed by Licklider and then Taylor, who saw this responsibility as an opportunity to implement their conception of computers as tools for communication.

Douglas Engelbart, an ARPA contractor at SRI International in California, the individual who created the computer mouse (and who developed other important means of improving human-computer interface), envisioned applying computers to augment human intellect, and sought to design technologies to advance this vision. Two dozen other ARPA contractors, mainly university-based computer scientists, were located around the United States. In 1969, Taylor, then the director of the Pentagon's computer research, established ARPANET as a computer network to link the ARPA contractors so that they could exchange computer software and databases. Instead, by far the most popular use of ARPANET was for electronic mail (e-mail), including jokes, personal information, and other types of non-defense-related message content. In other words, from the beginning, computer networks were utilized as a means of communicating messages between individuals.

As shown in Fig. 3.2, the number of adopters of the ARPANET, and its successors like BITNET and NSFNET, increased rather slowly during the the 1970s and 1980s. Finally, around 1990, the rate of adoption of the Internet began to take off very rapidly. Here we see a spectacular example of the critical mass in the rate of adoption of an innovation, a topic discussed shortly, along with other reasons for the suddenly hastened rate of adoption.

CAMELOT AT XEROX PARC

So by 1970, the concept of computers-as-communication was taking shape. However, access to expensive mainframe computers was limited. How did the miniaturization of computing—from mainframes costing several million dollars to affordable personal computers—occur? The first computer designed to be used by an individual (i.e., a "personal" computer) was created at Xerox PARC (Palo Alto Research Park), located on the Stanford University campus, and staffed by a few dozen brilliant, long-haired young computer scientists.[1] At PARC from 1970 to 1975, a Camelot of computing occurred, as many of the main computer technolo-

---

[1]One of these computer scientists was Alan Kay, whose doctoral dissertation at the University of Utah concerned his vision of the Dynabook (a laptop computer).

gies were created: pull-down menus, icons, laser printing, bit-mapped display, local area networking, and an improved mouse (several of Doug Engelbart's former researchers were hired at PARC, bringing the mouse technology with them). The Xerox Corporation fumbled the future by not commercializing these computer technologies into a product in the marketplace (Smith & Alexander, 1988). Instead, Apple Computer, Inc. transferred these technologies from Xerox PARC in the form of the Macintosh computer, released in 1984.

None of the main individuals involved in creating the new paradigm (Kuhn, 1962/1970) for computers-as-communication were communication scholars. Nor did they acknowledge any intellectual influence on their thinking from communication scholars, except for Engelbart, who credited his intellectual debt to Benjamin Lee Whorf, known (with Edward Sapir) for the concept of linguistic relativity (Rogers & Steinfatt, 1999). The role of communication scholars regarding these computer technologies was thus mainly limited to study of their diffusion, and of their consequences (Rogers & Malhotra, 2000).

BACKGROUND OF COMMUNICATION RESEARCH ON THE NEW MEDIA

Not only did communication scholars not have anything directly to do with creating computers-as-communication, they were remarkably hesitant to become engaged in investigating the new communication technologies. Acceptance of the new paradigm (Kuhn, 1962/1970) of communication research on the new media was a lengthy and deliberate process, approximating the familiar S-curve for the diffusion of innovations (Rogers, 1995).

One of the first communication scholars to realize the potential of studying the new media was Edwin Parker, then a faculty member at the Institute for Communication Research at Stanford University. Parker's early interests in the new media included the electronic newspaper, a computer-based information retrieval system (SPIRES), and the effects of a radio-based satellite system linking medical doctors at the University of Washington Medical School with village health aides in Alaska. Later, Parker studied satellite television systems in Third World development, and eventually left Stanford University to become an entrepreneur in the satellite communication industry.

Parker saw a major challenge for communication researchers in studying the new communication technologies, although at that time these new media were still in the process of evolving. It was not yet clear what form the new media would eventually take, although Parker was sure that a wave of such computer-based technologies was coming and that they would have strong impacts on society. He wanted communication scholars to play an active role in designing the new communication technologies, and in investigating their diffusion and consequences.

Origins of Scholarly Work on the New Media

I recall arguing with Ed Parker in 1974 about directing communication research toward the study of the new communication technologies (I was then a doubter). Parker asked me how much people's lives could be improved by the effects of the development communication programs that I was then studying in Latin America, Africa, and Asia. I allowed that it might be as much as 2% or 3%. In comparison, Parker argued, he was measuring much larger effects of the new media on people's lives, perhaps 15% to 20%. I insisted that study of the new media should be a task for electrical engineers, computer scientists, and other communication technologists, but not for communication scholars (I expect this was a conventional viewpoint of most communication scholars at that time).

Shortly thereafter, I changed my mind. By the late 1970s, I was investigating the diffusion of personal computers and their impacts, and in the early 1980s I wrote *Silicon Valley Fever* (Rogers & Larsen, 1984) about the high-technology community that was creating the computer-communication technologies. By the mid-1980s, one of my main scholarly interests was in the diffusion and impacts of the new communication technologies (Rogers, 1986). Many other communication scholars (e.g., Fred Williams, William Paisley, Ronald Rice, Rolf Wigand, Frank Biocca, Byron Reeves, and others) also devoted their scholarly attention to the new media, and to training a new set of scholars who specialized in investigating the new communication technologies. Thus, in the past 25 years, a new scholarly specialty has arisen in communication study, as a rapid growth has occurred in the number of users of computers-as-communication.

APPLICATION OF THE DIFFUSION MODEL

The diffusion of innovations is the process through which an innovation is communicated via certain channels over time among the members of a social system (Rogers, 1995). An *innovation* is an idea that is perceived as new by an individual or some other unit of adoption (such as an organization). Because of its newness, an innovation is usually perceived by individuals with a greater degree of uncertainty than are communication messages about other ideas. As a result, the communication of innovations is usually a relatively slow process, and subject to unexpected events, such as a rate of adoption of the new idea that plateaus at an early level.

When communication scholars began to investigate the new media, one of the important research questions was how rapidly the new communication technologies would be adopted and used. Communication scholars were already familiar with the diffusion model, which had been formulated several decades previously from research on the spread of technological innovations (and, to a lesser extent, on the diffusion of major news events). So it was natural for communication scholars to apply the diffusion model in their investigations of the diffusion and adoption of the new media.

However, as soon became evident from diffusion research on the new communication technologies, certain unique aspects of the new media meant that the diffusion model had to be revised in important ways. The rate of adoption of a new communication technology over time often displayed a long tail to the left (i.e., a very slow rate of initial adoption), which might then be followed by a sudden spurt of rapid adoption (see Fig. 3.2).

In the context of diffusion theory, *critical mass* is a sudden increase in the rate of adoption of an innovation that occurs when a sufficient number of individuals have adopted so that the further diffusion process becomes self-sustaining. As shown in Fig. 3.3, the rate of adoption for a new medium proceeds slowly for a fairly lengthy period of time, until the critical mass is reached. Then, the rate of adoption shoots upward very rapidly in a self-sustaining manner. Compared to the usual diffusion curve, the rate of adoption for a new communication technology starts more slowly, but then increases more rapidly once the critical mass is reached.

Interactivity of the New Media

Why is the critical mass particularly pronounced for the diffusion of the new media? One important reason is because of their *interactivity,* the degree to which the participants using a new medium have a high degree of control over the communication process and can exchange information in a mutual discourse (Williams, Rice, & Rogers, 1988). Mutual discourse is the degree to which a given communication act is based on a prior series of communication acts. An individual's response to another individual depends not just on the immediately previous statement, but on all of the past exchanges that have been made. Human communication via e-mail on the Internet, for example, has a degree of interactivity, one that is similar to face-to-face communication (see Walther & Boyd, chap. 6; Rice &

The Rate of Adoption (1) for a Usual Innovation, and (2) for an Interactive Innovation, Showing the Critical Mass.

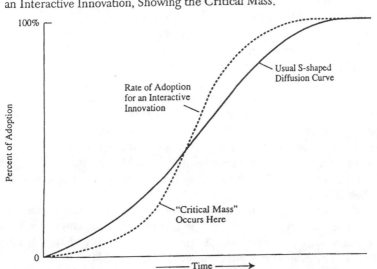

Figure 3.3. The critical mass occurs in the diffusion process when the number of adopters increases suddenly, so that the rate of adoption becomes self-sustaining

Webster, chap. 7; Steinfield, chap. 8, this volume). In fact, some scholars call the new communication technologies *interactive communication*.[2]

The new media provide a means for individuals to interact with each other via computer networks. This interrelationship creates a technological interdependency linking all of the individuals connected by a computer network like the Internet. Each individual's actions become somewhat dependent on the actions of all others who are interlinked. The concept of critical mass in this context has its roots in mob behavior and network externalities. Bates et al. (chap. 4, this volume) discuss how economists and telecommunications policy researchers analyze the concept of network externalities in the context of telephone networks. Markus (1987) helped make this work accessible to new media scholars, suggesting that, as each additional individual adopts use of interactive media, the

[2]Other names used to distinguish communication via the new technologies are *machine-assisted interpersonal communication* and, more commonly, *computer-mediated communication*.

innovation has greater utility for every individual who is already an adopter (and for those individuals who may adopt in the future). Now the adoption decision, although still mainly a matter of individual choice, begins to have a "lumpy" quality in that when one individual adopts, the perceived utility of the innovation is changed slightly for everyone else.[3] The situation in which an individual decides to adopt an interactive communication innovation is one in which everyone is watching everybody else, while being watched (Allen, 1988).

Imagine the first person to have a telephone in the 1800s. This interactive communication technology had zero utility until a second person (that the first person wanted to talk to) also had a telephone. Hence, the interactive nature of the telephone slowed its diffusion during the early decades of its availability. Many individuals held off from adopting because the other people with whom they wanted to communicate had not yet adopted. Only very venturesome individuals (innovators) with a very low resistance to the innovation (and adequate slack resources) adopted at this early stage.

With each additional adopter, the telephone gained increasingly more value as a convenient device for information exchange. Eventually, the telephone was perceived as having so much utility that it became a necessity. Today almost every business and household has one.

A *threshold* is the number of other individuals who must be engaged in an activity before a given individual will join that activity (Granovetter, 1978). One can think of 100 student protesters milling in front of a university administration building. Finally, one student (with a threshold of zero) throws a stone through a window of the building. Then, another protester with a threshold of one throws a stone. Soon, everyone is throwing stones. But had there not been at least one individual with a threshold of one in the crowd, the stone-throwing contagion process would have stopped at that point. An innovator has a very low threshold (perhaps zero) to adopting an innovation. So innovators play an important role in launching the diffusion process.

However, there are relatively few innovators in the total population (Rogers, 1995). Furthermore, innovators are perceived as being of low credibility by the more average member of a system. So, the decision to adopt the telephone by the innovators in the 1800s did not convince others to follow their lead (see Bates et al., chap. 4, this volume). Becoming a new adopter was much more expensive, as there was no pre-

---

[3]This quality of interactive innovations is referred to as *externalities* by economists, in order to indicate that the value of the innovation depends upon external qualities as well as internal qualities. Many telecommunications services have relatively high externalities, and a critical mass usually occurs in their rate of adoption (Mahler & Rogers, 1999).

existing infrastructure; all new subscribers had to be wired to each other. For many years (decades in the case of the telephone), the rate of adoption of an interactive communication technology is essentially a straight line with a very modest increase each year.

Finally, however, when enough individuals have adopted, the innovation is perceived as having utility for a broader set of individuals. This perceived value of the innovation becomes greater than the resistance to the innovation on the part of these individuals. At this point, a typical individual in the population knows several other people who have adopted the interactive innovation. At this point, a more-or-less average person begins to think, "Hmmm, maybe I should adopt telephone service so that I could talk to these friends of mine." One can see from this illustration that most people evaluate an innovation subjectively through the experiences of other individuals like themselves (Allen, 1988; Rogers, 1995). So, diffusion is essentially a social process of people communicating with, and influencing, other people about the innovation (Rogers, 1995).

Other factors, in addition to the installed base of users of a new communication technology (and factors that are complexly interrelated with the number of users), influence the critical mass. For example, the cost of the new technology usually becomes much lower as the product gains a mass market. Also, the innovation may be improved by means of technological advance, making adoption easier. For instance, personal computers by the early 1990s came with built-in modems and with Windows software that supported Internet browsers. Development of MOSAIC in 1989 was a technological improvement that encouraged the rapid rate of adoption of the Internet. Furthermore, separation of the public/commercial Internet from the military Internet, a policy decision, boosted the rate of adoption. Thus, the critical mass, at least in the case of the Internet, represents a combination of externalities factors like an improved technology and public policy decisions, and of individual/social factors based on the interactive nature of this new communication technology. The Internet circa 1989 was quite different than the Internet in 2001. The innovation changed in important ways as it diffused.

Getting to Critical Mass

Obviously, a crucial issue in the diffusion of the new media is reaching critical mass. Thereafter, further diffusion is mainly self-sustaining. Is it possible to avoid the lengthy tail to the left in the rate of adoption of interactive innovations (see Fig. 3.3)? Why did the idea of computer-networked communication take 20 years to catch on? Why did facsimile (fax), invented 125 earlier by a Scottish engineer, require such a lengthy period before it achieved critical mass in the United States in 1986?

Considerable research in recent years has been devoted to identifying effective strategies for reaching critical mass. One example is the case of Minitel, a telecommunications innovation launched by the government telephone and telegraph agency in France in 1981. Initially, Minitel was designed to serve as an electronic telephone directory, allowing a subscriber to request a telephone number by typing in the name of any individual or organization in France on the Minitel keyboard.

The French PTT provided a Minitel unit (costing about $125 U.S.) to several hundred thousand heavy telephone users, instead of a paper directory. Thus, these innovators were forced to adopt in order to receive an essential service (Rogers, 1995). Furthermore, the Minitel was first introduced in upper middle-class suburbs of Paris, in Strassbourg, and in other sites characterized by a low degree of resistance to this new telecommunications service. Then, after a critical mass in the rate of adoption of the Minitel was reached in one geographical area, the service was expanded to other areas. Within a 5-year period in the 1980s, all of France was covered by Minitel service.

Nevertheless, the rate of adoption was relatively slow until some hackers in Strassbourg discovered that they could use their Minitels to exchange messages via a computer messaging unit that they established. Much of the message content dealt with sex, as the users of the system exchanged titillating information, made dates, and set rendezvous for liaisons. The user-created uses of this telecommunications innovation led it to be called *Minitel Rosé* (Pink Minitel). When the Minitel became an interactive technology, the critical mass was reached and the number of adopters began to increase rapidly. By the early 1990s, a decade after the launch of this interactive communication technology, more than one third of all French telephone subscribers were adopters. Here, we see an example of how certain users reinvented a communication technology system so that it became more interactive, which in turn led to reaching a critical mass, and to its further rapid rate of adoption.

Similarly, for computer communication, users had to sense the critical mass was sufficient to begin offering online services. As explained previously, the development of MOSAIC, the separation of the public/commercial Internet from the military Internet, computers with modems and Windows supporting browsers, were necessary for the general public to become adopters, as well as for providers to sense the critical mass. Early adopters were mainly paid information researchers and academics who were users because they had the technical expertise to use difficult interfaces and ftp/unix commands, and they could afford (or did not have to pay for) the necessary equipment and access fees.

Political economy aspects (such as a change in government policy), identified in the context of the Internet, are also instructive in helping to enhance understanding of the very slow growth of fax and voicemail, both of which had to wait for inexpensive and rapid transmission, processing, and digital storage. As in the Minitel example, these infrastructural issues must be managed before personal preferences and innovativeness can become salient.

Once diffusion scholars conceptualized the critical mass, investigated its functioning in the diffusion process of the new media, and began to understand its nature, research got underway on the critical mass in the diffusion of other types of innovations (Valente, 1994). Many innovations have a critical mass, although often it is somewhat less pronounced than in the case of the new communication technologies.

TECHNOLOGICAL DETERMINISM AND SOCIAL DETERMINISM

As various technologies reach their critical mass, it is useful to consider macro aspects of the diffusion process and their influences on society.

Technological determinism is the degree to which social changes in a society are believed to be caused by technology. Much of the public believes in technology as a cause of social changes. For example, the widespread adoption of the automobile in the United States is widely believed to have caused the dispersion of city populations to the suburbs, the construction of superhighways, and the decline of mass transportation. Although a technological innovation often plays an important role in the occurrence of social changes, the interrelationships of a technology and its accompanying changes in society are often more complicated than would be expected on the basis of a strict belief in technological determinism. For example, government regulatory changes (as in the case of the post-World War II growth of the FM radio, or, more recently, in the change to digital television broadcasting) may affect the rate of adoption of a communication technology, and ensuing social changes.

Furthermore, we might ask what caused a technology of study to be developed and diffused at the time that it was, and in what form. Often, social factors are very important in shaping a technological innovation that is created and diffused. *Social determinism* is the degree to which social factors are believed to be the causes of technological change. Hence, social determinism is the opposite of technological determinism. The reality is that both types of determinism may occur together. Think about the history of computers-as-communication, described previously in this chapter. This history seems to have begun with visionaries like Bush, Licklider, and Engelbart, who foresaw the use of computers as a special type of communication channel (in the case of Bush this vision was expressed when computers hardly existed). Certainly, these early visions shaped the directions in which computers eventually were utilized as tools for human communication (Rogers & Malhotra, 2000).

Another social factor, the post-Sputnik alarm about the technological power of the Soviet Union, led the U.S. Congress to establish the Advanced Research Projects Agency (ARPA) and to provide the massive funding to develop computers for networking purposes. Nor could the development of the personal computer (and its component technologies) at Xerox PARC from 1970 to 1975 have taken place without the resources (about $14 million per year) provided by the Xerox Corporation in the vague hope that "the architecture of information" could be advanced.

In essence, the important wave of computer-related technologies representing the new media of today came about for social as well as technological reasons. Their consequences in impacting contemporary society are the result of both technological determinism and social determinism.

LIFE IN THE INFORMATION SOCIETY

Now we turn from the diffusion of interactive technologies to their consequences on daily life in the Information Society of today and the future.

Welcome to the Technopolis

One means of glimpsing the society that lies ahead of us in the new millennium is to understand life at present in certain technologically advanced communities of today. A *technopolis* is a "technology city," a community in which the individuals and the companies that create new interactive communication technologies are concentrated. Examples of such technopolises are Silicon Valley in northern California; Route 128 around Boston; Austin, Texas; Tsukuba Science City, north of Tokyo; Cambridge, England; and Bangalore and Hyderabad, India.

What do these technopolises have in common? An attractive climate, an outstanding research university, easy access to international air transportation, and an entrepreneurial "fever" that is expressed in a high rate of spin-off companies. A *spin-off* is a new company that is formed when key technical individuals, and a technological innovation are transferred from a parent organization (Carayannis, Rogers, Kurihara, & Allbritton, 1998; Steffensen, Rogers, & Speakman, 1999). Spin-offs are the essential growth factor in a technopolis, providing the basis for new jobs and wealth. Silicon Valley has more than 3,000 microelectronics companies, most of which began as spin-offs from each other, tracing back to the Hewlett-Packard Company, which in turn was founded in 1938 as a spin-off from Stanford University (Rogers & Larsen, 1984).

Why do high-technology companies agglomerate in a technopolis? The basic reason is due to the nature of the spin-off process. The entrepreneur who launches the new venture usually wants to remain in the same area as the parent organization. Often, the needed infrastructural resources for the spin-off company are more easily available locally: legal advice, venture capital, research facilities, skilled manpower, and, perhaps, materials. Thus, high-technology companies in any industry tend to agglomerate in one or a few places. For example, in the mid-1980s, 79 of the 82 U.S. semiconductor companies were concentrated in Silicon Valley. Microcomputer companies also tended to be centered in this area, as were laser and biotechnology companies (Rogers & Larsen, 1984).

A technopolis is an engine for wealth creation. For example, Silicon Valley, which began its growth spurt in about 1960, had produced 15,000 millionaires (and two billionaires) by 1982, this out of a total workforce of around 350,000 (about half of whom were skilled manual laborers and half were university graduates). In 1999, 24 new billionaires were created in Silicon Valley, mainly in Internet-related companies. Most of these individuals were either Indian or of Chinese descent, with doctoral degrees in engineering, computer science, or other technical/scientific fields (Singhal & Rogers, 2001). In 2000, Silicon Valley produced an average of 63 new millionaires every day (Nieves, 2000).

Similarly, Microsoft has created a small army of millionaires in the suburb of Seattle in which the company is located. Bill Gates, the company president, is the richest billionaire in the world (with a net worth exceeding that of the poorest 40% of Americans combined). How is such vast wealth created? Through the entrepreneurial process of spin-off companies. The founders and the key technical employees of a new high-tech company are rewarded with shares. Then, when the company "goes public" (i.e., when its shares are sold on the stockmarket, perhaps 5 years after its founding), those who held many shares become wealthy. This process was happening in Silicon Valley with relentless regularity, especially for Internet-related companies (this despite the fact that many of these companies were not yet making a profit).

There is also a dark side to life in the technopolis. For instance, a large survey of high-tech employees in Silicon Valley, conducted by the *San Jose Mercury-News* in 1983, found that many individuals complained of high levels of stress and overwork. The average skilled employee (i.e., a university graduate) reported working more than 60 hours per week, on average. Many individuals, especially those in the "crunch period" of starting up a new company, said they worked 100 hours per week. Burnout is a common problem, as is a high rate of employee turnover (about

30% per year). One result of this high turnover is that Silicon Valley is a network of networks, characterized by technical information exchange. It is difficult to keep a secret in Silicon Valley, due to the many personal friendships that cross company lines.

Another problem facing Silicon Valley is the lack of available space for expansion. Since about 1980, rising real estate prices have made it difficult for high-tech companies to hire new employees from other locations. Companies cannot pay salaries high enough for the new employee to be able to afford local housing, which is exorbitantly priced. In 2000, a number of *employed* individuals were homeless in Silicon Valley; some were sleeping on busses (Nieves, 2000). As a result of housing prices (the highest of any U.S. city), high-tech companies headquartered in Silicon Valley retain their R&D function locally, but locate their manufacturing operations in Austin, Albuquerque, Phoenix, Portland, Colorado Springs, and elsewhere around the United States, and at overseas locations like the Philippines, Malaysia, and Indonesia. Through this dispersion process, high-tech lifestyles are spreading to other communities in the United States and abroad. The high real estate costs are an example of negative network externalities, as are slow downs in Internet access and usage when major online events occur.

High-technology companies invest a relatively high percent of sales in R&D, averaging about 10% (compared with 2% or 3% for all U.S. companies). The main basis for competition is technological innovation, to develop new products that are important improvements over that of a competitor. As a result of this focus on R&D, a relatively high percent of the workforce (usually about 10%) are scientists and engineers, many with graduate degrees. As a result, Silicon Valley and other technopolises are characterized by a high concentration of individuals with doctoral degrees. Brainpower is highly prized in the technopolis, as it is the quality that is transformed into wealth through high-technology entrepreneurship. India has important competitive advantages in the global marketplace for high-tech products and services, especially computer software: large numbers of highly skilled computer engineers who are English-speaking and who work for salaries that are 10% of what someone with similar skills would be paid in the United States (Singhal & Rogers, 2001).

Information Workers

An *information worker* is an individual whose work entails gathering, processing, and outputting information, as well as individuals who design and produce information-handling equipment. Examples of information workers include journalists, investment counselors, teachers, and computer software writers in Silicon Valley. Compared to other members of the workforce, information workers have more years of formal education, longer hours of work (including work at home), and higher pay. Most university students of today will become information workers.

In 1900, the U.S. workforce was predominantly composed of agricultural workers who produced food and fiber. At the millennium, only 2% of the U.S. workforce were farmers, as a result of mechanization, technological innovation, and increased labor efficiency, and of the movement of farming functions to agribusiness firms. What happened to the millions of individuals freed from farming occupations? Many, or their children, have become information workers. The United States became an Information Society in about 1955, the year when its workforce had more information workers than farmers, industrial workers, or service employees (Rogers, 1986).

What is the nature of daily life for information workers? They often use the interactive communication technologies to overcome the constraints of physical distance. For instance, an information worker may be a telecommuter, spending at least several workdays per week in an office at home, perhaps interacting with other employees by means of e-mail, fax, and telephone. Today, about 10% of the U.S. workforce work at home at least a couple of days per week, and 2% or 3% do not have any office outside of their home.

Not only is telecommuting facilitated by the new media, but so is teleworking in other forms. For instance, imagine five company employees, each located in a different city, linked by e-mail, jointly writing a 5-year plan. Here we see how electronic communication can overcome the former constraints of physical distance. Bill Gates, president of Microsoft, manages his company mainly by means of e-mail. As a result of e-mail, many organizations today are more open, as flows of information messages easily cross organizational boundaries and hierarchical levels within an organization (Rogers & Allbritton, 1997).

The new communication technologies have affected newspeople, who are one type of information workers. News professionals today write, edit, and publish the news on computer systems. News reporters utilize computer databases in writing their stories. They send requests, and respond to them, via e-mail (Fidler, 1997). Every news organization has a home page on the World Wide Web, to which they frequently refer their audience for further detail on news or entertainment.

Overcoming Social Distance

Not only can the new interactive communication technologies overcome the cost of communicating at a distance, but they also have the potential of negating social distance. *Social distance* is the perceived lack of intimacy between two or more individuals. The notion of intimacy versus distance in interpersonal communication has a long intellectual tradition, going back to the German sociologist Georg Simmel who wrote about the stranger at the turn of the century (Rogers, 1999), and tracing through Robert E. Park and his students (Emory Bogardus and Everett Stonequist) at the Chicago School in the 1915-1935 period of the beginnings of sociology in the United States (Rogers & Steinfatt, 1999).

An investigation of the potential of electronic communication in bridging social distance was conducted in Santa Monica, a seaside California community of about 90,000 homed residents plus several thousand homeless individuals (Schmitz, Rogers, Phillips, & Paschal, 1995). Santa Monica was one of the first U.S. communities to offer a free electronic communication networking system, Public Electronic Network (PEN), to its residents in 1989. Several thousand Santa Monicans soon became active users of PEN. One of the first topics discussed on the PEN chat groups was homelessness, an issue high on the agenda of the city. Many of these early entries complained about the laziness, smell, and unkempt appearance of the homeless in Santa Monica.

Although most individuals accessed the PEN system by means of their home or office computers and modems, several dozen public terminals were located in public libraries, the city hall, and recreation centers. Homeless people who accessed the PEN system via these public terminals responded to correct the stereotypes and missimpressions about the homeless that had been created on PEN by the homed. For example, several entries by the homeless stated that they actively sought jobs, but when they applied, they seldom got past the receptionist due to their lack of clean clothes. Because they were unemployed, they could not afford to purchase clothing or to clean themselves; hence they remained unemployed (Rogers, Collins-Jarvis, & Schmitz, 1994).

Even though the two groups passed each other every day on the street, they had never exchanged information in any meaningful way. As one homeless man stated in an entry on PEN: "I was considered human [on the PEN system]. . . . On the streets, one is looked on with varying measures of pity, disgust, hatred, and compassion, but almost always as something alien, from another world." Electronic communication is devoid of such nonverbal communication as appearance, smell, and socioeconomic status. A homeless individual said: "On PEN, I have been helped, rebuffed, scorned, criticized, considered, and, in most cases, respected—as a human. PEN is a great equalizer. . . . There are no homeless or homed unless we say we are."

Discussions between the homed and the homeless continued for several months, exploring the homeless issue in Santa Monica. Eventually, a small group of homed and homeless people began to meet on a regular basis in order to identify possible solutions. They created SHWASLOCK (for SHowers, WASHers, and LOCKers), a facility in which homeless people could wash their clothes, store their belongings, and clean themselves. A job-information bank on the PEN system was begun to inform the homeless about available positions. Later, in 1993, SHWASHLOCK was expanded to include a classroom equipped with computers to provide job-skills training to the homeless. The result of these collaborative activities was that several hundred homeless people in Santa Monica obtained employment (Rogers & Allbritton, 1997).

The new interactive technologies allow human communication to transcend time, space, and social distance barriers. The PEN system illustrates how information exchange across socioeconomic distance helped solve a social problem that could not otherwise be worked out. Each party (the homed and the homeless) possessed certain information and resources that the other needed to solve the problem. Note, however, that the PEN Homelessness Group had to meet on a face-to-face basis, once they were acquainted via the PEN system, in order to come up with the SWASHLOCK Project. A parallel experience occurred in the case of PEN-FEMME, a group of women users of the PEN system who organized to oppose male sexual aggression against them (Collins-Jarvis, 1993).

SUMMARY

This chapter has explored the special qualities of the diffusion of the new media. These new communication technologies were not created by communication scholars, and only very gradually, mainly since the 1980s, have communication scholars been attracted to studying the diffusion and consequences of these new media.

This study of the new media had champions like Edwin Parker of Stanford University and Fred Williams of the University of Southern California, and eventually became institutionalized in university departments of communication. Today, most schools and departments of communication offer a course or courses in the new media, and many units have at least one faculty member specializing in teaching and research on the new communication technologies. Study of the new media is now a central part of communication study. It was not always so.

Once communication scholars began studying the diffusion of interactive media, they realized that these innovations were usually characterized by a lengthy period of initially slow growth in the rate of adoption, until a critical mass occurred, after which the number of adopters increased sharply. An example is the diffusion of computer-based communication networks like the Internet. In this case, 20 years went by before the critical mass occurred in 1989. Thereafter, the rate of adoption of the Internet has displayed one of the most rapid rates of increase of any innovation in human history.

The interactive communication technologies have a unique ability to overcome physical distance and to bridge social distance. These technologies are changing the nature of daily life in the Information Society in which we live.

What does the new millennium hold? Certainly, information work will continue to dominate work life, as advancing technological change (e.g., computerized automation) further shrinks the number of people employed in agriculture, industry, and service occupations. The daily lifestyle of the present day technopolises will gradually infect much of the rest of society, bringing entrepreneurial fever, a high degree of work-related stress, and an emphasis on brainpower to a much larger population. Research universities, especially those specializing in R&D on computer-based communication technologies, will become the growth engines of the economy. The communication media in the typical household will become increasingly integrated into a single system of electronic equipment (after all, why have both a television screen and a computer screen?). Physical space will cease to be a barrier to human communication, as a result of the new media. Social distances may also shrink.

Thus life in the new millennium will be quite different from the past, although many trends are already underway. The new media will play an increasingly dominant role in the future society.

REFERENCES

Allen, D. (1988). New telecommunications services: Network externalities and critical mass. *Telecommunications Policy, 12*(5), 257-271.

Carayannis, E. G., Rogers, E. M., Kurihara, K., & Allbritton, M. M. (1998). High-technology spin-offs from government R&D laboratories and research universities. *Technovation, 18*(1), 1-11.

Collins-Jarvis, L. (1993). Gender representation in an electronic city hall: Female adoption of Santa Monica's PEN System. *Journal of Broadcasting and Electronic Media, 37*(1), 49-65.

Granovetter, M. S. (1978). Threshold models of collective behavior. *American Journal of Sociology, 83*(6), 1420-1443.

Hafner, K., & Lyon, M. (1996). *Where wizards stay up late: The origins of the Internet.* New York: Simon & Schuster.

Fidler, R. (1997). *Mediamorphosis: Understanding new media (journalism and communication for a new century).* Thousand Oaks, CA: Pine Forge Press.

Kuhn, T. S. (1970). *The structure of scientific revolutions.* Chicago: University of Chicago Press. (Original work published 1962)

Licklider, J. C. R., & Taylor, R. W. (1968). The computer as a communication device. *Science & Technology,* 21-31.

Mahler, A., & Rogers, E. M. (1999). The diffusion of interactive communication innovations and the critical mass: The adoption of telecommunications services by German banks. *Telecommunications Policy, 23,* 719-740.

Markus, M. L. (1987). Toward a "critical mass" theory of interactive media: Universal access, interdependence and diffusion. *Communication Research, 14,* 491-511.

Nieves, E. (2000, February 20). Many in Silicon Valley cannot afford housing. *The New York Times,* p. 16.

Rogers, E. M. (1986). *Communication technology: The new media and society.* New York: The Free Press.

Rogers, E. M. (1995). *Diffusion of innovations* (4th ed.). New York: The Free Press.

Rogers, E. M. (1999). Georg Simmel and intercultural communication. *Communication Theory, 9*(1), 58-74.

Rogers, E. M. (in press). *Diffusion of innovations* (5th ed.). New York: The Free Press.

Rogers, E. M., & Allbritton, M. M. (1997). The public electronic network: Interactive communication and interpersonal distance. In B. D. Sypher (Ed.), *Case studies in organizational communication 2: Perspectives on contemporary work life* (pp. 249-261). New York: Guilford Press.

Rogers, E. M., Collins-Jarvis, L., & Schmitz, J. (1994). The PEN project in Santa Monica: Interactive communication, equality, and political action. *Journal of the American Society for Information Science, 45*(6), 401-410.

Rogers, E. M., & Larsen, J. K. (1984). *Silicon Valley fever: Growth of high-tech culture.* New York: Basic Books.

Rogers, E. M., & Malhotra, S. (2000). Computers as communication. In K. L. Hacker & J.A.G.M. Dijk (Eds.), *Digital democracy: Issues for theory and practice* (pp. 10-29). Newbury Park, CA: Sage.

Rogers, E. M., & Steinfatt, T. M. (1999). *Intercultural communication.* Prospect Heights, IL: Waveland Press.

Schmitz, J., Rogers, E. M., Phillips, K., & Paschal, D. (1995). The public electronic network (PEN) and the homeless in Santa Monica. *Journal of Applied Communication Research, 23,* 26-43.

Singhal, A., & Rogers, E.M. (2001). *India's communication revolution: From bullock carts to cyber marts.* Delhi: Sage/India.

Smith, D. C., & Alexander, R. C. (1988). *Fumbling the future: How Xerox invented, and then ignored, the first personal computer.* New York: Morrow.

Steffensen, M., Rogers, E. M., & Speakman, K. (1999). Spin-offs from research centers at a research university. *Journal of Business Venturing, 21,* 24-39.

Valente, T. W. (1994). *Network models of the diffusion of innovations.* Cresskill, NJ: Hampton Press.

Williams, F., Rice, R. E., & Rogers, E. M. (1988). *Research methods and the new media.* New York: The Free Press.

4

The Difficult World of Predicting Telecommunication Innovations: Factors Affecting Adoption

Joey Reagan
Washington State University

CONVERGENCE: EXPECTED SERVICES

The future isn't what it used to be. That's certain. What is less certain is determining with accuracy what that future will look, sound, and feel like. In the telecommunication arena, the most popular conception is "convergence." That is, the services that are now provided by separate companies—cable TV, telephone, broadcasting, and so on—will be offered in tandem by each. In addition, some say there will be a plethora of new services—electronic commerce, 3-D video, virtual events, and others. Many innovations will merely offer new ways to access information and entertainment—using the cable TV line for local telephone calls, for example. Others will offer new devices for "better" service—such as digital video discs (DVD, often called digital versatile discs).

As pointed out by Price Waterhouse (1997), The Telecommunications Act of 1996 opened the markets of telecommunication services so that new services could be offered by phone, cable, wireless, and utility companies. Each is now free to offer cable or cablelike video services, local and long distance, and network services such as Internet access. Put another way, cable operators are now providing high-speed access to the Internet, telephone companies are providing home video services, and wireless operators will provide more than cellular phone service. In order to remain competitive, cable and phone operators often choose to merge operations, combining local telephone, Internet, and wireless access into "one-stop" offerings (Price Waterhouse, 1997, p. 107). Alternatively, direct broadcast satellite (DBS) services such as Direct TV will release the consumer from having to be tethered to a cable or wire. Moreover, access to telecommunication services will not be restricted to existing telecommunication providers; the local utility company might provide the access or consumers might access their own portion of the spectrum to connect to their telecommunication services through the use of "spread spectrum," much like the use of citizen's band radio today.

Flanagan (1998) predicted that by 2001 or 2002, there would be a host of new services. In his list are packet voice—connecting voice service from personal computer (PC) to phone, phone to phone, PC to PC; local multipoint distribution systems (LMDS) for broadband interactive to compete with cable MODEMs, wireless local loops to replace the current telephone wire; and Web-enabled call centers, where one can click on a "talk" button online to speak to a human.

When switched to a digital system, wireless telecommunications promises to bring more than cellular telephone or wireless cable video services (Zysman, 1995). The new digital personal communications services (PCS) will provide access to e-mail and the Internet, and artificial speech chips that will read incoming e-mail over the phone, faxes, personal data assistants, even video e-mail. The integration with the geopositioning system (GPS) will make emergencies easy to locate.

Stutzman and Deitrich (1998) predicted that wireless services will go beyond paging and cellular telephones to offer many new consumer and business services. These may include the GPS tracking of people, monitoring utility meters and vending machines, locating trucks and railroad cars, monitoring alarm systems, providing locations for 911 and other emergency calls, monitoring erosion of oil pipelines, and remote inspection of railroad crossings to see if they are working.

Evans (1998) and Pelton (1998) described satellite and other innovations that promise to provide worldwide telecommunication services, connection to any place in the world. Low and medium earth orbiting satellites (LEOS and MEOS) will be used with PCS in a global network. These satellites are expected to deliver multimedia services.

Some predict that in only a few years, high altitude long endurance (HALE) platforms will hover above cities at 20,000 meters

(Pelton, 1998). These space-based platforms will beam directly to consumers rather than an intermediary. What makes the HALE, LEOS, and MEOS valuable is that they eliminate the "last mile" problem faced by land-based carriers. Basically, the land-based carriers might upgrade their trunks for broadband applications, but the consumer is faced with a telephone wire with limited capacity.

Many innovative online uses are expected to start up or become more prevalent (Price Waterhouse 1997): streaming video and audio (essentially, real-time on-demand via Internet or similar network access); 3-D graphics; Internet telephony; online "silent auctions" where an individual might conduct an array of electronic commerce activities such as buying insurance or a used car, tracking a shipment, banking or tracking investment activity, receiving an education, booking travel tickets, participating in virtual events, retrieving information from magazines and newspapers, and checking phone directories. One can also expect electronic commerce (EC) in the form of online storefronts; ATMs; business requests for quotes; "just-in-time" inventory control, inventory monitoring, ordering, invoicing, and payment; customer support; sales and marketing; human resources (including job hunting and interviewing); electronic-cash (e-cash); and establishment of credit (Price Waterhouse, 1997). The recent AT&T-TCI merger promises 500 TV channels, voice, and video phone service (Kalish, 1998).

Although the over-hyped video on demand (VOD)—where one ultimately could watch *60 Minutes* or *Titanic* at any time on any day of the week via a two-way cable system—is on the rebound (Higgins, 1998; Kuhl, 1998). With three test sites and 1,000 subscribers, VOD is now starting to generate interest among many cable operators, and may prove very competitive to the video rental store.

Even local communities are getting into the convergence act. The city of Manning, Iowa, for example, already operates its own cable system, but it now plans to also offer telephone service and Internet access (Estrella, 1998).

Although "smart card," another highly touted innovation, is not a telecommunication service per se, it is capable of carrying credit card, e-cash card, medical and other information with better security than existing credit cards (Francher, 1996). This card could also provide customized access to PCS, with the user merely inserting his or her card into any PCS device rather than carrying his or her own unit (Francher, 1996; Zysman, 1995). Wells-Fargo is running a trial of smart cards in San Francisco with the expected cost to the future consumer at about $3 per month (Price Waterhouse, 1997).

This horde of innovations is summarized in Table 4.1. Market competition among comparable products and services aside, consumer

Table 4.1. Summary of New Access and Services.

New Access Modes	New Services
Local phone company	Electronic commerce (EC)
Local community	Electronic cash (e-cash)
Utility company	3-D video
Cable company	Video/audio streaming
Wireless Terrestrial:	Virtual events
PCS	Video on demand (VOD)
Wireless cable	
LMDS	Packet voice
Satellite:	Web-enabled call center
LEOS	GPS tracing of
MEOS	People
HALE	Trucks, railroad cars, etc.
Spread spectrum	911/other emergency locations
Smart Cards	Monitoring:
	Utilities
	Alarms
	Pipeline erosion
	Railroad crossings
	Inventory
	Voice e-mail/fax
	Video e-mail
	Online:
	Storefront
	ATM
	Credit
	Banking
	Insurance
	Travel
	Education
	News
	Directories
	Business quotes
	Invoicing
	Marketing
	Human resources
	Customer support
	JIT inventory control

demand is the key to the success of innovation adoption. Because consumers won't adopt all of these innovations, predicting which of these products or services will experience sustained market success is a difficult task.

MARKET PREDICTION

Most research on adoption of innovations explores those innovations that have already been successful. That is not surprising because one can follow the innovation (such as cable TV) as it penetrates more and more of the market. But it is also important to examine the failures, as well, to make sure that the factors that lead to success are not also the same ones that lead to failure.

Some Failures

If prediction were certain, most of us would have an analog videodisk and picture phone, notable failures of three and five decades ago. (For an excellent discussion of why forecasting with the videodisk failed, see Klopfenstein, 1989). Touted as "having high picture quality," "transmitted anywhere in the world in seconds," Sony (1986) claimed that its new still video camera "will be a successful still video communication tool." With a built-in floppy disc to record pictures and a converter to show those pictures on a standard TV set, how could this innovation be anything but a success? Not many of these still video cameras are in consumers' homes today, 12 years later.

A Success?

Digital versatile discs (or digital video discs), commonly known as DVDs, have the ability to store a full-length movie and are compatible with existing computer CD-ROM drives. It seems obvious that DVD will be successful because it has better quality audio and video and the potential for single disc computer storage. There is not a consensus that DVD will be successful. Writeable CDs will compete with DVD and current CD-ROM ("Emergence of CD-RW," 1998). The Electronic Industries Association (1998) reported that neither DVD nor laser disc (LD) has shown good market penetration. After 17 years, LD penetration is only at 2%. By comparison, after 10 years, TV was at 62%, and VCRs and CDs were at about 42%.

What is instructive about DVD, however, is how a consolidation in technical standards contributed to the elimination of standards—the type of indecision that can often stall the marketing of an innovation (Rogers, 1995); that is, consumers are often hesitant to adopt a technology when there's a risk that it will be made obsolete by a superior competing version. Two sets of companies had created their own DVD formats. Through a series of design talks, one format emerged incorporating aspects of each company's technology. Each company would share in the license, as government does not always have to be the arbiter. Without this agreement, DVD may not yet have hit the market (Bell, 1996).

Notable Misprognostications

Despite his past successes with forecasting, Martin (1977) also serves as an example of the difficulty in making predictions about adoption of innovations. Although Martin was a computer engineer, had worked for both IBM and the Bell System, and had written books on computer and network design, back in 1977 he still managed to miss some of the major innovations of the next 20 years. Although he correctly predicted wideband, rapidly switched communication networks and Internetlike services, he totally missed the PC and application software, instead predicting that users would all be using terminals hooked to mainframes and would have to master a minimum of two computer languages! (This is not the extent of his errors or his correct predictions. For a fun look back at the future see his "Future Scenario.")

What makes it difficult for the experts to make good predictions? More to the point, why don't people adopt innovations like they're supposed to? Martin (1977), a computer technology expert who predicted a network environment dominated by mainframes instead of network terminals and PCs with diverse applications of software, outlined some of the variables that must be considered.

Complexity. Even the development of digital broadcasting taking place today is fraught with technical problems. Recent tests (McConnell, 1998b) show that although digital technology is being introduced there may be residual technical difficulties plaguing consumers' reception of the signal on their set-top antennas. As of this writing, there remain 18 different technical standards for digital and/or high definition TV (HDTV) transmission (see Dupagne, chap. 10, this volume). The Federal Communications Commission (FCC) has decided to let the marketplace generate its most popular technical standards in digital broadcasting.

Legal and Political Problems. Legal challenges—such as the obscenity challenge against dial-a-porn 900 numbers (*Sable Communications v. FCC,* 1989)—have the potential to stop the development of a service or innovation. "Must-carry" legislation being considered for the Senate (Hearn, 1999a) would have an impact on the market for broadcasters by requiring DBS services to carry local television stations. Competition in the long distance arena is affected by legislation and court decisions, including the recent refusal by the Supreme Court to consider a challenge to the 1996 Telecommunications Act, which keeps Regional Bell Operating Companies (RBOCs) out of the long distance business (Vicini, 1999).

Market Constraints. Martin (1977) complained about the lack of voice messaging which, in 1977, would have been easy and cheap. He ascribed this to the fact that AT&T, then a monopoly, chose not to implement the service. With the break up of AT&T, markets changed and provided many key telecommunications innovations (see Bates et al., chap. 4, this volume). Even today, the RBOCs are trying to keep competitors, and perhaps their innovations, out of the market by limiting space on utility poles, freezing long distance accounts, simple delays, and so on (Estrella & Haugsted, 1996). It may, however, simply be that the market already provides competitive services that obviate the need for an innovation— such as the existence of a global system for mobile communication service (GSM) network protocol for wireless that is already in use—even though another protocol, code divided multiple access (CDMA), would give more efficient use of the spectrum (Price Waterhouse, 1997); that is, GSM enjoys first-comer advantages—having been used in Europe for several years—that enable it to prevail over superior protocals.

Market Growth Rates. Some innovations are slow to take off, and some never do hit that upward slope of the growth curve (e.g., LD and video phones). For most innovations, there is a need to develop ancillary services or technology. For example, the automobile needed roads, digital television (DTV) needs set-top converters, and a PCS needs more efficient use of spectrum. Rennie (1995) also noted that ancillary innovations often have to be introduced to make the main innovation practical— such as the application software that made personal computers valuable.

Capital. Without suitable development resources, many innovations cannot get off the ground. The convergence of services discussed here will never occur without a major infusion of capital. For example, the recent AT&T-TCI convergence is expected to cost between $2.7 billion and $6.2 billion just for the upgrades (Gibbons, 1998; Gibbons & Ellis, 1998; Kalish, 1998).

Long-Term Trends. Although one likes to think of innovations as following a smooth growth curve, Martin (1977) viewed development as a series of innovations, each replacing the previous one. Computer development, for example, is characterized by several innovations—from the replacement of vacuum tubes by transistors to the replacement of transistors by microchips. In the Bell system, the lead time from innovation to actual market implementation was on average 20 years. So whether the DVD of today is a success, we may have to wait another decade to find out.

Reasons for Failure. Rennie (1995) noted that many technologies or innovations fail because they were more complex than first expected. Most predictions are simplistic, and fail to take into account the many factors that account for success. Rennie cited several innovations that failed for various reasons. For instance, the use of robotics in manufacturing often failed because upgrading conventional machines was less expensive.

Rennie is perhaps the only author who lists moral standards as an issue in innovation development. He specifically pointed to resistance to development of the Human Genome Project, which aims to map the genetic code of mankind.

SEARCHING FOR A MODEL

Developing a model to predict adoption of innovations is difficult. Martin's (1977) description of the characteristics of failure can be considered a model. If one only knew how complex the innovation was, if one only knew what the trends were. Those are big ifs. Although researchers are not close to a general model today, there have been attempts to develop predictions surrounding either the nature of the consumer—such as social evolution theory (DeFleur & Ball-Rokeach, 1989) or early adopter models of Rogers (1983, 1986, 1995), or specific predictors for specific innovations or clusters of innovations—Lin (1994) for the home video environment, Reagan (1987) for videotex, cable TV, VCR, and PC, and many others.

Stanek and Mokhtarian (1998) developed a model for home-based telecommuting that included drives, attitudes, and information about the innovation. Presumably, these factors can prompt the consumer to make an appraisal of the innovation, which in turn lead to a consumer preference and eventually consumer choice of whether or not to adopt telecommuting (under circumstantial constraints such as monetary consideration, etc.).

Price Waterhouse (1997) identified the "modes of drivers of electronic commerce (EC)" (p. 374): societal, business, marketing, and technical. Although societal modes include the need to identify groups with different needs and preferences, business modes include looking for others to help develop a product more quickly, controlling the supplier relationship, speeding up design, and improving customer service. The marketing modes include a mind set that mass marketing is not optimal, but one needs to customize marketing strategy to individualized products. Finally, the technology modes include the use of the Internet and other telecommunications technologies to increase the ways to access customers and information.

Agarwal and Goodstadt (1997) proposed a model for the successful marketing of an innovation. The model factors in technical standards, sufficiency of capital, elimination of legal restraints, reasonable cost, product superiority, customer relationships, brand equity, and horizontal integration. Burt and Kinnucan (1990) identified different types of models for identifying adopters of information systems. These models include the user view (whether one is an expert or a novice), the mental view (differences between how experts and novices approach innovations), and task views (using psychology theories to examine how tasks are approached by different people).

The few examples given here illustrate the problems in trying to develop a general model of innovation adoption. Each of these studies examines different innovations and each uses different independent variables; each study also approaches the model from a different perspective, such as a business orientation versus a consumer orientation. Rarely do researchers examine multiple innovations with the same set of factors. Nonetheless, one can learn a lot about the success or failure of innovations in general, as each study contributes to the understanding of the myriad factors that foster or impede the development of an innovation. With this in mind, the next section presents a list of factors affecting innovation adoption. These factors are grouped into four areas based on where they have the most impact—at the technology development level, societal level, corporate level, or individual level. Clearly, each level is important in itself, but there is a hierarchy to the order of importance. For example, if the innovation simply does not work in the way it is intended, it would not pass on to the societal or corporate levels. Table 4.2 summarizes all these factors, along with the subcomponents of each factor.

Table 4.2. Factors Affecting Innovation Adoption.

Technical Level	Individual Level	Societal Level	Corporate Level
Available spectrum/bandwidth?	Advantages	Government policies	Capital
Complexity	Brand loyalty	Legal challenges	Competition
Does it work?	Communication needs	Long-term trends	Cost to produce
Standards in place?	Convenience	Overall economy	Joint ventures
	Cost	Social mores and morals	Marketing:
	Demographics	Societal needs and uses	Branding
	Fears		Customer relationship
	Habit		Niche development
	Knowledge/familiarity		Horizontal integration
	Media use:		Market restraints
	Repertoire		Timing
	Functional similarity		
	Innovation clusters		
	Motivations:		
	Innovativeness		
	Information seeking		
	Involvement		
	Drives		
	Interests		
	Necessity or luxury		
	Quality		
	Resistance to change		
	Substitutability and compatibility		

FACTORS AFFECTING INNOVATION ADOPTION

Technical Level

Of course, the innovation must do what it is supposed to do. In other words, does it work? Even with the innovations in the field, there may be other problems that must be solved. For example, the diesel-electric hybrid car that is capable of 80 miles per gallon has run into snags, namely, that charging up the cars may make neighbors' lights dim ("Rerouting electric cars," 1998). Similarly, recent tests of DTV have some stations realizing that, because the spectrum assigned to the new digital channels is near that used for home and car security systems, signal interference with garage door openers (which the station would have to replace) may occur (McConnell, 1998a).

Often, before an innovation can be marketed, standards must be in place. Wireless LAN standards have been set, making the development of wireless networks practicable (Hills, 1998). The fact that there are many different standards for various services (so-called "multiprotocols") makes such delivery "a mess," even if sufficient bandwidth were available (Dawson, 1998).

In many cases, the standards issue can be relieved by cooperation between manufacturers, as was the case for DVDs. In another case, various HDTV industry players generated standards as well as the National Cooperative Research Act, which allowed such cooperation to occur without antitrust intervention (Braun, 1995).

Standards must sometimes be imposed by the government, as was the case with DTV (see Dickson, 1997; "Summary Fact Sheet," 1998). Otherwise, standards can evolve or appear accidentally as the innovation develops, which continues to be the case for PCs and the Internet (Ellis, 1998).

As noted by Martin (1977), prognosticators often miss the *complexity* associated with an innovation because innovations do not work in a vacuum. Rennie (1995) observed that the personal jet pack that was going to make us all fly like James Bond was not practical; is the same true of Dick Tracey's two-way wristwatch. As for wireless PCSs, the fact that a hand-held device has a small non-dish antenna makes it more difficult to receive a signal of sufficient strength (Zysman, 1995).

The adoption of telecommunication innovations requires that a certain portion of the spectrum be set aside for their implementation. Spectrum and bandwidth are opposite sides of the same coin that ensure an appropriate transmission pipe is accessible.

In wireless communication, Zysman (1995) noted that a problem with market growth for various technology innovations is the lack of spectrum, and that there is pressure to allocate more bandwidth to accommodate the anticipated demand. When attempting to provide home video and high-speed Internet or data services, telephone companies are finding that installing the wire with broadband transmission capability to connect the consumer's home is a major obstacle (the "final-mile" problem). Tedesco (1998) also noted that "(The) biggest bottleneck is the connection to the home" (p. 23). The cable TV industry thus has a headstart in its ability to offer broadband services, as its coaxial cable system is a broadband system, as compared to the telephone companies' copper wire system, which transmits signals in an extremely narrow bandwidth (i.e., 4kHz).

Societal Level

In the late 1980s, DeFleur and Ball-Rokeach (1989) identified cultural and social conditions as important in innovation adoption, as more recently did Price Waterhouse (1997), who found societal needs and uses important to an innovation's success. Businesses are more likely to be concerned with organizational need than individual need.

Societal mores and morals also play a part in whether an innovation can be offered to society. Rogers (1995) noted that existing social norms play a role in the extent to which an innovation is accepted.

Controversies surrounding the content of the Internet have resulted in attempts to regulate such content (i.e., Communication Decency Act, 1998). If the only implications for decency regulation concerned content, then one wouldn't worry about its impact on Internet development. But the sale of sex over the Internet is the major funding source that keeps the network afloat ("Sex powers Internet," 1997). This poses a dilemma for those who believe in Free Speech and the right to market a legal product to consenting adults. Without that support, parts of the Internet may grow less rapidly, or perhaps stop growing altogether.

Both Rennie (1995) and Martin (1977) recognized that the overall economy plays an important role in innovation adoption. Not only does it affect the disposable income of consumers for innovation adoption, the overall economy affects investment levels in corporations, their available capital and the risks they are willing to take in developing and marketing innovations.

As Martin (1977) predicted, the diffusion of innovations does not often approximate a smooth growth curve; the process is instead compelled by an array of improved innovations—each replacing the previous one over time. Therefore, long term trends have an appreciable impact on innovations. If technological improvements do not continue, or if the innovation remains static, it may fall by the wayside to other innovations.

Government policies can help or hinder innovation development, depending on the nature of the intervention. The allocation of spectrum for wireless dictated the rate at which that innovation could proceed (Rennie, 1995). The FCC's set-top rules that require cable operators to accommodate the reception of both digital and analog broadcast signals might increase the cost of set-top converters by $50 to $80 (Hearn & Ellis, 1998); this may, in turn, slow adoption of DTV by consumers.

Innovations may be delayed or quashed by legal challenges. As noted previously, the legal challenge to dial-a-porn 900 services may have slowed the development of audiotex services had it succeeded (Neuendorf, Atkin, & Jeffres, chap. 5, this volume). The Playboy Channel's recent victory over limits on times adult movies can be shown opens a larger market to those services, while at the same time the Department of Justice is seeking to limit the impact of that ruling which, in turn, might limit the market for other adult services (Umstead, 1999). Competition between highly regulated cable TV and unregulated video distribution may occur should an appeals court ruling stand (the ruling exempts "cablelike" services carried via telephone wire that do not use local rights of way; Hearn, 1999b).

Corporate Level

Capital is essential in developing an innovation (Agarwal & Goodstadt, 1997; Kalish, 1998; Martin, 1977). Innovations usually require huge capital investments. The AT&T-TCI upgrade for telephone/cable TV convergence to the home has been estimated as high as $6.2 billion (Gibbons & Ellis, 1998). The satellite systems for worldwide wireless communication require from $1 to $12 billion per system and more than $60 billion for all the complete planned systems (Evans, 1998).

One way to ease the capital requirement is to engage in joint ventures. Obviously, if two or more companies can combine their financial resources, they can pursue innovations that require heavier capital investment. However, it is not just money that can be combined; it's also expertise or other nonmonetary assets. In the AT&T-TCI merger, TCI brings "reach" and AT&T brings technical expertise that can take the unacceptable noise out of cable telephony (Higgins, Coleman, Tedesco, McConnell, & Albiniak, 1998).

Price Waterhouse (1997) noted that the success of an innovation "will be determined more by *marketing* than by the merits of the technology" (p. 123). In the development of marketing strategies, Agarwal and Goodstadt (1997) noted that there are specific marketing techniques that make an innovation more likely to succeed. The first involves branding— people are more likely to respond well to a known computer brand such as "Dell" than an unknown brand. Another involves customer relationships—the use of online customer support for a consumer product can develop better customer relations. In addition, some consider niche development, which is targeting customers who have special service needs, as is the case with homes paying at least $110 per month for advanced services (Dawson, 1998). Finally, horizontal integration involves integrating the innovation with other innovations such as LD and video (Agarwal & Goodstadt, 1997).

Innovations are subject to market restraints whereby competitors attempt to keep the new players out of the market, or as Martin (1977) complained, a tactic similar to the old monopolistic AT&T's blocking of innovations because there were no competitors to force changes into the market. Recent attempts to enter the local telephone market by national long distance carriers have been thwarted or delayed by the RBOCs, whose anticompetitive methods include delays on unbundling local loops, having customers sign a service "freeze" agreement, keeping secret their interconnection agreements and limiting space on telephone poles, and other anticompetitive tactics (Estrella & Haugsted, 1996)

Timing is another crucial factor accompanying the introduction of an innovation. Doing so too soon or too late can cause companies to miss a "window of opportunity." Satellites and worldwide telecommunication "have perhaps a 10-year window of opportunity" (Pelton, 1998, p. 82). And, as media convergence develops, "speed and focus are key factors" (Ellis, 1998).

Once an innovation is in place, the cost to produce relative to the revenue earned determines whether entrepreneurs will continue to supply the innovation. Although the Internet seems to be vastly successful, Price Waterhouse (1997) noted that in 1997 only 20% of commercial sites were profitable. None of the major electronic commerce ventures—including such EC and Internet giants as Amazon.com, AOL, and Yahoo—has yet turned a profit, even though their stock market share prices soared dramatically in 1998 (see Klopfenstein, chap. 14, this volume).

The relative advantage accruing from the adoption of an innovation is also important. For example, although most cable and wireless operators choose not to adopt HDTV at present (Hogan, 1998), both industries foresee little added advantage to adopting it in the near term. Another example involves the low rate at which wireless telephony is penetrating the U.S. market. Some attribute this to the fact that people are already using and are familiar with wired telephones (Hills, 1998) and they perceive insufficient relative advantage to adopting a more expensive technology that provides a similar service that is already being provided by a more economical technology. Hills also extended this argument to the even poorer performance of wireless data services, noting that, although wireless voice service is merely an extension of the telephone, adopting wireless data services requires good familiarity with such services as computers or other data transmission operations.

Individual Level

Cost is almost always the primary factor mentioned when innovations are introduced. Whether consumers will opt for the new world of convergence is often met with skepticism, and begs the following question: "Can the promised gee whiz services be sold at a price people can afford?" (Kalish, 1998, p. A12). New services are normally costly to the average consumer. For example, the current cost to access spread spectrum is about $11,000 (Hughes & Hendricks, 1998), and the consumer cost of video streaming equipment may be $200 in addition to $100 for installation and $50 to $60 per month for subscribing to the service (Tedesco, 1998).

Consumers will not be willing to pay even low fees if the quality of the new technology service is inferior. Tedesco (1998) found that video streaming had a long way to go simply because, "The pictures are small, fuzzy and jerky" (p. 22).

Still, people may be willing to pay a lot of money if they perceive exceptional value in adopting an innovation. Likewise, they may ignore an inexpensive innovation if perceived benefits are not sufficiently compelling. Part of seeing the value of an innovation's value is determined by whether the innovation is judged to be advantageous to make the adoption. Richmond (1996) identified several advantages to on-line shopping that consumers considered crucial: (a) more convenient than traveling to a store, (b) time savings, and (c) online stores are always open. Of course, then, there can be disadvantages which might include lack of selection or quality. Lin (1998) and Rogers (1995) also noted that relative advantage can determine whether an individual uses a technology, including whether the innovation makes one more competitive in the workplace or whether it simply makes life easier.

Many studies have identified demographics as important in the adoption process. For example, James,Wotring, and Forest (1995) found that bulletin board (BBS) users tended to be better educated and wealthier professional males. However, demographics tend to become less important as the innovation penetrates beyond the early adopter (O'Keefe & Sulenowski, 1995). Lin (1994) categorically stated that "demographic analyses offer little insight" (p. 30) in those instances. Indeed, demographics have been inconsistent predictors when used for predicting the adoption of certain communication technologies (compare Atkin, 1995; LaRose & Atkin, 1992; Reagan, 1987). Some studies of the later stages of adoption find income and age to be the best demographic predictors (Lin, 1998), which is inconsistent with James et al. (1995), who found no age difference in electronic BBS use.

Media use is an important consideration in how the new innovation fits with existing consumer customs. For example, does an innovation like the VCR complement existing television uses (Atkin, 1993), or in Atkin's words, is it functionally similar to current habits? Likewise, Reagan, Pinkleton, Chen, and Aaronson (1995) suggested that people use a repertoire of media technologies, and that different sets of media serve different functions. So if an innovation fits into an existing functional set, is it more likely to be adopted? Rogers (1995) called these technology clusters (see also Neuendorf, Atkin, & Jeffres, 1998).

Aside from cost considerations and consumer desirability toward the innovation, there may be limits on how much the consumer is willing to adapt to the changes brought about by an innovation. In other words, there is resistance to change. More specifically, there are limits on the number of changes a consumer is willing to make. Batt and Katz (1998) found that, on average, a consumer is willing to make one and one-half to three changes per year.

Even within those tolerances for change, whether or not the innovation is perceived as a necessity or luxury also determines whether a consumer will adopt. Batt and Katz had consumers rate various dimensions (entertainment-information; primary-secondary; necessity-luxury) of telecommunication services. Primary necessities included local phone, long distance phone, heat, and electricity; secondary necessities included education, cable TV, and pets; luxuries included home security, call-waiting and call-forwarding, car phone, information services, PCs and software, video games, vacations, and CDs. Obviously, even luxuries can be adopted. But a luxury is lower on the list when one must decide which innovation to adopt next.

A person's knowledge or familiarity with an innovation also affects whether that person will adopt. Zysman (1995) worried that new wireless innovations run the risk of being seen as more complicated devices that might baffle the user. However, these problems might be countered by accessing innovations through intelligent devices like smart cards that could personalize each PCS to the user. As Neuendorf et al. (1998) pointed out, the use of audiotex (900 and 800 numbers) was facilitated by the familiarity the consumer had with existing phone technology, since "it was nothing more than picking up the phone and dialing" (p. 83).

A number of motivations within individuals also affects their decisions about innovation adoption. These include (a) innovativeness (Lin, 1998; Rogers, 1995)—wanting to learn new ideas and explore, (b) information seeking (Reagan, Pinkleton, Thornton, Miller, & Main, 1998)—or more active versus more passive information seeking, (c) involvement (Reagan, Pinkleton, Miller, & Main, 1998)—attitudes toward an innovation or use such as "boring" or "desirable," (d) drives (Batt & Katz, 1998)—one's instinctual needs, and (e) perceived needs (Lin, 1994)—how useful an innovation is for work or life. A person's interests also play a role in adoption. For example, Reagan (1996) found that those who had low interest in sports are less tolerant of those technologies that were more complex to use for sports information access (see also James et al., 1995).

More specific to telecommunication innovation adoption than general motivations are communication needs. Neuendorf et al. (1998) found that social indicators are less important than communication variables such as communication needs (frequency of communication interaction at work, home, etc.). Likewise, James et al. (1995) discovered that although paper letter writing among electronic bulletin board (BBS) users decreased, increased use of e-mail enhanced the overall communication activity. They also found that BBS use served the user's need to socialize.

Batt and Katz (1998) noted that the factors of substitutability and compatibility are complementary. In some cases, an innovation will replace an existing technology. That is a much more difficult process than if the innovation is compatible to existing products (in some cases, similar to the "familiarity" factor). Reagan et al. (1995), in support of "functional similarity," found that different sets of media—including new technologies—are compatible depending on the type of use to which the sources are being applied (in their study, information uses).

Much of the discussion here can be subsumed under the umbrella of habits (Batt & Katz, 1998), in other words, whether those are how one uses the media, the life style one pursues, the communication needs one has, and so on.

Price Waterhouse (1997) also pointed out that consumer fears could also be barriers to innovation use. For example, those less likely to access the Internet are more worried about security and less confident in the innovation as a result.

Like the development of branding at the corporate levels, there must be a concomitant brand loyalty on the part of the consumer (Agarwal & Goodstadt, 1997) in order for this branding effort to succeed. If one is loyal, for example, to AT&T and TCI, then one would be more likely to adopt the various services provided by the converged company.

An innovation that provides valued convenience to the user is also likely to be adopted. According to Hills (1998), "Cellular became popular once phones were small and light enough to slip into a pocket" (p. 87). Richmond (1996) found that online shopping was convenient because it saves time and can be done at any time of the day.

APPLICATION TO TELECOMMUNICATIONS

Several factors are involved in innovation adoption. In some cases, these factors could interact with each other to affect adoption decisions. For example, low cost may be insufficient to lure consumers if they are unfamiliar with the innovation or do not perceive a need for it. Furthermore, the perceived importance of these factors could change, depending on the application nature of the innovation or the relative importance of other adoption factors. For instance, high resistance to change may make innovation adoption unlikely, regardless of the perceived value of the innovation. A lack of understanding about the dynamics of these adoption factors could mean a loss of millions of dollars to the corporation that invests heavily in failed technology.

These multiple adoption factors can be further interpreted in a hierarchical flow. First, the innovation must work in the way that it's expected in a real-world application. Second, there must not be forceful interference at the societal level. For example, if the innovation generates controversy on moral grounds or government interference, these barriers would need to be overcome if the innovation is to proceed to consumer trial. Third, there must be sufficient corporate support, not just at the development stage with capital, but at crucial stages in developing the market and branding with the consumer. Finally, the consumer must overcome all of those potential barriers to adoption: cost, resistance, motivations, familiarity, and so on.

The innovations most likely to succeed—especially in the short term—include those with the least need for capital intensive investment, least dependency on existing spectrum or bandwidth, least subject to social norms or regulations, least complex, lowest cost to the adopter, the most advantageous, and most specifically applicable to needs. The PC is a prime example of this. With few regulatory, corporate, and societal limits, the PC has slowly become a fixture in our work and personal lives. The Internet provides another good case in point. Like PCs, use of the Internet has few regulatory, corporate or societal limits. It is relatively easy to create a web page. Still, a number of adoption barriers persist, such as lack of familiarity, fear, and so on. As a generation passes and people get used to using the Internet, its adoption rate should continue to increase.

When it comes to the issue of lack of familiarity with an innovation, there is often the "chicken-and-egg" dilemma. How does one become familiar with an innovation if one has not already used it? Moreover, how does one convince a consumer to use an innovation about which the consumer has a negative attitude and lacks proper motivations to adopt? As suggested by Jackson (1998) and Reagan, Pinkleton, Busselle, and Jackson (1998), these problems may have to be solved through marketing strategies at the corporate level. Promoting the ease of use and personal security for adopting an innovation may help alleviate some of those fears. Still, if an innovation is simply difficult to use—as some people find the Internet—then the innovation needs to be made more user-friendly.

RESEARCH NEEDS

In order to increase understanding of how innovations are diffused, several considerations need to be taken. First, there is a need to compare failures with successes. Although one might think that positive user adoption motivations equate with success of the innovation, such a positive relation—although not often found to be true—is not automatic. Hence, when adoption motivations do present themselves and the market fails the innovation, there is a need to search for the real cause of failure.

Second, there is too much single innovation-oriented research. For example, Stanek and Mokhtarian (1998) only analyzed telecommuting, and Price Waterhouse (1997) looked at EC for their innovation model. Comprehensive studies (perhaps meta-studies) with all adoption variables and hierarchies of adoption factors need to be conducted. After all, it does little good to know what factors predict the success of cable television, if those same factors cannot also help to predict convergence and emerging services that provide similar services.

Researchers need to establish a common terminology. Is it *drives, motivations,* or *advantages*? Is it *product superiority, advantages,* or *value*? Part of the problem is that different words are often used to mean the same thing due to different operationalizations for the same terminology. So, in order to better compare research findings, and so that marketers can more easily understand the meaning of those findings, a common terminology is in order.

Finally, research studies need to examine all relevant adoption factors to better assess their hierarchy of importance in the innovation adoption decision-making process. This entails adopting multiple theoretical elements for predicting innovation adoption and finding the interaction patterns and their order or predictive strength.

CONCLUDING NOTE

One must realize that it is nigh impossible to assess all factors on all potential innovations, certainly not in a single study. And this list of hier-

archical factors is also in no way an exhaustive one. Maybe there will
never be a general model of innovation adoption with high scientific reliability and validity. It is possible, however, to develop multiple models of
innovation adoption, each useful in explaining and predicting a set of
functionally similar innovation clusters. That is a goal researchers could
and should accomplish in the future.

REFERENCES

Agarwal, M. K., & Goodstadt, B. E. (1997). Gaining competitive advan-
    tage in the U.S. wireless telephony market: The marketing challenge.
    Telematics and Informatics, 14, 59-171.
Atkin, D. J. (1993). Adoption of cable amidst a multimedia environment.
    Telematics and Informatics, 10, 51-58.
Atkin, D. J. (1995). Audio information services and electronic media envi-
    ronment. *Information Society, 11,* 75-83.
Batt, C. E., & Katz, J. E. (1998). Consumer spending behavior and
    telecommunications services. *Telecommunications Policy, 22,* 23-46.
Bell, A. E. (1996). Next-generation compact discs. *Scientific American,
    275,* 42-46.
Braun, M. J. (1995). Research joint ventures and the development of digital
    HDTV. *Journal of Broadcasting and Electronic Media, 39,* 390-407.
Burt, P. V., & Kinnucan, M. T. (1990). Information models and modeling
    techniques for information systems. *Annual Review of Information
    Science and Technology, 25,* 175-208.
Communication Decency Act. (1998). *ACLU et al. v Janet Reno,* covered
    at: http://www.aclu.org/court/cdadec.htm; Reno v ACLU, 96-511.
Dawson, F. (1998). Sprint vows one-phone-line approach to new services.
    Multichannel News, 19, 3a, 19a-21a.
DeFleur, M. L., & Ball-Rokeach, S. (1989). *Theories of mass communica-
    tion.* New York: Longman.
Dickson, G. (1997). Networks have different views of DTV. *Broadcasting
    and Cable, 127,* 52-56.
Electronic Industries Association. (1998, June 2). Available online:
    http://www.ovda.org.
Ellis, L. (1998). Convergence redux: This time for real? *Multichannel
    News, 19,* 3a, 22a-24a.
Emergence of CD-RW pulls the brake on DVD adoption in the near term
    according to IDC. (1998, June 2). Available online: http://www.tech-
    mall.com/techdocs/TS980407-8.html.
Estrella, J. (1998). Muni cable op expands into telephony. *Multichannel
    News, 19,* 32.

Estrella, J., & Haugsted, L. (1996). How RBOCs stave off competitors. *Multichannel News, 17,* 1, 14.

Evans, J. V. (1998). New satellites for personal communication. *Scientific American, 278,* 70-77.

Flanagan, P. (1998). This year's 10 hottest technologies in telecommunications. *Telecommunications, 32,* 30-38.

Francher, C. H. (1996). Smart cards. *Scientific American, 275,* 40-45.

Gibbons, K. (1998). Reach out and touch TCI. *Multichannel News, 19,* 1, 122.

Gibbons, K., & Ellis, L. (1998). AT&T deal hangover. *Multichannel News, 19,* 1, 86.

Hearn, T. (1999a), McCain: Satellite bill excludes cable. *Multichannel News, 20,* 3, 16.

Hearn, T. (1999b). NCTA, NATOA, LFAs unite to fight ruling. *Multichannel News, 20,* 42.

Hearn, T., & Ellis, L. (1998). FCC extends set-top rules to analog. *Multichannel News, 19,* 1, 67.

Higgins, J. M. (1998). Will operators sing diva's tune. *Broadcasting and Cable, 128,* 30-31.

Higgins, J. M., Colman, P., Tedesco, R., McConnell, C., & Albiniak, P. (1998). AT&T makes local call (and six other news stories). *Broadcasting and Cable, 128,* 6-17.

Hills, A. (1998). Terrestrial wireless networks. *Scientific American, 278,* 86-91.

Hogan, M. (1998). Wireless won't embrace HDTV this year. *Multichannel News, 19,* 30, 32.

Hughes, D. R., & Hendricks, D. (1998, April). Spread-spectrum radio. *Scientific American, 278,* 94-96.

Jackson, K. (1998). *Factors affecting Internet use.* Unpublished master's thesis, Washington State University, Seattle.

James, M. L., Wotring, C. E., & Forest, E. J. (1995). An exploratory study of the perceived benefits of electronic bulletin board use and their impact on other communication activities. *Journal of Broadcasting and Electronic Media, 39,* 30-50.

Kalish, D. E. (1998). Jury out on AT&T-TCI deal. *The (Spokane) Spokesman-Review, 116,* A12, A15.

Kuhl, C. (1998). VOD returns to fast-forward. *Multichannel News, 19,* 14, 26, 28.

Klopfenstein, B. C. (1989). Forecasting consumer adoption of information products and services: Lessons from home video forecasting. *Journal of the American Society for Information Science, 40*(1), 17-26.

LaRose, R. K., & Atkin, D. J. (1992). Audiotex and the reinvention of the telephone as a mass medium. *Journalism Quarterly, 69,* 413-421.

Lin, C. A. (1994). Audience fragmentation in a competitive video market-place. *Journal of Advertising Research,* 30-38.

Lin, C. A. (1998). Exploring personal computer adoption dynamics. *Journal of Broadcasting and Electronic Media, 42,* 95-112.

Martin J. (1977). *Future developments in telecommunications* (2nd ed.). Englewood Cliffs, NJ: Prentice-Hall.

McConnell, C. (1998a). Must-carry draft expected. *Broadcasting and Cable, 128,* 17-18.

McConnell, C. (1998b). Sinclair tests multichannel DTV. *Broadcasting and Cable, 128,* 16.

Neuendorf, K. A., Atkin, D., & Jeffres, L. W. (1998). Understanding adopters of audio information innovations. *Journal of Broadcasting and Electronic Media, 42,* 80-93.

O'Keefe, G. J., & Sulenowski, B. K. (1995). More than just talk: Uses gratifications and the telephone. *Journalism and Mass Communication Quarterly, 72,* 922-933.

Pelton, J. N. (1998). Telecommunications for the 21st century. *Scientific American, 278,* 80-85.

Price Waterhouse (1977). *Technology forecast: 1997.* Menlo Park, CA: Author.

Reagan, J. (1987). Classifying adoptors and nonadoptors of four technologies using political activity, media use and demographic variables. *Telematics and Informatics, 4,* 3-16.

Reagan, J. (1996). The "repertoire" of information sources. *Journal of Broadcasting and Electronic Media, 40,* 112-121

Reagan, J., Pinkleton B., Busselle R., & Jackson, K. (1998). *Factors affecting Internet use in a saturate access population.* Unpublished manuscript.

Reagan, J., Pinkleton B., Chen, C., & Aaronson D. (1995). How do technologies relate to the repertoire of information sources? *Telematics and Informatics, 12,* 21-27.

Reagan, J., Pinkleton B., Thornton, A., Miller, M., & Main J. (1998). Motivations as predictors of information source perceptions: Traditional media and new technologies. *Telematics and Informatics, 15,* 1-10.

Rennie J. (1995). The uncertainties of technological innovation. *Scientific American, 275,* 57-58.

Rerouting Electric Cars. (1998, July). *Scientific American, 279,* 22.

Richmond, A. (1996). Enticing on-line shoppers to buy: A human behavior study. *Computers and ISDN Systems, 28,* 1469-1480.

Rogers, E. M. (1983). *Diffusion of innovations.* New York: The Free Press.

Rogers, E. M. (1986). *Communication technology.* New York: The Free Press.

Rogers, E. M. (1995). *Diffusion of innovations* (4th ed.) New York: The Free Press.

Sable Communications of California, Inc. v FCC, 492 US 115. (1989).

Sex powers Internet drive—Researchers. (1997, August 19). *Yahoo News.* Available online: http://www.yahoo.com//h...stories/cybersex_1. html.

Sony. (1986). Still video camera recorder (promotional brochure).

Stanek, D. M., & Mokhtarian, P L. (1998). Developing models of preference for home-based telecommuting: Findings and forecasts. *Technology Forecasting and Social Change, 57,* 53-74.

Stutzman, W. L., & Deitrich, C. B., Jr. (1998). Moving beyond wireless voice systems. *Scientific American, 278,* 92-93.

Summary Fact Sheet. (1998, July 12). Available online: http://fcc.gov/ nmb/prd/dtv.

Tedesco, R. (1998). Video streaming: Not ready for prime time medium. *Broadcasting and Cable, 128,* 22-28.

Umstead, R. T. (1999). DOJ to limit 505 ruling to Playboy. *Multichannel News, 20,* 4.

Vicini, J. (1999, January 19). Bell firms lose U.S. Supreme Court appeal over law. *Yahoo News.* Available online: http://www.yahoo.com// h...stories/telecom_1.html.

Zysman G. I. (1995). Wireless networks. *Scientific American, 273,* 68-71.

PART TWO

TECHNOLOGY
AND INTERPERSONAL
COMMUNICATION

5

Not Your Plain Old Telephone: New Services and New Impacts

Benjamin J. Bates
University of Tennessee

Kendra Albright
Information Associates, Inc.

Kadesha D. Washington
Department of the Interior

Following the telegraph, the telephone was the second major electronic communication technology to be developed in the 19th century. Like the telegraph, it utilized a land-based, wired network to send messages, yet differed by transmitting signals that were voice-based, offering a switched network for sending messages from one place to another. And for almost a century, that has what the telephone has meant: the ability to talk to one another over distances through a switched, wired network.

Such a simple definition is no longer sufficient. The telephone system is redefining itself, as the technology and the infrastructure reconstructs itself and as new social uses and impacts emerge. The basic telephone network is undergoing a transition from analog transmissions over copper wire to digital fiber optic transmissions (and even wireless delivery around the world), from a fully wired land-based system to a mix of wired and broadcast delivery systems. The telephone system provided an early foundation for, and now lies at the heart of, the emerging global information infrastructure (GII), sometimes referred to as the information superhighway. Furthermore, in this new era of convergence and competition, the old ubiquitous monopoly telephone network is also facing new competition from other electronic networks, both wired and wireless. What started with the opening of the long-distance and equipment markets to competition, and the licensing of multiple cellular and personal communication system[1] (PCS) operators, has now, with the deregulation of the industry under the 1996 Telecommunications Act, extended the potential for competition into the market for local phone service (Aufderheide, 1999). Continuing changes in technology, regulation, and uses are opening the door to myriad new systems and services, redefining telephony and its markets.

As an example of the expanding definition, the U.S. Department of Commerce (1998) in their 1998 U.S. Industry and Trade Outlook defined the telecommunications industry broadly to include "local exchange, cellular telephony and paging, long-distance (toll) and international services, whether provided by wire (coaxial or fiber cable) or wireless (terrestrial radio systems or satellite) technologies." Although the long-distance segment of the U.S. market has been open to competition for years, the industry's other basic service market, local exchange service, seems to be shifting from a natural regulated monopoly to an open competitive marketplace. Regulatory agencies are struggling not only over how to (and whether to) continue regulation (Baumol & Sidak, 1994), but over fundamental definitions of what is telephony and what should constitute "Universal Service" in the emerging information age.

Part of the problem in defining telephony these days results from the expansion of the kinds of network infrastructures through which services can be offered. There are three basic types of transmission systems: (a) wire technologies (both traditional narrow-bandwidth and emerging high-bandwidth networks such as ISDN, cable, and DSL; (b) terrestrially based radiotelephone technologies (including cellular, paging, and personal communications services; and (c) satellite technologies (including global mobile satellite). The rise of new digital networking and transmission options further increases the ability of others to enter telephony's traditional markets, as well as increasing the potential for new services to emerge, some of which are quite distinctive from what has traditionally fit the definition of telephony. For example, one of the current hot regulatory issues is how to treat Internet telephony, a new service that uses the Internet instead of the traditional switched network for voice (and video) communication. All of these changes and the emerging potential will impact telephony markets and the use of telecommunications, and thereby impact the social and economic impacts of telephony.

---

[1]Personal communication system, a sort of mini-cellular system with smaller cells and greater bandwidth.

This chapter examines some of the historical social and economic impacts of the telephone, examines the changing technological infrastructure, and considers some of the likely impacts of the new "telephony."

THE SOCIAL AND ECONOMIC EFFECTS OF THE TELEPHONE

The invention of the telephone had a dramatic impact on the U.S. public. Since its invention in 1876, the telephone gained an important place in the United States. Despite its original intended purpose of transmitting education via lectures, assisting the deaf, and offering entertainment broadcasts, the telephone quickly became a standard feature in both the office and the home. Today, we take its presence for granted and often forget the impact the telephone has on our everyday lives. The telephone has brought a way of communicating one-on-one without requiring the physical presence of those conversing. The impact of this technology is far-reaching, impacting work, home, and relationships.

We need to remember, however, that the impact of communication systems is generally held to be more than the technology it employs; any impact results primarily from the use (including unequal use, or non-use, or inappropriate use) of the medium. The patterns of use of communication, as well as the structures of telecommunications systems, can influence economic values (e.g., Bates, 1988; Beniger, 1986; Lipartito, 1989; Saunders, Warford, & Wellenius, 1983), as well as cultural values (e.g., E. Katz & Szecko, 1981; Lundstedt, 1990; Mulgan, 1991; Slack, 1984; Stern & Gwathmey, 1994; Williams, 1976) and society at large (e.g., Bates, 1990, 1993; Cherry, 1985; Fischer, 1992; Innis, 1950, 1964; Marvin, 1988; Mowlana & Wilson, 1990; Pool, 1977; Short & Christie, 1976; Slack, 1984; Winston, 1986; Woods, 1993). This suggests that any thorough examination of the impact of the telephone on people and society must also consider the impact of the use of telecommunications, the structures and operations of communication systems, and how those uses and operations can have social and economic influence.

Scholarship has suggested a variety of social, economic, and political impacts of telephony. Many are reviewed in Pool's (1977) *Social Impact of the Telephone* and Fischer's (1992) *America Calling*. Some impacts were predicted, others unforeseen, and many predicted impacts never came to fruition (Fischer, 1992; Pool, 1983a, 1983b). Many of these impacts center around the fundamental essence of telecommunications; that is, how it freed communication from location, making it possible to disseminate messages without being physically present, or having to carry them from one location to another. This separation of communication from distance and transportation had three general impacts. First, telecommunications expanded the geographical scope of practical communications. Telecommunications could reach isolated areas where transportation was problematic, costly, or slow. The second general impact was to speed the flow of information and communication. Communication was no longer tied to travel times. The third general impact was in increasing the scope of information; that is, expanding the amount and variety of information, and information services, available. The reduced cost and increased capacity of telecommunications encouraged the development of new uses, and the dissemination of greater amounts, and more diverse types, of information. What the rise and continuing development of telecommunication did was essentially to expand the range, speed, and scope of information and communication in society, and thus its impact.

These three basic impacts each had the potential for impacting social and economic development, both singly and in combination. Pool (1990), for example, argued that the expanded geographic range of telecommunications impacted on social geography, enabling and encouraging not only the process of suburbanization, but also the ability to expand vertical scope in the form of skyscrapers, thus enabling the growth of urban centers. Fischer (1992) argued that the telephone, in conjunction with the automobile, extended the scope and range of community. Beniger (1986) suggested that this also amounted to the extension of control over distance, providing a driving force for adoption, particularly in business and government. There were two main impacts in the area of social geography: the general rise in mobility, and an increase in opportunities. The expansion of telephone service to the rural population allowed people to move outside of cities and create smaller towns and suburbs while maintaining contact with cities. It also meant that people (and industries) no longer needed to be physically co-located to maintain contact and influence. Both urban and rural workers were no longer limited to the opportunities provided by the local industry, and could seek employment opportunities in other types of businesses (Short & Christie, 1976). Where cities had once been created to facilitate the process of human communication, the telephone (aided and abetted by the automobile) made physical proximity optional. The city of local neighborhoods—where social, work, and commercial needs were all within walking distance—became the city of segregated districts (financial, industrial, commercial, residential). The telephone promoted the population shift out of the inner cities while helping to expand business operations within cities (discussed in several chapters of Pool, 1977).

The expansion and adoption of the telephone also had many impacts on the individual, both psychologically and in social relationships (Fischer, 1992; Marvin, 1988). The telephone allows the rapid transmission of news and information. Illness, injury, and other emergencies are more readily attended to due to the widespread availability of this technology. The telephone also provided an alternative to other communicative activities such as travel and letter writing, reducing the amount of time that might otherwise have been spent. We use the phone to obtain information about products and services, plan activities, and for a range of educational and enlightenment purposes (Dimmick, Sikand, & Patterson, 1994; Neuendorf, Atkin, & Jeffres, chap. 6, this volume; O'Keefe & Sulanowski, 1995). In addition, the telephone has social value. It serves as a link to community by reducing loneliness, isolation, and separation (Aronson, 1986; Dordick & LaRose, 1992; Fischer, 1992). Others (e.g., Marvin, 1988) suggested that the telephone contributed to rising withdrawal from public life. Other research has also shown that the telephone promotes the strengthening of social ties (Fischer, 1992). The number of telephone calls has been positively correlated with the strength of a relationship (Wellman & Tindall, 1993).

The separation of communication from transportation meant that telecommunications could be used to improve transport efficiency. Telecommunications could coordinate supply and demand regionally, and improve transportation scheduling (Saunders et al., 1983). This could contribute not only to regional development, but telecommunications could also improve links to other nations and areas, thereby improving coordination of international activities, and expansion of markets (Saunders et al., 1983). Hudson (1984) and others expanded on this notion of using telecommunications to expand access by focusing on the ability of telecommunications to assist in rural development. The role and impact of telecommunication in development is discussed in more detail later.

The increased range, speed, and efficiency of telecommunications made it acceptable for use as a mechanism for control. Beniger (1986) and others demonstrated that telecommunications enabled and encouraged the formation of larger and more complex organizations by expanding the capacity to control. Telecommunication, by providing information quickly and efficiently, was also able to simultaneously permit both the centralization and decentralization of control which larger, more complex, organizational forms require. This increased capacity for communication and control was welcome in most developing societies. Larger organizations were able to take advantage of the economies of scale resulting from industrialization and related technological advances. The rise of more complex, industrial, societies brought with them more complex societal problems and a greater need for information and communication. The ability of telecommunications to extend coordination and control, particularly in a decentralized manner, provided the capacity to deal with many of these problems (Utsumi, 1978). This ability to extend control through telecommunications is an organizational function

(Cherry, 1977), one that permits order to be extended throughout larger social organizations. As Weber argued, it was the rationalization of organization that made industrialization, and development, possible (Varma, 1980; Webster, 1984). One general consequence of the expansion of communication and control was that it permitted the development of larger and more diverse corporate structures. This stimulated the rise of monopoly structures (DuBoff, 1983; Melody, 1988) and transnational corporations (Schiller, 1981).

It is important to note, however, that control can be exerted in several directions. Mulgan (1991) noted that with the rise of networked telecommunications, patterns of control also shifted. The technology and design of networks permitted and encouraged horizontal communication, and extension of forms of control other than the traditional "top-down" form normally associated with the concept of control. Mulgan and others (cf. Masuda, 1981; Radojkovic, 1984; Smith, 1983) suggested that such extensions can contribute to the advance of democratization, and the decline of authoritarian values. Lundstedt (1990) provided a useful set of readings on the impact of telecommunications on social and public values. On a final note, some authors (Czitrom, 1982; Maddox, 1977) have suggested that the rise of the telephone contributed significantly to the rise of the women's movement, by providing significant employment opportunities for young women (as did the invention of the typewriter, which opened up the office/secretarial profession).

TELECOMMUNICATIONS AND DEVELOPMENT

The area of effects that has been the source of the most theorizing and research has been the presumed impact of telecommunications on economic and social development. Communication, in general, has been held to be what makes economies and societies work, and thus any communication technology would likely have substantial social and economic impacts. It was not a great leap to then presume that investment in a technology that enhanced communication (such as the telephone) might help to advance social and economic development.

Economists initially suggested that economic development was predicated on two primary factors: capital acquisition and invention (Arndt, 1978). Communication initially became central to development as a mechanism to spread invention and innovation (Rogers, 1983), in addition to the central role played by information in economic theory (Babe, 1995). Communication and information about prices and markets is crucial to market operations and economic efficiency, making communication central to economics (Babe, 1995). Telecommunications, as a specific technology, was seen as essential to the control of economic activities over space (Babe, 1995; Beniger, 1986; Mulgan, 1991) and the expansion of markets.

Telecommunications could coordinate supply and demand regionally, and improve transportation scheduling (Hudson, 1984; Saunders et al., 1983), thus helping to expand markets by reducing transportation costs and other risks associated with trade. On the local level, telecommunication development was seen as helping to integrate rural areas, thereby expanding the benefits of development to traditionally neglected areas (Hudson, 1984; Singh, 1983). This contributed to regional development and, as telecommunications systems expanded in scope to coordinate international activities, the creation of global markets (Saunders et al., 1983; Singh, 1983).

Telecommunications also increased the speed (and) range of communication. This aided in making the larger markets and organizations of the industrial age more efficient and manageable, assisting in coordinating the expanding markets for goods and labor (Melody, 1988; Saunders et al., 1983), while also providing the mechanism for overseeing and controlling industrial production. Both the growth in markets and the growing capacity to handle larger organizations fostered the growth of capital acquisition, one of the two prime components of economic development. The increase in scope and speed also meant that more information and knowledge were available to more people. Expanding the information base can contribute to human development through improved education (Woods, 1993). Greater information bases and information flows also promoted discovery and invention. And according to the early economic development models, invention combined with capital acquisition promoted development. Telecommunication provided the foundation for economic growth and development, particularly if its services and benefits were widely diffused.

These factors led many to consider telecommunications, telephony in particular, to be crucial investments for economic development. Most early research concurred, finding generally positive relationships between investment in telecommunications and industrial development. While acknowledging in general the impact of telecommunications, scholars have more recently begun to critically examine previous theories and research into this area, and to question some of the assumptions made about what constitutes progress and development (Hudson, 1984; Mowlana & Wilson, 1990; Rogers, 1976). The perceptions of how communications, particularly the telephone, was tied to development went through three phases.

The first phase was based on the idea that communication was a prerequisite for economic and social development. Influenced in large part by Weber, scholars such as Daniel Lerner (1948, 1958) argued for the centrality of telecommunications to economic and social development. Their arguments stirred telecommunication investments and projects throughout the world. A second phase also stressed the value of telecommunications to development, but recognized that impacts might differ from country to country and from project to project. Thus, theories sought to examine these differences, and studies shifted to a more utilitarian, cost-benefit perspective to the value of communication investment (Hudson, 1984; Saunders et al., 1983). There has been extensive research in this area, much of which is indexed in bibliographies (Bracken & Sterling, 1995; Hudson, 1988; Snow & Jussawalla, 1986). In general, telecommunications was found to positively affect measures of economic development, although the size and scope of the effect did vary. The studies also tended to find positive relationships between the development of telecommunications and indicators of social and political development, although those relationships were weaker, more variable, and sometimes relied on problematic measures.

The third phase embodied the questioning of some of the basic assumptions of the Western development model. Part of this could be seen as a conceptual expansion of the model, through the recognition that other factors could contribute to the viability and success of development efforts. Economists, for example, began to recognize the role of social and cultural factors in fostering development (Arndt, 1978; Woods, 1993) noting that a key component in successful development is human development. Scholars also began to note that social and cultural factors also influenced how communication systems developed (Bates, 1997; Innis, 1950, 1964; Slack, 1984), and thus the nature of their impact on economic and social development (Fischer, 1992; Hudson, 1984; Mowlana & Wilson, 1990; Singh, 1983).

Some studies emerged from more critical roots, wondering if the benefits of telecommunication development were being fairly distributed (e.g., Becker, Hedebro, & Paldan, 1986; Gerbner, Mowlana, & Schiller, 1996; Maitland Commission, 1984), or whether the Western definition of development was necessarily the best model for non-Western nations to use in their efforts to advance. Hudson (1984) found that telecommunications developments in rural areas did permit more equitable distribution of benefits, but also noted that there needed to be a certain level of infrastructure and organizational development already in place for the benefits of telecommunications investment to be realized. Critical/Marxists and cultural studies scholars had, of course, been addressing the issue of how telecommunications development and policy served Western interests for some time (e.g., Schiller, 1981, 1989). The critical perspective has contributed scholarship on three other presumed social and economic impacts. One is the use of telecommunications as a political device used to empower some groups at the expense of others (e.g., Gonzalez-Manet, 1988; Mattelart, 1985). A somewhat related issue is the concern that telecommunications is contributing to the internationalization of both economies and cultures (Gerbner et al., 1996; Mosco, 1996; Mowlana, 1986). Finally, there is a concern over what is seen as the role of telecommunications in the "commodification" of information and culture (Mosco, 1996; Schiller, 1989).

There is a common thread weaving throughout these considerations of the various ways in which telecommunications can have an impact on development. That is the notion that whatever the source of influence, the impact is greater when the system is most widely diffused. The economic benefits of sector development are increased when the system is larger and more comprehensive. The economic benefits of efficiency and extended scope are greatest when there is uniform and total coverage. The educational, social, and political impacts are maximized when the system is extended to incorporate all members of society. As Pool (1990) noted, telecommunications development has been most successful when it expands access to the system.

There is often a tendency to think of technology as a simple causal agent; in this case, to think of telecommunications as causing development. Although certainly there are consequences of technological development and adoption, we also have to remember that social forces influence whether and how any technology is used. In the age of the inventor, these forces can even influence what is invented and created. Scholars such as McAnany (cited in Hudson, 1984), Slack (1984) and Williams (1976) argued that technologies depend as much on the development of appropriate social and economic conditions as on inventive and creative genius. Rogers (1983), in his review of diffusion research, amply illustrated the range of social, political, and economic forces that can influence the adoption of new technologies. Marxists and structuralists both suggest that social forces influence the utilization of telecommunications, as well as other media (McQuail, 1994). The growth and performance of the telecommunications sector are clearly affected by the political and economic environment in which it operates (Fischer, 1992; Hudson, 1984; Noll, 1986). For example, both democracies and free market economies tend to place greater emphasis on making information widely available, fostering both the growth and diffusion of telecommunications as communication media. This concurred with the sociologists' argument that certain values, norms, and organizational structures have also contributed to the development in the West (Badham, 1986; Etzioni, 1986; Varma, 1980; Webster, 1984).

Where does this leave us in our consideration of the effects of the telephone? Several conclusions can be reached. One is that, despite all of the theories and evidence of effect, there seems to be no single coherent approach to the study of the social impact of communications systems. Such an approach is proposed in the next part of this chapter. As to the actual impacts, we can conclude that the telephone changed communication patterns, and that change brought forth a range of social and economic impacts. Most of these related to the separation of communications from transportation, and the enlarging of the scope of communication and information effects. In doing this, the telephone has had significant impacts on economic development, on enabling social development, and in encouraging shifts in social geography. Furthermore, most of these changes had the additional consequence of promoting diversity and empowering previously marginalized groups, by increasing their ability to communicate with themselves and others. In fact, Pool (1990) argued that telecommunication was most successful where it was offered as a means of disseminating access (through expanding the reach of communications), rather than as a means of disseminating messages. In addition, as the telephone and telecommunications system continues to develop globally, these trends are likely to continue. Akwule (1992) phrased it succinctly: "Telecommunications is now recognized as a basic technology underlying the whole global information economy and society, with important implications for political, economic, social, and cultural development" (p. 6).

COMMUNICATION SYSTEMS AND SOCIETY: A MACROSOCIAL PERSPECTIVE

Traditionally, academic research has addressed and sought the social impact of mass media. To adequately address the question of future impacts, it helps to have a theoretical foundation for considering how still developing or emerging communication systems can have effects. The study of the broader social effects of communication and media is rooted in a range of theoretical scholarship ranging from the conceptualizations of McLuhan to the normative analyses of Marxist/criticalist and cultural studies to the positivist social science theories of diffusion, televised violence, and agenda-setting. All presume that media at least contribute to message effects in some form or another. There has been no lack of theory of the broader social effects of mass media; however, there has seemed to be a lack of a coherent organization of theory and effects that can provide a broad basis for analysis (McLeod & Blumler, 1987).

Recently, a move toward such an organization has been provided by Bates (1993), who argued that these theories suggest that the macrosocial effects of communication systems occur through one of three basic mechanisms, labeled *access, bias,* and *control.* The Bates model argues, based on a synthesis of critical and social scientific theories of social effects, that the structure and operations of communication systems can have broad social effects through the operation of one or more of three general mechanisms. The access mechanism is based on the notion that some social impacts come from a structure's inherent capacity to limit access to the communication system. The bias mechanism argues that system factors can exert influence by favoring certain types of content, or certain uses of the communication system. The control mechanism examines the structural factors allowing or regulating the ability of outside groups to exert control of all types on the communication system, and through that control have influence on system content and how the system is used.

These influences work, in essence, by helping to define and delimit relationships between various sets of users of the communication system. It is a systems approach, in that the model suggests that social and technological factors shape the development of communication systems, which shapes how those systems are used and thus shapes social and technological factors, which consequently affect media, *ad nauseum*. This systems approach is neither determinative nor definitive; rather it attempts to provide a mechanism for examining patterns and relationships, both in the communication system and within the social systems that utilize them. It focuses on preferences and tendencies, on stochastic patterns of mutual influence. Let's examine what this approach suggests about the basic structure of the telephone system and the implications for social effects, both in general and with specific reference to the evolution of the U.S. telephone system.

Access

When looking at telephone systems, there are two basic aspects of access to consider: access to the infrastructure itself, and access to the services provided by that infrastructure. The first of these clearly deals with the technological structure, or the network itself. However, aspects of organizational structure can have impacts in terms of decisions to wire certain areas, or in the decision to employ one type of network or technology over another. There are two ways in which this aspect of access can have impacts. Clearly, the most direct is the question of the presence of the network itself. Decisions to wire or not clearly impact on what areas are going to even be able to have the capacity to experience whatever effects are brought by the system. The second component of infrastructure access is the technological capacity of the network. Both technical and economic constraints influence the kind of network that is built. The kind of network and its capacity affects the types of information and information services which can be accessed. For example, a telegraph line lacks the physical ability to transmit switched video and a film projector cannot screen DVD movies.

Although access to services is determined in part by access to the network, factors such as organizational behavior, pricing and marketing strategies also play a role (see McCreadie & Rice, 1999a, 1999b). In other words, the industry makes decisions about what services to offer, and how to price those services, often in conjunction with regulatory agencies. Individuals then make decisions on whether access is worth the cost. Pricing is the primary device used to limit or promote access to, and use of, telephone services. Clearly, differential access is fundamental in determining how the costs and benefits of telephony are distributed. The early "Universal Access" focus of U.S. telephone regulation, subsidizing the construction of telephone systems in rural areas through below market rate construction loans, certainly contributed to the diffusion of the telephone in rural areas. Similarly, pricing policies (through cross-subsidies) initially helped to encourage residential access. By contrast, in countries where demand for telephone services outstrips the capacity of service, access costs have been inflated to curb demand and/or to keep the system benefits for the wealthy and powerful. Pricing is a significant policy issue today, as the earlier cross-subsidies cannot be maintained in an increasingly competitive environment.

Access can also be limited by what could be termed *literacy* requirements, or the diffusion of the skills necessary to use the communication system. The nature of the telephone as a communication system is one that places very few literacy requirements. Essentially, all that is required is to be able to converse with the connected party through speech. This does pose a difficulty for small segments of populations in most communities—primarily those with speech or hearing problems— and may have hampered communication between different language groups. Compared to most other communications systems, however, the telephone has minimal access restrictions.

However, even in the United States, access is neither complete nor uniform, raising the potential for equity effects. It took almost 100 years to reach the current market penetration of approximately 97% of homes and businesses passed, and only 95% of homes subscribe (McDermott, 1998). As late as 1960, one fourth of the U.S. population did not have a telephone (Mitchell & Donyo, 1994), yet the U.S. was a leader in telephone penetration rates. Currently, the lowest telephone penetration resides in households within central cities (McConnaughey, 1995). By race, Native Americans have the fewest telephones, followed by rural Hispanics, and rural Blacks. By age, those under 25 in rural areas have the lowest telephone penetration. Education also plays a role in telephone penetration, being negatively correlated with telephone, computer, and computer-household modem penetration (McConnaughey, 1995). Geographically, persons in central cities in the northeast have the least numbers of telephones, followed by those in central cities in the south, and then by rural areas in the south. And finally, the poor have fewer phones than any other income group. For example, Black families in the United States with incomes of less than $5,000 had a telephone penetration rate of 63.3% in 1991 (Organisation for Economic Co-operation and Development, 1995) and the penetration rate for female heads of households, living with children near or below the poverty line, was only about 50% (McDermott, 1998).

There is clearly a trend toward expanding access and services, as the telephone industry seeks to expand its markets. This trend is likely to continue as more telephone systems around the world privatize and as telephone markets open to competition. Competition and the drive for revenues will continue the push to increase access, and work to limit differential access, at least to the network structure. Access to services, on the other hand, will continue to be differentiated by pricing mechanisms. Those mechanisms are increasingly more likely to be influenced more by the degree of competition and actual costs than by regulatory pricing decisions. With competition increasing and actual costs of access tending to decrease, economic barriers to access should decline over time, although they are likely to remain to some degree.

Bias

The bias mechanism looks at how technological and organizational components of the system can favor certain types of uses, the transmission of certain types of content. Looking at this historically, there were clear biases inherent in early telephone systems. First, the analog bases of the network favored the transmission of analog forms of content, such as speech. Second, the channels on which the network was designed clearly favored the most narrow bandwidth signals (i.e., speech over video). Bell Labs, the research arm of AT&T, was experimenting with sending both video and facsimile content over the telephone system in the 1920s. However, the limits of the system, as designed and constructed at that time, made those types of messages costly and inefficient, and thus there was a strong bias against such uses. A third designed structural element that shaped the use and content of telephony was the decision to employ switched systems. The use of a switched network, providing a distinct line between two individuals, clearly favored interpersonal communication uses over mass communication applications.

As another example, the combination of a wired network and the old mechanical switching systems tied phones and numbers to physical locations. On one hand, this embodied a bias on uses involving reaching a place, or a person at a place, rather than reaching an individual regardless of location. This created a bias favoring business and family-oriented messages. The rise of wireless networks placed more emphasis on reaching individuals rather than places, and has fostered the rise of intra-family calls. The limits of the old mechanical switches also manifested a technological bias for linking a specific telephone number with a specific location, or at least with a specific switch. This limited the availability of services such as the ability to keep one's phone number when moving. Other limitations of mechanical switches made today's features such as caller ID and call forwarding impractical. Although technologically possible, such services would have been problematic and prohibitively expensive. Only with the advent of digital, computer-based switches were services like call forwarding and caller ID practicable. Today, the technological bias is less and such services are becoming more widely adopted.

As the telephone system converts to digital and fiber optic transmission systems, the bias of the system is changing. Digital systems, with their ability to convert, compress, and manipulate content through computer-based systems, offer the potential to transmit virtually any form of communication. To some extent, that ability is still constrained somewhat by bandwidth limitations. The diffusion of fiber optic networks is rapidly expanding channel capacity, however. As effective bandwidth increases, the bias in favor of low-information message forms will begin to disappear. The conversion to digital has also had impacts on the kinds of switching possible. In the early days of telephony, the limited intelligence of mechanical switching systems offered the industry only the stark choice of broadcast mass communication or switched interpersonal communication. Although some systems did opt for broadcast forms initially, telephony found its initial niche with one-to-one, real-time, interpersonal communication by voice. The advent and growth of intelligence in the system, however, has made it possible for the telephone system to accommodate the full range of communication, including one-to-one, group, traditional mass (one-to-many), and even new forms (many-to-many) through computerized switching. Voicemail and other store-and-forward services have even made asynchronous communication possible. Still, the high cost of high-bandwidth switches is the current limiting technology, leaving a strong bias against high-bandwidth uses in switched networks.

As of late, the addition of intelligence to user devices (the handset or terminal) has made it possible for addressable communications, bypassing the structural need for switches. The development of addressable packet switching transmissions and the new asynchronous transfer mode (ATM) and Internet protocol (IP) transmission standards threatens to remove the switching bottleneck completely. Many local phone companies are considering moving from switched systems to ATM and similar network infrastructures as they face competition from alternative digital transmission networks. What all this suggests is that the new telephony systems are quickly removing any old biases for content, enhancing the potential for communication of all types. Consequently, the emerging digital network will accommodate a much wider range of uses, with an enhanced potential for effects.

Although the technological biases are being removed with improved network systems design, there are still strong organizational biases at work. The industry still differentiates itself in terms of one-to-one interpersonal communication, exhibiting an organizational bias toward switched systems that may limit future options. The industry, and to a large extent policy and regulation, still differentiates local exchange services from other functional offerings and from long distance, seeming to segregate uses and services rather than embracing the flexibility and convergence that digital brings. This has placed an institutional bias against radically new services and uses, which, for instance, arguably slowed the development and adoption of consumer computer networks (Lansing & Bates, 1992).

Control

The control mechanism focuses on aspects of the structure of communication systems that enable or discourage others from attempting to exert control over operations. Again, there are mixed aspects to this control dimension when looking at the telephone system. One aspect of control is the ability to monitor communication, to intercept and possibly to prevent the message from getting through. Another aspect of control is the ability to prohibit certain uses, or to prohibit certain users from having access to the system. The infrastructure aspect of the system influences what types of control is possible, whereas a look at organizational structures can inform us more of the likelihood of such control, and who is most likely to be able to exert it.

On the infrastructure side, one must first acknowledge that wired systems are subject to more control than wireless systems, or at least are subject to a finer level of control. That is, control can be exerted on an individual level in a switched, wired telecommunications infrastructure. The switched nature of the early mechanical wired telephone network made control fairly easy. Similarly, the monopoly structure of telephony that prevailed in most areas certainly facilitated the ability to control. This structure gave the monopolist the power to exert control, and also made it relatively easy for state intervention through the monopolist, as monopoly structures gave states the excuse to exercise control. The state often tried to reduce the telephone system's ability to exercise control, by making the system a common carrier and enacting laws to preserve the privacy of telecommunications and limit the ability of the monopolist to act arbitrarily. Common carrier status prohibited the telephone system from being able to discriminate, that is, from being able to control users or uses of its system, while privacy laws attempted to prevent others from monitoring or disclosing messages.

On the other hand, the increased automation (and later digitization) prompted by the expansion of the system made it a bit more difficult to monitor or to exert control over specific messages. As the network became more redundant, with multiple paths between switches, and with increased traffic, it became more difficult to monitor specific traffic. Increased competition is further reducing the ability of both telephone firms and the state to control the system, as it invests more power in the user of the system. Digital transmission systems also made it more difficult to tap into specific lines, and to monitor specific messages. In fact, the "control" pendulum has swung back, to the point where states are now enacting legislation designed to protect their ability to exert control by monitoring messages and limiting uses.

One consequence of this systems approach to examining effects is the argument that one of the strong determinants of communication system structure, and thus of broad macrosocial effects, is policy. Policy decisions can determine or influence everything from fundamental industrial organization to individual pricing decisions, shaping how a communication system evolves and is used. Bates (1997) examined how the role of early policy decisions in the United States, Great Britain, France, and Germany shaped the evolution of telephony in those countries. One conclusion was that long-term social and economic benefits were highest under a general policy of maximizing the use and diffusion of telephony (the concept of Universal Service). Second, industry structures embodying competition, at least among communication technologies, were most likely to encourage diffusion and use (see Reagan, chap. 12, this volume). Finally, pricing and tariff policies had considerable impacts on who had access to the system, and the type and kind of use, and should be used with the goals of broader social policy in mind (rather than the narrower goals of industrial or economic policy). In other words, although the technology itself can lay a foundation for impacts, legislation and policy can also have an important role to play in determining the evolution and impact of telecommunication systems, emphasizing or even overriding the technological and structural biases of the system.

FROM POTS (PLAIN OLD TELEPHONE SERVICE) TO
PANS (PRETTY AMAZING NEW STUFF)—THE U.S. MARKET

The current telecommunications market in the United States grew out of a monopoly once held by AT&T. After periods of local competition in the early years of telephony, and in agreement with the government, AT&T and other local monopoly carriers provided near universal service to U.S. citizens in exchange for maintaining its unthreatened position in the marketplace. The high cost of building and maintaining a land-based, wired network, provided a "natural monopoly" argument in support of this status. The advantages offered by this relationship continued throughout much of this century. During this initial period, technological advances focused on improving the quality and efficiency of basic telephone service. The situation began to change in the 1960s, however, as technological advances opened up new types of network infrastructure. The building of a microwave long distance network lead to a rapid increase in efficiency in the long-distance market, which combined with declining costs and rates held artificially high by regulators (in order to subsidize other types of service); this led to the entry of new firms and the rise of competition. Once this competition was sanctioned by the courts and regulators during the 1980s, it was the beginning of the end for the all-inclusive monopoly telephone system in the United States.

Local exchange service was still considered a natural monopoly, due to the high costs of infrastructure development needed to provide a switched telecommunications system. The rise of the digital computer and improvements in the ability to use radio spectrum led to technological innovation that challenged that presumption. The combination of newly usable frequencies and intelligent networks made cellular and PCS systems possible. Although these wireless local service options did not have quite the capacity of land-based networks, the initial infrastructure investment was also significantly less, providing a cost-effective alternative to switched wired networks (Regli, 1997). The rapid growth of competition through cellular and PCS is reflected in Table 5.1 (for the United States) and Table 5.2 (globally). Continuing declining costs and technological innovations in network intelligence and in network capacity (i.e., fiber optic cable) encouraged other industries with wired infrastructures (principally cable and utilities) to consider the viability of offering interactive voice (telephone) services over their new networks. As infrastructure investment increases, and cost differentials decline, even local exchange services will be facing fiercely competitive markets, if permitted by their regulatory bodies (Baumol & Sidak, 1994). And the 1996 Telecommunications Act provides that permission (Aufderheide, 1999).

Table 5.1. U.S. PCS Marketplace (1st Quarter 1998).

Carrier	Subscribers
Sprint PCS	37%
PrimeCo PCS	16%
Pacific Bell	13%
AT&T Wireless	7%
Omnipoint Communications	6%
BellSouth Mobility DCS	5%
Aerial Communications	5%
Western Wireless	5%
Powertel PCS	5%
Other	1%

Strategis (1998b)
Note. PCS is a digital wireless service similar to cellular, but with smaller cells.

Table 5.2. World Cellular/PCS Subscribers by Region (in Millions).

	North America	Western Europe	Eastern Europe	Asia-Pacific	Latin America	Other	World Total
1993	17.3	8.9	0.1	6.6	1.2	0.3	34.4
1998	71.8	78.0	6.5	102.0	19.0	8.5	285.8
2003	139.2	168.5	28.6	266.8	64.0	25.9	693.0

Strategis (1998a)

The rise of potential (and real) competition was one of the primary reasons for the telephone industry to seek out new services and functions. New competitors would eat into their basic markets and revenues. On the other hand, the same kinds of technological innovations that are allowing entry into the telephone market allows the telephone industry to enter into other markets. Another reason was the fact that, in the United States at least, the market had reached near saturation penetration levels, and any further growth would have to come from new markets. To survive and grow would require the telephone industry to find and develop new markets and new services. Most of today's new services are the outgrowth of new technologies. In particular, the rise and diffusion of fax machines and the use of the telephone system for computer communications has fueled the huge increase in the number of phone lines in recent years. In addition, although there are few untapped markets for basic service available in the United States, some telephone companies are attempting to expand into new markets, either in new industries, such as cable, or in new parts of the world. Virtually all of the major U.S. telephone companies are involved in providing telecommunications services outside the United States, either through direct ownership or in partnership with other telecommunications firms. Most have also recently acquired interest in cable operators and/or Internet service providers or backbone operators. Foreign and international investments can contribute to the bottom line, but the focus for most of these companies remains with their main U.S. markets.

There was nothing fundamentally wrong with the basic telephone network. As it had been designed to do, the network did a wonderful job of allowing two people, at fixed locations, to talk to one another. What that network could not do was offer much to other markets, and once the primary markets reached saturation, further growth demanded the ability to enter or create new markets. Adding a bit of intelligence and digital technology to the existing network was a start, but was generally not seen to be the best long term solution. Of greater interest are the new services that are being explored and implemented. New services can be grouped into several categories: adding new types of content/uses that can utilize existing telephone networks (such as fax and computer-modem connections); value-added services complementing the basic service (call-waiting, caller ID, voicemail); new mechanisms for delivering existing and emerging services (cellular); and finally, those new uses which were not feasible under the technical limitations of the old networks, but which may be under new broadband networks (high-speed modems, DSL, video dialtone).

What the industry needed, in order to continue to grow and thrive, were ways to take advantage of the computer revolution and the fiber optic revolution. The first offered intelligence, the ability to do more than connect two fixed points, and a digital transmission system that could send content other than simple voice. The second offered a quantum leap in bandwidth, the ability to expand not only basic capacity, but to enter the emerging markets for high-bandwidth communications such as video, a market with considerable growth potential (see Tables 5.3 and 5.4). The key to the future lay with new network infrastructures and the new services they would support. There are basically two ways to grow new networks to reach new markets: to go wireless to reach the mobile market, and to construct a high-capacity network that allows entry into the various markets for high-bandwidth communications. Both directions offered the potential for considerable growth.

Table 5.3. U.S. Optical Fiber Access Market (in $Million).

Market	1998	2000	2005
Enterprise/MAN	22.40	141.94	1182.25
Interoffice	48.00	134.07	485.84
Local Loop	6.00	18.55	250.01
Total	76.40	294.56	1918.10

Meyers (1998)

Table 5.4. Business and Residential Global Broadband Service Revenues (US$ Millions).

Year	1998	1999	2000	2001	2002	2003
Business	65755.9	76249.8	89505.5	104379.5	122370.5	143110
Residential	1449.4	2901.0	5133.1	8035.1	12219.4	18056

Share of World Broadband Service Revenues

Latin America	Asia Pacific	Europe	North America
4%	24%	27%	45%

Strategis (1998c)

Goin' Mobile: Wireless Telephony

Wireless offered the "quick fix" (Regli, 1997) to extending existing wire networks. Wireless networks could be constructed more quickly and cheaply than a comprehensive wired network. Their inherent limitation, however, was bandwidth. The radio spectrum, although theoretically infinite, has practical limitations. One limitation is technical, in that not all of the radio spectrum can be efficiently used with existing technology, or for particular types of uses (see Lin, chap. 2, this volume). The second, more important limitation is that there is tremendous competition for viable bandwidth. Thus, the uses of radio spectrum are regulated, with specific segments of the spectrum assigned to particular types of uses. For practical purposes, the bandwidth available for a given use is fixed and finite. The effective bandwidth, however, can be increased by adding intelligence, the basic strategy used by cellular telephony and PCS systems.

Mobile telephony has been around since the 1960s, but the frequency limitations of the initial implementation severely limited the number of potential users. It wasn't until a new intelligent network structure was developed, enabled by improvements in computers and digital signal processing, that capacity permitted the general introduction of cellular service. The idea of cellular was that effective capacity could be increased by reducing the broadcast area for local cells, if there was a way of tracking where a cellphone was located and switching calls from cell to cell as the user traveled. Computer tracking and switching, combined with the use of a digital tracking signal along with the analog voice signal, made cellular telephony possible. The cellular industry started in the 1980s but took off in 1995 when the FCC added more frequencies and auctioned off PCS licenses, greatly enlarging both the capacity for mobile communications and the number of competitors. Since cell phones were introduced in 1983, demand for the service has risen between 26% and 35% each year. In 1998, fifty-three million people subscribed to wireless services, with about 6 million of those using digital and 3.5 million being PCS subscribers.

There are two basic transmission technologies at the heart of the wireless phone industry: analog and digital. Analog is the technology the phones were first introduced with, and are similar to standard radio broadcasts. Digital signals, however, transform the signal into digital packets before transmission, and offer significant advantages in clarity, privacy, and in the ability to compress signals, further enlarging the effective capacity of fixed bandwidth systems. Currently, the switch to all-digital systems in the United States is slowed by a debate over which compression and transmission system to use. Still, there is a predicted reduction of analog usage to under 25% in 2001, largely attributed to the growing acceptance of code division multiple access (CDMA) technology. In the meantime, expansion of cellular and PCS services continue, with the increased competition among wireless providers driving prices down. Wireless telephony can be a lot like wired telephone services, in terms of consumer perception concerning the product and what it does. However, wireless telephony will need to offer competitive flat-rate services and must be willing to appeal to the "least desirable" market segments to compete directly with wired systems. Still, domestic growth for many mobile services is expected to grow 35% a year through the year 2002 (Strategis, 1998a, 1998b).

There are currently a number of plans to offer global wireless telephone service by satellite. These systems propose using a fairly large number of low orbiting satellites, a sort of space-based cellular system, to provide worldwide coverage. Ideally, this system would allow any person, anywhere in the world, to talk to any other person, anywhere in the world. Initial marketing would target global businessmen, or people traveling in areas without reliable phone service. Perhaps the most well-known of these is Motorola's Iridium project, designed to use 66 low-cost low-earth orbit (LEO) satellites, which started offering satellite telephony and paging in 1998. Several other consortia have satellite telephony networks planned or under construction.

Getting Fat: Building the High-Capacity Network

With the growth of digital and computer communications, telephone companies began to realize that the biggest obstacle to the potential growth of telecommunications was limited bandwidth. The basic telephone system had been essentially designed at the start of the century to carry a 3kHz analog voice signal. Although improvements in equipment and digitization allowed for some improvements, the basic telephone network remains very limited in terms of bandwidth. Many of the potential new, and potentially very lucrative, services require significantly more bandwidth than the existing basic network could handle.

This drove the phone companies to explore ways in which they could increase bandwidth. One obvious solution was to rebuild the entire copper wire telephone network infrastructure using fiber optics. Furthermore, to fully take advantage of all that capacity, all existing telephone switches would have to be replaced with wide-band switches and digital conversion systems would have to be placed in every home and office. This would be an incredibly expensive and time-consuming operation, even if the necessary technology were available. Early estimates suggested that consumer payments for telecommunications services would need to be in the range of several hundred dollars a month for a fully digital, fiber to the home system to be commercially viable within the near future. Phone companies would need to find alternative paths to high bandwidth and/or generate a lot of new services and new demand to successfully make the transition to high-capacity networks.

Staying small, however, was not a long-term solution. Too many potential competitors were getting the capability to offer high-bandwidth services. The cable industry had a high-bandwidth network already passing 95% of the homes in the United States (even though actual cable subscription is only 65%), although much of their existing networks could not handle the bidirectional switched signals of telephony, or even the digital ATM/IP networks, without substantial reconstruction. They had the needed bandwidth in their network, and were already rebuilding their networks to meet increase consumer demand for channels and to incorporate the capacity for bidirectional signaling required for computer communications (cable modems), telephony, and related services. In addition, the combination of an already saturated market, increased competition for

cable, and the costs of rebuilding are putting cable companies in the position of also looking for new services to offer and new markets to enter
(like telephony). Additionally, the bandwidth available for satellite and
terrestrial broadcast communications increases annually, providing closer
competition for both telephone and cable companies.

Encouraged by the opening of competition in the 1996
Telecommunications Act, other industries were also building and rebuilding
networks that are likely to become future competitors for telecommunications revenues. Competitive access providers (CAPs), which started offering
business telephone services, in limited areas, in competition with local
phone companies, are expanding out of business areas, and the electric
companies have been laying large-scale fiber optics networks in urban areas
and have recently started offering alternative cable and telecommunications
services. Sprint has led a number of long-distance service providers in
expanding its long-distance network into local communities, offering subscribers a full range of telecommunication services. All of these threaten to
not only compete with the local phone companies for advanced services,
but to eventually challenge their main business sector—local service.

In the face of potential and real competition, several options
began to be explored by the local telephone companies. One was to make
smaller improvements to the system and offer improved, but only slightly
higher, bandwidth connections. Integrated Services Digital Network
(ISDN) is one outgrowth of that line of thinking. ISDN was initially based
on upgrading the existing network by switching to an all-digital signal,
and upgrading to digital switches. The improvements offered by ISDN
were minimal, however, limited to about a threefold increase in capacity
without adding new lines or replacing the basic phone line with coax or
fiber. A more compelling development is Digital Subscriber Line (DSL).
DSL consists of digital modems connected to the basic network, but
through integration of packet-switching techniques and flexible bandwidth
utilization DSL can offer effective bandwidth up to 300 times greater than
the plain old telephone service. Furthermore, as the heart of DSL is a signaling transmission technology and not a wiring technology, the advantages can be applied to any physical network structure. Variations of DSL
technology known as DSL promise even higher capacity when combined
with network improvements. ISDN is now widely available in the United
States, although adoption by subscribers has been minimal. Problems with
connections and high pricing strategies, when combined with only minimal
improvements in signal capacity, have kept demand low. DSL, being a
newer service, was just becoming publicly available in selected markets in
1998, yet is likely to have greater potential.

Another strategy was to seek alternative ways to deliver high-
capacity signals other than building a dedicated high-bandwidth switched

fiber optic line. One such strategy, ATM, emerged in the 1980s as the international standard for high-bandwidth, packet-switched, multiplexed transmission technology. Two key components are the use of fixed-length packets, which improves signal handling and switching, and its ability to dynamically allocate bandwidth, which allows the network to accommodate all kinds of electronic signals. ATM applications currently accommodate an effective capacity of more than 600 Mbps, roughly 80 times the capacity of DSL, and roughly equal to the capacity of a 100-channel cable system. Although some have argued that ATM technology is too expensive, too fast and not easily compatible with some of the existing technologies for it to be used as a general consumer service, there are those who are finding the switch to ATM not too difficult. Extensive use of ATM technologies are currently being made in telemedicine and distance education applications. Furthermore, Sprint announced in June 1998, that it would begin offering a high-bandwidth network based on ATM technology to businesses and consumers within a year. However the busiest sector that is using ATM technology is Europe, specifically France and Britain. AT&T announced in May 1998 that it would offer ATM service between the United Kingdom and the United States for customers operating in the United Kingdom. Many say the key to ATM success will be the offering of more services and that such services will include extensions connecting the outside line to local computer networks.

A further partial solution was to shift to a partially fiber optics network. The effective capacity of a wire or fiber is determined by both the channel itself and the distance the signal needs to travel. If you could get a digital signal within a couple of hundred feet of the various sets, a basic telephone twisted pair line could carry several phone, fax, and data signals, as well as a couple of video channels, instead of a single 3 kHz phone call. Moving the digital/analog conversions from the end user further up the line also meant that digital conversion equipment (and its high costs) could be shared by more users. Telephone companies have been rapidly converting their internal network infrastructure to fiber optics, while developing a variety of networking strategies that moved the digital fiber network closer and closer to the end user. These systems went under a variety of names: fiber to the curb (FTTC), fiber in the loop (FITL), hybrid fiber-coax (HFC). These differed mainly in terms of how close to the end user the digital fiber network went. Many local phone companies have been using these networking strategies in new construction, as well as replacing older copper-based networks in selected neighborhoods. Many cable companies have also adopted this strategy of combining fiber with coax cable. One way or another, the high-bandwidth network is being built, and the first to reach the consumer will have a significant advantage in this booming market.

New Wine for Old Bottlenecks

One way to expand demand is for companies to find new ways for people to use their basic products. For the telephone industry, the basic product has always been providing the capacity to send signals. For most of this century, voice signals have dominated network traffic. With the emergence of digital technologies, it became possible to use the basic telephone network to send digital as well as analog signals, and virtually any electronic content could be digitized and transmitted. Facsimile, computer data signals, and video are examples of other kinds of signals that can be accommodated. The rise of digital fax machines, computer modems, and video codecs have allowed those signals to be sent over basic telephone lines, and have led to the birth of several new services. One limiting aspect of these kinds of services, however, is that they are not fundamentally telephone services, and thus can also use non-telephone networks to provide similar or identical services. Another is the fact that these services are affected much more by bandwidth limitations than are basic voice signals. Many of these new uses for the basic telephone network are addressed in other chapters, so this section only briefly identifies new services and their impact.

Telephone company interest in facsimile and videophone services dates back to the 1920s. A variety of implementations were demonstrated and tested over the years, but it took the development of digital technologies to bring costs down sufficiently to encourage widespread adoption. Even so, although digital fax machines are now seen as a necessary business tool, and have contributed in a tremendous increase in the demand for telephone lines, there has been virtually no adoption of personal videotelephony. A somewhat higher quality videoconferencing service has been offered businesses with higher capacity connections, but was met with limited success.

As digital compression techniques improved, telephone companies started to investigate the possibility of offering a switched video service, called video dialtone service. Although conceptually an outgrowth of the idea of video-telephony, video dialtone proposed delivering one or more full-motion, full-screen, video signals (i.e., broadcast TV quality), which at present requires significantly greater bandwidth than permitted by the basic telephone network. Although DSL and some mixed fiber/wire systems can accommodate the signal, trials of video dialtone service have primarily been conducted with all-fiber systems, and have generated little interest in the service. Once seen as a means to challenge cable systems in their home markets, or as an alternative pay-per-view system, consumer interest has been so slight that most plans to introduce video dialtone have been scrapped.

The new service with perhaps the greatest long-term impact on the existing telephone systems is computer communications. The development of the modem and the personal computer created a strong demand for computer communications. The rise of the Internet and the new opportunities it offered for communication (the World Wide Web, e-mail, chat rooms, interactive gaming, videoconferencing, and Internet telephony, among others) has driven a tremendous increase in demand, both for telephone lines and for connections (see Neuendorf et al., chap. 6; Walther & Boyd, chap. 7; Rice & Webster, chap. 8; Klopfenstein, chap. 14, this volume). Although the phone companies have welcomed the added demand for lines, they are troubled by the shift in telephone usage patterns prompted by the use of the network for computer communications. The problem is that data service usage tends to be for longer periods of time than voice conversations, tying up more resources and increasing network operating costs. (Also, revenues are usually only for local access, not long-distance, even though the connection is long-distance.) Another concern is that the Internet can also provide competitive alternatives to traditional telephone services, possibly lowering demand for basic services. In fact, the possible shift in demand from voice to data services will reinforce the changing usage patterns and cost structures for the telephone industry.

Furthermore, those same computer communications are threatening the traditional telephone marketplace. Use of e-mails is starting to supplant not only traditional letter-writing, but also the telephone as a means of interpersonal contact. Furthermore, the Internet can accommodate real-time audio and video transmissions, providing a "virtual" telephone or even video-phone that bypasses the traditional telephone network (and its pricing structure). The structure of the Internet network also has some significant economic advantages over switched phone networks, turning Internet Telephony into a potentially major threat. We elaborate on Internet (IP) telephony more in a later section. Thus, the local phone companies are beginning to see this growing market as a mixed blessing.

Enhancing Value Through Derivative Services

The rise of digital switching allowed telephone networks to create intelligent networks, and that intelligence allowed them the flexibility to create a range of enhanced telephone services. Enhanced services generally refer to those services that add value, or features, in one way or another, to the basic voice service. These include things such as call-waiting, call-forwarding, caller ID, voice messaging and audiotext (see Neuendorf et al., chap. 6, this volume). There is a limit, however, as to how large a market there will be for what are essentially only enhancements to the basic market product.

PANS: Is it Still Telephony?

New technologies and a changing economic and regulatory environment are creating new services and new ways of providing old telephony services. One buzzword often applied to the changing telecommunication environment is *convergence*. What this generally refers to is the notion that that some of the old industry/media boundaries are breaking down through technological innovation (Baldwin, McVoy & Steinfield, 1996). The old switched narrow-bandwidth telephone network is being upgraded to a high-bandwidth switched network. The old high-bandwidth cable network is being upgraded to handle interactive, switched signals. Broadcasters are finding that the conversion to digital may provide them the opportunity, with cellular, to offer wireless data communications. The old distinctions are disappearing as previously separate industries gain the capacity to enter one another's markets. The emerging digital network is more flexible: it can handle a variety of messages, along a variety of channels, using multiple methods. This can raise the question of just what is telephony

Some of the new services are clearly extensions of telephony: cellular/PCS, enhanced services like call-forwarding and caller ID, videophones. Some seem to share aspects of traditional telephony, such as switched point-to-point communications (fax machines, video dialtone). For other new services, the ties to traditional telephony are weaker. In addition, there are some new services emerging outside of the traditional telephone industry that are providing functional alternatives to telephony. Internet telephony, computer videoconferencing, and virtual worlds all offer the potential for interpersonal and group communication at a distance.

There are now hot debates over whether two specific instances of convergence are actually telephony: Internet telephony and video dialtone. One can now use the digital addressable Internet network to engage in real-time audio (and video) interaction, totally bypassing the local telephone network, or, use the net to bypass the long-distance system and connect to a local phone system. The telephone industry is arguing that this is "telephone" service and should be subject to the same taxes (access fees) and regulation as the older switched telephone network. The Internet phone industry, however, argues that this is an enhanced computer service, which is not subject to regulation under current U.S. law. Conversely, several phone companies are proposing to provide their customers with television signals through the phone system, arguing that this is a enhanced telephone service that should not be subject to the regulation and local taxation faced by cable systems that deliver the same signals to the same household. From the user perspective, if the quality of the service is the same, it doesn't matter who provides it or what it is called. Although video dialtone has languished in the United States, Internet telephony has exploded in 1999, increasing twelvefold to some 2.5 billion minutes (Wong, 1999).

To further convolute matters, many of the new entrants into the telephony/data services/video delivery marketplaces are looking at the Internet as an alternative basic network structure. Internet network systems use an addressable, digital, packet-switched network, abbreviated as IP systems. These systems are flexible, accommodate any level of bandwidth in the wired system, and replace expensive switches with cheap computer processors. They are not only inherently significantly cheaper than traditional switched systems, but they are more easily upgradeable in terms of bandwidth, and the cost advantages of IP over switched networks increases as bandwidth increases. For the first time, local phone companies' heavy investment in switched networks is proving to be an economic disadvantage, as new entrants can build the newer, more efficient IP networks more cheaply (Sanford C. Bernstein and McKinsey & Company, 2000).

The answer to the question of just what new services are embodied in the new vision of "telephony" may well be resolved in the current debate over just what will constitute the goal of Universal Service in this new millennium. Since the 1930s, the goal of Universal Service has been phrased in terms of providing access to basic voice telephone service. With the 1996 Telecommunications Act, the FCC has been asked to revisit this definition, with an eye toward incorporating some level of new telecommunications services into the definition (Aufderheide, 1999). Among the primary considerations are adding Internet access (computer communications) and/or some version of wideband video (cable). It has been virtually accepted that basic voice telephony is no longer the minimally acceptable level of telecommunications service for modern society.

CONCLUSION

As Pitsch (1996) noted, the changes in telephony sometimes referred to as the information superhighway are in large part a manifestation of the same digital revolution that is driving the computer industry. One of the clear trends is toward the convergence of voice, data, and video communication services in the digital network, a trend symbiotically enhanced by the conversion to wide-bandwidth network structures. These trends are now fostered by a new policy emphasis promoting competition and convergence rather than seeking to micromanage monopoly service providers. Competition is already starting to drive prices down significantly, with further cuts clearly coming.

Although there remain important questions about costs and user demand, there are important economic impacts that can be confidently predicted. These are likely to be driven by three fundamental trends now under way: Telecom services will become cheaper and more mobile; bandwidth and addressability will improve; and the network will become increasingly interconnected and global. Pitsch (1996) suggested that one of the biggest impacts of these trends will be in increasing the scale, scope, and speed of innovation and information flows. The scope, many believe, is rapidly becoming global (Akwule, 1992). This will have the impact of reducing transaction costs (particularly based on distance) and in further increasing the market for information goods and intellectual property (often referred to as the "commodification" of information). In this last, Pritsch is joined by many others (Babe, 1995; Mosco, 1996; Schiller, 1981, 1989; Sussman, 1997). One of the continuing issues will be whether, or how fast, these changes will diffuse around the world. Akwule (1992) noted that there are a number of constraints to the creation of new telecommunication networks and the adoption of new telephony services: limited economic resources for investment, scarcity of prerequisite power sources and technical expertise, and problematic geography. Although these are obstacles that may slow down the diffusion of new networks and services, demand for information and communications services is growing at a tremendous pace and will continue to push the expansion of telecommunications.

Nowhere is the impact of increased competition and convergence, driven by continuing technological advances, more evident than in the telephone industry. The telephone industry is being radically transformed as it searches for new markets and services in the face of increased competition and the implications of digital wideband telecommunications. People are building this new network now, and many of them are not traditional phone companies. More and more, central players in telephony speak of abandoning the ubiquitous switched network so identified with the telephone in favor of Internet-flavored network structures. What we think of today as the telephone is increasingly just one piece of telecommunication goods and services being offered by an ever-increasing variety of suppliers.

REFERENCES

Akwule, R. (1992). *Global telecommunications: The technology, administration, and policies.* Boston: Focal Press.

Arndt, H. W. (1978). *The rise and fall of economic growth: A study in contemporary thought.* Chicago: University of Chicago Press.

Aronson, S. H. (1986). The sociology of the telephone. In G. Gumpert & R. Cathcart (Eds.), *Intermedia: Interpersonal communication in a media world.* New York: Oxford University Press.

Aufderheide, P. (1999). *Communications policy and the public interest: The Telecommunications Act of 1996.* New York: Guilford.

Babe, R. E. (1995). *Communication and the transformation of economics: Essays in information, public policy, and political economy.* Boulder, CO: Westview Press.

Badham, R. J. (1986). *Theories of industrial society.* New York: St. Martin's Press.

Baldwin, T. F., McVoy, D. S., & Steinfield, C. (1996). *Convergence: Integrating media, information & communication.* Thousand Oaks, CA: Sage.

Bates, B. J. (1988). Information as an economic good: Sources of individual and social value. In V. Mosco & J. Wasko (Eds.), *The political economy of information* (pp. 76-94). Madison: University of Wisconsin Press.

Bates, B. J. (1990). Information systems and society: Potential impacts of alternative structures. *Telecommunications Policy, 14*(2), 151-158.

Bates, B. J. (1993, May). *The macrosocial impact of communication systems: Access, bias, control.* Paper presented at the 43rd annual conference of the International Communication Association, Washington DC.

Bates, B. J. (1997). Learning from the evolution of telecommunications in the developed world. In P. S. N. Lee (Ed.), *Telecommunications and development in China* (pp. 21-54). Cresskill, NJ: Hampton Press.

Baumol, W. J., & Sidak, J. G. (1994). *Toward competition in local telephony.* Cambridge, MA: MIT Press.

Becker, J., Hedebro, G., & Paldan, L. (1986). *Communication and domination: Essays to honor Herbert I. Schiller.* Norwood, NJ: Ablex.

Beniger, J. R. (1986). *The control revolution: Technological and economic origins of the information society.* Cambridge, MA: Harvard University Press.

Bracken, J. K., & Sterling, C. H. (1995). *Telecommunications research resources: An annotated guide.* Mahwah, NJ: Lawrence Erlbaum Associates.

Cherry, C. (1977). The telephone system: Creator of mobility and social change. In I. Pool (Ed.), *The social impact of the telephone* (pp. 112-126). Cambridge, MA: MIT Press.

Cherry, C. (1985). *The age of access: Information technology and social revolution.* London: Croom Helm.

Czitrom, D. J. (1982). *Media and the American mind: From Morse to McLuhan.* Chapel Hill: University of North Carolina Press.

Dimmick, J. W., Sikand, J., & Patterson, S. J. (1994). The gratifications of the household telephone: Sociability, instrumentality and reassurance. *Communications Research, 21*(5), 643-663.

Dordick, H., & LaRose, R. (1992). *The telephone in daily life: A study of personal telephone use.* East Lansing: Department of Telecommunications, University of Michigan.

DuBoff, R. (1983). The telegraph and the structure of markets in the United States, 1845-1890. *Research in Economic History, 8,* 253-277.

Etzioni, A. (1986). The American way of economic development. In O. F. Borda (Ed.), *The challenge of social change* (pp. 57-74). London: Sage.

Fischer, C. S. (1992). *America calling: A social history of the telephone to 1940.* Berkeley: University of California Press.

Gerbner, G., Mowlana, H., & Schiller, H. I. (1996). *Invisible crises: What conglomerate control of media means for America and the world.* Boulder, CO: Westview Press.

Gonzalez-Manet, E. (1988). *The hidden war of information* (L. Alexandre, Trans.). Norwood, NJ: Ablex.

Hudson, H. E. (1984). *When telephones reach the village: The role of telecommunications in rural development.* Norwood, NJ: Ablex.

Hudson, H. E. (1988). *A bibliography of telecommunications and socio-economic development.* Norwood, MA: Artech House.

Innis, H. A. (1950). *Empire and communications.* Toronto: University of Toronto Press.

Innis, H. A. (1964). *The bias of communication.* Toronto: University of Toronto Press.

Katz, E., & Szecko, T. (Eds.). (1981). *Mass media and social change.* London: Sage.

Lansing, K. P., & Bates, B. J. (1992). Videotex as public information systems: The French and American experience. *Southwestern Mass Communication Journal, 7*(1), 22-34.

Lerner, D. (1948). Communication and development. In D. Lerner & L. M. Nelson (Eds.), *Communication research: A half-century appraisal* (pp. 148-166). Honolulu: University of Hawaii Press.

Lerner, D. (1958). *The passing of traditional society.* New York: The Free Press.

Lipartito, K. (1989). *The Bell System and regional business: The telephone in the South, 1877-1920.* Baltimore: Johns Hopkins University Press.

Lundstedt, S. B. (1990). *Telecommunications, values, and the public interest.* Norwood, NJ: Ablex.

Maddox, B. (1977). Women and the switchboard. In I. De S. Pool (Ed.), *The social impact of the telephone* (pp. 262-280). Cambridge MA: MIT Press.

Maitland Commission. (1984, December). *The missing link* (Report of the Independent [Maitland] Commission for Worldwide Telecommunications Development). Geneva: ITU.

Marvin, C. (1988). *When old technologies were new: Thinking about electric communication in the late nineteenth century.* New York: Oxford University Press.

Masuda, Y. (1981). *The information society as post-industrial society.* Bethesda, MD: World Future Society.

Mattelart, A. (1985). *Communication and information technologies: Freedom of choice for Latin America?* Norwood, NJ: Ablex.

McConnaughey, J. (1995). *Falling through the net: A survey of the "have nots" in rural and urban America.* Washington, DC: U.S. Department of Commerce.

McCreadie, M., & Rice, R. E. (1999a). Trends in analyzing access to information, Part I: Cross-disciplinary conceptualizations. *Information Processing and Management, 35*(1), 45-76.

McCreadie, M., & Rice, R. E. (1999b). Trends in analyzing access to information, Part II: Unique and integrating conceptualizations. *Information Processing and Management, 35*(1), 77-99.

McDermott, P. (1998). (HYPERLINK http://ombwatch.org/www/ombw/info/infortun.html). Accessed 27 July 1998.

McLeod, J. M., & Blumler, J. G. (1987). The macrosocial level of communication science. In C. R. Berger & S. H. Chaffee (Eds.), *Handbook of communication science* (pp. 271-322). Newbury Park, CA: Sage.

McQuail, D. (1994). *Mass communication theory: An introduction* (3rd ed.). Thousand Oaks, CA: Sage.

Melody, W. H. (1988). Dealing with global networks: Some characteristics of international markets. In G. Muskens & J. Gruppelaar (Eds.), *Global telecommunications networks: Strategic considerations* (pp. 59-73). Dordrecht, Holland: Kluwer Academic Publishers.

Meyers, J. (1998, June 8). Today's networks of tomorrow. *Telephony,* pp. 40-60.

Mitchell, B. M., & Donyo, T. (1994). *Utilization of the U.S. telephone network.* Delft, The Netherlands: RAND.

Mosco, V. (1996). *The political economy of information.* London: Sage.

Mowlana, H. (1986). *Global information and world communication: New frontiers in international relations.* New York: Longman.

Mowlana, H., & Wilson, L. J. (1990). *The passing of modernity: Communication and the transformation of society.* New York: Longman.

Mulgan, G. J. (1991). *Communication and control: Networks and the new economics of communication.* New York: Guilford.

Noll, R. G. (1986). The political and institutional context of communications policy. In M. S. Snow (Ed.), *Marketplace for telecommunications: Regulation & deregulation in industrialized democracies* (pp. 42-65). New York: Longman.

O'Keefe, G. J., & Sulanowski, B. K. (1995). More than just talk: Uses, gratifications, and the telephone. *Journalism and Mass Communications Quarterly, 72*(4), 922-933.

Organisation for Economic Co-operation and Development (OECD). (1985). *Universal service obligations in a competitive telecommunications environment.* Series: Information Computer Communications Policy, 38. Paris: Author.

Pitsch, P. K. (1996). *The innovation age: A new perspective on the telecom revolution.* Washington, DC: Hudson Institute/Progress & Freedom Foundation.

Pool, I. S. (Ed.). (1977). *The social impact of the telephone.* Cambridge, MA: MIT Press.

Pool, I. S. (1983a). *Forecasting the telephone: A retrospective technology assessment.* Norwood, NJ: Ablex.

Pool, I. S. (1983b). *Technologies of freedom: On free speech in an electronic age.* Cambridge, MA: Harvard University Press.

Pool, I. S. (1990). *Technologies without boundaries: On telecommunications in a global age.* Cambridge, MA: Harvard University Press.

Radojkovic, M. (1984). Eight considerations on new information technology and the development of democracy. *Gazette, 33*(1), 51-58.

Regli, B. J. W. (1997). *Wireless: Strategically liberalizing the telecommunications market.* Mahwah, NJ: Lawrence Erlbaum Associates

Rogers, E. M. (Ed.). (1976). *Communication and development: Critical perspectives.* Beverly Hills, CA: Sage.

Rogers, E. M. (1983). *The diffusion of innovations.* New York: The Free Press.

Sanford C. Bernstein & Co., Inc., & McKinsey & Co., Inc. (2000, January). *Broadband! A joint industry study* (Research report). New York.

Saunders, R. J., Warford, J. J., & Wellenius, B. (1983). *Telecommunications and economic development.* Baltimore: Johns Hopkins University Press.

Schiller, H. I. (1981). *Who knows: Information in the age of the Fortune 500.* Norwood, NJ: Ablex.

Schiller, H. I. (1989). *Culture, Inc.: The corporate takeover of public expression.* New York: Oxford University Press.

Short, J., & Christie, B. (1976). *The social psychology of telecommunications.* London: Wiley.

Singh, I. B. (1983). *Telecommunications in the year 2000: National and international perspectives.* Norwood, NJ: Ablex.

Slack, J. D. (1984). *Communication technologies and society: Conceptions of causality and the politics of technological intervention.* Norwood, NJ: Ablex.

Smith, A. (1983). Telecommunications and the fading of the industrial age. *Political Quarterly, 54*(2), 127-136.

Snow, M. S. (Ed.). (1986). *Marketplace for telecommunications: Regulation & deregulation in industrialized democracies*. New York: Longman.

Snow, M. S., & Jussawalla, M. (1986). *Telecommunication economics and international regulatory policy: An annotated bibliography*. Westport CT: Greenwood Press.

Stern, E., & Gwathmey, E. (1994). *Once upon a telephone: An illustrated social history*. New York: Harcourt, Brace.

Strategis (1998a, May 28). *World cellular/PCS subscribers to surpass one-half billion at the millennium*. Press release. (http://www.strategis-group.com/press/worldcell98.html. Accessed 25 August 1998.)

Strategis (1998b, June 5). *PCS vs. PCS: Competitive climate to intensify based on newest PCS market entries*. Press release. (http://www.strategisgroup.com/press/uspcs98.htm. Accessed 25 August 1998.)

Strategis Group, (1998c, August 7). *$160 billion global broadband market in 2003*. Press release. (http://www.strategisgroup.com/press/globbrdband.html. Accessed 25 August 1998.)

Sussman, G. (1997). *Communication, technology, and politics in the information age*. Thousand Oaks, CA: Sage.

U.S. Department of Commerce. (1998). Telecommunications services. In *U.S. Industry and trade outlook 1998* (pp. 30-1-30-23). Washington, DC: U.S. Government Printing Office.

Utsumi, T. (1978). Need for a global information system. In A. S. Edelstein, J. E. Bowes, & S. M. Harsel (Eds.), *Information societies: Comparing the Japanese and American experiences* (pp. 79-83). Seattle, WA: International Communication Center.

Varma, B. N. (1980). *The sociology and politics of development: A theoretical study*. London: Routledge & Kegan Paul.

Webster, A. (1984). *Introduction to the sociology of development*. London: Macmillan.

Wellman, B., & Tindall, D. B. (1993). How telephone networks connect social networks. In W. D. Richards & G. A. Barnett (Eds.), *Progress in communication sciences* (Vol. XII). Norwood, NJ: Ablex.

Williams, R. (1976). *Communications* (3rd ed.). Hammondsworth, Middlesex, England: Penguin.

Winston, B. (1986). *Misunderstanding media*. Cambridge, MA: Harvard University Press.

Wong, W. (1999, December, 29). Net phone calls could soon catch on. CNET News.com. (Available online at: http://news.cnet.com/category/0-1004-200-1509350.html. Accessed April 4, 2000.)

Woods, B. (1993). *Communication, technology and the development of people*. London: Routledge.

6

Adoption of Audio Information Services in the United States: A Bridge Innovation

Kimberly A. Neuendorf
David Atkin
Leo W. Jeffres
Cleveland State University

The recent focus on the information superhighway has crystallized the nation's attention on media convergence. What may come as a surprise, however, is that the telephone company has been integrating prototypical mass-audience information services—in one form or another—for several decades now (see Bates, Albright & Washington, chap. 4, this volume). Observers contend that these services "constitute the first widely used interactive medium, allowing users to retrieve information, complete transactions or answer questions with touch-tone phones" (LaRose & Atkin, 1992, p. 413). In some respects, telephonic applications have paved the way for the information superhighway, preparing users for interactivity and scalability.

Some distinguish between 1-900 telepolls and audiotext services, pointing out that the latter typically "requires the user to pay a fee to access any of a wide variety of vendor-supplied information services" (Neuendorf, Atkin, & Jeffres, 1998, p. 81). Such reports suggest that ongoing deregulatory measures, such as the Telecommunication Act of

1996, should hasten the arrival of telephony as a dominant player in the electronic media environment. This chapter outlines adopter characteristics for audiotext, broadly defined to encompass such vehicles as most 1-900 systems, many 1-800 numbers and related audio-information services.

The realization of audiotext as a mature medium implies a need to revisit some of the earlier work that examined the characteristics of telephone subscribers (Atkin, 1995). The purpose if this chapter is threefold: (a) to profile audiotext in terms of its structure and regulatory evolution; (b) to review the evolution of earlier work that contributed to our current understanding of audiotext subscribership; and (c) to introduce some new theoretical perspectives to the problem of understanding audiotext's role in the changing information environment, including the identification of audio information services as a bridge innovation.

BACKGROUND

As scholars (e.g., Marvin, 1988; Poole, 1983) recount, audio information services featuring one-to-many messaging strategies can be traced back to the earliest applications of the telephone, such as Budapest's one-way public information line (circa 1885). Customers in the United States will be more familiar with recorded services for time, which date back to the 1920s. Other services such as weather were added in the decades to follow, but no wide expansion of these facilities existed until the telephone industry was deregulated during the 1970s and 1980s. As Neuendorf et al. (1998) outlined, a defining aspect of these services is their common-carrier, pay-per-use structure, requiring the user to pay a fee to access any of a wide variety of vendor-supplied information services.

At present, mass media phone services heavily rely on "media-stimulated" users for their audiences because their advertisements or promotions in print and broadcast media are often the only means potential users have of learning about them. More recently, Internet sites have proven a popular vehicle for 1-900 promotion, with hundreds of individual lines promoted in dedicated Web sites, and scores of others noted in topical listing services.

The $1 billion audiotext industry is already a major provider of mass audience phone services:

> About two-thirds of the content accessed through national 900 numbers is entertainment, another 15 percent is live conversation (on so-called Group Access Bridging or "GAB lines"), 10 percent is polling and the rest consists of news and information programs, promotions and user-supported customer service lines. . . . There are also audiotext services that allow their callers to learn about the activities of

their favorite entertainers or to take part in trivia contests, to confess their sins or to hear confessions recorded by others, or to talk to the undead. (LaRose & Atkin, 1992, p. 414)

Print and electronic media have become, in turn, heavy users of phone-delivered text services. Kamerer and Bergen's (1995) study of a media-stimulated audiotext system run by a large metropolitan daily newspaper identified two categories of user inquiry—functional (the most popular), including weather and financial information; and "fun," including soap opera updates, horoscopes, and trivia. Audiotext is being used in a variety of media promotion schemes, including play-along audience participation games and instant polls: "By keying in personal identification information, home participants in game shows or tune-in promotions can enter drawings for 'valuable prizes,' and become part of an extended audience that is actively in the game" (Neuendorf et al., 1998, p. 81).

One of the largest segments of entertainment services involves dial-a-porn (Glascock & LaRose, 1993), nonobscene versions of which are constitutionally protected (*Sable Communications, Inc. v. FCC*, 1989). Persistent court challenges to indecency services take a toll on adult-oriented market providers, however, as industry leader Carlin Communications filed for bankruptcy during the early 1990s. (For a discussion of moral values as an impediment to diffusion, see Reagan, chap. 12, this volume). Segments outside of this realm also have shown vulnerability, as the Psychic Friends Hotline ultimately went out of business; apparently they didn't see the end coming (Atkin, 1998)!

Even so, LaRose and Atkin (1992) found that 60% of respondents in a national survey reported using audiotext, dubbing it the "reinvention" of the telephone as a mass medium. Comparable demand levels have been borne out in more recent work (Bates et al., chap. 4, this volume; Neuendorf et al., 1998), prompting the observers to conclude that, although the telephone is commonly taken for granted as a low technology, one-to-one, culturally integrated voice medium, recent changes in technology and policy render it an ideal pathway for new information and entertainment services. As they conclude, this is one of many ways in which the phone industry helps blur traditional distinctions between conventional communication media and their high-tech counterparts.

Audiotext thus presents an intriguing convergence of conventional, entertainment-oriented mass media—including broadcasting—and more information-oriented point-to-point media, such as telephony. In the parlance of diffusion theory, the telephone has been reinvented to operate in a manner more characteristic of mass media, as a sender of mediated information and entertainment. At the same time, its introduction of *interactivity*—reacting to user prompts—evokes comparisons with newer, higher tech cousins such as the Internet.

The study of audiotext audiences has been limited. Like the Internet that followed, the 1-900 industry was characterized by unbridled and undocumented expansion. No coherent "1-900 phonebook" has existed. This folkloric existence carries a couple of implications. First, for users accustomed to comprehensive documentation (e.g., in the form of telephone directories, television guides, and library indexes), the ephemeral nature of the structure and content of the 1-900 industry could act as a barrier to adoption. Potential adopters receive only scattered information about the availability of 1-900 services.

Second, the loosely structured audiotext industry does not easily lend itself to academic study. Indeed, Glascock and LaRose (1992) lamented the difficulty in securing the cooperation of telephone providers. In their content analysis of 1-900 numbers hosted by four major providers, they were unable to construct a complete sampling frame, persuading only two providers to supply subscriber lists. For the two who refused to provide lists, they resorted to random-digit dialing (RDD) methods, using Bellcore's catalog of 800/900 prefix assignments, a very time-consuming and expensive option (approximately 6,000 numbers were randomly dialed). Their content analysis found that services fall into seven functional categories: informational (38%), mature (20%), adult (6%), credit (10%), general entertainment (9%), contests (9%), and sales promotion (8%).

A symbiotic relationship seems to have developed between the 1-900 industry and Internet commerce. A systematic search via a dozen Internet search engines reveals an interesting mix of sources on 1-900 telephone services: (a) hundreds of individual 1-900 numbers advertised, (b) several 1-900 "phonebooks" (with very limited coverage—self-selected entirely), (c) a number of regulatory guides to the legalities involved in the administration of 1-900 numbers (including cautions about unscrupulous services; e.g., the FTC's guide and a number of statements from state attorneys general), and (d) scores of sites providing information on "how-to" establish 1-900 businesses, including companies that provide "pre-packaged" 1-900 services and "011" services. Additionally, some services offering standard advertising plans for existing 1-900 services are promoted on the Internet. These "ad plan" sites, as well as the 1-900 phonebooks and "pre-packaged 1-900" plans, follow a standard template or outline of 1-900 service types: psychics, astrology/horoscopes, sex lines, chat lines, date lines, sports scores and trivia, advice (e.g., medical, cooking, car repair), technical support (e.g., word-processing, WWW help), fund-raising, soap opera information, and other (e.g., Dial-a-laugh, Dial-an-insult, Dial-a-prayer, UFO sightings, "Dream line").

Interactive Polling as a Special Case of Audiotext

Often classified alongside audiotext, 1-900 polling is a related call-in service that allows callers to "vote" in media-stimulated plebiscites by pressing buttons on their keypads. For instance, the media make extensive use of unscientific self-selected listener opinion surveys (SLOPs), and have been heavily criticized for doing so (Gollin, 1992). These SLOP surveys are susceptible to "rigging" by blocks of organized voters, multiple voting, and demographically skewed respondent pools (Atkin & LaRose, 1994b). Yet the same might be said of rallies, the Internet, and other public settings in which various groups jockey to present their views (Bates & Harmon, 1991, 1993). As LaRose and Atkin (1992) noted, 1-800 numbers typically differ in that a live operator rather than a computerized answering system provides the content of the call. As they recount, media-stimulated calling is a related service that was created for media promotion purposes, allowing users to register their responses to questions or to ring through to a live operator. Fig. 6.1 summarizes the typical differences in these various phone-based services.

These phone applications—as progenitors to online media—can help individuals gain a better understanding of the adoption dynamic for emerging applications along the information superhighway.

UNDERSTANDING AUDIOTEXT ADOPTION

Despite the recent and smooth diffusion of audiotext into most U.S. households, an understanding of the factors that contribute to its use is incomplete. As such, a theoretical model for audiotext subscribership is in order. Market research (e.g., Yankee Group, 1988) has examined the media and demographic characteristics that distinguish audiotext users from nonusers, but has not left much in the way of theoretical insight into audiotext usage.

	Operator-Assisted	Computer-assisted
INTERPERSONAL	1-800	Voicemail
MASS	1-900 polling	Audiotext

Figure 6.1. Typical phone-based innovation applications

As scholars (LaRose & Atkin, 1992; O'Keefe & Sulanowski, 1992) noted, audiotext adoption would seem to provide an excellent place to start looking for the convergence of theories of mass media behavior and other domains of telecommunications behavior. It makes use of the oldest and most pervasive form of mediated voice communication (i.e., the telephone), which provides interpersonal linkages to virtually every home in the country (see Bates et al., chap. 4, this volume).

Because academic research addressing audiotext did not begin until the 1990s—and has only encompassed a handful of contributors beyond us—it is useful to consider parallels with more widely studied media innovations such as cable. Becker, Dunwoody, and Rafaeli (1983), for instance, underscore the utility of uses and gratifications variables in helping to explain cable subscribership. LaRose and Atkin later observed that satisfaction with service is the most powerful predictor of cable adoption, which Reagan (1989) confirmed was the case for several new media, including videotext. Although O'Keefe and Sulanowski (1992) confirmed that a consideration of user motivations is also useful for understanding attendance to audiotext, hybrid mass communication, telecommunication, and interpersonal communication perspectives of that sort have been rare.

Part of the gulf between these literatures might be explained by the distinct functions traditionally provided by media in each realm. As reviewed at the onset, the telephone has long been taken for granted as a relatively low-technology, culturally familiar, two-way voice medium. To the extent that telephone adoption research was conducted, it was often steeped in the annals of the Bell system monopoly, and hence remained proprietary. Moreover, the period of "take-off" for the telephone as an innovation—in the first half of the 20th century—predated the diffusion of television (and the research traditions that emerged to study its influence). Research on cable adoption, for instance, did not begin until the 1970s (e.g., Barnes & Kelloway, 1978; Collins, Reagan, & Abel, 1983; Sparkes, 1983; Sparkes & Kang, 1986). And, given that so much diffusion research has been conducted via telephone, telephone adoption has performed as a constant, rather than a variable, in diffusion study databases.

Even so, the recent convergence of these traditionally distinct media necessitates a wider cross-pollination of the research traditions that arose around each (Heeter, 1989). Although Steinfield, Dutton, and Kovaric's (1989) study is representative of work that considers distinctions between new and conventional media, LaRose and Atkin (1988) noted that the telephone emulates cable in that it is delivered to the home by wire, requires substantial initial effort to obtain, engenders a recurring monthly purchase decision, is shared by the entire household and acts as a carrier for a variety of services provided by third parties.

When tracing the route through which the telephone has assumed utility status (i.e., something one cannot do without), those authors drew from several early telephone studies focusing on interpersonal dynamics (Dunn, Williams, & Spivey, 1971; Mahan, 1979; Perl, 1978, reviewed in Taylor, 1980; Pousette, 1976; Train, McFadden, & Ben-Najiv, 1987). This work exemplifies how the telecommunication literature introduces new variables that have been neglected in the mass communication literature—the cost of telephone service and the quality of service (operationalized as single vs. multi-party service availability). As Bates et al.'s (chap. 4, this volume) review suggests, these variables have been found to be important predictors of telephone access and a wide variety of other telecommunications behaviors. Perhaps the most important perspective that might unify these disparate media use domains involves the diffusion of innovations perspective.

DIFFUSION THEORY

As other reviews (e.g., Rogers, chap. 3, this volume) recount, the diffusion of innovations perspective has been widely studied during the past century, originating from the disciplines of anthropology and rural sociology, and becoming firmly ensconced in the discipline of communication during the 1960s and 1970s. Rogers' (1995) review links innovativeness to several certain attitudinal and sociodemographic factors that might determine consumer patronage of new products and services.

Krugman's (1985) review of early studies on new media adoption confirmed the adoption profile noted in diffusion research generally (Rogers, 1995). Earlier adopters of such media as cable, personal computers, and videotext generally have been found to be upscale, educated, younger adults who express greater interest in adopting new products (see Atkin & LaRose, 1994a; Dutton, Rogers, & Jun, 1987a, 1987b).

Although formal meta-analyses (Dutton et al., 1987a, 1987b) have reviewed diffusion trends for new media ranging from personal computing to cable communications, point-to-point media have generally been absent from those discussions. When trying to fashion a theoretical model for adoption of phone-based information services, scholars (Mahan, 1979; Train et al., 1987) have distinguished adopters from nonadopters in media use and demographic terms.

Others in the marketing literature (e.g., Dickerson & Gentry, 1983) have explored the concept of *consumer creativity,* which emphasizes *origence* (the personality trait of originality) and *intellectence* (intellectual ability). They found the latter was linked to personal computer adoption.

As Rogers (1995) noted, a century of research encompassing more than 10,000 studies has yet to yield empirical support for a concept of innovativeness that is generalizable over a wide range of products and other innovations. He also noted (see chap. 3, this volume) that some of these inconsistencies can be attributed to variations in products under study and the limited scope of empirical research in communication.

Past work on media adoption typically addresses descriptive hypothesis testing rather than conceptual theory building to explain and predict consumer behavior. Applied studies on diffusion, for instance, are representative of a larger marketing literature whose failures are reaching "crisis" proportions (e.g., Clancy & Shulman, 1993). As Wolfe (1998) noted:

> Multivariate statistics that describe personality traits can account for no more than 7 percent of purchasing behavior. . . . An increasingly desperate search for cause-and-effect explanations leads many psychologists to retreat to abstract ideas and ignore contexts completely. (p. 25)

In order to expand explanatory power, Wolfe (1998) recommended that researchers expand the range of psychological variables to include biological variables:

> Many research questions fail to deeply stimulate consumers' somatic markers or "hot buttons." Instead, they invite respondents to develop a reason-based explanation that often distorts reality. Instead of the real reason for buying or not buying something, researchers get a rationalization based on the respondent's idealized self-image. (p. 26)

Rogers' (1995) work includes the linkage of cosmopoliteness and innovativeness: Those with an orientation toward the greater world (rather than toward solely local concerns) are more likely to be innovators. Although this variable has yet to be investigated in relation to phone information services adoption, cosmopoliteness has been addressed in relation to the adoption of companion Internet services. In particular, Atkin, Jeffres, and Neuendorf (1998) found that adoption of online information services was related to a more localized communication, but not to a larger "cosmopolite" need for information about the larger city or national community.

Characteristics of the Innovation

Researchers (e.g., Dozier, Valente, & Severn, 1986; Robertson, 1967, 1971; Rogers with Shoemaker, 1971) outline four categories of innovation: the *continuous,* the *dynamically continuous,* the *discontinuous,* and the *dynamically discontinuous.* Communication scholars have classified a wide range of new media according to the typology (Atkin & LaRose, 1994a), defining a continuous innovation as one that modifies an old product in some small way, but does not disrupt established behavior patterns (Dozier et al., 1986). A dynamically continuous innovation is rather more differentiated from past technologies, prompting a greater disruption in behavior patterns. Finally, the greatest degree of disruption accompanies the discontinuous innovation, which typically requires some new behavioral patterns and new hardware acquisition, and the dynamically discontinuous innovation, which entails a *major* shift in behavior and hardware adoption.

Phone-based innovations may be assessed using this categorization scheme (Atkin & LaRose, 1994a): Voice (plain old telephone service [POTS]) as continuous, audiotext as dynamically continuous, the answering machine as discontinuous, and modem/use of T1 data lines as dynamically discontinuous. We maintain that most phone delivered services are dynamically continuous with traditional telephony; thus, few barriers to adoption exist.

Other dimensions have been set forward for classifying innovations, many of which are discussed in other chapters in this volume. In the first edition of his treatise on diffusion, Rogers (1962) outlined five characteristics: relative advantage, compatibility, complexity, divisibility (later termed trialability), and communicability (later termed observability). Others (e.g., Fliegel & Kilvin, 1966) added such characteristics as financial cost risk associated with the product, return to the investment, and efficiency of the product (in terms of time saving and avoidance of discomfort).

In evaluating these attributes in wide ranging product areas, Rogers (1995) noted that the adoption process is positively related to the product's relative advantage, compatibility, trialability, and observability, and negatively related to its complexity and cost. Focusing on the personal computer, Dickerson and Gentry (1983) found that the relative advantage of adopting high-technology innovations derives from functional needs, whereas adoption of lower technology, high symbolism innovations is driven by a buyer's need to appear fashionable.

A main relative advantage for most audiotext users seems to be the technology's *reliability*—the provision of consistent and ready information on demand, often 24 hours a day. A major relative disadvantage is the lack of opportunity for feedback. On the dimension of compatibility, audiotext scores are quite high. Its dependence on existing hardware and user skills make it a unique adjunct to traditional telephone use. But, compatibility may not obtain in limited cases where, say, an adult-oriented service conflicts with an individual's personal mores. Similarly, trialability is high; users may sample 1-900 offerings, for example, without capital outlay. The perceived complexity of audiotext will vary with its scalability. That is, the "deeper" the tree structure of an automated audiotext system, the more complex it may seem to the user. However, simple human-contact 1-900 numbers (e.g., many psychic lines, sex lines, and chat lines) will be perceived as no more complex than "reaching out and touching someone" via an ordinary phone call. The use of audiotext services requires negligible capital investment, but often entails rather high recurring costs, as any parent of a 1-900-frenzied teen can attest. This "low apparent cost/high real cost" dynamic has been a threat to the longevity of 1-900 services.

Adopter Profiles

As reviews by Rogers (1995) and Dutton et al. (1987a, 1987b) suggest, diffusion studies find a fairly consistent positive relationship between early adoption and income, education, and higher status occupations (e.g., Adcock, Hirschman, & Goldstucker, 1977; Robertson, 1971). With regard to income, adoption is a natural function of the disposable financial resources one has available; higher costs of course present a less imposing barrier for wealthier households. As commentators (Atkin & LaRose, 1994a; Lin, 1994; Zerbinos, 1990) note in conjunction with videotext, online services are now more attractive, as they provide better content for only half the cost of defunct 1980s pioneers such as Viewtron. The value of the Internet should continue to increase as more users connect to it (see Rogers, chap. 3, this volume), as it reaches "critical mass" (Markus, 1987; Rogers, 1995) and the high "connectivity" levels now enjoyed by audiotext.

Similarly, educational attainment is linked to a higher need to process and understand information services. As other chapters in this volume detail, this was traditionally perceived as a daunting barrier to the adoption of computer services, but has recently been ameliorated by the drive to provide more user-friendly systems. Related to these attributes, higher occupational status can drive adoption owing to a professional's greater work-related need to receive constantly updated information, such as stock reports.

As Rogers' (1995) seminal review suggests, innovation studies often yield conflicting results with respect to age. Although the confluence of research suggests that the elderly are relatively slow to adopt innovations, younger consumers are typically only able to adopt low-cost innovations. So, to the extent that age is a proxy for income, middle-aged consumers are often among the earliest to adopt new media, although younger segments typically express the highest levels of adoption intention (Lin, 1998).

In the realm of interactive media, for instance, younger consumers are among the most receptive for low-cost, high-technology products such as automatic teller machines (Adcock et al., 1977; LaRose & Atkin, 1992). Studies of 1-900 polling service adoption suggest a modest inverse relationship involving age (Atkin & LaRose, 1994b). Yet neither age nor any of the other commonly studied social locators has been powerfully related to audiotext adoption.

Generally, innovativeness has been positively linked to several personality factors not widely considered in the communication literature, including achievement motivation, receptivity to change and venturesomeness. Innovators are also typically less inner-directed and dogmatic than their nonadopting counterparts (Rogers, 1995).

Hirschman (1980) argued that the causes for innovativeness can be traced back to the underlying construct of novelty-seeking motives. These novelty-seeking motives, as noted by Flavell (1977), may serve two purposes: enhancement of self-preservation and problem-solving skills. Individuals with stronger novelty-seeking motives may proceed to either develop a novelty-seeking orientation (or willingness to adopt) or actualize this novelty-seeking intention (or engage in actual adoption). Building on that work, Lin's (1998) study of computer adoption found support for an intermediate category of "likely" adopters.

Rogers (1995) noted that adopters are less likely to perceive risk in the process of innovation, which he sees as driven by an actor, orienting to a situation. As he outlined, adoption behavior is oriented toward ends or goals, normally regulated, and involves the expenditure of effort or motivation. As Atkin and LaRose's (1994a) review suggests:

> Security is the ultimate goal, defined as the state of being that minimizes tension. Early adopters gain such security by being more venturesome (i.e., willing to try new products). This venturesomeness emerges as the dominant value among adopters, generally superseding concerns such as risk. In accordance with this model, security would represent the motivational force determining innovator adoption of phone delivered information services. (p. 97)

Indeed, in one of the very few studies to focus on audiotext and its adjuncts, Neuendorf et al. (1998) found that the use of audio information services was best predicted by patterns of personal communication, perceptions of quality of life, and film-going, rather than by social indica-tors (e.g., age, income, gender, education). In contrast, use of fax technol-ogy fit the profile of the early adopter articulated by Rogers (1995) fairly closely—the heavy fax user was younger, of higher income and more con-servative, engaging in more workplace and other cosmopolite personal communication, and was more likely to engage in computer use. The researchers concluded that the uniquely *continuous* nature of audio infor-mation services circumvents the "obstacles to adoption identified as criti-cal by other new-technology scholars" (p. 91) (e.g., expense that "tends to favor economic and intellectual elites"; Garramone, Harris, & Pizante, 1986, p. 446), and the print-based nature of many interactive media that discriminates against the less educated. Thus, audiotext and other infor-mation services emerge as conspicuously egalitarian, providing new infor-mation opportunities to users regardless of social status or other demo-graphic markers.

Given the limited empirical work on diffusion of audiotext, it is useful to review the adoption literature on the broader telephone medium.

Understanding Telephone Adoption

As reviews of the telephone adoption literature (Bates et al., chap. 4, this volume; LaRose & Atkin, 1994a; Taylor, 1980) recount, the telephone subscription phenomenon has given rise to a distinctive research tradition, addressing reasons for the acquisition and maintenance of telephone sub-scriptions. This tradition addressing what prompts users to obtain and maintain a telephone subscription is commonly termed demand for access. As LaRose and Atkin (1988) noted:

> This literature is found largely in the annals of the Bell System and is steeped in microeconomic theory. It relies heavily on aggregate data and was developed around the planning needs of the telephone com-panies that sponsored it. Time series models that predict growth in the demand for WATS lines and interstate telephone service or cross-sec-tional analyses of demand using city pairs as the units of analysis are typical of the research problems that are addressed. (p. 107)

These studies thus treat adoption issues differently than, say, the commu-nication literature, which focuses on the individual in its treatment of new media adoption. A rare behavioral perspective on telephone access demand was offered by Perl (1978), who found that age, income, educa-tion, employment, and urban residence were related to telephone access. Similarly, Mahan's (1979) work revealed that telephone subscribership was positively related to income, education, age, and status as head of household. Those less likely to have a phone included minority homes and homes with young children. These attributes were also inversely related to telephone subscription in Perl's (1978) study, along with male-headed, single-person, and southern and spouse-absent households.

There are, nevertheless, similarities in the ways access demand has been conceptualized for the latter two media (i.e., cable and telephony). For instance, Taylor faults the demand for access literature for its lack of theoretical rigor, echoing Krugman's (1985) major criticism of cable research. And, just as access demand has been marginalized in the telephone literature, scholars (Atkin & LaRose, 1994a; Rogers, chap. 3, this volume) maintain that new media adoption has been marginalized in the communication literature.

But when research on new media adoption was moving past the exploration of demographics (e.g., Becker, Dunwoody, & Rafaeli, 1983), Taylor (1980) advocated a wider consideration of attitudinal and economic variables in the area of telephony. Some of the more recent nonproprietary work on telephone access addresses the impact of cost and service quality variables. Consistent with expectations derived from the cable literature (LaRose & Atkin, 1988), telecommunication services judged higher in quality and lower in cost were consistently found to be more popular (Dunn, Williams, & Spivey, 1971; Perl, 1978; Pousette, 1976; Taylor, 1980; Train et al., 1987).

In this manner, communication scholars have drawn from Taylor's (1980) criticism that the benefits conferred by telephone access deserve wider consideration. Specifically, benefits conferred are conceptualized as the perceived utility of the telephone connection, a utility that is related to the connectivity of the network (LaRose & Atkin, 1988). Thus, as other chapters in this volume (e.g., Rogers, chap. 3) point out, the utility of a given network increases as more parties can be reached by it. LaRose and others maintain that this conceptualization echoes expectancy value theory as it is used to explain attendance to the media (e.g., Fishbein & Ajzen, 1975). In this manner, media behavior (in this case, telephone subscribership) can be related to the perceived benefits of engaging in the behavior.

Despite the diffusion literature's finding that earlier adopters of new technology tend to be upscale (e.g., Ettema, 1989), adopters of phone-polling services have been found to be lower in socioeconomic status (Atkin & LaRose, 1994b; LaRose & Atkin, 1992). This paradoxical finding prompted those researchers to conclude that, in this instance, the issue of complexity overrides constraints owing to financial resources. In particular, these phone-based services were inexpensive substitutes for those not skilled in accessing other two-way polling alternatives (e.g., online services).

In order to gain a better understanding of adoption intentions, it is useful to consider allied traditions that examine media choice in light of audience uses and gratifications and media substitution dynamics.

THE USES AND GRATIFICATIONS PERSPECTIVE

Given the increasing diversity of today's multimedia environment, an examination of attendance to audiotext service from the perspective of audience uses and gratifications is warranted. Dating to early applications with radio audiences a half-century ago, this framework assumes that content choices are motivated by certain internal needs and gratification-seeking motives (see, e.g., Charney & Greenberg, chap. 15, this volume). This tradition has uncovered a wide range of uses and needs served by media (Blumler, 1978; Levy, 1978; Rubin, 1983). In their seminal work, Katz, Gurevitch, and Haas (1973) identified the following five needs:

1. Cognitive needs, such as the need to understand.
2. Affective needs strengthening aesthetic or emotional experience.
3. Integrative needs strengthening one's confidence, credibility, stability.
4. Needs relating to strengthening contact with family, friends, and the world.
5. Needs related to escape or tension release (Jeffres, 1994, p. 247).

Following those intentions, audiences can fashion their own content selection and use patterns for the purposes of fulfilling various gratification expectations. As Lin (1993) noted, the strength of those needs, motives, and expectations ultimately determines modality or media content selection.

Although traditionally applied to the study of one-way, mass audience media, this approach is now favored by scholars (e.g., Lin, 1998; Perse & Dunn, 1998; Williams, Phillips, & Lum, 1985) for application to the study of new media. Here, the need for gratification assumes that an individual's media use behavior is motivated by the expectation to fulfill certain self-actualization needs (independent of the innovativeness need), such as entertainment.

This consideration of internal need is particularly important for a hybrid mass interpersonal vehicle like audiotext. For instance, Jeffres and Atkin (1996) found support for a model suggesting that use of visual media would be related to the traditional audience role, whereas the need to send messages was linked to interpersonal communication needs.

In that regard, the area of uses and gratifications theory that is perhaps most instructive here involves functional equivalence. Akin to notions of displacement and relative advantage discussed elsewhere in other chapters, this construct states that media content, channels, or modalities may be functionally equivalent in fulfilling audience needs (Jeffres, Atkin, & Neuendorf, 1995; Levy & Windahl, 1984; Lin, 1993; Rosengren, Wenner, & Palmgreen, 1985). Dimmick and his associates (e.g., Dimmick, Patterson, & Sikand, 1996) rephrased this concept in terms of gratification opportunities, finding distinctive patterns associated with the telephone.

As Lin's (1998) review suggests, dimensions of audience selectivity have been explored amidst a wide variety of mediated communication environments (see LaRose & Atkin, 1991; Lin, 1993; Perse & Courtright, 1993; Rubin & Rubin, 1990). These studies are representative of several in the mass communication literature that explore the multifaceted "needs," "motivations," or "gratifications sought" (i.e., expectations) in relation to the subsequent content selection and uses.

In the only comprehensive analysis of uses and gratifications associated with audiotext use, O'Keefe and Sulanowski (1992) found support for the dualistic approach common to uses and gratifications research on television. In particular, they discovered a range of audiotext gratifications patterns that fall into two broad dimensions: ritualistic (entertainment-oriented) and instrumental (information-oriented). They also found support for their expectation that audiences seeking higher levels of gratification would express greater interest in adopting. These parallel Kamerer and Bergen's (1995) classification of instrumental and "fun" audiotext service categories, and Dozier and Rice's (1984) identification of distinct audiences for videotext services—mature newsreaders who engage in ritualized play while reading newspapers, and nonpleasure readers who seek specific information from the newspaper and show significantly greater interest in videotext.

So it would seem that mass audience audiotext services are bridging a utilitarian gap between the entertainment-oriented television and the more instrumental telephone (Dimmick et al., 1996). Outside of that framework, researchers (Jeffres & Atkin, 1996; Neuendorf et al., 1998) confirm that attitudinal variables—particularly those addressing communication needs served by technology—are the most powerful predictors of audiotext as well as Internet adoption intentions. These studies collectively establish the value of considering need for gratification alongside more traditional demographic predictors of information service adoption. Even so, Perse and Courtright (1993) found that gratifications associated with computer use are not clustered along gratifications connected with traditional media (e.g., TV) and interpersonal communication channels (e.g., telephones). It is useful, therefore, to explore media-specific perceptions and patterns of use.

MEDIA SUBSTITUTION

Media scholars long have viewed the relationship between old and new media as a functional one, with new media forcing existing media to change their form and function in order to to persist. A new medium does not supplant existing media, but rather supplements them as they adapt to the changed environment. As Schramm (1988) noted, mass media never seem to die, although single units—individual newspapers or TV stations, for example—may cease to exist. All media available in the 17th century are still with us today.

Economic theory also has been applied to the relationship between media. The principle of relative constancy first enunciated by McCombs (1972) says that the pattern of economic support for mass media is relatively constant, so that the appearance of a new medium means further division of the pie. The complementary nature of print and visual/audio media is supported by an analysis that matches a decline in spending on print with a relative growth in spending on visual/audio media (Fullerton, 1988). Even within a media group—such as print media—tradeoffs are noted. Support for this principle has been found in the United States (McCombs, 1972) and other countries (Werner, 1986), but Wood (1986) and colleagues (Wood & O'Hare, 1991) found mixed results using the concept of "share of income constancy" in other historical periods.

Regardless of the historical pattern of adjustment between media as a whole, we need to examine how audience reactions (measured as uses and gratifications and in economic terms) allow us to examine the evolution of technologies that figure into more than a single medium. Whereas the distinction between books and newspapers is fairly clear, the boundaries between more recent innovations in media and technology are less definitive. Although it has taken many shapes and forms, media substitution theory maintains that the introduction of a new medium encourages a restructuring in the way consumers view established media (e.g., Henke & Donohue, 1989; Lin, 1994). Reagan (1987, 1989), for instance, found that adoption of most telecommunication technologies studied was most powerfully predicted by use of other such technologies and attitudes toward them.

Other applications of this concept encompass such elements as expectancy value theory (Fishbein & Ajzen, 1975), which may provide fruitful linkages to demand for telecommunication services. Accordingly, it may be possible to predict the adoption of one medium (e.g., phone-delivered text) on the basis of attitudes people hold toward competing modes of communication. Drawing from parallel work in cable, we would expect that positive attitudes toward competing modalities (e.g., the Internet) and/or negative attitudes toward audiotext would predict discontinuance of audiotext use. For instance, LaRose and Atkin (1991) examined media modality choice in light of perceived benefits associated with media use, finding that adoption of pay-per-view modalities is linked with negative attitudes toward competing modalities.

As those scholars noted, behavioral intention to adopt a service would be a function of attributes of the innovation, evaluations of attributes, belief strength of attributes, and the number and nature of competing modalities. Reagan (1996) further refined notions of perceived benefit, discovering that adopters are more tolerant of complexity in technologies when they satisfy a particular user interest (see Reagan, chap. 12, this volume).

These notions are akin to the concept of relative advantage, as derived from diffusion theory. In that regard, consumers will not adopt a new media alternative unless its advantages—in terms of cost or function—are sufficiently compelling to justify the adoption effort. Yet, although this dynamic might explain television's success in competition with radio for audiences, programming, and advertising revenues, research on audio information services finds displacement effects in only two cases—personal computer use (Neuendorf et al., 1998) and Internet use (LaRose & Atkin, 1992). Although these relationships are weak in magnitude, they may signal the beginning of a displacement dynamic, whereby the Internet emerges as a substitute for audio information services (see Klopfenstein, chap. 14, this volume).

Of course, as Reagan (chap. 12, this volume) indicates, the demand for functionally similar goods can also be either orthogonal (unrelated) or complementary. The latter dynamic is consistent with Rogers' (1995) notion of technology clusters, which suggests that users may adopt groups of innovations that fulfill similar functions, as well as Rice and Case's (1983) notion of "media styles," which indicate either personality-related preferences or job-related requirements for different communication channels. For instance, Neuendorf et al. (1998) found several distinctive cluster patterns of use among phone technologies: Fax use is uniquely predicted by workplace communication and long-distance phoning; 1-900 service use is predicted by home communication and public neighborhood communication (and, to some extent, long-distancing phoning).

THE REAL AND THEORETICAL SIGNIFICANCE OF AUDIOTEXT

Increasing Internet use may erode the major relative advantage of audiotext in relation to online substitutes—namely, its unique status as a low complexity, "continuous" information utility, where:

> the delivery system is not simply "compatible" with older established technologies, it *is* the century-old technology of telephony. And, in terms of Rogers' criterion of innovation trialability, "adoption" of audiotext . . . consists of nothing more than "picking up the phone and dialing"—something virtually all Americans are accustomed to doing from childhood. (Neuendorf et al., 1998, p. 83)

Drawing from that analysis, as younger generations grow to perceive computers and user-friendly computer-mediated communication as being low in complexity, we may soon reach the time when there are no discontinuous computer innovations.

In the same way that recent work finds few socioeconomic differences between adopters and nonadopters of audiotext, we would posit that future studies will identify a similar pattern for computer-based innovations. A nonprobability survey provides startling evidence that those under age 25 are as comfortable with computers as previous generations were with the telephone. The study found 99% of people born after 1971 to have used a computer before the age of 10 (compared with 7% of those older). More than 66% of those born after 1971 call themselves "intermediate," "expert," or "power" PC users (compared with 19% of older respondents; Beniger, 1996).

When all is said and done, audiotext may eventually occupy a niche for those seeking information utilities where an Internet hook-up is not feasible (in either proxemic or economic terms). For the present, audiotext has served as a useful "bridge" innovation, acclimating audiences to the benefits of phone-delivered information using a familiar, low-technology vehicle.

Audiotext as a Functional Bridge Innovation

We introduce the concept of the *bridge technology,* one that conceptually or technically connects an old, familiar innovation with an emergent innovation, usually one with high perceived complexity or incompatibility. The bridge innovation has commonalities with the original innovation, and also with the emergent innovation, but the original and emergent innovations have little overlap. This type of "stepping-stone" innovation may be short-lived, at least in its wide use and application. But it is essential to the process of diffusion of certain replacement innovations, when there exists a wide gap between the initial innovation and a final, replacement technology—strong technical or functional discontinuity.

In the case of a bridge innovation, new attributes are introduced within a context of technical and/or functional continuity. Then, user comfort with the new attributes, perhaps accompanied by a growing use of and dependence on the bridge innovation, allows the successful introduction of a sequential, functionally continuous but technically discontinuous (or, technically continuous but functionally discontinuous) innovation that replaces the original technology. The bridge innovation also may be replaced. This "sacrificial" function of some bridge innovations is an interesting characteristic. It may take the form of "planned obsolescence," although this is not necessarily the case.

For example, the dedicated word processor extended the capabilities of the typewriter, and prepared users for the full-blown personal computer experience. It shared some attributes with the typewriter (functional aspects such as its operation), and some with the personal computer (functional characteristics such as data storage and rapid retrieval), but shared specific hardware with neither. It performed as the mode of introduction for such key attributes as data storage and retrieval (see Johnson & Rice, 1987).

Some bridge innovations are ahead of their time, failing at one point only to reappear later, after parallel technologies enhance their functions and help find an audience. The laserdisc is one such example. First appearing as a consumer product in the late 1970s, it faded as videocassettes captured the public's fancy. This competition pitted two uses against each other—superior playback versus the ability to record content. Although the laserdisc also promised superior permanence, there was a price differential, and consumers opted for the innovation that offered more functions at a lower price—functions that included time shifting, archiving (recording for long-term collection), and playback of new movies via rented or purchased tapes.

The laserdisc emerged again in the 1990s, gaining a niche but remaining secondary to VHS tape. The introduction of DVD came close on the heels of the "second era" of the laserdisc. This cousin of the laserdisc had somewhat lower quality (i.e., compressed video) but held certain advantages viewed as important to the public—a smaller disc and some merging of computer technologies (and, when the recording function is added, it will have co-opted the advantages of laserdisc's original competitor). Importantly, its operation and function were highly similar to those of the laserdisc—laser "primed" the public to accept and adopt DVD.

Thus, the laserdisc has served as a discontinuous bridge that appeared more than once across three decades. In that regard, media technologies should not be viewed as one-shot creations, but rather bundles of hardware/software that evolve through time to meet user needs and provide user gratifications. Other notable examples of bridge innovations include 8-track audiotape (bridging reel-to-reel tape and audiocassette, with an additional functional bridge to CD technology) and pagers (bridging traditional human "paging" and cell phones).

In the case of audiotext, the innovation bridges a gap between telephony and the Internet, as shown in Fig. 6.2. This figure introduces a model of "continuities" (i.e., commonalities) between telephone and audiotext (sharing user hardware) and between audiotext and the Internet (both enjoy a high degree of interactivity or user control/flow, and both allow designs with a wide range of scalability, that is, levels through which the user navigates). These continuities place audiotext as a continuous innovation with regard to the older telephone, given shared hardware and few changes in user behavior patterns. The continuities between audiotext and the Internet indicate a discontinuous innovation shift, with new hardware acquisition required.

Our model also indicates sets of adaptations, attributes that distinguish the two newer innovations. Audiotext technology extends telephony with certain characteristics:

1. Reliability (the capacity to make consistent information available on a more regular—perhaps even on-demand—basis; Goodhue & Thompson, 1995).
2. The capacity to engage in mass messaging (i.e., to construct and access messages created for relatively large, undifferentiated audiences).
3. A reduction in the ready availability of user feedback.

In shifting from audiotext to Internet use, several new characteristics are introduced, in addition to the requisite hardware:

1. The potential for text and/or video material.
2. The capacity for fairly random access to information; while often structured in similar "branching" fashion, Web sites typically offer more "links" that accommodate horizontal and upward flow than do audiotext systems, and the use of URL addresses allows true nonlinearity.
3. Multiple modes of communication are possible, from point-to-point interpersonal contact to mass-distributed mass messaging.

Such modeling of the bridging function of an innovation allows us to explore the integration of disparate theoretical perspectives. The var-

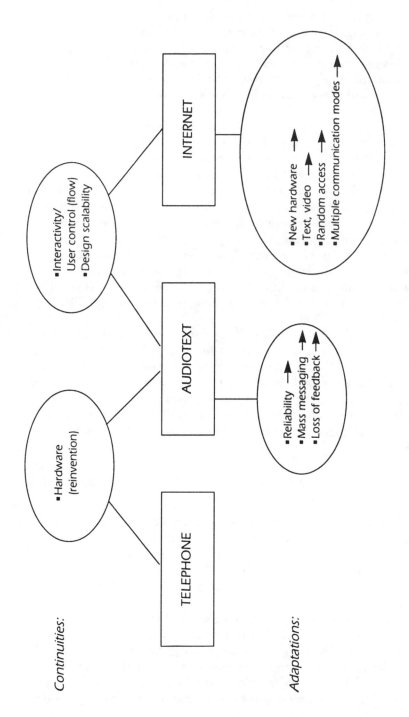

Figure 6.2. Audiotext as bridge innovation

ious continuities and adaptations introduced in Fig. 5.2 may all be viewed as innovation attributes á la Rogers (1995). The low cost of audiotext use, assuming access to the telephone, facilitates its adoption. Characteristics of the Internet that may speed its adoption include the relative advantage of random access when compared to audiotext, and the compatibility of the Internet with the earlier audiotext systems with regard to user control and scalability.

In a parallel fashion, continuities and adaptations may be seen as manifestations of appeals to gratifications sought by users. In particular, each succeeding innovation in the model demonstrates an incremental increase in instrumental (information-oriented) gratifications fulfilled (O'Keefe & Sulanowski, 1992). The functional equivalence construct may be applied to the striking similarities between complex audiotext systems and the Internet, notably with regard to user control, scalability, and reliability of information access. This merging of functions will be furthered by the rise of wireless phone/Internet devices, known as personal communication systems. The largest merger in the world, a $180 billion deal between Germany's Mannesmann AG and Britain's Vodafone AirTouch PLC, is intended to capture first mover advantages in the wireless Web world (Niak & Raghavan, 2000).

Finally, the model also allows for a media substitution analysis (McCombs, 1972), whereby the rapid diffusion of Internet use will substitute for most audiotext functions. Then, a "restructuring" in the way users view audiotext will be stimulated—audiotext may be relegated to "backup" status, for use in situations in which Internet connection is not possible (e.g., when computer access is impossible), although the growing use of personal digital assistants (PDAs) may intervene (Seaman, 2001).

CONCLUSION

On balance, audiotext adoption—or the act of paying a toll to access information over the telephone—adds an important dimension to an understanding of attendance to the telecommunication and information services media. As the gateway to a wide variety of new content choices, audiotext adoption is a major contributing factor for attendance to information media in general, and one that can only become more important as the number of homes passed by high-capacity fiber optics cable increases.

Given the likely demise of bridge technologies, does that make audiotext another likely case of roadkill along the information superhighway? Although media substitution theory (e.g., Lin, 1994) might predict such displacement, we may instead see a retrenchment comparable to that experienced by radio after it was beset by competition from television. So, just as competition for audiences and program inputs forced radio into a secondary niche capitalizing on its relative advantage in terms of mobility, we might expect audiotext to fulfill similar functions with mobile telephony. And, its utility as an information system within the large organization will most probably continue. An alternative to the niche-fitting of audiotext, and to its virtual elimination, is the possibility of its evolution into a hybrid form. Indeed, a *merging* of key audiotext characteristics with Internet systems may well be underway. With advances in voice-recognition software, emergent "voice portals" (Eisenberg, 2001) allow users to "talk" with computer systems over the phone, providing users with access to everything from stock quotes to their e-mail. Onboard automobile adjuncts provide hands-free phone calling and voice-driven access to news, e-mail, and more. Further work should continue to investigate the relative appeal of audiotext in relation to online substitutes, as audiotext finds its fit within the "integrated grid" (Dizard, 1989) of interdependent innovations.

REFERENCES

Adcock, W. O., Hirschman, E. C., & Goldstucker, J. L. (1977). Bank credit card users: An updated profile. In W. D. Perreault (Ed.), *Advances in consumer research* (Vol. 4, pp. 537-541). Atlanta, GA: Association for Consumer Research.

Atkin, D. (1995). Audio information services and the electronic media environment. *The Information Society, 11,* 75-83.

Atkin, D. (1998). Local and long distance telephony. In A. Grant & J. Harman (Eds.), *Communication technology update* (6th ed., pp. 200-212). Boston: Focal Press.

Atkin, D. J., Jeffres, L. W., & Neuendorf, K. A. (1998). Understanding Internet adoption as telecommunication behavior. *Journal of Broadcasting & Electronic Media, 42,* 475-490.

Atkin, D. J., & LaRose, R. (1994a). A metaanalysis of the information services adoption literature. In J. Hanson (Ed.), *Advances in telematics* (Vol. 2, pp. 91-110). Norwood, NJ: Ablex.

Atkin, D. J., & LaRose, R. (1994b). Profiling call-in poll users. *Journal of Broadcasting & Electronic Media, 38,* 217-227.

Barnes, J. G., & Kelloway, K. R. (1978). Cable television viewership: An examination of innovative behavior. Memorial University of Newfoundland Working Paper 78-14.

Bates, B. J., & Harmon, M. (1991, November). *Prodigy goes to war: Public opinion and videotex polling during the Persian Gulf War.* Paper presented at the annual meeting of the Midwest Association of Public Opinion Research, Chicago.

Bates, B. J., & Harmon, M. (1993). Do "instant polls" hit the spot?: Phone-in vs. random sampling of public opinion. *Journalism Quarterly, 70,* 369-380.

Becker, L. B., Dunwoody, S., & Rafaeli, S. (1983). Cable's impact on use of other news media. *Journal of Broadcasting, 27,* 127-140.

Blumler, J. G. (1978). The role of theory in uses and gratifications studies. *Communication Research, 6,* 9-36.

Clancy, K. J., & Shulman, R. S. (1991). *Marketing revolution: A radical manifesto for dominating the marketplace.* New York: Harperbusiness.

Collins, J., Reagan, J., & Abel, J. D. (1983). Predicting cable subscribership. *Journal of Broadcasting, 27,* 177-183.

Dickerson, M. D., & Gentry, J. W. (1983). Characteristics of adopters and non-adopters of home computers. *Journal of Consumer Research, 10,* 225-235.

Dimmick, J. W., Patterson, S., & Sikand, J. (1996). Personal telephone networks: A typology and two empirical studies. *Journal of Broadcasting & Electronic Media, 40,* 45-59.

Dizard, W. P. (1989). *The coming information age: An overview of technology, economics, and politics* (3rd ed.). New York: Longman.

Dozier, D. M., & Rice, R. E. (1984). Rival theories of electronic newsreading. In R. E. Rice et al. (Eds.), *The new media: Communication, research, and technology* (pp. 103-127). Beverly Hills, CA: Sage.

Dozier, D. M., Valente, T. W., & Severn, J. J. H. (1986, May). *The impact of interconcept networks on perceived attributes and projected adoption of discontinuous innovations.* Paper presented at the annual conference of the International Communication Association, Chicago.

Dunn, D. M., Williams, W. H., & Spivey, W. A. (1971). Analysis and prediction of telephone demand in local geographic areas. *Bell Journal of Economics and Management Science, 2,* 3.

Dutton, W. H., Rogers, E., & Jun, S. H. (1987a). The diffusion and impacts of information technology in households. In P. I. Zorkoczy (Ed.), *Oxford surveys in information technology* (Vol. 4, pp. 133-193). New York: Oxford University Press.

Dutton, W., Rogers, E. M., & Jun, S. H. (1987b). Diffusion and social impacts of personal computers. *Communication Research, 14,* 219-250.

Eisenberg, D. (2001, March). Dial tone 2.0: This phone talks back. *Time Bonus Section,* pp. B2-B4.

Ettema, J. S. (1989). Interactive electronic text in the United States: Can videotex ever go home again? In J. L. Salvaggio & J. Bryant (Eds.), *Media use in the information age: Emerging patterns of adoption and consumer use* (pp. 105-123). Hillsdale, NJ: Lawrence Erlbaum Associates.

Fishbein, M., & Ajzen, I. (1975). *Belief, attitude, intention and behavior: An introduction to theory and research*. Reading, MA: Addison-Wesley.

Fliegal, F. C., & Kilvin, E. (1966). Attributes of innovations as factors in diffusion. *American Journal of Sociology, 72*, 235-248.

Flavell, J. H. (1977). *Cognitive development*. Englewood Cliffs, NJ: Prentice-Hall.

Fullerton, H. S. (1988). Technology collides with relative constancy: The pattern of adoption for a new medium. *Journal of Media Economics, 1*, 75-84.

Garramone, G. M., Harris, A. C., & Pizante, G. (1986). Predictors of motivation to use computer-mediated political communication systems. *Journal of Broadcasting and Electronic Media, 30*, 445-457.

Glascock, J., & LaRose, R. (1992). A content analysis of 900 numbers. *Telecommunications Policy, 16*, 147-155.

Glascock, J., & LaRose, R. (1993). Dial-a-porn recordings: The role of the female participant in male sexual fantasies. *Journal of Broadcasting & Electronic Media, 37*, 313-324.

Gollin, A. E. (1992). AAPOR backs RIC statement on call-in "polls." *AAPOR News, 20*, 1-2.

Goodhue, D. L., & Thompson, R. L. (1995). Task-technology fit and individual performance. *MIS Quarterly, 19*, 213-236.

Heeter, C. (1989). Implications of new interactive technologies for conceptualizing communication. In J. L. Salvaggio & J. Bryant (Eds.), *Media use in the information age: Emerging patterns of adoption and consumer use* (pp. 217-235). Hillsdale, NJ: Lawrence Erlbaum Associates.

Henke, L. L., & Donohue, T. R. (1989). Functional displacement of traditional TV viewing by VCR owners. *Journal of Advertising Research, 29*(2), 18-23.

Hirschman, E. C. (1980). Innovativeness, novelty seeking and consumer creativity. *Journal of Consumer Research, 7*, 283-295.

Jeffres, L. W. (1994). *Mass media processes*. Prospect Heights, IL: Waveland.

Jeffres, L. W., & Atkin, D. (1996). Predicting use of technologies for communication and consumer needs. *Journal of Broadcasting & Electronic Media, 40*, 318-330.

Jeffres, L. W., Atkin, D., & Neuendorf, K. (1995). The impact of new and traditional media on college student leisure preferences. *World Communication, 24*(2), 67-73.

Johnson, B. M., & Rice, R. E. (1987). *Managing organizational innovation: The evolution from word processing to office information systems*. New York: Columbia University Press.

Kamerer, D., & Bergen, L. (1995). Patterns of use, exposure in paper's audiotex system. *Newspaper Research Journal, 16,* 48-59.

Katz, E., Gurevitch, M., & Haas, H. (1973). On the use of mass media for important things. *American Sociological Review, 38,* 164-181.

Krugman, D. M. (1985). Evaluating the audiences of the new media. *Journal of Advertising, 14*(4), 21-27.

LaRose, R., & Atkin, D. (1988). Cable subscribership as telecommunications behavior. *Telematics and Informatics, 5,* 105-113.

LaRose, R., & Atkin, D. (1991). An analysis of pay-per-view versus other movie delivery modalities. *Journal of Media Economics, 3,* 3-21.

LaRose, R., & Atkin, D. (1992). Audiotext and the re-invention of the telephone as a mass medium. *Journalism Quarterly, 69,* 413-421.

Levy, M. R. (1978). The audience experience with TV news. *Journalism Monographs, 55.*

Levy, M. R., & Windahl, S. (1984). Audience activity and gratifications: A conceptual clarification and exploration. *Communication Research, 11,* 51-78.

Lin, C. A. (1993). Modeling the gratification-seeking process of television viewing. *Human Communication Research, 20,* 224-244.

Lin, C. A. (1994). Exploring potential factors for home videotex adoption. In J. Hanson (Ed.), *Advances in telematics* (Vol. 2, pp. 111-120). Norwood, NJ: Ablex.

Lin, C. A. (1998). Exploring personal computer adoption dynamics. *Journal of Broadcasting & Electronic Media, 42,* 95-112.

Mahan, G. P. (1979). *The demand for residential phone service.* Unpublished doctoral thesis, Michigan State University, East Lansing.

Markus, M. L. (1987). Toward a "critical mass" theory of interactive media. *Communication Research, 14,* 491-511.

Marvin, C. (1988). *When old technologies were new: Thinking about electric communication in the late nineteenth century.* New York: Oxford University Press.

McCombs, M. E. (1972). Mass media in the marketplace. *Journalism Monographs, 24.*

Niak, G., & Raghavan, A. (2000, February 4). Mannesmann agrees to Vodafone bid. *Wall Street Journal,* p. A3.

Neuendorf, K. A., Atkin, D., & Jeffres, L. W. (1998). Understanding adopters of audio information innovations. *Journal of Broadcasting & Electronic Media, 42,* 80-93.

O'Keefe, G., & Sulanowski, B. (1992, November). *Audiotex as an informational medium: Public uses and perspectives.* Paper presented to the Midwest Association for Public Opinion Research, Chicago.

Perl, L. J. (1978, March). *Economic and demographic determinants of residential demand for basic telephone service*. Washington, DC: National Economic Research Associates, Inc.

Perse, E. M., & Courtright, J. A. (1993). Normative images of communication media: Mass and interpersonal channels in the new media environment. *Human Communication Research, 19,* 485-503.

Perse, E. M., & Dunn, D. G. (1998). The utility of home computers and media use: Implications of multimedia and connectivity. *Journal of Broadcasting & Electronic Media, 42,* 435-456.

Poole, I. D. (Ed.). (1981). *The social impact of the telephone.* Cambridge, MA: MIT Press.

Pousette, T. (1976, August). *The demand for telephones and telephone services in Sweden.* Paper presented at the European Meetings of the Econometric Society, Helsinki, Finland.

Reagan, J. (1987). Classifying adopters and nonadopters for technologies using political activity, media use and demographic variables. *Telematics and Informatics, 4,* 3-16.

Reagan, J. (1989, November). *Technology adoption: Is satisfaction the best predictor?* Paper presented to the Midwest Association for Public Opinion Research, Chicago.

Reagan, J. (1996). The "repertoire" of information sources. *Journal of Broadcasting & Electronic Media, 40,* 112-121.

Rice, R. E., & Case, D. (1983). Electronic message systems in the university: A description of use and utility. *Journal of Communication, 33*(1), 131-152.

Robertson, T. S. (1967). The process of innovation and diffusion of innovation. *Journal of Marketing, 31,* 14-19.

Robertson, T. S. (1971). *Innovative behavior and communication.* New York: Holt, Rinehart & Winston.

Rogers, E. M. (1962). *Diffusion of innovations.* New York: The Free Press.

Rogers, E. M. (1995). *Diffusion of innovations* (4th ed.). New York: The Free Press.

Rogers, E. M., with Shoemaker, F. F. (1971). *Communication of innovations: A cross-cultural approach.* New York: The Free Press.

Rosengren, K. E., Wenner, L. A., & Palmgreen, P. (Eds.). (1985). *Media gratifications research: Current perspectives.* Beverly Hills, CA: Sage.

Rubin, A. M. (1983). Television uses and gratifications: The interactions of viewing patterns and motivations. *Journal of Broadcasting, 27,* 37-51.

Rubin, A., & Rubin, R. (1990). Social and psychological antecedents of VCR use. In M. R. Levy (Ed.), *The VCR age* (pp. 92-111). Newbury Park, CA: Sage.

Sable Communications, Inc. v. FCC (1989). Slip Opinion No. 88-15.

Schramm, W. (1988). *The story of human communication: Cave painting to microchip.* New York: Harper & Row.

Seaman, B. (2001, March 26). No hands, no harm. *Time,* p. 61.

Sparkes, V. M. (1983). Public perception of and reaction to multi-channel cable television service. *Journal of Broadcasting, 27,* 163-175.

Sparkes, V., & Kang, N. (1986). Public reactions to cable television: Time in the diffusion process. *Journal of Broadcasting & Electronic Media, 30,* 213-229.

Steinfield, C. W., Dutton, W. H., & Kovaric, P. (1989). A framework and agenda for research on computing in the home. In J. L. Salvaggio & J. Bryant (Eds.), *Media use in the information age: Emerging patterns of adoption and consumer use* (pp. 61-85). Hillsdale, NJ: Lawrence Erlbaum Associates.

Taylor, L. D. (1980). *Telecommunications demand: A survey and critique.* Cambridge, MA: Ballinger.

Train, K. E., McFadden, D., & Ben-Najiv, M. (1987). The demand for local telephone service choices. *Rand Journal of Economics, 18,* 1.

Werner, A. (1986). Mass media expenditures in Norway: The principle of relative constancy revisited. In M. L. McLaughlin (Ed.), *Communication Yearbook 9* (pp. 251-260). Beverly Hills, CA: Sage.

Williams, F., Phillips, A. F., & Lum, P. (1985). Gratifications associated with new communication technologies. In K. E. Rosengren, L. A. Wenner, & P. Palmgreen (Eds.), *Media gratifications research: Current perspectives* (pp. 241-252). Beverly Hills, CA: Sage.

Wolfe, D. B. (1998, February). What your customers can't say. *American Demographics,* pp. 24-29.

Wood, W. C. (1986). Consumer spending on the mass media: The principle of relative constancy reconsidered. *Journal of Communication, 36*(2), 39-51.

Wood, W. C., & O'Hare, S. L. (1991). Paying for the video revolution: Consumer spending on the mass media. *Journal of Communication, 41*(1), 24-30.

Yankee Group. (1988). *Local area signalling services.* Boston, MA: Author.

Zerbinos, E. (1990). Information seeking and information processing: Newspapers versus videotext. *Journalism Quarterly, 67,* 920-929.

7

Attraction to Computer-Mediated Social Support

Joseph B. Walther
Rensselaer Polytechnic Institute

Shawn Boyd
University of St. Thomas

OVERVIEW

One of the most interesting and controversial phenomena in the recent explosion in computer-mediated communication (CMC) and Internet use involves the development of "virtual communities" in which people meet, share interests, and exchange social support via text-based messages on computer networks. As Rheingold (1993) described them, "virtual communities are social aggregations that emerge from the Net when enough people carry on those public discussions long enough, with sufficient human feeling, to form webs of personal relationships" (p. 5). Although the Internet has its share of idle and banal chat, it is also a viable and vital conduit for valuable information and interpersonal affect. Although critics have raised questions about the "communal" nature of the Internet and its subnetworks, and the validity or utility of these personal relationships (e.g. Critical Art Ensemble, 1996; Fernback & Thompson, 1995; Kraut et al., 1998), there is a great deal of social support activity taking place online, appealing to its users.

In contrast to a view of unlimited bounty and a bonanza of benefits from online support, research on traditional social support offers "two well-established empirical generalizations," according to Ford, Babrow, and Stohl (1996): "First, not all ostensibly supportive social interactions are experienced as supportive. . . . Second, the supportee's perception of the quality or substance of social support is a better predictor of successful coping than the sheer number or quantity of support at one's disposal" (p. 189). For these reasons, a systematic exploration into the perceived benefits to adopting online social support is especially warranted.

This chapter examines why face-to-face (FtF) personal relationships may offer disadvantages for social support in some contexts and revisits arguments about the advantages of weak-tie networks—as happen to occur over computer networks—in their affordances for support seekers and givers. We also consider the special capabilities of CMC, the factors influencing its adoption and use and how these features also facilitate social support processes. This review led to an empirical investigation among Usenet support users, attempting to assess the social and technological dimensions of online support that make it attractive to users, the results of which conclude this study.

SOCIAL SUPPORT

Social support communication is traditionally considered to be the exchange of verbal and nonverbal messages conveying emotion, information, or referral, to help reduce someone's uncertainty or stress, and "whether directly or indirectly, communicate to an individual that she or he is valued and cared for by others" (Barnes & Duck, 1994, p. 176). Conventional social support is thought of as taking place most often within established, multidimensional, and primarily dyadic close personal relationships (Cutrona & Suhr, 1992; Leatham & Duck, 1990), although it may also take place in therapeutic relationships (e.g., Robinson, 1988) as well as through informal social networks (Albrecht & Adelman, 1987).

In growing numbers, social support is being exchanged via CMC, in relatively large networks among people who do not know each other and do not communicate FtF. The communication process is thus changed in some dramatic respects. Unlike FtF support relationships, most CMC support exchange begins by discussing the topic of concern, immediately and often in very personal terms, rather than leading up to these concerns after establishing relationships based on other commonalities. Electronic social support develops among strangers whose primary connection is their common affliction or concern over a source of personal discomfort, in a "uniplex," rather than "multiplex," relationship. As Rogers (chap. 3, this volume) suggests, these online connections sometimes lead to FtF encounters.

To gain a better understanding of CMC use dynamics, we explore its adoption in the context of electronic venues, social support functions, weak-tie networks, and support mechanisms (including self-esteem, emotional support, social networks, and tangible aid). FtF versus CMC social support mechanisms are then examined within the context of mismatching as well as costs of giving and receiving. Further comparisons involving weak-tie networks versus CMC support are then examined in the context of stigma management and validation/intimacy, with special attention paid to advantages of CMC and electronic support (including lurkers, access, hyperpersonal aspects, and anonymity).

Electronic Venues

The main electronic venues in which people exchange social support solicitations and responses include the worldwide Internet and proprietary commercial online systems. Additionally, some private electronic support systems have developed with the specific and exclusive purpose of providing peer-to-peer and/or expert advice on personal, medically related, or other issues (e.g., Scheerhorn, Warisse, & McNeilis, 1995). Steve Harris (1996) keeps an up-to-date list on the World Wide Web of hundreds of online sources for "emotional support" on his World Wide Web site, *Emotional Support on the Internet.* These sources include Usenet newsgroups, electronic mailing lists, discussion groups available through commercial CMC providers such as Prodigy and America Online, as well as real-time chat sessions through Internet Relay Chat (IRC) and several multi-user discussions (MUDs). Harris lists these services as venues for emotional support as well as information support, devoted to discussion of a wide range of illnesses, social problems, psychological issues, and other topics around which users may seek company. They are places in which to share feelings and experiences.

Most dedicated electronic support spaces work via asynchronous communication. These venues primarily work on a "bulletin board"-type arrangement of messages (see Rafaeli, 1986; Rapaport, 1991). That is, users post messages that are stored online for some period of time for others to read, with readers logging in and responding at different times. Alternatively, mailing lists ("distribution lists") form another method to communicate asynchronously with many others. List systems involve multiple-addressing remailers, so when someone sends a message to the one official e-mail address for the group, a host computer system re-sends the mail message out to everyone who has subscribed to the list. Whereas a bulletin board keeps messages in virtual space until perused, list-based systems deliver the messages to each subscriber's electronic mailbox. It should be noted that there is a distinction between bulletin boards/threaded systems and distribution lists. The former involves the easy reviewing of past messages, whereas distribution lists offer no common or easy way to review past messages, especially for newcomers.

In addition to such asynchronous systems, fewer synchronous "chat" spaces allow participants to type messages to one another simultaneously and read them in "real time." Hybrid systems exist as well; one such system is the SANCTUARY multi-user domain—a chat space for survivors of physical abuse—that also contains an asynchronous bulletin board system. The chat capacity provides a valuable environmental ambiance: According to Moursund (1997), "in spite of having only words and one's own imagination to create an environment, the sense of being in a familiar place, interacting with people you know and care about, is astonishingly vivid in SANCTUARY" (p. 61). The bulletin board facilitates other social support exchanges: in order of frequency, expressions of companionship (talking about problems, sharing experiences), information, positive feedback, motivational support, and belongingness (Moursund, 1997).

Perhaps the largest and most accessible asynchronous venues are the support spaces transmitted via Usenet. Although Usenet was not originally part of the Internet, it is now commonly accessible through the Internet in such a seamless way as to be almost indistinguishable to users. Usenet feeds are sorted into topical "newsgroups," with topics now reaching the ten thousands, ranging from scientific discussions to erotica. Within each newsgroup, people post written messages, and others read and sometimes reply. Chains of replies (i.e., messages with the same subject line) are known as *threads,* and many readers' computer systems sort these messages by thread and then by date and time of posting. Thus, following a thread, a continuous discussion takes shape.

Like the Internet proper, participation in these discussion groups may be international in scope. Among these are several newsgroups particularly focused on support, often indicated by name (e.g., alt.support.depression). Some of these support groups are estimated to be very heavily trafficked, with thousands of readers, if not writers, participating. It should also be noted that social support takes place within electronic groups without a support theme name. For instance, in the alt.sex related Usenet groups, so maligned as prurient by the press and politicians, it has been found that sexually oriented (bulletin) boards act as a kind of support group for . . . especially individuals whose sexual orientations are very marginalized. . . . In addition . . . college-aged students who might find the information posted in the newsgroups . . . to be practical guides to sexuality and safe sex practices . . . which students might not have recourse to otherwise. (Shade, 1996, p. 18)[1]

Table 7.1 lists the 10 most popular Usenet support-related groups and their readership estimates as of March 1995 (after which time the data were no longer updated for public dissemination; see also Galagher, Sproull, & Kiesler, 1998).

Social Support Functions

Although several typological approaches have been made to defining the scope of support activities (see for review Barbee & Cunningham, 1995), we describe social support by means of the list Cutrona and Suhr (1992) offer. These activities include informational support, emotional support, esteem support, tangible aid, and social network support. This typology was found to have provided a useful classification scheme for Braithwaite, Waldron, and Finn (1999) to content analyze the types of electronic support messages for the disabled (findings of which are also reflected here). Readers are encouraged to verify for themselves the extent of each activity taking place in online venues that they may observe.

With regard to offline interactions, Schwarzer and Leppin (1991) demonstrated that support relationships may provide both cognitive social support as well as behavioral social support. Wellman and Wortley (1990) found that females tend to exchange verbal and nonverbal messages of

---

[1]Indeed, a vehement objection to attempts by the Prodigy network to censor certain words, and to the potential of the Communications Decency Act enacted by the U.S. government in 1995, was that it could as equally prohibit discussion of "breasts" as related either to breast cancer as well as in lascivious discussions. Just such issues over the censorship of language with the potential for prosocial or lascivious discussion were part of the U.S. District Court's reasoning in striking down the CDA (*ACLU v. Reno*, 1996, Sec. III, Dalzell, C.):

> Yet, this is precisely the kind of speech that occurs, for example, on Critical Path AIDS Project's Web site, which includes safer sex instructions written in street language for easy comprehension. The Web site also describes the risk of HIV transmission for particular sexual practices. The FCC's implication in In the Matter of King Broadcasting Co., 5 FCC R. 2971 (1990), that a "candid discussion of sexual topics" on television was decent in part because it was "not presented in a pandering, titillating or vulgar manner" would be unavailing to Critical Path, other plaintiffs, and some amici. These organizations want to pander and titillate on their Web sites, at least to a degree, to attract a teen audience and deliver their message in an engaging and coherent way. [11]

Table 7.1. Top 10 Support-Oriented Usenet Readership Estimates, March 1995 (from news.lists on Usenet).

Usenet Newsgroup	Estimated Monthly Readers Worldwide
alt.support.depression	22,000
alt.dads-rights	21,000
alt.support	21,000
alt.support.diet	20,000
alt.support.cancer	18,000
soc.support.youth.gay-lesbian.bi	16,000
alt.support.shyness	11,000
alt.support.eating-disord	11,000
alt.support.divorce	11,000
alt.support.arthritis	8,100

emotional support, whereas males tend to give support by way of doing instrumental activities to assist others. Such emotional support and instrumental activities may potentially be less available through online discussions among relative strangers, no matter what else the benefits might be.

Informational support comes in the form of advice, factual input, and feedback. Such messages may discuss symptomatology, medications, legal issues, and so on. Information support helps people make decisions and attributions, and judge actions. According to Braithwaite et al. (1999), this type of support message was one of the two most frequently exchanged online (along with emotional support).

Emotional support is given through expressions of caring, concern, empathy, and sympathy, according to Cutrona and Suhr (1992). These messages are less about decisional issues and more about psychological well-being. Examples of emotional support would include statements of affection, emotional understanding, and statements geared toward relieving pain and stress.

Esteem support comes through expressing admiration, understanding another's worth, or both. This can come through complimentary statements about another's skills and abilities, or through expressions of genuine admiration and telling someone that he or she is a good or normal person. This type of support appears highly personal and is psychologically oriented.

Tangible aid is support in the form of actual physical assistance. It provides needed goods and services. An example of tangible aid would be buying groceries for a friend who is sick. We should expect that this type of support is very infrequent among computer-mediated support groups, whose members tend not to share the requisite geographic proximity to exchange such support. Indeed, Braithwaite et al.'s (1999) analysis found this type of support among the least frequently exchanged. Nonetheless, Rheingold (1993) described how one user community activated enough expertise and finances to mount a medical airlift for an injured colleague, and how even the beginnings of "the Well"—network home to his "virtual community"—relied on financial contributions and credit from early users to upgrade and maintain the system. Although such anecdotes may stand out because of their very rarity, they point out that tangible aid indeed may be mobilized, even if it is not common, via electronic networks.

Finally, social network support involves directing or referring someone to a another person or group of people who share a common set of experiences or expertise. This type of support allows an individual to feel tied in to a larger community.

Because electronic social support is exchanged in network "spaces" involving numerous participants, it is therefore instructive to consider how this milieu parallels a support or therapy group. According to Braithwaite et al. (1999), "the majority of face-to-face self help groups have also been duplicated online" (p. 126). Offline groups of this nature are formed explicitly to help members cope with or solve their common concern. Robinson (1988) suggested several characteristics of these groups, many of which are evidently occurring online (and as we have seen informally in the comments of our respondents). These include (a) common experience of the members, whereby all members of self-help groups face the same problem issue; (b) mutual help and support, assuring that groups meet regularly and provide mutual aid; (c) the helper principle, where those providing support to others may be the ones deriving the greatest benefit; (d) differential association, emphasizing a healthy self-concept to encourage members' separation from previous deviant self-concepts; (e) collective belief, members drawing validation from one another; and (f) the importance of information, promoting "factual understanding of the problem as opposed to intrapsychic understanding" (p. 119).

In several ways, support or self-help groups seem most comparable to that which occurs in electronic social support. Yet the most drastic difference between FtF and electronic support groups is that FtF meetings imply spatio-temporal and sociological arrangements that are not relevant in electronic space. According to Galagher et al. (1998), online support groups function much the same way as FtF support groups, but with the additional benefits of greater access (discussed later), and greater confidentiality:

Confidentiality regarding the (FtF) group's proceedings may be expected, but one's physical presence and the possibility of encountering others in one's community create a risk of unwanted public exposure. Furthermore, these groups often exert social pressure on members to participate actively and to disclose their thoughts and feelings. Small size, local geography, and social pressure make these groups less private, less anonymous, and more conformist than are electronic social support groups. (p. 497)

Aside from formal groups, however, day-to-day FtF social support takes place within personal relationships. In the following, we examine some disadvantages posited to accompany support exchange in close personal relationships, identify how CMC support brings support partners in contact with people outside such relationships, and how these different types of connections affect support exchange.

FtF VERSUS CMC SOCIAL SUPPORT

Although the feeling of social support may be a cornerstone to psychic health and functioning, some commentators have pointed out that the exchange of social support ironically may bring with it serious harmful effects to autonomy and relational well-being. In particular, according to La Gaipa (1990), support exchange encapsulates a struggle between autonomy and dependence, both for providers as well as for receivers of social support. When the exchange of social support leads to dependence, unhealthy outcomes result. It is our contention that support exchange in electronic venues, and the types of social systems they encompass, attenuate some of the negative effects liable to appear in FtF personal relationships. In the following, we review several aspects of the "dark side of support" (Albrecht, Burleson, & Goldsmith, 1994), and contrast them to electronic support, leading to hypothetical attractions to online support.

Mismatching

Difficulties can arise when efforts to help one in need are not well matched to the recipient's needs, and these difficulties can affect relationships adversely (see for review Goldsmith, 1992). According to La Gaipa (1990), "when, for example, members of one's social network have no personal experience with a particular crisis, such as cancer, their efforts to be helpful are likely to be strained and clumsy" (p. 124). Different types of support may be most helpful at different stages in a problem, yet nonexpert sources may be more or less directive or blindly reassuring than needed at various points in dealing with a problem. Should they persist, their efforts at assistance may be ineffective, annoying, or counterproductive.

By comparison, friends may be of no help in relation to a particular problem one may experience as they may be reluctant or inappropriate sources to go into much depth in the case of a personal issue. When they do, they may be ineffectual (La Gaipa, 1990). As online social support is exchanged among those with similar experiences or concerns, without the multiple concerns and filters that close relationships impose, these issues may be ameliorated.

Gender role, also, seems to affect what kinds of support messages are given and what will be perceived as effective. Research by Mickelson, Helgeson, and Weiner (1995) found that women provide more emotional support messages than do men, and more so in mixed-gender dyads than in same-gender interactions, in FtF conversations. And more negatively oriented and trivializing messages are directed toward males who discuss their problems FtF. By contrast, in the online social support group examined by Egdorf and Rahoi (1994), very little communication was coded as negative. It is not known whether the medium alters the kinds of messages that are produced by men and women, or whether they adhere to the same patterns as they do FtF, or whether gender demographics account for the overall tone of support. Although Mickelson (1997) also found a higher proportion of females (52.3%) than males (47.7%) online in a study of electronic social support for parents of developmentally disabled children, a comparison group of non-electronic support group members was 98% female. Hence, gender effects may pervade social support. A research question is thus posited:

RQ1: Is candor—both less harshness and less sparing of feel-ings—an attraction to computer-mediated social support?

Costs of Giving

To provide social support to others may risk "high costs associated with caring," according to La Gaipa (1990, p. 126), or a "drainage of resources, particularly when the need for support is great or extends of a long period of time," according to Albrecht et al. (1994, p. 433). These commentators reviewed several studies showing that those with numerous network links and who are more supportive may experience great stress and emotional strain. If the provision of support becomes extended and emotionally demanding, "caregiver burden" may result, leading to numerous mental health problems such as depression, sleeplessness, anxiety, and frustration. Other symptoms may include emotional exhaustion, impatience, and irritation. These outcomes would appear to be counterproductive to the support relationship in the long run.

Costs of Receiving

One of the great costs in soliciting and accepting social support in FtF personal relationships has to do with the presentation of self and the self-evaluations that follow the admission of a problem or uncertainty. According to Albrecht et al. (1994, p. 433), asking for help may make people "appear weak or less competent"; undesirable information may be disclosed in seeking support; and "the problem for which help is needed results in stigmatization." (We address the special affordances of CMC for stigma management later.)

Another cost of disclosing has to do with the judgments providers may make about other social actors related to the problem. La Gaipa gave the example of a mother's hostility toward her daughter's husband should the daughter seek counsel about a marital issue. This is not the case of a support receiver wishing to avoid negative social judgments, but wishing to forestall negative judgments of other close network members. Such paradoxes can inhibit potential recipients from seeking support in the first place. These types of concerns are rarely associated with electronic social support.

RQ2: Is less personal *judgment* an attraction to electronic social support?

A further cost of receiving social support is the potential to be called on to reciprocate. There is a norm of reciprocity in close relationships. To deny reciprocation is to violate relational equity; yet to be "on call" to provide support when one is ill-disposed, unable, or inexpert, may be equally disturbing (see for review Albrecht et al., 1994). The potential reciprocity debt, like the obligation to provide support in close relationships mentioned above, may be an unattractive aspect of FtF support exchange in close personal relationships.

RQ3: Is the lack of *obligation* to provide social support an attractive aspect of online support exchange?

However, more costly may be the relational dependency that may accompany a support seeker's admission of concern, fear, or incompetence, and the acceptance of advice from others (La Gaipa, 1990). So resentful of this reduced autonomy accompanying support needs, persons may reject otherwise useful advice in order to restore a balance of relational power.

RQ4: Does the reduced *dependency* on others provide an attraction to electronic social support?

By comparison, aspects of CMC social support may ameliorate a number of the disadvantages associated with support in close relationships. For one thing, one need not build a relationship to a point of a problem disclosure as one may in FtF relationships. In CMC support venues, it is expected that one is seeking support. Relational dependency and obligation are less likely to be a factor in this environment. It is quite easy to extricate oneself from the support group—one simply quits posting and responding to messages.

RQ5: Is the ability to garner support immediately *without the establishment an extensive personal relationship* an attraction of electronic social support?

WEAK TIE NETWORKS VERSUS CMC SOCIAL SUPPORT

One way to view the way that CMC reduces the costs of support through personal relationships is to assume that not only the medium, but the sources of support have different characteristics. One contention of the present work is that the exchange of social support in virtual support "spaces" on computer networks constitute weak-tie, rather than strong-tie, relationships (as has also been discussed by Egdorf & Rahoi, 1994; Wellman & Gulia, 1999). Strong-tie relationships are those within which interactions typically revolve around more than one kind of topic, that is, they are multiplex. They are typified by friends, loved ones, work associates with whom one also socializes, confidantes, family, and so on. It is these kinds of relationships in which social support is usually exchanged, according to most sources (see for review Albrecht & Adelman, 1987; Leatham & Duck, 1990; Rice, 1994).

Weak-tie relationships differ from strong ties in several structural and social respects. Structurally, in offline realms, weak ties are not originally known to a person directly, but may be known through secondary associations (e.g., a friend of a friend) in a social network, or through some social agency. Weakly tied persons are themselves embedded in other social networks. In the case of electronic support networks, we would argue that the association to other people is offered by the agency of the electronic space rather than a secondary social link; people come to the space for support, rather than coming to meet a specific person. In social terms, the overlap of weak ties onto one's primary network of close ties is relatively small. That is, although our closest associates or strong ties are often likely also to know one another, weak ties are less likely to know and interact with each other, or with our primary network members.

Maintaining contact with weak ties is often accomplished via mediated communication channels such as telephones or electronic bulletin boards. As a result, when information rests with a weak tie, it is less likely to be commonly known among strong ties. Adelman, Parks, and Albrecht (1987) attributed special facilitation to restricted channels; they assert that "restricted communication channels . . . provide individuals with a comparatively anonymous way to disclose highly personal or potentially embarrassing information" (p. 133).

Expertise

It is the dynamic of the separation of close from weak networks, and the greater number of weak links to strong ones, that undergirds the "strength of weak ties" hypothesis (Granovetter, 1973). In its simplest form, there is often more information to be found in the extended network than in the primary one. This is due to several factors. There are more individuals available through weakly linked associations (secondary links, tertiary links, etc.) than there are within one's primary network of close ties. Moreover, there tends to be greater diversity among weak ties than close ones; close ties tend to be homogenous in many respects, whereas heterogeneous people know more different things. Thus, locating and using expertise is highly facilitated by the technology as well as the loose confederation of users in a single support space, where there may be more expertise than in one's primary network. Thus, the following research question:

RQ6: Is *expertise* an attraction to computer-mediated social support?

Stigma Management

Stigma management refers to the discussion of incidents or topics with others in such a way that others do not become aware of it (Thompson & Seibold, 1978). For instance, it is common in depression-related electronic support groups to ask, "Does anyone else experience sexual dysfunction as a side-effect of certain antidepressants?" This type of information, when imparted to weak links, is less likely to feed back to one's close network as extensively as information shared within a close, more densely connected link. As Adelman et al. (1987) surmised, "This network distance enhances perceived anonymity and allows people to seek information and support without having to deal with the uncertainty of how those in primary relationships might respond" (p. 131). In this way, they argued, weak links facilitate "low-risk discussions about high-risk topics" (p. 133). Thus the following research question is posed:

> RQ7: Does the ability to *manage stigma* by having support conversations with others than our closer ties, provide an attraction to computer-mediated social support?

Validation and Intimacy

Another benefit of weak-tie interaction is its capability to foster community, according to Adelman et al. (1987). Two processes relate to this dynamic. First, they allow participants to conduct "reality checks" by comparing their own reactions and feelings to others who have had similar experiences. To detect similar reactions among others would help attribute normality to one's reactions. Indeed, in online support, one may observe numerous disclosures about critical events and participants' psychological and physical reactions to them. Many messages begin or end with "me, too" (see also Galagher et al., 1998). As Adelman et al. (1987) projected, "Self-evaluation is facilitated by comparison to weak ties because they provide a greater variety of information and thus a better ability to judge how typical or normal our own behavior is" (p. 135).

A secondary effect—a great degree of inferred "intimacy"—seems to develop through electronic social support, as individuals engage in self-disclosure to discuss these conventionally personal issues. Validation by others often follows the disclosure of personal issues, manifesting highly rewarding outcomes from what Millar and Rogers (1976) called a "vulnerability pattern," online. Among weak ties, "discussion about intimate topics occurs . . . within highly limited contexts" according to Adelman et al. (1987, p. 130). Here our research asks:

> RQ8: Does the *intimacy* inferred provide an attraction to computer-mediated social support?

The strength of weak ties has been examined directly in relation to computer networks contexts other than social support. A network analytic study by Feldman (1987) established that an electronic network increased communication among both familiar and unfamiliar members within an organization. Focusing on two primary characteristics of such networks—asynchrony and multiple addressability—she noted that electronic message exchange has a much lower cost in time, effort, and resources, than other means of communication. A byproduct of this affordance is the easy emergence of mailing lists focused on specific interests, especially to those unknown directly to one another. Feldman argued that these lists are driven by interests, some of which are not business-related and therefore are less likely to emerge in typical organizational conversations constrained by place, time, and purpose. Because these extra-organizational interests are as likely to be shared by people who do not share place, tasks, or other topical interests, they lend themselves to weakly tied electronic links (Feldman, 1987).

Feldman's analysis of organizational e-mail messages lends support to her contention. Although most messages originated from members at least slightly known to one another, such messages were predominantly (64%) related to work topics. Among the smaller set of weak-tie messages, however—messages from users not at all known to one another with no other link than computers—the proportion was reversed, with 65% of messages related to nonwork topics, including personal issues, political, recreational, or humorous remarks. These messages were communicated almost exclusively by distribution list rather than e-mail addressed to identifiable recipients. Distribution list messages—messages sent to "topics" rather than "persons"—dominate these interactions.

Constant, Sproull, and Kiesler (1996) also conducted research on the utility of weak versus strong ties available through e-mail distribution lists, in a large multinational corporation. Their research was limited to work-related information exchange, and the technical questions and answers commonly sent via lists crossing departmental and geographic distances. Many questions were of the type, "Does anyone know . . . ?", and most replies—particularly the most helpful ones—were returned by users who had no personal acquaintance with the question-asker. The study does not therefore inform the question of whether users actually preferred closer ties to weaker ones, as no effort was made to determine that question. In contrast, in relation to social support and the dynamics of weak ties just articulated, we would expect some distinct advantages of weak ties to make online support preferable to asking one's closest associates even if they did have potential answers.

ADVANTAGES OF CMC AND ELECTRONIC SUPPORT

Different aspects of the CMC support process may affect the temporal and content aspects of communication. Some simple technical properties of CMC use are identified that may also facilitate social support exchange. Moreover, the hyperpersonal perspective of CMC may help to identify more complex CMC benefits. These aspects, taken together, suggest dimensions of CMC exchange that may make online support attractive and beneficial to its users.

Access

Easy access to electronic support appears to be the first advantage articulated by many researchers (e.g., Braithwaite et al., 1999; Egdorf & Rahoi, 1994; Rheingold, 1993). Temporally, Internet-supported support spaces, as well as those on most commercial electronic services, are available by modem connection 24 hours a day, 7 days a week. Potential support providers are never awakened or disturbed by a message placed on such a discussion board because users often use the system to post queries or responses asynchronously, without expectation for real-time interaction. Support providers, in turn, reply at their convenience. Although these are not instantaneous conversations, they build over time, and such interaction may gradually achieve the same interpersonal intimacy and depth as FtF meeting provides (Walther & Burgoon, 1992). Geographically, interactants half way across the globe may build conversations, and one's own location is irrelevant, and in many cases unknown (see Mitchell, 1995).

This differs substantially from FtF support, which is less readily available anyplace, any time. In dyadic, offline social support, a potential provider may not be available at the precise time when a support seeker needs help (Leatham & Duck, 1990). A critical mass of experienced or expert sources may also not exist within one's normal geography. Scheerhorn et al. (1995), for instance, detailed the barriers to FtF support faced by hemophiliacs and their families in small rural Ohio towns, who may have had no access to social support without electronic assistance, leading to the establishment of the HIGHNet, the Hemophiliacs in Good Health Network. And when sources of support do exist within geographic proximity, temporal issues may interfere with access. As a participant in the Usenet alt.sexual-abuse.recovery group wrote about trying to access FtF support,

> Well I finally called this councelling center for sexual asault and abuse victims. It was really hard. The woman on the phone was very nice though and she tried to put me at ease. I was told that there is a nine month waiting list. Can you belive that? I was not prepared for the questions that they ask and to my embarrasment, I cried. I really hate that. I can't seem to talk about the abuse without bursting into tears. (Anonymous note posted in Usenet alt.sexual-abuse.recovery, February 1996; rept. with permission of author)[2]

---

[2]In this and other direct quotations from respondents or online sources, all text is reproduced as originally appeared without corrections to spelling, punctuation, and grammar. Permission obtained by e-mail through anonymous remailer.

The Internet, on the other hand, is not limited by capacity. CMC interactions offer "a rolling present" (Hiltz, 1992) in which time and location are discretionary. As CMC groupware stores messages for perusal at the discretion of the user at least for some period of time, participants thus may come and go when they choose and respond at their own pace. Conversational coherence (McGrath & Hollingshead, 1993) or meaningful dialogues is built through the use of threads, and quoting previous messages (sometimes automatically), enabling subsequent participants to add comments (Black, Levin, Mehan, & Quinn, 1983; Walther & Tidwell, 1995).

Although most electronic support interaction is asynchronous, people all over the network, around the world, may be available with help at a moment's notice (as illustrated in Rheingold, 1993). Or one may peruse what others have said on related topics regardless of whether one actively queries or not. One method is by reading answers to "Frequently Asked Questions (FAQ lists), which are posted periodically in a variety of Usenet groups for discretionary reference (Hersch, 1996). Another is by *lurking*.

Lurkers

A relatively unique aspect of online support has to do with lurking (Egdorf & Rahoi, 1994). Lurking (and lurkers who do it) refers to reading messages posted by others on electronic spaces, without also posting one's own messages or in any way signaling one's vicarious observation. Some estimations place the number of lurkers to active posters as a hefty majority of users who frequent a particular group (see Sproull & Faraj, 1997). It is not only acceptable in this context not to "speak" when one has nothing to say, it is encouraged that those who are new to a particular group spend considerable time observing the interaction of established members (Moraes, 1996). This observation period allows two things: the opportunity to learn the norms and "netiquette" of the group, and the chance to see if answers to FAQs are already available in some electronic file that is periodically posted. In a sense, it is very efficient to see if anyone is discussing one's concerns already (with perhaps a week's worth of replies already posted) without the additional effort of writing them up, posting, and returning over some period of time to see what responses have been generated.

In FtF personal relationships, of course, it is almost inconceivable to "listen" only to a support exchange, or to "eavesdrop" surreptitiously on others' intimate self-disclosures or discussions of serious concerns. Yet, according to Mickelson (1997), online lurkers "can obtain comparison information or vicarious support without having to disclose anything about themselves . . . (and) obtain validation for their feelings of stigma without having to communicate those feelings to others" (p. 172). It is acceptable and preferable online in some ways to seeing many people raise the same or similar question over and over (McLaughlin, Osborne, & Smith, 1995).

Whether as a "poster" or a "lurker," a research question asks

RQ9: Is virtually unlimited *access* an attraction to computer-mediated social support?

Production Blocking

Research in the domain of electronic group decision making has pointed out another advantage to online interaction—the ability of such systems to reduce "production blocking" relative to FtF communication (Diehl & Stroebe, 1987; Valacich, Dennis, & Nunamaker, 1992). In CMC, participants may type their comments at any time, regardless of what any other participant may be doing. Unlike FtF groups and dyads, there is no need to take turns or to manage conversations in the usual manner. As a result, participants may not suppress or forget their comments as they might during a delay that could even preclude an FtF utterance. There is no limit on the time a group has for a meeting in CMC; everyone gets a chance to speak. Thus the research question:

RQ10: Is the ability to *write uninterrupted* an attraction to computer-mediated social support?

Hyperpersonal Aspects

Although much early research on CMC characterized it as "cold" relative to FtF interaction, recent research has found it quite tenable for establishing impressions and interpersonal relations (Walther, 1993; Walther & Burgoon, 1992). Indeed, recent work finds that previously unknown interactants are able to achieve greater intimacy via CMC than they do in parallel FtF interaction (Walther, 1996, 1997). Although this outcome is not universal, there are certain affordances of CMC and some combinations of social context factors that are known to affect relational communication and interpersonal perceptions in extraordinarily positive directions.

The hyperpersonal model of CMC suggests that extraordinary intimacy levels depend on activation of psychological processes related to receiving, sending, channel, and feedback in ways that can be enhanced by CMC (Walther, 1996). When message receivers assume that they are part

of a group of similars, messages stimulate idealization of group and interpersonal perceptions (Spears & Lea, 1992). CMC can hide certain personal traits that would be more easily detected and more salient through FtF
interaction. As senders, CMC users engage in selective self-presentation,
imbuing in their written messages highly preferred personal and relational
cues. The impressions these may garner may be especially friendly, knowledgeable, pathetic, or otherwise, as the sender may prefer; they are
arguably more deliberative and effective than one might manage offline.

Another component of the model addresses the affordances of the
asynchronous channel in the processes just discussed. This has particular
importance for electronic social support. As CMC does not demand real-
time utterance, participants may craft their messages and their self-presen-
tations with greater care than may be possible in spontaneous FtF settings.
They may stop and think, edit, rewrite, even abort and re-start a message
that is not to their liking. Additionally, Walther (1996) argued, CMC
users need not maintain any other expressive system than writing (i.e.,
they need not monitor their gestures, facial expressions, voice, or physical
appearance). They may in turn reallocate greater cognitive resources to
the articulation of their desired message. These possibilities, along with
the relative solitude accompanying CMC use, have been found to heighten
users' self-awareness (Matheson & Zanna, 1988). These advantages allow
CMC users to present whatever degree of vulnerability or wisdom that
their verbal skills are able to muster. In this way, it is easy to imagine that
requests for support, and its provision—especially for emotional support—may be enhanced.

By contrast, it is easy to imagine that FtF conversants may not
have at their disposal relevant references, addresses, or contact information during a specific, impromptu support conversation. Online, however,
because the "conversation" does not continue until each participant is
ready, there is no apparent interruption while one searches for external
information (Altman, Walther, & Edelson, 1997). Hence, the asynchronous and electronic nature of CMC allows time to craft a good request or
a good response. Thus, the actual quality of support may be increased.
This, in turn, may enhance interpersonal perceptions; as Rice (1987) suggested, one's image in cyberspace is likely to be a function of the quality
of one's information, and the character one reveals through one's writing.
Based on these aspects of the hyperpersonal model we ask:

RQ11: Does the ability to *craft and edit* a message asynchronously, with the potential for *more desired expression,* provide
an attraction to computer-mediated social support?

Anonymity

CMC, over the Internet to Usenet news groups, can offer absolute, objective anonymity, which many social support participants use in discussing their situations. Soliciting support or reflecting common experience in the provision of social support often reflects a personal concern that many might consider to be problems for the individual offline; they include inadequacy, maladaptation, weakness, or other stigma. It may be inappropriate to attribute these problems to their offline personal or professional identity. Participants often disclose extremely personal details online in seeking social support, and others sometimes respond with equally intimate details as they relate similar experiences or traumas of their own. Anonymity, although infrequently used, may be one of the most dramatic things about CMC in the realm of social support.

Anonymity may be achieved by several means. Some commercial online systems allow users to adopt "screen names" that are marginally traceable to one's actual identity. The Internet goes a step farther: Using one or more of the freely available anonymous remailer systems, one can post messages to Usenet newsgroups in such a way that one's real user name and e-mail address are not apparent and are virtually untraceable (Bacard, 1995, 1996). Although such systems have raised concerns about information security and a cloak of anonymity for subversive communication (see Lee, 1996), they remain available on the difficult-to-regulate Internet environment.

It is through low sociometric density or actual anonymity, said Rheingold (1993), that online venues are "a place that people often end up revealing themselves far more intimately than they would be inclined to do without the intermediation of screens and pseudonyms" (p. 27). Thus the research question:

> RQ12: Is *anonymity* a source of attraction to computer-mediated social support?

METHOD

Questionnaire

An original questionnaire was developed and distributed by e-mail to people who had posted messages to selected Usenet support groups. Based on the 12 research questions and background reviewed here, 33 scale items were developed reflecting hypothetical aspects of the electronic support advantages and disadvantages of FtF support. Items were constructed with a mixture of positively and negatively worded items, scaled as five-interval Likert-type items.

The questionnaire was formatted for e-mail in such a way that respondents could simply execute a "reply" command to return it with their scores. They were asked to type their 1 to 5 response to the left of each item as it appeared on their screens. A key with the semantic values for each number 1 to 5 was repeated twice, as it might be at the top of a printed page in a multipage questionnaire, so that respondents did not lose sight of the response anchors as they scrolled down the questionnaire on their computer screens. Additionally, scale items were consecutively lettered, rather than numbered, to avoid confusion or bias that numbers might otherwise introduce appearing adjacent to the blanks where numerical responses were requested.

Additionally, demographic items were included, as well as single items indicating experience with FtF support groups, use of anonymous remailers, and whether respondents pay for their Internet access. Finally, respondents were invited to add their own thoughts on the value of electronic social support by means of a single, open-ended question.

Sampling

Sampling procedures in organic electronic spaces raise a number of troubling issues. The first one apparent in this research is estimating the size of the potential participant population, despite readership estimates, and determining how to access it. One has very little idea how many people passively participate by lurking in these spaces. Additionally, there is no simple way to determine, of those who do post, whether they represent one person or more (as people may share e-mail addresses), or whether more than one address corresponds to what is in actuality a single individual (because an individual may have more than one way to access Usenet). In some cases, we have observed what appears to be multiple personalities of the same individual person (or at least the same address) posting messages that are related but in different "voices" or age-related styles. We also consider the possibility that some postings are exercises in creative writing and/or attempts to gain attention in which the posters may not actually manifest the symptoms or experiences about which they write (see e.g., Hellerstein, 1990). Concerns over deception on the Internet are not new (see e.g., Van Gelder, 1985). The fluidity of one's identity presentations, whether as a game (see Curtis, 1992), a reflection of psychological multiplicity (Stone, 1995), or as a rather normal and strategic affordance of the medium (Walther, 1996), is an issue that occupies a great deal of discussion and inquiry of late (e.g., Allen, 1996; Turkle, 1995).

Acknowledging that we would miss the lurking subpopulation by this strategy, we collected the e-mail addresses of posters from several Usenet groups.

Newsgroups were identified on the basis of their compatibility with social support topics. All groups containing the word *support* and *recovery* in their names were selected within both the alt.* and the soc.* newsgroup hierarchies (with the exception of alt.support.jockstrap, due to its lack of activity). On the basis of other pointers such as support-related web pages and FAQs, we were able to locate other pertinent groups without "support" in their names (e.g., alt.sexual-abuse.recovery) that we verified through observation as involving social support exchange.

Based on typical response rates to mail surveys and a similar methodology for online questionnaires (Parks & Floyd, 1996), we projected a 33% response rate to the questionnaire distribution. In order to achieve some stability for subsequent factor analyses, we aimed for at least 10 subjects per questionnaire item, necessitating the use of 1,000 addresses. In order to get both a diversity of responses as well as to be sensitive to similarities within groups, a randomized block sampling method was adopted to obtain these addresses. Once identified as pertinent, the groups' names were arrayed in a list. Every fifth group was identified, and within these groups, we recorded up to 50 unique user name/addresses from the messages posted to that group. Addresses were added from the next consecutive group on the list, until fifty were gathered. Then the next group, of the original every fifth group, was examined similarly. A list of all groups sampled appears in Table 7.2. The same method was used to gather additional addresses for each original set that we learned were not valid. The sampling method makes the groups unequal at the stage where we solicited responses, and imperfect response rates skew the representation of various groups in the final sample even more. However, the randomized approach to subject recruitment should bolster the generalizability of our results.

As we do not have knowledge of the base of potential subjects, either because they did not happen to post messages, or they do not post but rather read only during our data-collection period; this sample thus differs from census block. Despite the uncertainties of the sampling method, however, response rate was very typical compared to other electronic and nonelectronic research. Of the 1,000 questionnaires sent out, 340 were returned sufficiently completed for most analyses.

Table 7.2. Usenet Newsgroups Sampled.

alt.abuse.recovery	alt.support.headaches.migraine
alt.recovery	alt.support.learning-disab
alt.recovery.aa	alt.support.loneliness
alt.recovery.addiction-sexual	alt.support.menopause
alt.recovery.catholicism	alt.support.mult-sclerosis
alt.recovery.codependency	alt.support.pco
alt.recovery.compulsive-eat	alt.support.personality
alt.recovery.na	alt.support.post-polio
alt.recovery.religion	alt.support.prostrate.prostatitis
alt.sexual-abuse.recovery	alt.support.schizophrenia
alt.support	alt.support.shyness
alt.support.anxiety-panic	alt.support.skin-diseases.psoriasis
alt.support.arthritis	alt.support.sleep-disorder
alt.support.asthma	alt.support.step-parents
alt.support.attn-deficit	alt.support.stop-smoking
alt.support.big-folks	alt.support.tall
alt.support.breastfeeding	alt.support.tinnitus
alt.support.cancer	alt.support.tourette
alt.support.crohns-colitis	soc.support.depression.manic
alt.support.depression.manic	soc.support.depression.treatment
alt.support.depression	soc.support.depression.family
alt.support.diet	soc.support.depression.crisis
alt.support.diet.rx	soc.support.depression.seasonal
alt.support.dissociation	soc.support.depression.misc
alt.support.divorce	soc.support.fat-acceptance
alt.support.eating-disord	soc.support.loneliness
alt.support.epilepsy	soc.support.pregnancy-loss
alt.support.ex-cult	soc.support.transgendered
alt.support.grief	

RESULTS

Demographics

Initial analyses revealed an interesting profile of respondents. Their ages were extremely diverse, ranging from 16 to 79. Of the sample, 5% was below 20 years of age; 23% was in their 20s; 33% in their 30s; 22% in their 40s; 8% in their 50s; and the remaining 2% in their 60s or 70s. The mean age was 36.29 years. There were slightly more females (55%) than males (44%) in this sample. Two subjects identified themselves as transgendered.

Many of these subjects (65%) paid for their Internet access and 73% of these respondents reported having participated in some form of organized FtF support groups at some point. In general, the descriptive demographic data reveal a diverse and knowledgeable population for purposes of this research.

Analyses

Scores were subjected to principal components factor analysis with orthogonal rotation, in order to determine the most parsimonious set of dimensions of attraction to electronic social support. Criteria for the acceptability of a solution included the following: eigenvalues of 1.5 or greater for as many factors as would be accepted; items having a primary loading of .50 or greater on the primary factor, and less than .30 on any other factor; that any dimension has a minimum of three items meeting the loading criteria, and that factors be readily and meaningfully interpretable. Eigenvalues indicated as many as eight factors, but initial statistics indicated that no substantial increments in variance would be accounted for beyond four or five. A final four-factor solution met all analytic criteria and accounted for 51% of the variance. The items and factor loadings are presented in Table 7.3. In presenting the final factors and their interpretation, illustrative comments from the open-ended question are offered.

The first factor, which accounted for the greatest variance, appears to reflect a notion of social distance (see Rogers, chap. 3, this volume), and clusters together concepts from several areas reviewed for this research ($M = 2.69$). The items include advantageous aspects of the strength of weak ties, as well as disadvantageous aspects related to autonomy and dependence issues from FtF support relationships. In particular, items related to stigma management are included, dealing with the embarrassment one might experience if offline acquaintances were to know of the users' concerns. Dependency issues surfaced in items dealing with dependency, giving up control, and feeling obligated in FtF social support. Items reflecting CMC partners' gentler and more expert treatment than that provided FtF were also included. Overall, this dimension suggests a more distant rather than close relationship offers certain benefits, and the detriments of unmediated support and the benefits of mediated support are indeed complementary. Respondents' comments reflected this dimension. Concurrence with the notion of reduced obligation/dependency may be seen in the comments of a 17-year-old male from alt.support.shyness:

Table 7.3. Subscale Alpha Reliability, Means, Standard Deviations, and Rotated Factor Matrix.

Factor	Alpha Reliability	Mean	St Dev	I	II	III	IV
Factor I: Social Distance	α = .88	2.69	0.82				
* I'm afraid to talk to my close, personal, face-to-face contacts about this topic.		2.37	1.23	.73	.24	.05	-.01
* My face-to-face acquaintances might think less of me if we talked about this issue		2.56	1.24	.72	.11	.17	-.01
* I would feel embarrassed if people I know offline knew I had these concerns.		2.59	1.33	.69	.32	-.03	-.06
* My face-to-face relationships hold things back to spare my feelings.		2.99	1.19	.65	.33	-.03	-.06
* In face-to-face support relationships, you get too dependent on others.		2.55	1.15	.64	.09	.05	-.01
* People I know face-to-face are too harsh about this topic.		2.45	1.17	.64	.10	.02	.08
* In seeking support in my face-to-face relationships, I give up a measure of control over my life.		2.49	1.12	.63	.09	.31	.11
* I wouldn't want some of my friends and family to be aware of this issue.		2.80	1.40	.63	.36	.03	-.05
* My online acquaintances are *less* likely to judge me negatively.		3.02	1.17	.54	.29	.05	.22
* After I receive face-to-face social support I feel obligated to return the support even though I may not want to.		2.68	1.14	.52	.01	.23	-.01
* The advice I receive from my face-to-face relationships is not as objective.		2.76	1.15	.50	.22	.24	.23
The advice I receive from people I may not know is more objective than from people I know well.		3.12	1.15	.42	.25	.01	.29
My face-to-face social support network does not have enough expertise in this area.		3.26	1.24	.35	.03	.08	.24
Factor II: Anonymity	α = .75	3.28	0.83				
* Online, I can say personal things without others knowing who I really am.		3.37	1.17	.21	.76	.09	.04
* I can say things anonymously online.		3.27	1.24	.16	.66	.26	.03
Others can say personal things because we don't know who they are online.		3.50	1.14	.40	.59	.01	.15
* There is less embarrassment being anonymous online.		3.25	1.13	.29	.54	.27	.08

Table 7.3. Subscale Alpha Reliability, Means, Standard Deviations, and Rotated Factor Matrix (cont'd).

Factor	Alpha Reliability	Mean	St Dev	I	II	III	IV
* I always get an opportunity to express myself online.		3.87	0.96	-.10	.52	.26	.32
* No one knows my true identity online.		2.65	1.28	.19	.52	.23	-.12
Factor III: Interaction Management	α = .72	3.53	0.71				
* Face-to-face interactions do not always allow me time to compose my thoughts.		3.50	1.16	.28	.09	.67	.08
* It's hard to put my thoughts into words on the spot face-to-face.		3.12	1.19	.35	-.04	.65	-.04
* I have time to craft a well-thought message online.		4.00	0.92	-.05	.30	.65	-.01
* There's plenty of time to say exactly what I mean online.		3.93	0.86	-.09	.28	.59	.15
* I am not expected to continue my interaction/relationship after I receive online support.		3.14	1.03	.14	.22	.56	.05
I do not always get a chance to speak in face-to-face support.		3.06	1.18	.36	-.09	.41	.26
I cannot receive anonymous support face-to-face.		3.38	1.22	.29	.26	.38	.09
In seeking support here, I do not give up any control over my life.		3.50	1.11	.12	.35	.37	.16
Factor IV: Access	α = .72	3.92	0.78				
* Online support is always there when I need it.		3.89	0.99	-.04	.15	.02	.70
* Face-to-face social support is not available 24 hours a day.		3.72	1.17	.19	-.02	.16	.66
* It is available any time of day or night.		4.23	0.92	-.06	.05	.21	.65
I cannot always receive face-to-face social support when I want it.		3.84	1.19	-.01	.05	-.12	.57
This online group has enough expertise to be helpful in this area.		3.75	1.02	.43	-.08	.14	.56
Compared to face-to-face relationships, you don't have to get to know people as long before you can ask for help.		3.75	1.07	.24	.34	.16	.37

Note. * indicates items reflecting the greatest reliability, retained for dimensional analyses to be reported elsewhere.

> I often feel uncomfortable asking my friends/acquaintances for help
> with being shy because I don't want this fact to ruin my friendships,
> as it sometimes has done in the past. I received more diversified opin-
> ions and support when online, and this also helps me—I ask for help
> "into the air" (one might say) and receive many replies, as opposed
> to asking one person for help and getting one reply—which is usually
> not enough to help. In short, I prefer asking for help online than ask-
> ing my friends for help.

A 33-year-old female from soc.support.transgendered seems to concur:
"You get a wider spectrum of people. People from more diverse backgrounds and experiences. You get a larger *number* of people as well,
increasing the likelihood of hitting it off with someone, or getting the
answer you need (provided that you're capable of weeding through the
chaff)." A 27-year-old female participant from soc.support.depression.cri-
sis stated, "Usenet has given me the opportunity to communicate with
people I would not ordinarily meet. And yes, sometimes it is a great help
to be able to bare your soul to someone who has some *understanding*
of what you're going through, which many of my actual friends do not."

The second factor related to *anonymity* ($M = 3.28$). Items mentioned that no one knows who one is online, and that people can say personal things without knowing one another. One item in this cluster
implies that anonymity, too, precludes embarrassment. Given that the
anonymity factor factored separately from the social distance factor—
which also contained items about embarrassment and stigma-related
issues—it appears that respondents saw differently the social distance of
weak ties than the technological distance anonymity may provide.

Factor 3 appears to focus on *interaction management* ($M = 3.53$).
Most of these items reflect the hyperpersonal perspective's notions about
the medium's relative advantage in terms of message composition. CMC
users taking the time and putting into words what they really desire, is
reflected here. An additional item stating, "I am not expected to continue
my interaction/relationship after I receive online support," broadens this
dimension beyond message composition to interaction management somewhat more generally.

Another respondent's comment illustrates the hyperpersonal
notion of message management reflected in this factor. A 47-year-old male
contacted through alt.support.loneliness observed:

> Writing is a lot different means of communicating than we are all used
> to. Our questions and answers are more articulate, more meaningful,
> and can be viewed over and over again until we get the message. It is
> my belief that the discussion is easier and healthier, and the computer
> does not interrupt us during our story or questions, and we do not

have a chance to interrupt the response. That means there is a purer form of communication going on. Each person has a chance to deal with their own issues—then move on to others issues, after they are finished.

The fourth and final factor relates to *access* (M = 3.92). It is somewhat surprising that this factor was not more prominent, given the salience of the access issue in discussions about the benefits of online support and virtual communities. The item ratings on the overall factor did show a generally high appreciation for this dimension. That online support is available any time, and that nonelectronic support is not, is the essence of this dimension.

DISCUSSION

The present research attempted to ascertain some dimensions of participants' attraction to social support transacted through CMC. The numerous potential benefits of online social support were suggested by the social support literature, both from disadvantages of close personal relationship for support exchange, and from the benefits of weak-tie interaction as affect social support. CMC research and theory also offered several potential benefits, as online support may offer connections to different kinds of people, through different communication behaviors, than is traditionally associated with support exchange. This background yielded 12 research questions identifying potential attractions of electronic social support: candor (both less harsh and more forthright responses to problems), less negative judgment, reduced obligation to reciprocate support, less relational dependency, more immediate ability to seek support, greater expertise in the network, stigma management, intimacy, access, uninterrupted composition, more expressive communication, and anonymity. The findings from an online survey of Usenet support group users indicate that these specific attributes combine to form four overall factors of attraction, some of them exclusive and some combining attributes of CMC in unanticipated ways.

Findings suggest that users recognize several benefits of online social support: (a) they are aware of the kinds of people and relationship in which they transact their concerns, as seen in social distance; this distance provides greater expertise, stigma management, and more candor; (b) the level of anonymity with which their actual identity may be associated; (c) the affordances of the medium in optimizing their expressiveness, turns, and ongoing obligations, in interaction management; and (d) the ability to seek or provide support anytime, in terms of access.

Judging by the variance in the statistical analysis, the users who responded to our research appeared to vary in the degree to which they valued each of these dimensions. At the same time, specific support groups may have particular rewards that, like their own norms of conduct, evolve and develop over time among their own user communities. Although general research on social support or electronic interaction would not necessarily benefit through attempts to delineate specific groups' unique attractions, such work may be useful in "site-specific" concerns. That is, practitioners, therapists, system designers, and those in need of support would be well-advised to attempt to understand the communication patterns and dynamics of divergent groups. Although such an approach may address certain applied questions, it remains to be seen whether our knowledge about the support process online will be advanced by empirically examining these diverse online support activities without basing these studies on alternative or varied theoretical perspectives.

There are other aspects of electronic social support that deserve exploration. One aspect is the manner in which many online participants seek social support, in ways that are not considered in the FtF (see e.g., Barbee & Cunningham, 1995).[3] For instance, a common online support-seeking strategy is disclosing a very personal narrative and/or revelation of feelings and concluding with a question, asking if anyone else has similar experiences. It is quite common to send a narrative "into the air, so to speak" (as one respondent put it), in electronic support groups. This is also the case in other domains of CMC such as organizational electronic mailing lists or Usenet newsgroups on other topics, such as technical issues to hobbies, where users frequently send messages along the lines, "does anybody know/have any experience with . . ." whatever issue (e.g., Constant et al., 1996). Although this type of social support information request tends to be met with less success than those prefaced with an indication of familiarity with the group, according to Galagher et al. (1998), this remains an interesting support seeking strategy. Whether it is relatively undocumented in FtF encounters, or something relatively unique to online support remains to be seen.

Although we have argued that there may be many advantages to exchanging social support in electronic networks, we are hesitant to speculate whether this kind of support alone may be comparable to the known

---

[3]The closest we have noted is the support-seeking strategy Barbee and Cunningham (1995) called "tell details," which suggests some disclosure as a seeker describes a problem: A seeker "describes entire situation; explains the reasons for the problem; talks openly and states factual evidence; sticks to the facts . . ." (p. 394). Yet, this approach seems overly rational compared to the intimate, personal, subjective narratives we have frequently observed informally as calls for response in many support newsgroups.

benefits that are associated with traditional social support. Even if information and shared experience exchanged among similar participants may be useful, it may not satisfy other needs often met through FtF support exchange.

The benefits of these types of support activities to psychological and physical health and well-being remain unknown. A direct implication for future research is to assess the use of online social support to the extent that it correlates with an "individual's subjective sense of being supported by others as well as the appraisal of adequacy . . . of that support" (Albrecht at al., 1994, p. 423), as implied by any of several existing measures (see Albrecht et al., 1994; Sarason, Sarason, & Pierce, 1990). This type of research will be difficult, however. It is not clear whether the majority of posters to online social support groups are seeking or providing support. If the latter, sampling addresses of message posters, as this study did, may skew results toward exaggerated levels of social adjustment. On the other hand, if, once feeling supported, online support seekers tend not to use the system, polling recent posters may skew results to reflect people disproportionately experiencing problems.

In a recent field study by Kraut et al. (1998), despite negative effects of Internet use on depression and loneliness, there were no negative effects obtained on an assessment of self-reported social support access online. They found that previous nonusers showed a slight increase in depression and loneliness (R^2 = .0225) in association with hours of Internet use per week; and although their interaction in geographically close social circles and families was reduced, their conversations in larger social circles increased. These results were not anticipated, and the authors speculated that the replacement of strong relationships with weak ones—paralleling the sociometric definition of links, and as suggested by Egdorf and Rahoi (1994), taking them to connote qualitative values—leads to the negative psychological reactions. The report suggests that weakly linked, virtual support partners do not deliver adequate support when one is ill, typifying the superficiality of online relations that eventually disappoint or depress the user. It is thus unclear what, if anything, caused users to become more depressed with greater Internet use. Our own research suggests that online social support may make up for, or supplement, such a gap in offline life.

Although we share the concern over online support system abilities to transact tangible aid or instrumental support, we have doubts about Kraut et al.'s suggestion that these online relations lack meaning for their participants or that they are emotionally shallow compared to "close-tie" relationships. There are several bases for our skepticism. First, empirical work by Parks and Floyd (1996) found that most Usenet users "make friends" online and that many of these friendships are comparable to offline friendships on a variety of relationship assessment dimensions (a notable exception being how much time partners spend together). Furthermore, just as FtF social support relationships may become multiplex friendships (Burleson, 1990; Burleson, Albrecht, Goldsmith, & Sarasen, 1994) where as many as 60% meet FtF (Parks & Floyd, 1996), it is not clear the extent to which subjects in the Kraut et al. study used Usenet per se—the 1998 research looked primarily at e-mail and Web use, whereas a 1995 report (Kraut, Scherlis, Mukhopadhyay, Manning, & Kiesler, 1995) focused on Usenet, but in other contexts. We would be surprised if these contrary findings are that channel-specific, and the comments of our respondents, as well as other research about online relationships, don't reconcile the depiction of a "sad, lonely world" of Internet use (see Harmon, 1998) and displacement from one's family that Kraut et al. (1998) suggested. We maintain that discussions with one's family may not be the best place, for example, for a woman to ask how she can maintain a healthy sexual relationship with her husband; or one's circle of close friends may not be a comfortable venue in which to ask for advice about a possible divorce and custody fight. The Internet affords certain benefits in such cases.

Indeed, the present research demonstrates how new technology can be appropriated to address needs that may go unmet through the use of traditional communication channels. It offers some evidence to Egdorf and Rahoi's (1994) suggestion that electronic social support helps to satisfy unmet needs in nonmediated relationships. Whether it is because one doesn't have access to a critical mass of similar (expert) others, or one's close relations might deteriorate in response to a request for help—or one needs respite from the double-edged sword of dependency and obligation accompanying support in close relationships—accessing social support via CMC and electronic networks offer a potent alternative. It will be useful to bear this in mind as new developments in multimedia telecommunications are increasingly resembling FtF communication. Such innovations as "desktop video" would undermine the affordance of anonymity that, to some electronic support participants, is highly valuable (but see O'Sullivan & Levine, 1999).

In their comprehensive review of support communication, Albrecht at al. (1994) suggested that researchers "should be especially interested in the features of situations, messages, interactions, relationships, and networks that can alleviate or reduce dilemmas" (p. 435). That is, the dilemmas of meeting support needs while avoiding the negative aspects of FtF personal social support. Internet and CMC users have found this interesting as well, as their frequent usage and self-reflective comments about online social support demonstrate. The notion is ironic, to say the least, but worthwhile nonetheless: Sometimes FtF communication is not what is wanted or best suited to a situation, especially when the topic is personal, delicate, requiring support. In such cases, different aspects of new electronic communication venues can be an attractive alternative.

ACKNOWLEDGMENTS

We thank several individuals who contributed to conceptual development or data, including Sadhana Chandramouli, Kim Ludwig, Knight Hinman, and Chris Marsh. Additionally, our thanks to Malcolm Parks, Terrace Albrecht, and Michael Burgoon, for their helpful comments in various stages of the preparation of this research. Previous elements of this research were reported at the annual meetings of the International Network on Personal Relationships (1996) and the International Communication Association (1997).

REFERENCES

ACLU v. Reno, No. 96-963, 1996 U.S. Dist. Retrieved September 2, 1999 from the World Wide Web: http://www.aclu.org/court/cdadec.html (E.D. Pa. June 11, 1996).

Adelman, M. B., Parks, M. R., & Albrecht, T. L. (1987). Beyond close relationships: Support in weak ties. In T. L. Albrecht & M. B. Adelman (Eds.), *Communicating social support* (pp. 126-147). Newbury Park, CA: Sage.

Albrecht, T. L., & Adelman, M. B. (1987). Communication networks as structures of social support. In T. L. Albrecht & M. B. Adelman (Eds.), *Communicating social support* (pp. 40-63). Newbury Park, CA: Sage.

Albrecht, T. L., Burleson, B. R., & Goldsmith, D. (1994). Supportive communication. In M. L. Knapp & G. R. Miller (Eds.), *Handbook of interpersonal communication* (2nd ed., pp. 419-449). Thousand Oaks, CA: Sage.

Allen, C. L. (1996). *Virtual identities: The social construction of cybered selves.* Unpublished doctoral dissertation, Northwestern University, Evanston, IL.

Altman, M., Walther, J. B., & Edelson, D. C. (1997). *Electronic collaboration and problem-based learning.* Paper presented to the Computers in Healthcare Education Symposium, Health Sciences Libraries Consortium, Philadelphia.

Baccard, A. (1995). *The computer privacy handbook: A practical guide to e-mail encryption, data protection, and PGP privacy software.* Berkeley, CA: Peachpit.

Baccard, A. (2001). *Anonymous remailer FAQ.* Retrieved April 4, 2001 from the World Wide Web: http://www.andrebacard.com/remail.html.

Barbee, A. P., & Cunningham, M. R. (1995). An experimental approach to social support communications: Interactive coping in close relationships. In B. R. Burleson (Ed.), *Communication yearbook 18* (pp. 381-413). Thousand Oaks, CA: Sage.

Barnes, M. K., & Duck, S. (1994). Everyday communicative contexts for social support. In B. Burleson, T. Albrecht, & I. G. Sarason (Eds.), *Communication of social support: Messages, interactions, relationships and community* (pp. 175-194). Thousand Oaks, CA: Sage.

Black, S. D., Levin, J. A., Mehan, H., & Quinn, C. N. (1983). Real and non-real time interaction: Unraveling multiple threads of discourse. *Discourse Processes, 6,* 59-75.

Braithwaite, D. O., Waldron, V. R., & Finn, J. (1999). Communication of social support in computer-mediated groups for persons with disabilities. *Health Communication, 11,* 123-151.

Burleson, B. R. (1990). Comforting as social support: Relational consequences of supportive behaviors. In S. Duck (Ed.), *Personal relationships and social support* (pp. 66-82). London: Sage.

Burleson, B. R., Albrecht, T. L., Goldsmith, D. J., & Sarason, I. G. (1994). Introduction: The communication of social support. In B. R. Burleson, T. L. Albrecht, & I. G. Sarason (Eds.), *Communication of social support: Messages, interactions, relationships, and community* (pp. xi-xxx). Thousand Oaks, CA: Sage.

Constant, D., Sproull, L., & Kiesler, S. (1996). The kindness of strangers: The usefulness of electronic weak ties for technical advice. *Organization Science, 7,* 119-136.

Critical Art Ensemble. (1996). *Utopian promises—net realities.* Retrieved September 2, 1999 from the World Wide Web: www.well.com/user/hlr/texts/utopiancrit.html.

Curtis, P. (1992). Mudding: Social phenomena in text-based virtual realities. In D. Schuler (Ed.), *DIAC-92: Directions and implications of advanced computing* (pp. 48-68). Palo Alto, CA: Computer Professionals for Social Responsibility.

Cutrona, C. E., & Suhr, J. A. (1992). Controllability of stressful events and satisfaction with spouse support behaviors. *Communication Research, 19,* 154-174.

Diehl, M., & Stroebe, W. (1987). Productivity loss in brainstorming groups: Toward the solution of a riddle. *Journal of Personality and Social Psychology, 53,* 497-509.

Egdorf, K., & Rahoi, R. L. (1994, November). *Finding a place where "We all want to hear it": E-mail as a source of social support.* Paper presented at the annual meeting of the Speech Communication Association, New Orleans.

Feldman, M. S. (1987). Electronic mail and weak ties in organizations. *Office: Technology and People, 3,* 83-101.

Fernback, J., & Thompson, B. (1995, May). *Computer-mediated communication and the American collectivity: The dimensions of community within cyberspace.* Paper presented at the annual meeting of the International Communication Association, Albuquerque, NM. Rpt. as *Virtual communities: Abort, retry, failure?,* http://www.well.com/user/hlr/texts/VCcivil.html.

Ford, L. A., Babrow, A. S., & Stohl, C. (1996). Social support messages and the management of uncertainty in the experience of breast cancer: An application of problematic integration theory. *Communication Monographs, 63,* 189-207.

Galagher, J., Sproull, L., & Kiesler, S. (1998). Legitimacy, authority, and community in electronic support groups. *Written Communication, 15,* 493-530.

Goldsmith, D. (1992). Managing conflicting goals in supportive interaction: An integrative theoretical framework. *Communication Research, 19,* 264-286.

Granovetter, M. (1973). The strength of weak ties. *American Journal of Sociology, 78,* 1360-1380.

Harmon, A. (1998, August 30). Researchers find sad, lonely world in cyberspace. *New York Times on the Web.* Retrieved August 30, 1998 from the World Wide Web: http://www.nytimes.com/library/tech/98/08/biztech/articles/ 30depression.html.

Harris, S. (1996, June). *Emotional support on the Internet V1.07.* Available online: http://www.compulink.co.uk/~net-services/care/.

Hellerstein, L. (1990). Electronic advice columns: Humanizing the machine. In G. Gumpert & S. L. Fish (Eds.), *Talking to strangers: Mediated therapeutic communication* (pp. 112-127). Norwood, NJ: Ablex.

Hersch, R. (1996). *FAQs about FAQs.* Message posted to news.announce.newusers.

Hiltz, S. R. (1992). Constructing and evaluating a virtual classroom. In M. Lea (Ed.), *Contexts of computer-mediated communication* (pp. 188-208). London: Harvester Wheatsheaf.

Kraut, R., Lundmark, V., Patterson, M., Kiesler, S., Mukopadhyay, T., & Scherlis, W. (1998). Internet paradox: A social technology that reduces social involvement and psychological well-being? *American Psychologist, 53,* 1017-1031.

Kraut, R., Scherlis, W., Mukhopadhyay, T., Manning, J., & Kiesler, S. (1996). The Home Net field trial of residential Internet services. *Communications of the ACM, 39,* 55-65.

La Gaipa, J. J. (1990). The negative effects of informal social support systems. In S. Duck & R. C. Silver (Eds.), *Personal relationships and social support* (pp. 122-139). London: Sage.

Leatham, G., & Duck, S. (1990). Conversations with friends and the dynamics of social support. In S. Duck & R. C. Silver (Eds.), *Personal relationships and social support* (pp. 1-29). London: Sage.

Lee, G. B. (1996). Addressing anonymous messages in cyberspace. *Journal of Computer-Mediated Communication, 2*(1). Available online: http://www.usc.edu/dept/annenberg/vol2/issue1/anon.html.

Matheson, K., & Zanna, M. P. (1988). The impact of computer-mediated communication on self-awareness. *Computers in Human Behavior, 4*, 221-233.

McGrath, J. E., & Hollingshead, A. B. (1993). Putting the "group" back in group support systems: Some theoretical issues about dynamic processes in groups with technological enhancements. In L. M. Jessup & J. Valacich (Eds.), *Group support systems: New perspectives* (pp. 78-96). New York: Macmillan.

McLaughlin, M. L., Osborne, K. K., & Smith, C. B. (1995). Standards of conduct on Usenet. In S. G. Jones (Ed.), *Cybersociety: Computer-mediated communication and community* (pp. 90-111). Thousand Oaks, CA: Sage.

Mickelson, K. D. (1997). Seeking social support: Parents in electronic support groups. In S. Kiesler (Ed.), *Culture of the Internet* (pp. 157-178). Mahwah, NJ: Lawrence Erlbaum Associates.

Mickelson, K. D., Helgeson, V. S., & Weiner, E. (1995). Gender effects on social support provision and receipt. *Personal Relationships, 2*, 211-224.

Millar, F. E., & Rogers, L. E. (1976). A relational approach to interpersonal communication. In G. R. Miller (Ed.), *Explorations in interpersonal communication* (pp. 87-104). Beverly Hills, CA: Sage.

Mitchell, W. J. (1995). *City of bits: Space, place, and the infobahn.* Cambridge, MA: MIT Press.

Moraes, M. (1996). *A primer on how to work with the Usenet community.* Monthly posting to news.announce.newusers.

Moursund, J. (1997). SANCTUARY: Social support on the Internet. In J. E. Behar (Ed.), *Mapping cyberspace: Social research on the electronic frontier* (pp. 53-78). Oakdale, NY: Dowling College.

O'Sullivan, P. B., & Levine, K. J. (1999, May). *Mediated support groups: A bona fide group perspective.* Paper presented at the annual meeting of the International Communication Association, San Francisco.

Parks, M. R., & Floyd, K. (1996). Making friends in cyberspace. *Journal of Communication, 46*, 80-97.

Rafaeli, S. (1986). The electronic bulletin board: A computer-driven mass medium. *Computers and the Social Sciences, 2*, 123-136.

Rapaport, M. (1991). *Computer mediated communications: Bulletin boards, computer conferencing, electronic mail, information retrieval.* New York: Wiley.

Rheingold, H. (1993). *The virtual community: Homesteading on the electronic frontier.* Reading, MA: Addison-Wesley.

Rice, R. E. (1987). Communication technologies, human communication networks and social structure in the information society. In J. Schement & L. Lievrouw (Eds.), *Competing visions, complex realities: Social aspects of the information society* (pp. 107-120). Norwood, NJ: Ablex.

Rice, R. (1994). Network analysis and computer-mediated communication systems. In S. Wasserman & J. Galaskiewicz (Eds.), *Advances in social and behavioral science from social network analysis* (pp. 167-203). Newbury Park, CA: Sage.

Robinson, D. (1988). Self-help groups. In R. S. Cathcart & L. A. Samovar (Eds.), *Small group communication: A reader* (5th ed., pp. 117-129). Dubuque, IA: Wm. C. Brown.

Sarason, B. R., Sarason, I. G., & Pierce, G. R. (1990). Traditional views of social support and their impact on assessment. In B. R. Sarason, I. G. Sarason, & G. R. Pierce (Eds.), *Social support: An interactional view* (pp. 9-25). New York: Wiley.

Scheerhorn, D., Warisse, J., & McNeilis, K. (1995). Computer-based telecommunication among an illness-related community. *Health Communication, 7,* 301-325.

Schwarzer, R., & Leppin, A. (1991). Social support and health: A theoretical and empirical overview. *Journal of Social and Personal Relationships, 8,* 99-127.

Shade, L. R. (1996). Is there free speech on the net? Censorship in the global information infrastructure. In R. Shields (Ed.), *Cultures of Internet* (pp. 11-32). London: Sage.

Spears, R., & Lea, M. (1992). Social influence and the influence of the "social" in computer-mediated communication. In M. Lea (Ed.), *Contexts of computer-mediated communication* (pp. 30-65). London: Harvester-Wheatsheaf.

Sproull, L., & Faraj, S. (1997). Atheism, sex, and databases: The net as social technology (pp. 35-52). In S. Kiesler (Ed.), *Culture of the Internet.* Mahwah, NJ: Lawrence Erlbaum Associates.

Thompson, T. L., & Seibold, D. R. (1978). Stigma management in normal-stigmatized interactions: Test of the disclosure hypothesis and a model of stigma acceptance. *Human Communication Research, 4,* 231-242.

Turkle, S. (1995). *Life on the screen.* New York: Simon & Schuster.

Valacich, J. S., Dennis, A. R., & Nunamaker, J. F. (1992). Group size and anonymity effects on computer-mediated idea generation. *Small Group Research, 23,* 49-73.

Van Gelder, L. (1985, October). The strange case of the electronic lover. *Ms. Magazine*. Reprinted in C. Dunlop & R. Kling (Eds.), *Computerization and controversy: Value conflicts and social choices* (pp. 364-375). Boston: Academic Press.

Walther, J. B. (1993). Impression development in computer-mediated interaction. *Western Journal of Communication, 57*, 381-398.

Walther, J. B. (1996). Computer-mediated communication: Impersonal, interpersonal, and hyperpersonal interaction. *Communication Research, 23*, 3-43.

Walther, J. B. (1997). Group and interpersonal effects in international computer-mediated collaboration. *Human Communication Research, 23*, 342-369.

Walther, J. B., & Burgoon, J. K. (1992). Relational communication in computer-mediated interaction. *Human Communication Research, 19*, 50-88.

Walther, J. B., & Tidwell, L. C. (1995). Nonverbal cues in computer-mediated communication, and the effect of chronemics on relational communication. *Journal of Organizational Computing, 5*, 355-378.

Wellman, B., & Gulia, M. (1999). Net surfers don't ride alone: Virtual communities as communities. In P. Kollock & M. Smith (Eds.), *Communities in cyberspace* (pp. 167-194). Berkeley: University of California Press.

Wellman, B., & Wortley, S. (1990). Different strokes from different folks: Community ties and social support. *American Journal of Sociology, 96*, 558-588.

PART THREE

TECHNOLOGY
AND ORGANIZATIONAL
COMMUNICATION

8

Adoption, Diffusion, and Use of New Media

Ronald E. Rice
Rutgers University

Jane Webster
University of Waterloo

This chapter reviews the forms of, and influences on, the diffusion, adoption, and uses of computer-mediated communication (CMC) in organizational settings, from e-mail to desktop videoconferencing to collaborative systems. It does not explicitly consider outcomes or consequences of such usage, but, rather, considers adoption and uses of new media as important "dependent variables" in and of themselves (Rogers, 1995).

Research and models of the adoption, diffusion, and use of new communication media have arisen from several research streams—*diffusion of innovations* (e.g., Rogers, 1995), *media choice* (e.g., Daft & Lengel, 1986), and *implementation of information systems* (e.g., Saga & Zmud, 1994). The diffusion of innovations literature suggests that characteristics of an innovation (such as relative advantage and complexity) and communication networks (such as opinion leaders and informal interactions) influence media diffusion. The media choice literature posits that interactions between characteristics of the message and the task, and peer attitudes and use, will affect media choice and performance. The implementation literature proposes that management policies, technology design, ease of use, and user participation in design will affect media use, satisfaction, and effects.

"The" dependent variable has varied across research streams and individual studies. For example, in the diffusion of innovations literature, media adoption, usage or reinvention are generally the dependent variables (Agarwal & Prasad, 1997). In the media choice literature, choice or evaluation may be the dependent variables (Trevino, Webster, & Stein, 2000). And in the information systems literature, acceptance (measured as attitude toward use, intentions to use, or frequency of use), routinization (i.e., normal, standardized, or administrative use), user satisfaction (with respect to information, the system, and support staff) and infusion (extended, integrative, or emergent use) may be the primary dependent variables (DeLone & McLean, 1992; Saga & Zmud, 1994).

BACKGROUND

Adopters, Adoption, Use

Type and Level of Adopters. Simple dichotomizations of adoption type such as adopters or rejecters, adoption or nonadoption, usage or nonusage, are by now inadequate and misleading. For instance, Lin (1998) introduced the middle category of *likely adopters,* between non-adopters and adopters. O'Callaghan (1998) noted the distinction between *innovators*—those who make their decision to adopt independently of others' decisions or social influence—and *imitators*—those influenced by the nature and timing of others' decisions.

There may be a variety of *levels of adopters.* Often an "organization" decides to purchase or design, and implement, a new media system, which can be considered the "adoption." But that says little about the decision processes or adoption and usage levels within different units, much less by different groups or individuals. Influences on adoption by organizations and individuals may be quite different (Tornatzky & Klein, 1982). Even "organizational" adoption may be a product of prior actors' decisions, and user feedback, concerning technical and regulatory standards, designs, infrastructure, political factors, vendor and supplier strategies, and cultural constraints or national policies, as considered by the "social shaping of technology" perspective (Williams & Edge, 1996).

Adoption, Reinvention, and Infusion. A crucial distinction in kinds of adoption, especially for organizational communication media, is the extent of *voluntariness* of the innovation (Agarwal & Prasad, 1997), or how much individual (or unit, organizational) choice is involved in the adoption and usage of the system. For example, large-scale integrated systems typically require specific technical features and well-defined kinds of usage (perhaps even limited to entering data and responses to online forms). These necessary system boundaries reduce the variety of uses and applications by potential adopters. In addition, managerial policies may limit certain kinds of usage, such as barring unjustified use of internal phone in favor of e-mail (Markus, 1994a). The kinds, amount, and forms of usage may not be very "voluntary" in these conditions. It is also the case that adoption, however defined, at one time does not necessarily imply continued usage or acceptance; an innovation not rejected initially may later be *discontinued,* such as after the primary technology champion of organizational e-mail usage leaves (Markus, 1994a), or when one desktop video system attracts another system's potential user base (Kraut, Rice, Cool, & Fish, 1998).

Another distinction is between *adoption* (allocation of resources to acquire an innovation) and *infusion* (use of the system leads to increased organizational effectiveness at a more integrated level; Cooper & Zmud, 1990). As partial evidence of the conceptual distinction between initial use and intentions for future usage, Agarwal and Prasad (1997) found that predictors of the two (concerning use of the World Wide Web) differed: for initial use, compatibility, visibility, trialability, and external pressure; for intended future use, relative advantage, result demonstrability, and current usage. In between are *adaptation* (the system is installed, maintained, and revised, people are trained and begin using the system), *acceptance* (the system is applied to work), and *routinization* (usage becomes normal and system application implications become embedded in organizational governance). A new technology may be widely acquired but only sparsely used within "adopting" firms, generating what Fichman (1995) called the *assimilation gap,* or what Hiltz and Johnson (1989) distinguish as *usage* versus *acceptance.*

Infusion may be an outcome of high levels of *reinvention* (Johnson & Rice, 1987; Rice, 1987), which is the adaptation of an innovation after its adoption. For example, Markus (1994a) noted a creative and collective reinvention of e-mail, of using the "forward" feature with the prior message included as well as an annotation, to foster group discussions, with chained annotations allowing newcomers to enter into the conversations (Rice & Shook, 1990a, found a similar use of voicemail, and Rice & Steinfield, 1994, reported similar chained annotations in e-mail messages).

Tyre and Orlikowski (1994) argued that the general implementation or adoption process actually involves a *discontinuous process* of mutual adaptation among technology, users, and organizational contexts, where stable utilization periods are punctuated by both external and internal change triggers during "windows of technological opportunity." These changes may or may not be incorporated into work processes, leading to a new stable state, whereas stabilization in systems may cause user attitudes and usage patterns to become habituated and make it difficult to achieve higher levels of reinvention. Gasser (1986) discussed informal microlevel processes that help to integrate computing into work and sustain computing over the long term, such as *working around,* or "intentionally using computing in ways for which it was not designed or avoiding its use and relying on an alternative means of accomplishing work" (p. 216).

Levels and Types of Uses. Typically, utilization is conceptualized as amount of use, dependence on the technology, or diversity of functions used (Trice & Treacy, 1988). But adoption of a new medium involves more than just its use, and includes *acceptance, adaptation, resistance,* and *avoidance* (Hiltz & Johnson, 1989; Poole & DeSanctis, 1990), with wide variations in application and use of the innovation. Simple measures of adoption do not take into consideration advanced uses, applications, and reinvention of the technology (Majchrzak, Rice, Malhotra, King, & Ba, 2000; Rice & Shook, 1990b; Rogers, 1995; Stewart, 1992).

Usage may be distributed unequally, with "hard core users" as well as those reluctant to use or experiment with applications (Bowers, 1995). Webster (1998) distinguished among *complete, wary* and *nonusers* of desktop videoconferencing. Panko (1985) termed limited e-mail usage as *stunted use* and recommended choices in interfaces for different kinds of users. Unequal usage may be most apparent at a structural level. For example, McKenney, Zack, and Doherty (1992) revealed that density of communication among e-mail users was greater than for FtF communicators, but that there were more subsets of isolates among the e-mail users than among face-to-face interactants. Similarly, Rice's (1994a) analysis of summer interns' usage of e-mail found that those who received the lowest evaluation after their internships also participated less in the research group's wider socialization and task network via e-mail. Rice, Grant, Schmitz, and Torobin (1990) showed that membership in various communication groups strongly predicted those who used e-mail and those who didn't, whereas Haythornthwaite and Wellman's (1998) study of media use among members of a university group found that communication in general between two members was highly correlated with the number of media that that pair used.

Given a measure of adoption or usage, even "successful" adoption is an ambiguous concept. Emphasizing the distinction between organizational and individual adopters, Manross and Rice (1986) concluded that *organizational* definitions of the success of diffusion (there, an "intelligent" telephone system) are not necessarily the same as how the *users* actually respond to the innovation. A study of the implementation of an experimental networked computer-supported cooperative work system in a "best practice" government organization concluded that it is very difficult to define adoption success; it depends on what the system is being compared with, what constitutes the full complement of applications, what level of adopter is being considered, and what is defined as a core technology by "outsiders" (Bowers, 1995).

Regardless of the level of adoption or usage, there are also variations in the kinds of usage. Kettinger and Grover (1997) found three primary uses for e-mail:

1. Task: distribute, provide or receive info, messages, files, programs, or feedback.
2. Social/Entertainment: learning about events/things that interest me, taking a break from work, and keeping in touch.
3. Broadcast: broadcast requests for information.

Rice and Steinfield (1994) reported the same three general kinds of e-mail usage, and Kaye (1998) found that greater hours using the Web was correlated with entertainment, social interaction, and escape. Note that these kinds of usage are in line with uses and gratifications theory's propositions about influences on media use (see Charney & Greenberg, chap. 15, this volume).

OVERVIEW OF CMC: CAPABILITIES AND DIFFUSION

This section summarizes a range of trade and professional surveys on the adoption and use of several new and emerging media, specifically e-mail, voicemail, desktop videoconferencing, collaborative shared tools, facsimile (fax), and intranets.

New Media: Brief Definitions and Usage Surveys

E-Mail. E-mail, a computer-based messaging system, generally is asynchronous (although it may be invoked in synchronous "chat" or "talk" mode), quick, text-based (although it is becoming multimedia), and allows written messages to be composed and edited on a computer screen and then sent either individually addressed or to a predefined list of recipients.

Forty million Americans (15% of the U.S. population) used e-mail in 1997; this is expected to rise to 135 million (50%) by 2002 (Levins,

1997). Surveys noted by Klopfenstein (chap. 14, this volume) reported that more than 25% of all U.S. adults had an e-mail address by early 1998. These adopters are not equally distributed throughout society. An August 1998, survey of more than 50,000 households by Techserver (NUA, 1999) found that although 49.2% of homes with incomes of $75,000 were online, only 13.9% of homes with incomes of under $35,000 were.

The 1995 annual *Fortune Monitor* survey (1996), based on responses from top- and mid-management subscribers, showed a jump from 54% in 1993 to 70% in 1994 of those who used computers as part of a network, implying communication, data transfer, and information retrieval. Seventy-five percent reported their companies used e-mail (with 88% using at work and 47% connecting from home, for 5.8 hours online per week). In a 1995 survey (American Society of Association Executives, 1996), CEOs reported that their companies had e-mail for internal use (70%), external connections (49%), and international connections (13%). Nearly 80% of the Society for Human Resource Management members in 1996 said they used e-mail (McCune, 1997). By mid-1998, according to a survey of 1,000 small businesses by Cyberdialogue/FINDSVP (NUA, 1999), e-mail was the most used online business application, with more than 14.7 million business users. Of the 400 executives surveyed by Ernst & Young in early 1998 (NUA, 1999), 36% reported they use e-mail more frequently than any other communication tool, 26% preferred the telephone, whereas 15% indicated they preferred communicating by FtF in a meeting. A similar survey of 400 executives by the American Management Association also found e-mail to be the primary medium of business communication.

The Electronic Messaging Association (1997) estimated the number of e-mail messages sent overall in 1997 was 2.7 trillion; by 2000 this grew to 6.9 trillion. A study of a cross-section of Fortune 500 companies (Frazee, 1996) found an average user receives approximately 15 e-mail messages per day, spending almost 50 minutes just reading them. Half of the messages are likely to require a response; in-depth responses requiring considerably more time are frequent. A U.K.-based study of British and Irish employees (Condon, 1998) reported that junk e-mail costs businesses $8 billion a year, due to the time employees spend dealing with unwanted e-mail. E-mail overload was reported by 60% of 1,000 executives in a Pitney Bowes' survey (NUA, 1999), with greater levels perceived by those higher up in the organization. Reuters' study of 1,000 senior management in 11 countries indicated, however, that 49% felt the Internet actually helps to manage information overload (NUA, 1999). Other problems reported in the Cyberdialogue/FINDSVP survey included difficulties in prioritizing mail, attaching files, and spelling e-mail addresses.

E-mail may provide an alternative to newspapers as a major commercial medium, based on interviews by Forrester Research with executives of 50 U.S. corporations that support large-scale e-mail activities (Levins, 1997). Bill paying, prescription ordering, and vendor interactions through e-mail will become routine. E-mail management software will be able to filter out unwanted junk mail and organize incoming mail, such as putting news service messages into a news folder (Levins, 1997), and allowing browsing of an interactive, multimedia format.

According to a Human Resource Management member survey, 67% of the companies warn their employees that they should not expect privacy in their e-mail communications, 39% said that they monitor e-mail content routinely, whereas 31% indicated the company sets some parameters for respecting an employee's privacy in e-mail communications. Moreover, 42% explicitly restrict e-mail use to business purposes, but most do not heavily enforce this limitation. Only 36% of the respondents have outlined proper e-mail usage to employees (McCune, 1997).

Voicemail. Voicemail, another computer-based messaging system, accessible asynchronously from touch-tone telephones, allows digitized audio messages to be transmitted to one or more persons. However, voicemail often is conceptualized as similar to a voice answering system—that is, people use the phone expecting to talk to someone but are then requested to leave a message. This severely limits the technical and organizational capabilities of voicemail (Rice & Danowski, 1993; Rice & Tyler, 1995; Stewart, 1992). Proactively or intentionally using the messaging features allows intentional asynchronous messaging among those who have accounts on the system, forwarding, annotation, distribution lists, personalized messages and mailboxes, temporal tickler files, prioritizing of messages, storing messages for transmission at a later date, and so on (Rice & Shook, 1990b).

Voice-messaging services are available from local telephone companies, service bureaus, PC-based voice messaging, a dedicated system, or a digital system that integrates with other business and intraorganizational phone systems. Several drivers have raised the awareness and adoption of voice-messaging services, including the ability to (a) manage all messages from one mailbox from any phone or workstation, (b) manage wireless and wireline messages from the same mailbox, and (c) send and hear messages over the Internet (Landes & Harrod, 1997).

In 1997, Boston Technology, Centigram, Digital Sound, Lucent Technologies, Northern Telecom, Octel and Unisys supported more than 60 million mailboxes; Bell Atlantic's Home Voice Mail had 1.6 million residential subscribers; and U.S. West's residential service had another 1.5 million messaging subscribers (Landes & Harrod, 1997). A study by the

Voice Messaging Educational Committee reported that voicemail is used in 75% of Fortune 2000 U.S. corporations (Rodewald, 1997).

A 1996 survey of 150 executives found that 62% of business managers checked on their voicemail messages first, compared to 36% preferring e-mail ("For call-backs," 1997). *INC.* (1996) reported how frequently CEOs check their voicemail when they are away from their office: 0 to 1 times per day, 32%; 2 to 4 times, 47%; 5 to 9 times, 10%; more than 10 times daily, 3%. They logged in to their e-mail much less frequently: 0 times 56%, 1 to 3 times daily, 32%.

Future enhancements include speech recognition, mailbox management via the Internet, and a greeting card message using a celebrity voice to wish someone a happy birthday or anniversary. Other developments entail linking voice messaging to other services such as pager notification, fax messaging, broadcast distribution and routing capabilities, and the emergence of groups such as The Messaging Alliance (jointly owned by Ameritech, Bell Atlantic, Nynex, and Pacific Bell Information Services), which aims to enable private branch exchange (PBX) and network-based voicemail systems in North America to perform nonreal-time messaging communications (Rodewald, 1997). Two future challenges remain: first, adding audio menus and responsiveness design, so that callers won't be automatically cutoff or fail to reach a live respondent; and second, enhancing the voicemail system by implementing auto attendant (answering calls, allowing informed users to transfer to a specific extension, coverage during busy times), audiotext (broadcast frequently requested information in audio form on request), transaction boxes (navigation through menu prompts), and fax-on-demand (requesting print information through voice or fax requests; Rice & Shook, 1990b; Rodewald, 1997).

Desktop Videoconferencing. Desktop videoconferencing allows for audio and video communication between multiple locations through users' personal computers. It is a technology that integrates several media. For instance, some desktop systems also include collaborative shared tools that allow remote individuals to jointly (and often synchronously) share applications, such as spreadsheets (Alavi, Wheeler, & Valacich, 1995), graphics, computer displays, databases, and other features and resources necessary to accomplish joint activities. A more general term for combined groupware and desktop video is *media space,* which uses "integrated video, audio, and computers to allow individuals and groups to work together despite being distributed spatially and temporally" (Mantei, Baecker, Sellan, Buxton, & Milligan, 1991, p. 803). In accord with Bly, Harrison, and Irwin (1993) and Dourish, Adler, Bellotti, and Henderson (1996), Mantei et al. argued that media spaces are more than just "poor substitutes" for FtF: they offer unique conditions of richness and complexity.

The business market for desktop video will remain small until a variety of factors converge (Dixon, 1998). Real-time, full-motion desktop videoconferencing is expected to be technically and economically feasible in the next few years, overcoming today's complex configurations and low video quality. High-speed and/or broadband technologies such as Digital Subscriber Line (a derivative of ISDN digital phone transmission), coaxial cable TV lines, wireless systems, low-orbit direct-broadcast satellite systems (with Internet uplink connections), "streaming" video (where multiple users view the same one-way transmission) and switched LANs, will help make this possible (Korostoff, 1996; Poole, 1997).

Of 853 *Fortune* top management subscribers in 1996, 24% reported their companies were currently using videoconferencing, and 13% were actively investigating its use; for desktop video, the figures were 7% and 10%. *Electronic Market Trends* (1996) noted a Yankee Group report that 28,000 desktop video units were sold in 1995, and this jumped to 3.8 million in 1999. In 1996, only $180 million was spent in the United States on dedicated desktop videoconferencing hardware, whereas in the consumer market, Intel shipped more than 5 million ProShare cards in less than a year between 1997 and 1998 (Poole, 1997). According to Telespan Publications (Hamblen, 1996), business desktop videoconferencing units reached 6 million by 2000, and home units 14 million.

Facsimile. Facsimile captures and transmits the graphic image (typically as a series of digitized symbols indicating lighter or darker areas of the original) through telephone lines between fax machines that scan the original or print out the image on paper, whether to one recipient or to a distribution list of recipients. Computer fax can take a computer document and convert it into a fax image, transmit it over computer networks, receive other faxes, and use optical character recognition to convert images of alphanumeric symbols into editable text and numbers for use in word processing or spreadsheet applications. As the hardware for copying, faxing, and printing can now be one, the new fax systems, combining with intelligent telephone systems, are turned into a single desktop appliance.

A 1996 Gallup survey of Fortune 500 and mid-sized companies found that 60% of daily users were faxing more than in 1995 ("What paperless," 1997). In a 1996 *Fortune* uppermanagement survey (*Fortune Monitor,* 1996), 18% reported their organizations were intending to purchase computer-based fax, and 13% new fax machines. A 1996 Cablevision survey of 1,000 respondents noted that fax was used 2.7 hours per week for business purposes compared to .6 for home purposes (*Cablevision,* 1996). From a 1995 survey of 1,596 association management CEOs (PPAM, 1996), 68% said their company used fax broadcasting, 70% used faxes for in-house use, and 20% had fax-on-demand, mostly for in-house use; 20% offered for-fee information about associations through fax. In 1995, 5.8% of direct marketing organizations indicated that they used fax as their primary system for both consumer and business audiences; 7.1% indicated they used fax for secondary sales, and 10.3% used it for non-sales communication (DMA, 1996).

Respondents from *Fortune* and mid-sized organizations reported selecting fax over e-mail, voice mail, and overnight courier as the most reliable method of communication ("What paperless," 1997). The average time estimated to fax five pages created on a personal computer was less than required to send the pages by e-mail, and response rates from broadcast fax campaigns were quicker and higher than for mail, e-mail, and other media in almost every case, beyond the fact that many small businesses do not have e-mail addresses. A mid-1997 Gallup poll (NUA, 1999) found that although 65% of organizations had provided e-mail accounts for their employees, company staff still preferred fax to e-mail, largely because of a perceived greater reliability and simplicity of fax delivery.

Internet and Intranets. The use of the global Internet, or "the set of networks using multiple network technologies that can intercommunicate" (Leiner, 1994, p. 32), has exploded with the application of World Wide Web (WWW) technology. The WWW allows users to find and use information in a standard way across different platforms, and represents an integrated technology, as it can provide such services as e-mail, file transfer, and discussion groups (Scheepers & Damsgaard, 1997). Intranets, or "organizational Internets," are closed-user-group networks, whether limited to the physical boundaries of a single organization, or shared among members of dispersed organizational units. Some intranets may be "firewalled" off from the Internet, whereas others may provide gateways and even external access to the internal resources.

Approximately $19 billion was spent by end-users on Internet and Intranet products in 1996 (*Information Interactive Services Report* [IISR], 1997). By the end of 1997, 62 million Americans (30% of those over 16) were users of the Internet and online services (Intelliquest, 1998). Klopfenstein (chap. 14, this volume) reported that, by 1998, as many as 100 million Americans, and over half of all American and Canadians between 16 and 34, had used the Internet. LaRose and Hoag (1996) argued that use of the Internet is still primarily an organizational innovation. For instance, half of the users in 1994 were teachers and executives (Bournellis, 1995) who probably used the Internet from their institutions. Of the 853 upper level management respondents to the annual *Fortune* (1996) survey, 48% used commercial online services, 42% used the

Internet, and 21% used online financial services—at work and home—both for approximately 3 hours per week each. During April 1997, an ongoing panel of business users of the Web spent almost two thirds more time per week on the Web than did home users (5.75 hours per person vs. 3.5; NPD, 1998). Forty percent of 1,596 CEOs reported their companies had an Internet address, and 39% had a web page (PPAM, 1996).

The use of Intranets in organizations also is growing: 59% of U.S. companies and 38% of European companies had an Intranet in 1997, with about 75% expected in both regions by 1998, leading to 133 million Intranet users by 2001 (NUA, 1999). E-mail is the primary application for 50% of companies with Intranets, according to a survey of 3,000 companies with Intranets (NUA, 1999). Business-to-business companies were the highest adopters (37%) with government organizations the lowest (3%).

Not all of this organizational Internet use is necessarily productive or even healthy! Half of the 1,000 respondents in a survey by Reuters Ltd. actually "crave" information, and 54% said they experience a "high" when they find the information they have been seeking (King, 1997). More than one third of respondents believe their colleagues are obsessed with gathering information, and 65% said that makes their work environment more stressful. Eighty-four percent of respondents also recommended information management classes, yet 58% said their companies did not offer them. Nearly two-thirds of human resource executives report that employees are spending more time surfing the Internet as diversion (Sunoo, 1996), whereas 85% of Association for Information Technology Professionals (1998) are somewhat or very concerned about non-productive use of the Internet by workers.

Integrated/Other Communication Media. Media are becoming integrated today, rather than consisting of a single medium. Although forecasters have predicted that collaborative technologies like videoconferencing, groupware, and integrated messaging will become widely diffused, currently the most frequently used collaborative tools continue to be voicemail, e-mail, and audio conferencing (Borthick, 1997). Groupware may actually be used largely as fancy e-mail. For example, only about 50% of the 1,500 Notes end-users in a 1996 Arthur-Anderson survey regularly use Notes discussion databases; only 14% use workflow applications at least three times a week (Cole, 1996). Orlikowski (1993) explained the limited and simple use of Lotus Notes in a consulting organization as due to (a) an implementation that did not develop users' mental models of Lotus Notes as anything more than a limited, personal application; and (b) a competitive climate that mitigated against sharing information. However, more companies are switching from simple e-mail systems to software that also provides groupware—from 60% in 1997 to an estimated 80% in 2001, based on a 1997 survey by International Data Corp (Cole-Gomolski, 1997). This is due to increased integration of programs (such as Lotus Notes, Microsoft Outlook, and Novell's Groupwise), increased interoperability, and cross-program standards among groupware systems.

Some media, although valuable in themselves, are not sufficient for integrated communication activities. For example, newsgroups, threaded discussions, chat, and e-mail are necessary for virtual workspaces but are not sufficient, as they provide little support for convergence, consensus, focus, and joint creation of an outcome (Romano, Nunamaker, Briggs, & Vogel, 1998). Trends are toward strong integrated messaging (involving computer-telephony integration [CTI]), which includes a combination of e-mail, fax, and voicemail, with support for not only retrieving any of these forms of messages, but also filing and managing the messages (Franklin, 1997).

Other new media are becoming more prevalent in organizations. A *Fortune Monitor* survey (1996) reported that companies were either currently using (8%-32%), or were actively investigating (5%-12%), use of personal digital assistants, wireless data communication, and multimedia. For instance, pager sales rose from $139 million in 1991 to $300 million in 1995 (Electronic Market Trends, 1996) and cell phones were used for business activities 7.3 hours per week compared to 6 for home activities (Cablevision, 1996). International Data Corporation's survey of 600 executives reported that 70% owned a 3Com PalmPilot hand-held computer, most frequently using it for personal information and e-mail (Investor's Business Daily, 1998).

Diffusion in the Literature

Table 8.1 shows rough trends in coverage of new organizational media in business and social science literatures. These searches were conducted for 1990, 1995, 1997, and 2000 to show recent trends, first on the full record and then on the title only, as the title is a more explicit indicator of coverage of specific media. In the business literature, e-mail coverage grew rapidly from 1990 to 1995, with the most overall coverage except the recent emphasis on Intranets. Voicemail coverage remained essentially stable at a moderate level over the time period. Groupware interest jumped in 1995, but dropped off since then (possibly because of the use of different terms as group applications become more integrated). Fax has shown a steady increase in interest until recently. Academic coverage has been much lower in terms of sheer numbers of article title word retrievals, although e-mail coverage similarly rose in 1995 and has leveled off. Interest in groupware reached a peak in 1995, as in the business literature. Intranets are just now appearing.

Table 8.1. Diffusion of New Organizational Media as Indicated by Online Database Coverage, 1990-2000.

Database	E-mail	Voicemail	Video	Groupware	Fax	Intranet
			New Media			
ABI/Inform						
1990-all	276	101	4	42	—	0
1990-title	11	23	2	13	85	0
1995-all	809	186	89	594	—	8
1995-title	26	24	18	109	121	3
1997-all	876	173	46	428	—	432
1997-title	17	18	58	57	250	34
2000-all	867	17	3	166	—	183
2000-title	121	1	0	16	7	27
Wilson Business Abstracts						
1990-all	97	67	5	21	—	0
1990-title	17	19	3	13	136	0
1995-all	173	61	28	33	—	5
1995-title	12	14	8	104	47	1
1997-all	296	101	35	96	—	368
1997-title	11	12	6	19	35	94
Dissertation Abstracts						
1990-all	15	4	0	7	—	0
1990-title	3	1	0	2	1	0
1995-all	72	4	1	38	—	0
1995-title	24	1	0	12	2	0
1997-all	69	4	5	12	—	3
1997-title	20	0	1	9	2	0
2000-all	98	1	0	0	—	2
2000-title	14	0	0	0	0	1
PsychInfo						
1990-all	19	3	0	5	—	0
1990-title	8	3	0	2	0	0
1995-all	19	6	1	5	—	0
1995-title	7	4	0	4	2	0
1997-all	27	2	2	14	—	0
1997-title	6	2	1	1	0	0
2000-all	87	0	0	9	—	5
2000-title	24	1	0	4	0	1
Wilson Social Sciences Abstracts						
1990-all	2	0	0	1	—	0
1990-title	1	0	0	1	4	0
1995-all	21	2	0	2	—	0
1995-title	3	0	0	0	2	0
1997-all	27	5	0	2	—	0
1997-title	1	0	0	1	2	0

Table 8.1. Diffusion of New Organizational Media as Indicated by Online Database Coverage, 1990-2000 (con't.).

Database	E-mail	Voicemail	Video	Groupware	Fax	Intranet
			New Media			
2000-all	51	1	0	5	—	5
2000-title	9	0	0	0	2	0
Sociology Abstracts						
1990-all	4	0	0	1	—	0
1990-title	1	0	0	0	1	0
1995-all	21	1	3	1	—	0
1995-title	7	0	0	0	1	0
1997-all	11	4	1	2	—	0
1997-title	3	0	0	1	0	0
2000-all	24	0	0	1	—	3
2000-title	6	0	0	0	0	0

Notes. Term sets used in the searches were: (a) e-mail, electronic mail, electronic messaging, computer-mediated communication; (b) vmail, voicemail, voice messaging; (c) desktop video, desktop videoconferencing, computer videoconferencing; (d) groupware, collaborative technology, computer -supported collaboration, GDSS, group support system, group decision support system; (e) fax, facsimile; and (f) intranet.
Only feature articles in periodicals.
All = search on title, abstract, descriptor; Title = title only.
Fax: "All" not used because word "Fax" listed in abstracts for ordering.
ABI/Inform: 1,000 business, management, trade journals.
Wilson Business Abstracts: 345 business periodicals.
Dissertation Abstracts: PhD and master's theses; for 2000, *Digital Dissertations*.
PsychInfo: 1,300 journals in psychology, physiology, linguistics, medicine, nursing, sociology, education, pharmacology, psychiatry.
Wilson Social Sciences Abstracts: 350 social science journals (no mention of communication or information systems); for 2000, *ProQuest Social Sciences Abstracts*.
SocioFile: 2,000 journals; w/dissertations, conference abstracts.

INFLUENCES ON ADOPTION AND USE

As described earlier, influences on media adoption and use have arisen from multiple theoretical perspectives, relating to individual, rational, organizational, technology, and social factors (see Fjermestad & Hiltz, 1998; Kettinger & Grover, 1997, for recent reviews of influences on CMC system adoption and use). Individual factors often reflect persons' technology-related skills, such as their computer skills. Rational factors relate to the situation and reflect objective characteristics of the specific incident, such as message equivocality or access to the medium, that may constrain or guide behavior. Organizational influences relate to such factors as management support and organizational structures. Objective technology influences relate to such factors as transmission quality, while perceived technology influences relate to more subjective characteristics of the technology such as ease of use. Social factors relate to the social environment and reflect such forces as others' attitudes and symbolic cues.

Each of these factors may only explain a small amount of variance in adoption and use (e.g., critical mass, Rice, 1990; Sanderson, 1996; Steinfield, 1992; social influence, Rice et al., 1990; Rice, 1994b). For instance, Donabedian, McKinnon, and Bruns' (1998) analysis of responses from managers explained 15% of the variance in media choice by variables related to task and medium. One explanation is that certain factors may be more important for different media (Webster & Trevino, 1995) or at different times. For instance, Astebro (1995) found that peer communication helped explain diffusion and adoption for more innovative people (earlier), whereas social and political influences by management provided better explanations for less innovative people (later). Rice (1993b) analyzed social influences across time for a variety of media in several organizations, and found a significant effect only for the new medium (desktop videoconferencing) and only for users communicating through that medium.

A more fruitful approach is to examine influences of multiple factors drawn from a variety of perspectives (Webster & Trevino, 1995), as the following sections do. This complementary approach integrates influences on adoption, diffusion, and use, rather than examining them as competing explanations (Bozeman, 1993; Sitkin, Sutcliff, & Barrios-Chopin, 1992; Webster & Trevino, 1995).

Individual Influences

Most research has focused on individual characteristics of the sender (although Kraut & Attewell, 1997, and Zmud, Lind, & Young, 1990, noted the separate roles of sender and receiver). For instance, Schmitz and Fulk (1991) proposed that those with lower medium experience, computer experience, and keyboard skills would be inhibited from using a technology-based medium. Fulk (1993) posited that those who are younger and more educated would be more receptive to a newer medium. Older members may find it harder to learn new technologies, have more invested in the current status and environment, and have more equivocal tasks because of their higher organizational level (Rice & Shook, 1990a). For example, a study of more than 1,000 voicemail users in 75 different agencies and departments of state government agencies (Caldwell & Uang, 1995) found differences in preferences for voicemail across various situational constraints by gender, age, and experience.

Leonard-Barton and Deschamps (1988) suggested that several individual characteristics would influence usage of a system; for example, those who perceive themselves as higher performers would have stronger intrinsic motivation to adopt an innovation and those higher in personal innovativeness would be more likely to use an innovation without management urging. More innovative individuals are not only more likely to adopt a new medium earlier and use it more, but also to use it in more varied ways with more benefits. For example, voicemail users who were more innovative reported a greater ability to obtain information (Rice & Shook, 1990b). However, perceived organizational innovativeness was a stronger influence than individual innovativeness in a study of voicemail adoption in two organizations (Rice & Tyler, 1995).

Compeau and Higgins (1995) suggested that those with higher computer self-efficacy beliefs would exert greater efforts to master a system than those with lower self-efficacy beliefs. Webster (1998) proposed that those higher in introversion would have a greater need to maintain their privacy, and thus would use desktop videoconferencing systems less than those lower in introversion. Other individual characteristics studied for their influences on new media adoption and use have included communicator style (Rice, Chang, & Torobin, 1992), cognitive style (Trevino, Lengel, Gerloff, & Muir, 1990), and self-monitoring (Alexander, Penley, & Jernigan, 1991).

In addition to demographic and personality factors, researchers have suggested that user participation in the development process will positively affect user knowledge, and thus beliefs about usefulness and intentions to use (Saga & Zmud, 1994). Involvement or participation in implementation or the diffusion process increases users' perceptions of control, thus reducing perceived threats (Baronas & Louis, 1988), as well as fostering a variety of other intervening processes such as commitment and satisfaction (Johnson & Rice, 1987).

Task Influences

In explaining organizational use of new media, researchers argue that technologies must fit well with job tasks in order for positive impacts on individual performance to occur (Cooper & Zmud, 1990; Goodhue & Thompson, 1995). Based on organizational information-processing and contingency theory, this approach posits that the task demands of information-processing and communication content interpretation interact with technical capabilities of media to influence outcomes such as communication effectiveness and work (as well as organizational) performance.

The primary task-medium characteristics theories are social presence (Short, Williams, & Christie, 1976) and media richness (Daft &

Lengel, 1986). These explain how communication media differ in the extent to which (a) they can overcome various constraints over time, location, permanence, distribution, and distance; (b) transmit the social, symbolic, and nonverbal cues of human communication; and (c) convey equivocal information. A better fit between the medium's characteristics (such as higher social presence or richness in desktop videoconferencing compared to text-based e-mail) and the task demands (such as equivocality, as in negotiating) will foster greater communication performance. For instance, Rice and Shook's (1990a) meta-analysis demonstrated that managers at different levels would prefer or need to use different media, due to different task environments. Many studies show positive relationships between task analyzability and new media use (such as e-mail, Rice et al., 1990; or voice mail, Rice & Tyler, 1995).

Rankings of perceived media richness or social presence scales are usually quite consistent. However, correlations of those perceptions with levels of new media usage (generally e-mail) at the individual level are typically weak (Rice, 1993a; Rice et al., 1992; Rice, D'Ambra & More, 1998; Rice, Hughes, & Love, 1989). Furthermore, nonverbal cues and socioemotional content are possible in CMC (Rice & Love, 1987) and e-mail and voicemail are sometimes used by managers for equivocal situations (Markus, 1994a; Rice & Shook, 1990b).

Contextual Influences

Communication is an interdependent phenomenon. Hence, whether a critical mass of users exists or whether other relevant participants have access and will respond via the medium is a significant influence (Markus, 1994a). Markus (1987) summarized diverse literatures to show that the value of an interactive communication medium is related not just to the attributes of the system, but to the number of other users. As possible interactions escalate with additional users, later users gain more immediate value than do earlier users. Thus, she also highlighted the importance of different benefits, and different resources, of early and later adopters. Alternatively, rejection of an interactive medium by some groups may prevent an organization-wide critical mass from forming, reducing the value of the innovation for those who do choose to adopt (as found by Harper, 1996, in his study of use and rejection of "active badges" in two research labs). Kraut et al. (1998) analyzed the use of two similar desktop videoconferencing systems, showing that user migration to one system lead to the disuse and "death" of the other system. They pointed out that systems technically unprepared for critical mass may well become overloaded or too public, leading to rejection by earlier adopters. Similarly, individuals will benefit from new media such as voicemail in proportion to the degree that it is used by other members of the group (Beswick

& Reinsch, 1987; Rice & Tyler, 1995), and voicemail tends to be adopted or rejected by an entire work group (Stewart, 1992). Other studies addressing e-mail, voicemail, and fax (Bikson & Law, 1993; Ehrlich, 1987; Kaye & Byrne, 1986; Rice & Danowski, 1993; Rice et al., 1990; Soe & Markus, 1993), some controlling for a variety of other factors, have shown the impact of critical mass on influencing adoption, usage, and evaluation of new media.

Other factors, such as time pressures and geographic distances, also reflect the sociocontextual influence of the interdependent nature of communication. For instance, because of its ability to overcome situational constraints of time and space, e-mail is more likely to be used as the geographical distance between communication partners is greater (Rice, Hughes, & Love, 1989; Trevino, Daft, & Lengel, 1990). This relationship would hold more for cross-organizational communication, because within organizations task interdependencies, cost factors, and local usage norms are strong influences on use of e-mail even among physically close unit members (Eveland & Bikson, 1987; Markus, 1987; Rice, 1994a). Furthermore, according to Bly et al. (1993), work is fundamentally social, so collaborative technologies are defined by the social setting (such as group size, commonality of purpose, and degree of openness about work). Intragroup and intergroup task interdependence also have been identified as positive influences on e-mail, voicemail, and collaborative media use (Kraut & Attewell, 1997; Rice, 1994b; Rice et al., 1990; Rice & Shook, 1990b; Rice & Tyler, 1995; Steinfield, 1986).

Media/System Influences

Objective Characteristics. Characteristics of the media themselves and their availability affect adoption and use. Media richness (a perceived characteristic), reviewed earlier in connection with task characteristics, represents one key attribute. Other attributes include transmission quality of the medium, especially for those involving compressed video image transmission (e.g., video compression, half-duplex, and lack of synchronization of video and audio for desktop video; Anderson et al., 1997; Whittaker & O'Conaill, 1997). Familiar norms and habits can be disrupted by technical and design aspects in media spaces, such as audio degradation and limited dimensionality of sound, limited control of spatial orientation and how one's video image appears to others, and tradeoffs between detailed and wide views (Bly et al., 1993). Obstacles to successful use of desktop video include interaction differences between those in the same room and those in mediated spaces, misaligned eye gaze, loss of status information associated with traditional seating arrangements, minimized cues for in-meeting coordination of turn-taking, impact on discussion of participants' image sizes, misleading perceptions of personal or impersonal proximity due to small and asymmetric video image sizes and positioning, and issues of privacy and surveillance (Mantei et al., 1991). However, some research suggests that users will choose an image of some relevant object instead of others' facial views (Whittaker & O'Conaill, 1997). Similarly, Abel (1990) found that users of a videowall and cross-site office videoconference were more oriented toward audio than to video, and Egido (1990) summarized research showing that the visual channel does not really add much in terms of either content or outcomes.

Access and reliability of a medium influence adoption and use. For instance, visual access to an e-mail terminal reduces some uncertainty associated with the costs of checking for e-mail messages and thus influences e-mail use and evaluation (Rice & Shook, 1988). The time required for access, and ease of access, can influence employees' intentions to use a technology, especially with newer technologies such as desktop videoconferencing that may not support fast-enough connections (Webster, 1998). Higher reliability, or "dependability and consistency of access and uptime" (Goodhue & Thompson, 1995, p. 235) of the system, should lead to more medium use.

In situations involving time pressures, synchronous communication becomes important. People may turn to the telephone instead of e-mail to meet this task demand (Sproull & Kiesler, 1986; Trevino, Daft, & Lengel, 1990). It also may be necessary to know if the message has been received or not, and media that provide this notification may be needed.

The characteristics of the communication technology, in terms of containing single or multiple media, will also affect adoption and use. Employees do not use media in isolation; they sometimes combine several media or use an integrated technology, such as desktop videoconferencing, to get their message across (see Reder & Schwab, 1989, and Valacich, Paranka, George, & Nunamaker, 1993, for a conceptual discussion of sequencing and interdependence among media). Use of one or more media is clearly an influence on the adoption and use of other media. For instance, Markus (1994a) found that employees might first send a message through e-mail because of its ability to transmit text, and then follow up through the telephone because of its ability for two-way discussion. Ramsay, Barabesi, and Preece (1996) studied desktop videoconferencing software for informal communication, finding that it was used to share perspectives and discuss shared objects, whereas users adopted combinations of media (here, audio, video, and typed text) in sequenced activities for informal communication. They also discovered that as half of the pairs spontaneously displayed behavior indicating a need for shared activity space, such as drawings, tools, text editors, many of the pairs used mixed media exchanges—by simultaneously engaging in typing, annotating, talking, or a combination of these methods. A shared record (here, a text-messaging window process) was sometimes desired because audio and video media provided a shared reference point for nontextual abstract representations that were only transitory attention-getters. Finally, LaRose and Atkin (1992) showed that adoption of audiotext was associated with adoption of related innovations that provided information on demand, such as 800 numbers, automatic teller machines, and conference calling.

Perceived Characteristics. A communication medium's perceived characteristics may be equally or more important than their objective characteristics. For example, media richness perceptions may be based on both the objective properties of the medium and others' views in the social environment. Markus (1994a) was careful to note that social definitions of media do not discount material characteristics that constrain and foster some behaviors, but those constraints may not be permanent, and not all features will be used. Thus, differences across organizations in perception and use of e-mail are likely, due to the differences that exist in the social definitions of the medium and the technical functions of the medium derived at individual organizations. Research has demonstrated that perceived richness relates to use (Fulk, 1993), and that the more rich a medium is perceived to be, the more it is preferred and used for any communication task (Schmitz & Fulk, 1991).

Other perceptions of the communication medium's attributes (such as innovation attributes of relative advantage, compatibility, trialability, communicability, complexity, ease of use, voluntariness, result demonstrability, image, usefulness, effectiveness, and perceived accessibility—Agarwal & Prasad, 1997; Davis, Bagozzi, & Warshaw, 1989; Moore & Benbasat, 1991; Rogers, 1995; Saga & Zmud, 1994) influence technology diffusion. For example, Agarwal and Prasad (1997) concluded that more perceptual factors, such as compatibility, visibility and pressure to use, were the primary predictors of initial use of the Web, but more benefit evaluations and personal experience were the primary predictors of intentions to continue using.

Communication flow represents another perception of the human-technology interaction experience, and is measured as the extent to which (a) the individual perceives a sense of control over the interaction, (b) the individual perceives that his or her attention is focused on the interaction, (c) the individual's curiosity is aroused during the interaction, and (d) the individual finds the interaction intrinsically interesting (Trevino & Webster, 1992). Trevino and Webster found that employees experienced higher flow with e-mail than with voicemail, and that flow related positively to attitudes toward the medium and to employees' perceptions of communication effectiveness and quantity. Agarwal, Sambamurthy, and Stair (1997) integrated the concepts of perceived ease of use, flow, and computer playfulness into what they call cognitive absorption. This cognitive absorption is influenced by self-efficacy (a person's belief in ability to do a certain activity, fostering learning, and actual ability) and personal innovativeness.

Social Influences

One's perceptions of ambiguous stimuli such as a new medium are likely to be influenced by the opinions, information, behaviors, and rewards or sanctions of salient others, as individuals attempt to reduce uncertainty, respond to rewarded behaviors, and become socialized (Fulk, 1993; Fulk, Schmitz, & Steinfield, 1990; Howell & Higgins, 1990; Rice, 1993b). Schmitz and Fulk (1991) found, for example, that the attitudes and usage of a respondent's supervisor and the five closest communication partners positively influenced the respondent's attitude toward and use of an e-mail system. Rice and Shook's (1990a) analyses indicated that the number of voicemail messages sent by supervisors was influenced by the number of messages received by subordinates, and the number of voicemail messages sent by a respondent's work group influenced the number of voicemail messages that the respondent sent. Peer use, consulting, and advice have been significant influences on information system adoption (Leonard-Barton & Deschamps, 1988).

Saga and Zmud (1994) found that levels and forms of system usage tend to be compatible with one's group, social, and organizational norms (a straightforward diffusion of innovations principle). Salience and strength of norms influencing the adoption and use of a new medium, and the extent of potential influence (depending in part on individuals' varying innovation thresholds) changes as a new medium diffuses (O'Callaghan, 1998). For example, Dourish et al. (1996) found that new social arrangements for "office-sharing" through desktop video emerged over time, both with respect to how users' office behaviors became new norms for nonusers, and how nonusers' norms influenced the participants' adoption and usage (see also Fish, Kraut, Root, & Rice, 1993).

Another traditional source of social influence on adoption is the technology champion. Through ownership of the idea, activation of informal networks, articulation of the innovation's organizational potential, and risk to one's prestige (Howell & Higgins, 1990), technology champions lead the effort in overcoming resistance and indifference to major innovation. For instance, Markus' (1994b) study of a multisite organization identified the chairman as the primary e-mail champion. After 4 years of usage, e-mail was the primary medium of work-related communication, with the telephone a distant second. However, when the champion left, the new CEO did not use e-mail, and overall e-mail usage declined.

Researchers have also suggested that media choices have symbolic meanings in social settings (Sitkin et al., 1992; Trevino, Lengel, & Daft, 1987). Trevino, Daft, and Lengel (1990) proposed a symbolic interaction model of media choice, involving message equivocality, context (location, time, use by sender, and use by receiver), and the symbolic meanings represented by the medium and its use in particular contexts. That is, the medium itself, independent of its content, may come to represent symbolic values and meanings in its organizational and cultural setting. For example, letters have been found to symbolize formality, whereas meetings carry meaning about desire for involvement and teamwork. There often is no commonly accepted understanding of the symbolic meanings for newer and emerging technologies. Similar to the period when the telephone was first introduced, "current and emerging technologies come with many rough edges in need of the sandpaper of manners" (Marx, 1994, p. 540; see also Kraut et al., 1998, for an analysis of the development of social norms during the diffusion of a desktop videoconferencing system). For instance, at different times, e-mail has signaled technological innovativeness and at other times, a low priority message (Markus, 1994a; Trevino et al., 1990). Webster and Trevino (1995) found that the symbolic meaning of "when you want to be casual or informal" influenced e-mail choice within one organization.

To the extent that social influence matters, it seems to be more of a factor in the early stages of diffusion, and when new media are involved, because those situations involve more uncertainty (Rice, 1993a, 1993b). For example, Kraut et al. (1998) found that influences of usage and attitudes by one's group on one's own use of a desktop video system disappeared after the first few months of the year-long trial.

Organizational Influences

Organizational characteristics can facilitate or inhibit the use of a particular communication medium. For instance, Leonard-Barton and Deschamps (1988) suggested that managerial behaviors supporting or directly urging use of a medium would positively affect use. Similarly, Trevino and Webster (1992) proposed that employees who felt supported with resources and guidance on how to use a medium would exhibit more positive attitudes and use of the medium, and Saga and Zmud (1994) posited that employee training and managerial intervention would positively affect implementation success.

Alavi and Joachimsthaler's (1992) meta-analysis reinforced the commonsense belief that training increases the likelihood of successful implementation of an information system. For instance, Okolica and Stewart's (1996) study of voicemail users in a Fortune 500 company showed that the amount of training had a significant effect on the use of voice messaging, and Webster (1998) noted that limited training and documentation was associated with low levels of users' awareness of the full range of a desktop videoconferencing system's features (such as application sharing and privacy choices).

Zack and McKenney (1995) examined the influence of the social context of two ongoing daily newspaper management groups on the patterns of FtF and CMC. Different groups used the same functional structure, engaged in the same task processes, and used the same group-authoring and communication system, but operated in different social contexts (i.e., communication climate, management-leader philosophy, cooperation norms, communication networks). The two groups appropriated "the communication technology differently and in a way that was consistent with and reinforcing to their existing social structure" (p. 394).

Organizational structures affect adoption and use (Rice, 1994a; Rice & Gattiker, 2000). For instance, Schein (1994) argued that an innovative culture is necessary for achieving the potential of information technology in organizations. Taking a sociotechnical approach, he proposed that organizational structures, underlying cultural assumptions, and organizational processes, as well as the nature of information technology, influence the extent and type of organizational innovation in the information systems domain. Furthermore, Grover and Goslar (1993) found that greater decentralization, environmental uncertainty, and dispersion of information technology support throughout the organization affected diffusion.

Obviously, political factors in organizations, such as control over implementation policies, resources, and intended beneficiaries, and strategic and manipulative uses of new media (such as copying an e-mail message to others to increase pressure on an e-mail recipient), will influence the kinds, extent, and distribution of adoption of new media (Rice & Gattiker, 2000). For instance, Harper (1996) studied the attitudes of two groups of a corporate research lab toward "active badges." These transmit the location and computer activities of all individuals who wear the badges within the sections of a building where the information is transmitted by the badges. One lab group supported and wore the badges, whereas the other group vehemently opposed the badges. Each lab group had their own sets of attitudes, views, and beliefs, even though the technology was identical. Here, issues concerning badge-wearing were really a manifestation of organizational conflict—in particular, the labs' boundaries, and associated rights to research, but, more importantly, what was sacred concerning their research, autonomy, and ownership of ideas. Harper suggested that failure to respect community or group beliefs "can lead to the rejection of systems on grounds well removed from the purported purpose of those systems" (p. 297).

External Influences

A wide variety of external factors, such as economic, industry, and regulatory criteria, influence how people interpret, and organizations adopt, new media (Rice, 1987). Diffusion of a technology throughout an industry—another aspect of critical mass—can also change perceptions through increased knowledge of the technology, applications, and benefits, and reduced risk, influencing later adaptations and likelihood of adoption by others (O'Callaghan, 1998).

Two other significant external influences are standards (e.g., a stable and well-understood, but proprietary and slow-changing one versus a currently incomplete but rapidly improving one) and interoperability (such as the tradeoff of internal security versus the ability to interconnect with Internet resources and future business partners; Ginsburg & Duliba, 1997).

National culture also can affect the relationship between influences and usage. For example, Kwon and Chidambaram (1998) found that South Koreans were more likely to use cellular phones because of their perceived usefulness, whereas Americans were more likely to use them due to reasons of security, enjoyment, and social pressure. However, Rice et al. (1998) found only a few slight associations between high-context/collective and low-context/individualist cultural membership and perceptions of traditional or new media.

CONCLUSION

Based on the preceding review, Fig. 8.1 presents a comprehensive framework of factors influencing the adoption, diffusion, and use of new media in organizational settings. Two key attributes of this model should be noted.

First, perceived media characteristics and beliefs act as mediators between other influences (including objective aspects of the technology) and adoption, diffusion, and use. Consistent with previous models, for example, those of Agarwal and Prasad (1997), Bozeman (1993), Fjermestad and Hiltz (1998), Fulk (1993), Leonard-Barton and Deschamps (1988), Saga and Zmud (1994), Sitkin et al. (1992), Trevino and Webster (1992), and Webster and Trevino (1995), we include a complex array of influences, including these mediating variables. For example, Fulk (1993) proposed that perceived medium richness mediates between medium expertise and medium use, Trevino and Webster (1992) suggested that flow mediates between technology characteristics and use, and Saga and Zmud (1994) indicated that beliefs about the medium mediate between user knowledge and acceptance.

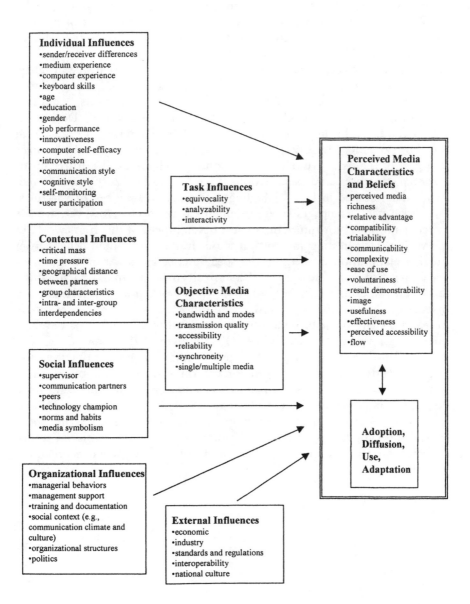

Figure 8.1. A general framework of influences on adoption, diffusion, and use of new media

Second, the figure includes recursive relationships between the mediating variables and adoption, diffusion, and use. For example, although higher perceived richness may result in more use of a medium, more use (especially more successful use, as usage norms develop) of a new medium over time may also result in higher perceptions of its richness. This reasoning is congruent with other researchers, such as O'Callaghan (1998), who emphasized that there is no predetermined causal order between organizations and technology—so that, for instance, choices about organizational redesign could influence technology adoption choices. Indeed, newer theoretical approaches such as "adaptive structuration theory" (DeSanctis & Poole, 1994; Poole & DeSanctis, 1990) and "technology/structure duality" (Orlikowski, 1992, 1993; Orlikowski & Robey, 1991) have proposed that CMC uses and outcomes are part of the recursive relationships among technological features, institutional structures, and users' actions (Rice & Gattiker, 2000). The framework diagrammed in Fig. 8.1 highlights the main categories of variables. We hope it will help guide future empirical research. However, we see three major areas for future theoretical development of this framework, in particular. First, testing any portion of our framework would benefit from further elaboration concerning the specific constructs within these main categories of variables, as well as specifying any interrelationships between the constructs. Second, our framework does not present the nature of the relationships between adoption, diffusion and use; future researchers will want to build on past research to continue this development (e.g., see Andriessen, 1994; O'Callaghan, 1998; Saga & Zmud, 1994). Third, our framework does not distinguish those influences that are differently and dynamically important to the stages of adoption, diffusion, and use. However, some research has addressed this important issue (e.g., see Andriessen, 1994; O'Callaghan, 1998; Saga & Zmud, 1994) and should be continued. In conclusion, there is significant practical and theoretical rationale for, prior empirical results about, and potential of future research on, the adoption, diffusion, and use of new media in organizational settings.

ACKNOWLEDGMENTS

We thank Carolyn Lin and Marilyn Mantei for comments on an earlier draft of this chapter.

REFERENCES

Abel, M. (1990). Experiences in an exploratory distributed organization. In J. Galegher, R. Kraut, & C. Egido (Eds.), *Intellectual teamwork: Social and technological foundations of cooperative work* (pp. 489-510). Hillsdale, NJ: Lawrence Erlbaum Associates.

Agarwal, R., & Prasad, J. (1997). The role of innovation characteristics and perceived voluntariness in the acceptance of information technologies. *Decision Sciences, 28,* 557-582.

Agarwal, R., Sambamurthy, V., & Stair, R. (1997). Cognitive absorption and the adoption of new information technologies. In L. Dosier & J. B. Keys (Eds.), *Academy of Management Best Papers Proceedings* (pp. 293-297). Madison, WI: Omni Press.

American Society of Association Executives. (1996). *Policies and procedures in association management.* Washington, DC: Author.

Andriessen, J. H. E. (1994). Conditions for successful adoption and implementation of telematics in user organizations. In J. H. E. Andriessen & R. Roe (Eds.), *Telematics and work* (pp. 411-441). Hillsdale, NJ: Lawrence Erlbaum Associates.

Alavi, M., & Joachimsthaler, E. A. (1992). Revisiting DSS implementation research: A meta-analysis of the literature and suggestions for researchers. *MIS Quarterly, 16*(1), 95-116.

Alavi, M., Wheeler, B. C., & Valacich, J. S. (1995). Using IT to reengineer business education: An exploratory investigation of collaborative telelearning. *MIS Quarterly, 19,* 293-312.

Alexander, E., Penley, L., & Jernigan, E. (1991). The effect of individual differences on managerial media choice. *Management Communication Quarterly, 5,* 155-173.

Anderson, A. H., O'Malley, C., Doherty-Sneddon, G., Langton, S., Newlands, A., Mullin, J., Fleming, A. M., & Van der Velden, J. (1997). The impact of VMC on collaborative problem-solving: An analysis of task performance, communicative process, and user satisfaction. In K. E. Finn, A. J. Sellen, & S. B. Wilbur (Eds.), *Video-mediated communication* (pp. 133-155). Mahwah, NJ: Lawrence Erlbaum Associates.

Association for Information Technology Professionals. (1998). *AITP education foundation member Internet survey.* Available online: http://www.edfoundation.org/detail.htm.

Astebro, T. (1995). The effect of management and social interaction on the intra-firm diffusion of electronic mail systems. *IEEE Transactions on Engineering Management, 42*(4), 319-331.

Baronas, A., & Louis, M. (1988). Restoring a sense of control during implementation: How user involvement leads to system acceptance. *MIS Quarterly, 12*(1), 111-123.

Beswick, R., & Reinsch, N. (1987). Attitudinal responses to voice mail. *The Journal of Business Communication, 24*(3), 23-25.

Bikson, T., & Law, S. (1993). Electronic mail use at the World Bank: Messages from users. *The Information Society, 9,* 89-134.

Bly, S., Harrison, S., & Irwin, S. (1993). Media spaces: Video, audio, and computing. *Communications of the ACM, 36*(1), 28-47.

Borthick, S. L. (1997). Reaching into today's collaborative toolkit. *Business Communications Review, 27*(9), 47-53.

Bournellis, C. (1995). Internet '95. *Internet World, 6*(11), 47-52.

Bowers, J. (1995). Making it work: A field study of a "CSCW Network." *The Information Society, 11,* 189-207.

Bozeman, D. (1993). Toward a limited rationality perspective of managerial media selection in organizations. *Academy of Management Best Paper Proceedings* (pp. 278-282). Madison, WI: Omni Press.

Cablevision. (1996, January 22). *20*(13), 16-25.

Caldwell, B., & Uang, S. (1995). Technology usability and utility issues in a state government voice mail evaluation survey. *Human Factors, 37*(2), 306-320.

Cole, B. (1996). Groupware not reaching its potential yet. *Network World, 13*(41), 37, 48.

Cole-Gomolski, B. (1997). E-mail, groupware converge. *Computerworld, 31*(39), 12.

Compeau, D. R., & Higgins, C. A. (1995). Computer self-efficacy: Development of a measure and initial test. *MIS Quarterly, 19,* 189-211.

Condon, R. (1998, April 29). Coping with spam costs billions, study finds. *Computerworld, Internet news.*

Cooper, R., & Zmud, R. (1990). Information technology implementation research: A technological diffusion approach. *Management Science, 36*(2), 123-139.

Daft, R. L., & Lengel, R. H. (1986). A proposed integration among organizational information requirements, media richness, and structural design. *Management Science, 32,* 554-571.

Davis, F., Bagozzi, R., & Warshaw, P. (1989). User acceptance of computer technology: A comparison of two theoretical models. *Management Science, 35*(8), 982-1003.

DeLone, W., & McLean, E. (1992). Information systems success: The quest for the dependent variable. *Information Systems Research, 3*(1), 60-95.

DeSanctis, G., & Poole, M. (1994). Capturing the complexity in advanced technology use: Adaptive structuration theory. *Organization Science, 5,* 121-147.

Direct Marketing Association (DMA). (1996). *1996 Statistical fact book.* New York: Author.

Dixon, G. (1998). Desktop videoconferencing. *Presentations, 12*(1), 83-88.

Donabedian, B., McKinnon, S., & Bruns, W., Jr. (1998). Task characteristics, managerial socialization, and media selection. *Management Communication Quarterly, 11,* 372-400.

Dourish, P., Adler, A., Bellotti, V., & Henderson, A. (1996). Your place or mine? Learning from long-term use of audio-video communication. *Computer Supported Cooperative Work: The Journal of Collaborative Computing, 5,* 33-62.

Ehrlich, S. (1987). Strategies for encouraging successful adoption of office communication systems. *ACM Transactions on Office Information Systems, 5*(4), 340-357.

Electronic Market Trends. (1996). Arlington, VA: Electronic Industries Association.

Electronic Messaging Association. (1997, April 28). Online summary of Electronic Messaging Association report. *Web Week.*

Eveland, J. D., & Bikson, T. E. (1987) Evolving electronic communication networks: An empirical assessment. *Office: Technology and People, 3,* 103-128.

Fichman, R. G. (1995). *The illusory diffusion of innovation: An examination of assimilation gaps.* Unpublished paper, MIT Sloan School of Management, Cambridge, MA.

Fish, R., Kraut, R., Root, R., & Rice, R. E. (1993). Video as a technology for informal communication. *Communications of the ACM, 36*(1), 48-61.

For call-backs from clients, voice mail tops E-mail. (1997). *The Practical Accountant, 30*(1), 10.

Fjermestad, J,. & Hiltz, S. R. (1998). An assessment of group support systems experimental research: Methodology and results. *Journal of Management Information Systems, 15*(3), 7-149.

Franklin, C. F., Jr. (1997). Integrated messaging. *CIO, 10*(8), 90-96.

Fortune Monitor. (1996). *133*(8), 8-13, 18-21, 66-70.

Frazee, V. (1996). Is e-mail doing more harm than good? *Personnel Journal, 75*(5), 23.

Fulk, J. (1993). Social construction of communication technology. *Academy of Management Journal, 36*(5), 921-950.

Fulk, J., Schmitz, J., & Steinfield, C. (1990). A social influence model of technology use. In J. Fulk & C. Steinfield (Eds.), *Organizations and communication technology* (pp. 117-140). Newbury Park, CA: Sage.

Gasser, L. (1986). The integration of computing and routine work. *ACM Transactions on Office Information Systems, 4*(3), 205-225.

Ginsburg, M., & Duliba, K. (1997). Enterprise-level groupware choices: Evaluating Lotus Notes and intranet-based solutions. *Computer Supported Cooperative Work: The Journal of Collaborative Computing, 6,* 201-225.

Goodhue, D. L., & Thompson, R. L. (1995). Task-technology fit and individual performance. *MIS Quarterly, 19,* 213-233.

Grover, V., & Goslar, M. (1993). The initiation, adoption, and implementation of telecommunications technologies in U.S. organizations. *Journal of Management Information Systems, 10*(1), 141-163.

Hamblen, M. (1996). Desktop video surge forecast. *Computerworld, 30*(42), 85.

Harper, R. (1996). Why people do and don't wear active badges: A case study. *Computer Supported Cooperative Work: The Journal of Collaborative Computing, 4*(4), 297-318.

Haythornthwaite, C., & Wellman, B. (1998). Work, friendship and media use for information exchange in a networked organization. *Journal of the American Society for Information Science, 49*(12), 1101-1114.

Hiltz, S.R., & Johnson, K. (1989). Measuring acceptance of computer-mediated communication systems. *Journal of the American Society for Information Science, 40*(6), 386-397.

Howell, J., & Higgins, C. (1990). Champions of technological innovation. *Administrative Science Quarterly, 35,* 317-341.

INC. (1995, December). *17*(18), 132.

INC. (1996, February). *18*(2), 108.

Information & Interactive Services Report (IISR). (1997, May 2). (citing International Data Corp.)

Intelliquest. (1998). http://www.internetnews.com/IAR/1998/02/0905-intelli.html.

Investor's Business Daily. (1998, July 28).

Johnson, B., & Rice, R.E. (1987). *Managing organizational innovation: The evolution from word processing to office information systems.* New York: Columbia University Press.

Kaye, A. R., & Byrne K. E. (1986). Insights on the implementation of a computer-based message system. *Information & Management, 10,* 277-284.

Kaye, B. (1998). Uses and gratifications of the world wide web: From couch potato to web potato. *New Jersey Journal of Communication, 6*(1), 21-40.

Kettinger, W., & Grover, V. (1997). The use of computer-mediated communication in an interorganizational context. *Decision Sciences, 28*(3), 513-555.

King, J. (1997). Info addicts wreak havoc on workplace. *Computerworld,* *31*(50), 0-1, 106.

Korostoff, K. (1996). Desktop video is coming. Really! *Computerworld,* *30*(38), 35.

Kraut, R., & Attewell, P. (1997). Media use in a global corporation: Electronic mail and organizational knowledge. In S. Kiesler (Ed.), *Culture of the Internet* (pp. 323-342). Mahwah, NJ: Lawrence Erlbaum Associates.

Kraut, R., Rice, R.E., Cool, C., & Fish, R. (1998). Varieties of social influence: The role of utility and norms in the success of a new communication medium. *Organization Science, 9*(4), 437-453.

Kwon, H. S., & Chidambaram, L. (1998). A cross-cultural study of communication technology acceptance: Comparison of cellular phone adoption in South Korea and the United States. *Journal of Global Information Technology Management, 1*, 43-58.

LaRose, R., & Atkin, D. (1992). Audiotext and the re-invention of the telephone as a mass medium. *Journalism Quarterly, 69*(2), 413-421.

LaRose, R., & Hoag, A. (1996, May). *Organizational adoptions of the Internet and the clustering of innovations.* Paper presented to the International Communication Association Conference, East Lansing, MI.

Landes, C., & Harrod, K. (1997). Please leave a message at the beep! *Telephony, 232*(24), 18-24.

Leiner, B. M. (1994). Internet technology. *Communications of the ACM, 37*(8), 32.

Leonard-Barton, D., & Deschamps, I. (1988). Managerial influence in the implementation of new technology. *Management Science, 34*, 1252-1265.

Levins, H. (1997). Growing impact of e-mail. *Editor & Publisher, 130*(9), 26-27.

Lin, C. (1998). Exploring personal computer adoption dynamics. *Journal of Broadcasting & Electronic Media, 42*, 95-112.

Majchrzak, A., Rice, R. E., Malhotra, A., King, N., & Ba, S. (2000). Technology adaption: The case of a computer-supported inter-organizational virtual team. *MIS Quarterly, 24*(4), 569-600.

Manross, G. G., & Rice, R. E. (1986). Don't hang up: Organizational diffusion of the intelligent telephone. *Systems, Objectives, Solutions, 10*, 161-175.

Mantei, M., Baecker, R., Sellan, A., Buxton, W., & Milligan, T. (1991). Experiences in the use of a media space. *Proceedings CHI '91 conference on human factors in computing systems* (pp. 803-808). New Orleans.

Markus, M. L. (1987). Toward a "critical mass" theory of interactive media: Universal access, interdependence and diffusion. *Communication Research, 14*(5), 491-511.

Markus, M. L. (1994a). Electronic mail as the medium of managerial choice. *Organization Science, 5*(4), 502-527.

Markus, M. L. (1994b). Finding a happy medium: Explaining the negative effects of electronic communication on social life at work. *ACM Transactions on Information Systems, 12*(2), 119-149.

Marx, G. (1994). New telecommunications technologies require new manners. *Telecommunications Policy, 18*(7), 538-551.

McCune, J. (1997). Get the message. *Management Review, 86*(1), 10-11.

McKenney, J., Zack, M., & Doherty, V. (1992). Complementary communication media: A comparison of electronic mail and face-to-face communication in a programming team. In N. Nohria & R. Eccles (Eds.), *Networks and organizations* (pp. 262-287). Boston, MA: Harvard Business School Press.

Moore, G. C., & Benbasat, I. (1991). Development of an instrument to measure the perceptions of adopting an information technology innovation. *Information Systems Research, 2*, 192-222.

NPD. (1998). *Business users spend 65 percent more time on the web than home users, says PC meter.* Port Washington, New York: Author.

NUA. (1999). http://www.nua.ie/surveys. NUA Ltd., NY, NY 10003.

O'Callaghan, R. (1998). Technology diffusion and organizational transformation: An integrative framework. In T. Larsen & E. McGuire (Eds.), *Information systems innovation and diffusion: Issues and directions* (pp. 390-410). Hershey, PA: Idea Group.

Okolica, C., & Stewart, C. (1996). Factors influencing the use of voice messaging technology: Voice mail implementation in a corporate setting. *Central State Business Review, XV*(1), 52-59.

Orlikowski, W. (1992). The duality of technology: Rethinking the concept of technology in organizations. *Organization Science, 3*(3), 398-427.

Orlikowski, W. (1993). Learning from Notes: Organizational issues in groupware implementation. *The Information Society, 9*, 237-250.

Orlikowski, W., & Robey, D. (1991). Information technology and the structuring of organizations. *Information Systems Research, 2*, 143-169.

Panko, R. R. (1985). Electronic mail. In K. T. Quinn (Ed.), *Advances in office automation* (pp. 191-228). New York: Wiley.

Poole, J. (1997). Standards, price push video apps to corporate desktops. *Infoworld, 19*(10), 49-50.

Poole, M. S., & DeSanctis, G. (1990). Understanding the use of group decision support systems: The theory of adaptive structuration. In J. Fulk & C. Steinfield (Eds.), *Organizations and communication technology* (pp. 173-192). Newbury Park, CA: Sage.

Ramsay, J., Barabesi, A., & Preece, J. (1996). Informal communication is about sharing objects and media. *Interacting with Computers, 8*(3), 277-283.

Reder, S., & Schwab, R. (1989). The communicative economy of the workgroup: Multi-channel genres of communication. *Office: Technology and People, 4*(3), 177-198.

Rice, R. E. (1987). Computer-mediated communication and organizational innovation. *Journal of Communication, 37*(4), 65-94.

Rice, R. E. (1990). Computer-mediated communication system network data: Theoretical concerns and empirical examples. *International Journal of Man-Machine Studies, 32*(6), 627-647.

Rice, R. E. (1992a). Contexts of research on organizational computer-mediated communication: A recursive review. In M. Lea (Ed.), *Contexts of computer-mediated communication* (pp. 113-144). London: Harvester-Wheatsheaf.

Rice, R. E. (with Hart, P., Torobin, J., Shook, D., Tyler, J., Svenning, L., & Ruchinskas, J.). (1992b). Task analyzability, use of new media, and effectiveness: A multi-site exploration of media richness. *Organization Science, 3*(4), 475-500.

Rice, R. E. (1994a). Relating electronic mail use and network structure to R&D work networks and performance. *Journal of Management Information Systems, 11*(1), 9-20.

Rice, R. E. (1994b). Network analysis and computer-mediated communication systems. In S. Wasserman & J. Galaskiewicz (Eds.), *Advances in social and behavioral science from social network analysis* (pp. 167-203). Newbury Park, CA: Sage.

Rice, R. E. (1993a). Using network concepts to clarify sources and mechanisms of social influence. In W. Richards, Jr. & G. Barnett (Eds.), *Advances in communication network analysis* (pp. 43-52). Norwood, NJ: Ablex.

Rice, R. E. (1993b). Media appropriateness: Using social presence theory to compare traditional and new organizational media. *Human Communication Research, 19*(4), 451-484.

Rice, R. E., & Case, D. (1983). Computer-based messaging in the university: A description of use and utility. *Journal of Communication, 33*(1), 131-152.

Rice, R. E., Chang, S., & Torobin, J. (1992). Communicator style, media use, organizational level, and use and evaluation of electronic messaging. *Management Communication Quarterly, 6*(1), 3-33.

Rice, R. E., D'Ambra, J., & More, E. (1998). Cross-cultural comparison of organizational media evaluation and choice. *Journal of Communication, 48*(3), 3-26.

Rice, R. E., & Danowski, J. (1993). Is it really just like a fancy answering machine? Comparing semantic networks of different types of voice mail users. *Journal of Business Communication, 30*(4), 369-397.

Rice, R. E., & Gattiker, U. (2000). New media and organizational structuring of meanings and relations. In F. Jablin & L. Putnam (Eds.), *New handbook of organizational communication* (pp. 544-581). Newbury Park, CA: Sage.

Rice, R. E., Grant, A., Schmitz, J., & Torobin, J. (1990). Individual and network influences on the adoption and perceived outcomes of electronic messaging. *Social Networks, 12*(1), 27-55.

Rice, R. E., Hughes, D., & Love, G. (1989). Usage and outcomes of electronic messaging at an R&D organization: Situational constraints, job level, and media awareness. *Office: Technology and People, 5*(2), 141-161.

Rice, R. E., & Love, G. (1987). Electronic emotion: Socio-emotional content in a computer-mediated communication network. *Communication Research, 14*(1), 85-105.

Rice, R. E., & Shook, D. (1988). Access to, usage of, and outcomes from an electronic message system. *ACM Transactions on Office Information Systems, 6*(3), 255-276.

Rice, R. E., & Shook, D. (1990a). Relationships of job categories and organizational levels to use of communication channels, including electronic mail: A meta-analysis and extension. *Journal of Management Studies, 27*(2), 195-229.

Rice, R. E., & Shook, D. (1990b). Voice messaging, coordination and communication. In J. Galegher, R. Kraut, & C. Egido (Eds.), *Intellectual teamwork: Social and technological foundations of cooperative work* (pp. 327-350). Hillsdale, NJ: Lawrence Erlbaum Associates.

Rice, R. E., & Steinfield, C. (1994). New forms of organizational communication via electronic mail and voice messaging. In J. E. Andriessen & R. Roe (Eds.), *Telematics and work* (pp. 109-137). Hillsdale, NJ: Lawrence Erlbaum Associates.

Rice, R. E., & Tyler, J. (1995). Individual and organizational influences on voice mail use and evaluation. *Behaviour and Information Technology, 14*(6), 329-341.

Rodewald, E. (1997). Message masters: Voice mail says it all. *Office Systems, 14*(7), 30-32.

Rogers, E. M. (1995). *Diffusion of innovations* (4th ed.). New York: The Free Press.

Romano, N., Jr,. Nunamaker, J., Briggs, R., & Vogel, D. (1998). Architecture, design, and development of an HTML/Javascript web-based group support system. *Journal of the American Society for Information Science, 49*(7), 649-667.

Saga, V. L., & Zmud, R. W. (1994). The nature and determinants of IT acceptance, routinization, and infusion. In L. Levine (Ed.), *Diffusion, transfer and implementation of information technology* (pp. 67-86). Amsterdam: North-Holland.

Sanderson, D. (1996). Cooperative and collaborative mediated research. In T. Harrison & T. Stephen (Eds.), *Computer networking and scholarly communication in the twenty-first-century university* (pp. 95-114). Albany: State University of New York Press.

Scheepers, R., & Damsgaard, J. (1997). Using Internet technology within the organization: A structural analysis of Intranets. In S. C. Hayne & W. Prinz (Eds.), *GROUP 97, Proceedings of the International ACM SIGGROUP Conference on Supporting Group Work* (pp. 9-18). Phoenix, AZ: Association for Computing Machinery.

Schein, E. (1994). Innovative cultures and organizations. In T. Allen & M. Scott-Morton (Eds.), *Information technology and the corporation of the 1990s: Research studies* (pp. 125-146). New York: Oxford University Press.

Schmitz, J., & Fulk, J. (1991). Organizational colleagues, information richness and electronic mail: A test of the social influence model of technology use. *Communication Research, 18*(4), 487-523.

Short, J., Williams, E., & Christie, B. (1976). *The social psychology of telecommunications.* London: Wiley.

Sitkin, S. B., Sutcliff, K. M., & Barrios-Chopin, J. R. (1992). A dual-capacity model of communication media choice in organizations. *Human Communication Research, 18*, 563-598.

Soe, L., & Markus, M.L. (1993). Technological or social utility? Unraveling explanations of e-mail, vmail, and fax use. *The Information Society, 9*, 213-236.

Sproull, L., & Kiesler, W. (1986). Reducing social context cues: Electronic mail in organizational communication. *Management Science, 32*(11), 1492-1512.

Steinfield, C. W. (1986). Computer-mediated communication in an organizational setting: Explaining task-related and socioemotional uses. In M. McLaughlin (Ed.), *Communication yearbook, 9* (pp. 777-804). Newbury Park, CA: Sage.

Steinfield, C. (1992). Computer-mediated communications in organizational settings: Emerging conceptual frameworks and directions for research. *Management Communication Quarterly, 5*(3), 348-365.

Stewart, C. M. (1992). Innovation is in the mind of the user: A case study of voice mail. In U. E. Gattiker & L. Larwood (Eds.), *Studies in technological innovation and human resources, vol. 3. Technology-mediated communication* (pp. 151-186). Berlin: de Gruyter.

Sunoo, B. (1996). This employee may be loafing: Can you tell? Should you care? *Personnel Journal, 75*(12), 54-62.

Tornatzky, L. G., & Klein, K. J. (1982). Innovation characteristics and innovation adoption-implementation: A meta-analysis of findings. *IEEE Transactions on Engineering Management, 29*(1), 28-45.

Trevino, L., Lengel, R., & Daft, R. (1987). Media symbolism, media richness and media choice in organizations: A symbolic interactionist perspective. *Communication Research, 14*(5), 553-574.

Trevino, L., Daft, R., & Lengel, R. (1990). Understanding managers' media choices: A symbolic interactionist perspective. In J. Fulk & C. Steinfield (Eds.), *Organizations and communication technology* (pp. 71-94). Newbury Park, CA: Sage.

Trevino, L., Lengel, R., Gerloff, E., & Muir, N. (1990). The richness imperative and cognitive styles: The role of individual differences in media choice behavior. *Management Communication Quarterly, 4*(2), 176-197.

Trevino, L., & Webster, J. (1992). Flow in computer-mediated communication: Electronic mail and media choice in organizations. *Communication Research, 19*(5), 539-573.

Trevino, L., Webster, J., & Stein, E. (2000). Making connections: Complementary influences on communication media choices, attitudes, and uses. *Organization Science, 11*, 163-182.

Trice, A., & Treacy, M. (1988, Fall/Winter). Utilization as a dependent variable in MIS research. *Data Base,* pp. 33-41.

Tyre, M., & Orlikowski, W. (1994). Windows of opportunity: Temporal patterns of technological adaptation in organizations. *Organization Science, 5*(1), 98-120.

Valacich, J., Paranka, D., George, J., & Nunamaker, J. (1993). Communication concurrency and the new media. *Communication Research, 20*(2), 249-276.

Webster, J. (1998). Desktop videoconferencing: Experiences of complete users, wary users, and non-users. *MIS Quarterly, 22*(3), 257-286.

Webster, J., & Trevino, L. K. (1995). Rational and social theories as complementary explanations of communication media choices: Two policy capturing studies. *Academy of Management Journal, 38*, 1544-1572.

What paperless office? Fax use is up! (1997). *Managing Office Technology, 42*(1), 39.

Whittaker, S., & O'Conaill, B. (1997). The role of vision in face-to-face and mediated communication. In K. Finn, A. Sellen, & S. Wilbur (Eds.), *Video-mediated communication* (pp. 23-50). Mahwah, NJ: Lawrence Erlbaum Associates.

Williams, R., & Edge, D. (1996). The social shaping of technology. In W. Dutton (Ed.), *Information and communication technologies* (pp. 53-67). New York: Oxford University Press.

Zack, M., & McKenney, J. (1995). Social context and interaction in ongoing computer-supported management groups. *Organization Science, 6*(4), 394-422.

Zmud, R., Lind, M., & Young, F. (1990). An attribute space for organizational communication channels. *Information Systems Research, 1*(4), 440-457.

9

Organizations and External Telecommunications Networks: The Adoption of Wide Area Networks and Their Impact on Organizational Structure and Strategy

Charles Steinfield
Michigan State University

Advances in telecommunications have had far-reaching implications for all organizations, influencing many aspects of organizational form and function. Small, medium and large organizations all extensively rely on communication technologies, both for internal communications and to transact with customers and other businesses. Who today could imagine running a business without telephones, voicemail, and fax machines? Increasingly, we can add e-mail, Internet access, a Web site, and even video conferencing to the list of "must-haves" for today's organizations.

As business reliance on communication technology grows, so too does the requirement for a robust, reliable, secure, and capable telecommunications infrastructure. Most medium and large-sized firms, and even many smaller ones, lease elaborate private network services from telecommunications operators. Increasingly, however, these networks do more than interconnect dispersed branches and other internal organizational sites. Extending a trend that began to grow significantly in the mid-1980s, organizations today interconnect via advanced networks with a variety of *external* constituents, including suppliers, downstream partners, and customers. We call such telecommunications linkages to external partners *interorganizational* or *external* networks.

The rapid growth of interorganizational networks today, however, is qualitatively different from the earlier 1980s versions. In the past, firms leased expensive private networks, and could only do this with major trading partners who generated enough business to justify the expense of the private link. Although many large firms today still maintain expensive private enterprise-wide networks for internal communications traffic, few extend leased private networks to outside organizations and consumers. Rather, links to external constituents today most often occur via public network infrastructures, such as the Internet. Even firms that do not have enterprise networks will lease a high-capacity telecommunications link to an Internet service provider (ISP). This guarantees access to a global digital highway for information and communication flows, which, like the public telephone network, potentially enables connections with all of a firm's constituents. Indeed, the changing technological infrastructure has lowered the costs to participate in the emerging global digital infrastructure, extending the benefits of interorganizational networks to smaller firms. The Internet-based digital infrastructure now even includes consumers, especially in those countries with significant personal computer penetration.

In this chapter, the first section provides a brief overview of major technological advances in wide area telecommunications networks, followed by an analysis of the implications of these developments for organizations. My focus is on interorganizational uses of telecommunications networks, emphasizing data and multimedia applications rather than simple telephone and fax use. Elsewhere in this volume, intraorganizational network use (e.g., local area networking and Intranets for sharing data, voice-related services, and video applications) is covered (see Klopfenstein, chap. 14, this volume).

In the second section, the research on uses and impacts of wide area, external networks is divided into three broad areas. First, I briefly review the traditional thinking about the situations in which people in organizations use computer-mediated communications (CMC). This is followed by an introduction to the use of interorganizational networks for competitive advantage. These two reviews establish the central business motivation for adopting and investing in such networks, and provides a heuristic perspective for understanding corporate strategic behavior vis-à-vis telecommunications network use. I then turn to the literature emanating from transaction cost economics addressing the structure of interorganizational relationships because wide area networks are thought to have considerably altered the very premises for the formation of firms and firms' trading relationships. Included here is a discussion of the evolution of virtual firms, networked firms, and electronic markets.

WIDE AREA NETWORKING TECHNOLOGIES

Transmission Media

All telecommunications transmission media can be broadly classified into bounded or wire-based media and unbounded or wireless media. Space does not permit a discussion of all types of media; only the most significant media over which interorganizational network applications are carried are mentioned. This includes optical fibers and higher capacity twisted pair copper wire now in widespread use, and emerging satellite constellation systems that may soon play a role in the future global digital infrastructure. Many other transmission technologies, formerly in widespread use in corporate networking, such as terrestrial microwave, geosynchronous satellites, and analog leased copper circuits are not discussed.

Optical Fiber

Perhaps no technology has changed the face of business telecommunications as much as optical fibers. Introduced more than two decades ago into the public network, optical fibers have now largely replaced coaxial cables and terrestrial microwave radio for long distance transmission. Today, optical fibers have moved into city and local networks as well.

Most optical fibers transmit information digitally in the form of short pulses of light emanating from semi-conductor laser diodes or small light-emitting diodes (LEDs). Individual fiber strands can carry several billion bits per second. Even more significant, however, is the emergence of wave division multiplexing (WDM). WDM allows multiple transmissions down the same single mode fiber, separated from each other by their wavelength (essentially the color or frequency of the light wave). Packing these separate light signals closer together is called dense WDM or DWDM. This has allowed fiber trunks in the public network to ramp up their capacity from 2.5 gigabits per second (Gbps) to 40 Gbps. For corporate networking, DWDM makes bandwidth cheaper than ever, making multimedia and advanced digital services more affordable.

With the new transmission speeds that optical fiber is capable of delivering, new digital transmission switching and multiplexing (i.e., combining multiple signals on the same channel) standards are becoming available to corporate users. However, today, a new multiplexing hierarchy designed for optical fiber and called Synchronous Optical NETwork (SONET) has become widely available. Attributes of this and other transmission systems are outlined in Table 9.1.

Copper-Based Wire Media

For several decades, telephone companies have provided leased digital access over copper wires to firms on a monthly rental basis. These services were rather costly, however, and would generally be used only when there was a great amount of traffic between locations. Rarely could a firm justify leasing T1 service, for example, to its suppliers or customers.

Today, innovations in coding techniques have transformed the ubiquitous twisted pair copper wire that connects most homes and businesses to the public network. One service uses the existing telephone access line, with new terminating devices to provide the equivalent of two channels (each equivalent to the standard digital voice rate), plus an additional channel for data. This service is known as the Integrated Service Digital Network (ISDN), and is available for a relatively low monthly fee—about twice the cost of a standard telephone line in most places.

Like regular telephone service, ISDN is used on a switched basis, so that, besides the low monthly fee, subscribers pay only for the time they actually use it. Combined with a video compression device (i.e., a device that codes the video information more efficiently so that the video information can be sent with fewer bits, albeit with lesser quality), two B channels can also easily support low grade videoconferencing. Hence, ISDN makes interorganizational networking with more than a small number of trading partners quite possible.

Other higher speed digital services running over twisted pair copper wire are just becoming available, mainly for Internet access and for multimedia services. Collectively called digital subscriber line (DSL) services, they enable existing access lines to carry many megabits per second, depending on such factors as the distance from the telephone central office and the quality of the line. The need for conditioning lines, and installing expensive terminating equipment has slowed the deployment of these services, however.

Table 9.1. Attributes of Selected Transmission Media.

Fiber Optics

In the past, the U.S. public network used the T or DS (for digital signal) multiplexing hierarchy to combine separate transmissions onto a higher capacity carrier. Common transmission services in this multiplexing hierarchy were T1/DS1 (1.544 megabits per second), and T3 (44.736 Mbps).

SONET systems start at about 51 Mbps in what is called an OC-1 (Optical Carrier). Other common services now in use in the digital infrastructure include OC-3 (155 Mbps), OC-12 (622 Mbps) and, recently, OC-24 (1.2 Gbps). Along with this new digital transmission hierarchy are new switching services, and most notably a technique called asynchronous transfer mode (ATM). ATM-based switches can easily accommodate the types of speeds now carried by fiber, and are designed to support the integration of many different types of communications traffic—voice, video, or data.

Copper Wire

Transmission rates for leased digital access over copper wires have traditionally ranged from 56 kilobits per second (kbps) to 1.544 Mbps. Firms seeking high-speed connections leased a service called a T1 line (1.544 Mbps), and could lease T1 connections or fractional T1 (in increments of 64 kbps) for their long distance private network needs.

The terminating devices utilized for ISDN provide the equivalent of two 64kbps channels (each equivalent to the standard digital voice rate), plus an additional 16kbps channel for data. Each 64 kbps ISDN channel is called a B (or bearer) channel, and together two B channels provide fairly high speed Internet access. One highly publicized service known as Asymmetric Digital Subscriber Line (ADSL) offers as much as 9 Mbps downstream (i.e., from the central office to the subscriber), with 640 kbps upstream (i.e., from the subscriber back up to the central office).

Satellites

Iridium was the most prominent of the low orbit satellite systems. Now bankrupt, it was first proposed with 77 satellites (the atomic number of Iridium—hence the name), which was subsequently reduced to 66 satellites in its constellation.

The best known of the emerging systems, Teledesic, is backed by Bill Gates of Microsoft. It will offer Internet access at speeds of 2 Mbps, as well as Internet backbone services, especially to parts of the world that lack adequate terrestrial networks. This may especially help firms in less developed countries engage in network-based transactions with their trading partners around the world. Teledesic would require 288 satellites (down from an initial plan of more than 800) in its constellation.

Satellites

For a time in the 1980s, large firms built corporate networks using leased capacity on geosynchronous satellites. These satellites, placed over the equator at an orbital height of 22,300 miles, orbit at a speed that allows them to remain stationary with respect to the earth stations receiving their signals. Hence, any receiving antennae in their "footprint" do not require expensive tracking capability. For services like television broadcasting, geosynchronous satellites have strong advantages because the cost to reach one receiver is no different than reaching 1 million receivers. However, such satellites suffer from latency (or delay) in the transmission up to and back from the satellite, making them undesireable for many real-time applications like telephone calls or video conferencing. Users complained about the delayed interaction in phone calls or videoconferences, and some data communications protocols are negatively affected. They were thus not heavily utilized as a medium for interorganizational transactions. Business television—that is, sending business-oriented programming direct to various subscribing company sites—and videoconferencing were the primary interorganizational applications for geosynchronous satellites.

Several new types of satellite systems are becoming available that do not suffer from the same latency problems as geosynchronous satellites. There are two primary differences: First, orbits are much lower, so that signals do not have to travel as far, and second, they operate in constellations of satellites, rather than on their own. As a result, these systems are called Low Earth or Medium Earth Orbit systems (LEO and MEO, respectively). It means that they are no longer in geostationary orbits around the equator, with LEO systems designed to use polar orbits. Hence, each satellite will pass out of view of any individual antenna on the ground for a period of time. To maintain full-time service, another satellite in the constellation must come into view of an Earth station (antennae on the ground) before the first satellite passes out of view and loses communications. Then, like a cellular telephone system on the ground, a call in progress would be handed off to the incoming satellite.

The first of these systems to begin providing service are all narrowband (i.e., providing only a limited bandwidth with a focus mainly on carrying telephone conversations and low speed data). Iridium, a system developed by Motorola, is probably the best known LEO system. It is not likely to be used extensively as an interorganizational networking platform, but rather as a means for traveling businesspeople to complete telephone calls from anywhere in the world. (As of 2000, Iridium was in bankruptcy proceedings.) However, in the development stages are new systems that may, indeed, become interorganizational networking systems because they are being designed to carry much higher data rates (e.g., Teledesic, see Table 9.1).

Communications Protocols: The Success of TCP/IP

In addition to the dramatic advances in the underlying physical transmission capability of networks, there has been a profound shift in the logic by which networks operate. In particular, with the growth of the Internet (and its associated protocol, Transmission Control Protocol/Internet Protocol or TCP/IP), many telecommunications services are moving to a packet-based, rather than circuit-based connection logic.

In the past, most networks relied on circuit-switching, where a temporary, but dedicated, connection is made between a sender and receiver. This is ideal for applications like a telephone call or a videoconference, where there is always a constant flow of information to transmit. Yet it is wasteful for data communication, where transmissions often occur in bursts (e.g., when downloading a file), followed by periods where no information is transmitted over the network. Hence, data networks have traditionally been packet-based, where information is broken into chunks (or packets) of data. These packets can then be independently routed to destinations, and other users' packets could flow over the same links without disrupting users' communications.

TCP/IP is the world's leading packet networking approach. Packet networks formerly could not handle real-time traffic like telephone calls, because bandwidth was not reserved, and if the network was busy, packets would be held or discarded until congestion abated. As networks become faster, however, more and more real time applications can be carried over packet networks, enhancing the efficiency of the global telecommunications infrastructure.

The prevalence of TCP/IP, and the corresponding widespread connection of firms and consumers to the Internet, has meant that a global, public data network infrastructure now exists. New protocols, such as the hypertext transfer protocol (HTTP) and hypertext markup language (HTML), have added new capabilities to the Internet, which formerly was used mainly for e-mail and file transfers. These new protocols are responsible for the creation of the World Wide Web, which supports the transmission of rich graphics and interactive services, and is responsible for the rapid growth of electronic commerce.

With so many potential trading partners accessible via the Internet, it is not at all surprising that many are turning to it as an interorganizational networking platform, in place of expensive private leased line connections, or dial-up circuit switched ones. The main advantage of the Internet is that firms only directly pay for their access to the public data

network, rather than the backbone long distance connections. The backbone costs are shared across the many millions of Internet subscribers. Of
course, concerns about Internet security have inhibited many firms from
relying on the open, public Internet for critical data. This has led to the
rapid growth of private Internets known as Intranets (for connection to
internal company locations), and Extranets (for connection to external
partners).

SUMMARY

New transmission media and new communications protocols have significantly lowered the costs and increased the capabilities for external voice,
video, and data communications. Interfirm telecommunications-based
transactions are no longer limited to telephone calls, fax, and simple e-
mail. Today, the public Internet and private Extranets support rich, multimedia communications and data sharing. The implications for the way
organizations engage in economic exchange activity with each other are
tremendous.

FRAMEWORKS FOR UNDERSTANDING ORGANIZATIONAL ADOPTION, USE, AND IMPACTS OF WIDE AREA NETWORKS

Organizational theorists have incorporated the new information technology and telecommunications network environment into their research.
They have realized that the new network infrastructure may potentially
alter traditional assumptions about how organizations should be structured and should do business. Major research foci are reviewed in this section. First, we introduce the factors that help explain why people in organizations choose to adopt and use new interorganizational communication
media. This research is comprehensively reviewed elsewhere in this volume (see Rice & Webster, chap. 7, this volume), and so is only briefly
touched on here. From the organizational point of view, however, I note
that one primary reason for adoption of interorganizational networks is to
improve the competitive position of the firm. Hence, we focus more on
the implications of wide area telecommunications networks for business
strategy and *competitive advantage*. I then review the impact of wide area
networks on firm structure and location decisions, with an emphasis on
the increasing viability of *virtual organizations*. In the fourth section, I discuss the emerging impact on business-to-business market structures,
emphasizing the potential for *electronic markets*. Finally, a brief discus-

sion of the potential impact of the Web on *intermediation* in interorganizational transactions is provided. Here, I address the question of the need for traditional and/or new intermediaries to facilitate business-to-business transactions.

Adopting and Using New Media in Organizations

As noted by Rice and Webster (chap. 7, this volume), a great deal of new media research considers the adoption and use of new media in organizations as a dependent variable, in and of itself. Although most of this research does not explicitly focus on interorganizational communications, it certainly can be applied in this context. Here, I focus on three sets of factors to show their applicability: *characteristics of new media, social influences,* and *critical mass.*

Interorganizational networks can support a wide range of transactions and modes of communication. Hence, the same theoretical frameworks that attempt to link media choice to the communication task are as relevant when communicating across firms as when communicating within a firm. Short, Williams, and Christie (1976), for example, summarized a number of laboratory and field studies showing that the physical differences in the *characteristics of communication media* may make them more or less well-suited for particular tasks. They developed the concept of *social presence,* arguing that such channels as video or face-to-face (FtF) meetings better convey a sense of the other persons' presence than text-based or audio media. They noted, however, that a large number of in-person meetings involving travel could be held via lower cost computer conferencing or audio media, because the communication tasks were mainly information exchanges. Daft and Lengel (1986) introduced the notion of *media richness* to explain how effective managers choose from among different media. Richer media such as FtF interaction or videoconferencing support nonverbal cues, immediate feedback, and other forms of information that can help resolve potentially ambiguous situations. Effective managers choose rich media for ambiguous or conflictful situations, and lean media for routine situations. Interorganizational linkages that mainly support data transactions, therefore, might be put into place once firms are more certain about the nature of the data that is to be shared and the situations that are likely to arise.

However, in more ambiguous situations, firms might use less-structured and richer communications, such as videoconferencing over an ISDN connection to meet with a potential client. One problem with this theoretical perspective is that people's perceptions of how rich or lean a medium is changes with their experience and the context in which use is embedded (Fulk, Schmitz, & Steinfield, 1990). Moreover, this literature tends to focus on individual media use decisions, but given the infrastructure costs associated with interorganizational networking, decisions about which media to make available often occur at the firm or industry level (Steinfield, 1992). Systems such as expensive videoconferencing rooms may, therefore, be put into place by upper management, but avoided by employees because of their perceptions that it cannot adequately substitute for in-person meetings (Ruchinskas, Svenning, & Steinfield, 1990).

Social influences such as group and organizational norms, technology champions, overt statements of co-workers, and the observed behavior of co-workers have also been considered to affect an individual's choice of media for particular situations (Fulk et al., 1990; Markus, 1994), especially for new media where habits have not yet fully formed. From the point of view of interorganizational networks, we might consider the social influences arising from peer or interdependent organizations. Saunders and Hart (1993), for example, examined how power and trust influences adoption of Electronic Data Interchange (EDI), a technology for completing electronic transactions through standardized business forms over networks. Organizations can be influenced by their peers in the same industry by observing their behavior (cf. Bradley, 1993, for a discussion of how imitation of information technology strategies quickly mitigates any "first-mover" advantage), as well as by firms in their own network of suppliers and clients (Powell, 1990). These organizational influences are the parallel of social influence processes within firms, as factors affecting media usage (Steinfield, 1992).

Interorganizational network use, particularly over public data network infrastructures, is particularly sensitive to a third factor noted in the media use literature: *critical mass.* Markus (1990) referred to the notion that use of any communications medium is dependent upon others also adopting the same medium. This reciprocal interdependence imposes a constraint on the early adopters of any medium, who have fewer partners with whom they can potentially interact (see Rogers, chap. 3, this volume). New media reach a critical mass when there are enough users that the benefits derived from using it exceed the costs, and therefore more and more people choose to adopt it. In essence, each new user adds a new benefit for all existing users. Markus explained e-mail adoption in organizations using this framework. However, it applies even more so in the arena of interorganizational network use. Few firms would choose to invest in an infrastructure to reach their external trading partners and customers if they felt that only a small fraction of them could actually be reached by the technology in question. Indeed, the history of public telecommunications networking illustrates that people prefer to join larger, rather than smaller networks due to the immediate benefit (often called a *network externality*) from access to a larger population (Mueller, 1997).

Hence, critical mass phenomena are particularly relevant for understanding interorganizational network adoption, and most observers use this concept to explain the widespread adoption of the Internet as the platform for interorganizational data communications.

External Networks and Competitive Advantage

The growth of interorganizational networks since the 1980s has not gone unnoticed by the organizational and management science research communities. Numerous case studies and conceptual articles and books have proclaimed the competitive advantages of information technology in general, and interorganizational systems in particular (Bradley, 1993; Cash & Konsynski, 1985; Johnston & Vitale, 1988; Keen, 1988; Malone & Rockart, 1993; Porter & Millar, 1985; Rockart & Short, 1991; Wigand, Picot, & Reichwald, 1997). The main emphases in this literature are the ways that information technologies can *lower the costs* of coordination across the various value chain activities of the firm, improve a firm's ability to *differentiate its products and services* from competitors, and enable the firm to *expand into new markets*.

Using the competitive advantage conceptualization largely developed by Porter (1985), management strategists have urged firms to seek ways to use information technologies to reduce the costs of important value-chain activities. Following Porter, these *value-chain* activities are all the ways that firms convert raw materials into value-added products, and include inbound logistics (obtaining raw materials from suppliers), operations, outbound logistics (delivering products to distributors), marketing, and customer service.

Widely discussed case examples demonstrate how the use of cooperative telecommunications networks to link firms to their suppliers and distribution chains conveyed important competitive advantages to such firms as American Hospital Supply, Benetton, McKesson, Wal-Mart, and Xerox (see Bradley, 1993). The reported benefits to the firms deploying such interorganizational networks included increased efficiency of order processing, reduced costs due to just-in-time inventory management, locking in trading partners because of the difficulties competitors faced once a network is in place, and greater ability to customize products and services based upon information arising from the transactions carried by the network (Cash & Konsynski, 1985; Johnson & Vitale, 1988). Wal-Mart, for example, built an enterprise network based upon low cost satellite antenna known as VSATs (very small aperture terminals) at each store. This allowed them to use EDI to link to important suppliers so that inventory levels at stores could be continuously monitored. This enabled suppliers to know when deliveries should be made, and prevented Wal-

Mart from carrying too much inventory or from losing business due to being out of stock. Xerox used its network to reduce its supplier base from more than 5,000 to fewer than 300 (Bradley, 1993), improving quality and reducing defects. American Hospital Supply and McKesson offered buyers (hospitals in the former case, independent drug stores in the latter), terminals through which orders could be made. This reduced order processing costs and helped to lock in buyers.

Finally, Benetton relies on its global data network to streamline production operations, but also to gather market demand data rapidly from retailers so that it can be instantly integrated into production decisions. Their network facilitates what has come to be called "quick response" in the retail industry. For example, rather than dye sweaters prior to the start of a season, they can wait until sales reports indicate buying trends. Then the colors in demand by buyers can be acquired form suppliers, produced, and shipped on an as-needed basis to their retailers.

In order to gain such competitive advantages, large firms such as GM or Wal-mart would often pressure suppliers to switch to the organization's proprietary EDI system, or risk losing valuable contracts. Power relations among firms, as noted above, often came into play in the adoption of interorganization networks for competitive advantage.

Today, the growth of public data networks like the Teletel system in France and the Internet worldwide extend these advantages to more than just the largest firms able to afford expensive private networks (Streeter, Kraut, Lucas, & Caby, 1996). The Minitel system was first deployed in France as a low-cost online information service. Using cheap terminals (the Minitel) that included a modem, monitor, and keyboard, French citizens and companies could connect to a wide range of information services through their local telephone line. The French telephone company built a national packet-switched network with local access nodes in each region so that from anywhere users only needed to make a local call. The phone company also worked with information service suppliers by providing a billing and collection service. Any telephone subscriber can use a Minitel to retrieve information and complete transactions, for which they are billed on their regular telephone account.

Research that focuses on the Minitel/Teletel system as a public data network is appropriate because of its long history of supporting commercial transactions. It nicely illustrates how competitive advantage theories can be powerful explanatory frameworks for understanding adoption and use of wide area networks. Several case studies summarized by Steinfield and Caby (1997) illustrate how firms used France's inexpensive Minitels for business-to-business networking to enhance competitive advantage. For example, one office supply company used the records of Minitel orders to develop detailed purchase history databases for its clients, allowing their clients better manage their own inventory processes. BMW France used Minitels to collect parts orders from dealers. They recorded the proportion of next day rush orders to routine orders and fed this information back to dealers; and with this feedback system, they were able to maintain the desired ratio of rush to routine orders annually and improve stocking practices of dealers (Steinfield, Caby, & Vialle, 1993). Resinter, a subsidiary of a large hotel and restaurant holding company, accepted hotel bookings by Minitel. From these transactions, they were able to tell which travel agencies were sending certain hotels the most customers. They then marketed this information to hotels (Steinfield et al., 1993).

As a final example, the supplier of parts for appliances mentioned earlier enhanced their Minitel service, and increased revenue directly from it, by offering a diagnostic service that helped technicians determine the problems with faulty appliances. This "just-in-time" training service meant that repair people did not need expensive and lengthy in-person training, a difficult task given the short life cycle of new electronics products. The expert system also accumulated data on repair problems and provided feedback to the design and manufacturing divisions of the company in order to help detect and correct potential structural flaws in their products (Steinfield & Caby, 1993).

Today, many of these same types of applications routinely occur over the public Internet or private extranets. Business-to-business transactions over the Internet are considered to dwarf those involving home consumers ("Real force," 1999; U.S. Department of Commerce, 1998). The ease of establishing interfirm networks, however, also means that competitive advantages are difficult to sustain, and now become an essential component of nearly all firms' competitive strategy.

Interorganizational Networks and the Boundary of the Firm

In their popular book, *The Virtual Corporation,* Davidow and Malone (1991), heralded the arrival of a new form of company—one that relies on advanced networks and innovative relationships to become more flexible in a changing business environment and more responsive to rapidly evolving customer needs and demands. There appears to be some consensus that telecommunications networks facilitate the rise of such *virtual organizations,* which are described as smaller focal firms that rely on data networks to coordinate a range of up and downstream transactions with globally distributed partners (cf. Bradley, Hausman, & Nolan, 1993; Clemons, 1993; Malone & Rockart, 1993; Miller, Clemons, & Row, 1993; Monge & Fulk, 1999).

Organizational theorists have begun to formalize the structure and function of virtual enterprises. Wigand et al. (1997) highlighted three characteristics of a virtual company and corresponding design principles associated with each:

- Modularity and the Open-Closed Principle. Virtual companies are made up of small, modular units having their own specific competencies and potentially belonging to different legal institutions. These modular units can be assembled on an as-needed basis, allowing a dynamic reconfiguration of the company based on market demands. The open-closed principle means that, to customers, the enterprise appears to be a closed, cohesive system that they know and trust. In reality, however, it is an open, custom-built enterprise that is constructed after an order from a customer is initiated.
- Heterogeneity and the Complementarity Principle. Heterogeneity implies that each modular unit of a virtual organization has a different set of core competencies, enabling a more flexible assembly of just the right mix of skills to address varying customer requirements. Heterogenous, separate nodes on the network in a virtual organization actually perform activities that are complementary.
- Time and Spatial Distribution and the Transparency Principle. In a virtual enterprise, units are spatially distributed, freeing organizations from the former requirement that all members of a firm be geographically proximate. They can be located where resources or customers dictate. They are distributed in time in that they only belong to the virtual enterprise when their specific skills are required. The complexity of a virtual enterprise is transparent to customers, who see it as a sort of "black box," not knowing where exactly the unit is that is providing service, while perceiving it to be tailored to their needs.

From these characteristics, we can see that advances in telecommunications can influence organizational structures, leading to the *disaggregation* of a firm into a smaller focal unit that essentially outsources much of its production activities. To coordinate with this complex set of modular units, high capacity networks are essential. They support the rapid flow of information in the form of computer data, as well as the ability to hold meetings that can help sustain strong relationships among the disparate entities.

Empirical research on the structure and function of virtual enterprises is only just beginning, and conclusions about their overall effectiveness are still emerging. One study of more than 500 firms in the United States and France, for example, found that electronic transactions between producers and suppliers were more efficient when supplemented with strong interpersonal linkages among the players (Kraut, Steinfield, Chan, Butler, & Hoag, 1998). It may be that lack of legal relations between units leads to employee commitment problems (Wigand et al., 1997). Indeed, the Kraut et al. study also found that greater use of electronic networks to procure goods and services was not associated with more outsourcing. Rather, when firms have some ownership interest in their trading partners, they will use electronic networks more. Perhaps this is necessary to protect themselves from potential opportunistic behavior. Allowing another firm to link to company databases and networks does create vulnerabilities; some means of establishing trust is therefore essential.

External Networks and Electronic Markets

As organizations come to rely more on external networks, and as those networks become more prevalent, many researchers expect profound changes in the way markets are structured. For more than a decade, organizational theorists have questioned whether networks like the Internet are leading to the rise of *electronic markets*. An electronic market is one where consumers and firms obtain the goods and services they need electronically, using the network for search and evaluation, negotiation, delivery and after-sales service. The conceptual framework relevant to this area begins with an understanding of firms' make versus buy decisions, and is based on a branch of study known as transaction cost economics.

Why look at "make" versus "buy" decisions? Essentially, it has to do with the distinction between an organization and a market. According to transaction costs economics (Williamson, 1975, 1985), firms elect to make a good or a service only when it is cheaper to do so than buying it from the market. They consider their own internal production costs weighed against the costs of obtaining this good from an outside supplier. Note that this is more than just the price it includes search costs, contract costs (e.g., they may need a lawyer to draw up a contract), monitoring costs (ensuring that what they buy is of the needed quality), and after-sales related costs (returns, repairs, etc.).

Collectively, these are called *transaction costs*. Markets can fail under certain conditions leading to high transaction costs, such as when there are only a small number of suppliers of a good, and these suppliers behave opportunistically. Hence, even though a firm may not be able to produce some good or service as cheaply as an outside supplier, their transaction costs involved in *coordinating* with the market are too high, and they move production in-house to avoid opportunistic behavior of suppliers. In the transaction cost literature, this is known as the *market versus hierarchy* tradeoff.

Economic theory suggests that, were it not for the costs of coordination, markets would generally be more efficient mechanisms for production than hierarchies. By being able to sell to many customers in a market, a producer could acquire more experience, level the load of production across many customers, and capitalize on economies of scale, all of which generally lead to more efficient production. Similarly, in a market, customers can shop around for the best combination of price, quality, or other desirable attributes. Customers, due to choice opportunities, are not held hostage to the opportunistic behavior of any single supplier. Moreover, competition among suppliers would also lead to efficiencies.

How does this relate to telecommunications and wide area networks? According to Malone, Yates, and Benjamin (1987), telecommunications networks reduce the costs of coordinating with the market, and therefore increase the likelihood that firms will use market over hierarchy. They suggest that interorganizational electronic networks improve coordination between firms in two contrasting ways: (a) by providing *electronic brokerage* services and (b) by facilitating *electronic integration.*

By using wide area networks to reduce the costs of searching for appropriate goods and services, firms can achieve an electronic brokerage effect. The network, in effect, acts as the broker, bringing together buyers and sellers. Examples of using electronic interorganizational electronic networks to reduce search costs include the following:

1. The NASDAQ system, which creates an electronic market for over-the-counter stocks.
2. The EasySabre airline reservation system, which allows consumers to search for and compare ticket prices and availability before ordering.
3. Online multiple listing services, which help real estate agents and customers to narrow down the houses they visit.
4. CommerceNet, which allows firms in Silicon Valley to order computer supplies on the World Wide Web.

These services all connect different buyers and sellers through a shared information resource and provide tools for searching the data. They help the buyers to quickly, conveniently, and inexpensively evaluate the offerings of various suppliers. The electronic brokerage effect can increase the number of alternatives as well as the quality of the alternative ultimately selected, while decreasing the cost of the selection process. To the extent that firms use electronic networks for their brokerage effects, they will tend to develop electronic market relationships with their trading partners.

When electronic networks are used to reduce the costs of tightly integrating a particular buyer and seller, they achieve an electronic integration effect. An example would be an EDI system that connects a retailer's point of sale terminals to a supplier's delivery system, decreasing the likelihood of the retailer going out of stock on popular goods. This effect is manifested when technology is used not only to facilitate communication but also to tightly couple processes at the interface between stages of the value chain. To the extent that firms deploy electronic networks for their electronic integration effect, they will tend to develop long-term hierarchical relationships with trading partners. These are termed *electronic hierarchies* because the control of the supplying firm's behavior is more a function of management than the invisible hand of the market.

Malone and colleagues (1987) suggested that in the long run, for many types of products, electronic marketplaces will become more common than electronic hierarchies as networks become more standardized. The Internet would thus become an ideal platform for the growth of electronic marketplaces. We are beginning to see new new types of electronic markets, where firms can search among many suppliers for such goods as computer equipment, travel services, real estate, stocks, and more.

Empirical research suggests that electronic marketplaces, with multiple buyers and sellers participating, are not as easy to establish as we would expect (see Steinfield, Kraut, & Plummer, 1995, for a review of this argument). Case studies illustrate the role that such networks play in enabling suppliers to reinforce existing trading relationships, capture new business, and increase the costs their customers incur if they wish to switch to new suppliers (Steinfield & Caby, 1993; Steinfield et al., 1993). Some quantitative evidence exists to support the prediction that electronic hierarchies will remain commonplace, even on ubiquitous public data networks. In their survey of more than 600 firms in both France and the United States Streeter et al. (1996) found that firms seemed to use interorganizational data networks to bind customer and supplier firms. The survey also found that the more firms used external data networks of any sort, the more enduring were the trading relationships with their customers and the more frequent were their transactions with them.

More recent research suggests that lock-in effects, where networks are used to bind buyers to sellers, are even prevalent on the Internet (Chan, Steinfield, & Kraut, 1998). In their survey of 500 firms in the United States and France, Chan et al. found that firms became more integrated with their suppliers, and provided a larger share of business to those suppliers with which they traded electronically.

Finally, many theorists argue against using a simple market versus hierarchy dichotomy. Many different structures are feasible, as evidenced by the proliferation of complex webs of alliances between firms. Powell (1990) referred to networked forms of organization, where trusted relationships between firms—along different points in a value chain—can substitute for market transactions. A supplier, for example, realizes that its own economic health is a function of how well its buyers fare in the marketplace. If a retailer is struggling, for example, then it cannot buy as much, and the supplier suffers as well. Using a network of collaborating firms that compete against other larger firms or other networks provides the incentives for the supplier to help the retailer become more efficient and more successful, increasing the supplier's fortunes as well (Johnston & Lawrence, 1988). In addition, a network of smaller firms in combination can achieve the same economies of scale as larger firms, and compete more effectively against them. External telecommunications networks are a key ingredient for supporting such networked forms of organization (Monge, Fulk, Kalman, Flanagin, Parnassa, & Rumsey, 1998; Nouwens & Bouwman, 1995).

Intermediaries and External Networks

The final area of research to be reviewed is the emerging literature on the Internet and intermediation. An *intermediary* is an entity that comes between a buyer and seller, and facilitates an economic exchange in some way. Retailers are intermediaries, for example, who help sellers (the manufacturers of goods) reach consumers, and vice versa. A real estate agent is an intermediary who brings home sellers in contact with home buyers. Traditional intermediaries include wholesalers, distributors, retailers, and various types of agents and brokers. As more and more firms use the Internet as their wide area network, however, a restructuring of the value chain may occur, because the network allows direct linkages between producers and their customers. The central question here is whether or not a global infrastructure like the Internet encourages firms to bypass traditional middlemen such as wholesalers and retailers, and sell directly to their end customers or buy directly from distant suppliers. Many researchers believe that because the Internet has made network-based connections between producers and customers so affordable, firms may seek to bypass their traditional intermediaries such as their retail channels, and capture value that otherwise would be lost (Benjamin & Wigand, 1995). In essence, as alluded in the discussion of the electronic brokerage effect, the wide area network substitutes for traditional intermediaries.

The essential argument is that a network infrastructure connecting both businesses and end consumers allows producers to internalize activities that were traditionally performed by intermediaries. They can sell directly to end customers at a higher than wholesale price, therefore capturing more of the value in their goods. Benjamin and Wigand (1995) argued that both producers and consumers will benefit because the markup in price caused by intermediaries disappears; that is, the producers retain a higher portion of surplus value or profits that are generated along the value system, whereas the consumers benefit from both a larger choice and lower prices. In other words, the network's ability to efficiently support direct exchanges will increase both producer and consumer welfare. Thus, it is predicted that producers will sell directly to consumers, and consumers will prefer to buy directly from producers.

Examples of direct selling from producer to consumer abound on the Web. Many companies buy computers and telecommunications equipment direct from manufacturers such as Dell and Cisco (U.S. Department of Commerce, 1998). Of course, many producers also now sell directly to end consumers on the Web. Yet, at the same time, there exists an increasing number of Web-based businesses that play no role at all in the production of a good, but exist simply by adding some form of intermediary service, such as helping buyers find sellers. Many new Internet businesses, such as Amazon.com, are *new intermediaries* who have appeared only since the Web has come into existence, and are largely virtual businesses with little physical counterpart outside the Web. Of course, there are also many traditional intermediaries—such as existing retailers like Macy's, or catalogue sales companies like L.L. Bean—on the Web as well.

Even a closer examination of the transaction cost literature, on which the "threatened intermediaries" hypothesis is based, raises a paradox. If reduced costs of coordination indeed favor market approaches over hierarchy, producers should be more likely, rather than less, to outsource distribution activities. Hence, there should be a greater, rather than a smaller role for intermediaries.

Two recent papers by Sarkar, Butler, and Steinfield (1995, 1998) attempt to reconcile the "threatened intermediaries" hypothesis with the continued presence of traditional and new intermediaries on the World Wide Web. They noted that transaction costs of all sorts can be influenced by electronic networks, including producer to consumer, producer to intermediary, and intermediary to consumer varieties. In fact, bypassing existing intermediaries is only one of four possible outcomes, illustrated in Fig. 9.1, adapted from Sarkar et al. (1995).

The first box in Fig. 9.1 depicts the situation where it was formerly less expensive for producers to maintain direct linkages to customers before the Web, and producers use their Web presence to supplement this direct market. The scenario described by Box 2 is the threatened intermediaries situation, where the use of electronic commerce on the Web reduces direct marketing costs and encourages a producer to bypass traditional distribution channels. The two lower boxes describe situations where intermediation is likely to flourish due to Web-based electronic commerce. Box 3 notes the interesting situation where new electronic intermediaries, termed *cybermediaries* by Sarkar and colleagues, appear. Cybermediaries are simply intermediaries that take advantage of the Web to create economies of scale and scope. And Box 4 suggests the situation where existing intermediation is reinforced by the Web.

	T1 < T2 + T3	T1 > T2 + T3
T1 < T2 + T3	1 Web Supplemented Direct market	2 Threatened Intermediaries
T1 > T2 + T3	3 Cybermediaries	4 Web Supplemented Intermediaries

Post-Web

Figure 9.1. Possible outcomes of Web-based commerce (adapted from Sarkar et al., 1995)

As Wigand et al. (1997) suggested, cybermediaries encompass the role of the broker, auctioneer, or arbitrager. Sarkar and colleagues (1995, 1998) outlined the diverse functions that intermediaries fulfill both for producers and customers. In traditional consumer markets, intermediaries provide a variety of explicit and implicit services for their customers. For example, by patronizing a store, consumers implicitly choose a bundle of services for which they pay through the retailer's margin. Intermediary functions that benefit consumers include assistance in search and evaluation, needs assessment and product matching, risk reduction, and product distribution or delivery. Intermediary functions that benefit producers include disseminating product information and creating product awareness, influencing consumer purchases, providing customer information, reducing exposure to risk, and reducing costs of distribution through transaction scale economies. Their analysis suggests that, even though selling through the Web can lower the costs of direct interaction between producers and consumers, many functions (e.g., bias-free product matching) are best handled by intermediaries without a direct stake in any particular product.

It is clear that a great deal of service innovation is occurring because of the new economies and interaction possibilities provided by the World Wide Web. Many new types of intermediaries have appeared, including a type referred to long ago by Malone et al. (1987) as the *market maker*. Electronic auctioneers such as ebay, for example, demonstrate the power of ubiquitous networks to create real-time spot markets for specialized goods and services (see Klein, 1997, for a review of auctions on the Web). When computer networks connect as many potential trading partners as telephone networks, many new forms of commerce become feasible, not limited by the constraints of space and time.

SUMMARY AND CONCLUSIONS

This chapter has focused on the continuing growth of robust telecommunications networks that extend beyond the confines of a single firm. Such networks offer more than simple telephone, fax and voicemail, and link together more than a few close trading partners. They have become rich data networking platforms interconnecting a firm with potentially all of its present and future suppliers, distributors, and even end customers. Based on this review of the technological developments, and the theoretical literature examining electronic networks and organizational structure and strategy, a number of tentative conclusions can be drawn.

Expanded External Connections By More Firms

Technological developments, coupled with competitive pressures introduced by the global liberalization in telecommunications markets, will result in the continued proliferation of a vast global digital infrastructure. There will be many competing networks using a wide variety of technologies, all interconnected and all vying to attract businesses and consumers. This suggests that earlier limitations on external networking, caused by expensive bandwidth limitations, will be ameliorated. The conversion to Internet protocols as the fundamental internetworking approach means that communications costs no longer will prevent firms from interlinking with other businesses and with customers around the world. Moreover, with the growth of public data network infrastructures, interorganizational networks are now feasible even for smaller and medium-sized enterprises.

Media Characteristics, Social Influences and Critical Mass Effects Can Help Explain Organizational Adoption of Wide Area Network Technologies and Applications

Organizations might invest in infrastructure, but individuals ultimately choose to use one medium or another to communicate with others. Given the nature of the relationship between firms, such as whether the linkage is for automating routine transactions or negotiating complex business deals, different media are more likely to be used. Rich media, high in social presence, are more likely to be used for complex and ambiguous communication tasks. Social influences can also occur between firms to shape wide area network use, such as when firms that are dependent on others agree to link to their network. Finally, because of the high costs of wide area networks, there will be significant critical mass effects, in which firms link up to networks that are already joining a large number of other firms.

Network Applications Yield Short-Term Competitive Advantages

Organizations use external networks to reduce costs, differentiate products, offer new types of products and services, and access new markets. All of these are strategies to achieve competitive advantage. However, because networking costs are less expensive today, many of these competitive strategies can be imitated. It is thus more difficult to sustain competitive advantage, and the use of networks in turn becomes necessary for survival.

New Forms of Organization Dependent On Networks Are Emerging

With the greater connectivity provided by the Internet, organizations can engage in external networking on a much shorter lead time, and with many more trading partners. The review here suggests that this has been linked with the potential disaggregation of firms into modular units, creating virtual enterprises that are dynamically configured based on customer needs. The network is the glue that binds together these distributed units. However, at the same time, there is some evidence to suggest that such virtual organizations face serious obstacles. Ensuring adequate trust and commitment, when units belong to legally separate institutions can inhibit reliance on truly virtual enterprises. Moreover, empirical evidence suggests that it is not appropriate to rely on electronic transactions as a full substitute for interpersonal linkages that can both establish and maintain trust and commitment.

Open External Networks May Encourage the Evolution of Electronic Markets, But Electronic Hierarchies Are Also Likely

This review suggests that open external networks can allow firms to access a much larger and more distant set of trading partners, effectively aggregating buyers from global markets and finding the best sources of supply on an as needed basis. Thus, one effect of open external networks is the growth of electronic markets that bring together multiple buyers and sellers. Yet, although many interesting new Web-based marketplaces have emerged, there is also empirical evidence to suggest that network-based transactions tend to map onto pre-existing trading relationships. These practices also tend to lock-in trading partners by raising the costs each faces when switching to a new supplier or buyer. Interestingly, this appears to occur even over low cost public network infrastructures like the Internet.

Contrary to the Expectation That Open External Networks Would Eliminate Intermediaries, Many New Intermediaries Have Flourished

The prevailing wisdom is that external networks like the Internet permit producers of goods and services to directly access their customers, bypassing the need for intermediaries like wholesalers and retailers. Our review suggests, however, that many new forms of intermediaries are appearing, and are necessary for electronic markets to emerge and be sustained. New intermediaries can serve as market makers, matching buyers with sellers, and avoiding the biases associated with a producer selling direct to a consumer. The World Wide Web is filled with such new intermediaries that use the power of a ubiquitous, open network to add value to multiple producers' goods and services through providing information and accessibility.

In conclusion, developments in networking technologies have indeed had important implications for organizational structure and strategy. They have been creating new possibilities for managers, and new questions for organizational researchers. The adoption of wide area networks and the impacts of use of such networks often are counterintuitive and the result of complex social forces that interact with technology.

REFERENCES

Benjamin, R., & Wigand, R. (1995). Electronic markets and virtual value chains on the information highway. *Sloan Management Review*, 36(2), 62-72.

Bradley, S. (1993). The role of IT networking in sustaining competitive advantage. In S. Bradley, J. Hausman, & R. Nolan (Eds.), *Globalization, technology and competition: The fusion of computers and telecommunications in the 1990s* (pp. 113-142). Boston, MA: Harvard University School Press.

Bradley, S., Hausman, J., & Nolan, R. (Eds.). (1993). *Globalization, technology and competition: The fusion of computers and telecommunications in the 1990s*. Boston, MA: Harvard University School Press.

Cash, J. I., & Konsynski, B. R. (1985). IS redraws competitive boundaries. *Harvard Business Review, 63*(2), 134-142.

Chan, A., Steinfield, C., & Kraut, R. (1998, October). *Public vs. private networks: The effect on market structures in electronic commerce*. Paper presented to the Telecommunications Policy Research Conference, Washington, DC.

Clemons, E. (1993). Information technology and the boundary of the firm: Who wins, who loses, who has to change. In S. Bradley, J. Hausman, & R. Nolan (Eds.), *Globalization, technology and competition: The fusion of computers and telecommunications in the 1990s* (pp. 219-242). Boston, MA: Harvard University School Press.

Daft, R. L., & Lengel, R. H. (1986). A proposed integration among organizational information requirements, media richness, and structural design. *Management Science, 32,* 554-571.

Fulk, J., Schmitz, J., & Steinfield, C. (1990). Social information and media use: A theoretical framework and empirical evidence. In J. Fulk & C. Steinfield (Eds.), *Organizations and communication technology* (pp. 117-140). Newbury Park, CA: Sage.

Davidow, W., & Malone, M. (1991). *The virtual corporation*. New York: Harper.

Johnston, R., & Lawrence, P. (1988, July-August). Beyond vertical integration: The rise of the value-adding partnership. *Harvard Business Review,* 94-101.

Johnston, H. R., & Vitale, M. R. (1988, June). Creating competitive advantage with inter-organizational information systems. *MIS Quarterly,* 153-165.

Keen, P. (1988). *Competing in time: Using telecommunications for competitive advantage*. Cambridge, MA: Ballinger Press.

Klein, S. (1997). Introduction to electronic auctions. *Electronic Markets, 7*(4), 3-6.

Kraut, R., Steinfield, C., Chan, A., Butler, B., & Hoag, A. (1998). Coordination and virtualization: The role of electronic networks and personal relationships. *Journal of Computer Mediated Communication, 3*(4).

Malone, T., & Rockart, J. (1993). How will information technology reshape organizations? Computers as coordination technology. In S. Bradley, J. Hausman, & R. Nolan (Eds.), *Globalization, technology and competition: The fusion of computers and telecommunications in the 1990s* (pp. 37-56). Boston, MA: Harvard Business School Press.

Malone, T., Yates, J., & Benjamin, R. (1987). Electronic markets and electronic hierarchies. *Communications of the ACM, 30,* 484-497.

Markus, M. L. (1990). Toward a critical mass theory of interactive media. In J. Fulk & C. Steinfield. (Eds.), *Organizations and communication technology* (pp. 194-218). Newbury Park, CA: Sage.

Markus, M. L. (1994). Finding a happy medium: Explaining the negative effects of electronic communication on social life at work. *ACM Transactions on Information Systems, 12*(2), 119-149.

Miller, D., Clemons, E., & Row, M. (1993). Information technology and the global virtual corporation. In S. Bradley, J. Hausman, & R. Nolan (Eds.), *Globalization, technology and competition: The fusion of computers and telecommunications in the 1990s* (pp. 283-307). Boston, MA: Harvard University School Press.

Monge, P., & Fulk, J. (1999). Communication technology for global network organizations. In J. Fulk & G. DeSanctis (Eds.), *Shaping organizational form: Communication, connection, and community* (pp. 71-100). Newbury Park, CA: Sage.

Monge, P. R., Fulk, J., Kalman, M. E., Flanagin, A. J., Parnassa, C., & Rumsey, S. (1998). Production of collective action in alliance-based interorganizational communication and information systems. *Organization Science, 9*(3), 411-433.

Mueller, M. (1997). *Universal service.* Cambridge, MA: MIT Press.

Nouwens, J., & Bouwman, H. (1995). Living apart together in electronic commerce: The use of information and communication technology to create network organizations. *Journal of Computer Mediated Communication, 1*(3). Available online: http://www.usc.edu/dept/annenberg/vol1/issue3/vol1no3.html.

Porter, M., & Millar, V. (1985). How information gives you competitive advantage. *Harvard Business Review, 63*(4), 149-160.

Porter, M. E. (1985). *Competitive advantage.* New York: The Free Press.

Powell, W. (1990). Neither market nor hierarchy: Networked forms of organization. In B. Staw & L. Cummings (Eds.), *Research in organizational behavior* (Vol. 12, pp. 295-336), Greenwich, CT: JAI Press.

Real force in e-commerce sales is business-to-business. (1999, January 5). *The New York Times.* Available online: http://www.nytimes.com/library/tech/99/01/cyber/commerce/05commerce.html.

Rockart, J., & Short, J. (1991). The networked organization and the management of interdependence. In M. Scott Morton (Ed.), *The corporation of the 1990s: Information technology and organizational transformation* (pp. 189-219). New York: Oxford University Press.

Ruchinskas, J., Svenning, L., & Steinfield, C. (1990). Video in organizational communication: The case of ARCOvision. In B. Sypher (Ed.), *Case studies in organizational communication* (pp. 269-281). New York: Guilford.

Sarkar, M. B., Butler, B., & Steinfield, C. (1995). Intermediaries and cybermediaries. *Journal of Computer Mediated Communication, 1*(3). Available online: http://www.ascusc.org/jcmc/vol1/issue3/vol1no3.html.

Sarkar, M. B., Butler, B., & Steinfield, C. (1998). Cybermediaries in the electronic marketspace: Towards theory building. *Journal of Business Research, 41*(3), 215-221.

Saunders, C., & Hart, P. (1993). *Electronic data interchange across organizational boundaries: Building a theory of motivation and implementation* (Working Paper No. 7-93). Boca Raton, FL: Decision and Information Systems, Florida Atlantic University.

Short, J., Williams, E., & Christie, B. (1976). *The social psychology of telecommunications.* London: Wiley.

Steinfield, C. (1992). Computer-mediated communications in organizational settings: Emerging conceptual frameworks and directions for research. *Management Communication Quarterly, 5*(3), 348-365.

Steinfield, C., & Caby, L. (1997). Changing relationships in the information society: The effect of information infrastructures on relations among business users. *Trends in Communication, 3,* 93-115.

Steinfield, C., & Caby, L. (1993). Strategic organizational applications of videotex among varying network configurations. *Telematics and Informatics, 10*(2), 119-129.

Steinfield, C., Caby, L., & Vialle, P. (1993). Internationalization of the firm and the impacts of videotex networks. *Journal of Information Technology, 7,* 213-222.

Steinfield, C., Kraut, R., & Plummer, A. (1995). The effect of networks on buyer-seller relations. *Journal of Computer Mediated Communication, 1*(3). Available online: http://www.ascusc.org/jcmc/vol1/issue3/vol1no3.html.

Streeter, L. A., Kraut, R. E., Lucas, H. C., & Caby, L. (1996). The impact of national data networks on firm performance and market structure. *Communications of the ACM, 39*(7), 62-73.

U.S. Department of Commerce. (1998). *The emerging digital economy.* Washington, DC: Author.

Wigand, R., Picot, A., & Reichwald, R. (1997). *Information, organization and management: Expanding markets and corporate boundaries.* New York: Wiley.

Williamson, O. (1975). *Markets and hierarchies: Analysis and antitrust implications.* New York: The Free Press.

Williamson, O. (1985). *The economic institutions of capitalism.* New York: The Free Press.

10

Electronic Commerce: Going Shopping with QVC and AOL

August E. Grant
Focus25 Research & Consulting

Jennifer H. Meadows
California State University, Chico

Electronic commerce (EC) is changing the face of retailing. Just 25 years ago, most shopping required a trip to the store; today many consumers can shop from their home using a variety of communication media, ranging from the catalog, telephone, and the fax machine to television and personal computers. The general definition of commerce is the exchange of goods and services for a profit. With EC an electronic form of communication is used to facilitate this exchange of goods and services. In this chapter, we examine EC through two forms of interactive media, personal computers and television.

From the first time that anyone realized that computer technology could be combined with television to create interactive media, engineers and media practitioners have attempted to introduce interactive television programming. Although most of these efforts have met with only limited or no success, one interactive application has grown to become a multi-billion dollar business: television shopping.

Television shopping is important not only because of the role it plays in the television industry but because it is one of the best examples of successful EC. Online shopping is the fastest growing form of EC currently and provides an excellent example of a form of EC still in relative infancy. As EC continues to proliferate, primarily through the Internet, application of theory becomes one of the best mechanisms by which to understand and compare all forms of EC. This chapter, therefore, applies a variety of theories to explore the dimensions of EC.

Electronic commerce is one of the most important types of interactive media to study for at least four reasons:

1. EC is one of the best examples of interactive media.
2. EC is playing an increasingly important role in the economy.
3. EC's rapid evolution provides a dynamic object of study to aid in understanding a variety of new media.
4. EC provides a vehicle for applying theoretical lessons in a new context, thereby extending the understanding of media theories.

The chapter begins with a brief exploration of the current and projected impact of EC on the U.S. economy, followed by an exploration of the concepts of interactivity and EC. Theories of consumer behavior are then used to differentiate shopping behaviors so that similarities and differences can be observed across media. The chapter then applies a range of theories to explain the process by which individuals become "electronic shoppers," how and why they continue to shop, and how the mediated shopping relationship may be different from conventional shopping.

THE EC INDUSTRIES

The two basic types of EC explored here are direct response television (DRTV) and online (Internet) shopping. *Direct response television* is a generic term that includes three types of commerce: television shopping, infomercials, and direct response advertising. Television shopping includes services such as the Home Shopping Network, QVC, and Shop at Home Network, and may be defined as continuous streams of programming selling a variety of products directly to consumers. Although groups of product pitches may be aggregated into "programs," this genre is typified by offering a virtually continuous stream of sales pitches for products. Each "program" usually centers around a theme such as gemstone jewelry, fitness, or cooking and features a host. There is a regular group of hosts with whom the television shopper can become familiar. In addition, the hosts often have guests who help sell particular products. These guests range from celebrities (such as Joan Rivers selling her line of jewelry on QVC) to "experts" or spokespeople for the products. Audiences watch the shopping programming and when an item they want to purchase appears on the screen, they obtain the item number and phone number from the programming and call to order the item. Customers can also talk to the host and guest about the product, often giving testimonials about the product or asking questions. The item is paid for with either a credit card or check and then the order is packed and shipped to the customer.

Infomercials, on the other hand, are television programs that are designed to sell a single product or service, which are inserted into the flow of television programming on traditional broadcast or cable television outlets. Infomercials actually began in the 1950s with what were called "long running commercials." Eventually, the FCC outlawed these program-length commercials in 1973, but this guideline was struck down in 1984 (Elliott & Lockard, 1996). Generally, these commercials are seen at times when cable and broadcast stations need to fill time—late night or early morning on the weekends. Infomercials are generally made up of two parts: a program component and a direct response segment. The program segment attracts the potential buyers and generates interest in the product while the direct response segment asks for consumer action (call now!) (Elliott & Lockard, 1996). The purchaser can then call and order the product using a credit card or mail a check or money order.

In cable systems with a two-way interactive capability, shoppers need only keypunch their order into an addressable converter. The information is then fed upstream via the same cables that are used to deliver downstream programming. Early shopping services available via two-way cable in Warner Amex's Qube system, offered during the late 1970s and early 1980s, did not attract much interest in Columbus, Ohio and Milwaukee (Baldwin & McVoy, 1988). Baldwin, McVoy, and Steinfield, (1996) noted that scaled-down versions of two-way services—utilizing addressable converters to place orders—provided a more sustainable pattern of demand growth. As Martin (1998) concluded, the growth of pay-per-view markets during the 1990s spurred cable operators to began rebuilding their systems, providing upstream data to manage these new services. Of course, once cable lines are used to deliver data and Internet services, a growth in home shopping via cable is expected.

However, even as of late 1997, only about 20% of cable operators were capable of doing two-way data transfer; 7 million households are expected to subscribe to a cable modem service by 2001 (Martin, 1998). In order to enhance their two-way capabilities, cable operators will need to upgrade from coaxial cable to fiber-optics. Presently, only telco-delivered cable services possess fiber-to-home networks on a regional scale. Perhaps the most aggressive entrant into this area is Ameritech, whose "Ped and Rex" two way services carry several home shopping options.

Finally, direct response advertisements are short advertisements designed to sell a specific product or service that are inserted within another program. Almost all direct response advertisements are 2 minutes or less in length, with common lengths being 30, 60, and 90 seconds. These advertisements urge the viewer to call and order the product directly rather than a traditional commercial that urges the viewer to go elsewhere and purchase the product or service.

Online shopping uses quite different technology. With online shopping, a shopper needs a personal computer, a modem, and an Internet service provider (ISP). The shopper then shops on the World Wide Web (WWW), going to a specific shopping Web site. There are online shopping sites that offer a wide range of products (buy.com), and those that cater to specific products such as books (books.com), music (cdnow.com), and software (outpost.com). Many traditional retailers also offer Web sites such as gap.com and walmart.com. There is a multitude of choices for the online shopper, ranging from auctions (ebay.com) to stock trading (etrade.com). Once shoppers arrive at a shopping site, they then select the product or service they wish to purchase. This purchase generally goes into a virtual shopping basket. When the shopper has finished making selections, the invoice is processed and the shopper then has the choice to pay through the Web site using a credit card. Often, the shopper can also phone or fax the order. Most shopping Web sites offer secure credit card transactions. Most secure transactions use virtual private networks (VPNs) or a secure http. VPNs use a "tunneling protocol" to protect data between the sender and receiver. The data is encrypted such that if a packet-sniffing program tried to obtain the data, it would receive nothing but garbage. With a secure http, the Web browser and the web server create a coded conversation that can only be understood by each other (Urbaczewski & Jessup, 1998). The order is then processed and shipped.

Closely related to television shopping and online shopping is interactive television shopping, which could best be described as a hybrid between the two. With interactive television shopping, the viewer uses a remote to make purchases directly by selecting items displayed on the television. Most trials of interactive television have been failures (Traudt, 1998). The Time Warner Full Service Network was one such trial of interactive television. The service offered electronic shopping, but few subscribers took advantage of the service. Time Warner discontinued the service in 1997 (Meadows, 1998). Microsoft's WebTV is often described as interactive television. Users attach a set-top box to their televisions and use a keyboard. They can then access the Web to shop. For the purpose of this chapter, the shopping that occurs on WebTV can best be described as online shopping.

Interactive television shopping is not a dead idea, however. Wink Communications, Inc. now offers Wink Enhanced Broadcasting. This interactive system uses a portion of the broadcast called the vertical blanking interval in analog signals and the data channel of a digital signal. When one is watching a television program or commercial, a small icon will appear on the screen. The user can click on the icon using a remote and a menu will appear; the user can then access information, order samples of products, or even make a purchase. Users need a Wink-enabled set-top box and networks will have to provide Wink-enhanced signals for the system to work. Purchasers will be billed through their cable company much like a pay-per-view program. When the item is purchased, servers operated by Wink at the cable company process the order and billing (Desmond, 1998). This system is interesting in that it allows advertisers to directly reach customers, much like a banner ad on a web page. In addition to Wink, there is a renewed interest in establishing interactive television in the United States. This interest is spurred by the founding of the Advanced Television Enhancement Forum (ATVEF) and the Advanced Television Systems Committee (ATSC). Both groups are attempting to create a set of industry standards for interactive television (Foremski, 1999). Thus, the nature of interactive television shopping services that will be available in the future remains to be seen (Glazer, 1999).

DEFINING EC

Electronic shopping may be defined as the process of using communication technology to select and purchase goods and services. The process of selecting the product or service must be mediated by an electronic communication technology to fit this definition, as most purchasing processes already involve technologies such as the telephone (for catalog orders) and computer networks (for credit card purchases in retail stores).

It is possible for the "selection" process to be electronic, even if the purchase process is not, as consumers may use electronic resources to help make a purchase decision, but then make the purchase through traditional, unmediated means. Indeed, the fact that communication media are implicated in so many areas of product selection, evaluation, and purchase is indicative of the role that these media play in our society. Some in the direct response television industry argue that estimates of the total value of EC transactions should include the value of all goods sold as a result of promotion through product advertising (A. Eads, personal correspondence, October 1997). This chapter, however, uses the more conservative measure of the value of sales made from direct and immediate responses (such as through a toll-free telephone number or immediate Internet response).

Revenues and Demographics

As might be expected, the sheer volume of products offered for sale through television shopping channels makes it the most lucrative medium. Television shopping grossed almost $4 billion in 1998, with most of that total accounted for by QVC (approximately $2 billion) and the Home Shopping Network (approximately $1 billion). Gross sales through infomercials were estimated at $1 billion and direct response advertising accounted for roughly $1 billion more.

For comparison purposes, consider that gross revenues for each of the four major broadcast networks was about $4 billion in 1998. Television shopping may be a small part of the $150+ billion catalog market, but it compares favorably to the revenues from advertiser-supported television.

Online, or Internet shopping, on the other hand, had estimated revenues of $7.8 billion in 1998 (Radosevich & Tweney, 1999) These revenue numbers are outstanding, considering that online shopping revenues were only $400 million in 1997. The rapid growth of Internet shopping is expected to continue, with one analyst predicting that EC sales would reach $18.2 billion in 1999, far exceeding those of all forms of direct response television combined (McMillan-Tambini, 1999a).

Forrester Research forecasts that, in 1999, 4.4 million households were expected to shop online for the first time (McMillan-Tambini, 1999a). The 1998 holiday shopping season clearly showed that online shopping is a viable form of commerce. In fact, online retailers were caught by surprise during the 1998 holiday season, as purchases greatly exceeded expectations. Many online shoppers were unable to get onto popular online shopping sites or experienced long waits, backordered stock, and down Web sites. ISP America Online (AOL) reported that 1.25 million of its 15 million members made their first online purchase during the 1998 holiday season. One million new shoppers made purchases through online book-selling giant Amazon.com, during the 1998 holiday season (McMillan-Tambini, 1999a). The growth of online shopping is an important phenomenon, especially considering that 60% of the buying power in the United States is held by Internet users ("Consumers cite," 1999).

The growth curve of online shopping is quite steep, resembling the growth curve of television shopping in the mid-1980s (see Fig. 10.1).

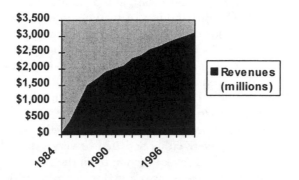

Figure 10.1. TV shopping revenue growth

Television shopping experienced a similar dramatic growth, from about $45 billion in 1984 to $450 billion in 1985, hitting $2 billion by 1990. At that point, however, growth slowed dramatically, increasing only 50% over the next 6 years. The key question regarding Internet shopping is where the growth curve will level off. It is easy to project an indefinite growth in online commerce, but lessons from other technologies, including television shopping, suggest that the growth rate has to level off.

It may be instructive to compare the run-up in stock prices for companies engaged in online commerce with the similar run-up in stock prices for television shopping services in the mid-1980s. For example, the stock price of Home Shopping Network shot up from $18 a share when the company first went public to more than $90 a share. After two splits (3:1 and 2:1), the stock price came crashing down, settling at $3 per share—the equivalent of the initial $18 price per share after controlling for stock splits (Knight, 1988). As of mid-1999, the same type of run-up in stock price had become typical for companies involved in online commerce. The stock prices for most of these companies then declined dramatically during 2000.

Analysis of revenues and stock prices clearly indicates the importance of time in understanding the behavior of any organization involved in EC. Just as time is a critical variable in understanding the business, it is also a key variable in understanding the behavior of audiences. Time is thus a major variable in the theoretical discussion of EC later in this chapter.

Before discussing other dimensions of electronic shopping, it is useful to examine the demographics related to different forms of EC. According to a 1993 study commissioned by Deloitte & Touche (see

Grant, 1997), 48% of all TV shoppers are between the ages of 25 and 44. Minorities are disproportionately represented among regular TV shoppers, as 20% are African American (vs. 14% in the U.S. population), 17% are Hispanic (vs. 8% in the U.S. population), and 55% are White (vs. 72% in the U.S. population). The distribution of income among TV shoppers is skewed toward both the lowest and highest income categories, with middle-income consumers less likely to buy. Finally, TV shoppers watch about half an hour more television per day than the average viewer, and are more likely to make purchases from catalogs and direct mail (Braun, 1993).

NIMA International profiled infomercial customers, reporting that the majority were married women between the ages of 26 and 45 with household incomes of between $20,000 and $50,00. The vast majority—92%—indicated they were either satisfied or very satisfied with their purchases, and 27% indicated repeat buying from the same company. The study indicated that repeat viewing was a major factor in infomercial purchases, with almost three quarters of the respondents reporting that they watched an infomercial two or more times before ordering the product, whereas 15% watched the same infomercial five times or more before purchasing (Levin, 1993).

A 1999 survey of online shoppers commissioned by the Consumer Electronic Manufacturers Association found that online shoppers are more likely to be women from a high income household (Convenience, 1999); these shoppers use both online and in-store shopping and are impulse buyers. Four categories of shoppers were identified: convenience lovers, money savers, smart shoppers, and selection seekers. The largest category of shoppers is the primarily female convenience lovers. Money savers see online shopping as a way to obtain bargains. These shoppers were mostly male and within the Generation X age range.

Encompassing both genders, smart shoppers see online shopping as a tool to research products before they buy. Finally, selection shoppers are those people who shop at specific online shopping sites. These shoppers were more likely to be from lower income groups. The study also found that almost 30% of the respondents indicated that they plan to double their online purchasing in the next year ("Convenience," 1999).

A study by E-Marketer examined male and female online shoppers and found differences in shopping behavior but not much difference between types of purchases. Men tend to browse more while online shopping, whereas women go online with a specific purchase or task in mind. Both men and women purchase books, music, and software and both men and women ranked convenience as the main reason they shop online. The study also projected that women would spend more than $18 billion on online shopping by 2002. That figure is over half of the total projected online shopping revenues ($35.3 billion; McMillan-Tambini, 1999b).

It is much more hazardous to profile the users of online shopping. The universe of users is much more limited, with the online community skewing toward higher income and education. Although 99% of U.S. households have a television, only about one half have personal computers with access to the Internet. As online services become more widely used, the demographic characteristics of online shoppers will certainly change, following the pattern of later adopters of almost any technology.

DEFINING INTERACTIVITY

Before exploring interactivity in EC, it is necessary to define the term *interactive*. Numerous definitions of interactivity have been offered. At the most basic level, most definitions of interactivity refer to the fact that the user provides some input into ("interacting" with) media content. In the process, the user gains some degree of control over the content of programming received.

The choice to engage in EC engages the user at a deeper level, typically implicating monetary resources (as well as time and mental effort) in the transaction. Levy and Windahl's (1985) three dimensions of audience activity—selectivity, involvement, and utility—can be taken a step further in relation to EC. In this case, selectivity is extended beyond choice of the program to a deeper level of cognitive involvement each time a purchase decision is made. The commitment of time and money, along with the effort that must be devoted to completing a purchase, is a strong indication of involvement. Finally, an indicator of utility is the fact users choose to commit resources to acquire specific products (although some might argue that many of the items offered for sale through such outlets as television shopping have minimal utility). The issue of whether the audience member is "active" or "passive" is clear—this is one form of media use in which audience members are clearly active.

The definition of interactivity in media use, however, must go beyond the issue of audience input in the messages received. Indeed, interactivity may be conceived as a continuous variable, with the question becoming not whether a medium or its use is interactive or not, but to what degree interactivity exists. There is clearly a difference between viewer involvement in choosing content (changing channels, etc.) and in providing direct feedback that affects the content seen (as in a video game or interactive video presentation).

The type of activity in television shopping is slightly different, as the viewer rarely "changes" the content of the presentation through their interactivity. Rather, the process of purchasing a product through the medium requires a commitment of time, money, and effort, yielding a different type of relationship between user and medium.

This level of interactivity also has an intertemporal component; that is, the user not only has an immediate interaction, but also has a delayed interaction through the process of receiving the product or service purchased.

Online shoppers have a different level of interactivity. An online shopper changes the content of the presentation by moving throughout a Web site or going to a different Web site altogether. A shopper on the Dell Computer Web site is able to construct a list of the components he or she will want in a new computer. The shopper could have also done the same thing on the Gateway 2000 online shopping site. In this case, the online purchasing process requires a commitment of time, money, and effort— much like television shopping—but also requires the purchaser to provide direct feedback into what is seen. With online shopping, there can be an intertemportal component similar to television shopping. There can be a delayed interaction through the process of receiving the product or service purchased. With online shopping, the purchaser can also receive the product or service immediately, depending on the product. For example, online shoppers can purchase software that can be downloaded to their computer immediately, or they can trade stocks or purchase information and receive that service immediately.

It could be argued that in TV shopping, often there are phone calls being broadcast at the same time, representing an interactivity in program content that approaches that of online transactions. But the latter can be enhanced by chat rooms, or at least bulleting boards, where users can post their comments about various products (e.g., a book review section on Amazon.com).

As of 2000, no research instruments have been identified that measure the specific level of interactivity between a user and the medium, allowing comparison of different forms of EC with each other and with other interactive media such as video games. Development of such a continuous measure of interactivity will surely add to our understanding of these different types of interactivity.

DIFFERENTIATING SHOPPING BEHAVIORS

Catalog Versus DRTV

Virtually all forms of EC can be divided into two categories: catalog-type shopping and direct response-type shopping. The difference between the two is the power of the consumers to select which items they will review for possible purchase. In the catalog model, shoppers can choose from an array of products available at their leisure. In the direct response model, on the other hand, shoppers are presented with only one item for possible purchase at a time, with their only decision being whether to purchase the item or not. To these traditional models we might add an emerging brand of shopper—the auction shopper—where one's actions are not clearly either catalog or DRTV; such shoppers actually reflect a consumer network component.

The fact that the catalog model offers a much greater array of choices and significantly greater control might, at first glance, suggest that electronic catalog shopping would be more important than direct response shopping. In traditional (nonelectronic) shopping, the catalog model is indeed popular, with an estimated U.S. market of more than $150 billion in 1997.

Most online shopping uses the catalog model. Shoppers can access a variety of products in their own time, when it is most convenient. The catalog model fits well with online shopping, to the point where many online shopping sites are seen as electronic versions of catalog. Prominent catalog retailers, such as Land's End and L. L. Bean, have large online shopping sites. In many cases, the online shopping sites can offer shoppers more information and services than the traditional paper catalog. Shoppers for music can download music samples to listen to before purchasing. Shoppers at Land's End can put together a "virtual wardrobe" to see how clothing goes together. A study by the market information group, Taylor Nelson Sofres, found that high-income, female, catalog shoppers were four times more likely to make online purchases than high-income females who do not catalog shop. The reasons for online and catalog shopping were the same for these women: convenience, time savings, and the ability to shop anytime ("Survey reveals," 1999).

Television shopping, on the other hand, is dominated by the direct response model. DRTV, in all of its forms, totaled more than $4 billion in 1998, with the bulk of that sum ($3 billion) coming from television shopping channels. The linear nature of television shopping channels prevents this genre from providing as wide a range of products or services, and hence possesses lower utility than the catalog model. But an exploration of shopping motivations and behaviors, combined with theoretical perspectives on the television-viewing process, helps indicate why the direct response model has, to date, been more successful than the electronic model. The following section explores and applies these theoretical perspectives.

Theoretical Perspectives on Relationships Between Shoppers and the Media

Rather than applying a single theoretical perspective, this section applies a variety of theoretical perspectives to various aspects of EC. Because each theory focuses on a different process, dimension, or variable, application of all of these theories provides a more detailed understanding than can be achieved by using any single theory. These theories help explain the adoption, uses, and effects of EC.

Rogers' (1963, 1995) classic diffusion of innovations theory is a great place to start. This theory attempts to explore the process by which an innovation is communicated over time through a social system. The most often quoted aspects of Rogers' theory can be summarized into three important lists: five categories of adopters, five attributes of innovations, and five steps in the diffusion process.

According to Rogers (1995), the process of adopting an innovation begins with (a) knowledge of the innovation, followed by (b) persuasion, (c) decision-making, (d) implementation of the innovation, and (e) confirmation. (Rogers also discussed a sixth step that occurs after adoption and use of the technology: reinvention, which is the process of finding a new use for an innovation.)

Understanding that these steps occur at different times for different adopters, Rogers further examined characteristics of different types of adopters, developing a typology of adopters including innovators, early adopters, early majority, late majority, and laggards. One of the keys to applying diffusion theory to EC is identifying the stage of adoption of a particular innovation. It is easy to look back at the diffusion pattern of an innovation over time to assess the specific stage of diffusion at any particular point in time, but it is extremely difficult to do so during the diffusion process, as the asymptote for the diffusion curve is then unknown (representing 100% of potential adopters, not 100% of the population).

For instance, Atkin, Jeffres, and Neuendorf (1998) found evidence of an Internet adopter profile that seems reminiscent of a medium in its early stages of diffusion (attracting users who are younger and upscale). Internet adopters were also likely to make greater use of other media and adopt other new technologies such as the computer (for a discussion of academic and industry profiles; see Klopfenstein, chap. 14, this volume). In addition to the adopter-nonadopter dichotomy of diffusion theory, Lin's (1998) study of computer adoption uncovered a third category: likely adopters.

Rogers' five attributes of innovations are relative advantage, compatibility, complexity, trialability, and observability. Analysis of these five attributes allows a particular innovation to be studied in relation to other innovations and the system within which the innovation diffuses. By thus placing innovations in the larger context of the competitive, regulatory, and technological environments it becomes easier to assess the prospects for success of these innovations.

The strength of the diffusion paradigm is its ability to explain the most observable factor related to new technologies—the fact that usage changes over time. The first target of researchers studying a new technology is frequently the pattern of diffusion, as understanding how the innovation spreads throughout a system provides a great deal of information about the innovation and its attributes (see, e.g., Klopfenstein, chap. 14; Rice & Webster, chap. 7, this volume).

Diffusion studies are typically followed by studies of the manner in which innovations are used. In studying mass media, the most common perspective is uses and gratifications, which was originated by researchers who were more interested in what people did with media than with what media did to people. This focus on the individual makes uses and gratifications a logical avenue for the study of new media, where the manner and frequency of use change as individuals discover new capabilities and limits of technology. Katz, Blumler, and Gurevitch (1974) summed up the approach, indicating that studies in this tradition are concerned with "(1)the social and psychological origins of (2) needs, which generate (3) expectations of (4) the mass media or other sources, which lead to (5) differential patterns of media exposure (or engagement in other activities), resulting in (6) need gratifications and (7) other consequences, perhaps mostly unintended ones" (p. 20). This approach has been applied to almost every medium ever introduced. Examples of new technologies researched from this perspective include VCRs (e.g., Levy, 1989; Lin, 1990; Rubin & Bantz, 1989) and cable television (e.g., Heeter & Greenberg, 1988; Sparkes & Kang, 1986). Most recently, Internet adoption has provided an extensive focus for research on media uses (e.g., Atkin et al., 1998; James, Wotring, & Forrest, 1995; Lin, 1999; Morris & Ogan, 1996), including user predispositions to use it as vehicle for electronic commerce (Jeffres & Atkin, 1996).

Understanding Differences. One of the most important steps in understanding electronic shopping is identifying the different dimensions of electronic retailing. Just as Rubin (1981) defined instrumental and ritual definitions of television viewing, Babin, Darden, and Griffin (1994) defined two dimensions of shopping: hedonic and utilitarian. The hedonic dimension (comparable to ritual television viewing) refers to the practice of shopping whereby a person primarily engages in shopping behavior for relaxation, enjoyment, or both. The utilitarian dimension (comparable to instrumental television viewing) refers to the practice of shopping whereby a person primarily engages in shopping behavior for the express purpose of acquiring a specific product or service. (It should be noted that these dimensions are not dichotomous categories, but rather independent dimensions—it is possible for an experience to have a high hedonic and utilitarian component at the same time, or to be high on one and low on the other.)

The two dimensions are especially useful in differentiating different forms of electronic shopping. Television shopping has a strong hedonic component, as it can be likened to "window shopping" in that it is a ritual event, often shared, in which the process of watching the program yields a set of gratifications even if no purchase is made. The fact that some television shopping services offer regular "program" schedules so that viewers can plan viewing around the purchase of a particular item or type of item indicates that there can be an instrumental dimension as well.

Online shopping differs from television shopping and in-store shopping in that it usually occurs with one person and a computer. Rarely does online shopping occur with several people gathered at a computer. Just because the shopping is solitary does not mean it does not have a hedonic component; shoppers can window shop online while engaged in hedonic behaviors that are simply less robust than television shopping. As noted earlier, a study of male and female online shoppers found that men were more likely to browse when shopping online and women were more likely to shop online for a specific purpose or item (McMillan-Tambini, 1999b). This study clearly shows both the hedonic and utilitarian dimensions of online shoppers. These gender roles can converge online as well, as in the case where a woman and her fiance were able to browse a common shopping site from different offices, using their phone to simultaneously discuss potential purchases.

The direct-to-consumer model that characterizes online shopping is viewed by many online retailers and EC professionals as a possible block for potential shoppers. Urbaczewski and Jessup (1998) summed up this problem by noting "direct-to-consumer electronic commerce may not succeed, primarily because consumers will shun its perceived convenience for the social benefits of shopping in person and interacting directly with sales personnel and other shoppers" (p. 10). The authors go on to examine some strategies that online retailers use to boost the hedonic/social component, such as the creation of virtual communities, chat rooms, and customer reviews.

Passive Audience. One strong indicator of the hedonic nature of television shopping is the finding that a large number of viewers watch television shopping programming on a regular basis without buying anything from the programs. Grant, Meadows, and Handy (1996) reported that the number of people watching without purchasing was almost equal to the number of people who actually bought merchandise from shopping channels. The group of watchers (12% of the sample) was as large as the group of buyers (11%; the other 77% did not watch or buy from any television shopping service). The presence of such a large audience for television retail programming suggests that these programs may fulfill goals other than making purchases.

These "watchers" could be playing a number of important roles. They could be "watching" to obtain product information for a purchase through a traditional retail channel. It is also possible that they are "passively" watching the program to fulfill gratifications and goals, such as the parasocial relationships discussed later.

Diffusion theory presents another possibility. For most people, it typically takes more than one exposure to a television shopping program for a person to make a purchase. The key question is how many times a person must watch a television shopping program before making a purchase. Just as different categories of adopters choose to adopt technology sooner or later in its diffusion process, it is logical to assume that the threshold number of exposures varies across individuals. Those individuals who have not yet crossed this threshold may be considered "buyers in training" (Grant et al., 1996), or potential adopters (Lin, 1998).

In discussing these buyers in training, Grant et al. (1996) suggested that the passive consumption of television shopping may have analogues in other interactive technologies. In essence, they stated that enabling users to observe the purchase process before actually making a purchase can facilitate the long-term success of any interactive technology. Part of the success of online shopping might thus be attributed to the fact that it provides the opportunity for prospective users to "shop," getting information about products, features, and prices without having to complete a purchase. If online shopping is analogous to television shopping in this fashion, it should be expected that there will be a wide range in the number of times a person accesses an online shopping site on the Internet before actually making a purchase.

Parasocial Interaction. As discussed earlier, parasocial interaction, the relationship that viewers develop with television personalities, is one of the most important variables in understanding the relationship between consumers and any form of television retailing (Horton & Wohl, 1956). Grant, Guthrie, and Ball-Rokeach (1991) developed a model of television shopper behavior that demonstrated that strong parasocial relationships led to increased viewing, which in turn led to an increase in the number of purchases from television shopping programs (see Fig. 10.2).

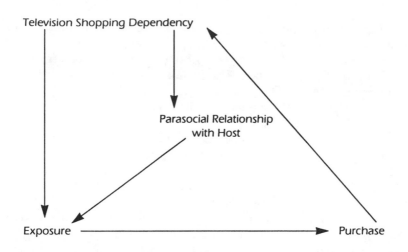

Figure 10.2. Model of television shopping relationships (adapted from Grant et al., 1991)

One strong piece of evidence on the importance of the parasocial relationship between viewers and television shopping hosts is the success of celebrities as hosts of infomercials and television shopping segments. Interestingly, the strongest parasocial relationships reported by Grant et al. (1991) were not with celebrities, but with the regular hosts of the television shopping programs. Regular viewers spend more time with these hosts than with many of their closest friends, and the result is a continuing psychological need to interact with these hosts, both by watching and by making purchases from the service.

Media Dependency. In addition to parasocial interaction, the Grant et al. (1991) model of television shopping behavior examined the role played by two different types of "dependency" relationships that viewers have with television. In understanding the importance of these relationships, it is useful to examine the theory underlying the relationships. In her explication of media system dependency theory, Ball-Rokeach (1985) indicated that individual audience members develop dependency relationships with a medium over time. The relationship develops as a person learns that the medium can help him or her fulfill a specific goal or set of goals.

Grant et al. (1991) identified two different types of dependency relationships. The first is the dependency relationship on television programming in general that viewers develop to fulfill their personal goals of play, orientation, and understanding. The second is a specific dependency on television shopping programming to fulfill these personal goals. The Grant et al. model (confirmed by Skumanich & Kintsfather, 1998) indicates that television dependency (in general) leads to parasocial interaction, that both dependency and parasocial interaction relationships between a viewer and television shopping program lead to strong media dependency upon such fare. Television shopping dependency, in turn, leads to purchase behavior, which leads back to increased dependency on television in general.

One key lesson from this model is the cycle that develops with dependency leading to purchasing behavior, which in turn leads to greater dependency. If it can be assumed that a similar cycle of dependency exists with other forms of EC, the first purchase made establishes the dependency relationship with the medium. Thus, an airline passenger's first attempt to buy a ticket online through Priceline.com will be crucial for acclimating them to a behavior pattern that's likely to endure over time.

Parasocial Behaviors. Although most research on EC focuses on the user, a few scholars have focused on the presentation forms. Auter (1996) extended the study of parasocial interaction to examine the behaviors of television shopping hosts and how these behaviors contribute to the formation of parasocial relations between viewers and the hosts. By changing the focus of the parasocial relationship away from the viewer's one-way relationship with the program—to focus on the behaviors of the hosts that foment those relationships—Auter's work provides a deeper understanding of the roots of the parasocial relationship. To date, the potential effects of parasocial interaction and parasocial behaviors have not been addressed in relation to online shopping. The utility of parasocial relationships, however, suggests that online marketers should consider means to utilize celebrities or other personalities to help users establish relationships with specific Internet "storefronts." This has been done with such celebrities as Ray Charles, who is featured on an interactive Web site promoting Diet Pepsi. But it is online music sales that provides the best example of online selling, as the medium is used to help singers "chat" with their fans to help market their music.

FUTURE

Although it is too early to predict the ultimate role that Internet shopping will play in the retail arena, the rapid growth in Internet shopping has already established this form of electronic shopping as one to watch. As of

1998, all forms of DRTV (including television shopping) easily outsold online shopping, but the growth rate of online shopping caused a reversal in the relative position of the two forms of EC before the end of 1999.

Perhaps the most important lesson from the rapid growth of online shopping is that the electronic media have a tremendous potential to play a role in retailing. The rapid growth of online shopping suggests that other electronic retailing services will be developed over the next decade, and that shoppers may be eager to embrace those new forms of shopping that compete favorably with traditional retail forms, including the so-called "brick and mortar" stores, DRTV, and online shopping.

One conclusion that may be drawn from this chapter is the importance of considering two key variables in understanding EC and consumers: The first of these is time. It is not only important to realize the role of time in the diffusion and development of relationships, but also to avoid simple extrapolation of trends over time. Instead, detailed understanding of an emerging interactive technology can be obtained by drawing lessons from fully diffused technologies, enabling a more comprehensive set of predictions about different types of adopters and motivations for adoption at different stages in product diffusion.

The second set of variables that should be examined involves the relationships that users develop in the process of using interactive technologies. These include parasocial relationships with celebrities and other personalities, dependency relationships, and such other audience uses and gratifications dimensions as entertainment, personal identity, companionship or diversion or escape (Lin, 1999). As more EC technologies emerge, researchers and marketers alike should be able to expand the list of relationships related to technology use, further expanding our understanding of the role that these media play in society.

The final lesson from this chapter is a practical one: The theories that have been applied in this chapter to help understand the underlying motivations, relationships, and processes implicated in electronic shopping can be applied by entrepreneurs and marketers to generate additional business for virtually any type of EC. As Kurt Lewin stated, "There is nothing so practical as a good theory" (Marrow, 1969).

REFERENCES

Atkin, D., Jeffres, L., & Neuendorf, K. (1998). Understanding Internet adoption as telecommunications behavior. *Journal of Broadcasting & Electronic Media, 42,* 475-490.

Auter, P. J. (1996). TV that talks back: An experimental validation of a parasocial interaction scale. *Journal of Broadcasting & Electronic Media, 36*(2), 173-181

Babin, B. J., Darden, W. R., & Griffin, M. (1994, March). Work and/or fun: Measuring hedonic and utilitarian shopping value. *Journal of Consumer Research, 20,* 644-656.

Baldwin, T. F., & McVoy, D.S. (1988). *Cable communications.* Englewood Cliffs, NJ: Prentice-Hall.

Baldwin, T. F., McVoy, D. S., & Steinfield, C. (1996). *Convergence: Integrating media, information and communication.* Thousand Oaks, CA: Sage.

Ball-Rokeach, S. J. (1985). The origins of individual media-system dependency—A sociological framework. *Communication Research, 12*(4), 485-510.

Braun, H. D. (1993). Just what kind of people buy from TV-shopping shows? *Retail Market Analysis, 2,* 1.

Consumers cite convenience as lure to on-line shopping. (1999). *Discount Store News, 38*(8), 20.

Convenience, bargains motivate online shoppers—study. (1999). Available online: http://www.newsedge.com.

Desmond, E. (1998, February 2). Interactive TV has arrived. *Fortune,* p. 3.

Elliott, M., & Lockard, P. (1996). An analysis of information content in infomercial programs. *Journal of Direct Marketing, 10*(2), 44-55.

Foremski, T. (1999, March 3). Busier life ahead for couch potatoes: Interactive TV. *Financial Times,* p. 1.

Glazer, R. (1999). Case study: OpenTV, Inc. *Journal of Interactive Marketing, 13*(2), 74-89.

Grant, A. E. (1997). Television IS the store: Direct response television. In R. A. Peterson (Ed.), *Electronic marketing and the consumer* (pp. 39-60). Thousand Oaks, CA: Sage.

Grant, A. E., Guthrie, K. K., & Ball-Rokeach, S. J. (1991). Television shopping: A media system dependency perspective. *Communication Research, 18*(6), 773-798.

Grant, A. E., Meadows, J. H., & Handy, S. L. (1996). The passive audience for interactive technology. *New Telecom Quarterly, 4*(1), 48-51.

Heeter, C., & Greenberg, B. S. (1988). *Cableviewing.* Hillsdale, NJ: Lawrence Erlbaum Associates.

Horton, D., & Wohl, R. R. (1956). Mass communication and para-social interaction. *Psychiatry, 19,* 215-229.

James, W., Wotring, C. E., & Forrest, E. (1995). An exploratory study of the perceived benefits of electronic bulletin board use and their impact on other communication media. *Journal of Broadcasting & Electronic Media, 39,* 30-50.

Jeffres, L., & Atkin, D. (1996). Predicting use of technologies for communication and consumer needs. *Journal of Broadcasting & Electronic Media, 40,* 318-330.

Katz, E., Blumler, J. G., & Gurevitch, M. (1974). Utilization of mass communication by the individual. In J. G. Blumler & E. Katz (Eds.), *The uses of mass communications: Current perspectives on gratifications research* (pp. 19-32). Beverly Hills, CA: Sage.

Knight, J. (1988, June 20). HSN, the story: Schlock, stock, and barreling. *The Washington Post National Weekly Edition,* pp. 21-22.

Levin, G. (1993). Infomercial demos get lift in new survey. *Advertising Age, 65*(4), 3, 62.

Levy, M. R. (1989). *The VCR age: Home video and mass communication.* Newbury Park, CA: Sage.

Levy, M. R., & Windahl, S. (1985). The concept of audience activity. In K. E. Rosengren, L. A. Wenner, & P. Palmgreen (Eds.), *Media gratifications research: Current perspectives* (pp. 109-122). Beverly Hills, CA: Sage.

Lin, C. A. (1990). Audience activity and VCR use. In J. R. Dobrow (Ed.), *Social and cultural aspects of VCR use* (pp. 75-92). Hillsdale, NJ: Lawrence Erlbaum Associates.

Lin, C. A. (1998). Exploring personal computer adoption dynamics. *Journal of Broadcasting & Electronic Media, 42,* 95-112.

Lin, C. A. (1999). Online-service adoption likelihood. *Journal of Advertising Research, 39,* 79-89.

Marrow, A. J. (1969). *The practical theorist: The life and work of Kurt Lewin.* New York: Basic Books.

Martin, D. R. (1998). Cable distributed telephone and data services. In A. E. Grant & J. H. Meadows (Eds.), *Communication technology update* (6th ed., pp. 242-247). Boston: Focal Press.

McMillan-Tambini, A. (1999a). On-line shopping soars into '99. *Discount Store News, 38,* 2, 3.

McMillan-Tambini, A. (1999b). Web woos women shoppers. *Discount Store News, 38,* 1, 19.

Meadows, J. H. (1998). Pay television services. In A. E. Grant & J. H. Meadows (Eds.), *Communication technology update* (6th ed., pp. 21-30). Boston: Focal Press.

Morris, M., & Ogan, C. (1996). The Internet as mass medium. *Journal of Communication, 46,* 4-13.

Radosevich, L., & Tweney, D. (1999). Retooling retail. *Infoworld, 21*(12), 1, 62.

Rogers, E. M. (1963). *Diffusion of innovations*. New York: The Free Press.

Rogers, E. M. (1995). *Diffusion of innovations* (4th ed.). New York: The Free Press.

Rubin, A. (1981). An examination of television viewing motivations. *Communication Research, 8,* 141-165.

Rubin, A., & Bantz, C. R. (1989). Uses and gratifications of videocassette recorders. In J. Salvaggio & J. Bryant (Eds.), *Media use in the information age: Emerging patterns of adoption and use* (pp. 92-111). Newbury Park, CA: Sage.

Skumanich, S., & Kintsfather, D. P. (1998). Individual media dependency relations within television shopping programming: A causal model reviewed and revised. *Communication Research, 25*(2), 200-220.

Sparkes, G., & Kang, S.H. (1986). Public reactions to cable television: Time in the diffusion process. *Journal of Broadcasting & Electronic Media, 30,* 213-229.

Survey reveals relations between traditional and online catalog shoppers. (1999). Available online: http://www.digitrends.com.

Traudt, P. (1998). Interactive television. In A. E. Grant & J. H. Meadows (Eds.), *Communication technology update* (6th ed., pp. 31-37). Boston: Focal Press.

Urbanczewski, A., & Jessup, L. (1998). A manager's primer in electronic commerce. *Business Horizons, 41*(5), 5-17.

PART FOUR

TECHNOLOGY AND
MASS COMMUNICATION

11

Adoption of High-Definition Television in the United States: An Edsel in the Making?

Michel Dupagne
University of Miami

With the first consumer sets hitting the stores in August 1998, high-definition television (HDTV) has finally made its formal entrance into U.S. homes after a tortuous journey that began in 1981. Technical standards and station conversion schedules have been specified for the deployment of HDTV, but ultimately it is up to consumers to decide on the success or failure of this technology in the marketplace. With billions of dollars at stake, the consumer electronics industry appears buoyant about the future of HDTV in the United States. The Consumer Electronics Association (CEA; formerly called Consumer Electronics Manufacturers Association or CEMA) predicts that 30% of U.S. households will have bought a digital TV set by the year 2006 (CEA, 2000b). But some industry observers are less optimistic, contending that HDTV holds little appeal for the consumer (Tedesco & Dickson, 1998) and even alluding to the possibility that HDTV could become the Edsel of the information age (Glick, 1998). In the industrial vernacular, the ill-fated Ford Edsel of the 1950s has come to symbolize the "modern American antisuccess story" (Brooks, 1963, p. 19). Will HDTV end up as the Edsel of the information age, unable to capture the interest of the American public? What does the empirical evidence reveal about consumer awareness and predispositions toward HDTV? Do consumers prefer HDTV over conventional television? Which of the key attributes, if any, do consumers find most desirable? How much of a premium are consumers willing to pay for an HDTV set? At initial retail prices ranging from $5,000 to more than $10,000 (Brinkley, 1998b), is it wishful thinking to expect, as CEA does, that 30% of U.S. households will own an HDTV receiver by 2006?

To address these questions and to shed some light on the issue of HDTV demand, this chapter reviews 21 quantitative pre-adoption HDTV-related consumer studies conducted in the United States between 1987 and 2000. Research findings in four topical areas are explored: HDTV awareness, preference for HDTV over National Television System Committee (NTSC), desirability of HDTV attributes, and willingness to pay for HDTV. The chapter begins with a brief overview of HDTV technology, policy, and economics to set the context for the literature review. The second section presents the key elements of diffusion theory so that empirical findings can be interpreted relative to a theoretical framework. The next section reviews available HDTV audience studies according to the four variables just cited. The fourth and final section discusses the practical implications of the empirical findings as well as describes four external factors that may influence the diffusion of HDTV in the United States.

HDTV BACKGROUND

Ever since the first public U.S. demonstration in February 1981, HDTV has been touted as the eventual replacement of the existing NTSC standard in the United States (for reviews, see Dupagne, 1995; Dupagne & Seel, 1998; Seel, 1996; Seel & Dupagne, 1998). It was designed to offer consumers three major technical improvements: sharper picture resolution using the 1,080-line interlaced or the 720-line progressive format instead of NTSC's 525 lines; multichannel distortion-free sound using six digital channels instead of NTSC's analog stereophony; and wider and bigger images using 16:9 aspect ratio instead of NTSC's 4:3 and approximating the theatrical motion picture experience.

Of course, the implications surrounding the conversion from analog to digital transmission extend far beyond improved picture and sound quality. As other chapters in this volume outline, digital signal processing enables a host of other capabilities—encompassing voice, video, and data applications—and is the major breakthrough for the development of complete digital integration of household communication.

Also at stake in the debate over HDTV formats is leadership in a half-trillion dollar market for TV set manufacturing, which the United States relinquished to Asian competitors in the second half of the 20th century. As observers (Dupagne & Seel, 1998; Schaefer & Atkin, 1991) suggest, HDTV proved a key trade battleground between the United States and Japan. The latter, under the auspices of NHK and the Ministry of Trade and Industry (MITI), pursued an "industrial policy" aimed at developing a global HDTV standard based on an advanced analog system utilizing 1,125 scanning lines.

Fearing the displacement that such a standard would present to U.S. broadcasters, the Federal Communications Commission (FCC) encouraged the development of a compatible (and, by implication, American) HDTV standard. In 1990, the FCC settled on a simulcast approach requiring broadcasters to transmit both HDTV and NTSC feeds (FCC, 1990). Their aim was to facilitate the development of a digital standard that would enable the U.S. manufacturers to "leapfrog" ahead of their Japanese counterparts by harnessing the advantages of digital media integration mentioned previously (Schaefer & Atkin, 1991).

On December 24, 1996, after countless tests and rule-making initiatives, the FCC approved a digital television (DTV) standard that would enable broadcasters to air either one HDTV program or multiple lower resolution standard-definition television (SDTV) programs within the confines of the allocated 6 Mhz channel width (FCC, 1996). Therefore, like advanced television, DTV is an umbrella term that encompasses several DTV technologies. To avoid confusion, and because most of the empirical literature deals with HDTV, I use the term *HDTV* instead of *DTV* throughout the chapter unless the context dictates otherwise.

On April 3, 1997, the FCC adopted a *Fifth Report and Order* requiring stations affiliated with ABC, CBS, Fox, and NBC in the top 10 television markets to construct their DTV facilities by May 1, 1999 and those in the top 30 markets to do so by November 1, 1999 (FCC, 1997a). It mandated that all full-power commercial stations be on the air with a digital signal by May 1, 2002. Surprisingly, the FCC declined to require that local broadcasters air a minimum amount of HDTV programming and instead left this decision to the discretion of the licensees. The FCC is expected to phase out NTSC broadcasting in 2006, unless it determines that 15% or more of television households in local markets have not subscribed to a multiple video programming distributor providing terrestrial DTV programming and have not acquired a DTV receiver or a digital-to-analog converter box by that date (Balanced Budget Act, 1997). In such a case, the FCC will be required to extend the deadline if petitioned by any local station.

On the same day, April 3, 1997, the FCC adopted a Table of Allotments for DTV, assigning a second 6 Mhz channel to nearly 1,600 full-power broadcasters in 900 U.S. communities. According to this table, more than 93% of the broadcasters received an allotment that would reach at least 95% of their existing coverage areas (FCC, 1997b). On February 17, 1998, the FCC (1998a) amended the DTV Table of Allotments and established the final DTV core spectrum between Channels 2 and 51.

In the early 1990s, many local broadcasters expressed concerns at the cost of converting their facilities from NTSC to HDTV, especially within the then 15-year transition window. By 1996, however, they had resigned themselves to accept the inevitability of HDTV for political and competitive reasons (McConnell, 1996). Some stations are now eagerly embracing the digital future (see Brinkley, 1997). Estimated conversion costs range from $2 million for pass-through equipment (i.e., to retransmit the network signal) to as high as $10 million for complete local production facilities (Ashworth, 1998). By July 1998, 16 stations were already broadcasting DTV programs or test signals (Dickson, 1998c). In August 1998, the first consumer HDTV sets went on sale in the United States at prices ranging from $5,499 to $5,999 (Snider, 1998). But, as indicated in fine print at the bottom of the SoundTrack advertisement (Fig. 11.1), buyers of these first Panasonic 56-inch rear-projection sets had to acquire an additional $1,500 decoder box to receive digital signals. In January 2000, prices began to drop, with fully integrated (DTV decoder included) 30-inch and 57-inch HDTV models costing $3,500 and $6,000, respectively (Kerschbaumer, 2000). In 1999, 121,226 DTV sets were sold (CEA, 2000c). But this number only represented .5% of the 23.2 million color TV units sold that year (CEA, 2000a). By the end of January 2000, 117 television stations in 44 markets were on the air with a digital signal (National Association of Broadcasters, 2000).

THEORETICAL FRAMEWORK

Although diffusion theory deals specifically with actual diffusion of goods and services, not potential diffusion, it provides a valuable theoretical framework to guide this chapter and situate the empirical findings of the HDTV audience studies. The key points of the theory are summarized here.

Rogers (1995) defined *diffusion* as "the process by which an *innovation* is communicated *through certain channels* over *time* among the members of a *social system*" (p. 5, italics added). The first element of this definition presupposes the existence of an innovation, which refers to an idea that is perceived as new by an individual. People evaluate an innovation in terms of five main attributes—relative advantage, compatibility,

Figure 11.1. Advertisement for the first consumer HDTV sets, *The Denver Post,* July 30, 1998, p. 8A. Reprinted with permission

complexity, trialability, and observability, which account for 49% to 87% of the variance in rate of adoption. For instance, if consumers consider HDTV's (sharper) pictures, (crisper) sound, and (wider and larger) screen size as superior to that of conventional television, then it could be concluded that HDTV enjoys a relative advantage over the existing NTSC television system. Consumers' perceived importance or desirability of these HDTV attributes will probably exert a powerful impact on purchase intention and rate of adoption.

The second element, communication channels, involves both interpersonal (e.g., word of mouth) and mass media (e.g., television) channels. Although mass media channels offer the most effective means to create awareness and knowledge (i.e., to inform the widest possible audience of individuals about the existence of an innovation), interpersonal channels are best to persuade potential adopters about the merits of an innovation.

The third element is time, which is an important dimension in determining the innovation-decision process and measuring the adopters' degree of innovativeness. The innovation-decision process is "the process through which an individual (or other decision-making unit) passes from first knowledge of an innovation to forming an attitude toward the innovation, to a decision to adopt or reject, to implementation and use of the new idea, and to confirmation of this decision" (p. 20). Therefore, it contains five steps: knowledge (e.g., HDTV awareness), persuasion (e.g., reactions to HDTV and its attributes), decision (e.g., willingness to pay for HDTV), implementation, and confirmation. Implementation and confirmation stages do not really apply to this review of the literature because virtually all studies were conducted prior to the introduction of HDTV sets on the consumer market. Rogers (1995) classified adopters into five groups according to their level of innovativeness: innovators (2.5% of adopters), early adopters (13.5%), early majority (34%), late majority (34%), and laggards (16%). Earlier adopters (innovators, early adopters, early majority) differ from later adopters (late majority, laggards) in terms of socioeconomic status, personality values, and communication behavior. Among other things, they are better educated, have higher income, and are more exposed to mass media channels than later adopters (Rogers, 1995).

Finally, the fourth element of diffusion is the social system, which, according to Rogers (1995), is "a set of interrelated units that are engaged in joint problem-solving to accomplish a common goal" (p. 23). Members of a social system can be individuals, groups, or organizations. Within the HDTV policy arena, Schaefer and Atkin (1991) noted that HDTV technology's diffusion is influenced by regulators, economic conditions, and industry players—both domestic and international—including content producers. The acceptability of a policy favoring a given format (e.g., compatible digital systems) is thus contingent on the support it receives from a critical mass of policymakers in government and industry circles (see also Dupagne & Seel, 1998). Some of the issues impacting the social system are addressed in the Discussion section.

EMPIRICAL FINDINGS

The third and main section of this chapter reports the findings of 21 quantitative HDTV-related consumer studies that were conducted in the United States between 1987 and 2000 (see Table 11.1). A review of studies carried out in Japan and Europe is available from Dupagne and Seel (1998). Research findings in four topical areas are explored: HDTV awareness, preference for HDTV over NTSC, desirability of HDTV attributes, and willingness to pay for HDTV. Not all studies specifically focus on HDTV's potential diffusion and adoption, but all investigate empirically at least one aspect of the technology. A brief methodological description introduces the findings of each study.

Awareness of HDTV

The American public's level of HDTV awareness has slowly risen from less than 25% in February 1987 to 55% in July 1998. In February 1987, a marketing study conducted by Advanced Television Publishing (ATP) at the Hecht Company department store, Washington, DC, concluded that less than 25% of the 90 shoppers or visitors who saw the HDTV demonstration had heard about HDTV (Bush, 1987). In the Home Box Office (1988) study, 27% of the 820 surveyed respondents in Danbury, Connecticut, reported prior awareness of HDTV. But Lupker, Allen, and Hearty (1988) found that 63% of their 91 Seattle participants were aware of HDTV. The methodology used in both the HBO and the Lupker et al. studies is detailed below. In March 1995, Dupagne (1999) conducted a telephone survey with a random sample of 193 Miami respondents to determine predictors of HDTV awareness based on demographics, mass media exposure, ownership of home entertainment products, and importance of television attributes. He found that 32% of the respondents had heard of HDTV at the time. Significant (positive) predictors of HDTV awareness included income, gender (male), and importance of picture sharpness. This study also revealed a significant positive relationship between HDTV awareness and interest ($r = .23$, $p. < .01$). A similar telephone survey conducted in spring 1999 with 321 Cleveland adults

Table 11.1. Summary of U.S. HDTV-Related Consumer Adoption Interest Studies.

Author	Year	N	Method	Variables
Atkin et al.	2000	321	Survey	Awareness, willingness to pay
Book	1999	630	Survey	Awareness, willingness to pay
Bush	1987	90	Survey	Awareness, preference
CEMA	1998	1,000	Survey	Awareness
CTAM[a]	1998	1,000	Survey	Awareness
Detenber and Reeves	1996	132	Experiment	Screen size
Dupagne	1999	193	Survey	Awareness, willingness to pay
Harris Corporation	1997	104	Survey	Preference, willingness to pay
HBO	1988	820	Survey	Awareness, preference, willingness to pay
Lombard	1995	32	Experiment	Screen size, viewing distance
Lombard et al.	1997	80	Experiment	Screen size
Lombard et al.	2000	65	Experiment	Screen size
Lupker et al.	1988	91	Survey	Awareness, preference, willingness to pay
McKnight et al.	1988	356	Experiment	Screen size, screen shape
Neuman	1988	613	Experiment	Preference, viewing distance, willingness to pay
Neuman	1990	214	Experiment	Picture quality
Neuman et al.	1987	367	Experiment	Sound quality
Pitts and Hurst	1989	180	Experiment	Screen shape
Reeves et al.	1992	32	Experiment	Screen shape, viewing distance
Reeves et al.	1993	40	Experiment	Picture quality, sound quality
Reeves et al.	1999	38	Experiment	Screen size

Note. Year = year of publication or presentation. *N* = sample size
[a]The Marketing Society of the Cable and Telecommunications Industry.

revealed that only 30% of the respondents knew something about DTV (Atkin, Neuendorf, Jeffres, & Skalski, 2000).

In May 1998, a CTAM telephone survey indicated that 50% of 1,000 randomly selected adults reported knowing what DTV is. When probed further, about one third of the interviewees did not know what DTV is and about one quarter heard that DTV provides better technical quality than analog television (The Marketing Society of the Cable and Telecommunications Industry, 1998). In July 1998, CEMA (1998a) conducted a telephone survey with a random sample of 1,000 adults and found that 27% were familiar with the term *HDTV*, 45% were familiar with the term *high-definition TV*, 19% were familiar with the term *DTV*, and 63% were familiar with the term *digital TV*. Overall, 55% of the respondents were aware of the term *HDTV* or *high-definition TV*. Consistent with diffusion theory, those familiar with digital TV were more likely to have acquired their knowledge from mass media sources (television, newspapers, magazines, internet; 53%) than from interpersonal sources (friends, family members, retailers: 27%; see also Book, 1999).

Finally, a face-to-face survey conducted at the North Carolina State Fair in October 1998 revealed that 73% of the 630 respondents had "heard that our country is making a transition to provide Americans with over-the-air digital television" (Book, 1999, p. 7). Awareness of the transition to DTV was significantly related to ownership of communication technologies, gender (male), age (younger), educational level, income level, home ownership, perceived picture quality, and willingness to pay for a new HDTV set. Although this question did not measure HDTV awareness per se, it produced a profile that is consistent with previous research.

In summary, these various studies suggest that the level of HDTV awareness has risen in the United States since the mid-1980s, although these levels vary widely across different monikers for the technology.

Preference for HDTV Versus Conventional Television

In February 1987, as noted previously, ATP conducted a survey at a Washington, DC department store, with 90 shoppers or visitors to assess public reactions toward the NHK 1,125-line HDTV system (Bush, 1987). Programming segments originated from *Top Gun* (a U.S. theatrical movie), *Dream* (an Italian music video), and *Chasing Rainbows* (a Canadian miniseries). These segments were displayed simultaneously on three monitors of different sizes (32-inch CRT, 54-inch rear projection, and 120-inch direct projection). After 2 to 5 minutes of exposure, respondents were asked to complete a questionnaire. Of the respondents, 87% rated the quality of HDTV better than that of conventional (NTSC) television.

When asked to report their favorable impressions about the HDTV demonstration, respondents singled out picture clarity (59% of all positive reactions), followed by color rendition (36%) and picture brightness (35%). Only 18% and 11% of the favorable reactions referred to the large (i.e., 54-inch) and wide (i.e., looks like a movie screen) picture, respectively; only 27% of the respondents felt that having a 54-inch HDTV set at home was very important for them. Dislike of the projected picture (26%) and size of the set (i.e., too big; 19%) topped the list of unfavorable mentions (Bush, 1987).

In October 1987, as part of the Committee for the North American High Definition Television Demonstrations to the Public, Lupker et al. (1988) surveyed 91 respondents in Seattle, Washington, to determine how well viewers discriminate between HDTV and NTSC. These participants were recruited by local advertisements, personal invitations, mall intercept, and telephone interviews. Program material included excepts from *Oniricon,* an Italian production, *Chasing Rainbows,* a Canadian miniseries, and *Around the World in HDTV,* a Japanese documentary. NTSC sets were 25-inch models, and HDTV sets were either 28-inch or 30-inch models. On average, 73% of the respondents judged HDTV to be better than NTSC in overall picture quality. In addition, respondents preferred HDTV to NTSC in terms of sense of depth (78%), screen shape (74%), picture sharpness (72%), color quality (69%), picture brightness (61%), and motion quality (e.g., lack of blur; 57%). As to sound quality, 60% expressed no preference.

At about the same time, HBO (1988) conducted a related survey in Danbury, Connecticut, to compare consumer responses to HDTV versus NTSC. Eight hundred twenty American consumers were surveyed in one of two settings: the living room (LR) situation (n = 507) and the walk-through (WT) situation (n = 313). In the LR situation, recruits were selected randomly by telephone and paid $15 for their participation. Groups of about 15 respondents entered a room in which rows of seats were arranged according to three different viewing distances (3H-three screen heights, 5H, and 7H). In the WT situation, "intercepted" consumers were asked to watch an HDTV versus NTSC demonstration for a few minutes and complete a short questionnaire on the future of television. In both situations, programming was displayed in studio-quality NTSC format on a 25-inch NTSC monitor and in reportedly less-than-studio-quality MUSE HDTV format on a 28-inch HDTV monitor. In the LR situation, programs included *Oniricon* (Italy), *Chasing Rainbows* (Canada), and *Around the World in HDTV* (Japan). The WT situation used the same programs plus four additional materials. Of the LR respondents, only 39% stated that HDTV was better in overall picture quality, whereas 45% preferred the overall picture quality of NTSC (Lupker et al., 1988).

Likewise, fewer than a majority of LR respondents preferred HDTV along seven technical characteristics: screen shape (46%), sense of depth (43%), color quality (43%), picture sharpness (41%), picture brightness (41%), motion quality (36%), and sound quality (30%). In the WT situation, however, 56% stated that HDTV was better than NTSC, and 34% preferred NTSC (Lupker et al., 1988).

In December 1987, Neuman (1988) conducted an experiment at the Massachusetts Institute of Technology's (MIT) Audience Research Facility in the Liberty Tree Mall, Danvers, Massachusetts, to assess viewer preferences for HDTV versus NTSC. The 613 participants were recruited by mall intercept and telephone. Each session consisted of two tests. In the first test, called the conservative test or the single stimulus test, participants were randomly assigned to either the HDTV sets condition or the NTSC sets condition. They were asked to evaluate the quality of the respective sets. The two screen sizes were 18 inches and 28 inches. In the second test, called the comparison test or the dual stimulus test, participants were asked to view and evaluate programming on two sets (HDTV vs. NTSC) side by side. Participants were seated at three different distances: 1 meter, 2 meters, and 3 meters (18-inch sets: 3H, 7H, 10H; 28-inch sets: 2H, 5H, 7H). Programming included six clips: *Carly Simon* (concert), *Olympics, Football, Long Gone* (comedy-drama), *Mandela* (drama), and *Lions of Africa* (drama). Viewing exposure totaled about 15 minutes.

The author found that in the side-by-side comparison test, 62% preferred the overall picture quality of HDTV to that of NTSC. However, preference for HDTV was highly context-dependent (e.g., program type, set size, viewing distance). For instance, 95% of the participants in Group 2—viewing the *Olympics* clip on 28-inch HDTV and NTSC monitors from a distance of 1 meter (2H)—preferred the quality of HDTV. On the other hand, 89% of the participants in Group 1—viewing the *Football* segment on 18-inch HDTV and NTSC sets from a distance of 3 meters (10H)—preferred NTSC to HDTV. Neuman (1988) found a clear relationship between viewing distance and preference for HDTV: The closer the viewers sat, the more they preferred HDTV to NTSC. This and other findings (HBO, 1988; Lupker et al., 1988) support the contention that three picture heights (3H) is the optimal viewing distance to discern the attributes of HDTV, although it remains to be seen whether viewers would want to watch television that close in normal viewing situations (see Lombard, 1995).

In the conservative test, Neuman (1988) found no significant differences between the HDTV and NTSC groups in their evaluations of program liking, program interest, program involvement, and screen quality. In the same vein, there were few evaluation differences based on content, and there were no differences in evaluations of technical characteristics (color quality, screen shape, picture sharpness, picture brightness, sense of depth, and motion quality). All in all, Neuman (1988) concluded that "HDTV is not the same kind of revolutionary shift in technology as experienced in the transition to color in the 1950s and 1960s in the United States. To the mass audience, the difference between NTSC and HDTV is perhaps more akin to the difference between monophonic and stereo sound" (p. 7).

In March 1997, Harris Corporation commissioned a survey with 104 participants to assess consumer reactions to the characteristics of the U.S. digital HDTV system versus those of NTSC. These respondents were recruited from the Washington, DC area based on specific screening criteria (e.g., at least 6 hours of TV viewing per week, VCR ownership). The same material was shown simultaneously on an HDTV monitor and an NTSC monitor. Of the respondents, 98% felt that HDTV was superior to traditional television in picture quality; 96% stated that they liked the shape of the 16:9 receiver; and 97% reported that the six-channel digital HDTV sound was superior to NTSC stereophonic sound (Harris Corporation, 1997).

Taken together, these studies suggest that a majority of viewers prefer HDTV—whether it appears in analog or digital form—to conventional television. Even so, the intensity of this consumer demand for HDTV does not seem to be as great as that for color TV over its black-and-white counterpart several decades earlier.

Desirability of HDTV Attributes

This section reviews experimental studies that examine further the impact of the three main HDTV characteristics (picture quality, sound quality, and screen size and shape) on audience acceptance.

Picture Quality. Neuman (1990) investigated the interactions between three levels of resolution as measured by the number of scanning lines (525-line NTSC, 1,125-line HDTV, and 3,000-line simulated very HDTV) and three screen sizes (25-inch, 35-inch, and 180-inch diagonals). The 180-inch screen size was intended to correspond to a flat-screen display. Neuman set out to determine whether there is "a saturation threshold under normal viewing conditions, beyond which increased resolution is unnecessary and imperceptible" (p. 9). A representative sample of 214 adults were recruited from the Greater Boston area. Neuman found the expected interaction between resolution and screen size. At any given resolution, subjects preferred larger screen sizes. For both the 35-inch and 180-inch displays, the higher the resolution, the more positive the overall evaluation of the display. For the 28-inch display, however, participants preferred the 525-line NTSC to the 1,125-line HDTV resolution. This finding suggests that consumers may not perceive the incremental value of a higher resolution picture when displayed on a small- or medium-sized TV set. But when asked to rate the picture quality of the programs, subjects preferred the 28-inch display to either the 35-inch or 180-inch display for the 1,125-line resolution. Neuman explained this apparent contradiction as follows: "The line-structure and artifacts are increasingly evident, and though people express a preference for the larger display, they have to acknowledge that the picture quality is, from a subjective point of view, lower" (p. 23; see also Lombard, 1995). He concluded that resolution beyond 1,125 lines (HDTV) makes a difference but that there is no ideal screen size for advanced television.

Reeves, Detenber, and Steuer (1993) examined the effect of video fidelity on attention, memory, and content evaluation. Forty undergraduate students viewed 16 one-minute clips from four entertainment movies (*Casualties of War, Days of Thunder, Indiana Jones and the Last Crusade,* and *Total Recall*). In this within-subjects experiment, subjects were exposed to both low-fidelity video (low resolution, low signal-to-noise [S/N] ratio) and high-fidelity video (high resolution, high S/N ratio). The authors found significant effects for some of the content-based measures (i.e., subjects preferred high-fidelity video to low-fidelity video), but not for attention or memory.

Sound Quality. Neuman, Crigler, Schneider, O'Donnell, and Reynolds (1987) investigated the impact of audio fidelity on viewer perceptions of television programming and technical features. A sample of 367 people was recruited at the Liberty Tree Mall in Danvers, Massachusetts to participate in this experiment. Each session included a conservative test, which measured the subject's response across several conditions, and a comparison test, which measured the subject's response to two sequentially contrasting stimuli. The tests were performed sequentially. In the conservative test, participants watched a 2-1/2-minute television clip of one of three content types (*Miami Vice* [action adventure], *Cheers* [situation comedy], *Basketball*) in one of four conditions (mono/low-fidelity; mono/high-fidelity; stereo/low-fidelity; stereo/high-fidelity). After exposure, participants were asked to rate liking, interest, involvement, picture quality, audio quality, and overall quality of TV set for the clip on evaluation scales. In the comparison test, each participant watched and evaluated two 30-second clips that were identical except in audio quality (e.g., mono/low-fidelity vs. stereo/low-fidelity).

In the conservative test, the authors found significant differences in evaluation scores of program liking, interest, and involvement but only when comparing extreme audio conditions. Participants in the stereo/high-fidelity group liked the program content better and found it more involving and more interesting than those in the mono/low-fidelity group. As would be expected, participants in the stereo/high-fidelity condition also rated the sound quality of the program significantly higher than those in the mono/low-fidelity condition. But differing audio quality had little or no impact on evaluations of picture quality and overall quality of the TV set. Findings from the comparison tests reflected those of the conservative tests. The authors concluded that subjects were "willing to report the overall quality and sound quality of one set as better than another, but [the results did] not provide clear support for the hypothesis that respondents prefer 'high' quality over 'low' quality sound" (pp. 9-10).

Reeves et al. (1993) assessed the impact of audio fidelity and audio spaciousness on attention, memory, and content evaluation. Using a within-subjects design, 40 participants were exposed to a low-fidelity condition (altered frequency spectrum, lower S/N ratio) and a high-fidelity condition (unaltered frequency spectrum, higher S/N ratio). The second independent variable, audio spaciousness (i.e., dimensionality), was manipulated between subjects. Participants were assigned either to the surround sound condition (five speakers) or the monophonic sound condition (one speaker). Contrary to expectations, attention was significantly higher, and memory was significantly better, when subjects were exposed to the low-fidelity stimulus rather than to the high-fidelity one. Audio fidelity yielded significant main effects for seven of the eight content items. But for five of these measures, the low-fidelity condition was rated more highly than the high-fidelity condition. The results for audio spaciousness were mixed for the three dependent variables, but there were several significant interactions. For instance, women in the mono group responded more slowly to the audio tone (to measure attention) than those in the surround group. On the other hand, men were more attentive in the surround condition than in the mono condition.

Screen Size and Shape. Reeves, Lombard, and Melwani (1992) conducted a within-subjects experiment with 32 students, manipulating screen size (small = 15-inch; large = 41-inch) and viewing distance (near = 4 feet; far = 10 feet). The dependent variables were attention, memory accuracy, and evaluation. Each subject saw a series of faces. The authors found that subjects were more attentive to large images than to small ones and better remembered images at 4 feet than at 10 feet. On the other hand, screen size and viewing distance had no significant effect on evaluative measures—subjects did not rate large images more positively than they did small images; nor did they evaluate near-distance images more positively than they did far-distance images.

Reeves et al. (1993) also investigated the effects of screen size on attention, memory, and content evaluation, but found results contradicting those of Reeves et al. (1992). Screen size was manipulated using a between-subjects design. The 40 participants were either assigned to the small screen size condition (35-inch) or the large screen size condition (70-inch). Presentations on the larger screen yielded lower attention and memory scores than those on the smaller screen. Of the 10 evaluative items (8 content-oriented, 2 quality-oriented), only 1 proved to be statistically significant for screen size. Subjects felt more a part of the action when they viewed the clips on a 70-inch set than they did on a 35-inch set.

Lombard (1995) administered an experiment to measure responses to viewing distance and screen size. The design was a within-subjects 2 (close vs. normal viewing distance) x 3 (10-inch, 26-inch, and 42-inch screen sizes), yielding six viewing conditions. The dependent variables included emotional responses to and impressions of people on television, both measured by a series of bipolar semantic differential items (e.g., calm-anxious). At each of the six viewing stations, 32 subjects from the Stanford University community watched four excerpts of television news broadcasts featuring an anchor speaking to the camera. Contrary to expectations, subjects' emotional responses to and impressions of people on television were not more positive when they watched television from a close viewing distance (10 inches, 24 inches, and 38 inches for the small, medium, and large screens, respectively) than from a normal viewing distance (30 inches, 72 inches, and 115 inches). But the screen size manipulation had a significant effect on the dependent variables. Subjects' emotional responses to and impressions of people on television were significantly higher when the stimuli were displayed on the large screen (42-inch) than on either the small (10-inch) or medium (26-inch) screen. Interestingly, although subjects preferred viewing these broadcast news excerpts on a large or medium screen than on a small screen, they favored watching television from a normal viewing distance over a close viewing distance. This finding suggests that just because consumers may prefer a large screen over a small one does not necessarily mean that they are willing to sit at a closer distance to the screen than they currently do. One should wonder whether this finding would hold with higher resolution displays.

Detenber and Reeves (1996) conducted an experiment to measure the effect of image size (22-inch vs. 90-inch) on three dimensions of emotion (valence, arousal, and dominance). Participants ($N = 132$) were randomly assigned to a small or large image condition, viewed 60 six-second pictures, and then rated their emotional responses after each one. The authors found a significant main effect of image size on arousal and dominance, but not on valence (measured with a pleasing-unpleasing scale). Participants rated large pictures as more arousing and as eliciting more "in control" responses than small pictures.

Lombard, Ditton, Grabe, and Reich (1997) conducted a between-subjects experiment with 80 undergraduate students to compare evaluative responses to small versus large screen sizes. The first half of the sample (20 males and 20 females) viewed 17 short scenes from current television programming fare on a 12-inch CRT direct view TV set. The other half (20 males and 20 females) watched the same program segments on a 46-inch rear projection TV set. After controlling for the effect of perceived picture quality, the authors found that participants in the large screen condition reported responses of greater intensity than those in the small screen condition. However, there were no significant differences in reported level of enjoyment between the two groups.

Reeves, Lang, Kim, and Tatar (1999) administered a between-subjects experiment to 38 female college students to assess the effects of screen size (2-inch, 13-inch, and 56-inch picture heights) on attention (measured by heart rate deceleration) and arousal (measured by skin conductance). All participants viewed 60 six-second video clips taken from television and film. Results revealed that participants were more attentive to, and aroused by, the large screen (56-inch) than to the medium (13-inch) and small (2-inch) screens. The authors also found a significant difference in skin conductance level measures (for attention) between medium and large screens, but not between small and medium screens.

Lombard, Reich, Grabe, Bracken, and Ditton (2000) conducted a between-subjects experiment with 65 undergraduate students to assess presence responses (measured with a paper-and-pencil questionnaire) and physiological arousal (measured by recording electrodermal activity) to two screen sizes (12-inch and 46-inch). Participants viewed 10 short scenes selected for their rapid point-of-view movement. Those in the 46-inch receiver condition reported more intense presence responses (e.g., "How exciting was the scene?") than those in the 12-inch receiver condition. Viewers' physiological arousal was also significantly higher for the large screen than for the small screen.

In addition to investigating the impact of screen size on evaluative responses, a few researchers have looked into the effects of screen format. In 1986, Pitts and Hurst (1989) conducted a side-by-side comparison test with 180 nonexpert RCA employees to determine preferences for widescreen (16:9) versus conventional (4:3) television formats. Two 35-inch 4:3 NTSC monitors were modified to reproduce video images in 4:3 and 16:9 formats. Ninety percent of the respondents chose widescreen over 4:3. When the 26-inch diagonal was reduced to 20 inches, preferences did not change in favor of the 4:3 format. The authors concluded that "people would buy smaller widescreen sets; the market would not need to be limited to the largest displays" (p. 163).

In early 1988, McKnight, Neuman, Reynolds, O'Donnell, and Schneider (1988) administered an experiment to assess viewer responses to variations of aspect ratio (5:3 vs. 4:3) and screen size (35-inch vs. 20-inch). Three hundred fifty-six subjects were recruited at the Liberty Tree Mall, Danvers, Massachusetts. In the single stimulus test, subjects watched two 2-minute clips (*Cheers* [situation comedy] and 1984 *Olympics*) from a distance of 2 meters. The aspect ratio, screen size, and program order were varied randomly. In the dual stimulus test, the same subjects were asked to view the same two clips on two NTSC sets side by side, which were varied either in screen size or aspect ratio. The results from the dual stimulus test revealed that 67% of the subjects preferred the 5:3 format to the traditional 4:3. They also favored 5:3 in overall picture quality and sense of depth (but not in color quality and picture sharpness). In addition, 87% of the subjects exposed to the two screen sizes preferred the 35-inch monitor to the 20-inch monitor. But they rated the smaller screen as superior in color quality, picture sharpness, and picture brightness. In the single stimulus test, there were few significant differences in affective responses (e.g., was the program clip emotionally involving) either between aspect ratio conditions or between screen size conditions.

In summary, the most important perceived benefit of HDTV is picture sharpness, as subjects seem less concerned about improved sound quality and larger screen size. Consumer acceptance of the widescreen format may depend on the receiver's size and weight.

Willingness to Pay

In the Lupker et al. (1988) study, only 11% of the Seattle respondents reported that they definitely or probably would buy an HDTV set for $2,500 within the next 2 years. This percentage rose to 20% when the price was set at $1,500. In addition, the authors ran a series of multiple regression analyses with the entire North American sample to identify possible early adopters based on demographics and ownership of consumer electronics products. The dependent variables were five purchase scenarios of HDTV (e.g., "Currently, a high-quality television or a high-quality VCR costs $800. If they were available at $2,500 each, how likely would you be to buy each of the following within the next 2 years?"). The only variable that was a significant predictor for all five questions was ownership of a compact disc player. Three variables predicted responses to four of the five questions: number of TV devices owned (positive), educational level (negative), and employment in a television-related industry (negative). Contrary to adopter characteristics expectations, those with a higher educational level were less inclined to purchase HDTV. Lupker et al. (1988) concluded that "the best initial market would be those individuals who already have a reasonably strong orientation towards buying technology (owners of TV and non-TV equipment and pay movie subscribers, but not television industry people)" (p. 50).

In the HBO study, only 17% of the LR respondents indicated that they definitely or probably would purchase an HDTV set at a price of $2,500, but this percentage climbed to 23% when the price was dropped to $1,500. For the WT respondents, the percentages were 24% and 30%, respectively (Lupker et al., 1988). In the 1988 MIT study (conservative test), Neuman (1988) found that 57% of the subjects in the HDTV viewing condition would be willing to pay an additional $100 over the price of their current set for the HDTV set on display. But only 6% would do so if the increment were $500. By comparison, 41% of the subjects in the NTSC viewing condition expressed willingness to pay a premium of $100 for the exhibited NTSC set, and 3% were willing to pay an extra $500.

In March 1995, Dupagne (1999) found that 15.5% of his respondents indicated that they would be likely to purchase an HDTV receiver at $3,000, a rather low-end estimate for the price of the first digital HDTV receivers in the United States. As mentioned earlier, the first consumer HDTV sets went on sale in August 1998 with a price tag of at least $7,000. In March 1997, only 6% of the Harris survey respondents were ready to pay $1,000 or more on top of the price of their current television set for an HDTV set (Harris Corporation, 1997). In October 1998, Book (1999) reported that her respondents would be willing to pay an average of $1,262 for a DTV set. Willingness to pay was significantly related to perceived picture quality, but unrelated to any of the demographic variables. In spring 1999, Atkin et al. (2000) discovered that fewer than one fifth of their Cleveland respondents were willing to pay $5,000 for first-generation digital sets. In summary, all these findings suggest that consumers are unwilling to pay even a modest premium for HDTV.

DISCUSSION

This literature review points out several important observations about the potential diffusion and adoption of HDTV in the United States. First, although the degree of HDTV awareness grew significantly in the 1990s, it has yet to reach saturation. By July 1998, only half of the U.S. public was familiar with HDTV, and this despite extensive coverage by print and electronic media organizations in recent years. Awareness is the first step in the innovation-decision process of diffusion (Rogers, 1995). Consumers must first possess some knowledge about HDTV before being able to form opinions toward the product and consider its purchase.

Second, consumers prefer HDTV to conventional NTSC in over-all picture quality. However, percentages from the preference studies are quite volatile, ranging from 39% to 98% with an average mean of 69%. As such, one may argue that these results hardly provide consistent and overwhelming evidence for this claim. Critics might even go further by contending that these findings cannot be projected to the U.S. population at large because participants have not been selected randomly and may have been predisposed toward advanced television and new communication technologies. All these points are well taken. On the other hand, we must realize that these results are only preliminary, based on limited HDTV exposure. Had the participants been able to watch HDTV programs for hours or days instead of minutes, the results might have been more conclusive. Perhaps they did not have sufficient experience with HDTV to discriminate adequately between HDTV and NTSC (see Carey & Elton, 1996). It is equally important to note that all but one (Harris Corporation, 1997) of the preference studies were conducted in the late 1980s using the Japanese analog 1,125-line HDTV system as the stimulus. Today's newer digital HDTV systems may yield better image and sound quality, which in turn may result in more definitive consumer perceptions. Furthermore, as noted in Dupagne and Seel (1998), highly favorable attitudes toward new products do not necessarily translate into fast diffusion, and this is certainly the case of color television in the United States. Following a color television demonstration in 1953, 98% of the respondents reported that color television was more enjoyable than black-and-white television and 87% felt that the overall quality of the color pictures was either excellent or very good (Opinion Research Corporation, 1953). Yet, it took about 20 years for color television to pass the 50% home penetration mark in the United States (Television Bureau of Advertising, 1987).

Third, consumers consider improved picture quality as the most desirable attribute of HDTV, followed by wider screen size, improved sound quality, and larger set size. Both survey and experimental studies clearly indicate that respondents prefer high-resolution images to low-resolution images. Likewise, a substantial majority of respondents favor the widescreen 16:9 format to the conventional 4:3 format. But with regard to improved sound quality, the experimental evidence is ambiguous. Contrary to expectations, Reeves et al. (1993) found that subjects rated more highly the low-fidelity condition than they did the high-fidelity condition for five of the eight content-based measures. Obviously, this experiment was conducted prior to the recent boom in sales of home theater systems, which offer viewers a movie theaterlike experience at home with a minimum of a large-screen TV set, five or more speakers, a video player, and a multichannel receiver. CEMA (1998b) reported that in 1997 one out of four households owned the basic equipment needed to assemble a home theater system and that sales of home-theater-in-a-box units grew from 621,000 in 1996 to 979,000 in 1997.

On the other hand, it is clear that many respondents expressed reservations toward set size. Again, the growing popularity of large-screen television receivers may force us to rethink these findings. For instance, CEMA indicated that sales of large-screen sets 30 inches and over rose by 14% from May 1997 to May 1998 ("May color set sales," 1998). Today, consumers may not necessarily view a 25-inch TV set as a large-screen receiver, although they probably did a decade ago. But perhaps more than anything else, the advent of flat-panel-display technology should resolve the issue of receiver bulkiness and encourage consumers to acquire larger television sets.

Finally, consumers are unwilling to pay a high premium for HDTV. Aside from the validity issue of the question (see Klopfenstein, 1989), few respondents are prepared to pay $2,500 for HDTV—a rather low-end figure for the first consumer HDTV sets. In January 2000, the cheapest fully integrated HDTV set retailed for $3,500 (Kerschbaumer, 2000). The case of the HDTV diffusion in Japan offers compelling evidence to support this claim. Despite positive attitudes toward the technology and the availability of a full-time programming schedule, sales of Hi-Vision sets have remained sluggish (829,000 in December 1999; Hi-Vision Promotion Association, 2000). In June 1997, after 8 years of diffusion, a 28-inch HDTV set still cost more than $3,000 (Dupagne & Seel, 1998). The Japanese experience demonstrates that favorable predispositions toward the technology and software availability are no substitutes for low hardware prices.

Even if the empirical evidence suggests that HDTV has the potential to succeed in the marketplace on its own technical merits, its diffusion could be adversely affected by a number of issues beyond consumer control. These external factors include indoor reception, digital must-carry, cable boxes, and programming. A brief description of each factor follows. First, there are some concerns about adequate digital reception using an indoor antenna. In April 1998, tests conducted for the Association for Maximum Service Television by the Model HDTV station WHD-TV in Washington, DC, revealed that only 16 out of 46 reception sites produced digital pictures with a bowtie antenna (McConnell, 1998). WHD-TV's unusually short transmitting antenna (400 feet) may have confounded the results, however. In August 1998, Tribune Broadcasting released test findings indicating that an indoor antenna can successfully receive DTV signals sent from a 1,200-foot antenna (Dickson, 1998a). This controversy led the Sinclair Broadcast Group and 250 television stations to petition the FCC to incorporate the European-based coded orthogonal frequency division multiplexing (COFDM) modulation technology in addition to 8-

VSB (vestigial sideband) in the DTV standard. Armed with demonstration results, Sinclair argued that COFDM would provide better indoor reception capability than 8-VSB. In February 2000, the FCC denied the petition, contending that the reception problems encountered in the first-generation DTV sets will be solved with new chips in future products (see Brinkley, 2000; Dickson, 1999a). As of mid-2001, the viability of indoor reception is still an open question, and consumers may have to install rooftop antennas at least in some locations.

Second, there is the matter of digital must-carry and whether in light of *Turner Broadcasting System, Inc. v. FCC* (1997), the FCC could obligate cable operators to carry both the analog and digital signals of local broadcasters during the transition period to DTV broadcasting. In a five to four decision, the Supreme Court upheld the constitutionality of the 1992 Cable Act's must-carry provisions, but it did not address the mandatory carriage of local broadcasters' DTV signals. On July 9, 1998, the FCC launched a *Notice of Proposed Rule Making* to explore this and other cable-related issues (FCC, 1998b). The must-carry rules have become a staple of litigation in telecommunications policy for more than 10 years, and unless broadcasters and cable operators agree on a compromise, they are likely to be reargued in court. The FCC issued a decision in the spring of 2001 (no dual carriage).

Third, there is the controversy over whether the digital cable set-top boxes will be able to pass through the HDTV signal, either 1080I or 720P, to HDTV receivers. Cable executives have assured Congress that these boxes will deliver all HDTV signal formats, although "the 15 million digital set-top boxes that TCI has on order cannot pass through an HDTV format higher than 720P at 24 frames" (Albiniak, 1998, p. 6). In addition, technical work on the compatibility of the cable jack needed to transmit the HDTV signal from the cable box to the set has yet to be completed (Brinkley, 1998a). In January 2000, FCC Chairman William Kennard warned the consumer electronics industry that the FCC will step in and mandate its own compatibility rules if the industry is unable to reach an agreement by April 2000 (Beacham, 2000).

Finally, as of this writing, it is unclear how truly committed the broadcast networks are to offer programs in high definition. CBS broadcast four football games in high definition between November 1998 and January 1999 instead of 5 hours of HDTV programming a week in prime time (Dickson & Albiniak, 1998). During the 1999-2000 season, CBS aired 12 hours of prime-time HDTV programming underwritten by Mitsubishi Electronics (Dickson, 1999b). Under a production deal with Panasonic, ABC broadcast *Monday Night Football* and the Super Bowl in 720P. But NBC only televised *The Tonight Show with Jay Leno* and an occasional movie feature film. As of December 1999, Fox had not announced a single

HDTV production (Glick, 1999). It is difficult to understand why the major networks are not more active on the programming front, provided that about 70% of their prime-time programming is shot on 35mm film and can be easily converted to an HDTV format. This minimal network commitment is reminiscent of the dearth of color television programming between 1954 and 1963. Eleven years after the FCC adopted the color NTSC standard in 1953, the three networks collectively only broadcast 6 hours of color programming a day (or 2 hours a day per network) ("How television color," 1965). Garvey (1980) argued that "color television might have reached the American home far faster if networks and stations had been more aggressive in using color programming" (p. 519).

In the final analysis, HDTV will not follow the path of the Edsel not just because empirical studies show that consumer responses to this technology are generally positive, but also because consumers ultimately will have little choice but to acquire an HDTV receiver. Because of the FCC deadlines, the issue of HDTV adoption is not a matter of "if" but "when" and "how fast." Yet, optimism must be tempered with realism. Classic visionary aphorisms, such as IBM Chairman Thomas Watson's "I think there is a world market for maybe five computers," are constant reminders of our own fallibility in predicting the evolution of new communication technologies (see Klopfenstein, 1985). Specifically, high retail prices and the four external obstacles discussed in this chapter, if not overcome, could seriously slow down the growth of HDTV in the United States. By the end of 1999, the retail appliance chain Circuit City had predicted that 1 million of HDTV sets would be sold (Dickson, 1998b), but only 121,226 sets were sold that year (CEA, 2000c). Therefore, this and other HDTV forecasts should be viewed with a certain dose of skepticism. Indeed, as a lesson of humility, it is opportune to remember that three HDTV forecasting studies in the late 1980s had predicted household penetrations ranging from 2% to 43% by the year 2000 (see Dupagne & Seel, 1998). Forecasting demands prudence and a careful examination of assumptions and factors that might impact the diffusion of a product.

ACKNOWLEDGMENTS

I am grateful to Peter B. Seel for his comments. An earlier and enlarged version of this chapter was previously published in *High-Definition Television: A Global Perspective,* by Michel Dupagne and Peter B. Seel, 1998, Ames: Iowa State University Press. Reproduced with permission. All rights reserved. This chapter was completed in February 2000.

REFERENCES

Albiniak, P. (1998, April 27). HDTV no problem, says cable. *Broadcasting & Cable*, p. 6.

Ashworth, S. (1998, March 23). Finding funds for the transition. *TV Technology*, pp. 10, 12.

Atkin, D., Neuendorf, K., Jeffres, L., & Skalski, P. (2000, June). *Predictors of audience interest in adopting digital television.* Paper presented at the annual meeting of the International Communication Association, Acapulco, Mexico.

Balanced Budget Act of 1997, Pub. L. No. 105-33, 3003, 111 Stat. 251, 265 (1997).

Beacham, F. (2000, February 9). Kennard warns of FCC action on TV/cable standards. *TV Technology*, pp. 12, 22.

Book, C. L. (1999, April). *The impact of consumer education on public response to digital television.* Paper presented at the annual meeting of the Broadcast Education Association, Las Vegas, NV.

Brinkley, J. (1997, November 24). Getting the picture. *The New York Times*, pp. C1, C12.

Brinkley, J. (1998a, August 26). FCC wants HDTV glitch solved soon. *The New York Times*, p. C4.

Brinkley, J. (1998b, January 12). They're big. They're expensive. They're the first high-definition TV sets. *The New York Times*, p. C3.

Brinkley, J. (2000, February 7). F.C.C. denies Sinclair's request to modify digital TV standard. *The New York Times*, p. C6.

Brooks, J. (1963). *The fate of the Edsel and other business adventures.* New York: Harper & Row.

Bush, S. (1987). *A survey of audience reaction to NHK 1125 line color television.* Portland, OR: Advanced Television Publishing.

Carey, J., & Elton, M. (1996). Forecasting demand for new consumer services: Challenges and alternatives. In R. R. Dholakia, N. Mundorf, & N. Dholakia (Eds.), *New infotainment technologies in the home: Demand-side perspectives* (pp. 35-57). Mahwah, NJ: Lawrence Erlbaum Associates.

Consumer Electronics Manufacturers Association. (1998a). *A consumer perspective of the transition to digital TV.* Arlington, VA: Author.

Consumer Electronics Manufacturers Association. (1998b). *U.S. consumer electronics industry today.* Arlington, VA: Author.

Consumer Electronics Association. (2000a). *December caps strong year in video sales.* Retrieved February 4, 2000 from the World Wide Web: http://www.ce.org/newsroom/newsloader2.cfm?id=1286.

Consumer Electronics Association. (2000b). *DTV market.* Retrieved January 30, 2000 from the World Wide Web: http://www.dtvweb.org/about/market.cfm.

Consumer Electronics Association. (2000c). *1999 a banner year for DTV sales.* Retrieved January 30, 2000 from the World Wide Web: http://www.dtvweb.org/news/press_release.cfm?RecordID=142.

Detenber, B. H., & Reeves, B. (1996). A bio-informational theory of emotion: Motion and image size effects on viewers. *Journal of Communication, 46*(3), 66-84.

Dickson, G. (1998a, August 3). Good DTV news from Chicago. *Broadcasting & Cable,* p. 10.

Dickson, G. (1998b, January 12). HDTV sweeps CES floor. *Broadcasting & Cable,* pp. 6-7.

Dickson, G. (1998c, July 6). WKOW-TV goes digital. *Broadcasting & Cable,* p. 43.

Dickson, G. (1999a, August 2). Back to the future. *Broadcasting & Cable,* pp. 22, 24.

Dickson, G. (1999b, August 30). HDTV rolling at CBS, ABC. *Broadcasting & Cable,* p. 10.

Dickson, G., & Albiniak, P. (1998, October 12). Where's the HDTV? *Broadcasting & Cable,* pp. 10, 14.

Dupagne, M. (1995). High-definition television. In A. E. Grant (Ed.), *Communication technology update* (4th ed., pp. 101-117). Boston, MA: Focal Press.

Dupagne, M. (1999). Exploring the characteristics of potential high-definition television adopters. *The Journal of Media Economics, 12*(1), 35-50.

Dupagne, M., & Seel, P. B. (1998). *High-definition television: A global perspective.* Ames: Iowa State University Press.

Federal Communications Commission. (1990). *Advanced television systems and their impact on the existing television broadcast service* (First Report and Order), 5 FCC Rcd. 5627.

Federal Communications Commission. (1996). *Advanced television systems and their impact on the existing television broadcast service* (Fourth Report and Order), 11 FCC Rcd. 17771.

Federal Communications Commission. (1997a). *Advanced television systems and their impact on the existing television broadcast service* (Fifth Report and Order), 12 FCC Rcd. 12809.

Federal Communications Commission. (1997b). *Advanced television systems and their impact on the existing television broadcast service* (Sixth Report and Order), 12 FCC Rcd. 14588.

Federal Communications Commission. (1998a). *Advanced television systems and their impact on the existing television broadcast service* (Memorandum Opinion and Order on Reconsideration of the Sixth Report and Order), 13 FCC Rcd. 7418.

Federal Communications Commission. (1998b). *Carriage of the transmissions of digital television broadcast stations* (Notice of Proposed Rule Making), 13 FCC Rcd. 15092.

Garvey, D. E. (1980). Introducing color television: The audience and programming problem. *Journal of Broadcasting, 24,* 515-525.

Glick, E. (1998, June 22). Digital TV: Do consumers really care? *Cable World,* pp. 1, 47.

Glick, E. (1999, December 13). The DTV debacle. *Cable World,* pp. 149-150.

Harris Corporation. (1997). *Consumer DTV screening survey.* Melbourne, FL: Author.

Hi-Vision Promotion Association. (2000). *More HDTV receivers.* Retrieved February 12, 2000 from the World Wide Web: http://www.hpa.or.jp/english/0002/shukka.html.

Home Box Office. (1988). *Consumer response to high definition television.* New York: Author.

How television color has grown. (1965, November 29). *Advertising Age,* p. 109.

Kerschbaumer, K. (2000, January 10). In search of DTV's magic price point. *Broadcasting & Cable,* pp. 52, 54.

Klopfenstein, B. C. (1985). Forecasting the market for home video players: A retrospective analysis (Doctoral dissertation, The Ohio State University, 1985). *Dissertation Abstracts International, 46,* 03A.

Klopfenstein, B. (1989). Problems and potential of forecasting the adoption of new media. In J. L. Salvaggio & J. Bryant (Eds.), *Media use in the information age: Emerging patterns of adoption and consumer use* (pp. 21-41). Hillsdale, NJ: Lawrence Erlbaum Associates.

Lombard, M. (1995). Direct responses to people on the screen: Television and personal space. *Communication Research, 22,* 288-324.

Lombard, M., Ditton, T. B., Grabe, M. E., & Reich, R. D. (1997). The role of screen size in viewer responses to television fare. *Communication Reports, 10,* 95-106.

Lombard, M., Reich, R. D., Grabe, M. E., Bracken, C. C., & Ditton, T. B. (2000). Presence and television: The role of screen size. *Human Communication Research, 26,* 75-98.

Lupker, S. J., Allen, N. J., & Hearty, P. J. (1988). *The North American high definition television demonstrations to the public: The detailed survey results.* Montreal, Canada: Committee for the North American High Definition Television Demonstrations to the Public.

The Marketing Society of the Cable and Telecommunications Industry. (1998). Digital TV: What does it mean to consumers? *Pulse, 5*(2).

May color set sales roll despite oncoming DTV debut. (1998, June 29). *Video Week,* p. 5.

McConnell, C. (1996, April 22). Broadcasters ready for digital switch. *Broadcasting & Cable,* pp. 10, 14.

McConnell, C. (1998, April 27). "Bowtie" no invite to digital reception. *Broadcasting & Cable,* p. 4.

McKnight, L., Neuman, W. R., Reynolds, M., O'Donnell, S., & Schneider, S. (1988). *The shape of things to come: A study of subjective responses to aspect ratio and screen size.* Cambridge: Massachusetts Institute of Technology, The Media Laboratory.

National Association of Broadcasters. (2000). *Broadcasters delivering on digital television to over 60% of U.S. audience.* Retrieved February 19, 2000 from the World Wide Web: http://www.nab.org/PressRel/Releases/0300.ASP.

Neuman, W. R. (1988, April). *The mass audience looks at HDTV: An early experiment.* Paper presented at the annual meeting of the National Association of Broadcasters, Las Vegas, NV.

Neuman, W. R. (1990). *Beyond HDTV: Exploring subjective responses to very high definition television.* Cambridge: Massachusetts Institute of Technology, The Media Laboratory.

Neuman, W. R., Crigler, A., Schneider, S. M., O'Donnell, S., & Reynolds, M. (1987). *A study of television sound.* Cambridge: Massachusetts Institute of Technology, The Media Laboratory.

Opinion Research Corporation. (1953). A survey of audience reaction to RCA color television. In J. T. Cahill, R. T. Werner, R. B. Houston, & E. R. Beyer, Jr. (Eds.), *Petition of Radio Corporation of America and National Broadcasting Company, Inc. for approval of color standards for the RCA color television system* (pp. 41-86). New York: Radio Corporation of America.

Pitts, K., & Hurst, N. (1989). How much do people prefer widescreen (16 x 9) to standard NTSC (4 x 3)? *IEEE Transactions on Consumer Electronics, 35,* 160-169.

Reeves, B., Detenber, B., & Steuer, J. (1993, May). *New televisions: The effects of big pictures and big sound on viewer responses to the screen.* Paper presented at the annual meeting of the International Communication Association, Washington, DC.

Reeves, B., Lang, A., Kim, E. Y., & Tatar, D. (1999). The effects of screen size and message content on attention and arousal. *Media Psychology, 1,* 49-67.

Reeves, B., Lombard, M., & Melwani, G. (1992, May). *Faces on the screen: Pictures or natural experience?* Paper presented at the annual meeting of the International Communication Association, Miami, FL.

Rogers, E. M. (1995). *Diffusion of innovations* (4th ed.). New York: The Free Press.

Schaefer, D., & Atkin, D. (1991). An analysis of policy options for high definition television. *Telecommunications Policy, 15*, 411-428.

Seel, P. B. (1996). High-definition and advanced television. In A. E. Grant (Ed.), *Communication technology update* (5th ed., pp. 101-113). Boston, MA: Focal Press.

Seel, P. B., & Dupagne, M. (1998). Advanced television. In A. E. Grant & J. H. Meadows (Eds.), *Communication technology update* (6th ed., pp. 64-78). Boston, MA: Focal Press.

Snider, M. (1998, August 3). HDTVs hit the market this week. *USA Today*, p. 1D.

Tedesco, R., & Dickson, G. (1998, March 9). HDTVs: One (big) size will fit all. *Broadcasting & Cable*, p. 42.

Television Bureau of Advertising. (1987). *Trends in television.* New York: Author.

Turner Broadcasting System, Inc. v. FCC, 117 S.Ct. 1174 (1997).

12

International Satellite Television Networks: Gazing at the Global Village or Looking for "Home" Video?

Joseph D. Straubhaar
University of Texas

Elizabeth Burch
California State University, Sonoma

Luiz Guilherme Duarte
Michigan State University and Hughes Corporation

Patrice Sheffer
Brigham Young University

Although the satellite was borne of military necessity against the backdrop of superpower rivalry during the late 1950s, its primary importance in the 21st century lies in peacetime applications as a communication device. Yet, as the Cold War subsided, fears of military hegemony associated with the technology gave way to concerns over cultural hegemony, as the communication satellite offers the prospect of turning the world into a "global village" (McLuhan & Powers, 1989). As the United States enters the new millennium in a position of unrivaled dominance, it is useful to ask whether the satellite represents (a) the latest in a series of tools by which it can control the essential grammar of global discourse, and/or (b) a vehicle for other nations to express their own cultures alongside (or in opposition to) global cultural themes, or (c) a combination of the two.

This chapter examines three of the new theoretical directions for examining the production and flow of television: globalization, cultural-linguistic regionalization, and cultural proximity. Those theoretical perspectives are examined in terms of media imperialism—including program genres and media models—in addition to current developments in Asia, Latin America, NAFTA and the Middle East.

SATELLITE TECHNOLOGY AND INFORMATION FLOW

Satellite television, like cable TV, VCRs, and even video or film recording for sale abroad, has consistently expanded the possible penetration of television created in one culture across borders into other cultures. By the 1970s, most countries imported most of their television fare from the United States (Nordenstreng & Varis, 1974; Varis, 1984), a trend that was intensified by the global spread of satellite and cable TV channels in the 1990s. This unequal exchange was termed *media imperialism* by Boyd-Barrett (1980), Lee (1980), and others. Subsequent studies saw changes, increasing national production and regional trade in programs and looked for other theoretical explanations (Rogers & Schement, 1984; Straubhaar, 1984, 1991; Tracey, 1988; Tunstall, 1977).

Critics perceived a massive potential effect of cross-border satellite-based television in the 1960s and 1970s, long before direct satellite broadcasting (DBS) or even satellite delivery to cable systems became technological realities (McPhail, 1989; Nordenstreng & Schiller, 1979) . Fears that cross-border television controlled by other countries would find and affect mass audiences was reflected in policy debates in the U.S. Commission on the Peaceful Uses of Outer Space in the 1960s (de Sola Pool, 1979) and in academic work by Mattelart and Schmucler (1985) and others in the 1970s and 1980s.

Because satellites can technologically cover a good part of the globe, many people expected them to produce a global village, of the sort anticipated by McLuhan and Powers (1989). It was supposed to be an American village, as proclaimed in Tunstall's (1977) book, *The Media are American* or Collins' (1986) anticipated "Wall-to-wall *Dallas*." But as subsequent work on *Dallas* (Ang, 1985; Liebes & Katz, 1990) demonstrated, different audiences could "read" or interpret *Dallas* in quite diverse ways, not reflecting the anticipated linear mass effects of cross-border TV. The next section discusses technical aspects facilitating these program flows.

Satellite and Television Program Flow

Satellites have impacted international television distribution in several stages. In 1975, Home Box Office (HBO) exemplified this stage of the process by achieving national impact by putting its channel on a satellite for distribution to cable systems all over the United States. The international impact of television satellites started then, too, as cable systems in Canada, Mexico, and the Caribbean also began to pull down HBO and other channels primarily intended for domestic U.S. distribution. The main international impact of satellites probably has been distribution of cable programs across borders. This cross-border distribution took place in North America, from Japan to Taiwan, and within Europe and from Europe to the Mediterranean region starting in the 1970s and early 1980s. Satellite signal spill-over was accentuated as people in a number of countries covered by the footprints of television and cable distribution acquired C-Band satellite dishes (1.5-2 meters across), which permit direct reception of satellite signals by individual homes. This type of direct-to-home (DTH) satellite service became the de facto DBS service until the 1990s, when true DBS service became technologically viable. The latter differs from C-Band in that it utilizes higher (K or Ku-band) frequencies and is designed expressly for transmission to home antennas (as opposed to "spill-over" intended for cable feeds).

Millions of DTH dishes sprouted across the globe to capture satellite spill-over channels from other countries. But there were only a few channels that were distributed globally (such as CNN, the U.S. Armed Forces Radio-Television Network, and USIA's WorldNet), and regular national broadcast channels that were distributed to affiliates by satellite, especially in large countries with vast rural areas unserved by television, like Brazil, India, Indonesia, and Mexico (Holaday, 1996). For example, India's first major experience of widespread national television distribution and reception was via large satellite dishes to community reception centers and schools in the Satellite Instructional Television Project in 1975-1976.

However, cable systems are probably the dominant means by which satellite-delivered channels are actually carried to the viewer in most countries of the world. Cable systems are cheaper in many countries, costing only a few dollars a month in some countries, like India, where systems are "informal" or illegal (Greenwald, 1993). Cable systems have been favored by governments as diverse as Canada, China, and France, because they offer greater national control for governments trying to mitigate the inflow of foreign culture or political information. Government policy can control hundreds or thousands of cable companies more easily than they can control millions of individual home or apartment block dishes. It is helpful, now, to explore the influence of this technology development on programming.

Satellite and Television Program Development

Just as some researchers tend to see economic relations as determinant of world cultural systems, including television, others sometimes slip into seeing technology as the prime determinant (de Sola Pool, 1983). Some, such as de Sola Pool, think technology will tend toward being localized and liberating. Other researchers, such as Mattelart and Schmucler (1985), tend to think that technology—such as VCRs or satellites—will expand the outflow and domination of U.S. television programming. We see both of these trends at work in a complex, contradictory or dialectic process. It seems as though technology, empirically, is both increasing the outflow of U.S. television programs and films on VCR, cable TV and DBS, and making local production cheaper and easier with lower cost television production, recording and transmission equipment, especially as television production is integrated with low-cost digital computer technologies.

Regional television markets, such as Latin America and Asia, became accessible thanks to the development of new satellite systems. Since the late 1980s, satellite communications in the region have been dramatically increased as an indirect result of the development of satellite systems in the United States, where nine domestic systems were in operation as early as 1981. The multiplication of the offer in the United States is estimated to have caused the rental costs of transponders to drop by half between 1975 and 1985 (Katz & Liebes, 1984). U.S. satellite operators were eager to continue to expand and explore less competitive markets, thus the U.S. government started to oppose the internationally controlled satellite system represented by Intelsat.

In 1986, the FCC authorized several satellite companies to launch separate systems bypassing Intelsat, and 2 years later the PanAmSat I was launched by the Alpha Lyracom group, with 18 of its 24 transponders focused on Latin America. A number of other private satellite ventures in various parts of the world have been launched subsequently. Various national government-owned systems, such as those in Brazil, Indonesia and Mexico have also been used for regional satellite television. It is useful, then, to explore the global dimensions of these new information flows.

MEDIA IMPERIALISM

Media imperialism described a situation of one-way, severely unequal relationships: Television programs flowed almost exclusively one way from the United States to other countries; models for how to create and operate television flowed out from the United States, the United Kingdom, France, and the Soviet Union to adopting countries; and investment and advertising from the same countries controlled the structure of broadcasting. This theoretical model was challenged by empirical work in the area of television flow. Research in Latin America (Antola & Rogers, 1984; Straubhaar, 1984) and Asia showed that many countries were producing much more, often a large majority, of their own programming. The Latin American research also showed the beginning, since the 1970s, of a regional market in some programs, such as *telenovelas* (serials), comedies, and variety shows. However, many still feared that the emergence of the satellite technologies for direct broadcasting would overwhelm those national and regional developments (Beng, 1994). The new reality of television flow might be better described as asymmetrical interdependence, where the United States is still the main exporter (and an absolutely minimal importer) but a number of other exporters are partially displacing the U.S. in global, cultural-linguistic regional, and national television markets and viewing habits (Straubhaar, 1991).

Satellite TV and the Flow of Genres and Media Models

One way that international satellite television can affect national television and the overall array of options for viewers is to place commercial pressure from international commercial channels on to national markets. If a strong international commercial channel suddenly comes into a primarily noncommercial national system, it tends to force the national channel into a more commercialized mode of operation, to shifting national programming away from news, public affairs and development toward entertainment. A current example of this is in India, where satellite-based competitors, like Zee TV, have created entertainment programs specifically targeted to the Indian culture. Under this competitive pressure, Indian national television (Doordarshan) had already begun to move away from the non-commercial development-oriented programming that characterized its origins under the SITE Project (i.e., the direct to home broadcast satellite project) in the 1970s (Mody & Shingi, 1976). Doordarshan moved toward a more commercial style, to gain revenue, and meet the demand by urban, middle-class audiences who are uninterested in development programming (McDowell, 1996; Rajagopal, 1993).

Program genre models, such as the soap opera, action series, or variety show, are frequently imported from other countries. But they are usually heavily adapted and changed, such as the Latin American *telenovelas* or the martial arts historical costume drama soaps that are produced by Hong Kong (Allen, 1995). Certainly, they have become more popular with domestic audiences.

In many ways, the international flows of genres and ideas may be more influential now than direct flows of programs, per se. Satellite television facilitates both. Programs do flow across borders now in even greater number via satellite channels like TNT, Cartoon Channel, MTV, and Discovery. Satellite television channels, along with international sales meetings like National Association of Programmers for Television (NAPTE), seem to be places where national programmers get ideas for copying or adapting international programs, even when they do not buy those programs for direct transmission to national audiences (interviews by author with Brazilian, Dominican, and Chilean program executives, 1989-1998). Maybe media imperialism is currently genre imperialism.

Global media models now are not so much imposed by colonial or near colonial relationships of imperialism, as by the demands of a globalizing economy in which global firms wish to run advertising everywhere around the world (Mattelart, 1991). "What globalization means in structural terms, then, is the *increase in the available modes of organization*: transnational, international, macro-regional, national, micro-regional, municipal, local" (Pieterse, 1995, p. 50). Tomlinson (1991) argued that much of what was labeled *cultural imperialism* is in fact a broader spread of a globalized pattern of modernity. This new discourse argues, in particular, that much of what was seen as Americanization or Westernization was a more general, deeper globalization of capitalism.

Media management models and program genres flow globally, through a series of adaptations. For example, one can trace the soap opera from the United States to its adaptation to Latin America by local professionals working for Colgate-Palmolive in Cuba in the 1950s (Straubhaar, 1984), to its spread and further adaptation throughout Latin America, to its use by the Mexican government in the 1970s-1980s to stress population planning themes, to the Indian government's decision to adapt that Mexican version of soap opera to India (Singhal & Rogers, 1989), to the subsequent (re)discovery that such development-oriented Indian soaps are still successful as advertising vehicles in India.

The local adaption of an increasingly global form of commercialized, entertainment television illustrates that "the concept of globalization has involved the simultaneity of what are conventionally called the global and the local" (Robertson, 1995, p. 30), who proposes that many cultural phonemona are now "global." In particular, we see a diffusion of some basic global or cultural forms related to the expansion of the world economy, but those globalized forms co-exist and even promote local adaptations and the expression of unique local content. In this mode, globalization is not equal to global homogenization. As the following section details, global diffusion of certain elements of consumer culture may well be more effective when those consumer elements are cast in local terms and adapted to local economic realities.

Satellite TV at Global, Regional and National Levels

The Latin American experience with the rapid regional spread of soap operas, transformed into *telenovelas,* opens the next layer of necessary theory: the development of cultural-linguistic regional media markets. There are now major spheres of television production and consumption at the global level, at the level of regions or cultural-linguistic markets, and the national level, where most television is still produced and consumed.

All three of these spheres or levels of television distribution, global, cultural-linguistic "regional," and national, are facilitated by satellites. The satellite can be used to cover the entire globe for CNN, using three or four satellites, or to cover Latin America or Asia. It can also be used to make sure that all Brazilians or Indonesians get a national television signal, either through DBS dishes or, more commonly, through receiving dishes hooked to local retransmitters or cable systems.

A major trend since the 1980s has been the "regionalization" of television into multicountry markets linked by geography, language, and culture. We argue that these might be more accurately called the cultural-linguistic markets, rather than regional markets, since not all these linked populations, markets, and cultures are geographically contiguous. There have been several notable attempts to use the regional-technical reach of satellites to create or address television audiences or markets defined by geographic region but spanning multiple cultures and languages.

For example, the European Economic Community (EEC) has made a pronounced effort to promote a Europewide television market, beginning with its report "Television without Frontiers: Green Paper on the Establishment of the Common Market for Broadcasting, Especially by Satellite and Cable" (Commission of the European Communities, 1984). Critics such as Schlesinger (1987) think that success for the EEC efforts is unlikely because what they are attempting to define as "European" is in fact an uneasy geographical alliance of several very distinct language and cultural groups, English-, German- and French-speaking groups, among others, which comprise both countries and subnational minority populations. Experiences to date with satellite-delivered cable TV or DBS programming in Europe indicates that there will be considerable resistance by non-native speakers of English to receiving satellite channels consisting largely of U.S. television (Tracey, 1988). For instance, one of the first "regional" satellite television channels, Sky Channel, which was programmed almost entirely in English, made very few in-roads in the European market, except in the smaller countries where cable systems were relatively hungry for new material (Straubhaar, 1988).

Another example comes from Star TV's initial attempt to cover the entire "region" of Asia, requiring two different satellite beams and footprints, with five channels, four of which were largely in English. That programming line failed to capture much of an audience, so the programming focus was later shifted to stress localization targeting specific cultural-linguistic markets (Man Chan, 1994).

Cultural-linguistic television markets are typically unified by language (even though different accents and dialects may divide countries somewhat). Beyond language, however, such markets are also defined by shared history, religion, ethnicity (in some cases), customs, and culture in addition to geographic location and climate. Geo-cultural markets are often centered in a geographic region, hence the tendency to call them regional markets, but they have also been spread globally by colonization, slavery, and migration. In Latin America and the Middle East, cultural linguistic markets are in fact centered on a geographic region, although immigrants and migrant workers have carried the Arabic market into Europe and the Latin American market into North America. In Asia, a satellite permits a television channel to address the audience of "Greater China" even though the audiences in question are spread across East Asia, South East Asia, and the considerable extent of China itself (Man Chan, 1996).

Pieterse (1995) observed that "Globalization can mean the reinforcement of both supranational and sub-national regionalism" (p. 50). Although one of the main arguments of this chapter is that the role of cultural-linguistic regions need to be emphasized more, that can be fit into the more sophisticated interpretations of globalization that are emerging, such as Pieterse (1995). The next section explores how satellites influence these expressions of culture.

Satellite Reach Versus Audience Preference: Toward Cultural Proximity

As television producers create television genres based on audience preferences, those preferences essentially reflect the audiences' interest in maintaining cultural proximity (Straubhaar, 1991). This represents a desire to see either national or similar, regional culture on television most of the time. Building on de Sola Pool (1979), this argument suggests that all other things being equal, audiences will tend to prefer programming that is closest or most proximate to their own culture: national programming if it can be supported by the local economy, regional programming in genres that small countries cannot afford to produce for themselves. The United States continues to have an advantage in genres that even large Third World countries cannot afford to produce, such as feature films, cartoons, and action-adventure series. Even in these genres, however, in Asia one must note the incredible productivity in feature films of India, in cartoons in Japan, and in action-adventures series and serials in Hong Kong.

We anticipate that when national production is available, audiences tend to prefer it (driving an increase in national production). This is reflected in an increase over time in the proportion of national productions appearing in prime time, reflecting audiences' primary preferences. Audience data, such as ratings, tend to support this idea in several Asian countries (see later). We might also anticipate a rise in regional production for cultural-linguistic markets, like the increase in television program production and export out of Hong Kong, India, and Japan. Work in Latin America and Asia seems to indicate that if audiences cannot find the genres they want to watch within national production, the desire for cultural proximity seems to lead them next to regional productions (Straubhaar, 1991). Other scholars in Latin America (Wilkinson, 1995) and Asia (Man Chan, 1994) are observing the tentative emergence of regional markets for television programming. Wilkinson (1995) moved, however, to look at these markets as based in language and culture, not the geography of a region. Next, we review how satellite technology has facilitated the rise of new geographical and cultural TV markets.

Satellite Technology and Global Access

Recent writing on the effects of technological changes in video media on media imperialism and the flow of media products has often assumed the worst, predicting that technology would simply reinforce the unequal flow between countries by adding a new set of channels that would favor U.S. exports over other television possibilities (Mattelart & Schmucler, 1985). In fact, VCRs, cable TV, and home satellite dishes do open new channels for the flow of U.S. feature films and, to lesser degree, U.S. television programs and music videos (Boyd, Straubhaar, & Lent, 1989).

The first major cross-border satellite-to-cable TV flows of programming tended to take U.S. cable channels into Canada and the Caribbean. However, although U.S. cable programming did have an extensive impact in English-speaking Canada (Raboy, 1990), the English-speaking Caribbean (Hoover & Britto, 1990) and Belize (Oliveira, 1986), it had less impact in the Spanish-speaking Caribbean, where it tended to be used only by English-speaking elites (Straubhaar, 1989, 1991).

CNN is now increasingly available on cable systems or other multichannel delivery systems in a number of major European, Asian, and Latin American cities. However, research in Santo Domingo and São Paulo indicates that actual viewing is limited to a small fraction of the elite, due to lack of general audience interest and the fluency in English which is required (Straubhaar, 1991; Straubhaar et al., 1992). The Korean version of Armed Forces Radio Television Service, Armed Forces Korea Network, which was until recently broadcast on VHF frequencies for the U.S. military, did acquire what one study called a substantial "shadow audience," particularly among English-speaking students (Choi, Straubhaar, & Tamborini, 1988). In general, audience reports for Star TV's initial offering of English-language channels indicated that audiences tended to be younger, upper middle or upper class TV ("BBC launches," 1991).

In practical terms, most people in most societies are shut away from access to satellite television by a lack of economic capital and/or cultural capital, two critical aspects of social class in terms of media access and behavior (Bourdieu, 1984). Economic capital or disposable income basically determines to what communications media a person can afford access. Cultural capital, such as education, family experiences, language ability, exposure to foreign cultures, and travel, is more related to what a person chooses to watch over the channels that they can afford. In most developing countries, direct satellite reception or cable television is a middle-class or even upper middle-class technology that excludes most of the population. Although monthly fees for cable television tend to be in the $20 to $30 range even in developing countries, the $100 to $200 median monthly incomes for much of the population in "middle-income" countries like Brazil (and less in many poorer countries in Asia, Latin America, and Africa) then limit access to cable or satellite television to less than 5% in these countries. By contrast, almost 75% of homes in wealthy middle class Taiwan have cable TV.

When economic class and capital do give access to new television technologies, privileged audiences receive a far more globalized form of media consumption. The initial offerings of most of the current transnational DBS channels and cable channels tended to emphasize the existing American, British, or Japanese satellite/cable channels, although that is beginning to change. One reason cable TV is so popular in Taiwan is that there are a large number of domestic channels as well as channels from Hong Kong, China and Japan within the cultural-linguistic region, as is seen later.

Once access to satellite TV is obtained, cultural capital becomes the more important factor. Interviews with satellite system programmers in Brazil and Taiwan show that they are aware of the need to increase the local content of satellite and cable systems in order to increase the appeal of these systems to mass audiences. That process is well underway in Taiwan, where more than a dozen "local" Taiwanese satellite-delivered cable TV channels were available as early as 1993, plus Chinese channels from elsewhere in the Greater China cultural-linguistic region. A similar localization or nationalization of satellite/cable channels is taking place in Argentina, South Korea, and a few other places, mostly countries with well-developed middle classes and broadcast television systems that had been held back from proliferating broadcast channel options due to government control.

SATELLITE NETWORKS AROUND THE WORLD

The fears expressed by nations in the UN debates about DBS were largely about potential government propaganda satellites that might follow in the tradition of government propaganda radio stations, like Voice of America (VOA), Radio Free Europe, Radio Moscow, Radio Havana, and the like. Ambitious global satellite network ventures were made by the U.S. government's U.S. Information Agency with its WorldNet and by the British BBC, a public institution supervised by government boards. WorldNet was ultimately cancelled in 1988 due to a lack of targeted audience reach.

The BBC's World Service Television had created agreements with Star TV in Asia and Orbit in the Middle East to carry the BBC television world service on those commercial satellite TV operations, but the BBC channel was jettisoned by both after receiving country governments, such as China and Saudi Arabia, that restricted direct satellite reception, objected to some contents of the BBC news (Boyd, 1998; Man Chan, 1994). The BBC Worldwide's Arabic-language television channel was closed in 1996-1997, however, the channel seemed to prosper in Europe and South Asia.

> The BBC's international 24-hour news and information channel, wholly owned by BBC Worldwide, is distributed to 52 million homes, up 25 per cent on a year ago, in 187 countries and territories around the world. The channel's largest audiences are in Europe, where it can be seen in more than 33 million homes and where the audience has increased by 50 per cent in the last year, and in South Asia, where it can be viewed in around ten million homes. (BBC, 1998)

Global Commercial Satellite Channels

There are a number of global American and European commercial satellite television channels entering most of the world's major regions. These are dominated by the channels of five major transnational media groups. Time Warner ($25 billion in 1997 sales) has HBO International (in more than 35 countries), CNN International (in more than 200 nations), TNT, the Cartoon Network and Time Warner Entertainment. Disney ($24 billion in 1997 sales) has the Disney Channel in English and several language versions, and ESPN International (in 21 languages in more than 165 countries). Bertelsmann ($15 billion in 1996 sales) has RTL and other European regional channels. Viacom ($13 billion in 1997 sales) has MTV available in several localized regional and language versions (in 250 million homes worldwide) and Nickelodeon in several languages in more than 90 million TV households (in 70 countries other than the United States). News Corporation ($10 billion in1996 sales) has dominant regional operations with Star TV and music Channel V in Asia, British Sky Broadcasting (BSkyB) in Europe, and Sky Latin America (in partnership with TCI, TV Globo, and Televisa; McChesney, 1997). Other global channels include Discovery, and Asia Business News (owned by Dow Jones, Tele-Communications Inc.).

To win audiences as a global network, CNN's Ted Turner declared a prohibition against the word "foreign" in newscasts, making it clear that, for international broadcasters, "cultural sensitivity" was the order of the day. Today, the newest plan of attack is toward regionalization, where language and cultural similarity or proximity are major selling points, targeting cultural-linguistic markets. For example, MTV Asia has begun partial programming in Hindi, trying to catch up with Channel V and new Hindi-oriented networks. ESPN's original highly globalized approach has also shifted, "Our plan is to think globally but to customize locally," stated the senior vice president of ESPN International. In Latin America the emphasis is on soccer, in Asia it is table tennis, and in India, ESPN provided more than 1,000 hours of cricket in 1995 (McChesney, 1997).

Asia's Regional Satellite Networks

For a number of years, no one spoke much of a regional television market in Asia. Countries in Asia did not import much from each other, tending to either produce their own material or to import it from the United States or Europe. The policy of importing little from other Asian countries was strongly reinforced by several national governments that actively discouraged importation within the region, fearing largely political effects. Despite the original national focus of most Asian television systems, the growth of television audiences there seemed to offer the potential for a regional market. Both locally based companies like TVB of Hong Kong and Rupert Murdoch's Star TV began to pursue the regional market.

But even as cultural-linguistic regional markets develop, national audiences seem to still to prefer first national productions, then regional productions in most genres, for reasons of cultural proximity (Straubhaar, 1991). At the regional level, we tend to see more export and import of television programs within the region where large, relatively affluent population groups share languages across national borders. Regional exports and imports also further displace U.S. imports in many genres. The following sections outline some of the more prominent cases where satellites can actually serve to further cultural heterogeneity in different parts of the world.

Language and Cultural Heterogeneity in Asia

As a region, Asia has some degree of cultural homogeneity, based on the historic diffusion of Indian religions (especially Buddhism) and Chinese culture through much of the region. Asia contains several very large language and cultural groupings, which form the basis for different major cultural-linguistic television markets, such as Mandarin Chinese, Cantonese Chinese, Hindi, and Malay. However, there are also a number of smaller populations that do not share languages and cultures across national boundaries to major degree. Hence, Asia contains a great deal of cultural, language, ethnic, and religious diversity and ideological, political, and economic heterogeneity.

Huntington (1993) discussed divisions between very broad civilizations, the broadest level at which people share values and traditions: Western, Confucian, Japanese, Islamic, Hindu, Slavic-Orthodox, Latin American, and "possibly" African. For example, he defined Western culture in terms of cultural history (its classical legacy from Greece and Rome), religion (Western Christianity), language (European languages), cultural and political traditions (separation of spiritual and temporal authority, rule of law, social pluralism and civil society, representative bodies), and values (individualism; Huntington, 1996).

It is possible to try to imagine that such civilizations with very broadly shared values might form a basis for exchanging culture, like television. Some early satellite TV projects, such as Star TV, seemed to think that the similarities were sufficient to create a market. However, both the Western European case (Schlesinger, 1987) and the Asian case discussed here seem to show that although some values may be shared at that level, tastes specific enough to guide television viewing preferences are not. In both cases, ambitious regional satellite television projects, Sky TV in Europe and Star TV in Asia, were unsuccessful in reaching truly regional audiences and have to focus on smaller linguistic and cultural markets.

Star TV nevertheless remains one of the most prominent regional satellite and cable television operations in the world. Its coverage footprint reaches from the Arab world to South Asia to East Asia. It has helped define a new type of cultural-linguistic television market situated between the global market, dominated by the United States, and national television markets. In both news and culture, Star TV is even more challenging to some governments than U.S.-imported programs and news have been.

In 1990, Hong Kong granted a license to Hutchison Whampoa to begin a DBS service via AsiaSat. The Satellite Television Asia Region operation (Star TV) began transmissions in 1991. By 1995, Rupert Murdoch's News Corp. became the sole owner of Star TV. Star TV represents a very direct challenge to several Asian governments that have tended to restrict the inflow of information. Burma, Singapore, Saudi Arabia, and Malaysia have made reception of Star TV essentially illegal. China requires a restrictive license for dishes, although many individuals and cable systems continue to receive it. India and Taiwan supposedly require licenses but permit both individuals and cable systems to receive it openly. Most other countries regulate redistribution via cable TV or apartment building antenna systems (SMATV) but are essentially open to Star and other satellite channels (Man Chan, 1994).

Although, in 1994, Star TV covered 52 countries—from Saudi Arabia to Japan—the bulk of the channel's initial viewers were in India (7.3 million) and China (30.5 million; Karp, 1994a). In 1998, Star TV reached 260 million viewers in more than 61 million homes (McDaniel, 1998). Star TV has since begun to "localize" target audiences more narrowly in terms of genres, language, and culture. For example, Star TV offers Indian-produced Hindi-language programs via Zee TV. Zee reaches an audience of more than 25% of the TV households in India and a significant viewership among Indian nationals residing in the United Arab Emirates, Oman, Kuwait, Saudi Arabia and Pakistan (no audience statistics available). Another example involves Star TV's creation of a more localized music channel, Channel V, "a tamer offshoot of the music network with more Chinese language videos than Western" (Foster, 1995, p. 9). Carrying localization further, Star TV has begun to target several versions of Channel V to different regions of Asia. In early 1999, Star TV had 24 channels targeting various genres, languages, and cultures, particularly in Hindi-speaking India and Mandarin Chinese-speaking areas.

Television Broadcasts Limited (TVB) has also become a major actor in several of the Asian markets. It offers a very different model than Star TV. It began by growing to become the market leader of commercial broadcasting in Hong Kong and later exporting programming widely around the region. Producing at a rate of 12 hours per day or 5,000 hours per year of original programs, TVB has the world's largest Chinese language television program library (To & Lau, 1995). In this, it is similar to national producers turned exporters in Brazil, Egypt, India, and Mexico.

Above all, TVB's strategy for overseas business has shifted to satellite television in order to widen the footprint of broadcasting and to generate profits from transborder advertising. First is a satellite channel (TVBS) broadcast to Taiwan in 1993 (To & Lau, 1995). Later, TVB created four additional channels covering entertainment, sports, and female-oriented genres.

These channels are downlinked by Taiwan cable operators authorized by TVB. With the cooperation of more than 300 cable operators, TVBS reached 2.6 million homes in 1995, amounting to 90% of the cable viewers and 52% of television audience in Taiwan (To & Lau, 1995). TVBS in Taiwan was the first satellite channel to have a local emphasis in terms of culture and language. A TVB production center was set up in Taipei to provide locally produced programs tailored to the taste of the Taiwanese audience.

Another target region of TVB's expansion is China. At present, comprehensive cable networks are operating in major cities of Guangdong Province, especially in the Pearl River Delta, to redistribute television signals for satellite reception. It is estimated that TVB's Hong Kong Chinese channel, Jade Channel, has attracted an audience of more than 5 million people in Mainland China in 1994. With this far more localized strategy, TVB is reaching more Chinese more openly than Star TV. As an Asian-operated outfit, TVB offers Beijing's wary government a viable alternative from the "cultural invasion" of Star's foreign broadcasts. However, despite (or perhaps because of) the appeal of cultural proximity, it is not clear that all Asian-produced programming will pass political muster in China. In fact, China's Communist Party is said to be highly critical of Hong Kong and Taiwanese entertainment, which it views as overly violent and sexually promiscuous (Karp, 1994b).

Latin America's Regional Satellite Networks

In the 1990s, after decades of state control, many Latin American countries are opening their economies to competition and foreign investment by privatizing some channels, easing restrictions on cable and satellite services, and increasing protection for intellectual property. The decline of inflation rates in countries like Mexico and Argentina, and the recent consolidation of MercoSul and NAFTA agreements have also accelerated investments in Latin America.

Televisa, which has about 90% of the share in the Mexican market, has been the main force behind the regionalization of television programming via satellite operations. Televisa was the main regional program exporter, even before the arrival of satellite technology. It moved quickly into satellite operations by acquiring 49% of the American satellite operator PanAmSat in 1993 (Varis, 1984). With the control of half of PanAmSat holding company, Televisa planned to secure long-term contracts to distribute its Galavision programming—which corresponds to its Channel 2 in Mexico—to Latin America and Europe. It would also speed up satellite newsgathering for Televisa's world news service Eco and provide for more options in pay-per-view and special events programming. Televisa has bought stakes in leading TV stations in Peru, Chile, and the United States (through Univision[1]) and has production agreements in Argentina and Venezuela, besides a joint-venture in regional satellite TV operation Sky Latin America with Televisa (30%), American cable giant TCI (10%), Murdoch's News Corp. (30%), and Brazil's TV Globo (30%) to develop cable, DBS and pay-TV throughout the region[2] (Nordenstreng & Varis, 1974).

Pressured by Televisa's expansion, its rivals—DirecTV/Galaxy Latin America (a joint venture of the largest U.S. satellite firm Hughes Communications), Cisneros Group (the largest multimedia group of Venezuela), Multivision of Mexico, and TV Abril of Brazil—have also moved to form their own alliances. The main other group, DIRECTV/GLA, is currently available in 20 Latin American countries and has developed a network of program and marketing partners in every country within its service area. It has more than 400,000 subscribers in 15 countries ("Hughes moves," 1998).

Thanks to all the strategic alliances created between local media conglomerates and U.S. programmers, viewers from Buenos Aires to Guadalajara can now tune to Spanish versions of many U.S. channels, such as The Discovery Channel, MTV Latino, CNN, TNT, Cartoon Network, CBS, NBC, Fox, ESPN, and QVC, besides other uniquely Latin channels, such as Teleuno, CineCanal, HBO-Ol_, Canal Sur, GEMS, and so on. Disney, for example, has created a weekend programming package to be sold by GLA as a pay-per-view service or monthly premium, capitalizing on its well-recognized brand name.

So far, the actual penetration and impact of international satellite television in Latin America is limited, except perhaps in Argentina, which has more than 50% cable penetration. Michael Kleinberg of Kagan World

---

[1]Despite protests from many Hispanic groups, the FCC approved in September 1992 the Hallmark Cards sale of Univision for $550 million to a group led by Hollywood producer Jerry Perenchio and two minority investors, Grupo Televisa and Venezuelan Venevision International.

[2]TCI currently holds interests and joint ventures in nine countries, including Israel, New Zealand, United Kingdom, France, and Scandinavia serving approximately 1 million subscribers abroad (Varis, 1984).

Media estimated in 1998 that 14% of the 80 million television households in Latin America had multichannel service, which included wireless (multipoint microwave distribution systems) as well as ground-based service, compared to 68% in the United States (García, 1996). A number of industry estimates expected this proportion to grow significantly, but surveys by the authors and others indicate that many people remain much more loyal to broadcast television channels in a number of Latin American countries than in the United States or some other major nations (e.g., Duarte, 1997).

SUMMARY AND CONCLUSIONS

This chapter argues that satellite television is part of a very complex globalization phenomenon. Satellites do help project television programs and channels far beyond the borders within which they were created, but it is reductionist and deterministic to assume that they will automatically find mass audiences for foreign materials. This study examines the evidence on the reach and programming directions of several satellite television channels. It finds not one phenomenon, but several. The most globalized satellite channels, those that adapt least to the countries and cultures in which they are received, have the smallest audiences. However, those audiences may be very important postcolonial elites who continued to use their knowledge of the "cosmopolitan" language and culture as a basis for maintaining political and economic power class distinctions (Parameswaran, 1995); they hence reflect a hybrid of local, traditional culture and of colonial influence (Bhahba, 1994).

In contrast, those channels, which gain the largest audiences, are characterized by cultural localization of content and production sources. That localization is not the same as nationalization. More massive satellite television audiences do sprawl negligently across national borders, but they are still closely defined by language and culture, following cultural-linguistic markets.

The eventual success of global channels, such as TNT or ESPN, seems to be the biggest question mark of all. These U.S. program sources seem to be struggling to figure how to localize their contents sufficiently to compete for audiences beyond narrow segments interested in American sports, documentaries, music, and so on, far from overwhelming local audiences in a new wave of media imperialism.

The major Asian producers and channel providers, Star TV and TVB, have both embarked on what they would describe as a program of localization, quite similar to the theoretical concept of cultural proximity. They seem to be trying to fit their programming or channels as precisely to their major intended markets as possible. The main Latin American region-wide operations, Sky Latin America and DirecTV/Galaxy Latin America, have also begun to also localize somewhat in channels focused on music, weather, news and variety, but still rely heavily on U.S. and European channels and programs that appeal strongly to a largely elite audience.

The eventual success of global channels, such as TNT or ESPN, seems to be the biggest question mark of all. Far from overwhelming local audiences in a new wave of media imperialism, they seem to be struggling to figure how to localize their contents sufficiently to compete for audiences beyond narrow segments interested in American sports, documentaries, music, and the like.

REFERENCES

Allen, R. C. (1995). Introduction. In R. C. Allen (Ed.), *To be continued— Soap operas around the world* (pp. 1-21). New York: Routledge.

Ang, I. (1985). *Watching Dallas: Soap opera and the melodramatic imagination.* New York: Methuen.

Antola, A., & Rogers, E. M. (1984). Television flows in Latin America. *Communication Research, 11*(2), 183-202.

BBC. (1998). *BBC Worldwide Annual Report 1997/98.* London: Author. Available online: http://www.bbcworldwide.com/report/channels/page01.html.

BBC launches Asian news channel. (1991, October 21). *Broadcasting,* p. 58.

Beng, Y. S. (1994). The emergence of an Asian-centered perspective: Singapore's media regionalization strategies. *Media Asia, 21*(2), 63-72.

Bhabha, H. (1994). *The location of culture.* New York: Routledge.

Bourdieu, P. (1984). *Distinction: A social critique of the judgement of taste.* Cambridge, MA: Harvard University Press.

Boyd-Barrett, O. (1980). *The international news agencies.* Beverly Hills, CA: Sage.

Boyd, D. A. (1998). *Broadcasting in the arab world: A survey of the electronic media in the Middle East* (2nd ed.). Ames: Iowa State University Press.

Boyd, D. A., Straubhaar, J. D., & Lent, J. (1989). *The videocassette recorder in the third world.* New York: Longman.

Choi, J., Straubhaar, J., & Tamborini, R. (1988). *American armed forces television in Korea and its shadow viewers: Who views what for what reasons with what impact?* Paper presented to the International Communication Association meeting, New Orleans, LA.

Collins, R. (1986, May-August). Wall-to-wall *Dallas?* The US-UK trade in television. *Screen*, pp. 66-77.

Commission of the European Communities. (1984). *Television without frontiers: Green paper on the establishment of the common market for broadcasting, especially by satellite and cable* (No. COM, 84, 300 final). Brussels: Author.

de Sola Pool, I. (1979). Direct broadcast satellites and the integrity of national cultures. In K. Nordenstreng & H. Schiller (Eds.), *National sovereignty and international communication*. Norwood, NJ: Ablex.

de Sola Pool, I. (1983). *Technologies of freedom*. Cambridge, MA: MIT Press.

Duarte, L. G. (1992). *Television segmentation: Will Brazil follow the American model?* Unpublished Master's thesis, Michigan State University, E. Lansing.

Foster, C. (1995, March 25). MTV's footprint around the globe. *Christian Science Monitor*, pp. 1, 8-9.

García, J. E. (1996, September 1996). Wiring Latin America: Media companies look south. *HISPANIC*. Available online: http://www.hisp.com/sep96/wiring.html.

Greenwald, J. (1993, May). Dish-weallahs. *Wired*, pp. 74-75, 107.

Holaday, D. A. (1996). The social impact of satellite TV in Indonesia: A view from the ground. *Media Asia, 23*(2), 100-106.

Hoover, S., & Britto, P. (1990). *Communication, culture and development in the Eastern Caribbean: Case studies in new technology and culture policy*. Paper presented at the International Communication Association meeting, Dublin.

Hughes moves to solidify DIRECTV services in Latin America and Japan. (1998). *Direct Broadcast—Uplink*, 3.

Huntington, S. (1993). The clash of civilizations. *Foreign Affairs, 72*(3), 22-29.

Huntington, S. (1996). The west unique: Not universal. *Foreign Affairs*.

Karp J. (1994a, January 27). Cast of thousands. *Far Eastern Economic Review*, pp. 46-48, 50, 52-53.

Karp J. (1994b, April 21). Do it our way. *Far Eastern Economic Review*, pp. 16, 73-90.

Katz, E., & Liebes, T. (1984). Once upon a time in *Dallas. Intermedia, 12*(3), 28-32.

Liebes, T., & Katz, E. (1990). *The export of meaning: Cross cultural readings of Dallas*. New York: Oxford University Press.

Man Chan, J. (1994). National responses and accessibility to STAR TV in Asia. *Journal of Communication, 44*(3), 112-131.

Man Chan, J. (1996). Television in greater China: Structure, exports and market formation. In J. Sinclair, E. Jacka, & S. Cunningham (Eds.),

Peripheral vision: New patterns in global television. New York: Oxford University Press.

Mattelart, A. (1991). *Advertising international: The privatization of publicspace.* New York: Routledge.

Mattelart, A., & Schmucler, H. (1985). *Communication and information technologies: Freedom of choice for Latin America?* (D. Bruxton, Trans.). Norwood, NJ: Ablex.

McChesney, R. (1997, November). The global media giants: The nine firms that dominate the world. *EXTRA!* Available online.

McDaniel, D. (1998). *Broadcast globalization in Southeast Asia.* Paper presented at the Broadcast Education Association meeting, Las Vegas, NV.

McDowell, S. (1996). *Globalization and policy choice: Broadcasting in India.* Unpublished paper, Michigan State University, E. Lansing.

McLuhan, M., & Powers, B. (1989). *The global village: Transformations in world life and media in the 21st century.* New York: Oxford University Press.

McPhail, T. (1989). *Electronic colonialism* (2nd ed.). Newbury Park, CA: Sage.

Mody, B., & Schingi, P. (1976). *Communications Research.*

Nordenstreng, K., & Schiller, H. (1979). *National sovereignty and international communication.* Norwood, NJ: Ablex.

Nordenstreng, K., & Varis, T. (1974). *Television traffic—A one-way street.* Paris: UNESCO.

Oliveira, O. S. (1986). Satellite TV and dependency: An empirical approach. *Gazette, 38,* 127-145.

Pan American digital. (1992, November 30). *Broadcasting,* p. 51.

Parameswaran, R. E. (1995). *Colonial interventions and the postcolonial situation in India: The English language, mass media, and the articulation of class.* Paper presented at the AEJMC Conference, Washington, DC.

Pieterse, J. N. (1995). Globalization as hybridization. In M. Featherstone, S. Lash, & R. Robertson (Eds.), *Global modernities* (pp. 45-68). Thousand Oaks, CA: Sage.

Raboy, M. (1990). *Missed opportunities—The story of Canada's broadcasting policy.* Montreal: McGill-Queen's University Press.

Rajagopal, A. (1993). The rise of national programming: The case of Indian television. *Media, Culture and Society, 15,* 91-111.

Robertson, R. (1995). Globalization: Time-space and homogeneity-heterogeneity. In M. Featherstone, S. Lash, & R. Robertson (Eds.), *Global modernities* (pp. 25-44). Thousand Oaks, CA: Sage.

Rogers, E., & Schement, J. (1984). Media flows in Latin America. *Communication Research, 11*(2), 305-319.

Schlesinger, P. (1987). On national identity: Some conceptions and misconceptions criticized. *Social Science Information, 26*(2), 219-264.

Singhal, A., & Rogers, E. M. (1989). *India's information revolution.* New Delhi & Newbury Park, CA: Sage.

Straubhaar, J. (1984). The decline of American influence on Brazilian television. *Communication Research, 11*(2), 221-240.

Straubhaar, J. D. (1988). A comparison of cable TV systems. In T. Baldwin & S. McAvoy (Eds.), *Cable communication.* Englewood Cliffs, NJ: Prentice-Hall.

Straubhaar, J. (1991). Beyond media imperialism: Assymetrical interdependence and cultural proximity. *Critical Studies in Mass Communication, 8,* 1-11.

Straubhaar, J., Campbell, C., Youn, S., Champagie, K., Ha, L., Shrikhande, S., & Elasmar, M. (1992). *Regional TV markets and TV program flows.* Paper presented at the International Association for Mass Communication Research meeting, Guaruja, Brazil.

To, T., & Lau, T. (1995). Global export of Hong Kong television: Television broadcasts limited. *Asian Journal of Communication, 5,* 108-121.

Tomlinson, J. (1991). *Cultural imperialism.* Baltimore, MD: Johns Hopkins University Press.

Tracey, M. (1988). Popular culture and the economics of global television. *InterMedia.*

Tunstall, J. (1977). *The media are Anglo-American.* New York: Columbia University Press.

Varis, T. (1984, Winter). The international flow of television. *Journal of Communication,* 143-152.

Wilkinson, K. (1995) *Where culture, language and communication converge: The Latin-American cultural linguistic market.* Unpublished doctoral dissertation, University of Texas-Austin.

13

The Videocassette Recorder in the Home Media Environment

Alan M. Rubin
Kent State University

Keren Eyal
University of California, Santa Barbara

The videocassette recorder (VCR) is a communication technology that has greatly affected the home media environment. The VCR "makes the initially unretrievable and inevitably lost content . . . recordable, replayable, and archivable" (Comstock, 1991, p. 2). Since 1975, when it was first introduced as a home technology, the VCR has become widespread in U.S. households. Only 1.1% of U.S. households owned a VCR in 1980, yet by 1997, 85% of U.S. households owned at least one (A. C. Nielsen Company, 1997; U.S. Bureau of the Census, 1997). Several factors contributed to the growth of VCRs in the home. These include price decreases for equipment and tapes, improved sound and video quality, longer recording capabilities, standardized video formats, increased advertising and promotions, established legality of home recording, and availability of prerecorded software (Klopfenstein, 1989).

　　As the diffusion of VCRs to the home environment in the United States and around the world spread, researchers became intrigued by the place of this communication technology in the lives of individuals and families. VCRs have altered the home media environment by expanding people's flexibility and range of programming options. The availability of VCR and digital video (DVD) technologies has contributed to flexible and altered patterns of media use in the home, and has affected media regulatory policy and the economics of media industries. For example, the interaction of VCR and cable television penetration has had "a strong negative relationship with network [television] audience shares and revenues" in the United States (Krugman & Rust, 1993, pp. 72-73). We focus in this review on the body of audience research seeking to understand the role of VCRs as an innovation and as a communication medium in the home.

The VCR is a technology that encourages substantial choice in media consumption and greater power and control over what consumers choose to watch. It encourages active participation, choice behavior, and involvement. Research questions have focused on who uses the VCR and how they use it. Consequently, theoretical perspectives such as uses and gratifications have often been employed to study the VCR. Uses and gratifications emphasizes audience initiative and choice in examining how and why people communicate in various contexts (see Charney & Greenberg, chap. 15, this volume). It sees communication as motivated behavior, media as sources of influence among other communication sources, and "audiences as variably active communicators" (Rubin, 1994, p. 418). In addition, individual predispositions, interpersonal and family interaction, and context or environment mold expectations about the uses and effects of communication media.

As a newer technology in an individual's and a family's media surroundings, VCR use affects and is affected by individual needs and by patterns of traditional media use. Researchers, for example, have examined how this technology might intensify and diversify mainstream video exposure. VCR use can encourage cognitive and affective intensity (Levy, 1989). It also affects and is affected by existing family behaviors and attitudes. Thus, researchers have examined the role of the VCR in the family, exploring notions such as interaction and control in the family setting. In addition, investigators have addressed the diffusion of this innovation, and research conducted in different countries has examined the effects of culture and societal conditions on adaptation to the VCR. In this chapter, we explore VCR's diffusion in the home media environment, focusing on: (a) VCR uses in the home, including the motives for and effects of using the VCR; (b) the VCR's influence on families, including adolescents and children, parental mediation, and gender differences; and (c) international perspectives on VCR use.

USES OF THE VCR IN THE HOME

In this section, we examine how people use the VCR in their homes. This has been the primary emphasis of research about this media innovation. We focus on user motives for adopting the VCR and the effects on users.

Reasons for Using VCRs

Researchers who have examined VCR adoption have considered people's motives for using the technology, such as seeking to control or to alter the time and context of viewing, and building a collection of programs or tapes to watch. Consistent with the idea of more active and selective choice among communicators, Comstock (1991) suggested that the VCR liberates "broadcast and cable television from the boundaries of time," opens "the home to theater movies," and allows "households to create unique schedules" (p. 41).

In the introductory chapter to *The VCR Age,* Levy (1989) declared that VCRs are unlike pop-up toasters in the home and are a worthy technology to study. VCRs "make for an unexplored new set of problems and issues and a new challenge for communication scholars" (p. 17). Some of those challenges have included identifying the use, role, and place of VCRs in the home, family, and society. For example, VCR use both complements traditional television viewing via time shifting and provides new forms of viewing via prerecorded rentals and the like (Krugman & Rust, 1993).

VCR use reflects active audience involvement in the communication process. Using the VCR to watch rented movies, for example, has been found to be a more active experience than television watching; viewers prepare and structure their environments and pay more attention when watching the VCR movie (Krugman & Johnson, 1991). Building from such a paradigm of the active audience, Lin (1990) found that most among her sample of 233 midwestern U.S. VCR owners were selective in their viewing decisions, active in channel switching, and involved in program discussions.

Much VCR research has been descriptive of reasons for owning and using VCRs in the home. Harvey and Rothe (1985/1986), for example, identified several reasons why people purchased VCRs. These reasons included recording shows to watch at another time, recording a show when watching another, watching prerecorded rental tapes, and attending the theater less. Focusing on the influences on time and displacing other social activities, they also identified several effects of using VCRs at home. Owning a VCR at home led people to change their regular hours of watching television, to increase the time they spent watching television, and to increase the time they spent with their families and friends when watching television. In addition, Henke and Donohue (1989) concluded that VCR acquisition displaced other media forms. The convenience of taping favorite programs accompanied greater use of the VCR and reduced movie-going outside the home. Clearly, the availability and use of the VCR in the home have led to changes in the amount and type of media behavior and in patterns of interpersonal interaction.

Ram and Jung (1990) identified time shifting and movie rental as the two primary uses of VCRs among a U.S. sample (mean age = 31.1 years). According to Klopfenstein (1989), early VCR adopters used VCRs to shift program viewing to more convenient times. As prerecorded tapes became more readily available, later adopters used VCRs to play prerecorded tapes. Such distinct and goal-directed uses of the VCR were supported by Potter, Forrest, Sapolsky, and Ware (1988), who segmented 415 VCR owners into five groups based on their attitudes and behaviors about VCRs and television viewing. *Time-shifters,* for example, wanted to record televised programs to play at another time. They valued personal freedom and being in control. They planned their viewing schedules and zipped past commercials when watching. In contrast, *source-shifters* sought to use the VCR to play prerecorded tapes. They watched low levels of television, but spent substantial time watching tapes.

Levy (1987a) analyzed 247 home video diaries and observed that time-shifting (i.e., recording a show to view at a later time) was the dominant use of the VCR in U.S. homes. He found that, "what VCR households do is rearrange the broadcast schedule, making viewing more convenient or eliminating programming conflicts" (p. 405). Levy noted that people also used VCRs to record entertainment specials, mini-series, and sports programs, but did not treat all recorded materials in the same fashion. They tended to view the taped news, public affairs shows, and soap operas on the day of the recording. However, they tended to play back entertainment shows and children's programs on Sundays, especially during morning and afternoon hours. Thus, despite the use of this technology, VCRs did not seem to alter defining features of media programs such as the currency of local news, the continuing appeal of daytime dramas, and family viewing of entertainment programs.

Other researchers found that the VCR enabled people to control the viewing environment or messages by *zipping* or *zapping* unwanted content. Harvey and Rothe (1985/1986) sent questionnaires to 745 VCR owners and found that the VCR allowed people to shift time. VCRs also enabled people to (a) exercise greater choice about what and when to view, (b) establish a controlled environment for children's viewing, and (c) zip (i.e., rapidly move past content when viewing) and zap (i.e., delete content from the tape when recording) commercial messages.

Sapolsky and Forrest (1989) observed undergraduate students and adult VCR owners viewing television content and zipping through commercials. They noted that adults zipped to a greater extent than did students, and tended to engage in more zipping as the show progressed. Sapolsky and Forrest suggested that people zipped through commercials regardless of their attitudes toward those commercials. They explained that this resulted from "the viewer's escalating involvement in the story-line and the desire to avoid the distraction and delay brought on by commercial breaks" (p. 163). They concluded that people zip because they find it to be rewarding and convenient.

Olney, Batra, and Holbrook (1990), on the other hand, observed attitudinal differences toward advertisements in relation to zipping and zapping behavior. They reported a sizable correlation ($r = .75$) between zipping and zapping behavior, and combined the two behaviors into a single index of "looking time." They found that commercials judged to be interesting and hedonistic (i.e., enjoyable and fun to watch) garnered longer looking time than ads judged to be utilitarian (i.e., information and useful). The VCR has encouraged program producers to make their messages unique and interesting so that audiences using the VCR technology might pay attention to them.

In a somewhat different venture, Lee and Katz (1993) examined reactions to commercials included on videocassettes such as rental films. They found negative attitudes toward such ads. VCR owners tended to find such advertising intrusive and offensive. They tried to avoid the commercials by zipping past them when playing the videotapes.

Other researchers have identified another reason why people use VCRs in their homes: to build home libraries of recorded movies, shows, and videos. As Lull (1988) wrote, "the VCR permits ownership of programs in the form of videotapes. These tapes can be displayed in the house like books or magazines to project an image of the owner to family members and others" (p. 256). Some people used a video camera or camcorder to record different family events, such as birthday parties, weddings, and vacations, for these collections. Others recorded events such as sports teams' workouts and medical operations, which were later subjected to the participants' critiques of surgical techniques (Lindlof & Shatzer, 1990).

Based on the uses and gratifications perspective, Rubin and Bantz (1987, 1989) administered 424 questionnaires to 13- to 62-year-olds. Participants were asked to identify their perceived importance of different uses of the VCR. Consistent with uses and gratifications, Rubin and Bantz found that people used VCRs to gratify felt needs or desires, and that the VCR enabled people to be more active and to take control over their viewing patterns. People were motivated and intentional in their behavior and in their choice of what to view and when. The results supported the findings of others in that people used VCRs primarily for movie rentals, time shifting, library storage, and socializing with others. Somewhat less salient reasons included watching music videos, viewing critically, watching exercise tapes, and enabling children to view selected tapes. Consistent with the need to examine relationships among personal and mediated communication (see Rubin & Rubin, 1985), Rubin and Bantz suggested that VCR viewing connects mass and interpersonal communication, as people watch together and interact about the content.

Rubin and Rubin's (1989) study of 299 18- to 75-year-old VCR users provided further support for the interpersonal orientation of home video, and suggested that the VCR is a technology of mediated interpersonal communication. They proposed a model of VCR use suggesting that locus of control predispositions, life-position elements such as mobility, interaction, and life satisfaction, and motives to communicate interpersonally influenced why people used the VCR. They found that "social affiliation seems to be a salient interpersonal need whose gratification may be facilitated by using the VCR" (p. 107). Those who tended to use the VCR for social purposes exhibited greater desires for social interaction, reduced mobility, and more salient needs to communicate with others for purposes of seeking inclusion and affection and overcoming boredom. In addition, those who communicated interpersonally to control others tended to use the VCR to control their environment by time-shifting and storing tapes. Rubin and Rubin concluded that the VCR can be used to complement interpersonal communication.

Critical viewing is another use of the VCR (Rubin & Bantz, 1987). Related to critical viewing is the idea of using the VCR to review shows already seen in the past. Dobrow (1990) conducted 193 interviews to identify the characteristics of VCR use for repeat viewing. She found that the reviewing function gave people a sense of control over their viewing environment. People mostly repeat-viewed movies, followed by sports, games, news, situation comedies, and soap operas. They also repeat-viewed home videos (e.g., recordings of family events). Among the reasons for repeat-viewing were to notice additional details, to concentrate on film techniques, to learn English, to relax, to critique their own technique or performance (e.g., reviewing a surgical technique or a dance or acting performance), to develop a sense of relationship with the characters, to anticipate punch lines, and to sing along with the characters when songs are recognized. People also used the VCR to review taped shows and events with friends, to introduce others to important events, and to initiate outsiders into the family. The reviewing function of the VCR was an economical way of being entertained.

In a different study, Dobrow (1989) considered how one immigrant group used VCRs by conducting interviews with 62 U.S. immigrants or children of immigrants. Dobrow found that immigrants used home videos to watch content other than mainstream U.S. shows and movies, and to view non-American content. Immigrants used VCRs as an opportunity to interact socially and to form identity and solidarity. Dobrow concluded that "VCRs give ethnic group members the ability to experience their differences from the mainstream in a private setting" (p. 204). She suggested that viewing ethnic videocassettes might supplement or replace more public means of ethnic affiliation.

Effects of VCR Use

Besides displacing social and communication activities, increasing the amount of media exposure, exercising greater control, and altering social interaction patterns, surprisingly few VCR studies have addressed more traditional questions of media effects. The ones that have addressed audience effects have sought to identify cultivation effects. Morgan and Shanahan (1991), for example, conducted a longitudinal survey of 206 children and adolescents to explore the links among television viewing, VCR use, and cultivation. They suggested that: (a) "the VCR and other new technologies are arguably more likely to be used to consume 'more of the same,'" (b) "the VCR is essentially an expanded delivery system for preexisting types of messages," and (c) "the VCR may be more likely to actually extend and augment cultivation than to fragment the mainstream" (p. 126).

Morgan and Shanahan (1991) found a substantial increase in VCR ownership from Wave 1 (30% in 1985) to Wave 2 (nearly 90% in 1988). In addition, the students in their samples used VCRs mostly to watch rented movies and to time-shift. Overall, however, VCR use was mostly unrelated to mean world measures of mistrust and violence; correlations between VCR use and sexist attitudes were insignificant or very slight. The same patterns held when viewers were divided into light, medium, and heavy television viewers. Despite these patterns, the authors argued that using the VCR can potentially cultivate television images among heavy television viewers. In another analysis of these data, Morgan, Alexander, Shanahan, and Harris (1990) concluded that VCRs strengthen, rather than mitigate, television effects, and "cultivate 'television-type' conceptions mainly among those who are heavy television viewers" (p. 120).

Similarly, Perse, Ferguson, and McLeod (1994) reasoned that VCR use can shift social reality perceptions from the television mainstream. They expected negative links between VCR ownership and both fear and interpersonal mistrust; these relationships may differ based on different VCR uses such as time-shifting and video rental. Among their two random samples of 152 persons from a mid-Atlantic state and 615 persons in one Midwest U.S. town, about 80% owned or had access to a VCR. Given that only one slight negative relationship between VCR ownership and fear of

crime (in the second sample) was found, it would appear that VCR ownership was linked to less fear and VCR uses were irrelevant to either fear or
mistrust. Consistent with Levy (1987b), who noted that "VCR users
actively discount the reality of the videos they see" (p. 274), Perse et al.
found no support for a cultivation effect from using a VCR.

   In summary, the VCR is a tool that enables people to have more
control over their viewing environment. As outlined in Table 13.1, people
make active choices with regard to VCR content and use. The VCR is
used to diversify viewing content (as with immigrants' uses of the technology) and to intensify existing viewing patterns (as a result of time-shifting,
library building, and reviewing). Using VCRs may have long-term effects
on people's viewing habits and other media and social behavior. These
influences, however, seem to focus on rearranging or altering time, social
activities, and interpersonal interaction, rather than cultivating attitudes.

THE VCR AND THE FAMILY

A second research direction has focused on the role of the VCR in the family context, especially in the United States. In this section, we address this
dynamic in the context of adolescent and children's VCR uses, parental
mediation, and gender differences in VCR use. Researchers have sought to
identify responses of individuals and the family—as a unit—to home video,
and the patterns of family viewing. Lull (1988) suggested that this research
direction is important because "audience members are family members,
too, and their identities, interests, and roles are articulated, acted upon,
and played out in routine activity at home" (p. 237). Lin (1992) suggested
that users interact and negotiate VCR use with relatives and friends to min-
imize conflicts. Thus, using VCRs in the home may reflect, affect, and be
affected by familial and television-viewing behaviors.

Table 13.1. Summary of VCR Use Motives and Effects.

Motives for Using VCRs	Effects of Using VCRs
Time-shifting	Change TV viewing habits
Record one program when watching another	Increase viewing time
Attend the theater less	Increase time spent with family
Increase control over viewing time or fare	Increase parental mediation
View nonmainstream fare	Increase viewing of R-rated movies
Avoid TV commercials	Decrease off-air viewership
Mediated interpersonal communication	Enable video parties
Library building	Extend mainstream messages
Repeat or critical viewing of special tapes	Slightly enhanced cultivation effects

Adolescents and Children

Morgan, Alexander, Shanahan, and Harris (1990) conducted a survey of 910 students in Grades 7 to 12. Participants were asked about VCR and television use in their households and about relationships among family members. They conducted a second survey 3 years later, asking 642 students in Grades 9 to 12 about their family communication patterns, parental media orientations, and VCR use. When compared with television watching, Morgan et al. found that VCRs were used more for family viewing, and that VCR viewing was more of a social experience for adolescents. They also observed that the VCR strengthened, rather than changed, existing television and family patterns.

This latter finding provided support for Greenberg and Lin (1989), who administered questionnaires to students in Grades 7 to 10. Greenberg and Lin reported that having more technologies in the adolescents' homes did not necessarily mean that the adolescents spent more time with all the technologies. Rather, time previously devoted to television viewing was shared with the VCR. Adolescents with VCRs in their homes also preferred to view more sexual, R-rated, or X-rated material. Earlier, Greenberg and Heeter (1987) found that, among the 9th and 10th grade students in their sample, those with VCRs had different media experiences, namely watching more television, reading more, and enjoying greater access to cable television and computers.

Lindlof, Shatzer, and Wilkinson (1988) sought to understand children's relation to the technology. They found that children as young as age 3 understood that the VCR is a machine that enables one to view programs by pushing buttons on the VCR or the remote control. This suggests that even young members of the family can purposively and actively use the VCR. As Lull (1988) explained, "children's natural curiosity and their desire to take advantage of these machines stimulate their learning how to operate them" (pp. 255-256).

Parental Mediation

To define the uses that different families make of the VCR, Lindlof and Shatzer (1989) analyzed the viewing patterns of 14 families in one U.S. state. They identified VCR uses for different types of families: (a) families that used the VCR for time-shifting and for convenience tended to watch recordings only once, and usually did not build libraries of tapes or engage in other activities when viewing; (b) families of price-conscious consumers viewed their tapes in privacy, tended to watch favorite tapes more than once, and usually viewed tapes with their children; and (c) families of enthusiastic renters of VCR tapes tended to zip through commercials; parents in these families rarely previewed children's tapes before viewing. Although the VCR enabled all types of families to exercise greater control over television viewing, researchers found that adolescents, children, and women in different types of families relate to and use the VCR differently.

Other researchers looked at parent-child relationships surrounding the technology. Krendel, Clark, Dawson, and Troiauo (1993), for example, sought to identify characteristics of children's VCR access and how parents supported or instructed about children's viewing. They conducted individual interviews with 4- to 6-year-old children, observed the children in a naturalistic setting, and conducted in-depth interviews with the children and their parents. Krendel et al. found that children were mostly permitted to play tapes by themselves and that limited parental support severely limited their competence in using the VCR.

Based on interviews with 124 parents who had at least one child under age 12 living in the home, Heintz (1990) reported that children had their own libraries of recorded shows and movies. Parents of older children and boys said they owned significantly more tapes for their children than did parents of younger children and girls. Participants reported that older children usually owned family- or adult-oriented tapes, whereas younger children owned tapes labeled as children's (e.g., Disney and toy-related) tapes. Younger children spent more time than older children watching videos. Parents reported that they tended to tape shows especially for their children and to use the VCR to complement rather than to replace television.

Research examining children and the VCR has shown that parents feel that the VCR enables them to have more control over their children's television viewing. Parental mediation should play an important role in the viewing process. Jordan (1990), for example, conducted an ethnographic observation of 21 families in a northeastern U.S. city. She noted that the families used VCRs to control media time in four ways: "(a) to *shift* when a program is viewed, (b) to *adapt* how much and what portions of a tape are watched, (c) to *structure* time for the family (particularly, bedtime), and (d) to *fill* time that seems to be empty" (p. 170). Jordan suggested that parental control of the VCR was consistent with the overall manner of children's time, rules, and media use in the home.

Two other studies suggest that such mediation is selective on the part of the parent. Kim, Baran, and Massey (1988) found that, among 110 sets of children and parents, parents felt that they controlled their children's viewing even though they infrequently previewed tapes the children watched. Lin and Atkin (1989) also examined parental mediation or control of adolescents' television and VCR use. They administered questionnaires to 7th and 10th graders and found that parents exercised more mediation of younger adolescents and were more likely to set rules about VCR use for male than female adolescents. Parents, then, exercised selective mediation of children's and adolescents' viewing.

Gender Differences

As previously noted, parental attitudes about mediation of VCR use differ toward boys and girls. Moreover, in two relatively early studies, researchers observed gender differences in the family for using VCRs. Morley (1986) described a pilot project in which he conducted in-depth interviews with 18 VCR families about their viewing activities. He found that, most of the time, women in these families relied on their husbands or children to operate the machine. Lindlof et al. (1988) also found that most of the female family members in their study showed little interest in operating the VCR. The women's main pattern of VCR use was to organize social events surrounding VCR viewing.

Gray (1992) also found gender differences with regard to viewing videotapes. He interviewed 30 women and found that they were distracted viewers of rented movies. They reported usually being engaged in other activities such as household chores when watching tapes. Gray concluded that there is "evidence in the accounts of unwillingness on the part of the women to impose their choice on the rest of the household" (pp. 236-237). Lindlof et al. (1988), however, offered alternate explanations for male-female VCR differences. These included the possibility that differences result from spousal agreements within the household as to role-appropriate tasks. VCR use, then, would reflect the existing patterns of behavior within the family. Fig. 13.1 overviews some sociodemographic factors that influence VCR use and mediation factors in the family context.

Sociodemographics	=>	Mediation of VCR use	=>	VCR Uses
.Child's Age, Gender	=>	Guidance in VCR use		.Library of Child Tapes
				.Library of Adult Tapes
.Parent's Gender			=>	VCR Operation, Tape Selection and Use

Figure 13.1. VCR use in the family context

Overall, these studies suggest that families differ in the ways in which they relate to the VCR. The VCR is commonly used by young children and adolescents. Similar to adults, young audiences are capable of making active choices about the content and context of viewing. In addition, VCR use tends to reinforce existing patterns of family viewing. Parents tend to report that they appreciate the VCR for the control it offers them over their children's viewing, but findings suggest that such parental control is infrequent and selective. Research also suggests differences between the genders about this home video technology, although researchers differ in how they explain these differences.

INTERNATIONAL PERSPECTIVES ON VCR USE

Although there are common patterns across diverse cultures, researchers have observed some differences in adoption patterns and effects of the home VCR technology on existing viewing orientations in such countries as Israel, Germany, Sweden, the former Soviet Union, Hong Kong, and Saudi Arabia. Governments can often exercise control of the media system, either through ownership, regulation, or censorship, depending on the degree of democratization. As compared with the United States, many of these countries vary little in terms of program diversity and channel choice.

For example, the authors of an Israeli study suggested that the VCR is not a distinct communication medium for children and adolescents. Cohen, Levy, and Golden (1988) questioned 576 Israeli children (Grades 4-10). They found that, although the VCR was often used, it had not achieved a distinct position or a separate identity from other media in terms of its perceived ability to gratify people's needs. In their analysis, the VCR seemed to be "inextricably 'blended' with cinema and records and tapes and close to television" (p. 778). The VCR did not seem to be a separate communication medium.

Most international researchers have focused on identifying factors that affect the diffusion and adoption of VCRs. Several factors are common in the adoption process. At a time when VCR penetration ranged from less than 1% in Africa to 40% in the United Kingdom to 90% in Kuwait, Straubhaar and Lin (1989) considered the reasons for worldwide VCR penetration. They identified three groups of factors having an impact: (a) income- and price-related factors (e.g., per capita Gross National Product, income distribution, VCR prices, proportion of the population living in urban areas); (b) media-related factors such as media availability (e.g., telephone receiver, television set, and radio set penetration); and (c) television-content diversity.

In addition, Straubhaar (1990) examined the international context of VCR adoption and argued several points. First, social class, ethnicity, and cultural interests affect VCR access. Second, VCR use expresses class needs. Third, the "abilities of different classes to use VCRs to meet their needs will be powerfully affected by income level and distribution" (p. 141).

When considering the adoption and use of VCRs in Third World countries, Straubhaar and Boyd (1989) provided two levels of explanation of VCR diffusion in the Third World. First, policies of broadcast media and government tariffs both encourage and restrict the types of content made available. Second, "the aggregated interests of individuals" control and diversify available media content (p. 163). Audiences seek to add content diversity to their entertainment television viewing, to circumvent government controls on media content, and to exercise personal control over entertainment and information viewing. For example, Boyd and Straubhaar (1985) explained how people seek to circumvent government restrictions and to diversify their available content: "Airport passengers, who are usually not body-searched, need only place in a coat pocket a small Beta or VHS tape. This is how *Death of a Princess,* after first being shown on British television, was made available 24 hours later in Saudi Arabia" (p. 15).

Schoenbach and Hackforth (1987), who sought to consider attitudinal and behavioral differences among VCR owners and nonowners in West German samples interviewed in late 1983, supported this conclusion. Schoenbach and Hackforth found that, as opposed to nonowners, owners felt that VCRs belonged to a modern lifestyle, VCRs enabled watching movies not permitted on television, and the purpose of television viewing was for entertainment. Owners also frequented movie theaters to watch Italian westerns, science fiction films, and detective stories, and listened to records, tapes, or cassettes at home. This suggests that early VCR owners in Germany were fairly steady consumers of entertainment media, in general.

Roe (1987, 1989) reported on VCR use in Sweden. At the time, Swedish television consisted of only two channels, and cable television, which was introduced in 1983, reached only a small minority of households. Despite this, Johnson-Smaragdi (1989) found that the VCR was the most widely disseminated of the new media in Sweden. Access, however, was not evenly distributed. Access was greater for "male urban dwellers who are younger, well educated, and have higher incomes" (p. 113). However, being a "peer medium," the VCR was accessible to those other than owners, especially to children and adolescents. Except for adolescents, it was also more likely for the VCR to be used for time-shifting than for playing rented tapes. Men rented considerably more tapes than did women. In general, however, "the longer a household had a VCR, the less likely it is to rent such cassettes and the greater is the proportion of recorded TV programs viewed" (p. 118).

At a time when VCR penetration was 41% among Swedish households, Roe (1989) administered questionnaires to 1,334 students in Grade 9 in Sweden. He asked them about their school commitment, self-esteem, and VCR use. He suggested that VCR use was considered a threat to children and adolescents in Sweden because it was thought to promote aggressiveness and violent behavior. Regardless, VCR use was widespread among Swedish, just as it was among U.S. adolescents. Roe noted that "only 15% never use a VCR" (p. 169). Adolescents used VCRs to reinforce peer-group autonomy, to bypass cinema censorship, and to break free from parental authority.

Roe (1989) also found that school achievement predicted the Swedish adolescents' VCR use. Lower achievers, who were more socially active and less satisfied with their lives, had greater access to the VCR and used it more often than higher achievers. Lower achievers used the VCR to watch forbidden tapes and to express their own identities. Male adolescents used VCRs more often (mostly to watch prerecorded tapes) and achieved lower grades, as compared with female adolescents. Students who were more active with their peer group tended to use the VCR more than those less interpersonally involved with their peers.

Besides research in the United States and western Europe, research conducted in other countries suggests that people make different uses of the VCR in the home environment. Boyd (1989) examined VCRs in the Soviet Union and Soviet-Bloc countries. He recognized that some motives for purchasing a VCR in these countries differed from those reported by VCR owners in the United States. Among the reasons that people reported for purchasing VCRs were financial gain (i.e., conducting viewings of tapes and asking people for money for participating), learning about the West, and fostering a change in the country. Similar to the United States, Boyd found that owning a VCR increased the time people spent with their immediate families and close friends when watching television.

In contrast to this finding, McIntyre (1995) found that larger Hong Kong VCR households tended to rent fewer tapes and to view less often with friends. McIntyre suggested that the reason for this is that viewing a rented tape had higher status than watching a broadcast program or a prerecorded tape. As a result, watching a rented tape would offend the visitors in the house because "to view would call undue attention to the act itself" (p. 68). However, similar to findings in the United States, McIntyre found that VCR ownership complemented existing media use patterns. That is, people who spent more money on theater visits also reported spending more money on movie rentals. Moreover, total television viewing time increased in homes with VCRs.

Boyd (1987) reported that in the Arabian Gulf States (i.e., Kuwait, Saudi Arabia, Bahrain, Qatar, the United Arab Emirates, and Oman), the VCR became popular for two reasons. First, people were dissatisfied with what they had to watch on television. Second, VCR watching was an ideal means of getting the family together. Boyd characterized rural Saudi Arabian villages, for example, as being conservative, having few sources of entertainment open to women, not permitting cinemas and theaters, and having only two channels of government television available. Thus, the introduction of the VCR opened the country to the outside world, increased exposure to foreign cultures, and introduced Western values.

Subsequent research conducted in Saudi Arabia revealed that home video use was most common among women and the young. Al-Oofy and McDaniel (1992) interviewed 100 secondary school students. They found that, whereas male teenagers preferred U.S. videos, female teenagers preferred movies from India and Egypt to those from Western countries. Because females voiced more concern than males about the threat the VCR poses to Saudi culture, the researchers concluded that it is unlikely that the video will reduce the gap between men and women in that society as a result of the exposure to Western values. Al-Oofy and McDaniel also noted that females preferred romance videos. They suggested that "girls may use videos to vicariously act out relationships they are not permitted in real life, in fantasies well portrayed by Egyptian and Indian movies" (p. 222).

In summary, research conducted in countries other than the United States has shown both similarities and differences among nations in how people use the VCR. Despite cultural differences, in most countries the VCR encourages family viewing and is used by both adolescents and adults. However, those in Middle Eastern Arab nations, Third World countries, and some European countries use the VCR more for purposes of viewing prerecorded tapes. This is done mainly because the VCR exposes people to cultures and values other than their own and allows them to bypass certain restraints that exist in the national media environment.

CONCLUSION

The literature suggests that the VCR plays an important role in the home media environment. The VCR enables people to extend their viewing repertoire and to strengthen their existing patterns of television viewing. Consistent with the uses and gratifications perspective, people use the VCR actively, motivated by needs and desires. They use the VCR for purposes as diverse as time-shifting, movie viewing, library building, diversified choice-making, time-restructuring, social facilitation, and language learning. The VCR also is used to promote and to complement interpersonal relationships.

Several investigators have identified or described various motives for using the VCR. Some have examined how individual motives relate to frequency of VCR use, and to diffusion and adoption of the technology. Yet, few have considered the antecedents (e.g., social, psychological, economic) and the outcomes of use (e.g., satisfaction, cultivation), or the complexity of motivation or use. As with other media, this is an important direction to understand the role, process, and impact of audience use more thoroughly. It also allows us to examine the functional relationships among different modes of communication.

VCR research has relied more on diaries, interviews, and surveys. A few studies have used naturalistic observations in the homes. For example, Krendel et al. (1993) employed naturalistic observations and interviews with the children, and in-depth interviews with the parents. They were able to observe children in their home environment. Survey instruments alone may have had difficulty in detecting that limited parental support can inhibit a child's competence with the VCR. Thus, triangulated methods have proven useful for such research.

Moreover, we still need to investigate several issues relating to VCR use in diversified multicultural environments. For instance, Dobrow (1989) offered an interesting direction for future research following her investigation of ethnic minorities and the use of VCRs. She suggested that researchers examine the connection between viewing ethnic tapes and other rituals, such as dressing in traditional clothing and eating ethnic food. It would be interesting to see whether Dobrow's conclusion holds true. Has the VCR replaced more public forms of ethnic affiliation? If so, what are the effects of such uses of the VCR on ethnic groups.

We also lack a clear understanding of the social and cultural impact of VCR technology. How has the VCR affected the allocation of leisure-time activities? How have social uses of the VCR influenced interaction patterns among family and friends, and has VCR use led to the integration or isolation of family members? Are there functional relationships among negotiation and conflict-reduction strategies pertaining to using the VCR? How has the VCR contributed to the socialization of groups in societies, and how has it helped circumvent restrictions placed on the availability and flow of entertainment and information in these societies? What functional relationships exist among the VCR, satellite television, and the personal computer in this regard?

As discovered by Venkatraman (1991), VCR adopters "value the relative advantages of a VCR, are attracted by its newness [i.e., new,

unique, and different], but are concerned about enjoyment and performance and economic risk" (p. 62). Sensory innovation—which emphasizes play, enjoyment, and visual information processing—positively and
significantly predicted VCR adoption. Cognitive innovation—which
emphasizes careful thinking, problem solving, and verbal information processing—did not. If the VCR has been an ineffective tool for cognitive
innovation, will the greater flexibility offered by DVD and other technology alter that pattern of innovation and use?

Systematic exploration of involvement and characteristics of the
variety of uses should help provide a better understanding of the role and
process of using VCRs, DVDs, and newer communication technologies.
Future research needs to reconcile differences in the characteristics, adoption, and diffusion of such newer communication technologies. It also
needs to consider whether these technologies should be regarded as distinct
means of mediated communication or whether their primary consumer
role is to provide an enhanced means of using more traditional media. Will
the evolution of technology, such as VCRs giving way to DVDs and other
technology, change the nature and utility of the technology?

REFERENCES

A.C. Nielsen Company. (1997). *Nielsen report on television.* Northbrook,
    IL: Author.
Al-Oofy, A., & McDaniel, D. O. (1992). Home VCR viewing among ado-
    lescents in rural Saudi Arabia. *Journal of Broadcasting & Electronic
    Media, 36,* 217-223.
Boyd, D. A. (1987). Home video diffusion and utilization in Arabian Gulf
    States. *American Behavioral Scientist, 30,* 544-555.
Boyd, D. A. (1989). The videocassette recorder in the USSR and Soviet-
    bloc countries. In M. R. Levy (Ed.), *The VCR age: Home video and
    mass communication* (pp. 252-270). Newbury Park, CA: Sage.
Boyd, D. A., & Straubhaar, J. D. (1985). Developmental impact of the
    home video cassette recorder on third world countries. *Journal of
    Broadcasting & Electronic Media, 29,* 5-21.
Cohen, A. A., Levy, M. R., & Golden, K. (1988). Children's uses and
    gratifications of home VCRs: Evolution or revolution.
    Communication Research, 15, 772-780.
Comstock, G. A. (1991). *Television in America* (2nd ed.). Newbury Park,
    CA: Sage.
Dobrow, J. R. (1989). Away from the mainstream? VCRs and ethnic iden-
    tity. In M. R. Levy (Ed.), *The VCR age: Home video and mass com-
    munication* (pp. 193-208). Newbury Park, CA: Sage.

Dobrow, J. R. (1990). The rerun ritual: Using VCRs to re-view. In J. R. Dobrow (Ed.), *Social & cultural aspects of VCR use* (pp. 181-193). Hillsdale, NJ: Lawrence Erlbaum Associates.

Gray, A. (1992). *Video playtime: The gendering of leisure technology.* London: Routledge.

Greenberg, B. S., & Heeter, C. (1987). VCRs and young people: The picture at 39% penetration. *American Behavioral Scientist, 30,* 509-521.

Greenberg, B. S., & Lin, C. (1989). Adolescents and the VCR boom: Old, new, and nonusers. In M. R. Levy (Ed.), *The VCR age: Home video and mass communication* (pp. 73-91). Newbury Park, CA: Sage.

Harvey, M. G., & Rothe, J. T. (1985/1986). Video cassette recorders: Their impact on viewers and advertisers. *Journal of Advertising Research, 25*(6), 19-27.

Heintz, K. E. (1990). VCR libraries: Opportunities for parental control. In J. R. Dobrow (Ed.), *Social & cultural aspects of VCR use* (pp. 147-162). Hillsdale, NJ: Lawrence Erlbaum Associates.

Henke, L. L., & Donohue, T. R. (1989). Functional displacement of traditional TV viewing by VCR owners. *Journal of Advertising Research, 29*(2), 18-23.

Johnson-Smaragdi, U. (1989). Sweden: Opening the doors—cautiously. In L. B. Becker & K. Schoenbach (Eds.), *Audience responses to media diversification: Coping with plenty* (pp. 109-131). Hillsdale, NJ: Lawrence Erlbaum Associates.

Jordan, A. B. (1990). A family systems approach to the use of the VCR in the home. In J. R. Dobrow (Ed.), *Social & cultural aspects of VCR use* (pp. 163-179). Hillsdale, NJ: Lawrence Erlbaum Associates.

Kim, W. Y., Baran, S. J., & Massey, K. K. (1988). Impact of the VCR on control of television viewing. *Journal of Broadcasting & Electronic Media, 32,* 351-358.

Klopfenstein, B. C. (1989). The diffusion of the VCR in the United States. In M. R. Levy (Ed.), *The VCR age: Home video and mass communication* (pp. 21-39). Newbury Park, CA: Sage.

Krendel, K. A., Clark, G., Dawson, R., & Troiauo, C. (1993). Preschoolers and VCRs in the home: A multiple methods approach. *Journal of Broadcasting & Electronic Media, 37,* 293-311.

Krugman, D. M., & Johnson, K. F. (1991). Differences in the consumption of traditional broadcast and VCR movie rentals. *Journal of Broadcasting & Electronic Media, 35,* 213-232.

Krugman, D. M., & Rust, R. T. (1993). The impact of cable penetration and VCR penetration on network viewing: Assessing the decade. *Journal of Advertising Research, 33*(1), 67-73.

Lee, W., & Katz, H. (1993). New media, new messages: An initial inquiry into audience reactions to advertising on videocassettes. *Journal of Advertising Research, 33*(1), 74-85.

Levy, M. R. (1987a). Home video recorders and time shifting. *Journalism Quarterly, 58,* 401-405.

Levy, M. R. (1987b). VCR use and the concept of audience activity. *Communication Quarterly, 35,* 267-275.

Levy, M. R. (1989). Why VCRs aren't pop-up toasters: Issues in home video research. In M. R. Levy (Ed.), *The VCR age: Home video and mass communication* (pp. 9-18). Newbury Park, CA: Sage.

Lin, C. A. (1990). Audience activity and VCR use. In J. R. Dobrow (Ed.), *Social & cultural aspects of VCR use* (pp. 75-92). Hillsdale, NJ: Lawrence Erlbaum Associates.

Lin, C. A. (1992). The functions of the VCR in the home leisure environment. *Journal of Broadcasting & Electronic Media, 36,* 345-351.

Lin, C. A., & Atkin, D. J. (1989). Parental mediation and rulemaking for adolescent use of television and VCRs. *Journal of Broadcasting & Electronic Media, 33,* 53-67.

Lindlof, T. R., & Shatzer, M. J. (1989). Subjective differences in spousal perceptions of family video. *Journal of Broadcasting & Electronic Media, 33,* 375-395.

Lindlof, T. R., & Shatzer, M. J. (1990). VCR usage in the American family. In J. Lull (Ed.), *Television and the American family* (pp. 89-109). Hillsdale, NJ: Lawrence Erlbaum Associates.

Lindlof, T. R., Shatzer, M. J., & Wilkinson, D. (1988). Accommodation of video and television in the American family. In J. Lull (Ed.), *World families watch television* (pp. 158-192). Newbury Park, CA: Sage.

Lull, J. (1988). Constructing rituals of extension through family television viewing. In J. Lull (Ed.), *World families watch television* (pp. 237-259). Newbury Park, CA: Sage.

McIntyre, B. T. (1995). VCR use in Hong-Kong. *Communication Research Reports, 12,* 61-70.

Morgan, M., Alexander, A., Shanahan, J., & Harris, C. (1990). Adolescents, VCRs, and the family environment. *Communication Research, 17,* 83-106.

Morgan, M., & Shanahan, J. (1991). Do VCRs change the TV picture? VCRs and the cultivation process. *American Behavioral Scientist, 35,* 122-135.

Morgan, M., Shanahan, J., & Harris, C. (1990). VCRs and the effects of television: New diversity or more of the same? In J. R. Dobrow (Ed.), *Social & cultural aspects of VCR use* (pp. 107-123). Hillsdale, NJ: Lawrence Erlbaum Associates.

Morley, D. (1986). *Family television: Cultural power and domestic leisure.* London: Routledge.

Olney, T. J., Batra, R., & Holbrook, M. B. (1990). A three-component model of attitude toward the ad: Effects of the zipping and zapping of television commercials. In S. J. Agres, J. A. Edell, & T. M. Dubitsky (Eds.), *Emotion in advertising: Theoretical and practical explorations* (pp. 269-281). New York: Quorum.

Perse, E. M., Ferguson, D. A., & McLeod, D. M. (1994). Cultivation in the newer media environment. *Communication Research, 21,* 79-104.

Potter, W. J., Forrest, E., Sapolsky, B. S., & Ware, W. (1988). Segmenting VCR owners. *Journal of Advertising Research, 28*(2), 29-39.

Ram, S., & Jung, H. (1990). The conceptualization and measurement of product usage. *Journal of the Academy of Marketing Science, 18*(1), 67-76.

Roe, K. (1987). Adolescents' video use: A structural-cultural approach. *American Behavioral Scientist, 30,* 522-532.

Roe, K. (1989). School achievement, self-esteem, and adolescents' video use. In M. R. Levy (Ed.), *The VCR age: Home video and mass communication* (pp. 168-189). Newbury Park, CA: Sage.

Rubin, A. M. (1994). Media uses and effects: A uses-and-gratifications perspective. In J. Bryant & D. Zillmann (Eds.), *Media effects: Advances in theory and research* (pp. 417-436). Hillsdale, NJ: Lawrence Erlbaum Associates.

Rubin, A. M., & Bantz, C. R. (1987). Utility of videocassette recorders. *American Behavioral Scientist, 30,* 471-485.

Rubin, A. M., & Bantz, C. R. (1989). Uses and gratifications of videocassette recorders. In J. Salvaggio & J. Bryant (Eds.), *Media use in the information age: Emerging patterns of adoption and use* (pp. 181-195). Hillsdale, NJ: Lawrence Erlbaum Associates.

Rubin, A. M., & Rubin, R. B. (1985). Interface of personal and mediated communication: A research agenda. *Critical Studies in Mass Communication, 2,* 36-53.

Rubin, A. M., & Rubin, R. B. (1989). Social and psychological antecedents of VCR use. In M. R. Levy (Ed.), *The VCR age: Home video and mass communication* (pp. 92-111). Newbury Park, CA: Sage.

Sapolsky, B. S., & Forrest, E. (1989). Measuring VCR "ad-voidance." In M. R. Levy (Ed.), *The VCR age: Home video and mass communication* (pp. 148-167). Newbury Park, CA: Sage.

Schoenbach, K., & Hackforth, N. (1987). Video in West German households: Attitudinal and behavioral differences. *American Behavioral Scientist, 30,* 533-543.

Straubhaar, J. D. (1990). Context, social class, and VCRs: A world comparison. In J. R. Dobrow (Ed.), *Social & cultural aspects of VCR use* (pp. 125-143). Hillsdale, NJ: Lawrence Erlbaum Associates.

Straubhaar, J. D., & Boyd, D. A. (1989). Adoption and use of videocassette recorders in the Third World. In J. Salvaggio & J. Bryant (Eds.), *Media use in the information age: Emerging patterns of adoption and use* (pp. 163-178). Hillsdale, NJ: Lawrence Erlbaum Associates.

Straubhaar, J. D., & Lin, C. (1989). A quantitative analysis of the reasons for VCR penetration worldwide. In J. Salvaggio & J. Bryant (Eds.), *Media use in the information age: Emerging patterns of adoption and use* (pp. 125-145). Hillsdale, NJ: Lawrence Erlbaum Associates.

U.S. Bureau of Census. (1997). *Utilization of selected media 1970-1995. Statistical abstracts of the United States: 1997* (117th ed., p. 566). Washington, DC: Bureau of Census.

Venkatraman, M. P. (1991). The impact of innovativeness and innovation type on adoption. *Journal of Retailing, 67*(1), 51-67.

PART FIVE

TECHNOLOGY AND
INTERMEDIA COMMUNICATION

14

The Internet and Web
as Communication Media

Bruce Klopfenstein
University of Georgia

> Marshall McLuhan had it mostly right: The medium is, if not the message, heavily shaping the message. . . . Online news is different from all of those media, and oddly embraces them all. It offers the depth of a newspaper (or, with hypertext links and electronic archives, even more depth). It showcases the attitude and focus of a smart-mouthed magazine. It emulates the immediacy and interactivity of talk radio (with the added interaction of chat rooms, forums and e-mail). It approximates the visual impact of television. This seemingly chaotic medium is exploding with messages.
> —Lule (1998, p. B7)

BACKGROUND

The purpose of this chapter is to introduce the Internet and its greatest application, the World Wide Web (WWW or web), as a mediated communication technology. As of late 2000, approximately 80 million Americans had been on the Internet at some point (Pietrucha, 1998; United States Department of Commerce, 2000). The number of Internet users globally in 1998 easily may have exceeded 100 million (Woods, 1998). The emphasis of this chapter is on Internet and web diffusion in the United States, where a 1998 survey suggested that as many as 84% of global Internet users resided (Hamilton, 1998). Other estimates of global user figures take the U.S. user population and add 30% to 35% to it (Tchong, 2001). In fact, a major commercial research report indicates that more than half of all Americans and Canadians between the ages of 16 and 34 were Internet users as of mid-1998 (Johnson, 1998). By contrast, for example, only 10% of Germans and 18% of Britons had Internet access as of early 1999 (see http://www.nua.ie).

Although more than one quarter of all U.S. adults had an e-mail address by the start of 1998 (Taylor, 1998), a November 1998 national study found that 35% of all adult Americans used e-mail (Gearan, 1999). E-mail is often cited as the most "popular" use of the Internet. The Institute for the Future has found that the average white collar worker sends and receives an average of 30 e-mails per day ("The numbers," 1999). As the Internet has diffused to all segments of the population, more services are being made available to older citizens (Russell, 1998).

Rogers (1986) noted that research related to new communication technologies often lags behind their initial diffusion. Authors of scholarly articles about the Internet and the Web are only beginning to find their way into academic outlets (Smith, 1997). Early efforts have been made to define the Internet phenomenon from a communication perspective (e.g., James, Worting, & Forrest, 1995; Lin, 1999; Morris & Ogan, 1996; Newhagan & Rafaeli, 1996). Before discussing the implications of the Internet and the Web, some historical background is necessary.

Brief History of the Internet and World Wide Web

The term *Internet* is shorthand for "interconnecting networks" (Tappendorf, 1995). In the United States, the Internet is supported by commercial Internet backbone providers, such as MCI, UUNET, Sprint, PSINet and others who connect these networks (Klopfenstein, 1998). For a thorough review of the Internet history, see works done by such authors as Krol and Klopfenstein (1996), Sterling (1993), Hafner and Lyon (1996), Hauben and Hauben (1997), Leiner et al. (1998) and Zakon (1998). Brody (1998) included a look at where the Internet was headed as of 1998.

The first ARPANET e-mail message was sent in 1972 and Usenet, an electronic bulletin board system (BBS), was established in 1979 at the University of North Carolina. E-mail took on an unanticipated life of its own, as researchers quickly adapted it for applications beyond professional collaboration. This was not anticipated (as is probably the case for the later wide adoption of the web). IBM funded BITNET in the 1980s, but the network was displaced by the eventually more popular Internet and shut down on January 1, 1997. Fig. 14.1 depicts the growth of Internet servers beginning around January 1991 to July 23, 2001.

Researchers, such as those at the European Laboratory for Particle Physics (CERN), knew that text-based e-mail over the Internet was one thing, but sharing scientific documents over computer networks was another. By 1990, Berners-Lee (1999) developed a hypertext system that allowed linking of documents in multiple windows, and he publicly demonstrated it in 1991. The concept was envisioned much earlier by Bush (1945). Berners-Lee named the system of sharing documents over a network (e.g., the Internet)—the World Wide Web (Cailliau, 1995).

The National Center for Supercomputing Applications (NCSA) at the University of Illinois released their "browser," Mosaic, in early 1993, with Macintosh and Windows versions introduced shortly thereafter ("An overview," 1997). The original goal of creating the WWW to allow sharing (i.e., networking) of documents (regardless of original format) set the stage for the web to evolve into the multimedia file delivery and display system of today (Klopfenstein, 1997). The WWW uses the Internet to allow transmission of files from server (web site) to client (end user). As seen in Fig. 14.1, the introduction of the web had a dramatic impact on Internet growth, as defined by the number of linked computer "hosts" (Internet Domain Survey, 1998). The exponential growth of the Internet reflects the impact of the WWW from 1994 through 1998 (although not all Internet hosts are Web hosts; see Internet Domain Survey, 2001, for a complete explanation).

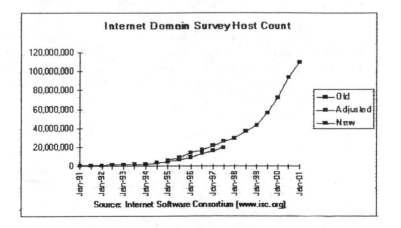

Figure 14.1. Internet Domain Survey Host Count (data for this graph is available in Appendix)

Media historians will note that the Web was responsible for the dramatic change from text-based online information to graphics-oriented content. Coincidental to the growth of the WWW was the diffusion of an enabling technology: relatively inexpensive home computers (Lin, 1998). In the 1990s, modems became standard features for these computers and many came with online access software preinstalled (e.g., America Online, Compuserve, and/or Prodigy). This helped set the stage for the impending Internet explosion. Table 14.1 displays the growth of personal computer (PC) penetration in the United States, but these data do not differentiate households that were buying replacement computers and first adopting households.

It is also true that penetration of PCs in households that have children is far higher than for those without (Lin, 1998; U.S. NTIA, 1998) and there is evidence that the children themselves influence the decision to adopt (McNeal, 1998). At least 70% of all households with home computers also had a modem as of the end of 1997 (U.S. NTIA, 1998). Research shows that there is a very strong relationship between household income and computer and modem penetration rates, and education exerts an influence independent of income (Clemente, 1998). Age has had important effects that are independent of income, and its influence will continue to be felt as the age distribution of the population changes in the future. Household composition is a predictor of PC adoption, and households in urban areas are better equipped than households in rural areas (Dickinson & Sciadas, 1998).

NATURE AND STRUCTURE OF THE INTERNET

Grappling with the structure of the Internet is like trying to get a good grip on Jello gelatin dessert. Who are the providers of conduit? Industry players include telephone companies, Internet service providers (ISPs), rural electric companies, cable television companies, and even newspapers, among others (Hakala, 1996). Although there have been around 5,000 ISPs in the United States, most experts expect this number to peak before significant consolidation begins ("Bringing home," 1999).

Table 14.1. Estimates for Household Personal Computer Penetration.

Personal Computers	1994	1995	1996	1997
U.S. Household penetration	33%	39%	41%	45%
Growth rate	—	18%	5%	10%

Source: Adapted from Vanderkay (1998)

The ISP industry is quickly approaching the cable television industry in size, with annual revenues nearing $10 billion as of late 2000 (Strow, 1997) and $32.5 billion in revenues predicted by 2001 ("National ISPs," 2000). This means that the ISP industry is already generating about as much revenue as the entire network television industry of ABC, CBS, NBC, and Fox. Industry analyst Paul Kagan predicted that "Internet/Interactive" media revenues will double those of radio broadcasting and be about two thirds those of television by 2007 as posted publicly on the Web by his company, as seen in Table 14.2. Also worth noting from these projections is the more optimistic tone sounded for newer media when compared to more established media (e.g., publishing and traditional broadcasting).

An ISP connects an Internet user to a web site or an Internet address (e.g., e-mail or newsgroup). A web portal, such as Yahoo!, Lycos, and so on, is a site where users may go to launch an online session, whether it be active (seeking information such as conducting research for personal, professional, or academic reasons) or passive (reading the latest weather, news, sports, entertainment, or other information). Although nothing like the oligopoly that guided the first four decades of broadcast television has emerged on the Web, a consolidation of formerly competing web portal sites was well underway by 1999. Just as commercial television programs bring viewers to advertisers, portals are doing the same by gathering users who then may be exposed to advertising messages. Portals take an additional step: they are moving into electronic commerce (EC) either directly (by allowing their own transactions) or indirectly (by serving as a window or portal to other EC vendors).

Major portal companies added new services (usually by acquisition) in an effort to stay a few weeks ahead of the field. Popular portal features included news headlines, weather, sports headlines, sports scores, near real-time stock tickers, company profiles, search engines, message boards, online games, automated reminder services, categorized links, free e-mail, and personalization of these services ("The portal wars," 1999).

Internet content providers are even more diverse than conduit providers. The amount of information on the Web has been growing exponentially. Alexa Internet, a company that archives the contents of the Web for future scholarly research, indicated that the following Web descriptors held true as of August 1998 ("Web spawns," 1998):

- Available public Web content was 3 terabytes, or 3 million megabytes.
- The Web was doubling in size every 8 months.
- There were approximately 20 million Web content areas (i.e., top-level pages of sites, individual home pages, and significant subsections of corporate Web sites).

Table 14.2. Entertainment and Communications Media Revenues.

		1997	2007	10-Year CAGR%
Internet/Interactive[a]	($ mil.)	6,104	63,100	26.3%
Wireless Telecommunications[b]	($ mil.)	33,489	111,662	12.8%
Cable and Satellite TV[c]	($ mil.)	33,838	91,188	10.4%
Out-of-home Entertainment[d]	($ mil.)	14,224	32,608	8.7%
Radio[e]	($ mil.)	13,595	30,868	8.5%
Television[f]	($ mil.)	45,016	91,046	7.3%
Direct Marketing[g]	($ mil.)	44,007	80,135	6.2%
Publishing[h]	($ mil.)	121,788	205,007	5.3%
Entertainment[i]	($ mil.)	52,636	87,839	5.3%
Total Media Revenues	($ mil.)	364,700	793,413	8.1%
Media Revenues by Category				
Total Consumer Spending	($ mil.)	191,634	460,231	9.2%
Total Media Advertising	($ mil.)	173,066	333,182	6.8%
Total Media Revenue per U.S. Home	$	3,622	7,259	7.2%
Total Media Spending per U.S. Home	$	1,902	4,211	8.3%

Note. Sectors ranked By 10-year compound annual growth rate (CAGR). (All figures are as of calendar year-end.)
aInternet access, Web retailing, Web telephony, Internet advertising
bCellular, PCS, ESMR
cIncludes wireless cable (MMDS)
dAmusement/theme/water parks, location-based entertainment, spectator sports
eLocal, syndicated & network radio ad billings
fBroadcast (local/network), barter, cable (local/network) and regional sports ad billings
gHome shopping, direct mail, outdoor/out-of-home advertising
hNewspapers, magazines, books, Yellow Pages, business and farm publications
iMovie theaters, home video, video games, computer games, entertainment merchandise, recorded music
Paul Kagan Associates, Inc. estimates. (Source. www.kagan.com/kmarket/mc08.html).

- 90% of all Web traffic was spread over 100,000 different host machines.
- 50% of all traffic went to the top 900 Web sites currently available.

The Web has been organizing itself into what is looking more and more like mainstream media. This is not surprising given the current media players and the resources they are pouring into their Web sites. The WWW, before 1996, was the domain of the web pioneers operating within a "frontier" atmosphere. The Web in the United States (for better or worse) is moving further away from its unique start and morphing into the existing commercial media industry structure. Users can recognize established media names like CNN and ESPN as well as new ones like Yahoo! and Excite.

Dreams of Internet commerce (sales and/or advertising/promotion of products) guide many Web investors today. Evidence of the parallel structure of the Internet to older media is seen by such commonalities as the role of TV ratings firm Nielsen in measuring Internet use (Tedesco, 1998) and the establishment in 1996 of the Internet Advertising Bureau (IAB). The IAB was "the first global association devoted exclusively to maximizing the use and effectiveness of advertising on the Internet" (see http://www.iab.net). This organization fits right in with its preceding industry counterparts: the Radio Advertising Bureau, the Television Advertising Bureau, and the Cable Advertising Bureau.

As noted at the outset of this chapter, there is no denying that the Web in 1999 had been driven by U.S. organizations (GVU, 1998). This is critical for understanding the current Web structure because of the unique case of media history in the United States where media content historically has been subsidized by advertising. Although Web content providers such as Gannet's *USA Today* tried to sell subscriptions to their services, many subscription-only Web services turned instead to advertiser support. Yahoo!, one of the oldest and most used portal sites, has never been subscription-based. Yahoo! was well on its way to generating $200 million in advertising revenues by the end of 1998 ("Web ad," 1998).

INTERNET USER PROFILE

As has been the case with the diffusion of previous new media such as the VCR (Klopfenstein, 1989a), the first research on users tends to focus on who the users are. The Internet and WWW are no exceptions (e.g., Nolan, 1998). One of the characteristics of the Web that distinguishes it from previous mass media is its inherently interactive nature. Because the Web allows easy interaction between sender (server) and receiver (surfer), setting up simple "audience measurement" tools that track Web site hits (file requests from unique users are automatically logged by web server software) was not difficult. Standards of web use management, however, had not been accepted as of 1998, and issues such as measuring Web use from the workplace have turned out to be difficult to resolve (Broersma, 1998; Brenneman, 1997; Court, 1997).

Many efforts have been made to find out who is using the Internet and why. Most notable of these efforts includes the impressive and widely publicized surveys of Georgia Tech's Graphics, Visualization & Usability (GVU) Center. As of late 2000, there have been 10 surveys of Web users. Respondents are self-selected, so the GVU survey results can not be projected onto the entire Internet/Web user population. The authors of the survey noted that their methodology's results "show a bias exists in the experience, intensity of usage, and skill sets of the users, but not the core demographics of users" (GVU, 1998).

Although the scientific limitations of the GVU surveys must be kept firmly in mind, they do offer insights into Web use over a 5-year period. For example, the data suggest that the Web has moved from the province of a male-dominated group of highly educated users to one that is much more closely in line with the demographics of the general population. This means that previously underrepresented demographic groups (e.g., women and people either below age 20 or over age 50) are coming online rapidly. The "gender gap" of Internet users was evident in the early 1990s according to every known scientific study. Even the unscientific GVU user surveys at Georgia Tech (http://www.gvu.gatech.edu/user_surveys/) showed this gap, which was negatively correlated with the date on which the survey was undertaken. The gap has declined over time to the point that in the United States, at least, there is no longer a gap ("Media metrix chronicles," 1999). Nielsen showed that the number of men and women online in 2001 matched the actual breakdown in the U.S. population ("Women," 2001)

Despite the rapidly growing size of the Internet population, average time spent online appears to be holding steady. More than one Internet measuring service found that Web users spent an average of 6 hours a week on the Web in 1997 and into 1998 (Hamilton, 1998). Average figures are not especially enlightening, of course, because of their sensitivity to outliers.

A useful perspective for studying Internet adoption is the diffusion of innovations paradigm. As other chapters in this volume (Dupagne, chap. 10; Rogers, chap. 3) detail, diffusion theory suggests that innovators—those relatively earlier to adopt a new product or service—are likely to spend more time with media, adopt other new media technologies, and be more upscale than later adopters. Atkin, Jeffres, and Neuendorf (1998) found some support for the upscale Internet adopter profile noted in earlier work, noting that adopters were younger and better educated than non-adopters. Internet adopters were also more likely to show an interest in adopting other new technologies—particularly the computer—and stay up to date with them. However, consistent with past work on media displacement (James et al., 1995), Atkin et al. (1998) found that Internet use is not consistently linked to uses of other media; in this case, adopters spent less time with TV, but expressed higher levels of use for magazines, theatrical movies, and videos. Time spent on the Web in the late 1990s was time that would have been spent some other way a few years earlier. One study documents that those who were spending more time on the Internet reported that they were spending less time with traditional media such as television (The Strategis Group, 1998). Other studies suggest that there is a correlation between heavier Web use and, for example, above average television use (i.e., in terms of time spent online, above average Web users also tend to spend more time watching television than average; Shapiro, 1998).

Diffusion theory also suggests that differences between adopters and nonoadopters of media tend to dissipate over time (e.g., Rogers, 1995). A survey by a noncommercial public interest group conducted in late 1998 confirmed the mainstreaming of Internet users in the United States (Pew Research Center, 1999). The nationwide telephone survey of 3,184 adults by the Pew Research Center found that 41% of U.S. adults were using the Internet, although the definition of Internet use was not dependent on extent of use. Pew also found that 46% of its sample of current Internet users started going online within the last year, and 52% of those were women.

According to the Pew Research Center, the weather was the most sought after news item on the Internet in 1998. Whereas 46% of experienced users (started using the Internet at least 1 year before the survey) were college graduates, 30% had some college experience, and 19% had graduated high school. Of those with a year or less experience on the Internet, only 29% graduated college, 32% attended college, and 33% graduated high school but never attended college. The survey indicated 80% of Internet users were under age 50 (compared with 63% of all Americans) and 39% of Internet users were college graduates (compared with 22% of the nation at large). Income levels of new users were lower than those of earlier adopters, as predicted by diffusion theory (Rogers, 1995).

An area of research relatively untouched thus far involves Internet "churn" (or disconnection). Internet churn can occur when someone tries the Internet and quits (Katz & Aspden, 1998). Another form of Internet churn occurs when an individual switches from one ISP to another. One

1997 study indicated that 40% of Internet users had switched ISPs at least once (Menefee, 1998).

SOCIAL SCIENTIFIC RESEARCH ON INTERNET USES

Web user research is in a nascent stage as of this writing. A recent study noted a phenomenon about Web use reminiscent of television use; that is, heavy use simultaneously occurring from a large number of users is event-driven (i.e., events like the death of Princess Diana and the release of the infamous Starr Report on the Clinton-Lewinsky affair), a term familiar to television broadcasters. When a special event occurred, online traffic doubled and often tripled at Web sites like MSNBC, Fox News Online, CNN.com, Associated Press Online, and others (Harper, 1999), as at least one in ten Americans tried to read the report online (Pew Research Center, 1998). Events such as the football Super Bowl and severe weather—including hurricanes—have also proven to generate significant web site traffic. Local television station Web sites have quickly found that weather radar images are among the most accessed files on the site.

Several studies have been produced on the uses and gratifications on the Internet and/or Web (Hunter, n.d.; Lin, 1999). Eighmey and McCord (1998) looked at how Web sites were rated by users in an exploratory study. Lin (1999) found that, although audience motives for access decisions could appear similar across both television and online media, differing perceptual links between the media content and audience/user motives dictate the actual media adoption choice.

Other related research is reported elsewhere in this volume, encompassing organizational (Rice & Webster, chap. 7, this volume; Steinfield, chap. 8, this volume) and interpersonal communication applications (Neuendorf et al., chap. 5, this volume; Walther, chap. 6, this volume) as well as audience uses and gratifications (see Charney & Greenberg, chap. 16, this volume). Outside of the communication field, computer scientists (e.g., Kiesler, Zdaniuk, Lundmark, & Kraut, 2000) have linked Web adoption to deeper personality measures, reporting that the new medium may serve as a depressant for heavy college student users (Coates, 1998). It remains to be seen whether these provocative findings stand the test of replication over time and more representative user groups. But, the confluence of these research approaches hold much promise for understanding Web user behavior.

For instance, an interesting area ripe for new research is Internet use in the workplace. Although radio listening in the workplace has long been the subject of commercial ratings firms, academic inquiries into radio listenership over the last several decades have been lacking. The Internet, as a conduit to all forms of communication content—whether work related or not—offers a new opportunity to examine media use in the workplace. Commercial researchers (e.g., see "August," 1998; and Internet at a Glance, 1998) are measuring some Web use at the work place.

Children on the Web

Access to the Web by children has emerged as an important and controversial issue for at least two important reasons: One is "equal access" to this immense storehouse of information and a second concern is limiting access to materials that are not appropriate for children. Research indicates that children may be one of the fastest growing segments of the population to be going online. It would seem that some time will pass before children have the same kind of access to the Internet as compared to television; it is not likely to occur until Web access is merged with the television (Lin, 1999). Even with that limitation in mind, one major commercial research firm predicted that nearly half of all children aged 2 to 12 will be online by 2002, as noted in Table 14.3.

INTERNET USE MEASUREMENT CHALLENGES

It is assumed that anyone who is accessing the WWW is an Internet user. Some Internet users theoretically may not be WWW users (e.g., e-mail only). One Internet market research company, eMarketer, has positioned itself deliberately as a conservative observer of Internet use. Going by its definition of "real" Internet users, as those who are online at least once or twice a week, and at least for a period of 1 to 2 hours per week, only an estimated 37 million (18.5% of the adult population) Americans were defined as users (Woods, 1998).

Definitions are joined by different methodologies for measuring who is online. Table 14.4 shows significant differences in estimates for U.S. Web users by four of the top Web ratings companies. Although the "growth per second" column may seem superfluous, it does serve as another indicator of just how varied the estimates were in 1998. NUA Internet Surveys listed 87 million Internet users between the United States and Canada as of September 1998 ("How many," 1998).

Other surveys of Internet use in the United States reached various conclusions on Internet use by 1998. Although there was a narrowing of the gender gap, as many as 60% or more of Internet users were male, and males may stay online longer than females. A recent study by publisher Ziff-Davis found men to more likely use the Web, to more frequently

Table 14.3. Estimated Number of Children Online, 1996-2002.

Children Online	1996	1997	1998	1999	2000	2001	2002
Total U.S. children age 2-12 (millions)	42.7	43.1	43.3	43.4	43.6	43.6	44.3
Total children online	1.4	2.7	5.1	7.9	11.5	15.9	20.9
Access only from home	1.4	2.6	4.6	6.7	9.0	11.6	14.9
Access only from school	0.0	0.1	0.5	1.2	2.5	4.3	6.0
Percent online	3%	6%	12%	18%	26%	36%	47%

Source. Jupiter Communications as cited in Thompson (1998).

Table 14.4. U.S. Internet Population Growth Estimates.

Researcher	Study 1	Study 2	Growth/Day	Growth/Sec
Cyber dialogue	41.5M Dec-97	53.5M Jul-98	60,914	0.7050
Nielsen	52.0M Sep-97	70.5M Jun-98	67,776	0.7843
IDC	49.4M Dec-97	66.0M Dec-98	45,611	0.5279
Relevant knowledge	51.3M Jun-98	53.4M Sep-98	22,978	0.2659
Overall average growth rate:			47,317	0.5708

Source. Iconocast (1998).

access the Web, and to spend more time online per session than women. Men and women shared instances of online purchasing behaviors, but items purchased differed by gender (Guglielmo, 1998).

Industry research helps to paint a picture of Web use through 1998. Indeed, one report indicates that online use appeared to be stable in use by time of day and day of week. Jupiter Communications noted that there is even a "prime time" for Internet use that lasts from noon to 4 p.m. (Harper, 1999). This coincides with the noon lunch hour across time zones. Despite significant growth in total Web usage, usage patterns by day of week and time of day have remained virtually identical to the patterns reported in 1996 ("August 1998").

Limitations of Web Measures

In the early days of the Web, server statistics were routinely kept. That is, server software automatically logged instances of file transfers. An administrator could check the logs in an "as needed" fashion and, for example, see which files were most frequently requested. The concept of the Web was created with the assumption of this model being in place. Computer networks included "clients," including such information as end users and "servers" with which users might send and receive files.

With the introduction of the Web, Web site developers quickly learned that such simple statistics were readily available. Rather than estimates of pages read or programs viewed, web server statistics showed precisely which files were taken and at what times. Soon, "click-throughs" became a legitimate Web advertising term.

Web usage terms are confusing. A *hit* on a Web server is a single request for content, a graphic or any other single element of a Web page. Assuming that the page in the example had one hit for the content, three graphics and a button, the log would record five hits for every one time the page was loaded. This grouping of all the hits on a particular page is known as one access. Just as hits can be grouped into accesses, accesses can be grouped into single sessions or visits. When a person visits www.business-name.com and looks at four separate pages (each with five single elements), that visit can be reported as 20 hits, four accesses, or one session. Because there is currently no standard in the way that statistics from Web servers are reported, it is imperative to know what the numbers being reported refer to in order to interpret correctly the traffic at a Web site (Sheets, 1998).

It is also possible to underreport exposures to a web page. To reduce download periods, Web browsers store recently visited pages in a user's cache on his or her hard drive. If a site is revisited, browsers may display pages from the disk instead of requesting them from the server. As a result, servers undercount the number of times a page is viewed (see also http://cyberatlas.internet.com/resources/glossary.html).

The Internet Advertising Bureau (IAB) has facilitated industry discussions on standardizing Web use measures (Media Measurement Task Force, 1997). These standards are based on the same statistical utilities available on Web server software. The following are some of the abstracted definitions promoted by the IAB at http://www.iab.net/advertise/content/mmtf3.html:

> *Visitor*
> Unique Registration: Where unique individuals who visit a site identify themselves via such methods as registration or completing a survey.

Unique Cookie: Where a Web server stores information uniquely identifying with a browser, the inactivity constrain on the calculation of visits (i.e. 30 minutes) should make it relatively safe to use cookies to determine the page requests associated with one.

Unique URL Tagging: The process of embedding Unique Identifiers into URLs contained in HTML content to allow for an acceptable calculation of visits, if caching is avoided.

Unique IP Addresses: A collection of http requests from an IP address grouped together to form a visit. The process of grouping requests to form visits from IP addresses associated with a visitor yields information that guides the grouping of requests to form visits from IP addresses associated with multiple users (e.g., proxies).

Visit
"A series of page requests by a visitor without 30 consecutive minutes of inactivity." Given the current stateless nature of the Web, a "visit" is an intrinsically arbitrary definition.

Return Visits
"The average numbers of times a visitor returns to a site over a period of time." Return visits rely on having a registration method in place.

Time
"The elapsed time from the first to the last page request that constitutes a visit, and adding the average time per page for such visit."

Average Time Per Page Request
"The elapsed time from the first to the last page request that constitutes a visit, divided by the number of page requests in that visit, minus one."

Sources of Commercial Internet User Research

A tremendous amount of data about Internet users is continually collected by commercial entities for general sale or, more often, for proprietary use. Unfortunately, most of this information is usually beyond the reach of scholars (Klopfenstein, 1989b). Moreover, when commercial information is released, users also need to be careful about possible author biases. Although it used this bias as a selling point for its own research, one company points out the potential problem with a research report showing large numbers of Internet users: "The original Nielsen survey, which projected a whopping 24 million users on the Internet in 1996, was sponsored by CommerceNet, a consortium of internet companies that are heavily invested in the internet's growth and development" (see http://www.emarketer.com/estats/estats.html).

There are a number of seemingly stable research Web sites where attempts are being made to catalog research about the Web and how it is being used (Klopfenstein, 1998). Information about Web use is being collected daily, and some of it is released via the Web. Table 14.5 presents a list of some of the most notable sources of current Internet research.

Table 14.5. Web Sites for User Research.

NUA Surveys http://www.nua.ie/surveys/Internet
This is an Irish Web site that maintains links to a plethora of Internet use surveys. Its researchers also attempt to analyze the results from these surveys into a more comprehensive picture of NUA Internet use. It has an outstanding track record.

ICONOCLAST http://www.iconoclast.com
ICONOCAST is the "definitive resource for facts, figures, trends and rumors in the Internet marketing industry." Like other sites listed here, it includes references to current Internet research data. Its founder also established http://cyberatlas. internet. com/.

eStats http://www.emarketer.com/estats/
eStats culls research from other sources and reports on it at their Web site. This group critiques available Web user research and also attempts to paint an overall picture of who's using the web. See also Net Geography (1999).

WilsonWeb Demographics of Web Users
http://www.wilsonweb.com/webmarket/demograf.htm
Wilson Internet Services provides links to current articles on a number of subjects including Web demographics and EC.

The Internet Society Market Research and Data on the Internet and World Wide Web
http://www.isoc.org/internet/stats/
The Internet Society is a professional association that provides leadership in addressing issues that confront the future of the Internet. This page lists other sites where data are reported on Internet users.

WWW User Research http://www.dowdencenter.org
This site at University of Georgia includes links to other Web sites where research on Internet use and users are posted. The author is an expert in new media diffusion.

RECENT DEVELOPMENTS

Study of Internet and Web use is a very fluid proposition. As 1999 began, it was not clear if the Web was reaching anything that approached a state of equilibrium. Major Web sites like CNN, ESPN, and *The New York Times* had undergone major redesigns. Certainly, as more people become more experienced online, content providers will learn from their users and will be able to employ design elements that promise to make Web sites easier to navigate.

Access to Web content will improve for two major reasons. First, Web designers have learned that the most eye-catching Web sites do not necessarily translate into intelligent Web design. Designs that allow reasonably fast (e.g., certainly less than 10 seconds) individual page downloads will become more of the rule than the exception. Second, increased bandwidth will continue to become available at lower cost per transmitted byte (Nielsen, 1998).

Although experts disagree about future pricing models, competition in the ISP industry (including the new cable television company entrants) will make increases in flat monthly charges difficult. It is possible, as some economists predict, that heavy users will be willing to pay a higher price for more reliable and faster Internet connections (Klopfenstein, 1998).

A key question into the future is how the Web will continue to evolve. If video has become the literature of our age, then it seems likely future Web applications may become even more graphics- and video-intensive. Video allows more passive consumption of media content than reading, and we are living in the video age. This prediction seems even more probable as the demographics of Internet users continues to reflect a more mainstream population than its more highly educated, higher income household predecessors. Interestingly, there is little evidence at present to suggest that many households would select the Networked Computer (NC) touted in 1996-1997, by such industry giants as Oracle (Haney & Weil, 2000). Just as consumers passed on the less expensive and more limited videodisc player in the 1980s for the more versatile and expensive VCR (Klopfenstein, 1989b). Corporate communication sectors have also passed on the NC thus far, but that may change depending on new advances and changes associated with the new generations of NCs.

The opportunity clearly exists for some convergence of media in the household. The technology to make this happen will be available, but that does not mean people will choose to use the same appliance for Web and television use. As of now, the television and the PC are two separate entities usually located in different rooms from one another (e.g., the console television in the den and the home computer in another room such as a home office).

WebTV, the product purchased by Microsoft in 1997 for nearly half a billion dollars (Lazarus, 1997), could be a sign of things to come. WebTV allows users to view the web on their television sets rather than a personal computer, using a standard telephone Internet connection. It also allows simultaneous viewing of television programs and web pages via a picture-in-picture option.

However, WebTV does have its limitations. For example, subscribers must use the Microsoft WebTV Networks to use WebTV and it does not support Java, a popular programming language that dominates the Web world today (Stirland, 1998). Any household that already has an Internet account will have to add the cost of access to the WebTV networks to their budgets.

Despite the virtually limitless promotional capabilities of Microsoft, WebTV had been adopted by few consumers by 1998. Interestingly, WebTV's limited success has come in baby-boomer households (in this case, ages 45 and older; Craig, 1998). Beyond WebTV, Microsoft also made its Windows 98 operating system television friendly. Microsoft's Windows 98 also allows the viewing of broadcast or cable television if the proper hardware (television tuner card) is installed.

Two recent phenomena on the Internet proved the system's resiliency when it was faced with unprecedented bandwidth demands. On September 11, 1998, the U.S. Congress released the contents of a 450-page document onto the Web—the aforementioned independent government counsel's detailed report on the sexual conduct of the U.S. president. News Web sites recorded their busiest days to that point, but Internet traffic continued to flow. Commercial Web sites handled the loads far better than government Web sites, but there was no digital gridlock (Walsh, 1998).

Another test of the Internet as well as people's media preferences of the time came on September 21, 1998, with the airing of a 4-hour video of President Clinton testifying about the physical nature of his extramarital liaison. Once again, Internet gridlock was generally avoided. Nevertheless, people seemed to turn to traditional broadcast and cable television outlets to hear the president's testimony. It is reasonable to assume that all the discussion about the video actually being available on the Web increased the public's awareness of this video streaming capability of the Web. Whether the Web ever becomes the medium of choice for video is analogous to asking in 1980 if cable television networks would ever match the dominance of broadcast networks. Nearly 20 years later, individual broadcast networks have their lowest ratings in history but those still dwarf the ratings of individual cable networks. The same may hold true for Web "versus" broadcast outlets for years.

In forecasting new media adoption, there are few certainties. The forecast horizon has also shortened: The more distant into the future one peers, the less clear the picture (Klopfenstein, 1989c). With this in mind, one more major factor emerges as we contemplate the future of the Web and the convergence of new media: the introduction of digital television (Dupagne, chap. 10, this volume; Dupagne & Seel, 1998; Whitaker, 2001). The broadcasting industry, as compared to other forms of mediated communication, will be the last to convert completely to digital technology (mandated to happen by 2006). This digital conversion would seem to all but guarantee the further convergence of mediated communication modalities that media scholars have been pondering since the 1970s (e.g., Robinson, 1978).

SUMMARY AND CONCLUSIONS

Certain aspects of the Web phenomenon appear to be typical of the evolutionary nature of new media in the United States, whereas other aspects seem unprecedented. Like other new media before it, the Web (and the Internet) had well-established technologies already in place before widespread diffusion started to take place in the general public. The key technologies for the Web were invented in an academic environment, as had been the case especially for radio broadcasting. The Internet was well known among the academic and research elites before the Web was launched for public consumption. The Internet's Web quickly rose in popularity, challenging the existing proprietary online services of Compuserve, AOL, and Prodigy to redesign their own services to take advantage of the layout and design of the Web as well as its growing number of users. Web usability (Nielsen, 1995; Rosenfeld & Morville, 1998) is a burgeoning area of applied research.

Content, too, matched the technological diffusion of Web access. Although the Internet included repositories of thousands of files of generally limited interest (weather information was one of the first to break this mold), the Web rapidly began to offer information of interest to a larger audience. Media historians will probably note the differences in how media organizations adopted the Web (Rosenfeld & Morville, 1998). Those who were more in tune with the long expected interactive electronic media future were in a better position to exploit the Web early. This was evident in both the newspaper and television industries, where the former has been involved in electronic publishing endeavors since the heyday of videotext (e.g., Knight-Ridder) and the latter have made a tremendous effort to establish a Web presence (e.g., MSNBC, etc.).

The Web is on its way toward matching audience access already available by cable television. Whether Web subscriptions will eventually reach that of the telephone is unknown, but seems probable as the conjoint effort between the telephone industry and the cable TV industry to create Web access via cable TV (e.g., the merger between AT&T and TCI). Critical issues remain, meanwhile, about the importance of relatively equal access to the storehouses of knowledge available on the Web through schools and libraries, if not through individual households.

As for how people use the Web and why, the question is being answered by academic researchers, as seen in other chapters in this volume. Will the Web become the next medium of mass entertainment, news and information, or some combination of the two? Will we find another Newton Minnow emerging with the new millennium to decry the Web as the new "vast wasteland" of unfulfilled content and functional potential? For how much longer will a television set and a PC be seen as two distinctly different media technologies? The emergence of digital television and the coming availability of near "bandwidth-on-demand" suggest that the questions will, once again, not be about technology. The ability to send and receive vast amounts of informative and entertaining material will be limited by the ability to produce content, not by limitations on the technological capabilities for accessing content. The Internet and the World Wide Web will continue to revolve around how we use technology as a tool, and if that use—when taken as a whole—is more beneficial than detrimental to our collective well-being.

APPENDIX: INTERNET SOFTWARE CONSORTIUM—
INTERNET DOMAIN SURVEY, JANUARY 2001

Number of Hosts advertised in the DNS

Date	Survey Host Count	Adjusted Host Count	Replied To Ping*	
Jan 2001	109,574,429		–	
Jul 2000	93,047,785		–	
Jan 2000	72,398,092		–	
Jul 1999	56,218,000		–	
Jan 1999	43,230,000		8,426,000	
Jul 1998	36,739,000		6,529,000	
Jan 1998	29,670,000		5,331,640	[first NEW Survey]
Jul 1997	19,540,000	26,053,000	4,314,410	[last OLD Survey]
Jan 1997	16,146,000	21,819,000	3,392,000	
Jul 1996	12,881,000	16,729,000	2,569,000	
Jan 1996	9,472,000	14,352,000	1,682,000	
Jul 1995	6,642,000	8,200,000	1,149,000	
Jan 1995	4,852,000	5,846,000	970,000	
Jul 1994	3,212,000		707,000	
Jan 1994	2,217,000		576,000	
Jul 1993	1,776,000		464,000	
Jan 1993	1,313,000			

[* estimated by pinging a sample of all hosts]

[adjusted host count was computed by increasing the old survey host count by the percentage of domains that did not respond to the old survey method]

Detailed Survey Data

- How the survey works -- what these numbers mean
- Distributions by Top-Level Domain Name (by hostcount)
- Distributions by Top-Level Domain Name (by name)
- Top 100 Host Names
- Top 100 Second-Level Domain Names
- Top 100 Third-Level Domain Names
- Host Count Graph (1991-2000)

Source: Internet Software Consortium (http://www.isc.org/)

REFERENCES

An overview of the World-Wide Web. (1997, December 3). Available online: http://www.cern.ch/Public/ACHIEVEMENTS/WEB/Welcome.html (September 3, 1998).

Atkin, D., Jeffres, L., & Neuendorf, K. (1998). Understanding Internet adoption as telecommunications behavior. *Journal of Broadcasting & Electronic Media, 42*(4), 475-490.

August 1998 new media highlights. (1998). New York: Media Metrixsm, The PC Meter(r) Company. Available online: http://www.pcmeter.com/interact_mmnewmedia.html (March 15, 1999).

Berners-Lee, T. (1999). *Weaving the web: The original design and ultimate destiny of the World Wide Web by its inventor.* San Francisco: HarperSanFrancisco.

Brenneman, K. (1997). Who's tops on the web? Advertisers want to know. *Boston Business Journal.* Available online: http://www.amcity.com/boston/stories/041497/focus1.html (September 5, 1998).

Bringing home the Internet. (1999, March). *IEEE Spectrum, 36*(3), 32-38.

Brody, H. (1998). Net cerfing: Q&A with Vint Cerf, one of the Internet's founding fathers. *Technology Review, 3*(101), 72-75.

Broersma, M. (1998, June 12). *Internet: Web ratings firms grilled for bad numbers.* Available online: http://www.zdnet.com/zdnn/stories/news/0,4586,2112010,00.html (July 11, 2001).

Bush, V. (1945). As we may think. *The Atlantic Monthly, 176*(1), 101-108.

Cailliau, R. (1995, November 2). *A short history of the Web.* Presentation to the launching of the European branch of the W3 Consortium, Paris, France. Available online: http://www.inria.fr/Actualites/Cailliau-fra.html (September 2, 1998).

Clemente, P. C. (1998). *The state of the net: The new frontier.* New York: McGraw-Hill.

Coates, C. (1998, August 31). *Study: Internet causes depression.* Available online: http://dailynews.yahoo.com/headlines/ap/technology/story.html?s=v/ap/980831/technology/stories/internet_isolation_2.html (August 31, 1998).

Court, R. (1997, November 24). *Truths about net use remain elusive.* Available online: http://www.wired.com:80/news/news/business/story/8745.html (March 3, 1999).

Craig, A. (1998, September 18). WebTV may vanish in two years. *TechWeb News.* Available online: http://content.techweb.com/wire/story/TWB19980918S00007 (July 12, 2001).

Dickinson, P., & Sciadas, G. (1998). *Access to the information highway.* Analytical Paper Series, Statistics Canada, No. 9. Ottawa, Ontario: Statistics Canada.

Dupagne, M., & Seel, P. B. (1998). *High-definition television: A global perspective.* Ames: Iowa State University Press.

Eighmey, J., & McCord, L. (1998). Adding value in the infomation age: Uses and gratifications of sites on the World Wide Web. *Journal of Business Research, 41,* 187-194.

Gearan, A. (1999, January 14). *Poll: Americans want weather news. The Associated Press.* Available online: http://www.washingtonpost.com/wp-srv/washtech/daily/jan99/weather14.html.

Guglielmo, C. (1998, May 4). *Survey tracks surfers, shoppers.* Available online: http://www.zdnet.com/intweek/print/980504/314052.html (July 11, 2001).

GVU WWW User Survey. (1998, April). Atlanta: Georgia Tech Research Corporation. Information and results available online: http://www.gvu.gatech.edu/user_surveys/survey-1998-04/.

Hafner, K., & Lyon, M. (1996). *Where wizards stay up late: The origins of the Internet.* New York: Simon & Schuster.

Hakala, D. (1996, June). Rural Internet access: Greening the digital desert. *Boardwatch,* pp. 70-72.

Hamilton, A. (1998, November 25). *Trouble deepens for traditional media. And it's only going to get worse. Here's why.* Available online: http://www.zdnet.com/anchordesk/story/story_2757.html (July 11, 2001).

Hamilton, B. (1998, APril 29). *The truth about the global Internet.* Available online: http://www.zdnet.com/anchordesk/story/story_2037.html (July 23, 2001).

Haney, C., & Weil, N. (2000, November 14). Oracle, Compaq team up on Net appliances. *Computerworld.* Available online: http://www.computerworld.com/cwi/story/0,1199,NAV47_STO539 90,00.html (July 12, 2001).

Harper, J. (1999, March 3). On-line news sites enjoy tidal wave of Internet surfers. *The Washington Times,* p. A8.

Hauben, M., & Hauben, R. (1997). *Netizens: On the history and impact of Usenet and the Internet.* Los Alamitos, CA: IEEE Computer Society Press.

How many online. (1998). Available online: http://www.nua.ie/surveys/how_many_online/index.html (July 11, 2001).

Hunter, C. (n.d.). *The uses and gratifications of the World Wide Web.* Available online: http://www.asc.upenn.edu/usr/chunter/webuses.html (July 11, 2001).

Iconoclast. (1998, August 26). Market update. Available online: http://iconocast.com/issue/19980826.html (July 14, 2001).

Internet at a glance: Users. (1998, November). Brisband, CA: Imagine Media, Inc. Available online: http://www.iconoclast.com (March 15, 1999).

Internet domain survey. (1998, July). Available online: http://www.nw.com/zone/WWW/report.html (September 3, 1998).

Internet domain survey. (2001, January). Internet software consortium. Available online: http://www.isc.org/ds/WWW-200101/index.html (July 23, 2001).

James, M., Worting, C., & Forrest, E. (1995). An exploratory study of the perceived benefits of electronic bulletin board use and their impact on other communication activities. *Journal of Broadcasting & Electronic Media, 39*(1), 30-50.

Johnson, D. (1998). Who's on the Internet and why. *The Futurist, 6*(32), 11-12.

Katz, J. E., & Aspden, P. (1998). Internet dropouts: The invisible group. *Telecommunications Policy, 22*(4/5), 327-339.

Kiesler, S., Zdaniuk, B., Lundmark, V., & Kraut, R. (2000). Troubles with the Internet: The dynamics of help at home. *Human-Computer Interaction, 15*, 323-351.

Klopfenstein, B. C. (1989a). The diffusion of the videocassette recorder in the United States. In M. Levy (Ed.), *The VCR age: Home video and mass communication* (pp. 21-39). Newbury Park, CA: Sage.

Klopfenstein, B. C. (1989b). Forecasting consumer adoption of information products and services: Lessons from home video forecasting. *Journal of the American Society for Information Science, 40*(1), 17-26.

Klopfenstein, B. (1989c). Problems and potential of forecasting the adoption of new media. In J. Salvaggio, & J. Bryant (Eds.), *Media use in the information age: Emerging patterns of adoption and consumer use* (pp. 21-41). Hillsdale, NJ: Lawrence Erlbaum Associates.

Klopfenstein, B. C. (1997). New technology and the future of the media. In A. Wells & E. A. Hakanen (Eds.), *Mass media and society* (pp. 19-49). Norwood, NJ: Ablex.

Klopfenstein, B. C. (1998). Internet economics: Pricing Internet access. *Convergence: The Journal of Research into New Media Technologies, 4*(1), 10-20.

Krol, E., & Klopfenstein, B. C. (1996). *The whole Internet user's guide and catalog.* Belmont, CA & Sebastopol, CA: Integra Media Group & O'Reilly and Associates.

Lazarus, D. (1997, April 7). *Microsoft buys WebTV.* Available online: http://www.wired.com/news/business/0,1367,2987,00.html (July 12, 2001).

Leiner, B. M., Cerf, V. G., Clark, D. D., Kahn, R. E., Kleinrock, L., Lynch, D. C., Postel, J., Roberts, L. G., & Wolff, S. (1998, February 20). *A brief history of the Internet* Available online: http://www.isoc.org/internet-history/brief.html (September 1, 1998).

Lin, C. A. (1998). Exploring personal computer adoption dynamics. *Journal of Broadcasting & Electronic Media, 42*(1), 95-112.

Lin, C. A. (1999). Online-service adoption likelihood. *Journal of Advertising Research, 39*(2), 79-89.

Lule, J. (1998). The power and pitfalls of journalism in the hypertext era. *The Chronicle of Higher Education, 44*(48), B7-B8.

McNeal, J. U. (1998). Taping the three kids' markets. *American Demographics, 20*(4), 36-41.

Media Measurement Task Force. (1997, September 15). *Metrics and methodology.* New York: Internet Advertising Bureau. Available online: http://www.iab.net/advertise/content/mmtf3.html (April 28, 1999).

Media Metrix chronicles the "history" of the Internet. (1999, March 18). Available online: http://www.findarticles.com/cf_0/m0EIN/1999_March_18/54145828/p1/article.html?term=%22internet+gender+gap%22.

Menefee, C. (1998, February 5). *ISPs could avoid churn as user profiles change—study.* Available online: http://library.northernlight.com/DG19980206040000119.html (July 11, 2001).

Morris, M., & Ogan, C. (1996). The Internet as mass medium. *Journal of Computer-Mediated Communication, 1*(4). Available online: http://www.ascusc.org/jcmc/vol1/issue4/morris.html (September 8, 1998).

National ISPs stand to gain most in growing U.S. market. (2000, September 25). Available online: http://www.instat.com/pr/2000/is0004sp_pr.html (July 23, 2001).

Newhagen, J.E., & Rafaeli, S. (1996). Why communication researchers should study the Internet: A dialogue. *Journal of Computer-Mediated Communication, 1*(4). Available online: http://www.ascusc.org/jcmc/vol1/issue4/rafaeli.html (September 8, 1998).

Nielsen, J. (1995, August). Generations of online services. *The alertbox: Current issues in web usability.* Available online: http://www.sun.com/950801/columns/alertbox/servicegenerations.html.

Nielsen, J. (1998, April). Nielsen's law of Internet bandwidth. *The alertbox: Current issues in web usability.* Available online: http://www.useit.com/alertbox/980405.html (September 5, 1998).

Nolan, S. (1998, July 15). *Counting heads internationally: What's the magic number?* Available online: http://searchz.com/wmo/071598.html (September 3, 1998).

The numbers behind e-mail. (1999, February 2). Westport, CT: internet.com. Available online: http://cyberatlas.internet.com/big_picture/traffic_patterns/email.html (March 15, 1999).

Pew Research Center. (1998). *Pew's poll numbers: 20 million go online for Starr Report* (1998). Washington, DC: Author. Available online: http://www.people-press.org/starrrpt.html (March 15, 1999).

Pew Research Center. (1999). *Online newcomers more middle-brow, less work-oriented* (1999). Washington, DC: Author. Available online: http://www.people-press.org/tech98sum.html (March 15, 1999).

Pietrucha, B. (1998, February 19). *Internet use jumps five-fold since 1995.* Available online: http://www.newsbytes.com (September 5, 1998).

The portal wars. (1999, April 14). *WebTomorrow.com.* Available online: http://www.webtomorrow.com/portals.html (April 25, 1999).

Robinson, G. O. (Ed.). (1978). *Communications for tomorrow: Policy perspectives for the 1980s.* New York: Praeger for the Aspen Institute for Humanistic Studies.

Rogers, E. (1986). *Communication technology: The new media in society.* New York: The Free Press.

Rogers, E. M. (1995). *Diffusion of innovations* (4th ed.). New York: The Free Press.

Rosenfeld, L., & Morville, P. (1998). *Information architecture for the World Wide Web: Designing large-scale web sites.* Sebastpol, CA: O'Reilly & Associates.

Russell, C. (1998). The haves and the want-nots. *American Demographics, 20*(4), 10-13.

Shapiro, E. (1998, June 12). Web lovers love TV, often watch both. *Wall Street Journal,* p. 1.

Sheets, S. (1998). Understanding WWW statistics. *Managing Office Technology, 43*(1), 18-27.

Smith, C. B. (1997, June). Casting the net: Surveying an Internet population. *Journal of Computer-Mediated Communication, 3*(1). Available online: http://www.ascusc.org/jcmc/vol3/issue1/smith.html (September 8, 1998).

Sterling, B. (1993, February). *A short history of the Internet. The magazine of fantasy and science fiction.* Available online various URLs including http://w3.aces.uiuc.edu/AIM/scale/nethistory.html (August 15, 1998).

Stirland, S. (1998). Real-time meets prime time on WebTV; or maybe not? *Wall Street & Technology, 16*(7), 72, 84.

The Strategis Group. (1998, June 29). *Internet users spend less time watching TV.* Available online: http://www.strategisgroup.com/press/Internetuser.html (September 3, 1998).

Strow, D. (1997, October 31). SISP industry consolidated amid boom, study shows. *The Business Journal.* Available online: http://triangle.bcentral.com/triangle/stories/1997/11/03/newscolumn4.html (July 23, 2001).

Tappendorf, S. (1995, July 30). *ARPANET and beyond.* Available online: http://clavin.music.uiuc.edu/sean/internet_history.html (August 13, 1998).

Taylor, H. (1998, February 18). The remorseless rise of the Internet. Available online: http://www.harris:interactive.com/harris_poll/index.asp?PID=204 (July 10, 2001).

Tchong, M. (2001). Internet at a glance. Available online: http://www.iconoclast.com/pdf/ataglance7-01.pdf (July 10, 2001).

Tedesco, R. (1999, January 18). Disney, Infoseek give it a go, *Broadcasting and Cable*, p. 133.

Tedesco, R. (1998). New yardstick for a new medium. *Broadcasting and Cable*, 6(128), 54.

Thompson, M. J. (1998, August 9). *Market perspective: Kids online.* Available online: http://www.thestandard.com/article/0,1902,9994,00.html (July 14, 2001).

United States Department of Commerce (2000, October). *Falling through the net: Toward digital inclusion.* Washington, DC: National Telecommunications and Information Administration. Available online: http://search.htia.doc.gov/pdf/fttn00.pdf (July 9, 2001).

United States National Telecommunications and Information Administration. (1998). *Falling through the net II: New data on the digital divide.* Available online: http://www.ntia.doc.gov/ntiahome/net2 (July 10, 2001).

Vanderkay, J. (1998). *Technology user profile.* Available online: http://www.metafactsusa.com (July 10, 2001).

Walsh, J. (1998). Internet withstands Starr test. *InfoWorld, 20*(39), 41.

Web ad revenue $219.4 million in 1998. (1998). *Media Daily, 4*(5).

Web spawns 1.5 million pages daily according to findings from Alexa Internet. (1998). Available online: http://www.alexa.com/press/press_releases/webfacts.html (July 13, 2001).

Whitaker, J. C. (2001). *DTV: The revolution in digital video.* New York: McGraw-Hill.

Women a formidable force on the web: Neilsen/Netratings. (2001, June 28). Available online: http://www.eratings/com/news/20010628.html (July 23, 2001).

Woods, B. (1998, July 21). *Five portals to be tops by 2000. Newsbytes news network.* Available online: http://www.newsbytes.com (accessed via www.elibrary.com, March 12, 1999).

Zakon, R. H. (1998, April 12). *Hobbes' Internet timeline v3.3.* Available online: http://info.isoc.org/guest/zakon/Internet/History/HIT.html (September 4, 1998).

15

Uses and Gratifications of the Internet

Tamar Charney
Bradley S. Greenberg
Michigan State University

As of August 1998, one third of all Americans over the age of 16 had access to the Internet, an increase of more than 18 million people in 9 months as reported by Nielsen Media Research (1998). This brings the total to 70 million adult Americans, as compared to estimates of 29 to 37 million just three years earlier when this study began (Nielsen Media Research, 1995). Although the origin of this access may be at work, at school, or at home, its location is less important than the mercurial growth curve for this information and entertainment technology, a growth curve that began at ground zero in 1991, when the World Wide Web was introduced (Kirsner, 1996).

The primary focus of this study is what motivates people to use the Internet. Knowing what needs people are looking to fulfill and what types of activities they prefer and participate in while online will enable companies, media producers, policymakers, and media effects researchers to better understand how to deal with this expanding technology. Understanding why people use new technologies can help researchers predict the impact the technology will have on society. As Cowles (1989) pointed out, the "use to which a medium is put helps determine its impact" (p. 84). Thus, it is important that energies be directed "to the study of interactive media because interactive media can be put to many different uses" (p. 84).

If the Internet is being used heavily for entertainment purposes, the way people allocate their time to other entertainment sources may shift. If the Internet is used mostly for research and information seeking, it may be less likely that the technology will achieve the degree of adoption as would a technology used for entertainment and other mass appeal purposes. As Williams, Phillips, and Lum (1985) noted, "we are seeing modifications in the choice environment. Some of these may be short lived . . . and others may change the media environment forever" (p. 243).

Knowledge about why people use the Internet will be helpful in business forecasting and decision making. Should companies be developing online video applications and games or reference and research tools or communication applications? Because "the proliferation of new communication technologies may affect the structure of communication in society" (Williams et al., 1985, p. 241), knowledge about the amount of use and type of use is important when policymakers and business leaders make decisions about the design and architecture of the information superhighway. Currently, there is much speculation about Internet use by business, academic, and government sectors. Business leaders want to know where to invest, the government wants to know how to regulate (or not), and academicians want to know how online services are going to affect society.

In addition to providing substantive information as to why a particular sample of users goes to the Internet, we offer evidence as to their activities and the frustrations they encounter.

We have chosen to examine these questions from a traditional uses and gratifications perspective, an approach that has as one of its fundamental principles the idea of an active audience. That idea has been challenged in other media contexts, where audiences have perhaps been considered at least as passive as they are active. The Internet, however, would seem to allow little passivity on the part of its users. Newhagen and Rafaeli (1996) argued that "the [uses and gratifications] perspective seems to hold some prospect for understanding the Internet because it addresses the problem of its mutability . . . the Internet offers the user a broad range of communication opportunities . . . [and] uses-and-gratifications offers a vehicle to lay out a taxonomy of just what goes on in cyberspace" (p. 11). At the same time, Morris and Ogan (1996) believe that the comprehensive nature of uses and gratifications makes the theory useful when studying the Internet because the Internet is "a media environment where [there are] not only home and business applications, but also work and play functions" (p. 47)

The uses and gratifications approach to media studies is described by Katz, Blumler, and Gurevitch (1974) as one that looks at "(1) the social and psychological origins of (2) needs, which generate (3) expectations of (4) the mass media or other sources, which lead to (5) differing patterns of media exposure, . . . resulting in (6) need gratifications and (7) other consequences" (p. 20). Lichtenstein and Rosenfeld (1984) explained that because people "choose their media experiences according to the particular gratifications, ... research has focused primarily on the exploration of audiences' decision making processes" (p. 393)

Currently, uses and gratifications seems to be most useful for describing the various reasons or motivations for choosing one medium over another. Lichtenstein and Rosenfeld (1984) found that "the decision to utilize mass communications channels involves a two part process. The first part involves the acquisition of normative expectations about gratifications from different media. The second part concerns individualistic decisions about how to seek gratifications" (p. 409). There is, of course, no single master list of the gratifications obtained from media use; instead, multiple lists, categories, and classification systems abound. Gratifications uncovered in past research on conventional media include a need for factual information, substitute companionship, social validation, relaxation, behavioral guidance, excitement, companionship, and affective guidance (Lometti, Reeves, & Bybee, 1977). Gratifications have been identified for television (Greenberg, 1974; Rubin, 1981), newspapers, books and magazines (Lichtenstein & Rosenfeld, 1984), the VCR (Rubin, 1987), and the telephone (O'Keefe & Sulanowski, 1995), among others. From these studies of conventional media came items and themes we adapted to develop a set of potential gratifications from using the Internet.

Some related research on newer media offer additional hints about potential gratifications that might be sought on the Internet. Perse and Courtright (1993), in a 1988 study (pre-Web) compared how 12 different communication media—television, VCRs, cable TV, movies, conversation, newspapers, telephones, music, books, magazines, radio, and computers—filled needs. Learning needs, passing time, and diversion were found to be the top three gratifications sought from computers. On the Internet, games, music, and videos, as well as browsing or exploring may exemplify opportunities for time passing, entertainment, and diversion. Further support for the entertainment or time-passing gratification come from Pitkow and Kehoe's (1995) Web study; 79% used the Web for browsing, 63% for entertainment, and 52% for work.

E-mail use has been researched fairly heavily, where a traditional assumption had been that e-mail systems were used primarily for task-related communication (Steinfield, 1986). However, a large portion of e-mail in work settings is social. Rice and Steinfield (1994) found that the use of office e-mail fell into three categories; two remind us of some common gratification factors—entertainment, consensus/control, and surveillance. In the cluster of entertainment-related uses, office e-mail was used to "fill up free time, take breaks from work, and participate in entertaining events." In other words, e-mail was used to pass time, for diversion, and for entertainment.

But what of motives and gratifications that are idiosyncratic to the Internet because of its alternative and original capabilities? Other common uses of the Internet include e-mail, discussions, and shopping. These are transactions or interactive Internet activities that do not easily fit into the conventional gratification dimensions and there has been speculation as to what satisfactions they provide. Palmgreen (1984) cautioned that in studying new communications technologies "researchers should not be wedded to gratification typologies that the very changes under study may have rendered incomplete, if not obsolete" (p. 49) For example, with many online services allowing users to choose aliases and Internet activities such as multi-user dungeons (MUDs) encouraging users to create the identity of their choosing, the use of new personas and identities is common on the Internet. Age, gender, and other elements of identity become "a property that can be reset with a line of code" (Bruckman, 1993, p. 5). How does the ability to transcend race, age, gender, and mobility motivate users? Parks and Floyd (1996) quoted Bruckman as noting that "cyberspace creates an 'identity workshop in which people learn and test social skills'" (p. 83).

What constitutes interactivity is unclear. Heeter (1989) posited that no definition per se exists, but there are dimensions of interactivity such as complexity of choice available, effort users must exert, responsiveness to the user, monitoring information use, ease of adding information, and facilitation of interpersonal communication. Thus, if the Internet and other "new media possess attributes not possessed by the traditional media, in particular, interactivity" (Cowles, 1989, p. 83), then the "consequences for audience members include greater selection, more personal control over selection, and the sense that one can be a communications source as well as a receiver. . . . Interactivity also provides opportunities for interpersonal-like transactions between individuals or among groups of communicators" (Williams et al., 1985, p. 247).

Specific utilitarian services such as banking, making airline reservations, and shopping may evoke satisfaction for work accomplished and/or frustration for an inability to complete such tasks (Williams et. al., 1985). The same authors suggest that some activities—namely, chat rooms and e-mail—are laden with emotional possibilities, not a characteristic found in prior gratification identification efforts.

Wellman and Gulia (1995) suggested that a large part of e-mail and other Internet use is socially motivated, "if the Net were solely a means of information exchange, then virtual communities . . . would mostly contain narrow, specialized relationships. However, there is evidence that information is only one of many social resources that is exchanged on the Net" (p. 5).

Netsurfing provides another avenue for exploring alternative media gratifications. Of Web users in a Nielsen (1995) study, 90% were "Netsurfing." Is surfing done to pass time, is it entertaining, is it a means of surveying the Internet environment, is it a way of coping with the large volume of options available? "New media use has created new audience activity dimensions such as grazing, or using the remote control device to graze over many viewing options" Lin (1993, p. 41) wrote about the multichannel television environment, but that quote could as easily be identified today as a reference to Netsurfing. Earlier, Heeter (1985) wrote that channel surfing with the remote control "when a viewer does not already know what they want to watch . . . may be an examination of program options (generating alternatives), accompanied by a covert matching of needs with programs that fulfill them (assessing consequences), leading eventually to selection of a matched needs-program option" (p. 129). Those needs become gratifications sought. In a somewhat different perspective on surfing, Hoffman and Novak (1994) posited that Netsurfing and time-passing ritualistic use characterize "early interactions with hypermedia" (p. 5). People Netsurf because they enjoy moving to mastery over the medium. The authors anticipated that more instrumental use will develop over time and the frequency of browsing will decrease. Another possibility suggested in the popular press is that Netsurfing is "a procrastinator's dream . . . [offering] us the opportunity to waste time, to wander aimlessly, to daydream about the countless other lives, the other people" also on the Internet (Gibson, 1996, p. 31).

Internet content providers continue to create an abundance, perhaps even an excess, of applications and content designed for entertainment, social, and time-passing activities. Chat groups, online comic strips, games, interactive extensions of television programs, audio and video selections, as well as the more bizarre efforts (e.g., cameras on fish tanks), abound in an environment once characterized by databases; search and retrieval programs, and academic, military, and government information. Services catering to diverse segments of society such as children and the elderly focus less on information germane to these groups and more on fostering a sense of community and providing time-passing activities targeted at the demographics of the user (Rigdon, 1994). Wellman and Gulia (1995) argued that one purpose of Internet use is the construction of a virtual community and society, wherein meeting people and becoming part of a community are focal goals. At the same time, Internet commerce through business transactions, product information, and advertising is also increasing. Of course, there remains a plethora of information and research tools available.

With so many different activities, types of content, and options on the Internet, how does someone decide or know what to do unless they come to the Internet seeking to gratify some felt need? We recognize the possibility as well that an Internet activity such as surfing might introduce users to content that creates needs or reminds them of needs they have or should have. An excellent venue for the latter is Internet advertising, of course. But that distinction begs to differ between motives going into the medium and motives induced by some Internet activities. Both scenarios require us to probe further into the identification of gratifications sought from the activity, and eventually to the identification of gratifications provided by the activity. We believe that those efforts can be informed and enhanced by the present study.

METHODS

Data were collected in 1996 through an in-class self-administered survey. Respondents were a purposive student sample in an introductory telecommunication class at Michigan State University. Although college student samples often are used only because they are convenient and free, such a sample was used in this project primarily because of the greater likelihood that they would have substantial Internet experience. That is, they are of a generation that is more oriented to computers and the university they attended provided free Internet access for all of them. Therefore, these college students provided a purposive sample whose experience would enable them to articulate their reasons for using the Internet. All respondents had free access to the Internet through the University. Out of the 216 questionnaires distributed, completed questionnaires were obtained and 168 respondents reported personal use of the Internet.

Instrument Development

In a preliminary study, data were collected from two groups. The survey was administered first to an office staff, all of whom had access to the World Wide Web. The instrument also was administered to an undergraduate class at Michigan State University, in which all students had free access to the Internet. Twenty-two people completed the instrument. Open-ended questions were used so as not to impose previous typologies nor to influence the manner in which respondents thought about the subject of study. Respondents detailed the different activities in which they engaged in online. For each activity listed, the respondent listed his or her main reasons or motivations. Responses were content-analyzed, and the resultant information was considered exploratory and qualitative. Those responses yielded eight categories of Internet activity: e-mail, chat rooms, work- and school-related research, job hunting, travel information, transactions (i.e., obtaining or delivering products), netsurfing, and games or "playing." The responses also suggested five motives: school/work necessity, social, entertainment, relieve boredom or pass time, and exploration-novelty seeking-surveillance.

Gratifications

The outcomes from the preliminary study were used to supplement and adapt items and factors from previous gratifications research. For each item, respondents indicated the frequency with which they use the Internet for that reason on a 5-point scale (1 = *not at all*, 2 = *rarely*, 3 = *sometimes*, 4 = *often*, 5 = *very often*). We began with the 10 a priori dimensions listed in Table 5.1.

The dimensions of social, entertainment, surveillance, and diversion motives, as well as many of the individual items under these headings, came directly from previous uses and gratifications research (Atwater, Heeter, & Brown, 1985; Dobos & Dimmick, 1988; Lin, 1993; Perse & Courtright, 1993). The social category was augmented heavily by the Wellman and Gulia (1995) research into the community-like aspects of the Internet. The acquisition category incorporates items from a study of uses and gratifications of the telephone (O'Keefe & Sulanowski, 1995) and our preliminary study. The remaining five dimensions—aesthetic, fame, identity, future, and peer pressure—merge ideas culled from responses in the preliminary study, from Wellman and Gulia, the popular press, and conversations with Internet users and media researchers. These categories attempt to tap some of the unique features and capabilities of the Net such as the ease of being a "publisher," the ability of the Internet to create "an identity workshop where people can learn and test social skills" (Parks & Floyd, 1996, p. 83), the fashionable status of the Internet, and the novelty of the Internet.

Computer Access and Use

Respondents were asked about their computer use. They were asked to answer yes or no to the question "Do you personally own a computer at this time?" They were also asked "How many hours per week do you use a computer for fun/play?" and "How many hours per week do you use

Table 15.1. Gratifications Items.

	Reliability	Mean[a]
Social	.81	2.17
I use the Internet to . . .		
• stay in touch with people I don't see very often.		
• get advice or support.		
• get information to pass on to other people.		
• meet new people.		
• find companionship.		
• find people like me.		
Entertainment	.87	2.77
I use the Internet to . . .		
• have fun.		
• feel good.		
• be entertained.		
• find excitement.		
• play.		
Acquisition	.73	2.32
I use the Internet to . . .		
• get information about products or services.		
• learn about how to do things.		
• order products or services.		
• make reservations.		
• find information.		
• deliver information or documents to someone.		
Surveillance	.87	2.51
I use the Internet to . . .		
• be informed about what is going on in the world.		
• get immediate knowledge of big news events.		
• keep up with news that isn't available elsewhere.		
• get information like time/weather/stock prices/sports scores .		
• find out about job opportunities.		
• get information I can trust.		
Pass time Diversion	.80	2.49
I use the Internet to . . .		
• relax.		
• combat boredom.		
• pass time.		
• satisfy a habit.		
• find new things.		
• avoid doing what I am supposed to.		

Table 15.1. Gratifications Items (cont'd.).

	Reliability	Mean[a]
Peer Pressure Status	.87	2.75
I use the Internet to . . .		
• feel important.		
• gain status.		
• be cool.		
• because I know I should.		
• because everyone else does.		
Future	.86	2.60
I use the Internet to . . .		
• develop new interests.		
• be a part of the information superhighway.		
• stay up to date for my career.		
• because I know it will be even more important in the future.		
• keep learning.		
• keep up with technology.		
Identity	.76	1.70
I use the Internet to . . .		
• try out new identities.		
• escape who I am.		
• be accepted for my ideas.		
• experience things I can't in the real world.		
• live out a fantasy.		
Fame	.67	1.95
I use the Internet to . . .		
• publish materials.		
• let people know who I am.		
• learn about famous people.		
• read home pages of other people.		
Aesthetic	.87	2.75
I use the Internet to . . .		
• look for visually interesting graphics and pages.		
• enjoy the sights and sounds.		
• look at graphics and animation.		

[a] 1 = *not at all*, 2 = *rarely*, 3 = *sometimes*, 4 = *often*, 5 = *very often*

your computer for work?" The response options for these two questions were *none, under 5 hours, 6-10 hours, 11-20 hours, 21-30 hours, 31-40 hours,* and *over 40.* These response options were guided by those used by Pitkow and Kehoe (1995).

Origin of Internet Use

Two questions were asked about the respondents' history with the Internet. The question, "How long have you been using the Net?" was asked. Response options were *less than 6 months, 6-11 months, 1-3 years, 4-6 years,* and *7 years or more.* For the question "How did you learn to use the Net?" respondents were asked to select one answer from: *junior high class, high school class, college class, extracurricular class, on my own, from a friend, from a parent or relative, from computer lab staff, at work,* or *other.*

Internet Use

Respondents were asked, "How many hours a week do you spend online?" by choosing from *less than one hour, 2-4 hours per week, 5-7 hours per week, 8-10 hours per week, 11-20 hours per week,* and *more than 20 hours per week.* To the question "Where do you most often use the Net?" respondents selected one answer from *home, school computer lab, work, friends home, relative's home, library, community center, other.* Respondents also circled *yes* or *no* to indicate whether they do each of the following activities on the Internet: research for school, research for work, browsing/surfing, learning, shopping, reading online news or magazines, doing work online, entertainment, e-mail, playing games, newsgroups/IRC, accessing general information (e.g., time, weather, stock prices, etc.), and accessing product information.

For the question "How much time do you spend Netsurfing each week?" respondents had the options of *less than 1 hour, 2-4 hours, 5-7 hours, 7-9 hours, 10 hours or more,* and *don't surf.* Reasons offered for surfing or browsing were "to find something in particular, to pass time, to see what's going on, for fun, to feel less lonely, to learn how to use the Net, I feel I should, and don't surf."

Frustration with the Internet

Respondents indicated the frequency with which they found themselves experiencing various frustrations with the Internet (1 = *not at all* to 5 = *very often*). Specific items are listed in Table 15.2.

Table 15.2. Frustration Items.

	Average[a]
I get frustrated because the Internet is running slowly.	3.16
I get frustrated having to wait while things are downloading.	3.13
The Internet graphics take too long to access.	3.12
I have trouble finding what I am looking for on the Internet.	2.73
I find I'm seeing the same stuff over and over.	2.65
I find the Internet is overrated.	2.58
I get bored using the Internet.	2.46
I get disconnected while I'm on the Internet.	2.24
I find myself thinking that the novelty of the Internet is gone.	2.20
I have trouble using the Internet.	2.18
I have trouble remembering how to get onto the Internet.	1.94

[a]1 = *not at all,* 2 = *rarely,* 3 = *sometimes,* 4 = *often,* 5 = *very often*
This set of items yielded an alpha reliability coefficient of .87.

Demographic Questions

Demographic questions included gender, age, class level (response options: freshman, sophomore, junior, senior, graduate student, continuing education, not an enrolled student), and current marital status (response options: single, domestic partnership/living with someone, married, widowed, divorced).

RESULTS

Following are some descriptive results, as to the sample's composition and its use and experience with the Internet. Two thirds of the respondents were male, and all but one were undergraduates, consisting of 56 freshmen, 49 sophomores, 36 juniors, and 21 seniors. Eighty one percent was between 18 and 21 years old, with an average age of 20; 93% were single.

Half of these college students personally owned a computer. On average, 60% to 70% used the computer less than 5 hours a week for work purposes, fun, or a combination of both. For amount of work time on the computer, 13% indicated no time at all, 47% less than 5 hours a week, 23% at 6 to 10 hours a week, and 16% more than 11 hours a week. For amount of fun time on the computer, 8% said they never use a computer for fun, 61% less than 5 hours a week, 22% at 6 to 10 hours, and 8% used the computer for fun in excess of 11 hours a week.

For most respondents, use of the Internet was a recent experience. More than 9 of 10 had been using it for less than 3 years (27% less than 6 months, 25% for 6 to 11 months, 41% for 1 to 3 years, 5% more than 3 years). Home (39%) and a school computer lab (43%) were the primary locations where most respondents used the Internet, with no other location greater than 9%. The major origins of their ability to use the Internet were more diffused; 26% said that they learned how to use the Internet on their own, 22% learned from a friend, 21% in a college class, and 11% from a high school class, with no other source greater than 7%. Three fourths of the respondents spent 4 hours or less each week using the Internet, whereas 11% spent more than 7 hours. Amount of time spent on the Internet correlates with owning a computer ($r = .25$, $p < .001$) and the amount of time the user has known how to use the Internet ($r = .48$, $p < .001$).

Internet Activities

Writing or reading e-mail, browsing or surfing, research for school, entertainment, research for work, and learning were frequent Internet activities for at least 75% of the students. Less common but still exercised by a majority were learning, reading online news, and playing games. About 33% reported accessing product information, working online, and using the newsgroups, whereas only 16% of the students used the Internet for shopping (see Table 15.3). These latter activities of course would be expected to be more common among older, nonstudent users.

Table 15.3. Frequency of Internet Activities.

Activity	% yes
E-mail	88
Browse or surf	79
Research for school	77
Entertainment	77
Research for work	75
Learning	73
Read online news	60
Access general information	52
Play games	49
Access product information	38
Do work online	36
Newsgroups /interrelay chat	35
Shop	16

Internet Frustrations

The sources of greatest frustration (with means slightly above the mid-point of 3.0) all related to the amount of time it takes to access Internet materials (see Table 15.2). The lowest frustration levels came from the respondents' mastery over using the Internet. The average score on the frustration scale was 2.6, which lies slightly below the midpoint (range = 1-5). Thus, these respondents were only *rarely* to *sometimes* frustrated by the Internet.

Gratifications

Examination of the gratification measures proceeded in two stages. First, the a priori gratification scales were examined for reliability and strength. Then, these scales were factor-analyzed to determine the nature of their interrelationships.

As Table 15.1 details, all 10 a priori gratification scales were generally reliable with alphas ranging from .67 for the fame scale to .87 for the surveillance, entertainment, and aesthetic scales; overall, the average reliability was .80.

Recalling that the range of each scale was from 5 (*very often*) to 1 (*not at all*), we can examine the relative magnitude of each dimension. The midpoint of this scale is 3 and no dimension exceeded that level. A major point of interest, then, is that no particular gratification is especially strong. Entertainment (mean = 2.77), aesthetic (2.75), future (2.60), surveillance (2.51) and pass time/diversion (2.49) order as the most frequent reasons for engaging in Internet use, and fall between scale responses of *rarely* and *sometimes*. Least strong were the motives of using the Internet for identification and peer pressure purposes.

These a priori scales then were reexamined to determine their independence from each other. A factor analysis was conducted with the SPSS/Windows 6.1.3 principal components solution using VARIMAX rotation. The procedure yielded 11 factors with eigenvalues greater than 1.0, but our interest centers on those eight factors whose reliability exceeded .7, and whose minimum item loading was .5. For the remainder of this presentation, the emergent factors are analyzed, rather than the a priori scales. Space limits prohibit using both for comparative purposes, and it seems preferable to use those dimensions that are empirically independent at this stage of inquiry. Table 15.4 provides the complete factor solution.

The first and largest factor, *Keep Informed*, had an eigenvalue of 20.1, explained 39% of the variance, and had a reliability of .94. No other factors explained as much as 10% of the variance. This factor con-

Table 15.4. Gratification Factor Analysis Results.

Factor	Meaning	Loading	Mean[a]	Alpha	Eigen	%Var.
Factor 1	Keep Informed		2.64	0.94	20.08	38.6
Surv	To get information like time/weather/stock prices/ sports scores	0.78	2.78			
Surv	To be informed about what is going on in the world	0.74	2.76			
Acq	To get information about products or services	0.71	2.40			
Surv	To get information I can trust	0.70	2.52			
Surv	To get immediate knowledge of big news events	0.68	2.34			
Acq	To find information	0.67	3.44			
Fut	To keep learning	0.66	2.89			
Div	To find new things	0.61	2.79			
Fut	To keep up with technology	0.57	2.64			
Surv	To keep up to date with new that isn't available elsewhere	0.57	2.58			
Fut	To develop new interests	0.55	2.43			
Soc	To get information to pass on to other people	-0.51	2.38			
Fut	Because I know it will be even more important in the future	0.46	2.75			
Fame	To read home pages of other people	0.44	2.26			
Factor 2	Diversion-Entertainment		2.80	0.92	3.81	7.30
Div	To pass tme	0.78	2.78			
Div	To combat boredom	0.75	2.88			
Ent	To play	0.73	2.98			
Ent	To be entertained	0.70	3.20			

Table 15.4. Gratification Factor Analysis Results (con't.).

Factor	Meaning	Loading	Mean[a]	Alpha	Eigen	%Var.
Factor 2	Diversion-Entertainment		2.80	0.92	3.81	7.30
Ent	To have fun	0.69	2.88			
Div	To relax	0.68	2.20			
Ent	To find excitement	0.62	2.86			
Fut	To be a part of the information superhighway	0.58	2.59			
Factor 3	Peer Identity		1.83	0.87	3.13	6.00
Peer	Because everyone else does	0.75	1.80			
Peer	To gain status	0.72	1.51			
Id	To live out a fantasy	0.71	1.46			
Id	To be accepted for my ideas	0.67	1.63			
Soc	To meet new people	0.59	2.02			
Div	To satisfy a habit	0.49	1.98			
Soc	To find people like me	0.48	2.17			
Soc	To get advice or support	0.45	1.57			
Factor 4	Good Feelings		1.59	0.79	1.90	3.70
Peer	To feel important	0.68	1.49			
Ent	To feel good	0.63	1.91			
Soc	To find companionship	0.60	1.51			
Id	To escape who I am	0.59	1.41			
Factor 5	Communication		2.74	0.76	1.71	3.30
Soc	To stay in touch with people I don't see very often	0.77	2.92			
Acq	To deliver information to someone	0.73	2.51			

Table 15.4. Gratification Factor Analysis Results (con't.).

Factor	Meaning	Loading	Mean[a]	Alpha	Eigen	%Var.
Factor 6	Sights & Sounds		2.72	0.84	1.33	2.60
Aesth	To look at graphics or animation	0.74	2.90			
Aesth	To enjoy the sights and sounds	0.62	2.67			
Aesth	To look for visually interesting graphics and pages	0.56	2.64			
Fame	To learn about famous people	0.51	2.24			
Factor 7	Career		2.33	0.77	1.23	2.40
Sur	To find out about job opportunities	0.64	2.15			
Acq	To learn how to do things	0.60	2.61			
Fut	To stay up to date for my career	0.53	2.26			
Factor 8	Coolness		1.74	.78	1.01	1.90
Peer	To be cool	0.68	1.62			
Peer	Because I know I should	0.67	1.86			
Acq[b]	To make reservations	0.40	1.51			

[a] 1 = *not at all*, 2 = *rarely*, 3 = *sometimes*, 4 = *often*, 5 = *very often*
[b] Item dropped dur to low reliability and conceptual reasons

tained 12 items with loadings of at least .5, combining items primarily from the surveillance and future scales, as well as information items related to acquisition. The average score for items on this factor was 2.6 on the 5-point scale, ranging from 3.44 (to find information) to 2.34 (to get immediate knowledge of big news events).

Diversion Entertainment was the second factor, with an eigenvalue of 3.81 and 7% of explained variance. The huge drop in variance explained indicates the overall dominance of the first factor across this complete set of items. Nevertheless, this dimension of eight items had an average item score of 2.8, making it at least as strong in importance to those expressing these motives, as was the first factor. The strongest motive averaged 3.2 (to be entertained) and the weakest was 2.2 (to relax). Reliability alpha was .92. All but one of the items on this factor came from the diversion and entertainment a priori groupings.

Peer Identity was the third strongest factor, in terms of eigenvalue (3.13) and variance accounted for (6%), but quite weak in terms of average item strength (1.83). The five primary items came from the social, peer pressure, and identity scales. The reliability was .87.

Good Feelings was the fourth factor (variance explained = 4%). It had the lowest average item score (1.59) of any factor, and therefore is a set of reasons minimally used by the sample. Furthermore, the four items representing this factor came from four different a priori scales. It is a stretch to identify a common element; the closest we can offer is use of the Internet for the purpose of improving one's mood or emotional state. Reliability was .79. It may be better to suggest that this is an unclear factor.

Factor 5, *Communication,* contains two items, each with loadings above .7, and a strong average score of 2.7. They explain 3% of the variance, with a reliability of .76.

Sights and Sounds characterize the sixth factor, also with 3% of the variance explained and with an average item strength of 2.7. All the items originate with the original aesthetics scale; reliability was .84. A fourth item (to learn about famous people) on the factor lacks a common theme.

Career, the seventh factor, contains three items (reliability = .77) that refer to career research and planning. This factor accounts for 2% of the variance with an average item score of 2.3.

The final factor, *Coolness,* also with 2% of the variance contains two items. This factor is weak in acceptance, with an average item score of 1.74, but strong in reliability at an alpha of .78.

Having established the set of basic gratifications sought from using the Internet, we then explored the relationships between Internet gratifications and Internet use, including time given to Internet activities and surfing time, as well as frustrations found in using the Internet. Without a priori hypotheses, we treated each issue as a research question.

Predicting Time Spent on the Internet

What accounts for the amount of time users spend on the Internet? The contributions of five groups of independent variables were used in multiple regression analysis to determine what accounts for time spent on the Internet: the sets of gratifications (8 variables), demographics (3 variables), how respondents learned to use the Internet (9 options), where respondents use the Internet most often (5 options), and the activities respondents engage in on the Internet (13 possibilities). The plan of analysis called for looking at each of these groups separately, to retain those which were significant, and to do a final regression analysis with all significant covariates. For Internet time use, two variables from the gratification dimensions were significant—the Keep Informed and Communication factors. No variables from any other groups were significant, so the final regression analysis contained only those two variables. Together, they accounted for 36% of the variance in Internet time used ($r = .60$, $p < .001$). However, the primary gratification, Keeping Informed, was itself correlated .56 with Internet time usage.

Predicting Netsurfing Time

What accounts for the variance in time spent Netsurfing? Seven groups of variables were regressed separately against the respondent's estimated time. These groups were the users' reasons for surfing: demographics, Internet time estimate for fun and for work, the set of Internet gratifications, how respondents learned to use the Internet, where respondents most often use the Internet, and Internet activities. Four of the users' reasons for surfing—to find something in particular ($B = .65$), to pass time ($B = .48$), to see what's going on ($B = .48$), and for fun ($B = .53$)—were significantly related to Netsurfing time (see Table 15.5). Gender, age and grade in school were not predictive. Two time variables—time spent using the computer for fun ($B = 48$) and using it for work ($B = .21$)—yielded significant relationships. One gratification—Keeping Informed ($B = .30$)—was a positive correlate. If one learned while in high school or on one's own were predictors. Location of use was not important. One of the 13 primary Internet activities—entertainment-seeking ($B = -.23$)—was the final correlate; it was the only one that was negatively related to netsurfing time.

These 11 variables were then entered into a single regression analysis. The result was a strong multiple correlation of .74 ($p < .01$), explaining 55% of the variance in Netsurfing time, substantially larger than that obtained for overall Internet time use. Seven variables retained statistically significant relationships at $p < .05$. These (in order of magnitude) were the motivation to keep informed, the time spent using the com-

Figure 15.5. Time Spent Surfing Regressions.

Surf Reason $(R-.41)$[a]	Beta
To find something in particular	.65
to pass time	.48
to see what's going on	.48
for fun	.53
Demographics $(R=.12)$	
Time $(R=.59)$[a]	
Time using computer for fun	.48
Time using computer for work	.21
Gratifications $(R=.67)$[a]	
Keep informed	.30
How Learned $(R=.29)$	
High school	.49
On own	.71
Location Internet Used $(R=.24)$	
Internet Activities $(R=.56)$[a]	
Entertainment	-.23

[a]$p < .05$; only significant Betas have been listed.

puter for fun, surfing to find something, surfing for fun, having learned in high school, time spent using the computer for work, and to surfing to feel less lonely. In addition, two covariates were significant at $p < .10$—surfing to pass the time, and using the Internet for entertainment (negatively related). Only two variables with individual relationships to Netsurfing time—surfing to see what' s going on and having learned on one's own—dropped completely from the predictive set.

Predicting Internet Frustrations

A parallel examination looked at causes of individual frustration with the Internet. Five groups of predictor variables for this analysis included the respondent's demographics, a set of time use variables (overall Internet time, surfing time, and time use for work and time use for fun), how respondents learned to use the Internet, where they most often use it, and the listing of Internet activities. From these several groupings, only three variables were identified as statistically significant—overall time spent using the Internet, time spent Netsurfing, and using the Internet for learning purposes. Unexpectedly, greater amounts of time spent using the Internet was associated with greater frustration, whereas greater amounts of time spent Netsurfing was associated with less frustration. In the final regression analysis, only these two time variables remained significant ($r = .26$, $p < .01$), but explained little of the variance. Overall, Internet frustrations have not been well explained in this study.

Predicting Gratifications

For each of the gratification dimensions found, the same five groups of variables previously identified for the Internet frustration analysis were used. Again, regressions were run for each variable group one at a time. Because of space limitations, we present only the results of the final regression analysis for each gratification dimension (see Table 15.6). The complete set of results can be found in Charney (1996).

   Keep Informed. Ten significant variables were used in the final regression analysis ($r = .76$, $p < 01$). Of those, four covariates accounted primarily for this outcome; they were the amount of time spent Netsurfing ($B = .34$), using the Internet for learning ($B = -.23$), for reading online news or magazines ($B = .-.20$), and for accessing information on products ($B = -.21$). Each of these was strongly related (correlations ranging from .49 to .62) to this motivation.

   Diversion/Entertainment. Ten variables were used in this multiple regression to explain variance in diversion-entertainment ($r = .71$, $p < .01$). The four significant covariates were time spent Netsurfing ($B = .27$), using the Internet for surfing or browsing ($B = -.18$), playing games ($B = -.14$), and seeking entertainment ($B = -.20$). The correlations for these variables ranged from .38 to .51. In addition, having learned on one's own was related to a marginally significant degree ($p < .06$).

   Peer Identity. No variables were significant predictors of the peer identity gratification.

   Good Feelings. One variable—engaging in entertaining activities—was significantly correlated with this gratification ($B = -.20$).

   Communications. Seven variables—age, grade, time using the computer for fun, using the Internet at home, browsing and surfing, e-mailing, and newsgroups/IRC—emerged from the individual regression analyses. The

Figure 15.6. Predicting Gratification Regressions.

	beta	p	multiple R
Keep Informed			.76, p < .01
time surfing	0.34	.001	
Using net for learning	-0.23	.001	
reading online news	-0.2	.001	
accessing product information	-0.21	.001	
Diversion Entertainment			.71, p < .01
time surfing	0.27	.001	
using Internet for surfing or browsing	-0.18	.015	
playing games	-0.14	.026	
seeking entertainment	-0.2	.008	
Good Feelings			
entertaining activities	-0.2	.05	
Communications			.60, p < .01
year in school	-0.18	.036	
amound of time computer used for fun	0.32	.001	
using e-mail	-0.22	.002	
using newsgroups	-0.26	.001	
Sights and Sounds			.56, p < .01
Using the Internet to learn	-0.18	.017	
time spent surfing	0.33	.001	
Career			.66, p < .01
amount of time using computer for work	0.25	.001	
using newsgroups	-0.26	.001	
using Internet to learn	-0.24	.001	
accessing information on products	-0.19	.013	
Coolness			
learned from parent or relative	0.38	.001	

Note. Only variables with statistically significant coefficients are tabled.

final regression accounted for 36% of the variance in use of the Internet for communication motives ($r = .60$, $p < .01$). The four critical variables were year in school (negatively related; $B = -.18$), the amount of time the computer is used for fun ($B = .32$), and pursuing e-mail ($B = -.22$) and newsgroup activities ($B = -.26$).

Sights and Sounds. The variables used in the final analysis for this gratification were year in school, time spent using the computer for fun, time spent Netsurfing, using the Internet to learn and to play games. They accounted for 31% of the variance in using the Internet to fulfill aesthetic needs (multiple $r = .56$, $p < .01$). Two of them were significant in this final analysis—using the Internet to learn ($B = -.18$) and time spent surfing ($B = .33$). Time spent surfing itself was strongly related ($r = .5$) with this motive.

Career. No less than 10 variables from the earlier regressions were used in the final analysis for this motive. From the time variable set, the amount of time spent using the computer for work was significant. From the set of activities on the Internet, using the Internet to learn, to access product information, and to use the newsgroups/IRC were all significant. Interestingly, six different origins of Internet training were each significant here—having learned in high school, college, from a parent, friend, at work, and on one's own were each significant. In the final regression, 44% of the variance in using the Internet to meet career needs was explained (multiple $r = .66$, $p < .01$). All six origins of learning lacked significance; the significant correlates of career motives were more time spent using the computer for work ($B = .25$), using the newsgroups/IRC ($B = -.26$), using the Internet to learn ($B = -.24$), and accessing information on products ($B = -.19$). The individual correlations for these variables all ranged between .42 and .47.

Coolness. A single variable—having learned to use the Internet from a parent or relative—was related to scores on this gratification ($B = .38$). Given the large set of predictors used and no apparent reason for this relationship, we attribute it to chance.

Overall, then, some major gratifications for using the Internet could be explained by the variables included in this study. Relatively strong predictions can be made for the dimensions of Keep Informed, Entertainment/Diversion, Communication, Sights and Sounds, and Careers. There was little power for the motives of Peer Identify, Coolness, and Good Feelings.

DISCUSSION

The first major dilemma these results provide stem from the factor analysis outcome. There is a single factor that overwhelms all the others; Keeping Informed is so dominant that it encompasses virtually all of the apparent uses, and accounts for two fifths of all the variance The second largest factor—Diversion/Entertainment—contains eight items, but reflects a fivefold drop in strength from the first factor. This limits the usefulness of the factor analysis results. For those who wish an overall assessment of how useful the Internet is for individual users, tapping the set of items from the Keeping Informed factor can provide that assessment. For those who want more particularized gratifications, the other factors may be used, but we are equally impressed by the 10 original item sets developed. Most form highly reliable scales, are logical, and they are derived from a variety of prior study sources. In subsequent research, we would choose to use them if they match up with the propositions we wish to test or research questions we wish to answer. We further suggest that alternative inasmuch as the average scores on some of the other scales/dimensions were larger than the mean for Keeping Informed, most notably the entertainment component. We are reluctant at this early stage in Internet gratification research to accept the idea that the motives are so unidimensional. Given the scale reliabilities reported, confirmatory factor analysis might be an appropriate approach.

A second possible explanation for this outcome lies with the sample in this study, that of university students. Indeed, their use of the Internet may be primarily for being/getting informed. Their use of the Internet may be primarily that of a coercive or compulsory context (e.g., that of class assignments). For them, that would not be entertaining, only information seeking, gaining, and offering. Information and surveillance functions might be stronger among this group, for example, whereas shopping and ordering services over the Internet would be stronger among a more senior, wage-earning group. We return to this possibility in the section on Netsurfing.

Let us review some other results of significance:

• Few respondents in this study spent much time with the Internet. Three out of every four spent 4 hours or less each week on the Internet, whereas at the other extreme, 1 of 10 spent more than 7 hours. Yet, access to the Internet was free for all of them. A recent study reported that adults were connected about 25 minutes per week, whereas their teenage sons were on for 4.2 hours and their teenage daughters for 1.4 hours (Mukhopadhyay et al., 1996). If anything, then, the Internet has not yet become addictive, even when freely available. Perhaps this again speaks to the issue of compulsory use at school or at work, rather than primarily for pleasure. The lack of heavy users, for example, precluded us from making definitive comparisons between heavier and lighter users; although the communication and keep informed motivations were predictors of a portion of the time spent on the Internet, the general low level of use makes it premature to say that very heavy Internet users have a higher than average need to keep informed and to communicate with others. Finally, the rate of acceptance and access since this study was completed make it more imperative to begin to better identify nonusers. We propose that superior information will come from a matrix of levels of Internet use crossed by individual motives for doing so, information that might originate in a diary form among Internet users, from beginners through expert levels.

• No gratification had an average acceptance score greater than 2.8 on the scale of 1 (*not at all*) to 5 (*very often*). The low absolute level of the means suggests that none of the needs identified here are uniformly accepted. This seems surprising at least for the one large factor related to information gain that appears. Instead, the entertainment/diversion factor provided the largest average score. It may be that the huge number of activities available on the Internet prevent any one gratification from being often or very often sought out by users. Respondents, instead, sometimes use the Internet for one purpose and sometimes use it for another.

• The factor results point out that reasons for using the Internet are not radically different from the motivations for using other media outlets (Lin, 1999). In some ways, the biggest difference may be that the Internet acts as a one-stop convenience outlet for a variety of different needs that no other single medium can provide. Perse and Courtright (1993) found that conversation best satisfies communication needs; telephones yield interpersonal needs; television, videos, and movies fulfill entertainment and escapist needs; and the print media best provide learning or informational needs. The Internet may do all of these, depending on what the user is seeking. Like television and radio, the Internet can be used for entertainment, information, and passing time. Like a newspaper, it can be used to learn, for entertainment, and to pass time (Lichtenstein & Rosenfeld, 1984). The interactive nature of the Internet makes it a communication tool like the telephone used by people to keep in touch. Additionally, the Internet like a telephone, is used for seeking information and entertainment (LaRose & Mettler, 1990). Television and radio are used for parasocial interaction or companionship (Conway & Rubin, 1991; Greenberg, 1974), and the Internet can be used for real interaction. Williams et al. (1985) suggested that new communication media "may affect the structure of communication in society and make available a greater range of choice for satisfying communication needs. New media uses may complement uses already studied. Previously identified uses may shift to new media from old media" (p. 241). This suggests a study in which alternative media, including the Internet, are concurrently assessed for their level of use and the nature of their gratifications.

• Somewhat more than half (55%) the sample appear to have learned how to use the Internet voluntarily rather than being compelled to do so. This portion either learned on their own or from a friend or relative, whereas slightly more than one third (36%) learned in a class in school or at work. Most of Net users self-selected themselves. Of course, those who learned in a class may have opted to take a class, or, a friend, parent, or relative may have compelled the respondent to learn to use the Internet. We raise this issue because no other mass medium would seem to have as an attribute being compelled to learn to use it. The implications of that possibility for subsequent enjoyment as well as continued use of the Internet remain for study. In addition, the basic gratifications sought may vary among individuals whose introduction to the Internet arose in such different contexts.

• Although the sources of frustration in using the Internet appear to be well delineated and concentrated in slowness of access, the elements used in this study could not explain those frustrations to a considerable degree. Furthermore, the finding that the more time spent Netsurfing, the less the frustration, is the antithesis of the relationship between frustration and total time on the Internet. It is less anomalous if Internet users conceive of surfing time as quite different from Internet time; that is, if surfing is for fun, then you wouldn't do it if it were frustrating, but if Net time is for work, you have to do it, and you get frustrated by the time and access problems that occur.

• Netsurfing remains to be better conceptualized and explained. Reasons for Netsurfing were to find something, for fun, to pass time, and to see what is going on. Time spent Netsurfing, not time spent using the Internet, was the measure that most often was a significant predictor of gratifications sought (i.e., to keep informed, for entertainment-diversion, and sights and sounds). Time spent using the Internet did not emerge as a significant predictor of any gratifications. Perhaps the uses and gratification notion better explains media use in a noncompulsory situation, which could characterize the surfing situation better than other net time activities. No scales measured motivations such as "because I had to" or "I was told to do it."

But just what is meant by Netsurfing has not been addressed well. It remains largely a free-floating concept to be defined by individual users. Is it the counterpart to channel-surfing in a multichannel cable system, do Internet users approach the Internet "with a variety of overt and covert potential goals (or needs) that might be satisfied by [accessing] any number of different available" (Heeter, 1985, p. 128) activities or services. Heeter was writing about cable channel choices, but the logic is the same.

We would be especially interested in determining if there are different styles of surfing, as indeed different maneuvers were identified in channel-choosing (Heeter & Greenberg, 1985). Do some surfers go through the same procedures while others engage in a greater variety of moves? Do some surf "more" before they are satisfied? How do they navigate? How much surfing is for fun and how much is task-oriented? Perhaps an adequate understanding of the surfing process requires intensive observation of Internet users, in part to determine their ability to articulate what they are doing and why.

• That demographics were of little value in understanding Net use in this study is due to the homogeneous nature of the student sample. But gender made no difference in these results, whereas prior research clearly identifies a male bias in computer access and use. Given this study was done only among users, we posit that once females have equal access, gender makes no difference in gratifications, in frustrations, nor in time spent with the Internet. There may, however, be a gender difference in content sought, an element not studied here.

Overall, the uses and gratifications approach explained a good deal of the variance in time spent using the Internet. Nearly 40% of the variance in time spent using the Internet was explained by the gratifications defined in this study. The Internet is used primarily to keep informed, for entertainment and diversion, to maintain communication, and to look at the sights and sounds of the Internet. Gratification items that tried to tap into new and unique features of the Internet did not fare as well as the gratifications uncovered repeatedly in earlier studies of traditional mass media, principally information, entertainment, diversion, and social gratifications. Or we have failed to identify the new dimensions.

What remains, however, is the need to better locate the gratification functions in a more general paradigm of the Internet use process. As a beginning, such a paradigm would attempt to integrate the elements of surfing, identified needs, Internet experiences (including frustrations, coping, search strategies, content choices), and gratifications obtained. We hope this study contributes to that beginning.

REFERENCES

Atwater, T., Heeter, C., & Brown, N. (1985). Foreshadowing the electronic publishing age: First exposures to viewtron. *Journalism Quarterly, 62*, 807-815.

Bruckman, A. (1993). *Gender swapping on the Internet.* Paper presented at the Internet Society, San Francisco.

Charney, T. R. (1996). *Uses and gratifications of the Internet.* Unpublished master's thesis, Michigan State University, East Lansing.

Conway, J. C., & Rubin, A. M. (1991). Psychological predictors of television viewing: Motivation. *Communications Research, 18,* 443-463.

Cowles, D. (1989). Consumer perceptions of interactive media. *Journal of Broadcasting & Electronic Media, 33,* 83-89.

Dobos, J., & Dimmick, J. (1988). Factor analysis and gratification constructs. *Journal of Broadcasting & Electronic Media, 32,* 335-350.

Gibson, W. (1996, July 14). The net is a waste of time: And that's exactly what's right about it. *The New York Times Magazine,* p. 31.

Greenberg, B. S. (1974). Gratifications of television viewing and their correlates for British children. In J. G. Blumler & E. Katz (Eds.), *The uses of mass communications: Current perspectives in gratifications research* (pp. 71-92). Beverly Hills, CA: Sage.

Heeter, C. (1985). Program selection with abundance of choice: A process model. *Human Communication Research, 12,* 126-152.

Heeter, C. (1989). Implications of new interactive technologies for conceptualizing communication. In J. L. Salvaggio & J. Bryant (Eds.), *Media use in the information age: Emerging patterns of adoptions and consumer use* (pp. 217-236). Hillsdale, NJ: Lawrence Erlbaum Associates.

Heeter, C., & Greenberg, B. S. (1985). *Cableviewing.* Norwood, NJ: Ablex.

Hoffman, D., & Novak, T. (1994). *Marketing in hypermedia computer-mediated environments: Conceptual foundations.* Nashville: Vanderbilt University Owen Graduate School of Management.

Katz, E., Blumler, J. G., & Gurevitch, M. (1974). Utilization of mass communication by the individual. In J. G. Blumler & E. Katz (Eds.), *The uses of mass communications: Current perspectives on gratifications research* (pp. 19-32). Beverly Hills, CA: Sage.

Kirsner, S. (1996, October). The ultimate webmaster: An interview with Tim Berners-Lee. *Webmaster,* pp. 38-44.

LaRose. R., & Mettler, J. (1990). *Social and antisocial uses of the telephone: An exploration of social learning explanations of personal telephone behavior.* Paper presented at the International Communication Association, Dublin.

Lichtenstein, A., & Rosenfeld, L. (1984). Normative expectations and individual decisions concerning media gratification choices. *Communication Research, 11,* 393-413.

Lin, C. A. (1993). Modeling the gratification-seeking process of television viewing. *Human Communication Research, 20,* 224-244.

Lin, C. A. (1999). Predicting online service adoption likelihood among potential subscribers: A motivational approach. *Journal of Advertising Research, 39,* 79-89.

Lometti, G. E., Reeves, B., & Bybee, C. R. (1977). Investigating the assumptions of uses and gratifications research. *Communication Research, 4,* 321-338.

Morris, M., & Ogan, C. (1996). The Internet as mass medium. *Journal of Communication, 46,* 39-50.

Mukhopadhyay, T., Kraut, R., Szczypula, J., Kiesler, S., Scherlis, W., & Buskirk, S. (1996). *Homenet: Residential internet use over time.* Available online: http://homenet.andrew.cmu.edu/progress/research.html.

Newhagen, J. E., & Rafaeli, S. (1996). Why communication researchers should study the Internet: A dialogue. *Journal of Communication, 46,* 4-13.

Nielsen Media Research. (1995). *Nielsen Media Research/Commercenet Internet Demographics Survey: Executive Summary.* Available online: http://www.nielsenmedia.com/whatsnew/execsum2.html.

Nielsen Media Research. (1998). *Number of Internet users and shoppers surges in United States and Canada, August 24, 1998.* Available online: http://www.nielsenmedia.com/news/commnet2.html.

O'Keefe, G. J., & Sulanowski, B. K. (1995). More than just talk: Uses and gratifications, and the telephone. *Journalism and Mass Communication Quarterly, 72,* 922-933.

Palmgreen, P. (1984). Uses and gratifications: A theoretical perspective. *Communication Yearbook 8,* 20-55.

Parks, M. R., & Floyd, K. (1996). Making friends in cyberspace. *Journal of Communication, 46,* 80-97.

Perse, E. M., & Courtright, J. A. (1993). Normative images of communication media: Mass and interpersonal channels in the new media environment. *Human Communication Research, 19,* 485-503.

Pitkow, J., & Kehoe, C. (1995). *Graphic, visualization & usability center's 4th WWW user survey.* Atlanta: Georgia Tech Research Corporation.

Rice, R. E., & Steinfield, C. (1994). Experiences with new forms of organizational communication via electronic mail and voice messaging. In J. H. Andriessen & R. A. Roe (Eds.), *Telematics and work* (pp. 109-134). Hillsdale, NJ: Lawrence Erlbaum Associates.

Rigdon, J. (1994, December 8). Homebound and lonely, older people use computers to get "out." *The Wall Street Journal,* pp. B1, B14.

Rubin, A. M. (1981). An examination of television viewing motivations. *Communication Research, 8,* 141-165.

Rubin, A. M., & Bantz, C. R. (1987). Uses and gratifications of videocassette recorders. In R. P. Hawkins, J. M. Wiemann, & S. Pingree

(Eds.), *Advancing communication science: Merging mass and interpersonal processes* (pp. 181-195). Newbury Park, CA: Sage.

Steinfield, C. W. (1986). Computer mediated communication in an organizational setting: Explaining task related and socioemotional uses. In M. L. McLaughlin (Ed.), *Communication yearbook 9* (pp. 777-804). Beverly Hills, CA: Sage.

Wellman, B., & Gulia, M. (1995). Net surfers don't ride alone: Virtual communities as communities. In P. Kollock & M. Smith (Eds.), *Communities in cyberspace.* Berkeley: University of California Press.

Williams, F., Phillips, A. F., & Lum, P. (1985), Gratifications associated with new communication technologies. In K. E. Rosengren, L. A. Wenner, & P. Palmgreen (Eds.), *Media gratifications research: Current perspectives* (pp. 241-252). Beverly Hills, CA: Sage.

16

Plugging Your Body Into the Telecommunication System: Mediated Embodiment, Media Interfaces, and Social Virtual Environments

Frank Biocca
Michigan State University

Kristine Nowak
University of Connecticut

> A naked human mind—without paper and pencil, without speaking, comparing notes, making sketches—is first of all something we have never seen.
> —Dennett (1997, p. 153)

> I am body entirely and nothing beside.
> —Nietzche, Thus Spake Zarathustra

The body, the first communication medium, is also the future communication medium. It is the frontier for technologically advanced communication systems. As transmission systems that feed the Internet increase their capacity by a thousandfold, the capacity for the human user to absorb the flow of information becomes the bottleneck in the communication system. There is more information than the user can absorb. Increasingly, information is coming at a rate that exceeds the capacity of the user. How can the user make better use of the bandwidth capacity of the telecommunication system? How do we better communicate with the mind of the user? There is only one transmission system in and out of the mind, the body. This chapter explores how advanced media interfaces are evolving to better connect the body of the user to the telecommunication system.

The rapidly evolving media have created various families of interfaces, for example, virtual reality (Biocca & Delaney, 1995; Durlach & Mavor, 1994) and augmented reality (Azuma, 1997). Although the specific configurations of computer processors, input and output devices, and telecommunication links change frequently, there are trends in media evolution that appear consistent. For example, a number of the new media interfaces increasingly immerse our senses in mediated multisensory and highly interactive environments. We can call this trend in media evolution the *progressive embodiment* of the user (Biocca, 1997), because these advanced interfaces allow the user's body to gradually and more fully "enter" the environments created by the computer. This trend is more important than any specific technological instantiation of the trend, say a specific virtual or augmented reality system. Specific interfaces come and go, but the process of progressive embodiment, the gradual immersion of the body into computer environments, continues unabated. The implications for this trend include issues such as how media can amplify and augment human learning (Biocca, 1996a), the psychophysical health of the user (see below), and the sociopsychological impact of communicating with others in and through immersive virtual environments.

This chapter also analyzes this increased connectivity between the body and the telecommunication system. We use an interdisciplinary approach common in human-computer interaction and some communication research. Where relevant, we integrate insights from psychology, interpersonal communication, and philosophy. Using these tools we do the following:

1. Define key *trends* that appear to characterize the *recent evolution of media interfaces,* especially the various forms of interactive media.
2. Examine one central trend in the evolution of advanced media interfaces, what we term *mediated embodiment,* the process of more tightly connecting the body and mind to the medium.
3. Outline the relative merits of three theoretical positions on how mediated embodiment creates the virtual body and influences

users' mental models of themselves and others, their sense of *social* or *co-presence.*

4. Explore some disturbing *psychophysiological effects* reported from users of interfaces that have a high level of mediated embodiment (e.g., virtual reality [VR] systems, military simulators, location-based entertainment simulators).

THE EVOLUTION OF TELECOMMUNICATION INTERFACES

What are telecommunication interfaces? Telecommunication interfaces are the devices such as telephones, computers, and television sets that allow the human user to transmit or absorb information. There are a number of different ways to conceptualize the idea of an interface (Shneiderman, 1998). One way is to consider the term *interface* using an interpersonal or spatial metaphor. According to the *American Heritage Dictionary,* the word, *interface,* is defined as "The point of interaction or communication between a computer and any other entity, such as a printer or human operator." We can think of the interface as the part of the system that "faces" the interactant, especially when that interactant is a human operator. The interface is quite literally the "face" of the telecommunication system, the only part of the weave of copper, silicon, and plastics that the user sees, hears, and touches. Alternatively, using a more spatial metaphor, the interface can be seen as a kind of door to cyberspace that the body can enter. It is a portal that turns digital information into a form that users can experience with their senses. It can also turn the users' text message, mouse movements, head motions, or other recorded actions into digital patterns, or a form that is easily read by the computer. The interface is always at an information transformation point where the structure of the information is changed as it moves from one system to another, as from the computer to the user, from the analog to the digital world, or from one code (e.g., spoken language) to another (e.g., written language).

There are a number of fundamental transformation points for information in a telecommunication system. Some of these are illustrated in Fig. 16.1. The interactive telecommunication interface senses the user's motor actions, physiological responses, or both. The interface then reacts to these motions by providing meaningful responses to them in the form of representations that the computer translates into energy patterns that can be interpreted by human senses. In this way, digital information (records of energy patterns and representational codes) are transmitted and received from the telecommunication network. For example, bits are assembled into images for a user to see, or a computer camera takes the light reflecting from a user's face and turns it into patterns for transmission to another user.

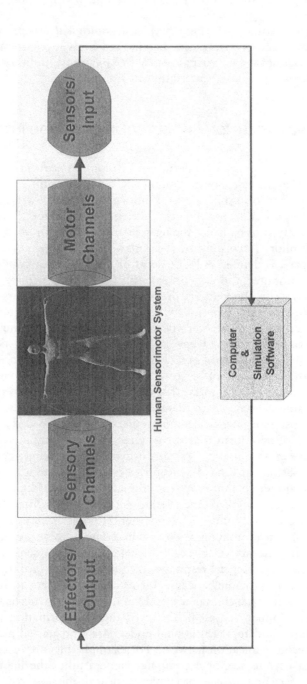

Figure. 16.1. Coupling of the body's sensorimotor system to the input-output devices of the computer interface

Many telecommunication interfaces, from the telephone to VR, are evolving to increase the information bandwidth (amount of information) exchanged between the average user and the telecommunication network (see Steinfield, chap. 8, this volume). One driving goal of interface designers is to better connect users to each other and to information. But when one talks about an interface, one is really talking about a connection between the user's senses and motor systems and the computer's programmed responses, or coded information. To do this, telecommunication interfaces are evolving to create better synchronous connections between the user's body (sensorimotor channels) and other users as well as remote physical environments (remote sensing of other physical environments in the form of video images, x-ray images, sound, tactile qualities, etc.). These interfaces are also connecting the body in a more efficient manner to networks of stored digital information. Table 16.1 illustrates the four principal dimensions that capture the telecommunication interface evolution, including embodiment, intelligence, ubiquity, and socialability.

Fig. 16.2 arrays the dimensions into one four-dimensional plot. The figure enables location of media along these four dimensions and allows one to see how they cluster. Fig. 16.2 includes more than traditional telecommunication interfaces such as the telephone, but also more general media interfaces as well such as books and television.

Mediated Embodiment

Media vary in terms of how much of the body is immersed into the medium (see Biocca, 1997; Biocca & Delaney, 1995; Durlach & Mavor, 1994). Media interfaces vary in how many sensory cues they provide (e.g., audio, visual, and tactile), how much the sensory channel is immersed in the mediated environment (e.g., small screen vs. IMAX screen), and how much of the user's body motions and responses the computer can sense (e.g., use of a mouse, head tracker, or eye camera). In some interfaces, input sensors also pick up a user's autonomic responses such as heart rate, blood pressure, and so on.

When we array media interfaces along this dimension, we can see a high degree of variation. On one end of the extreme are noninteractive media such as the book, which utilizes only a small part of the visual channel and is not interactive, as it does not sense and respond to the user's reactions to the messages. Furthermore, when there are no pictures, the book uses a small part of the sensory cues detectable by the visual channel to carry information. Closer to the other end of the dimension—specifically, at the visual extreme—are the widescreen outlets, such as IMAX theaters. These saturate the visual channel with information, filling all that the eyes can see with information from the virtual as opposed to

Table 16.1. Four Dimensions of Telecommunication Interface Evolution.

Dimension	Definition
Level of mediated embodiment	*Mediated embodiment* is defined as the degree to which the user's body is connected to the telecommunication system. Level of mediated embodiment is a combination of (a) the number of sensory, motor, and autonomic channels engaged (e.g., vision, hearing, taste, hand motion, heart rate); (b) display or sensor fidelity for each channel; and (c) amount of channel bandwidth used by the medium (i.e., 0-100%; see Biocca & Nowak, 1999b).
Level of interface intelligence	*Interface intelligence* refers to the ability of the interface to interact, sense, respond, and adapt to the user's behavior. Intelligent response to user behavior includes the interface's ability to simulate both the interactive properties of (a) physical environments (i.e., space and objects) and (b) intelligent beings (i.e., simulated animals, humans, and other sentient beings).
Ubiquity of access	*Ubiquity* refers to how many physical locations of the interface can be accessed. Ubiquitous access can be achieved by having many interfaces in the physical space (e.g., TV sets) or by making interfaces more portable (e.g., satellite phone).
Sociability	*Sociability* is defined as a combination of: (a) the number of users and (b) the quality of interpersonal interaction that the interface can support. Sociability is not exclusively a property of the interface. It is more dependent on other properties of the telecommunication system, such as the quality of the network and the nature application, than the other interface dimensions.

the physical environment. But still, the viewer cannot interact with virtual environments on the film screen.

At the absolute other end of the dimension is an immersive VR system that not only bathes the visual, aural, and sometimes the tactile senses, but also tracks every fine movement of the head, the hands, and other parts of the body to increase the ways in which the body can interact with the virtual environment (Biocca & Delaney, 1995).

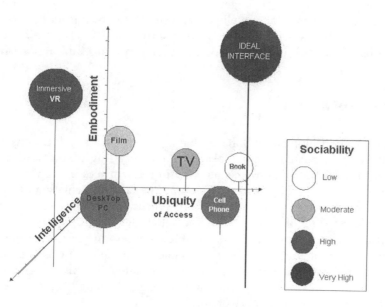

Figure 16.2. The four basic dimensions of media evolution

Looking at the graph, we see a clear trend where advanced media like virtual and augmented reality are steadily increasing the mediated embodiment of the user. This trend means that changes in the media involve more than the sensory, motor, and autonomic channels; it further means that sensors and displays increase steadily in their fidelity; and that media use more of the bandwidth of each channel.

Interface Intelligence

The interface has intelligence, or interactivity, when it can sense its environment (usually the user) and can respond in appropriate and varied ways to user behavior. At one extreme, we can consider the example of the book. It is true that books are written by intelligent people and filled with intelligent information. On the other hand, books have very little interface intelligence because they do not sense, respond to, or adapt to the user.

Desktop computers can display moderate to high levels of intelligence, depending on the way they sense the user and make use of that information to alter the display. Immersive virtual environments, especially those with sophisticated agent technologies, incorporate comparatively higher levels of interface intelligence. Virtual environments are continuously recalculated, with the user's perspective tracked. The display is continuously updated to account for the user's motions and actions in the environment.

Ubiquity of Access

Interfaces can be made mobile by having them in many locations or by making them portable. Film theaters have very low ubiquity of access. Their information can only be accessed in a few places in each town, and they are not portable. TV sets can display the same information as film (at lower levels of embodiment) in more places, in almost every home in America. Satellite phones also have very high levels of ubiquity. Although there are few of them, each user is able to access the telecommunication network from any place on earth. In general, ubiquity of access and level of mediated embodiment are negatively correlated. The user normally has to surrender some level of embodiment (e.g., the small screen size of a portable TV) to gain ubiquity of access.

Sociability

Finally, consider the dimension of sociability. Books are not sociable. They are designed for one user in isolation. McLuhan (1964) made much of the isolation of the printed work, and at the turn of the century, the lack of sociability of the book was considered a real social problem by critics (Lubar, 1993). They are rarely used for two people to interact synchronously. Although many people talk about books, they never interact *through* the book. Media may be sociable when people interact *around* the use of the medium, such as in film. But film is clearly passive interaction. Media are more "sociable" when more people can interact with each other through the medium, especially when the interaction is synchronous, or in real time.

Almost *all media interfaces* could be placed inside these four dimensions of embodiment, intelligence, ubiquity, and sociability. Furthermore, the simple four dimensions also capture fine differences between media interfaces that appear similar, such as the difference between a phone connected to a wall and a cell phone, a stone tablet (low ubiquity of access) and a printed piece of paper.

The Ideal Communication Interface?

To suggest trends in the evolution of the interface, we have extended all four dimensions into the future, and added a placeholder for the ideal interface. We are defining the ideal interface as one that is the optimal extension of these four dimensions, whether attainable or not. If we think of this four-dimensional space as the set of all possible interfaces, then we can also outline some properties of what might be an ideal interface. Table 16.2 suggests the features of an *ideal interface*.

If we summarize the features of this hypothesized ideal interface, we approach something like the Holodeck, the fictional communication medium seen on the TV series *Star Trek*. It could generate perceptual experiences of physical environments and intelligent others. Although beyond the capability of current VR and simulation software, it can be approximated crudely with today's interfaces. At present, the approximation is getting better and the interface is evolving toward this ideal. To understand the implications of these evolving media, we turn to focus on the dimension of mediated embodiment.

A CLOSER LOOK AT THE IDEA OF MEDIATED EMBODIMENT

Media alter the way the body, the primordial communication medium, interacts with the environment. In mediated embodiment, the medium interposes itself between the user's body and the (represented) environment. Here the body of the user is represented in many ways:

1. As a physical body connected the computer's sensors and effectors.
2. As a representation of the user's body (i.e., controls of effectors and sensors) inside the computer.

Table 16.2. Hypothesized Properties of an Ideal Interface.

Dimension	Hypothesized Properties of an Ideal Interface
Level of mediated embodiment	Information delivered at or beyond the band-width capacity of the senses. High levels of interactivity based on a sensing of the full range of motor and autonomic responses and a meaningful coordination of the motor actions and sensory feedback (Biocca & Delaney, 1995; Durlach & Mavor, 1994).
Level of intelligence	Simulate the physical dynamics and full morphology of physical environments (Sutherland, 1965) and simulate other intelligent beings.
Ubiquity of access	Allow access to virtual environment stimuli regardless of place and time. (Ideally at levels approximating full embodiment.)
Sociability	The interface would allow for synchronous interaction of individuals that at least matches, but most likely exceeds, the number of people who can interact in the physical environment. Quality of interaction should match, and possibly exceed, face-to-face communication for some aspects of interpersonal communication.

3. As an avatar representation inside the virtual environment which allows the user and others to experience the user's actions.
4. As user's internal representation of his or her body, the body schema, which may be altered by experience of one's body via the medium.

In communication research, the term *embodiment* is most often encountered in gender and cultural studies (e.g., Balsamo, 1995; Barnes, 1997; Featherstone & Burrows, 1995). Our treatment shares a common concern and some terminology with this work, but tends to be more grounded in perceptual and cognitive psychology (e.g., Biocca & Rolland, 1998), human-computer interface engineering (e.g., Biocca & Delaney, 1995; Durlach & Mavor, 1994), and artificial intelligence (Brooks & Stein, 1994; Kushmerick, 1998).

This perspective considers the body as a communication medium for a mind and a tool for thought. According to William James, "Each of

us lives within . . . the prison of his own brain. Projecting from it are millions of fragile sensory nerve fibers, in groups uniquely adapted to sample
the energetic states of the world around us: heat, light, force, and chemical
composition. That is all we ever know of it directly; all else is logical infer-
ence" (cited in Sekuler & Blake, 1994, p. 1). Sekuler and Blake suggested
that the human senses and motor systems are "communication channels to
reality."

The body is the primordial communication medium connecting
the mind to the environment. It allows the mind to not just think about
the environment, but, more importantly, from an interface-engineering
viewpoint, it allows the mind to think with the environment. Although
interactive, it engages the environment with and through the body
(Damasio, 1994; Gibson, 1966, 1979). These senses are not passive recep-
tors, but they are "interactive." Instinctively, the body's motor channels
propel them to interact with events in the world. This perspective assumes
that all communication is mediated to some degree.

Communication media interpose themselves on our senses
between our physical bodies and the physical environment. They mediate
our consciousness of the environment by interposing a virtual environment that supports our mental simulation (mental models) of the physical
and social world. In this way, communication media connect our body to
virtual environments, the mediated spaces and people of pictures, video,
and VR. The two forms of embodiment—physical and mediated embodiment—generate some interesting research issues for communication scholars interested in human-computer interaction. Table 16.3, summarizes the
three basic ways in which this concept is treated in the philosophical literature on embodiment.

Having introduced the concept of *mediated embodiment,* we can
now examine new media interfaces. In this section, we use only one
dimension of interface evolution, mediated embodiment, to gain insight
into the classification and evolution of VR interfaces, specifically, different
configurations of input and output (I/O) devices. Table 16.4 organizes
these interface types according to their level of the user's mediated embodiment.

Next, we consider how individuals perceive the environment, how
others perceive them in the virtual environment, and how they perceive
themselves. Each of these "perceptions" is based not on a single unified
representation of the body but on different representations of the same
user's body. When a user enters a virtual environment, especially an
immersive VR environment, different forms of the body are created. In
many advanced virtual environment systems, the hardware and software,
or input devices change the relationship between body movement (action
on objects and spaces) and sensory feedback. Part of the effect of this is

Table 16.3. Three Basic Theoretical Problems Associated With Physical or Mediated Embodiment.

Basic Problem To a Theory of Embodiment	Physical Embodiment in Philosophical and Psychological Studies	Mediated Embodiment in a Human-Computer Interaction Theory
Problem 1: How the body is a medium for a mind Ways in which the body of humans, animals, or an artificial intelligence provides an active medium that shapes the way consciousness experiences, manipulates, and constructs the world.	There is a fundamental question in all theories about physical embodiment: How does the body serve as a medium for thought? This question takes many forms. In philosophy the embodiment is a fundamental problem in epistemology (Clark, 1997; Haber & Weiss, 1996, O'Donovan-Anderson, 1997), especially for certain approaches to phenomenology (Merleau-Ponty, 1962). In cognitive psychology, this problem may lead researchers to focus on how meaning and symbolic representations emerge from bodily schema (Johnson, 1987). In neuroscience the body may be considered as a fully integrated representational device for a brain (Damasio, 1994). The question of embodiment takes on another form when we consider how different types of bodies mediate the experience of the world. In zoology and comparative epistemology, there is an interest in how different body forms mediate experience of the world differently and, thereby, generate different world models (e.g., Varela, Thompson, & Rosch, 1991; Von Uexkull, 1934). In artificial intelligence, the problem of embodiment involves understanding how the interaction of different robotic bodies and different physical or virtual worlds gives meaning to conceptualizations of the world and guides behavioral plans for action (Brooks, 1991, 1994)	In mediated embodiment, there is a concern about how the body is mediated by the medium. For example, a fundamental research problem focuses on how the user experiences the virtual world through a specific interface, the cybernetic extensions of the body. Specifically, how do combinations of input (sensors) and output (effectors) create different virtual bodies that mediate the way users experience the virtual world and how they create mental models of their environment and their virtual body within it (see discussion below).

Table 16.3. Three Basic Theoretical Problems Associated With Physical or Mediated Embodiment (cont'd.).

Basic Problem To a Theory of Embodiment	Physical Embodiment in Philosophical and Psychological Studies	Mediated Embodiment in a Human-Computer Interaction Theory
Problem 2: How an animated body is "evidence" of consciousness and agency Ways in which thought or consciousness is embodied or made manifest as an agent active in the world.	In theories of physical embodiment, researchers discuss how agency and intelligence is perceived in an active, animated, self-propelled body. How consciousness and agency is attributed to the animate forms such as the body (Dennett, 1997; Premack & Premack, 1996).	intelligence of users or by artificial intelligences (Benford, Greenhalg, Bowers, Snowdon, & Fahlén, 1995; Bowers, Pycock, & O'Brien, 1996; Palmer, 1995). Issues include the minimum cues necessary to create the illusion of agency: when and how users respond to artificial beings as sentient and intelligent (Reeves & Nass, 1996) and the effect on users of virtual environments where intelligence can be embodied in any form (i.e., chairs, rocks, or buildings, as well as human or animal virtual bodies) (Walser, 1991b).
Problem 3: How body shape and movement provides meaning for another Ways the body is an object for another, how body shape and motion are perceived or interpreted by another human, and how the body is a semiotically marked surface for a specific culture.	The body is the public form of the self (Argyle, 1988; Bull, 1983; Ichheiser, 1970). Viewed by another person or intelligence, the body is a moving surface that others automatically analyze, interpret, and stereotype (Argyle, 1988b; Bull, 1983; Ichheiser, 1970; Mehrabian, 1972). Others generate models of the unobservable consciousness or intelligence that "drives" the body, the source of movements, noises, and other actions that can be observed. At the level of cultural theory and feminist theory, this problem becomes how different cultures separated by time or space interpret, classify and stereotype human bodies, especially gender (Dietrich, 1997; Spender, 1996; Stafford & Reske, 1990).	Users of virtual environments are experienced by others through their virtual bodies (avatars or agents), their computer graphic representation inside the virtual environment. Work on this aspect of embodiment is concerned with how the morphology and behavior of the virtual body communicates meaning to others and how virtual bodies can be designed to help humans and artificial intelligences communicate with other users (e.g., Badler, Phillips, & Webber, 1993; Capin, Pandzic, Magnenat-Thalmann, & Thalmann, 1998).

Table 16.4. Types of Virtual Environment Interfaces Classified According to the Level of the User's Mediated Embodiment Classification.

Classification	Level of Mediated Embodiment	Description	User Experience	Typical Applications
W i n d o w interface	Very low	The basic personal computer where only the window display monitor and mouse connect the user's body to the virtual environment.	Limited field-of-view and limited sensorimotor interactions provide a modest experience of presence.	Internet 3D worlds, chat rooms, consumer computer games.
Mirror interface	Low	An image of the user's body is captured by video equipment. The image of the user's body is superimposed on the computer environment, which is projected onto a screen in front of the user.	Users see a video image of themselves on a large screen, often with other people. Cutout images interact with the environment. Can be compelling, but sense of presence is modest.	Walk-through museum or art experiences. Computer c o n f e r e n c i n g, arcade gaming applications.
Panoramic interface	Medium	Large wide-screen projection system fills the user's visual field. Often includes three-dimensional stereographic glasses and tracked, hand-held input devices, and high-end audio systems.	One or more users stand in front of large three-dimensional window on the virtual world. Motion effects and sense of depth can deliver higher levels of presence.	Corporate product v i s u a l i z a t i o n s. Scientific and medical visualization.
V i r t u a l rooms	Medium	Takes panoramic portals to their logical extreme. Users walk into a physical room that is a large display system. The motion and perspective of the user are continuously updated by tracking devices	Sense of space can be quite compelling. The virtual environment immerses the user's visual sensory system. Usually viewed	Scientific visualization. Corporate product and design visualization.

Table 16.4. Types of Virtual Environment Interfaces Classified According to the Level of the User's Mediated Embodiment Classification (cont'd.).

Classification	Level of Mediated Embodiment	Description	User Experience	Typical Applications
		as the user interacts with the virtual environment seamlessly projected on at least three walls and the floor.	through three-dimensional glasses. Expensive system ideal for multiple users.	
Vehicular interface	High	Users enter a mock vehicle (i.e., cars, planes, submarines, tanks, flying carpets, etc.) where they are allowed to operate input devices that control their vehicle inside the virtual environment. The vehicles often include motion platforms to simulate physical movement, and the computer graphics based world is projected onto the "windows" of the vehicle.	Sense of presence and motion can be quite compelling. The interface can faithfully reproduce a lot of detail, and a feeling of being inside the "real" vehicle.	Military and corporate training, simulation. High-end location-based entertainment rides.
Immersive VR interface	Very High	Users wear displays that fully immerse a number of the senses in computer-generated stimuli (e.g., vision, hearing, and touch). These systems often use the distinctive head-mounted, stereographic display, three-dimensional spatial audio. Input devices (sensors) immerse the motor actions of the user into the virtual environment. Trackers may register head and hand location. Data gloves may sense finger movement. Other sensors may track eye movement, walking, and so on. It is primarily	Arguably provides a significant "jump" in the level of "presence" because of the tight sensorimotor integration and the full immersion of at least the key senses of vision and hearing. Some purists argue that immersive environments are the only true VR systems because they that are the only systems	Scientific and medical visualization. Corporate product and design visualization. Military training. Some low quality systems used for gaming.

Table 16.4. Types of Virtual Environment Interfaces Classified According to the Level of the User's Mediated Embodiment Classification (cont'd.).

Classification	Level of Mediated Embodiment	Description	User Experience	Typical Applications
		the much higher levels of sensorimotor integration; the linking of sensory feedback to body movement that distinguishes immersive systems most differ from other VR systems.	that attempt to completely immerse the sensorimotor system into a virtual environment.	
Augmented reality interface	Medium to high	Some advanced augmented reality systems use hardware similar to that found in immersive VR. But rather than fully immerse the user in a virtual world, augmented reality systems overlay three-dimensional virtual objects onto real-world scenes. The goal here is to superimpose 2D and 3D graphics to enhance the user's experience with reality.	Few systems yet achieve a truly convincing integration of a stable three-dimensional virtual object and the real world, but many of these show promise with less compelling implementations and schematic virtual displays.	Medical imaging. Battle display systems. Manufacturing and equipment maintenance. Facilitating navigation with the natural environment.

the emergence of a virtual body, a mediated representation of our body that interacts with the sensory feedback afforded by the system. For example, the user in an immersive VR system is very much aware of the point of view of his or her virtual embodiment because the scene changes with head movement. The user may also see a computer graphic hand or body that occupies the same space as his or her own. Psychologically, the avatar or virtual body substitutes for or alters the boundaries of the physical body.

In this interaction, there are interconnected forms or representations of the user's body. Fig. 16.3 and Table 16.5 describe the different representational forms of the body active in a VR system.

THE VIRTUAL BODY IN TELECOMMUNICATION SYSTEMS

Virtual bodies, also called *avatars,* are digital representations of a person that are possible in networked immersive VR systems, and raise a number of new, compelling questions. The concept of avatars was originally discussed in Neil Stephenson's (1993) *Snow Crash.* Avatars can be seen in all visual interactive environments as two- and three-dimensional images. Essentially, virtual environments allow us, as a virtual body, to "exist in a world free from earthly physical constraints" (Paulos & Canny, 1997). The types and levels of avatars are as diverse as the people they represent. These can vary on a number of levels from representations of people to animals to inanimate objects. Their motion can vary from unmoving two-dimensional pictures, to fluidly moving avatars that walk or float through the environment in a variety of ways (Damer, 1997; Nowak, 2000).

The introduction and evolution of the virtual body opens up many possibilities for mediated interactions, including extending the question of how we experience the "other" in mediated interactions (Lea & Spears, 1992; Palmer, 1995; Rice, 1993; Rice & Tyler, 1995; Short, Williams, & Christie, 1976; Steinfield, 1986; Walther, 1996). As we are freed from our body, it opens up a number of new ways to experience both the self and the other. It further limits the capacity of others to categorize us based on traditional embodiment traits because "true" bodily information is not available. Nonetheless, categorization will occur when both the physical body and the virtual bodies are connected to the computer, but the question of which features of virtual bodies will be most salient in these environments remains unanswered.

Even so, research in this area has revealed that there is no ideal virtual body for all potential interactions (Benford, Greenhalg, Bowers, Snowdon, & Fahlén, 1995). The shape and capabilities of the virtual body might vary as to the function and communication setting. For example,

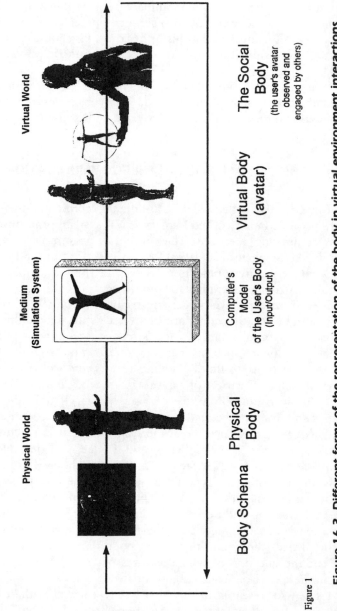

Figure 1

Figure 16.3. Different forms of the representation of the body in virtual environment interactions

Table 16.5. Interconnected Representations of the User's Body in Virtual Environments.

Body Representation	Selected Research Issues
1. The body schema: Our internal representation, mental model, of the body	Our body schema is not fixed or objective but influenced by experience and various disorders (e.g., anorexia and schizophrenia). Media use can trigger significant changes in body schema and this can occur in very ordinary circumstances to perfectly "normal" individuals. Issues include: • Effect of interface design and virtual body morphology on body schema (Biocca & Rolland, 1998). • Effect of the representation of other bodies on the user's body image (Meyers & Biocca, 1992). • Effect of other's interaction and reaction (the social body) to the virtual body on the user's body schema and identity (A. Stone, 1995).
2. The physical body: The sensorimotor system considered as (a) the part connected to the interface, and (b) the part not connected.	Advanced interfaces like VR connect the sensorimotor system of the user to mediated stimuli in various ways. The challenge of this connection generates the following research issues: • How do we engineer interfaces that fit the properties of the sensorimotor system (Biocca & Delaney, 1995; Durlach & Mavor, 1994). • The problem of spatial presence: Does connecting more of the body to the system make the user feel more present in the virtual as opposed to the physical environment (Biocca & Nowak, 1999a). • Possible damage to some aspect or function of the sensorimotor system as a result of prolonged interaction.
3. The computer's internal model of the user's body: A representation of I/O devices, including the logic for controlling effectors and sensors.	In VR systems, the computer programs must maintain an updated model of the location and perspective of the user's body (depending on sensor configurations) and use it to update the location and attitude of the virtual body (Bricken & Coco, 1995). • How to design more accurate tracking of the user's body in space (Azuma, 1997; Meyers & Biocca , 1992). • Psychophysical effects of errors in the spatial and temporal correspondence of the sensed body (input) and the display body (output; Biocca & Rolland, 1998).

Table 16.5. Interconnected Representations of the User's Body in Virtual Environments (cont'd.).

Body Representation	Selected Research Issues
4. The virtual body or avatar: The representation of the body movements and displayed as feedback to the user.	For the user to act in the virtual environment and to know he or she has acted, the user's motor actions need to be represented by a virtual body (Benford et al., 1995; Bowers, Pycock, & O'Brien, 1996). The virtual body can be as crude as a mouse arrow or hand and as sophisticated as a full three-dimensional articulated body. • How to design and move virtual bodies (Capin et al., 1998; Magnenat-Thalmann, Kalra, & Escher, 1998). • Ways in which the virtual body can better match the user's physical body. • Means of selecting, designing, and displaying various virtual bodies that are different from or fantastic forms of the physical body.
5. The social body: Other users' perceptions of the morphology and behavior of the virtual body.	In virtual environments, the user is represented by a virtual body that often varies dramatically in morphology and behavior from his or her physical body. This leads to research issues such as: • Opposition and play between relationship between the identity of the virtual body and the physical body: variations in gender, class, species, and form (Dietrich, 1997; McRae, 1997; Yates, 1997). • Confusions between avatars (virtual bodies "piloted" by humans) and agents (virtual bodies "piloted" by artificial intelligence; Oravec, 1996; Walser, 1991a) • Effects of unstable or uncertain body morphology or behavior on the behavior of workgroups (Benford et al., 1995; Bowers et al., 1996) or cultural communities (Dietrich, 1997; Lipton, 1996)

different forms of the virtual body may suit collaborative work environments such as those that support manufacturing, engineering, and medicine. The importance of our choice of avatar extends beyond any single interaction into the construction of self and relationship with the other, as the ideal representation of the body is dependent on the purpose of the interaction. Oravec (1996) drew a parallel between avatar choice and dressing appropriately for an interaction. To her, clothing is a vehicle of expression that has been linked to the construction of self. In the same way, "expression patterns (e.g., posture, gesture or tone of voice) are likely to be different in different settings" (Weiner & Mehrabian, 1968, p. 19). It is likely that one's choice of avatar and medium will have the same effect, framing both what one says and how the other hears it.

This fluid and adaptive body means it is no longer valid to assume that a body is an indicator of the person embodied by it. It is possible for a person to swiftly inhabit one virtual body, and just as swiftly switch to inhabit a completely different virtual body (Oravec, 1996). People will need to redefine how they understand and recognize others in these environments. It becomes a challenging theoretical problem to appreciate the impact of this fluid body on our ability to form relationships with others (Nowak, 2000). Designers around the world have developed some creative and expressive virtual humans capable of a wide variety of expressions for almost any type of interaction one could desire.

The next step for interpersonal researchers and media designers to address is whether virtual bodies need to look exactly like physical bodies, or whether as we predict, optimal communication in virtual environments may involve bodies that are intentionally distorted and amplified for specific communication needs. We suggest a functionalist approach to the design of the virtual body. Users and designers should seek to create an embodiment in mediated environments that supports and enhances the purposes of the interaction (e.g., see Palmer, 1995, on different levels of social presence).

VIRTUAL BODY HUMAN COMMUNICATION AND INTERACTION

Faced with arrival of the virtual body in cyberspace and VR environments, researchers in the 1990s began to formulate positions regarding the implications of the virtual body for human communication and social interaction. Three basic theoretical positions have emerged. These positions are outlined here and in Table 16.6. In the following sections, we examine evidence that supports or contradicts these positions, and discuss the future implications of the body's entrance in cyberspace.

Table 16.6. The Relationship of the Virtual Body to Human Communication and Social Interaction: Three Theoretical Positions.

Theoretical Position	Entailment	What the Position Emphasizes	What the Position Neglects
Theory 1: **The virtual body is disembodied, polymorphic, and free.**	*The virtual body can be ANYbody.*	▪ The arrival of the virtual body allows the mind to leave the physical body behind or transcends it in some way. ▪ The morphology of the virtual body is analogous to digital clothing, subject to alteration for whim, message emphasis, or fashion. ▪ Polymorphic "liquid" virtual body is a means to a quasi-utopian "democratizing cyberspace": social stereotypes of gender, race, class, disability, and other "restrictions" of the social body might "disappear" in cyberspace.	▪ Ignores concrete psychophysical link of the physical body to the virtual body in advanced virtual environments, or does not consider it a problem as would Theory 2. ▪ While aware of identity issues associated with the virtual body, this position rarely considers negative psychological effects of virtual body on the user's body image. ▪ Ignores research that shows judgments based on gender and race are still being applied in cyberspace.
Theory 2: **Virtual body is a sensorimotor extension of the physical body.**	*The virtual body can never be ANYbody.*	▪ In the more immersive and embodied media interfaces such as VR and augmented reality interfaces, there are increasingly direct psychophysical links of the physical body to the represented virtual body. Mapping of the physical body to the virtual body must be relatively faithfully or psychological and psychophysical disorders are likely.	▪ The focus on the body from a perceptual and psychophysical viewpoint, tends to ignore cultural issues regarding the semiotics of the virtual body.

Table 16.6. The Relationship of the Virtual Body to Human Communication and Social Interaction: Three Theoretical Positions (cont'd.).

Theoretical Position	Entailment	What the Position Emphasizes	What the Position Neglects
		▪ Emphasis on the user short-term and long-term body image, especially the effect of sensorimotor feedback on the user's motor processes and constructed identity.	
Theory 3: Virtual body as a social construction.	The virtual body is *never truly ANYbody and "free"* of all the restrictions of social judgement; like the physical body, the virtual is subject to social norms and constraints.	▪ Changing criteria for social hierarchy depends on the nature of human embodiment. ▪ Attempts by users to "see through" variations in virtual embodiment to the physical body, and decipher its social status in situ.	▪ Tends to ignore psychophysical links of the virtual body to the physical body, because most of this work is based on text based "embodiments" in chat environments. ▪ Tends to neglect empirical work on perception and psychophysical links of the physical body to the virtual body that might support the position.

Virtual Body as Polymorphic and Free

With the arrival of cyberspace and, especially, three-dimensional virtual embodiments in VR systems, theorists seized on the potential freedom that came from a virtual body that could take on any physical or social form. This belief includes the idea that a virtual embodiment allowed us the opportunity to be freed from earthly restraints and to overcome the limitations imposed by society based on our natural embodiment. If the virtual body can take any shape (i.e., morphology), then you can be ANYbody (i.e., any social role or identity). Advocates of this position hailed the "genderless," "classless," and "appearance-neutral" arena of cyberspace as a perfect opportunity to feel what is like to play the opposite gender, different social role, or even a different species. They argued that this freedom to be any virtual body provided the opportunity to experience what it "feels" like to be the opposite gender or to have no gender at all (Turkle, 1995). The issue of gender-swapping is one of the more visible and controversial form of the fluid representation of our embodiment in cyberspace. Some technological visionaries advocated researching and developing a dreamy surreal vision of virtual reality that included promises of social freedom and change (Lanier & Biocca, 1992).

Virtual Body as Sensorimotor Extension of the Physical Body

It may be impossible for us to be ANYbody in virtual environments, and even during virtual interactions, clues about who we "really" are leak out in a variety of ways (Nowak, 2000, Waskul & Douglass, 1997). For the utopian prediction that we can be ANYbody to be possible, it would mean we can overwrite a lifetime of embodied socialization by simply taking a different point of view during an interaction (Davis, 1995; Dietrich, 1997). It also ignores any significant hardware interface link of the physical body to the mind and to the virtual body, which reproduces the social structure people experience (Foschi, 1996; Stets & Burke, 1996). Thus, virtual bodies cannot be arbitrary because the shape, form, and type of connection of the virtual body to the physical body has significant psychological consequences.

Research on VR interface design examines closely how the human senses and actions are connected to the computer (Biocca & Delaney, 1995; Durlach & Mavor, 1994). There may be a strong psychophysical link to the virtual body, especially in media with very high levels of mediated embodiment. Research on effective interface design, simulation sickness, and perceptual adaptation (see later) suggest that psychophysical constraints require that the virtual body be mapped consistently to the physical body. So, how the body is connected to the computer can have significant psychological consequences (e.g., Biocca & Rolland, 1998), if not all the sweeping effects McLuhan predicted (1964, 1967; McLuhan & McLuhan, 1992). This does not mean that the physical body must be exactly the same as the virtual body. What it does mean is that gross inconsistent mapping of the physical body to the virtual body may have psychological cost, including psychomotor disturbances and physical illness (e.g., Biocca & Rolland, 1998).

Virtual Body as a Social Construction

In Position 3 the virtual body is socially constructed and constrained. We see the reemergence of social restraints in research and observation of users in cyberspace. In social virtual interactions, users frequently changed gender, class, and various other forms of identity. Role-playing seemed easy and free, but observations of how people used this freedom suggests that escapes from gender and class are limited. This observation has led researchers to retreat from the earlier utopian prediction of polymorphic freedom of the virtual body. One of the earliest utopian positions to be challenged by these observations was the notion that polymorphic freedom of the virtual body would create more equality and diminish the hierarchies of class. The first reports from cyberspace are not consistent with these utopian predictions. There is evidence of the entrenchment of traditional stereotypes (N. Clark, 1995; Yates, 1997).

Contrary to the original utopian predictions, the first questions in interactions in cyberspace are about gender or other cues of status and class (Spender, 1996; Turkle, 1995; Waskul & Douglass, 1997). Not only do people continue to make attributions of gender in these environments, but also the assumption appears to be that the interaction partner is male when in text-based interactions, especially when the interactions are task or negotiation (Matheson, 1991; Nowak & Anderson, 1999). Furthermore, these social classification schemes have held both their salience and their social meaning in these environments (Daly, Bench, & Chappell, 1996; Dietrich, 1997; Skitka & Maslach, 1996; Spender, 1996; Turkle, 1995; Waskul & Douglass, 1997). In other words, gender is salient in people's minds and meaningful during interactions in virtual environments. This is likely to be their attempt to bring things that are familiar and meaningful in previous experience to an unfamiliar and uncertain environment.

INTERACTING WITH OTHER VIRTUAL BODIES

As we just noted, interactions in some virtual environments remove the associations derived by others based on the appearance of our physical bodies (Hert, 1997; Turkle, 1995; Yates, 1997). It may be possible that others will judge us based on the avatar we choose. This does many things. It not only influences the perception that others have of "me" but it will also influence my self-perception, which is defined and redefined during interaction. Choosing an avatar is similar to selecting a costume to a party in that it filters out many of the physical features of one's identity. It is also similar to selecting clothing to wear for the day, in that people take it to be a representation of one's personality and lifestyle.

In the traditional physical world, we use people's faces to interpret a lot about them as individuals. It becomes a very different situation in virtual environments where there are no permanent features; all physical aspects are alterable and controllable by the individual. The virtual body, if not video-based, can be completely artificial, generated and presented by and through a computer. There are also few physical restraints in the current systems. For example, subconscious movements, such as twitches or blushing, are not recorded and do not influence social judgment.

THE COLLAPSE OF FREE VIRTUAL BODY

Advocates of the polymorphic freedom for the virtual body argued that the faceless and genderless interactions in cyberspace would force people to use other means to classify others. Research has not been very supportive of this utopian ideal associated with Position 1. It appears to incorporate "a naïve assumption" that unembodied communication is free from social markers (Yates, 1997).

If anything, instead of downplaying gender differences, the design and choice of avatars in cyberspace has served to exaggerate the distinction between the feminine and masculine in cyberspace (Nowak, 2000). This freedom to choose to be anybody has led users to take the already impossible body types of Hollywood and take them even further toward some gender ideal or caricature. Avatar designers have increased breast sizes and pectoral muscles to an even more unreasonable ideal (N. Clark, 1995). Examples can be seen in Stephenson's (1993) depiction of cyberspace in *Snow Crash*, by visiting any of several three-dimensional chat rooms (Damer, 1997), or even in the depictions of characters in video games, such as *Tomb Raider's* Laura Croft, or many other games with depictions of people.

We can attempt to be as "genderless" as we know how, but women and men may have recognizably different styles in posting to the

Internet and different ways of communicating (Witmer & Katzman, 1997; Yates, 1997). For example, men attempt to continue to dominate communication in cyberspace by interrupting and correcting. Also, women tend to use "emoticons," such as smiley faces (:)) more frequently during text-based interactions. Self-identity and gender can also be expressed via user names, phrasing choices, or signatures at the end of e-mail messages (Watson, 1997; Witmer & Katzman, 1997; Yates, 1997).

Preliminary reports from cyberspace support Position 3, that the virtual body is a social construction confined by conventions existing outside of cyberspace. But this issue has not yet addressed the impact of higher levels of sensorimotor embodiment. It may take more than technology to erase the stereotypes and distinctions that people use for classifying groups (Mitra, 1997; Watson, 1997; Yates, 1997). Could this need to identify one as female and know their physical location go back to our need to identify them as human?

Thus, it is unlikely that gender will cease to be significant, although society may redefine what it means to be male or female, and this may affect how individuals perceive themselves. Given the human mind's tendency to categorize, it is unlikely that we will cease to place others in categories (Bruner, 1957; Lakoff, 1987). But when there is no body to be identified, or when a virtual body can be manipulated and transformed at will, the codes that structure the meanings we make of bodies may take on new functions. It is possible that humans will create new categorization schemes that make sense in virtual environments, even though it will take time.

If it is true that users have a tendency to anthropomorphize all intelligent others (Reeves & Nass, 1996), especially if they take humanoid form, then it is quite possible that we will see the rise of various types of new and unique mediated relationships. In virtual environments, the other may or may not be human, and if human, may or may not be presented in a form easily recognized as humanoid. Thus, a new issue is raised about those we encounter in cyberspace. We may come in contact with a non-human mind, some form of artificial intelligence rather than a human intelligence (Nowak & Biocca, 1999). It is likely that the culture evolving in cyberspace will develop a social hierarchy based on different characteristics, such as whether the other is human or not, their technological ability and knowledge of issues that are only now beginning to emerge as important to people interacting in virtual environments.

CONFLICTING SENSORIMOTOR CUES

Should we be concerned about the psychophysical health and integrity of the body in immersive virtual environments? The coupling of motor action and sensation is part of the pattern of progressive mediated embodiment. More and more of the body is immersed in media that augment or substitute some aspect of our nonmediated sensorimotor interaction with the physical environment. Does the current generation of advanced telecommunication and simulation interfaces couple the sensorimotor system accurately (i.e., with high fidelity) and completely (i.e., with high levels of saturation and bandwidth utilization)? The simple answer is no (see Durlach & Mavor, 1994). So what happens when there is an imperfect coupling of the sensorimotor system to the interface? In media with low levels of user embodiment, such as television, distortions in visual cues such as optical distortions from off-center viewing or zoom lenses cause non-noxious distortions in the user's perception of the represented space, for example, distortions in depth perception and motion perception (Hochberg, 1986; Kraft, 1987). But, as the level of embodiment increases and the body is more tightly coupled to the interface, more disturbing psychophysical problems become evident. We discuss some of these problems here.

Sometimes, the virtual body is represented by a first-person viewpoint on the virtual environment. In this case, a computer graphic hand or even a full body may be seen by the user inside the virtual environment. It may appear to correspond in space to the felt body and motion of the user. The mouse arrow, the three-dimensional hand, and three dimensional, fully articulated bodies are just different instantiations of the virtual body. The mouse arrow or a full three-dimensional computer graphic body are just different sensory representations of the user's continuous motor movements and actions.

The link of the physical body to the virtual body is often accompanied by distorted perceptual cues. These cues are different from what the unmediated physical body would experience in the physical environment. Distorted perceptual cues in a medium can take the form of competing cues within a sensory channel (e.g., conflict between visual convergence and accommodation within vision) or competing cues across sensory channels (i.e., intersensory conflict, for example, conflict between the seen and felt position of the arm). Most commonly, there may be competing cues across and within the senses as to the location, depth, and characteristics of an object or scene. Welch (1998) listed a number of cues that can be different in virtual environments, including the following:

1. Inadequate sensory resolution.
2. An absence of certain sensory cues or entire sensory modalities.
3. Constricted range of stimuli (e.g., fields of view).
4. Sparse, ambiguous, or distorted object, motion, and depth cues from computer graphics.

5. Delayed, faulty, variable, or absent sensory feedback from the user's movements, and decorrelations of timing and spatial location of sensory cues.
6. Distortions of visual size, shape, and spatial orientation.

This and other properties of highly embodied interfaces have given rise to reports of a number of disturbances. Some of these are listed in Table 16.7. These reports come from research involving military simulators, VR systems, high-end arcade rides, and prototype augmented reality systems.

We see that virtual bodies that dramatically or even slightly alter the morphology of the virtual body can lead to intersensory conflicts. The effect seems more pronounced where there is a higher level of mediated embodiment, especially when there is tight sensorimotor integration. As the level of mediated embodiment increases conflict between the represented virtual body and the physical body, the interface can trigger more psychophysiological responses, some of which are noxious. Cue conflicts across sensory and motor channels can create nausea and simulation sickness.

Consider an example of how a users body image and coordination can be distorted by their interaction with an interface (see Biocca & Rolland, 1998). When the mediated sensorimotor loop is distorted by the inaccurate links between I/O devices, such that they cause conflict between a seen and felt hand position, for example, the user's hand-eye coordination may change. The after effect of this change can carry into the physical environment. This kind of effect can be seen with other forms of sensorimotor discoordination. Once they leave the simulator, their internal representation of their body may have changed. Using the language of embodiment, we can say that their altered body schema transfers properties of virtual body into the physical world!

SUMMARY AND CONCLUSION

In this chapter, we proposed that telecommunication interfaces are evolving along four dimensions: level of mediated embodiment, level of intelligence, ubiquity of access, and level of sociability. Using these four dimensions, we have seen how it is possible to organize and plot many existing media interfaces, including advanced virtual environments, and see distinctions between them.

We also explored the implications of the progressive embodiment of the user, the tighter coupling of the user's sensorimotor channels to the telecommunication interface's sensors and effectors. We have seen how embodiment gives rise to the virtual body, and how the virtual body has

Table 16.7. Physical Disorders Associated With Sensorimotor Conflicts and Other Problems Arising from a Tight Coupling of the Body and an Immersive Computer Interface.

Reported Problem	Description	Selected Studies/Reviews
Simulation sickness	A disorder similar to motion sickness associated with simulator and virtual environment use. Symptoms include sweating, stomach awareness, nausea, and vomiting.	(Biocca, 1992)
Perceptual-motor adaptation	Changes in the perception or motor function from adaptation to changes in environmental cues. Significant changes in hand-eye coordination reported with some VR systems.	(Biocca & Rolland, 1998)
Body image disturbances	Changes in the perceived morphology of the body due to simulator use or exposure to ideal or distorted body shapes, especially when these are seen a representations of the self or a social ideal.	(Meyers & Biocca, 1992)
Ocular disorders	Changes in eye function such as dark focus accommodation and eye strain associated with display use.	(Ebenholtz, 1992; B. Stone, 1993)
Ataxia	Postural instability or disequilibrium following simulator use.	(Baltzley, Kennedy, Berbaum, Lilienthal, & Gower 1989)

dramatic and unforeseen implications for human communication, cognition, and social action. It follows that in human-computer interaction, the cues from humanoid virtual bodies will be a powerful means to enhance the meaning and apparent co-presence of a human-to-human, and human-to-artificial intelligence interaction. This is likely to be especially true in any mediated interaction involving highly interactive virtual environments and expressive virtual bodies. Research has found that "a number of social conventions are carried over from our interaction in the physical world, are conveyed through the embodiment and positioning, and play a strong role in virtual interaction" (Henne, Mark, & Voss, 1998, p. 1).

Research in the traditional areas of interpersonal and mass communication have not fully considered the implications of the virtual body.

In networked virtual environments, mediated interaction brings the other's body "within range." Current interpersonal research that has looked at new technology, especially computer-mediated communication, has tended to focus on the lack of cues of mediated interactions. By emphasizing the cues that are missing, say in a telephone call or e-mail message, this line of research has prized the interactions that involve both participants in the same physical space (Burgoon, Buller, & Woodall, 1996; Kayany, Wotring, & Forrest, 1996; Steinfield, 1986; Suchman, 1987; Walther, 1996; Walther, Anderson, & Park, 1994).

Some have even narrowed the definition of *copresence* to two human bodies sharing the same physical space (see, e.g., Ciolek, 1982; Lipton, 1996). This link of virtual bodies inside virtual environments might well provide means of interaction and mutual self-discovery that might not only match, but potentially exceed the capabilities of face-to-face communication for certain kinds of collaboration and interaction. To understand and explore the implications of this technological opportunity, it is important to see copresence more broadly, as a psychological connection of two semiotically engaged minds (Goffman, 1963) via sensorimotor interaction in a physical environment or a mediated environment.

It still appears that the surface freedom of the disembodied virtual body is restrained. Higher levels of mediated embodiment make the virtual body far less disembodied, but rather increasingly tethered and connected to the physical body by sensorimotor links. Even in text-based chat rooms where there are few sensorimotor links of the physical body to the virtual body, the virtual body is increasingly linked to the physical body by social behavior that attempts to define the biological sex and class of the user. We have also seen how the morphology of the body and range sensory experience transmitted to the body is restrained as the body is more tightly coupled to the telecommunication interface. Tightly coupled interfaces that grossly violate the way the body connects motor activity to sensory feedback can lead to psychophysiological disorders.

The pattern of the evolution of the media and the early research discussed here suggests that the key to understanding the implications of immersive media will rest on an analysis of the boundaries and connections between the physical body and the virtual body. There is a fuzzy and changing boundary between the physical and virtual bodies, and ambivalence about how well each represents the "identity" of the user. There are questions about how consciousness increasingly embraces the two in those moments when we feel more present in the virtual environment than in the physical environment (Biocca, 1996b; Biocca & Nowak, 1999b). Finally, we have seen that the social virtual body is likely to influence how self and other are presented and defined and what this means for our ability to form and maintain interpersonal relationships (Nowak, 2000;

Nowak & Biocca, 1999). The forms, possibilities, and disturbances of the body are likely to continue to evolve in the same direction as people spend increasingly more time in immersive interfaces communicating with each other and accessing information via ubiquitous, high-speed telecommunication networks.

REFERENCES

Argyle, M. (1988). The explanation of bodily communication. In M. Argyle (Ed.), *Bodily communication* (2nd ed., pp. 290-304). New York: International Universities Press.

Badler, N., Phillips, C., & Webber, B. (1993). *Simulating humans: Computer graphics animation and control.* New York: Oxford University Press.

Balsamo, A. (1995). Forms of technological embodiment: Reading the body in contemporary culture. In M. Featherstone & R. Burrows (Eds.), *Cyberspace/cyberbodies/cyberpunk: Cultures of technological embodiment* (pp. 215-237). Thousand Oaks, CA: Sage.

Baltzley, D. R., Kennedy, R. S., Berbaum, K. S., Lilienthal, M. G., & Gower, D. W. (1989). The time course of postflight simulator sickness symptoms. *Aviation, Space, and Environmental Medicine, 60,* 1043-1048.

Barnes, S. (1996). Cyberspace: Creating paradoxes for the ecology of the self. In L. Strate, R. Jacobson, & S. B. Gibson (Eds.), *Communication and cyberspace: Social interaction in an electronic environment* (pp. 193-216). Cresskill, NJ: Hampton Press.

Barnes, S. B. (1997, November). *Ethical issues for a virtual self.* Paper presented at the National Communication Convention, Chicago.

Benford, S., Greenhalg, C., Bowers, J., Snowdon, D., & Fahlén, L. (1995, May). *User embodiment in collaborative virtual environments.* Paper presented at the CHI '95 Mosaic of Creativity, Denver, CO.

Biocca, F. (1992). Will simulator sickness slow down the diffusion of virtual environment technology? *Presence, 1*(3), 258-264.

Biocca, F. (1996a). Intelligence augmentation: The vision inside virtual reality. In B. Gorayska (Ed.), *Cognitive technology: In search of a humane interface* (pp. 59-75). Amsterdam: North Holland.

Biocca, F. (1996b). *What does it mean for consciousness to feel "presence" in virtual reality?* Paper presented at the Towards a Science of Consciousness "Tucson II," Tucson.

Biocca, F. (1997). The cyborg's dilemma: Embodiment in virtual environments. *Journal of Computer-mediated Communication, 3*(3).

Biocca, F., & Delaney, B. (1995). Immersive virtual reality technology. In F. Biocca & M. Levy (Eds.), *Communication in the age of virtual reality*. Hillsdale, NJ: Lawrence Erlbaum Associates.

Biocca, F., & Nowak, K. (1999a, May). *"I feel as if I'm here, inside the computer": Toward a theory of presence in advanced virtual environments*. Paper presented at the International Communication Association, San Francisco.

Biocca, F., & Nowak, K. (1999b). *"My body is connected to the computer": The body and the interface in highly immersive, social virtual environments*. Unpublished manuscript, Media Interface and Network Design Lab, East Lansing, MI.

Biocca, F., & Rolland, J. (1998). Virtual eyes can rearrange your body: Adaptation to visual displacement in see-through, head-mounted displays. *Presence, 7*(3), 262-277.

Bowers, J., Pycock, J., & O'Brien, J. (1996, April). *Talk and embodiment in collaborative virtual environments*. Paper presented at the CHI 96, Vancouver, BC Canada.

Bricken, W., & Coco, G. (1995). VEOS: The virtual environment operating shell. In W. Barfield & T. Furness (Eds.), *Virtual environments and advanced interface design*. New York: Oxford University Press.

Brooks, R. (1991). Intelligence without reason. *Proceedings of the 12th International Joint Conference on Artificial Intelligence* (pp. 45-61). San Francisco: Morgan Kaufman.

Brooks, R. (1994). Coherent behavior from many adaptive processes. In D. Cliff (Ed.), *From animals to animat 3*. Cambridge, MA: MIT Press.

Brooks, R., & Stein, L. (1994). Building brains for bodies. *Autonomous Robots, 1*(1), 7-25.

Bruner, J. (1957). On perceptual readiness. *Psychological Review, 64*(2), 123-151.

Bull, P. (1983). *Body movement and interpersonal communication*. New York: Wiley.

Burgoon, J., Buller, D., & Woodall, W. (1996). *Nonverbal communication: The unspoken dialogue* (2nd ed.). New York: McGraw-Hill.

Capin, T. K., Pandzic, I. S., Magnenat-Thalmann, N., and Thalmann, D. (Eds). (1998). *Realistic avatars and autonomous virtual humans*. Paper presented at the VLNET Networked Virtual Environments Virtual Worlds in the Internet.

Ciolek, T. (1982). Zones of co-presence in face-to-face interaction: Some observational data. *Man-environment Systems, 12*(6), 223-242.

Clark, A. (1997). *Being there: Putting brain, body, and world together again*. Boston: MIT Press.

Clark, N. (1995). Rear-view mirrorshades: The recursive generation of the cyberbody. In M. Featherstone & R. Burrows (Eds.), *Cyberspace/cyberbodies/cyberpunk; cultures of technological embodiment* (pp. 113-133). Thousand Oaks, CA: Sage.

Daly, N., Bench, J., & Chappell, H. (1996). Interpersonal impressions, gender stereotypes and visual speech. *Journal of Language and Social Psychology, 15*(4), 468-479.

Damasio, A. (1994). *Decartes' error: Emotion, reason, and the brain.* New York: Grosset/Putnam.

Damer, B. (1997). *Avatars!: Exploring and building virtual worlds on the Internet.* Berkeley, CA: Peachpit Press.

Davis, D. (1995). Illusions and ambiguities in the telemedia environment: An exploration of the transformation of social roles. *Journal of Broadcasting & Electronic Media, 39,* 517-554.

Dennett, D. (1997). *Kinds of minds: Towards an understanding of consciousness.* New York: HarperCollins.

Dietrich, D. (1997). (Re)-fashioning the techno-erotic woman: Gender and textuality in the cybercultural matrix. In S. Jones (Ed.), *Virtual culture: Identity and communication in cybersociety* (pp. 169-184). London: Sage.

Durlach, N., & Mavor, A. (1994). *Virtual reality: Scientific and technological challenges.* Washington, DC: National Research Council.

Ebenholtz, S. M. (1992). Motion sickness and oculomotor systems in virtual environments. *Presence, 1*(3), 302-305.

Featherstone, M., & Burrows, R. (1995). Cultures of technological embodiment: An introduction. In M. Featherstone & R. Burrows (Eds.), *Cyberspace/cyberbodies/cyberpunk: Cultures of technological embodiment* (pp. 1-21). Thousand Oaks, CA: Sage.

Foschi, M. (1996). Double standards in the evaluation of men and women. *Social Psychology Quarterly, 59*(3), 237-254.

Gibson, J. J. (1966). *The senses considered as perceptual systems.* Boston: Houghton-Mifflin.

Gibson, J. J. (1979). *The ecological approach to visual perception.* Boston: Houghton-Mifflin.

Goffman, E. (1963). *Behavior in public places: Notes on the social organization of gatherings.* New York: The Free Press.

Haber, H., & Weiss, G. (Eds.). (1996). *Perspectives on embodiment.* New York: Routledge.

Henne, P., Mark, G., & Voss, A. (1998). *Gestures for social communication in virtual environments.* Paper presented at the workshop on Presence in Shared Environments, Ipswich, Suffolk.

Hert, P. (1997). Social dynamics of an on-line scholarly debate. *The Information Society, 13,* 329-360.

Hochberg, J. (1986). Representation of motion and space in video and cinematic displays. In K. R. Boff, L. Kaufmann, & J. P. Thomas (Eds.), *Handbook of perception and human performance* (Vol. 2, pp. 22/1-22/64). New York: Wiley.

Ichheiser, G. (1970). *Appearances and realities: Misunderstanding in human relations.* New York: Jossey-Bass.

Johnson, M. (1987). *The body in the mind.* Chicago: University of Chicago Press.

Kayany, J., Wotring, C., & Forrest, E. (1996). Relational control and interactive media choice in technology. *Human Communication Research, 22*(3), 399.

Kraft, R. N. (1987). The influence of camera angle on comprehension and retention of pictorial events. *Memory & Cognition, 15,* 291-307.

Kushmerick, N. (1998). Software agents and their bodies. *Minds and Machines,* 7(2).

Lakoff, G. (1987). *Women, fire, and dangerous things: What categories reveal about the mind.* Chicago & London: The University of Chicago Press.

Lanier, J., & Biocca, F. (1992). An insider's view of the future of virtual reality. *Journal of Communication, 42*(4).

Lea, M., & Spears, R. (1992). Paralanguage and social perception in computer-mediated communication. *Journal of Organizational Computing, 2*(3&4), 321-341.

Lipton, M. (1996). Forgetting the body: Cybersex and identity. In L. Strate, R. Jacobson, & S. Gibson (Eds.), *Communication and cyberspace: Social interaction in an electronic environment* (pp. 335-349). Cresskill, NJ: Hampton Press.

Lubar, S. (1993). *Infoculture: The Smithsonian book of information age inventions.* Washington, DC: Smithsonian.

Magnenat-Thalmann, M., Kalra, P., & Escher, M. (1998, May). *Face to virtual face* [Proceedings of the IEEE] ACM. Available online: http://www.miralab.unige.ch/ARTICLES/art98.html.

Matheson, K. (1991). Social cues in computer-mediated negotiations: Gender makes a difference. *Computers in Human Behavior, 7,* 137-145.

McLuhan, M. (1964). *The Gutenberg galaxy.* New York: Signet.

McLuhan, M. (1967). *Understanding media.* New York: Harper Row.

McLuhan, M., & McLuhan, E. (1992). *Laws of media: The new science.* Toronto: University of Toronto Press.

McRae, S. (1997). Flesh made word: Sex, text and the virtual body. In D. Porter (Ed.), *Internet culture* (pp. 69-82). London: Routledge.

Mehrabian, A. (1972). *Nonverbal communication.* Chicago: Aldine Atherton.

Merleau-Ponty, M. (1962). *Phenomenology of perception.* New York: Routledge & Kegan Paul.

Meyers, P., & Biocca, F. (1992). The elastic body image: An experiment on the effect of advertising and programming on body image distortions in young women. *Journal of Communication, 42*(3), 108-133.

Mitra, A. (1997). Virtual commonality: Looking for India on the Internet. In S. Jones (Ed.), *Virtual culture.* Thousand Oaks, CA: Sage.

Nowak, K. (2000, May). *Creating a mental model of others: Implications for social virtual environments.* Paper presented at International Communication Association, Acapulco, Mexico.

Nowak, K., & Anderson, T. (1999, May). *Communicating emotions in CMC: In search of a sufficiency threshold.* Paper presented at the International Communication Association, San Francisco, CA.

Nowak, K., & Biocca, F. (1999, August). *"I think there is someone else here with me!": The role of the virtual body in the sensation of co-presence with other humans and artificial intelligences in advanced virtual environments.* Paper presented at the Cognitive Technology Conference, San Francisco, CA.

O'Donovan-Anderson, M. (1997). *Content and comportment: On emodiment and the epistemic availability of the world.* Latham, MA: Rowman & Littlefield.

Oravec, J. (1996). *Virtual individuals, virtual groups: Human dimensions of groupware and computer networking.* Cambridge: Cambridge University Press.

Palmer, M. (1995). Interpersonal communication and virtual reality: Mediating interpersonal relationships. In F. Biocca & M. Levy (Eds.), *Communication in the age of virtual reality.* Hillsdale, NJ: Lawrence Erlbaum Associates.

Paulos, E., & Canny, J. (1997). Ubiquitous tele-embodiment: Applications and implications. *International Journal of Human Computer Studies, 46,* 862-877.

Premack, D., & Premack, J. (1996). The origins of human social competence. In M. Gazzaniga (Ed.), *The cognitive neurosciences.* Cambridge, MA: MIT Press.

Reeves, B., & Nass, C. (1996). *The media equation: How people treat computers, television, and new media like real people and places.* Stanford, CA: CSLI Publications.

Rice, R. (1993). Media appropriateness: Using social presence theory to compare traditional and new organizational media. *Human Communication Research, 19*(4), 451-484.

Rice, R., & Tyler, J. (1995). Individual and organizational influences on voice mail use and evaluation. *Behavior and Information Technology, 14*(6), 329-341.

Sekuler, R., & Blake, R. (1994). *Perception* (3rd ed.). New York: McGraw Hill.

Shneiderman, B. (1998). *Designing the user interface: Strategies for effective human-computer interaction.* Reading, MA: Addision-Wesley.

Short, J., Williams, E., & Christie, B. (1976). *The social psychology of telecommunications.* London: Wiley.

Skitka, L., & Maslach, C. (1996). Gender as schematic category: A role construct approach. *Social Behavior and Personality, 24*(1), 53-74.

Spender, D. (1996). *Nattering on the net: Women, power and cyberspace.* Australia: Spinifex Press.

Stafford, L., & Reske, R. (1990). Idealization and communication in long-distance premarital relationships. *Family Relations, 39*, 274-279.

Steinfield, C. (1986). Computer-mediated communication in an organizational setting: Explaining task-related and socioemotional uses. In M. McLaughlin (Ed.), *Communication yearbook* (Vol. 9, pp. 777-804). Beverly Hills, CA: Sage.

Stephenson, N. (1993). *Snow crash.* New York: Bantam Books.

Stets, J. E., & Burke, P. J. (1996). Gender, control, and interaction. *Social Psychology Quarterly, 59*(3), 193-220.

Stone, A. R. (1995). *The war of desire and technology at the close of the mechanical age.* Cambridge, MA: MIT Press.

Stone, B. (1993). Concerns raised about eye strain in VR systems. *Real Time Graphics, 2*(4), 1-3, 6, 13.

Suchman, L. (1987). *Plans and situated actions: The problem of human machine communication.* Cambridge: Cambridge University Press.

Sutherland, I. (1965). *The ultimate display.* Paper presented at the Proceedings of the International Federation of Information Processing Congress, New York.

Turkle, S. (1995). *Life on the screen: Identity in the age of the Internet.* New York: Simon & Schuster.

Varela, A., Thompson, E., & Rosch, E. (1991). *The embodied mind: Cognitive science and human experience.* Cambridge, MA: MIT Press.

Von Uexkull, J. (1934). A stroll through the worlds on animals and men. In K. Lashley (Ed.), *Instinctive behavior.* New York: International Universities Press.

Walser, R. (1991a). Elements of a cyberspace playhouse. In S. Helsel (Ed.), *Virtual reality: Theory, practice, and promise.* Westport, CT: Meckler.

Walser, R. (1991b). Elements of a cyberspace playhouse. In S. Helsel (Ed.), *Virtual reality: Theory, practice, and promise.* Westport, CT: Meckler.

Walther, J. B. (1996). Computer-mediated communication: Impersonal, interpersonal, and hyperpersonal interaction. *Communication Research, 23*, 3-43.

Walther, J., Anderson, J., & Park, D. (1994). Interpersonal effects in computer-mediated interaction: A meta-analysis of social and antisocial communication. *Communication Research, 21*(4), 460.

Waskul, D., & Douglass, M. (1997). Cyberself: The emergence of self in on-line chat. *The Information Society, 13*(4), 375-397.

Watson, N. (1997). Why we argue about virtual community: A case study of the Phish.Net fan community. In S. Jones (Ed.), *Virtual culture: Identity and communication in cybersociety.* London: Sage.

Weiner, M., & Mehrabian, A. (1968). *Language within language: Immediacy, a channel in verbal communication.* New York: Appleton-Century-Crofts.

Welch, R. (1978). *Perceptual modification: Adapting to altered sensory environments.* New York: Academic Press.

Welch, R. (1998). *Adapting to telesystems.* Unpublished manuscript. Moffett Field, CA: NASA-Ames Research Center.

Witmer, D., & Katzman, S. (1997). On-line smiles: Does gender make a difference in the use of graphic accents? *Journal of Computer Mediated Communication, 2*(4).

Yates, S. (1997). Gender, identity and CMC. *Journal of Computer Assisted Learning, 13,* 281-290.

17

A Paradigm for Communication and Information Technology Adoption Research

Carolyn A. Lin
Cleveland State University

Throughout this volume, the contributors provided theoretical perspectives, empirical evidence, and economic forecasts as well as regulatory and policy analyses. This volume discusses the interlinkages between distinct communication research traditions and also showcases the unique theoretical as well as empirical contributions of these traditions. This emerging fusion or contrasting diversity in research traditions exemplifies the crossroads at which we have arrived contemporaneously. These crossroads represent an unforeseen opportunity for communication researchers to share, confer, and challenge the tradition that each has followed.

   Ideally, this cross-fertilization of research energy results in an integration of these different research traditions in ways that will help enhance the theoretical foundations of communication research and further legitimize its significance in an information society. In fact, one need only look to how this information society has become heavily reliant on technologies to perform all types of information-relevant tasks. Yet, the portal that facilitates interactions between technologies, people and technologies, and people themselves is "communication." Hence, one cannot overstate the role of communication in this technology-human sphere. For this very reason, communication research has been elevated to the forefront of this information-centric research arena.

If we view communication as a human behavior that occurs on a continuum within micro-social systems that exist in a larger macro-social system, then we need to define the relationships between all the technology-related communication activities within those microsystems and then link them to the macro-system. If we analyze both of these micro- as well as macro-systems, we are looking at a research paradigm that integrates systems, technology, social, audience, and use factors, where the input, output, and feedback derived from each component in the typology dynamically interacts in a reciprocal fashion.

This chapter explores each of the factors that contributes to technology adoption. It also explains how the integration of these different contributory factors in this typology can serve as a synthesis of a paradigm for mediated communication research. Figure 17.1 illustrates such a paradigm, which does not include either the outcomes or consequences of technology adoption.

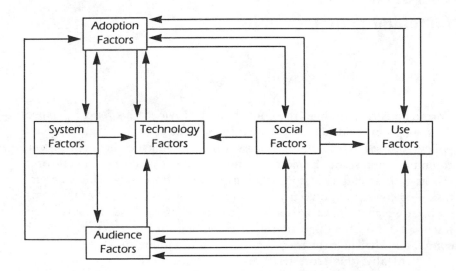

**Figure 17.1. A communication and information technology
adoption paradigm**

A DYNAMIC INTERACTIVITY PARADIGM

The structure of this paradigm is built on the principle of dynamic interactivity that interconnects and integrates a number of reciprocal social, technological, and human factors. In essence, this paradigm attempts to establish a research model where various components in the model can be studied individually or jointly to examine either a micro-aspect or a macro-perspective of the model.

Conceptually, each model component can be further examined through a series of communication research perspectives. These theories or constructs are summarized in Table 17.1.

To further explicate the interactivity between model components, the following discussion illustrates the relationships that link them together. The discussion starts with the system factor—the basis for technology development, marketing, and diffusion. It ends with adoption factors, which then loop back to the system factor, as they help shape and reshape the system factor.

System factors, designated as a combination of regulatory and policy tendencies and outcomes, technological culture in society, industry trends toward developing specific technology platforms, and market competition—all can help form or inhibit the market infrastructure for technology diffusion. In particular, system factors influence what kinds of technology products, features, uses, and interconnections will be developed and marketed within the given regulatory and policy environment as well as social and market trends toward technology adoption and uses.

Although these system factors, operating within their given social, economic, and political infrastructure, make technology products available or scarce to members of a society, the characteristics of one's social membership determine why, how, when, and which of these products would be adopted. These characteristics, referred to as *audience factors*, describe the beliefs, attitudes, and personality traits that are relevant to making innovation adoption decisions. They include audience beliefs and attitudes about the rationality for innovation adoption, beliefs about their ability to adopt and competence in using a technology innovation, personality traits that make the audience receptive to the idea of innovation adoption, and their self-actualization need for adoption (e.g., for work or pleasure). This model suggests applying the following four theories or constructs—self-efficacy theory (e.g., Bandura, 1983; Compeau & Higgins, 1995), theory of reasoned action (Fishbein,1980; Fishbein & Ajzen, 1975, 1981), the innovative attributes construct (e.g., Foxall & Bhate, 1991; Rogers, 1995), and the innovativeness need construct (Lin, 1998) to study these audience factors.

Table 17.1. Model Components and Communication Research Perspectives.

Model Component	Theories or Constructs
System factors	Regulation/policy Technological culture Industry trends Market competition
Technology factors	Innovation attributes Social presence Media richness Technology fluidity
Audience Factors	Innovative attributes Innovativeness need Self-efficacy Theory of reasoned action
Social factors	Opinion leadership Critical mass Media symbolism
Use factors	Uses and gratifications Expectancy value theory Communication flow
Adoption factors	Non-adoption Discontinuance Likely adoption Adoption Reinvention

These audience factors (or predispositions) regarding the innovation adoption don't function in a vacuum. On one hand, they can influence heavily how the audience perceives the role and functions of a technology innovation in a communication context, whether in a social or an organizational setting. On the other hand, they also can be readily mediated by a set of socialization factors that exist in their social environments. This type of socioenvironmental mediation, cast as social factors, can derive from such social structural sources as opinion leaders in a social or organizational setting and the availability of a critical mass of existing adopters that enables a sufficient level of communication applications associated with technology use. It can also be generated by other environmental factors that influence how the audience is socialized to perceive the degree of social interaction between the mediated communication participants associated with technology-use choice and the social symbolic meanings for such technology-use choice. These social factors can be further explored within the following theoretical frameworks: opinion leadership (e.g., Parks, 1977; Rogers, 1988), critical mass (e.g., Markus, 1987), and media symbolism (e.g., Trevino, Lengel, & Daft, 1987).

Both the audience and social factors can influence audience's beliefs and attitudes toward assessing the technical attributes of a technology when confronted with an adoption decision. That is, the audience normally develops a set of perceptions and expectations about a technology innovation, often through vicarious social learning (Bandura, 1986), based on a set of objective and subjective criteria—or technology factors. These objective criteria can include the audience's comprehension of the inherent technical characteristics (e.g., relative advantage, complexity) of a technology and the technology's built-in versatility level in terms of its transmutability from one communication modality into another—to perform multitasking (e.g., execute multiple audiovisual tasks simultaneously). By contrast, the subjective criteria can be formulated based on the audience's value-laden assessment of the technology's technical characteristics (e.g., ease of use, usefulness) and the technology's capability in transmitting and preserving interpersonal proximity and communication isomorphism. The criteria that help develop objective cognition can be examined separately by the innovation attributes construct (e.g., Rogers, 1995) and theory of technology fluidity (Lin, 2000b). Those criteria that allow for subjective cognition and affect formation can be more closely examined by social presence theory (e.g., Short, Williams, & Christie, 1976) and media richness theory (Daft & Lengel, 1984, 1986).

The accumulation and interaction of audience factors (reflecting audience predisposition), social factors (illustrating socialization effects), technology factors (depicting perceived technology attributes), and system factors (influencing availability and affordability of technology products), can thus shape the audience adoption decision. Such a decision can result in several different outcomes or adoption factors. The first outcome is nonadoption, where the audience decides not to adopt the technology. A parallel alternative of nonadoption is discontinuance, where the audience phases out an adoption and considers adopting a different technology as a replacement. By contrast, the third outcome, likely adoption, portrays the situation where the audience decides to delay their adoption decision, due to certain adoption barriers such as lack of financial resources or immediate needs. Alternatively, the fourth outcome can be an actual *adoption* act. Once a technology innovation is adopted, the audience may or may not utilize the technology for its originally intended purposes. When the latter occurs, the process is called *reinvention* (Johnson & Rice, 1987). An example for reinvention could be that e-mail is replacing paper memos at the workplace, even though the e-mail system is not designed or adopted to replace office memos.

Although audience use experience with the adopted technology can be influenced by whether the technology is used for its originally intended functional purposes, usage can also depend on the composition of audience factors and social factors. That is, there is an entire array of variables that can help frame use experience, whether such uses occur in a individualized, dyadic, group, or organizational level. This use experience, branded as *use factors*, can indicate a range of the audience's cognitive, affective, and behavioral responses. For instance, the audience can develop a set of perceptions associated with the following: (a) whether the expected reward attached to the technology's use is realized, (b) the level of psychological gratification received, and (c) their control over the use experience and the attention and interest the use experience generates. Individual and organizational uses and use patterns—in other words, use factors—can be formulated due to the motives and gratifications derived from actual uses of the technology. These use factors can be explicated with the following theoretical frameworks: expectancy-value theory (e.g., Rosenberg, 1956), the uses and gratifications perspective (e.g., Blumler, 1979), and the construct of communication flow (e.g., Trevino & Webster, 1992).

The cumulative effect of these use factors is then expected to reciprocally recreate, reinforce, or even convert a set of audience predispositions (audience factors) and technology socialization (social factors) that can directly impact how the audience perceives the technology's attributes (technology factors). These potentially recreated, reinforced, or converted audience, social, and technology factors, along with use factors, can loop back to shape future adoption decisions (adoption factors). The entire range of adoption factors—including nonadoption, likely adoption, adoption, and reinvention—as manifested in the marketplace, first and foremost—provides feedback to the social system that supplies the technology product.

This social system, dominated by a number of system factors, can be swayed by the technology's short- as well as long-term adoption patterns into maintaining or altering the technology's functional characteristics and marketing trends, as well as government's regulatory or policy directives. In the worst case scenario, a technology innovation can also be withdrawn from production, due to poor or insufficient adoption levels within a designated diffusion period. The net results perpetuated by the patterns of diffusion of innovations (or adoption factors) are instrumental in determining which technology products would thrive or wither in the marketplace, and which system factor(s) should be enhanced, modified, or discarded to ensure the continuous development and growth of a healthy technology marketplace. When and if these renewed system factors come into effect, a new adoption cycle can begin again, starting with perhaps a new set of technology products or marketing strategies that can help formulate a new or renewed set of audience factors (and the subsequent preadoption audience dynamics).

In summary, the research paradigm discussed here integrates its various model components into a coherent set of interrelated constructs. As each model component is linked to at least a theoretical tradition or an established theory, the model can be easily tested empirically. Most importantly, the interrelations between model components can also be examined with the application of these well-recognized theoretical frameworks. It would be most encouraging, when verifiable empirical evidence can be found to support the various interlinkages between model components that are proposed in this research paradigm. As this research paradigm presents a basis for empirical endeavors, the ultimate objective remains to theorize and hence legitimize the significance of communication technology diffusion research as a vital aspect of the communication- and information-centric digital technology era.

RESEARCH IMPLICATIONS FOR THE MODEL

The ensuing discussion reviews and explores each of the theoretical traditions and theories mentioned in conjunction with each model component in the research paradigm just discussed. Research implications and propositions relevant to each theoretical construct are also posited, where appropriate, to help guide future empirical research directions.

System Factors

The concept of system factors herein is based on a systems theory that describes a symmetrically regulated system where matter-energy and/or information flows is regulated for their input and output (Bailey, 1994, p. 49). In this regulated social system, some components are in the position to "design" and "monitor" feedback and thus are influential in controlling changes in the system itself (Lundberg, 1980, p. 251). In the present context, then, these selected components refer to the primary macrosocial forces in a society that facilitates or inhibits diffusion of communication technology innovations. These forces include public and private institutional policy and trends as well as the culture that assimilates technology and its associated implications into its social system and allows it to contribute to political, economic, social, and cultural changes. Rogers (1995), for instance, asserted that diffusion of innovations evolves within the confines of a social system, which in turn, provides regularity and stability through such social institutions as government bureaucracies to carry out policies that advance or inhibit the diffusion goals.

As a society, we have grown accustomed to such buzzwords as *information age, information technology, technocrat, techthusiasts, techies, IT workers,* or *computer-mediated communication.* According to Fisk (1990), these types of linguistic referrals for technology, as seen in marketing campaigns, trade and academic journals, and the news media, help construct the social meanings and the "public image" of this phenomenon in our culture. In fact, communication technology products are often marketed not only as a technical medium, but also as a distinct idea, lifestyle, image, social status, unique attitude to the world, affinity to a (technological) subculture, pledge of stake in the future, and so on (Dahlberg, Livingstone, Moreley, & Silverstone, 1989). Hence, technologies can, by dint of cultural assimilation, function as cultural symbols of the "(sub)cultural identity, position, image, self-perception, and world picture, social status, property rights, user competence, performance, 'techno-cultural capital,' and so on" (Jensen, 1993, p. 310)—in other words— the emblem of technological culture (Dahlberg, Livingstone, Moreley, & Silverstone, 1989).

Although these semiotic interpretations of technology as culture illustrate how technological culture is innate to the social system in which it thrives, they also raise the question of the causal relationship between culture and society. The *technological determinism* view, which regards technology as a "first cause" and all things human as its "effects" (McLuhan, 1964, 1967), lends credence to those prognosticative theories about information society, postindustrial society, and the like. By contrast, the *determined technology* view suggests that the development and distribution of technology encompasses a set of system effects spawned by such system factors as economic, political and social causes. These elements then represent an outgrowth of rational human will and control (Bell, 1973). This view is often operationalized as the *technology assessment* tradition that, by nature, is constantly evolving, changing, and formulating for the sake of making rational economic, political, and social forecasts.

In recent years, this technology assessment tradition has dominated the pursuit of technology development planning and forecasting. Hence, a technology assessment commission would gather and analyze facts to generate hypotheses and anticipated outcomes, based on the interaction effects of regulation/policy, industry trends, and market competition (Pepper, 1987). From a systems perspective, regulatory/policy decisions in effect serve as a "control mechanism" that is intended for regulating or legislating the communication technology industry's production and market structure, in addition to the industry's marketing practices (e.g., Lundberg, 1980). This type of systems control has a strong impact on the industry's research and development process, which directly influences the types of technology products produced and marketed.

Systems control notwithstanding, industry trends also reciprocally help shape regulatory and policy trends, as the government bureaucracies inevitably are compelled to address industry changes and emergent technology innovations as a function of time. Industry trends, as dominated by major producers or trend-setting producers, can also be a form of systems control mechanism. By favoring certain types of technical platforms (e.g., installing DVD drives in personal computers) or standards (e.g., deferring to a de facto standard such as VHS format), these industry trends can help foster or restrain the development or acceptance of a technology as the "next new thing" for the market. Additional examples in this area include the rise of the MPEG (i.e., Moving Picture Expert Group) standards for coding digitally compressed audiovisual information downloading, the adoption of ADSL (i.e., asymmetrical digital subscriber line) for high-speed Internet or data communication via a digital modem over a phone line instead of a fiber network, and so on. Hence, this type of industry favoritism or "bias" (see Bates et al., chap. 4, this volume) can forcefully decelerate the growth and adoption of communication technology (Lansing & Bates, 1992).

Systems control via industry trend-setting can, at times, be an attempt to control market competition or a result of the lack of or intense market competition. Therefore, market competition, by virtue of being the ultimate arbitrator of the economic success or failure of a technology, can both shape and reshape industry trends as well as regulation/policy. The break up of AT&T is a prime example of the government's effort to create market competition, which led to the exploding and competitive market of telecommunication and information technology innovations. On the other end, intense competition in the Internet service provider (ISP) market drove America Online and AT&T to seek a cable TV industry alliance for broadband service application expansions. Such cross-industry mergers then prompt new regulation/policy debates and considerations.

The deliberations just described clearly illustrate how the system factors interact in an open or adaptive system that has a dynamic structure, striving for homeostasis with elaboration and differentiation (Khandwalla, 1977). Moreover, these system factors are interdependent, dynamic, and vibrant social structural components that help lace the fabric of the overall technological culture. Yet, none of these system factors could stay afloat without being stifled by system entropy, if the audiences consuming these technologies lack the necessary technology savvy to be able to accept and embrace them.

Audience Factors

To study audience predisposition toward innovations and innovation adoption, the most direct route may be to review whether the audience in question, be they individual members in society or in an organization, have inherent personality traits that make them innately more receptive to new innovations. These personality traits may include such characteristics as venturesomeness (Foxall & Bhate, 1991), being independently receptive to new ideas (Midgley & Dowling, 1978), or being early adopters of innovations (Rogers, 1995). What these different dimensions of personality traits represent is a set of innovative attributes that propel an individual to adopt the original, unconventional, complicated, or even risky ideas or objects (e.g., technology products). Empirical evidence has born out the validity and reliability of this construct. For example, Rice and Shook (1990) found that more innovative voicemail users are more capable of utilizing the technology's ability to provide and obtain useful information.

These innovative attributes associated with an individual are good indicators of one's inclination toward innovation adoption. However, these attributes may not necessarily translate into actual adoption action if the individual is not motivated to adopt. According to Midgley and Dowling (1978), an innovative individual with strong novelty-seeking tendencies may either develop a novelty-seeking orientation (or willingness to adopt), or actualize this novelty-seeking orientation (or engage in actual adoption). Lin (1998) further explicates the distinction between *orientation* and *actualization* by testing the "need for innovativeness" construct, an indicator of an individual's need to reduce their novelty-seeking or venturesome drive as a means for self-actualization. She found that those individuals with a strong need for innovativeness are also more likely to adopt personal computers.

As innovative attributes are inherent to one's receptivity to innovations and need for innovativeness motivates one to make adoption decisions, one's self-confidence in executing adoption decision making may also be pertinent in the innovation adoption process. According to Bandura (1983), perceived self-efficacy is associated with how one makes judgments concerning whether one can apply their perceived skills or capability to deal with situations deriving from various circumstances. This suggests that an individual with higher self-efficacy will also be more willing to adopt a technology innovation, undeterred by any number of potential barriers, including the complexity involved in mastering the effective use of technology. Compeau and Higgins (1995) discovered that individuals with greater perceived self-efficacy in computer use are willing to devote a greater level of effort to learning and mastering the computer system.

Individuals imbued with innovative attributes, innovativeness need, and high self-efficacy in technology use are most likely to make an adoption decision when their beliefs about innovation adoption are consistent with their attitude. This assumption is based on Fishbein's (1980) theory of reasoned action, which suggests that one's judgment on whether to take an action is a result both of one's belief about the outcomes of that action and one's attitude about those outcomes. Therefore, an individual who believes that adoption and use of a technology would be costly and labor-intensive may still adopt it, if the individual is unconcerned about such hindrances (Fishbein & Azjen, 1975, 1981). Davis (1986, 1989) tested this theory of reasoned action with his technology acceptance model and found support for the relationship between one's beliefs and attitudes about innovation adoption. Other empirical studies also have shown that behavioral intention is a good predictor for actual technology adoption decision (e.g., Anandarajan, Simmers, & Igbaria, 2000; Davis, Bagozzi, & Warshaw, 1989; Sheppard, Hartwick, & Warshaw, 1988; Taylor & Todd, 1995).

Social Factors

Although audience factors portray the characteristics of an "adopter profile," external influences surrounding such units as the social or organizational groups with which the audience is affiliated also plays a pivotal role in the adoption decision. The most influential individual in these "groups" is usually the opinion leader whose topic-specific opinions are either influential or followed. The notion of opinion leadership, conceptualized by Lazarsfeld, Berelson, and Gaudet (1944) to explain how opinion leaders filter media messages and pass them on to others, often plays a role in whether certain innovations are adopted by their opinion followers.

According to Rogers (1995), opinion leaders may be more innovative than their followers but they are not necessarily innovators, as innovators are often "nonconformists" who are devoted to their elitist orientation toward change. These opinion leaders could be a salient other (e.g., Fulk, 1993), a peer or a colleague (e.g., Leonard-Barton & Deschamps, 1988), an administrative leader (e.g., Schmitz & Fulk, 1991) or even an organization. Opinion leaders can also be "key communicators," individuals who are in the position to communicate with a diverse set of people within or outside of their immediate social group or organizational setting. Through their frequent exchanges with group members, key communicators can emerge as influential opinion leaders in the technology adoption decision-making process (Friedkin, 1982; Marsden, 1981). If a key communicator is also an administrative leader, then the individual may also facilitate the technology adoption decision (Rogers, 1988). In other words, opinion leaders can exert strong "social influences," through either a formal or an informal communication channel over their opinion followers on their cognitive, affective, and behavioral tendencies toward technology (e.g., Fulk, 1993; Leonard-Barton & Deschamps, 1988; Rice, 1993; Schmitz & Fulk, 1991).

According to resource dependency theory (Preffer & Salancik, 1978), in an interorganizational setting, the organization that controls resources on which other organizations depend may also "obligate" them to adopt new innovations in order to facilitate effective interorganizational communication transactions. For instance, Powell (1990) suggested that the communication network involving suppliers and clients of an organization can be influential on an organization's communication technology adoption decision.

Above and beyond social influence via opinion leaders, individuals or organizations are also sensitive to the social context of mediated communication. In particular, as communication is a social behavior, the context of mediated communication intrinsic to the nature of a technology may figure prominently in the adoption decision.

When the adoption of a communication medium conveys a particular symbolic gesture and embodies an explicit message itself, then the choice medium itself can become a part of the message (Trevino et al., 1987). If this occurs, then the use of the medium is opened to social symbolic interpretation. For instance, a personalized voicemail message can convey a greater sense of urgency and social intimacy than an e-mail message with the same content, due to the presence of "personal involvement" via human speech. In fact, Webster and Trevino (1995) discovered that e-mail adoption choice can be a result of how casual or informal the communication is intended to be by the participants. Hence, individual adoption of a particular communication medium can bear a unique meaning in terms of the interpersonal distance and relationship present in the message—and thus a milieu adorned with social discourse symbolism.

Above and beyond the different social influences already discussed, there is at least one crucial social factor that can more fully capture the social nature of human communication in relation to technology adoption. Markus (1987) applied the critical mass theory, developed by Oliver, Marwell, and Teixeira (1985), to explain how the public good nature of communication technology can be fully distributed when universal access is made available. That is, later adopters of an interactive technology derive more benefit from the technology because they can make more efficient use of the technology, as an incrementally larger number of users become available. For instance, early e-mail adopters have few counterparts with whom to correspond, yet late e-mail adopters have a critical mass of correspondents to maximize the efficiency of their e-mail system usage. As Soe and Markus (1993) found, the existence of a critical mass of fax, voicemail and e-mail adopters has an impact on the subsequent diffusion rate, use patterns, and audience evaluation of the technology. In essence, human communication conducted via a media technology is an interdependent act whether it occurs at a dyadic or organizational level. Therefore, having a critical mass of existing adopters is instrumental in the continued diffusion of a technology. It is especially essential at an organizational level, as the "community" acceptance of an interactive technology determines whether a technology thrives or withers.

Technology Factors

Rogers defined (1995) innovation attributes as containing the following five dimensions:

1. Relative advantage (or benefits and costs) associated with adoption.
2. Compatibility among an innovation and existing values, past experiences and adopter needs.
3. Complexity associated with the use of the innovation.
4. Trialability feasible for the innovation.
5. Observability of the results from innovation adoption.

These innovation attributes, often identified by the technology expert, generally describe the objective characteristics of a technology innovation. They often can be found as the prescribed product attributes, when the technology product is being marketed. For instance, a wireless phone service advertising campaign would explain the benefits (that outweigh the costs) of the product, the compatibility with existing phone service, the ease of use, the free trial period, and the readily observable positive adoption results.

Nevertheless, even when technology attributes are genuine and positive, they can still be negatively perceived by potential adopters, and vice versa. These types of audience perceptions about technology attributes thus can formulate "subjective technology characteristics" that impact future adoption decisions (e.g., Agarwal & Prasad, 1997; Rogers, 1995).

One aspect of these subjective technology characteristics has to do with how users perceive the ability of a medium to "emulate" a face-to-face interpersonal communication experience. Short et al. (1976) consider mediated communication a phenomenon that falls along a "social presence" continuum, where the medium can help educe the awareness or "presence" of the participants and their interpersonal interaction. For example, when a group meeting is called, a videoconference has a higher social presence than an audio conference. Hence, to produce successful communication, it would be advantageous to choose a communication medium that can elicit the desired level of social interaction perspicacity for the communication tasks at hand (Rice, Grant, Schmitz, & Torobin, 1990). As such, the audience's socializing orientation and objective to inject a social atmosphere or a social setting in mediated communication can play a role in technology adoption choice.

An additional dimension of technology attributes that is not readily observable but weighs in the audience perception involves the concept of task equivocality. Daft and Lengel (1984) contended that mediated communication channels have different capabilities in processing equivocal information to transmit isomorphous meanings; although rich media have the greatest capacity to communicate shared meanings, lean media have the least capacity. The level of media richness associated with a particular communication technology can be evaluated in terms of whether the technology allows for an instant feedback mechanism, the transmission of multiple cues (e.g., body language, voice inflection), and the use of natural language and a personal focus. For instance, the telephone is ranked higher on the media richness hierarchy because e-mail lacks the capability of communicating nonverbal cues such as voice inflection. Thus, perceived media richness can be a crucial consideration in adoption decision making, when the successful communication of unequivocal information is quintessential. Empirical evidence has shown that the communication technologies that are perceived to be richer media are also preferred for more equivocal types of communication tasks (Rice, D'Ambra, & More, 1998; Schmitz & Fulk, 1991).

There is a unique dimension of technology attributes that is innate to the success of interactive media technologies such as the Internet. Lin (2000b) introduced the theory of fluidity to illustrate this particular technical attribute, which possesses the capacity to transform an interactive communication medium into different communication modes (encompassing interpersonal, organizational, and mass communication), different media platforms, and a multitasking unit. In essence, this technical attribute entails the capability of transforming itself from one communication modality into anther, shifting from one unique task to the next and operating in different communication modalities and tasks concurrently. For example, when accessing a Web site, the site allows the audience to alter its media modality from a primarily static text-based "information page" to a moving image-based "video screen," by downloading and viewing video or film clips. This same web site may also enable the audience to shift to a different task such as playing interactive video games. In addition, the audience can utilize this Web site's electronic messaging system to send and receive e-mail, voicemail, fax messages, and hear and view audio and video clips all at the same time, along with linking the audience to a hyperlink that leads to another Web site or page. Hence, in today's interactive media culture, the fluid nature of a communication medium in terms of its built-in functions to multilayering interactive platforms and multitasking interactive tasks can be effectual in impacting media technology adoption decisions. Lin's (2000b) initial empirical study provides support for this fluidity theory in that the audiences who consider the Internet a more highly fluid medium are also more likely to adopt videostreaming technology or online broadcasting service. Other examples of fluid technologies include, for example, a digital personal communication system (PCS) that can serve as a wireless phone, a miniature Internet personal computer, a pager and a global positioning system (GPS) device, or a desktop videoconferencing system that can provide audio, video, and typed text displays and exchanges. In their study of desktop videoconferencing system use, Ramsay, Barabesi, and Preece (1996) found that users utilize the system's multimedia modalities to set up shared space (e.g., text editors or drawings) for maintaining a shared record (of the communication transaction), while simultaneously engaging in other communication activities (e.g., annotating, talking). The communication benefits derived from technology fluidity appear to be clear. Further studies are needed to more fully investigate both the theoretical as well as practical meanings of this technology fluidity theory.

Adoption Factors

The mélange of antecedent variables—systems factors, audience factors, and social factors, as discussed here can all help contribute to interpose the outcome of the audience's technology adoption decision. When there is a nonadoption decision (Rogers, 1995), studies have found these antecedent factors are negative predictors or correlates (e.g., Agarwal & Prasad, 1997; Compaeu & Higgins, 1995; David, Bagozzi, & Warshaw, 1989; Fulk, Schmitz, & Steinfield, 1990; Markus, 1987). Similarly, when a discontinuance decision surfaces (Rogers, 1995), these negative relationships are indicative of why a technology adoption is discontinued and whether an alternative technology adoption is being considered as a replacement (Kraut, Rice, Cool, & Fish, 1998). When a likely adoption decision is reached, the audience generally has a positive response—adoption consideration—even though their adoption decision is a delayed one due to a perceived lack of available resources (i.e., the cost with which one is capable of and willing to part; Lin, 1998). If an actual adoption arises, then differential use patterns of the adopted technology will begin to emerge for different users or organizations. Depending on the use patterns and experiences, the prescribed technical functions of the adopted technology can be altered during the implementation stage (Rogers, 1995). That is, technology implementation can progress through several phases. These phases can include: (a) adaptation to make the technology compatible with existing technology systems or specific user needs, (b) acceptance via phasing in appropriate applications, and (c) routinization through infusing the technology as part of users' institutionalized or elemental use habit (Agarwal & Prasad, 1997; Rogers, 1995).

Reinvention, often conceptualized as "adaptation," should perhaps be conceptually distinguished from "adaptation," due to the different circumstances in which these two activities could occur. Specifically, reinvention is best manifested when new uses of a technology, engineered through purposeful functional (via adding or altering software, hardware, or peripheral devices) or application modification (via a new or unintended application), are created for the sake of making new applications available (e.g., Johnson & Rice, 1987). By contrast, the parameters of "adaptation" should be confined to technical modifications that occur for the purpose of successful implantation of the technology in the existing technology platform and application infrastructure.

Use Factors

Once the adoption occurs, as discussed earlier, the audience (an individual or an organizational unit) may learn to use the technology, adapt the technology for suitable application, routinize their technology use, and even reinvent new uses from existing functions. The cumulative use experience, whether limited or matured, is then evaluated by the audience from several different perspectives. For instance, users can judge their use experience by reviewing the degree of communication flow associated with the technical applications of the technology. Trevino and Webster (1992) suggested that the audience can evaluate their use experience based on their perceived sense of control, attentiveness, curiosity, and interestedness during their interaction with the technology. They found that their sample respondents perceive higher communication flow with the use of e-mail than voicemail; as a result, that perception is associated with a positive attitude toward the e-mail medium and their perception of the effectiveness and efficiency of their use experience.

This favorable perception and attitude, nevertheless, can be tampered by preexisting expectations, if the use experience fails to meet those expectations. Rosenberg's (1956) expectancy-value model argues that attitude is "accompanied by a cognitive structure made up of beliefs about the potentialities of that object for attaining or blocking the realization of valued states" (p. 367). Hence, for instance, if the audience believes that the adopted technology met their expectations for improving their communication efficiency (e.g., saving time and increasing productivity) and avoiding certain potential negatives (e.g., frequent system breakage or technical difficulties), then the audience will develop a positive attitude toward the technology (LaRose & Atkin, 1991).

A positive attitude toward the adopted technology, although dependent on the audience's expectancy values, can be further mediated by an additional perceptual element related to the audience's gratification with their technology use experience. The uses and gratifications perspective has been applied to study the adoption and uses of a variety of media and media technologies, including, most recently, interactive communication media such as the Internet. This theoretical perspective evolves from and builds on Maslow's (1943, 1970) hierarchy of needs, postulating that self-actualization needs motivate the audience to seek cognitive and affective fulfillment such as surveillance (of one's environment), entertainment, diversion, and personal identity through media content use (Blumler, 1979). Although the audience is presumed to be rather aware of these self-actualization needs, they are also presupposed to be goal-oriented in selecting and exposing themselves to media content that will satisfy these needs (Lin, 1996). As there is a wide variety of available literature that supports this theory's potency in predicting media content choice and use patterns, the theory's validity in explaining audience motives for mediated communication technology adoption has begun to solidify.

For instance, Lin (1999) verified the parallel audience adoption motives for TV programs and online service content, even though TV-use motives are insignificant predictors for likely online service adoption. Moreover, Lin (2001) also found statistically strong and significant predictive links between different audience motives (or needs for gratification) and the likely adoption of differential online service types. These findings are further affirmed by a recent study that also provides strong support for the predictive relationship between audience needs for gratification and online service adoption (Lin, 2000a). Other empirical studies similarly report statistically significant correlational or predictive relationships between audience gratification-seeking motives and the adoption and uses of interactive communication media, including interactive cable TV systems (Lin & Jeffres, 1998), personal computers (e.g., Perse & Dunn, 1998), electronic bulletin boards (James, Worting, & Forrest, 1995), electronic commerce (Eighmey, 1997), Web usage (Korgaonkar & Wolin, 1999), and Internet use intentions (Jeffres & Atkin, 1996).

THEORETICAL AND RESEARCH IMPLICATIONS

Research on innovation adoption and diffusion often involves some form of "technology forecast" or speculative foretelling about how and why a particular communication technology would be adopted and what the economic, social, or cultural outcomes will be due to such adoption. The principal reason that most technology adoption research appears to be tentative in explaining their research findings or justifying their rationale for predicting future outcomes is due to a lack of development in theories that directly address this social phenomenon. There most definitely is a dire need for technology adoption research to be theoretically based, so that the scientific process of inductive as well as deductive reasoning can take root, and the empirical verification process can be deemed valid and reliable. In other words, we need technology researchers to theorize and be theoretical.

Need for Theories

This need for communication-based theories is pressing because the pace of technological development and technology adoption has been greatly outpacing communication research. Although certain existing social science theories, communication-based or not, appear to be applicable or event pertinent to the explanation of the relationship between communication and innovation adoption, this opens up a window of possibilities for aspiring theorists. In particular, there are two basic approaches to undertake a productive theorizing task—applying existing theories and introducing new theories.

There are at least three different methods of applying an existing theory; they include adoption, adaptation, and integration. A direct adoption refers to a direct application of an existing theory that is compatible with the technology innovation adoption research. In the present model, the "systems theory" (e.g., Bailey, 1994; Lundberg, 1980) is inclusive enough to explain any number of social systems of interest here, the "self-efficacy theory" (Bandura, 1983) and "expectancy value theory" (Fishbein & Azjen, 1975) are time-tested cognitive theories that can explain how belief systems affect attitudinal and behavioral outcomes in any context. By contrast, "opinion leadership," as well as "innovation attributes" and "innovative attributes" (Rogers, 1995) have long been studied in conjunction with adoption of innovations, including technology innovation theories. They are also considered directly applicable conceptual frameworks.

An adaptation suggests that a theory may need further deduction and thus modification before it is theoretically valid for the study context in question. For instance, Davis (1986, 1989) adapted the "theory of reasoned action" by modifying the theoretical components and proposed a "technology acceptance model" to examine organization adoption of communication technologies. Markus (1987) extended the logic of the "theory of the critical mass" by recontexualizing its "public goods" and "physics" nature to make it meaningful for explicating the "social-physics" aspect of interactive media technology diffusion. The uses and gratifications perspective, a widely tested theory in explaining the affect and behavior associated with media content and medium choice, has been expanded to explore new media adoption by mass communication researchers. For instance, Lin (1999) and Eighmey (1997) utilized this theoretical perspective to explain online service adoption likelihood and motives for Web use.

A third means of applying an existing theory involves integrating it with a new theoretical dimension or a new theory. For instance, the "innovativeness need" construct (Lin, 1998) was introduced as a new dimension for studying the self-actualization needs as part of an individual's "innovative attributes" (e.g., Foxall & Bhate, 1991). By the same token, the "likely adoption" (or likely adopter) category (Lin, 1998) was coined to account for the group of individuals who are delayed adopters not due to the lack of innovative attributes or innovativeness need, but due to external resource constraints such as adoption cost. The construct is also meant to be considered as part of the adoption decision continuum, which may range from nonadoption (or rejection) to reinvention.

When it comes to introducing new theories, there have been some fruitful results. In particular, the "media richness" (Daft & Lengel, 1984), "media symbolism" (Trevino et al., 1987), and "social presence" theories (Short et al., 1976) were all developed to capture audience perceptions of how well the substantive and symbolic meanings of their communication is conveyed, and how "closely" their communication experience simulates an interpersonal discourse through the adoption of communication technology. Even though empirical evidence has provided uneven support for the validity or reliability of all three theoretical advents (e.g., Rice, 1993), they should be heralded as innovative "theoretical thinking" that is much needed in "new" communication research. In a similar vein, the construct of "communication flow" (Trevino & Webster, 1992) and the "theory of fluidity" (Lin, 2000b) tackle how cognitive response and physical experience of technology use help form audience acceptance or liking of technology. Although these two theoretical endeavors still need to be sufficiently validated by empirical studies, they signal a new frontier for future research.

IMPLICATIONS FOR RESEARCH

The complexity of studying the relationships between communication and information technology adoption and uses, the impact of technology adoption and uses on social systems, and the social's system's control over information technology diffusion is evidently illustrated in this research paradigm as well as in the chapters of this volume. Seetzen (1986) characterized the difficulties involved in evaluating the social and economic consequences of information technology as being rooted in the fact that "society is intrinsically based on communication—all cultural and economic affairs are intimately tied to communication process, i.e., the production and exchange of information" (p. 333).

Given these cautionary inklings, one is left with the question of what might be the most sensible approaches to formulate our theories and inquiries at this stage of the game. The logical means to arrive at an answer to this question seems to lie at the discovery of what is already out there that appears incomplete and what is still absent that may be essential. As this volume has provided a rather comprehensive review of the major theoretical frameworks and empirical findings relevant to the relationship between communication behavior and information technology adoption and uses, the ensuing discussion addresses what might be incomplete or omitted.

From a systems point of view, much of the regulation/policy research analysis tends to be ad hoc in nature due to a serious lack of valid, reliable, and definable theories or theoretical models from which the research could draw (e.g., McCool, 1995). As a result, the failures in optimal or effective policymaking abound, aversely affecting innovation diffusion. A good way to start theory-building in this area is to formulate a paradigm that both integrates and interrelates multiple schools of policy-analysis models devoid of such interfering systems factors as politicization. By theoretically and empirically separating these interactive system factors, we can allow for the study of the separate and combined effects of the policy-analysis model elements and those external systems factors.

As evidenced by the micro nature of the social factors previously discussed, there may be a dire need to study the social aspects of information technology adoption and uses in which these adoption and use activity take place. The Internet offers a good example of a fitting subject for this type of research, as its technical nature permits the audience to use it as an interpersonal, organizational, and mass communication medium. In other words, the Internet's fluid nature makes it an excellent choice to study, for instance, online social support groups that utilize both a one-on-one and group support modalities online (see Walther & Boyd, chap. 6, this volume), in addition to making mass media content available for single-to-multiple point information distribution. Succinctly put, we need to fully understand and define what makes a communication technology a social medium and what role that social medium plays in shaping the technological culture in a social system.

When assessing audience factors, the key remains maintaining a focus on the audience's cognitive, affective, and behavioral dispositions and intentions. Empirical studies should strive to establish a set of indices or scales based on the self-efficacy theory and theory of reasoned action that can be applicable to the study of various information technologies. In addition, audience characteristics that are relevant to their innovative nature—such as innovative attributes, innovativeness needs, and perceived external resources (i.e., perceived economic means)—should be the primary demographic/psychographic variables of interest. The significance of allowing these innovation-relevant internal personality traits to take precedence over certain conventional demographic and psychographic indicators (e.g., education, gender, or hobbies) is already manifest, due to declining technology costs and a rapidly growing "technological culture" influencing the entire social spectrum.

As technological culture progresses, the audience also may accept the ubiquitous "invasion" of technology products as a necessary evil. Hence, when communication technologies such as personal computers are widely perceived as a "technology appliance," the innovation attributes relevant to audience adoption decisions may involve perceived ease of use, usefulness (e.g., Igbaria, Schiffman, & Wieckowski, 1996), advantages (or benefits; Lin, 1998), and technology fluidity (Lin, 2000b). As the advancements in multifunctional-multipurpose multitasking communication technologies continue, technology fluidity may also emerge as the most important aspect of innovation attributes—both from a functional as well as user point of view. The fluidity of a medium may also directly influence audience perceptions of "media richness," as the medium's ability to concurrently deliver the communication content in multiple textual and audiovisual modes should enhance the audience perception of "information richness." Future research exploration of the validity and reliability of the theory of technology fluidity should help enhance our understanding of how the audience relates to these multitasking media.

The most obvious areas of research needed, when turning to the adoption factors, appears to be the concepts of "likely adoption" (Lin, 1998) and reinvention (e.g., Johnson & Rice, 1987; Rogers, 1995). As likely adopters are the next immediate wave of adopters to the medium, reinventing technical applications of a technology can be instrumental in lengthening its life span and retaining existing adopters.

Finally, use factors are the primary source for providing system feedback. The communication flow construct (Trevino & Webster, 1992) seems like a promising approach to examine user cognitive involvement with the technology use experience; additional studies are presently needed to help understand the full meaning of this conceptual framework. Although the uses and gratifications perspective has received more notice as a valid means of measuring audience cognitive and affective fulfillment via technology use, refinement in content as well as construct validity is much needed in empirical studies for the improvement of the overall validity of the theory. Likewise, Rosenberg's (1956) expectancy value theory, an extension of the theory of reasoned action, offers a well-grounded foundation for studying how positive belief leads to positive attitude and ultimately adoption action. Yet, this theory is waiting to be "rediscovered" as a legitimate conceptual basis for studying communication technology adoption, as it was once validated by earlier studies addressing media content choice (e.g., Galloway & Meek, 1981) and medium choice (LaRose & Atkin, 1991).

OBSTACLES AND OPPORTUNITIES

Above and beyond what has already appeared in this discussion thus far are the potential pitfalls that should be avoided when conducting communication technology adoption and uses research. McQuail (1986) summarized his observations as follow:

1. The volatile outcomes of "future-oriented" research.
2. The lack of a single dominant definition of the research problem.
3. The importance of focusing on perceptions and behaviors instead of content and effects.
4. The need to avoid overemphasizing either negative or positive research agenda formulation.
5. An awareness of the future values of the research subject.

It is true that "future-oriented" research results should be treated with caution, especially if forward-looking theories don't keep pace with technological development to reduce the reliability concerns of such findings. The multiplicity of communication research keeps the research questions and hypotheses original and comprehensive, even though it does create conceptual confusion and misunderstandings at times. McQuail's idea of prioritizing research objectives is a good rule of thumb, as he reminded us of the constancy in media content and effects (usually limited) over time, compared to the changing nature of perceptions and behaviors. More importantly, any attempt to "politicize" research problems to outfit a researchers' preexisting conceptual bias could produce the consequences similar to those of politicized policy research—lack of scientific objectivity and thus validity. Finally, thanks to advances in computer-mediated communication technology, we are transiting from a single platform (e.g., TV or radio) to a multiplatform (e.g., a personal computer/DVD unit) technology era. If we put all the communication technologies ever invented on a "technology continuum," it would become clear that later technologies are the extensions of older technologies either in hardware or software functions or designs. In other words, it is the "continuity" rather than "discontinuity" that helps push the progress of technology development. Thus, what will be valuable in the future can be found in what's valuable now. Good research then chooses the currently feasible continuity-oriented communication technologies (e.g., personal computer) as the study subject to help prepare for future research on the "next best things" (e.g., the Internet).

CONCLUSION

Bolter (1984) identified the computer as the "defining technology" in the 1980s; a defining technology then "resembles a magnifying glass, which collects and focuses seemingly disparate ideas in a culture into one bright, sometimes piercing ray" (p. 11). It would be fair to say that the defining technology in our current generation is communication/information technology. Metaphorically, communication/information technology can be seen as such defining technologies in their respective eras (e.g., the internal combustion engine or the personal computer) for affecting the unique qualities that help define all things human.

It is for this very reason that it is vital for communication/information technology research to take an interdisciplinary as well as an integrated approach, as advocated in this volume. McQuail's (1986) list of bipolar dimensions, ascribing the potential evaluative criteria for what technologies may bestow upon a "wired city," may serve as a good road map for communication researchers. These evaluative dimensions include more communication or less, freedom versus control, diversity versus uniformity access exclusion, interaction versus one-way communication, equality-inequality, centralization versus decentralization, and privatization or enlargement of the public sphere.

In conclusion, we need to carefully consider the nature of communication/information technology, as it increasingly comes to dominate every aspect of human activity. In fact, we need to avoid the fallacy of allowing technology to dominate our best asset—the ability to communicate—and to succumb to the "will" of the machine by becoming an "information processor" or the so-called "Turing's men" (Bolter, 1984, p. 13). The values of communication/information technology adoption research are thus immeasurable in that they reflect our desire to have control over technology and our ability to communicate, and henceforth our humanity and destiny.

REFERENCES

Agarwal, R., & Prasad, J. (1997). The role of innovation characteristics and perceived voluntariness in the acceptance of information technologies. *Decision Sciences, 28,* 557-582.

Anandarajan, M., Simmers, C., & Igbaria, M. (2000). An exploratory investigation of the antecedents and impact of Internet usage: An individual perspective. *Behaviour & Information Technology, 19,* 69-85.

Bailey, K. D. (1994). *Sociology and the new systems theory.* Albany: State University of New York Press.

Bandura, A. (1983). Self-efficacy determinants of anticipated fears and calamities. *Journal of Personality and Social Psychology, 45,* 464-469.

Bandura, A. (1986). *Social foundations of thought and action.* Englewood Cliffs, NJ: Prentice-Hall.

Bell, D. (1973). *The coming of the post-industrial society. A venture in social forecasting.* New York: Basic Books.

Blumler, J. G. (1979). The role of theory in uses and gratifications studies. *Communication Research, 6,* 9-36.

Bolter, J. D. (1984). *Turing's man. Western culture in the computer age.* London: Duckworth.

Compeau, D. R., & Higgins, C. A. (1995). Computer self-efficacy: Development of a measure and initial test. *MIS Quarterly, 19,* 189-211.

Daft, R. L., & Lengel, R. H. (1984). Information richness: A new approach to managerial information processing and organization design. In L. L. Cummings & B. M. Staw (Eds.), *Research in organization behavior* (Vol. 6, pp. 191-234). Greenwich, CT: JAI Press.

Daft, R. L., & Lengel, R. H. (1986). Organizational information requirements, media richness and structural determinants. *Management Science, 32,* 554-571.

Dahlberg, A., Livingstone, S., Moreley, D., & Silverstone, R. (1989, May). *Families, technologies and consumption: The household and information and communication technologies.* Paper presented to the ESRC Programme on Information and Communication Technology Conference, Brunel University.

Davis, F. D. (1986). *A technology acceptance model for empirically testing new end-user information systems: Theory and results.* Unpublished doctoral dissertation, Sloan School of Management, Massachusetts Institute of Technology, Cambridge.

Davis, F. D. (1989). Perceived usefulness, perceived ease of use, and user acceptance of information technology. *MIS Quarterly,* 319-340.

Davis, F. D., Bagozzi, R., & Warshaw, P. (1989). User acceptance of computer technology: A comparison of two theoretical models. *Management Sciences, 35*, 982-1003.

Eighmey, J. (1997). Profiling user responses to commercial web sites. *Journal of Advertising Research, 37*, 59-66.

Fishbein, M. (1980). A theory of reasoned action: Some applications and implications. In H. Howe & M. Page (Eds.), *Nebraska Symposium on Motivation* (Vol. 27, pp. 65-116). Lincoln: University of Nebraska Press.

Fishbein, M., & Ajzen, I. (1975). *Belief, attitude, intention, and behavior: An introduction to theory and research.* Reading: MA: Addison-Wesley.

Fishbein, M., & Ajzen, I. (1981). Acceptance, yielding, and impact: Cognitive processes in persuasion. In R. E. Petty, T. M. Ostron, & T. C. Brock (Eds.), *Cognitive responses in persuasion.* Hillsdale, NJ: Lawrence Erlbaum Associates.

Foxall, G. R., & Bhate, S. (1991). Psychology of computer use: XIX. Extent of computer use relationship with adaptive-innovative cognitive style and personal involvement in computing. *Perceptual and Motor Skills, 72*, 195-202.

Friedkin, N. E. (1982). Information flow through strong and weak ties in intraorganizational social networks. *Social Networks, 3*, 273-285.

Fulk, J. (1993). Social construction of communication technology. *Academy of Management Journal, 36*, 921-950.

Fulk, J., Schmitz, J., & Steinfield, C. (1990). A social influence model of technology use. In J. Fulk & C. Steinfield (Eds.), *Organizations and communication technology* (pp. 117-140). Newbury Park, CA: Sage.

Galloway, J. J., & Meek, F. L. (1981). Audience uses and gratifications: An exepectancy model. *Communication Research, 8*, 435-449.

Igbaria, M., Schiffman, S. J., & Wieckowski, T. J. (1994). The respective roles of perceived usefulness and perceived fun in the acceptance of microcomputer technology. *Behavior and Information Technology, 13*, 349-361.

James, M. L., Worting, C. E., & Forrest, E. J. (1995). An exploratory study of the perceived benefits of electronic bulletin board use and their impact on other communication activities. *Journal of Broadcasting & Electronic Media, 39*, 30-50.

Jeffres, L. W., & Atkin, D. J. (1996). Predicting use of technologies for consumer and communication needs. *Journal of Broadcasting & Electronic Media, 40*, 318-330.

Jensen, J. F. (1993). Computer culture: The meaning of technology and the technology of meaning. A triadic essay on the semiotics of technology. In P. B. Andersen, B. Holmqvist, & J. F. Jensen (Eds.), *The computer as medium* (pp. 292-336). New York: Cambridge University Press.

Johnson, B., & Rice, R. E. (1987). *Managing organizational innovation: The evolution from word processing to office information systems.* New York: Columbia University Press.

Khandwalla, P. (1977). *The design of organizations.* New York: Harcourt Brace Jovanovich.

Korgaonkar, P. K., & Wolin, L. D. (1999). A multivariate analysis of web usage. *Journal of Advertising Research, 29,* 53-68.

Kraut, R., Rice, R. E., Cool, C., & Fish, R. (1998). Varieties of social influence: The role of utility and norms in the success of a new communication medium. *Organization Science, 9,* 437-453.

Lansing, K. P., & Bates, B. J. (1992). Videotex as public information systems: The French and American experience. *Southwestern Mass Communication Journal, 7,* 22-34.

LaRose, R., & Atkin, D. (1991). Attributes of movie distribution channels and consumer choice. *Journal of Media Economics, 4,* 3-17.

Lazarsfeld, P., Berelson, B., & Gaudet, H. (1944). *The people's choice: How the voter makes up his mind in a presidential election.* New York: Duell, Sloan & Pearce.

Leonard-Barton, D., & Deschamps, I. (1988). Managerial influence in the implementation of new technology. *Management Science, 34,* 1252-1265.

Lin, C. A. (1996). Looking back: The contribution of Blumler and Katz's uses of mass communication to communication research. *Journal of Broadcasting & Electronic Media, 40,* 574-580.

Lin, C. A. (1998). Exploring personal computer adoption dynamics. *Journal of Broadcasting & Electronic Media, 42,* 95-112.

Lin, C. A. (1999). Online-service adoption likelihood. *Journal of Advertising Research, 39,* 79-89.

Lin, C. A. (2000a, August). *Predicting online use activity via motives, innovative traits and news media use.* Paper presented to the Association for Education in Journalism & Mass Communication, Phoenix, AZ.

Lin, C. A. (2000b). *Programming localism via online broadcasting* (Research report). National Association of Broadcasters, Washington, DC.

Lin, C. A. (2001). Audience attributes, media supplementation and likely online service adoption. *Mass Communication & Society, 4,* 19-38.

Lin, C. A., & Jeffres, L. W. (1998). Factors influencing the adoption of multimedia cable technology. *Journalism & Mass Communication Quarterly, 75,* 341-352.

Lundberg, C. C. (1980). On organization development interventions: A general systems-cybernetic perspective. In T. G. Cummings (Ed.), *Systems theory for organization development* (pp. 247-272). New York: Wiley.

Markus, M. L. (1987). Toward a "critical mass" theory of interactive media: Universal access, interdependence and diffusion. *Communication Research, 14,* 491-511.

Marsden, P. V. (1981). Introducing influence processes into a system of collective decisions. *American Journal of Sociology, 86,* 1203-1235.

Maslow, A. H. (1943). A theory of human motivation. *Psychological Review, 50,* 370-396.

Maslow, A. H. (1970). *Motivation and personality.* New York: Harper & Row.

McCool, D. C. (1995). *Public policy theories, and concepts: An anthology.* Englewood Cliffs, NJ: Prentice-Hall.

McLuhan, M. (1964). *Understanding media. The extensions of man.* New York: McGraw Hill.

McLuhan, M. (1967). *The medium is the message.* London: Allen Lane, Penguin Press.

McQuail, D. (1987). Research on new communication technologies: Barren terrain or promising arena. In W. H. Dutton, J. G. Blumler, & K. L. Kraemer (Eds.), *Wired cities: Shaping the future of communications* (pp. 431-445). Boston, MA: G. K. Hall.

Midgley, D. F., & Dowling, G. R. (1978). Innovativeness: The concept and its measurement. *Journal of Consumer Research, 4,* 229-242.

Oliver, P., Marwell, G., & Teixeira, R. (1985). A theory of critical mass, I, interdependence, group heterogeneity, and the production of collective action. *American Journal of Sociology, 91,* 522-526.

Parks, M. R. (1977). Anomie and close friendship communication networks. *Human Communication Research, 4,* 48-57.

Pepper, R. (1987). Competitive realities in the telecommunication web. In W. H. Dutton, J. G. Blumler, & K. L. Kraemer (Eds.), *Wired cities: Shaping the future of communications* (pp. 59-74). Boston, MA: G.K. Hall.

Perse, E. M., & Dunn, D. B. (1998). The utility of home computers and media use: Implications of multimedia and connectivity. *Journal of Broadcasting & Electronic Media, 42,* 435-456.

Powell, W. (1990). Neither market nor hierarchy: Networked forms of organization. In B. Staw & L. Cummings (Eds.), *Research in communication behavior* (Vol. 12, pp. 295-336). Greenwich, CT: JAI Press.

Preffer, J., & Salancik, G. (1978). *The external control of organizations.* New York: Harper & Row.

Ramsay, J., Barabesi, A., & Preece, J. (1996). Informal communication is about sharing objects and media. *Interacting with Computers, 8,* 277-283.

Rice, R. E. (1993). Media appropriateness: Using social presence theory to compare traditional and new organizational media. *Human Communication Research, 19,* 451-484.

Rice, R. E., D'Ambra, J., & More, E. (1998). Cross-cultural comparison of organizational evaluation and choice. *Journal of Communication, 48*(3), 3-26.

Rice, R. E., Grant, A., Schmitz, J., & Torobin, J. (1990). Individual and network influences on the adoption and perceived outcomes of electronic messaging. *Social Networks, 12,* 27-55.

Rice, R. E., & Shook, D. (1990). Voice messaging, coordination and communication. In J. Galegher, R. Kraut, & C. Egido (Eds.), *Intellectual teamwork: Social and technological foundations of cooperative work* (pp. 327-350). Hillsdale, NJ: Lawrence Erlbaum Associates.

Rogers, E. M. (1988). Information technologies: How organizations are changing. In G. M. Goldhaber & G. Barnett (Eds.), *Handbook of organizational communication* (pp. 437-452). Norwood, NJ: Ablex.

Rogers, E. M. (1995). *Diffusion of innovation* (4th ed.). New York: The Free Press.

Rosenberg, M. J. (1956). Cognitive structure and attitudinal affect. *Journal of Abnormal and Social Psychology, 53,* 367-372.

Schmitz, J., & Fulk, J. (1991). Organizational colleagues, information richness and electronic mail: A test of the social influence model of technology use. *Communication Research, 18,* 487-523.

Seetzen, J. (1986). The cultural implications of new telecommunications systems. In W. H. Dutton, J. G. Blumler, & K. L. Kramer (Eds.), *Wired cities: Shaping the future of communications* (pp. 331-336). Boston, MA: G. K. Hall.

Sheppard, B. H., Hartwick, J., & Warshaw, P. R. (1988). The theory of reasoned action: A meta-analysis of past research with recommendations for modifications and future research. *Journal of Consumer Research, 15,* 325-343.

Soe, L., & Markus, M. L. (1993). Technological or social utility? Unravelling explanations of email, vmail, and fax use. *The Information Society, 9,* 213-236.

Short, J., Williams, E., & Christie, B. (1976). *The social psychology of telecommunications.* London: Wiley.

Taylor, S., & Todd, P. A. (1995). Understanding information technology usage: A test of competing models. *Information Systems Research, 6,* 144-176.

Trevino, L. K., Lengel, R., & Daft, R. L. (1987). Media symbolism, media richness and media choice in organizations: A symbolic interactionist perspective. *Communication Research, 14,* 553-574.

Trevino, L., & Webster, J. (1992). Flow in computer-mediated communication: Electronic mail and media choice in organizations. *Communication Research, 19,* 539-573.

Webster, J., & Trevino, L. (1995). Rational and social theories as complementary explanations of communication media choices: Two policy capturing studies. *Academy of Management Journal, 38,* 1544-1572.

Author Index

Subject Index